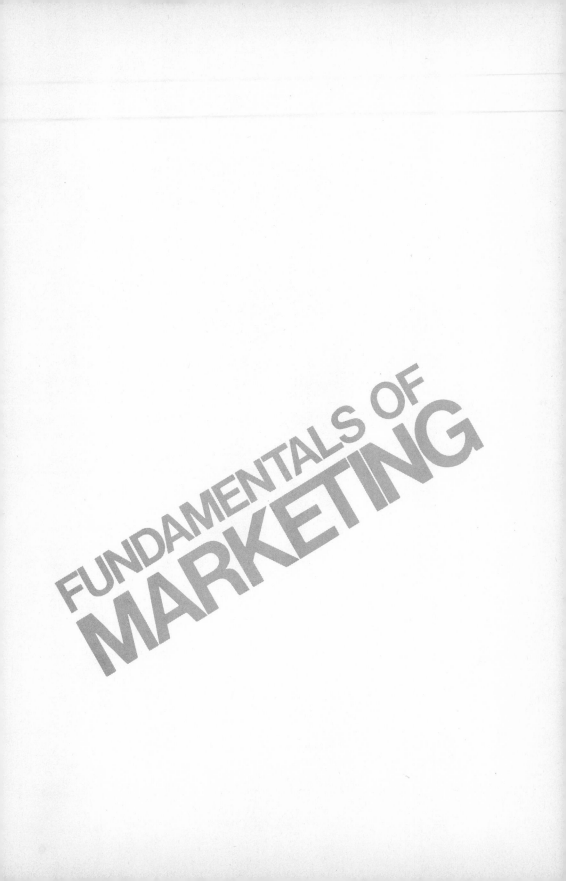

FUNDAMENTALS OF MARKETING

McGRAW-HILL BOOK COMPANY

New York   St. Louis   San Francisco   Auckland
Düsseldorf   Johannesburg   Kuala Lumpur   London
Mexico   Montreal   New Delhi   Panama   Paris
São Paulo   Singapore   Sydney   Tokyo   Toronto

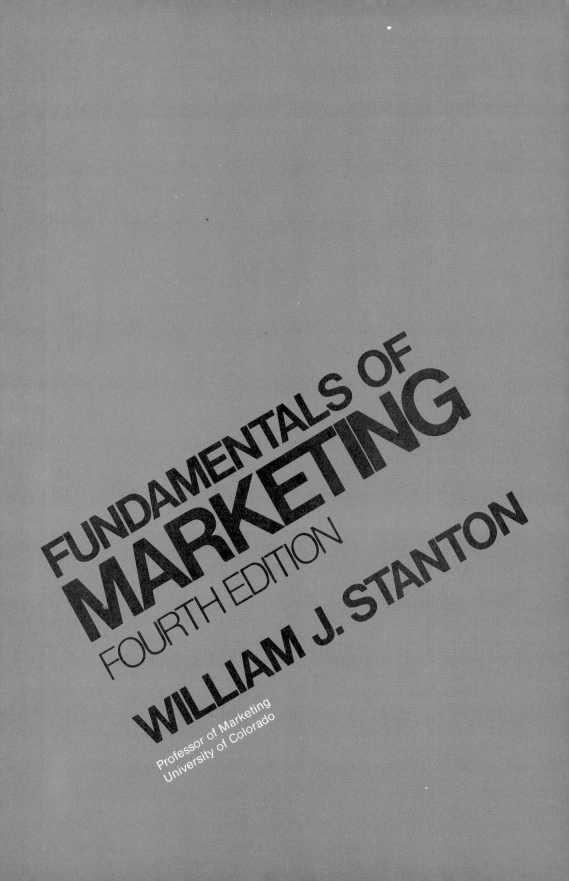

FUNDAMENTALS OF
MARKETING

FOURTH EDITION

WILLIAM J. STANTON

Professor of Marketing
University of Colorado

FUNDAMENTALS OF MARKETING
Copyright © 1964, 1967, 1971, 1975
by McGraw-Hill, Inc. All rights reserved.
Printed in the United States of America.
No part of this publication may be
reproduced, stored in a retrieval
system, or transmitted, in any form
or by any means, electronic, mechanical,
photocopying, recording, or otherwise,
without the prior written permission
of the publisher.

1 2 3 4 5 6 7 8 9 0 KPKP 7 9 8 7 6 5

This book was set in Helvetica by University Graphics, Inc.
The editors were Thomas H. Kothman and Matthew Cahill;
the designer was Anne Canevari Green;
cover photo by J. Paul Kirouac;
the production supervisor was Thomas J. LoPinto.
New drawings were done by J & R Services, Inc.
Kingsport Press, Inc., was printer and binder.

Library of Congress Cataloging in Publication Data

Stanton, William J
   Fundamentals of marketing.

  Bibliography: p.
  1. Marketing. I. Title.
HF5415.S745 1975   658.8   74-14510
ISBN 0-07-060862-8

TO KELLY AND LITTLE JOE

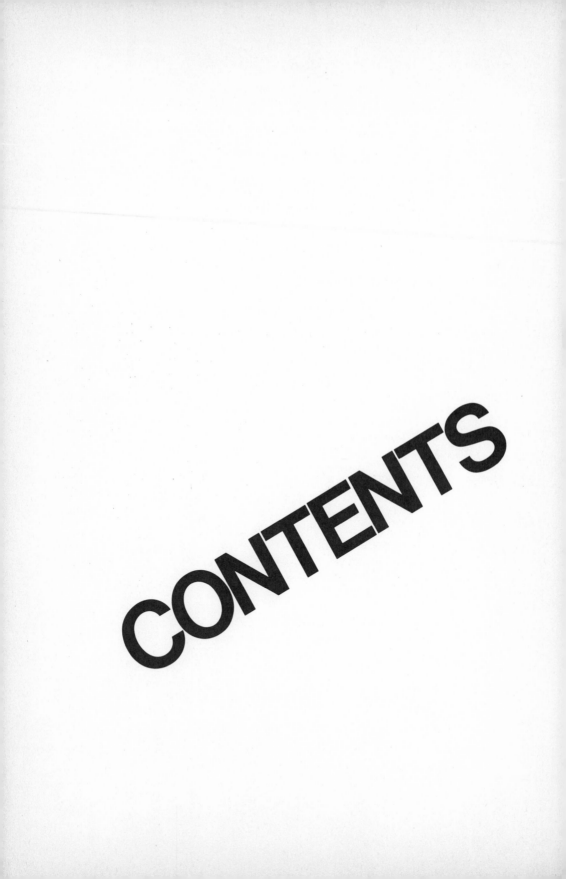

CONTENTS

PART FIVE. DISTRIBUTION STRUCTURE

CASES FOR PART FIVE

PART SIX. PROMOTIONAL ACTIVITIES

21. THE PROMOTIONAL PROGRAM   466

22. MANAGEMENT OF PERSONAL SELLING   488

23. MANAGEMENT OF ADVERTISING   506

CASES FOR PART SIX

PART SEVEN. MARKETING IN SPECIAL FIELDS

PART EIGHT. PLANNING AND EVALUATING THE MARKETING EFFORT

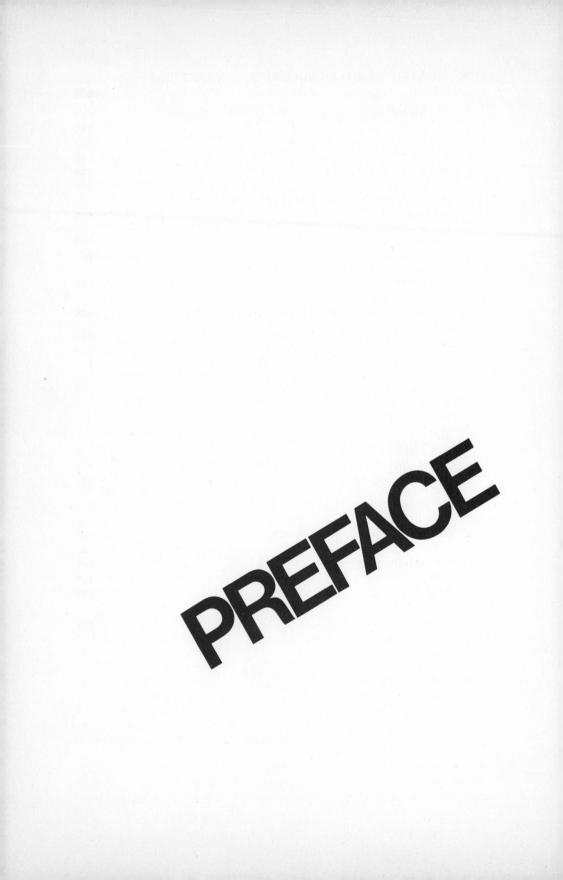

PREFACE

Marketing is a dynamic segment of a dynamic field—business administration. The last half of the 1970s is posing new environmental challenges to business in general and to marketing in particular. A societal orientation and an awareness by executives of their social responsibilities are growing in marketing. Also, for the first time in over 30 years, several industries are faced with product shortages. A textbook in marketing should reflect these challenges and offer some strategic guides to marketing's executive leadership in its problem-solving and decision-making responsibilities. Consequently, several changes have been made in this revision of *Fundamentals of Marketing* in order to keep it up to date. However, those who are familiar with the earlier editions will find that the basic theme, approach, and organization have been retained. The central theme is that marketing is a *total system* of business action rather than a fragmented assortment of functions and institutions, as it has often been treated in marketing literature and in practice.

In this edition the material has been updated, and several chapters have been completely or extensively rewritten. Fifteen of the 27 cases are new. The chapter on consumerism and marketing's social responsibility has been greatly expanded. The emerging societal orientation in marketing is reflected in the broadened definition of marketing, the revised evolution of marketing management, the broadening of the marketing concept, and in other topics. "Marketing in an era of shortages" is introduced, and the treatment of market segmentation and marketing information systems is expanded. Several other chapters have been partially rewritten to introduce recent developments and new concepts.

The sequence of some topics has been rearranged to effect a more logical order and to improve the teaching/learning experience. The sections on distribution structure and price systems have been reversed in order, reflecting the idea that a product typically is priced before it is distributed. The chapter on sociological influences on buying behavior is improved by bringing into that chapter the topics of diffusion of innovation (as a part of small-reference-group theory) and family buying behavior. Perhaps a controversial shift is the relocation of marketing information systems and marketing research to Chapter 26 from its former spot as Chapter 3. The change is a response to the suggestion of several people over the years. Fortunately, the topic is sufficiently free-standing and flexible that it can be treated in either location, as an instructor prefers. (In my own teaching, I still prefer the earlier location because throughout the course I refer to this managerial aid in decision making.)

For those not acquainted with the earlier editions, this is a basic textbook in the dynamic, complex field of marketing. While more attention is directed to the role of marketing in our socioeconomic system, the book is written largely from the viewpoint of management *in an individual firm*—either a manufacturer or a middleman. Emphasis is placed on the marketing problem solving and decision making required of a firm's executives. For the most part, the coverage is analytical and evaluative. At the same time, some descriptive material is certainly necessary in an introductory textbook. However, such material intentionally is limited to the amount needed by the student to undertake some intelligent analysis and evaluation.

Fundamentals of Marketing is intended for use in the introductory course in marketing. It is designed for students who plan to specialize in marketing and also for those who will be taking only one course in the field. Both of these groups are provided with a realistic treatment of marketing as it operates in American business today. The book may also be used in management training programs or for general reading by business executives.

The "systems" idea of marketing has become more meaningful in recent years with the acceptance of the marketing concept—a philosophy which stresses the need for a marketing (rather than production) orientation which is compatible with society's long-run interests. A company's managerial planning and operations should be directed toward satisfying the customers' long-run wants, considering societal interests, and obtaining profitable sales volume. In short, marketing is becoming recognized as an all-pervasive part of the system of business management, and all managerial activity in a firm should be directed toward making the marketing process more effective.

This philosophy may be seen in the framework of the marketing process, which, to be effective, requires that a firm first identify, study, and measure its markets. Management then has four elements—its product, price system, channels of distribution structure, and promotional activities—which can be used to build a program to reach its markets. The firm is seeking to achieve the most effective marketing mix—that is, the best possible combination of the four ingredients. Throughout these four areas, especially in channel structure and promotion, management makes extensive use of another element—the human factor. Manpower considerations often are paramount in marketing decisions. At all stages in the marketing process, management should use marketing research as an aid.

This framework of the marketing process is reflected generally in the organization of the book's content. The text is divided into eight parts. Part 1 serves as an introduction and includes a chapter on the role of systems and the management process in marketing. Part 2 is devoted to an analysis of the consumer and the industrial markets. Population, income, and buyer behavior are analyzed as factors affecting the market for products.

Parts 3 through 6 deal with the development and operation of a marketing program, and each of these parts covers one of the above-mentioned four components of the marketing mix. In Part 3 various topics related to the product itself are discussed, including product planning and development, product-line policies and strategies, and several characteristics of a product such as branding and packaging. A firm's price system is the subject of Part 4, where we study pricing objectives, price determination in practice, and some major price policies and strategies. Part 5 covers the distribution structure. Retailing and wholesaling institutions are described and appraised. Consideration is given to the selection of channels of distribution, the selection of individual middlemen, and the ever-present conflict within and among marketing channels. The management of physical distribution, in which this activity is viewed as a system of product flow, is studied in a separate chapter. Part 6 is devoted to the total promotional program, including the advertising and the personal selling programs.

The major portion of the book pertains to the *domestic* marketing of *manufactured goods*. In the interest of completeness, however, Part 7 is devoted to marketing fundamentals as they are applied in the special fields of international marketing and the marketing of services.

Part 8 covers marketing information systems, marketing planning, and the evaluation of the marketing program. Included are such topics as marketing research, demand forecasting; and marketing cost analysis. Chapter 29 is devoted to consumerism and marketing's social responsibility. Chapter 30—the final chapter—is an appraisal of the role of marketing in the economy and a look to the future in this field.

Special attention has been devoted to the preparation of the discussion questions found at the end of each chapter. These questions generally cannot be answered "right out of the book." Instead, they are intended to be thought provoking and to serve as an aid in applying the material in the chapter. Some of the questions require outside fieldwork, and thus have the merit of introducing the students to practical business applications of the textbook fundamentals.

Another feature of *Fundamentals of Marketing* is the inclusion of short cases at the end of each of the eight parts in the text. Each one focuses on a specific issue related to topic covered in the text. These cases serve as both a teaching tool and study guide. In line with the managerial approach in this book, the cases provide an opportunity for problem analysis and decision making by the student.

To complement this book as a teaching and learning tool, a study guide and a timely collection of readings has been prepared by Professors Jack L. Taylor, Jr., and James F. Robb (Portland State University). To give students a more realistic taste of a marketing executive's job, a marketing game built around the ski manufacturing industry has been developed by Professors Charles L. Hinkle and Richard C. Koza (University of Colorado).

Many people—business executives, publishers, students, present and past colleagues, and other professors—have contributed greatly to this book. Many of these debts are acknowledged in footnotes and other references in the text. However, for reviewing the manuscript and offering suggestions for its improvement, I especially want to thank Professors Bjorn Bergman (Castleton State College), Louis P. Bucklin (University of California at Berkeley), Richard C. Casey (San Jose City College), Cyril Cope (Centralia College), William Dickson (Green River Junior College), W. Richard Donaldson (County College of Morris), Stanley Garfunkel (Queensborough Community College), Barnett Greenberg (Georgia State University), Thomas I. Kindel (The University of Texas at Arlington), Richard Kuklis (University of Vermont), Thomas O'Connor (Louisiana State University at New Orleans), Sadaomi Oshikawa (University of Washington), Grover O. Phillips (Sam Houston University), Margaret Reid (Western New England College), Frank Roberts (California State University at Fullerton), Stephen E. Schneider (Laney College), Richard Skinner (Kent State University), James H. Underwood (Louisiana State University at Baton Rouge), and Philip R. Cateora, my colleague at the University of Colorado. Several of the cases were written by other professors, and in each instance the authorship is identified.

William J. Stanton

PART ONE

MODERN
MARKETING

MARKETING IN THE ECONOMY

Most of us probably consider ourselves rather well informed on the subject of marketing. After all, we watch television commercials and see how advertisers are trying to persuade us to buy. We purchase products on a self-service basis in a supermarket. We observe the quality of personal selling as we buy our clothes or gasoline. Many of us have friends who "can get it for us wholesale," or we ourselves may be shrewd shoppers who can ferret out bargains. Some us have worked as salesclerks in retail stores. In short, everybody knows something about marketing. It is on this perilous base of a little knowledge that we begin our study.

NATURE AND SCOPE OF MARKETING

While most people probably do know a little something about marketing, the word itself has often been misunderstood and used loosely even by those in the field. When a salesman or sales manager speaks of marketing, he is actually talking about selling, an advertising account executive means advertising, and a department store manager means retailing or merchandising. Each of these people is talking about *one part* of the total marketing activity.

NARROW INTERPRETATION

The American Marketing Association says that marketing is "the performance of business activities that direct the flow of goods and services from producer to consumer or user."[1] In its comments, the committee suggests a somewhat broader meaning than this, and for the purpose of modern marketing, a broader definition is certainly needed. Marketing processes begin long before the goods go into production. Marketing decisions must be made regarding the product and its market, its pricing, and its promotion. Should the product even be made? How should it be packaged and labeled? What is the composition of its potential market? What will be the initial price? Just as marketing does not begin at the end of the production line, it does not end with the final sale. The customer must be satisfied if we expect his repeat business or if we want him to speak well of our company. Thus a product guarantee and considerable servicing may be required after the sale is made.

This narrow definition reflects the production orientation which has permeated so much of American business. Products have been designed by engineers, manufactured by production men, priced by accountants, and then given to sales managers to sell. Just *building* a good product will not in itself result in a company's success, nor will it have much bearing on consumer welfare. The product must be *marketed* to consumers before its full value can be realized. Aggressive marketing practices have been largely responsible for the high material standard of living in America.

MARKETING AND THE STANDARD OF LIVING

Possibly the most expressive, all-encompassing, and yet short statement of modern marketing was made some years ago by Paul Mazur. He said that marketing is the delivery of a standard of living to society.[2] Malcolm McNair of Harvard added an important concept when he amended Mazur's fine definition to read that marketing is the *creation* and delivery of a standard of living to society.

SYSTEMS DEFINITION USED IN THIS BOOK

This broad concept of marketing gives us a feel for the "big picture," but it is not precise enough. Consequently, the following definition will be used in this text. *Marketing* is a total system of interacting business activities designed to plan, price, promote, and distribute want-satisfying products and services to present and potential customers.

> Marketing is:
> A system: A system of business activities
> Designed to: plan, price, promote, and distribute (the action)
> Object of the action: want-satisfying goods and services
> Beneficiaries of the action: the market—present and potential household consumers or industrial users

---

[1] Committee on Definitions, *Marketing Definitions: A Glossary of Marketing Terms,* American Marketing Association, Chicago, 1960, p. 15.

[2] See Paul Mazur, "Does Distribution Cost Enough?" *Fortune,* November, 1947, p. 138.

This concrete definition has several important implications. First, it is a managerial definition rather than a legalistic or economic one. Second, the entire system of business action should be market- or customer-oriented. Customers' wants must be recognized and satisfied effectively. Third, the definition suggests that marketing is a dynamic business process—a total, integrated process—rather than a fragmented assortment of institutions and functions. Marketing is not any one activity, nor is it exactly the sum of several; rather, it is the result of the *interaction* of many activities. Fourth, the marketing program starts with the germ of a product idea and does not end until the customer's wants are completely satisfied, which may be some time after the sale is made. Furthermore, market programming should be done with a maximum of effectiveness and a minimum of cost. Finally, the definition implies that to be successful, marketing must maximize profitable sales *over the long run.* Thus, customers must be satisfied in order for a company to get the repeat business which ordinarily is so vital to success.

Marketing and related terms. Sometimes marketing is confused or misunderstood in relation to some other terms, especially selling, merchandising, and distribution. Marketing is the comprehensive concept. The others are each only one part—one activity—in the total marketing system.

Marketing is:	The total of what we are talking about.
Selling is:	One part of promotion and promotion is one part of the total marketing program.
Merchandising is:	Product planning—the internal company planning to get the right product or service to the market at the right time, and at the right price, and in the right colors and sizes.
Distribution is:	Market coverage—the retailing and wholesaling structure—the channels used to get the product to its market.
Physical distribution is:	Materials-flow activities such as transportation, warehousing, and inventory control.

BROADER, SOCIETAL DIMENSIONS OF MARKETING

The systems concept of marketing is essentially a management activity in business firms. Of course, it is true that the marketing system in a company is influenced by external factors—for instance, economic conditions, customers' behavior, technology, and legal forces. In fact, it is marketing's job to evaluate and capitalize on changes and opportunities in this external environment. Nevertheless, our systems definition is oriented mainly toward marketing *within* a business enterprise. And because this book deals with the management of marketing as a business activity in a firm, this systems definition is useful for our purposes.

However, marketing is not solely a business activity. We need also to recognize that marketing has a social dimension far broader than may be apparent in the above systems definition. In fact, a societal perspective is more meaningful and

truly descriptive of marketing today. Any interpersonal or interorganizational relationship involving an exchange (a transaction) is marketing. That is, *the essence of
marketing is a transaction.* Consequently, marketing occurs anytime one social
unit strives to exchange something of value with another social unit.[3]

Within this societal perspective then, (1) the marketers, and (2) what it is they are
marketing, and (3) their potential markets all assume new and far broader dimensions. The category of *marketers* might include, in addition to business firms, such
diverse social units as: *(a)* a political party trying to market its candidate to the
public; *(b)* the director of an art museum providing new exhibits to generate greater
attendance and financial support; *(c)* a labor union which markets its ideas or
terms to its members and the company management. A professor is doing a
marketing job when he attempts to make his course interesting and meaningful
to his students. A young man is engaged in marketing when he tries to persuade
a girl to date him or marry him.[4]

In addition to the range of items normally considered as products and services,
in a broader sense *what* is being marketed might include: *(a)* ideas, such as
reducing air pollution, stopping smoking, or contributing to the Red Cross drive;
or, *(b)* people, such as a new football coach or a political candidate.

In a broad sense, *target markets* include more than the consumers of products,
services, and ideas. Thus, a state university's market includes the legislators who
provide funds, the citizens residing near the university who may be affected by
student and university activities, and the alumni. A business firm's market may
include government regulatory agencies, environmentalists, and local tax
assessors.[5]

---

[3]See Philip Kotler, "A Generic Concept of Marketing," *Journal of Marketing,* April, 1972, pp.
46–54; also see Philip Kotler and Sidney J. Levy, "Broadening the Concept of Marketing,"
Journal of Marketing, January, 1969, pp. 10–15; Philip Kotler and Gerald Zaltman, "Social
Marketing: An Approach to Planned Social Change," *Journal of Marketing,* July, 1971, pp. 3–12;
Leslie Dawson, "Marketing Science in the Age of Aquarius," *Journal of Marketing,* July, 1971,
pp. 66–72.

[4]For a small sample of studies illustrating the broader view of marketing, see Adel I. El-Ansary
and Oscar E. Kramer, Jr., "Social Marketing: The Family Planning Experience," *Journal of
Marketing,* July, 1973, pp. 1–7; John U. Farley and Harold J. Leavitt, "Marketing and Population
Problems," *Journal of Marketing,* July, 1971, pp. 28–33; William A. Mindak and H. Malcolm
Bybee, "Marketing's Application to Fund Raising," *Journal of Marketing,* July, 1971, pp. 13–18;
Steven A. Baumgarten, Santosh K. Choudhury, Tanniru R. Rao, and L. Winston Ring, "Study of
Nursing Homes: The Patient as Consumer," in Fred C. Allvine (ed.), *Combined Proceedings:
1971 Spring and Fall Conferences,* Series No. 33, American Marketing Association, Chicago,
1972, pp. 452–456; and Benson Shapiro, "Marketing for Nonprofit Organizations," *Harvard
Business Review,* September–October, 1937, pp. 123–132.

[5]For an opposite point of view which questions the propriety of this broader meaning of
marketing and which is concerned about the possible loss of marketing's identity, see David J.
Luck, "Broadening the Concept of Marketing—Too Far," *Journal of Marketing,* July, 1969, pp.
53–55.

On the question of whether there is an identity crisis in marketing—are we stressing the
management of the technology of marketing (product planning, promotion, etc.) rather than the
social-process concept, see Daniel J. Sweeney, "Marketing: Management Technology or
Social Process?" *Journal of Marketing,* October, 1972, pp. 3–10.

HISTORICAL DEVELOPMENT OF MARKETING

In this brief historical review, we shall see how marketing is born and grows as a society moves from a home handicraft economy of self-sufficiency into a socioeconomic system which involves a division of labor, factory industrialization, and urbanization of the population.

In an agrarian or backwoods economy, the people are largely self-sufficient. They grow their own food, make their own clothes, and build their own houses and tools. There is very little specialization of labor and very little need for trade of any sort. As time passes, however, the concept of division of labor begins to evolve, and craftsmen concentrate on the production of the item in which they excel. This results in each man producing more than he needs of some items and less than he needs of others. Whenever a person makes more than he wants or wants more than he makes, the foundation is laid for *trade,* and trade is the heart of marketing.

As exchange begins to develop in agrarian economies, it is on a simple basis. Most businesses are small-scale endeavors with no specialization in management. The emphasis is largely on production, and little or no attention is devoted to marketing. In fact, the general practice is to hand-make products to order.

In the next step in the historical evolution of marketing, small producers begin to manufacture their goods in larger quantities in anticipation of future orders. Further division of labor occurs as a type of businessman develops to help sell the increased output. This businessman—who acts as an intermediary between the producers and consumers—is the middleman. To facilitate communication and buying and selling, the various interested parties tend to assemble geographically. Trading centers are thus formed. There are nations or parts of nations in the world today going through these various stages of economic development. We may conclude that advancement and refinements in marketing generally go hand in hand with advancements in a civilization.

Modern marketing in the United States was born with the Industrial Revolution. Concurrent with, or as a by-product of, the Industrial Revolution there was a growth of urban centers and a decline in rural population. Home handicraft operations moved into factories, and people came to the cities to work in the factories. Service industries grew to supply the daily needs of factory workers, who were no longer self-sufficient. Marketing remained an infant during the last half of the nineteenth century and the first two decades of the twentieth. Emphasis was on the growth of manufacturing enterprises because the market demand generally exceeded the available supply of products.

Actually, mass marketing was a prerequisite for successful mass production. Only with a system of mass marketing could factories operate at optimum rates of output and thus enjoy the economies of scale. As the factory economy became more complex, the channels through which trade flowed became longer. Better methods had to be devised to market the industrial output. The growth of specialists in marketing was a natural step in this evolutionary development.

PRESENT-DAY IMPORTANCE OF MARKETING

Modern marketing came of age after World War I, when the words "surplus" and "overproduction" became increasingly common in our economics vocabulary. Since about 1920, with the exception of World War II and the immediate postwar periods, a strong buyers' market has existed in this country. That is, the available supply of products and services has far surpassed effective demand. There has been relatively little difficulty in producing most of these goods; the real problem has been in marketing them.

Ordinarily there cannot be a high level of economic activity without a correspondingly high level of marketing activity. During recession periods, people soon realize that it is a slowdown in marketing activity which is forcing cutbacks in production. (The deeper social, economic, and political factors which cause the slowdown in marketing activities are outside the scope of this book.) It becomes evident that in our economy "nothing happens until somebody sells something," and there are urgent requests for increased marketing not for increased production.

IMPORTANCE OF MARKETING IN OUR SOCIOECONOMIC SYSTEM

Some quantitative measures may help to point up the importance of marketing in our socioeconomic system. The gross national product—the measure of the total goods and services produced in the United States—rose from about $285 billion in 1950 to well over $1 *trillion* by 1975. It has been marketing's task to move the mountain of goods and nongovernmental services which constitute the bulk of the gross national product. There has been a tremendous increase in the volume of goods and services produced in the United States in the past 25 years, even after allowing for the inflation of prices. Also, there is every evidence that the economy will continue to grow and will require even more effective marketing.

Another indication of the importance of marketing in the economy is the number of people employed in the field. Between one-fourth and one-third of the civilian labor force is engaged in marketing activities. This includes all employees in retailing, wholesaling, transportation, warehousing, and communications industries and all people employed in marketing departments of manufacturers and engaged in marketing activities for financial, service, agricultural, mining, and other industries classified essentially as nonmarketing. Furthermore, over the past century jobs in marketing have increased at a much more rapid rate than jobs in production. Harold Barger pointed out that the number of people engaged in retailing and wholesaling activities increased more than twelve times from 1870 to 1950, as contrasted with a threefold increase in the number of production workers during the same period.[6] The great increase in the number of marketing workers is a reflection of marketing's expanded role in the economy and the increased demand for marketing services.

A measure often used to indicate marketing's importance is its cost. On the average, about 50 cents out of the total retail dollar goes to cover marketing costs. Marketing costs should not be confused with marketing *profits*, however, nor should it be assumed that products and services would cost less if marketing activities were not performed.

An economy of abundance. A brief comparison of the American economy with economies found elsewhere in the world further demonstrates the importance of

---

[6]Harold Barger, *Distribution's Place in the American Economy since 1869*, Princeton University Press, Princeton, N.J., 1955, pp. 4–5.

marketing. The type of economy we have largely explains why marketing as we know it is so much an American phenomenon, both in practice and as a field of study. Ours is not a raw-materials, "underdeveloped" economy, nor is it any longer a subsistence economy. It is not an economy of state capitalism, as is found in Russia, nor is it similar to the Western European economy of cartels and small shopkeepers. It most certainly is not the static, perfectly competitive economy of classical economic theory.

Instead, ours is an economy of abundance. This means that as a nation we produce far beyond our subsistence needs. We have an adequate national disposable income and considerable discretionary purchasing power. We are under no necessary compulsion to consume all that is produced, but unless we do, a severe economic decline can set in. While marketing exists in every type of *modern* economy, it is an especially important foundation stone for successful business performance in a highly competitive economy of abundance.

American marketing activity has the task of encouraging the consumption of the vast output of goods and services of American industry. Although modern marketing has been successful to a reasonably high degree, it has not been greeted with equal joy in all quarters. There are still many scarce social and economic resources in our economy, and a number of respected students of our social, economic, and political systems have raised serious questions concerning the influence which marketing activities have on the allocation of these resources. The question they raise is whether too much marketing is leading to a misallocation of these resources—is marketing accepting its responsibility for guiding our economic abundance into socially desirable channels? Possibly we may have been so successful in promoting the consumption of automobiles, fashionable dresses, and outboard motors that we have overlooked other more basic values such as education, savings, or metropolitan services—slum clearance, sewage disposal, and the elimination of air and water pollution.

In *The Affluent Society,* Prof. John K. Galbraith raised the resource-allocation question in a slightly different fashion.[7] He said that we are investing too much in things and not enough in people, that we are producing too much of some things and not enough of others. Galbraith also suggested that we decrease our emphasis on production and devote greater attention to a more rational use of what we produce. (This suggestion, it seems, would have the unfortunate effect of forcing us to relinquish greater economic growth only because we have not learned to use our abundance wisely.)

David M. Potter, in his book, *People of Plenty,* examined some of the influences which our economy of abundance has exerted upon the life and attitudes of the American people.[8] His analysis shows how the influence of abundance cuts across the fields of the behavioral sciences, history, and political science, how it has remade our social structure, and how it has made democracy in America different from democracy anywhere else in the world. He also points out that we have made mistakes in trying to get the American way of life adopted in foreign countries, largely because we do not understand how economic abundance has influenced our development. Truly the question of marketing and its influence on the allocation of resources in an economy of abundance is a very important one.

---

[7]John K. Galbraith, *The Affluent Society,* Houghton Mifflin Company, Boston, 1958.
[8]David M. Potter, *People of Plenty,* The University of Chicago Press, Chicago, 1954.

IMPORTANCE IN THE INDIVIDUAL FIRM

The vital importance of marketing in the successful operation of an individual firm was suggested in our definition of marketing. Marketing considerations are today the most critical factors in business planning and decision making. The National Association of Manufacturers put this cogently when it said:[9]

> In this exciting age of change, marketing is the beating heart of many operations. It must be considered a principal reason for corporate existence. The modern concept of marketing recognizes its role as a direct contributor to profits, as well as sales volume.
>
> No longer can a company just figure out how many widgets it can produce and then go ahead and turn them out. To endure in this highly competitive change-infested market, a company must first determine what it can sell, how much it can sell, and what approaches must be used to entice the wary customer. The president cannot plan; the production manager cannot manage; the purchasing agent cannot purchase; the chief financial officer cannot budget, and the engineer and designer cannot design until the basic market determinations have been made.

Many organizational departments in a company are essential to its growth, but marketing is still the sole revenue-producing activity. This fact sometimes seems to be taken for granted by other executives such as production managers who use these revenues, and financial executives who are responsible for managing them.

Several economic forces are pushing marketing to the fore in American business and industry. Product lines are becoming more diversified. Stiffer competition is coming both from substitute products and from directly comparable goods. Production operations are growing more costly and complex. Markets are ever growing and rapidly changing. More and more money is needed to develop and support marketing programs. Thus risks are increased, and the ability to make proper marketing decisions is at a premium

MARKETING IN AN ERA OF SHORTAGES

In the early 1970s many industries in the U.S. were faced rather abruptly with an economic situation which was quite new to management—there were shortages of materials with which to make their products and operate their factories, stores, and other institutions. Many students of the situation have been advancing the idea that the U.S. has reached the end of an era—characterized by economist Kenneth Boulding as a "cowboy economy"—an era which reflected the frontier philosophy of unlimited resources where a person could use products and waste them as he pleased.

The oil shortage in 1973 which triggered the so-called energy crisis generally epitomized the shortage situation. However, in the mid-1970s shortages seemed to occur suddenly not only in oil-based industries (plastics and other petrochemicals), but also in many other industries (wood, paper products, farm products, for example) where the shortages were not triggered by cutbacks in energy availability. This

---

[9]As quoted in "An Historic Marketing Paper," *Sales Management,* Mar. 20, 1959, p. 7.

is not the place to argue the political and economic causes underlying the shortages, but we should recognize the impact they have on marketing in our economy.

In preceding sections we made statements to the effect that for most products the real problem is marketing them, not producing them, and that marketing considerations are the most critical factors in business planning. In many industries today those statements must be modified. For the first time in about 60 years (with the exception of the World War II years) management is worried about how to *make* the products.

At the same time in most of those industries, management still has to worry about how to *market* the output. Industries faced with shortages will *not* find their marketing task easier, even though some executives have the short-sighted idea of "why spend money on marketing when we can sell all we can produce." Most firms still face substantial challenges in marketing. Competition within industries and between industries is still intense in most cases. Essentially the U.S. is still an economy of abundance, and consumers still have considerable disposable income.

It is just that our priorities are changing, and a company must be alert to adapt its marketing programs to these changes. In the 1950s and 1960s, for example, a guiding marketing strategy was to expand the product assortment—that is, to market a full line. In an abrupt about-face in the 1970s, companies have been slimming down their product mix by eliminating low-margin products and concentrating on the more profitable items. In the same vein, management should examine other parts of its marketing program with an eye toward pruning out unprofitable, wasteful segments. In advertising, for instance, total expenditures might be reduced, and a firm might shift from the direct-action type of ad (buy our product now) to the institutional and public-service type of advertising. Managing a sales force is different where the sales job is (1) to allocate a scarce supply among existing customers as contrasted with the job (2) of creative selling to develop new accounts. Management also might remember that shortages also create new marketing opportunities. Less building heat means more sweaters, and less gasoline means more bicycles.

Environmental forces such as inflation and shortages are changing the life style of the U.S. consumers in many instances. Looking to the next few years, consumers may very well decide to live more simply, cut back on their buying, and generally conserve. These attitudes carry significant implications for the marketing programs in many firms. At the time this is being written (1974) it is still too early to predict detailed changes. But we can rest assured that changes there will be and challenges there will be in marketing programs in the U.S.

THE MARKETING CONCEPT

As business administrators recognize that marketing is vitally important to the success of a firm and as they realize that a business is a marketing organization, an entirely new way of business thinking is evolving. It is called the *marketing concept,* and it has developed as production- and engineering-oriented firms have changed into market-oriented structures.

The marketing concept is based on three fundamental beliefs. First, all company planning, policies, and operations should be oriented toward the customer. Second, *profitable* sales volume should be the goal of a firm. Third, all marketing activities in a firm should be organizationally integrated and coordinated. In its fullest sense, the marketing concept is a philosophy of business which states that the customer's want-satisfaction is the economic and social justification of a company's existence. Consequently, all company activities in production, engineering, and finance, as well as in marketing, must be devoted first to determining what the customer's wants are and then to satisfying those wants while still making a reasonable profit.

A marketing executive at the General Electric Company, one of the first companies formally to recognize and activate the marketing concept, expressed the philosophy nicely when he said:[10]

> We feel that marketing is a fundamental business philosophy. This definition recognizes marketing's functions and methods of organizational structuring as *only the implementation* of the philosophy. These things are not, in themselves, the philosophy.
>
> Fundamental to this philosophy is the recognition and acceptance of a customer-oriented way of doing business. Under marketing the customer becomes the fulcrum, the pivot point about which the business moves in operating for the balanced best interests of all concerned. . . .
>
> The second fundamental on which the marketing philosophy rests is that it is rooted in the profit concept, not the volume concept. (I am not eliminating the use of volume as a rewarding way of obtaining profits from the efficiency of the service rendered; rather, I am referring to the profitless volume or volume - for - the - sake - of volume - alone concept.)

The marketing concept points up sharply the following contrasts between marketing and selling:

Selling	Marketing
1. Emphasis is on the product.	1. Emphasis is on customers' wants.
2. Company first makes the product and then figures out how to sell it profitably.	2. Company first determines what the customers want, and then the firm figures out how to profitably make and deliver a product to satisfy those wants.
3. Internal, company orientation.	3. External, market orientation.
4. Emphasizes company (seller's) needs.	4. Emphasizes market (buyers') needs.

The marketing concept calls for a management reorientation regarding what business a company is in. Typically, when an executive is asked, "What business are you in?" the answer is, "We make _____," or "We sell _____." These executives must start thinking in terms of what benefits they market—what needs (wants) are they satisfying.

---

[10]Fred J. Borch, "The Marketing Philosophy as a Way of Business Life," *The Marketing Concept: Its Meaning to Management,* American Management Association, Marketing Series, no. 99., New York, 1957, pp. 3–5.

In this vein, Universal Studios markets entertainment, rather than making movies. Union Pacific markets transportation rather than running a railroad. Mountain Bell markets a communication system rather than operating a telephone company. The Lennox Company provides home comfort, instead of making furnaces and air conditioners. The Head Ski Company should not think of itself as being in the business of making skis. Rather, it markets recreation, exercise, relaxation, ego-building, a chance to meet fun people, etc.

We hope that management will *not* implement the marketing concept as did the company in Fig. 1-1.

DISTINCTION BETWEEN THE MARKETING CONCEPT AND MARKETING

The marketing concept is a philosophy, an attitude, or a course of business *thinking,* while marketing is a process or a course of business *action.* Naturally, the way of thinking determines the course of action.

MARKETING MANAGEMENT: THE APPLICATION OF THE MARKETING CONCEPT

For a business enterprise to realize the full fruits of the marketing concept, the philosophy must be translated into practice. This means that (1) the marketing activities in a firm must be better organized, coordinated, and managed, and (2) the chief marketing executive must be accorded a more important role in total company planning and policy making than has been generally true in the past. As these two changes take place, we see emerging in American business the idea of marketing management. *Marketing management* is the marketing concept in action.

FOUR-STAGE EVOLUTION OF MARKETING MANAGEMENT

Marketing management has been evolving in American business since the Industrial Revolution. Roughly, it has gone through three stages of development, and a fourth era is emerging. However, the managerial philosophies and practices of many companies are still in one of the earlier stages. Only a few firms as yet have the organization and philosophy which are characteristic of the most advanced developmental stage of marketing management.

Production stage. During the first stage, a company typically is production-oriented. The executives in production and engineering shape the company's objectives and planning. The operating philosophies emphasize mass production of simplified product lines at low unit costs. The function of the sales department is to sell this output at a price set by production and financial executives.

Early in this period of development the marketing activity is organized in a simple fashion. Manufacturers have sales departments headed by a sales manager whose major responsibility is to operate a sales force. Advertising, marketing research, and sales analysis are generally unknown. Production planning and sales budgeting are handled in other departments.

Later during this first period, expanding markets typically encourage a manufacturer to expand into specialized marketing activities. Thus, separate organizational

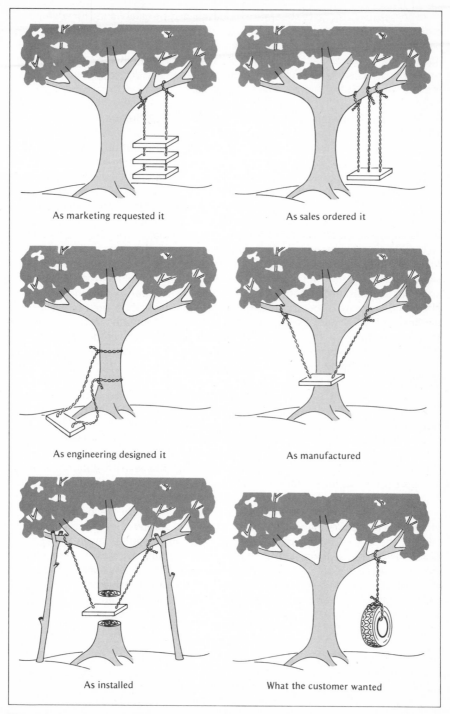

As marketing requested it

As sales ordered it

As engineering designed it

As manufactured

As installed

What the customer wanted

Figure 1-1

divisions, each assigned to separate executives, may be established for advertising, marketing research, export sales, etc. The department responsible for selling the company's output is called the "sales department," and its chief executive typically has the title of sales manager or vice president of sales. This form of marketing organization, as shown in Fig. 1-2, predominated in the United States until about the start of the Great Depression in the 1930s.

Sales stage. The depression made it quite clear that the main problem in the American economy no longer was one of being able to manufacture or grow enough products. Rather, the problem was in selling this output. Just producing a better mousetrap was no assurance of its market success; the product had to be sold. Thus, we entered a period during which selling and sales management were accorded new respect and responsibilities. Sales performance, however, still was measured primarily by the *sales volume* generated, and not by *marketing profits*.

During this stage a better understanding of the scope of sales management results in two significant organizational changes in many firms. See Fig. 1-3. First, all marketing activities such as advertising and marketing research are grouped under one marketing executive, although he is still typically called *sales* manager or vice president of *sales*. Second, activities such as sales training, product servicing, and sales analysis, which were formerly carried out in departments outside sales or marketing, now are put under the marketing umbrella. While each of the several divisions (advertising, sales analysis, etc.) may have a separate manager, all report to the chief sales executive. This type of organization—and the sales era itself—generally extended from the 1930s well into the 1950s, although no specific dates sharply define any of the four eras.[11]

Marketing stage. In the third stage of the evolutionary process, companies embrace the concept of integrated marketing management, directed toward the twin goals of a customer orientation and *profitable* sales volume. Attention is focused on marketing rather than on selling, and the top executive in this area is called a marketing manager, director of marketing, or vice president of marketing. He is aligned organizationally with the top executives in production, finance, and personnel, to work with the president as the company's top planning and policy-making group.

In this stage, several activities which traditionally were the province of the production manager, financial manager, or other executives become the responsibility of the marketing manager (see Fig. 1-4). For instance, inventory control, warehousing, and aspects of product planning are often turned over to the marketing manager. Obviously he must coordinate his efforts with those of the production manager and the top financial executive, but in the final analysis the marketing manager makes the decisions regarding packaging, design, color, and other product features. The position of the marketing manager is epitomized in General

---

[11]The conceptual foundations for scientific sales management and modern marketing management actually were laid in the literature of the 1920s and earlier, where we find a direct application of Frederick W. Taylor's scientific management concepts to early sales management. See Bernard J. La Londe and Edward J. Morrison, "Marketing Management Concepts Yesterday and Today," *Journal of Marketing*, January, 1967, pp. 9–13.

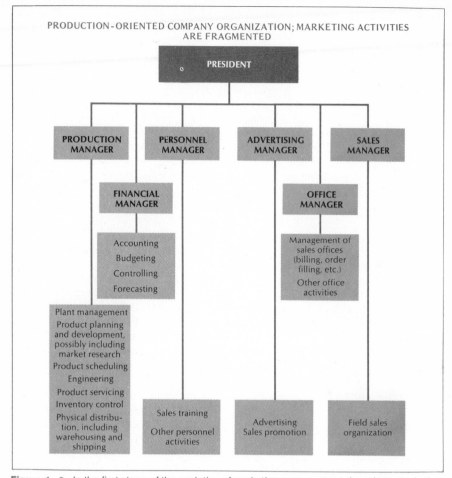

PRODUCTION-ORIENTED COMPANY ORGANIZATION; MARKETING ACTIVITIES ARE FRAGMENTED

Figure 1-2. In the first stage of the evolution of marketing management, there is no marketing department, and sales management involves only operating a sales force. When managerial responsibility for marketing is fragmented, consider the problems in planning, coordinating, and directing such marketing activities as advertising, sales forecasting, product planning, and personal selling.

Electric's philosophy that he should be introduced at the *beginning* rather than at the *end* of the production cycle. In this way he can integrate marketing into each stage of the operations.

We are now living in this third stage in the evolution of marketing management. The marketing concept has generally been adopted by both large and medium-size companies. In large industrial firms, for example, one typical study concluded that (1) the marketing division is being used as a training grounds for many top executives; (2) the marketing manager participates extensively in major policy decisions in virtually all companies studied; (3) the span of responsibilities of the marketing executive has greatly increased; and (4) his executive status and relative pay level

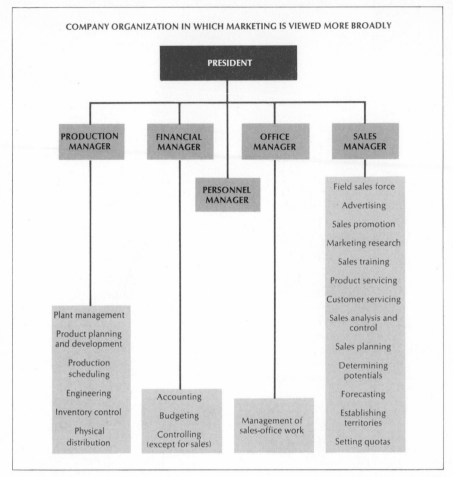

COMPANY ORGANIZATION IN WHICH MARKETING IS VIEWED MORE BROADLY

Figure 1–3. In this stage of the evolution of marketing management, most marketing activities are under the control of the sales manager. The personnel manager no longer handles sales training. But note that the production manager is still in charge of production scheduling, inventory control, and physical distribution, while the office manager still controls management of sales-office work.

have increased significantly.[12] Later studies show, however, that *(a)* consumer goods companies have tended to implement the marketing concept to a greater extent than have industrial goods manufacturers, and *(b)* large companies have tended to adopt and implement the marketing concept to a greater degree than is true in small and medium-size firms.[13]

In firms which have fully embraced the marketing concept, the entire company becomes a marketing organization. This position is reached when the attitudes of a company's executives change so that the entire company works to develop, man-

---

[12]Stanford L. Johnson and John J. Tenge, Jr., "The Man behind the Marketing Concept," *Sales/Marketing Today*, June, 1967, pp. 14–17.

[13]Carlton P. McNamara, "The Present Status of the Marketing Concept." *Journal of Marketing*,

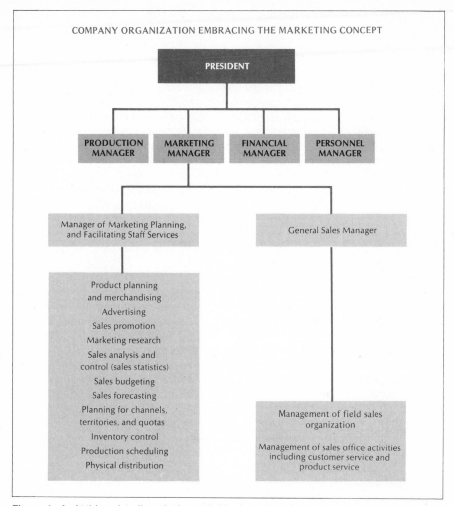

Figure 1-4. At this point all marketing activities have been integrated under a single marketing manager. Organizationally, the company has the "marketing concept."

ufacture, and sell a product from the marketing point of view. The president of the Burroughs Corporation caught the spirit of this when he said, "Any company is nothing but a marketing organization." Marketing becomes the basic motivating force for the entire firm, and marketing influences all short-term and long-range company policies. A top executive at Sylvania Electric Products observed: "Marketing faces the challenge of setting the leadership pace for the entire

January, 1972, pp. 50–57. For some examples of the marketing concept at work in specific companies, see "Why Philip Morris Thrives," *Business Week,* Jan. 27, 1973, p. 48; Don Korn, "The Best **?!≠z@ Sales Department in the Railroad Industry (Illinois Central Gulf R.R.)," *Sales Management,* Oct. 16, 1972, p. 21; "How Kodak Will Exploit Its New Instamatic," *Business Week,* Mar. 18, 1972, p. 46.

organization. . . . Marketing is charged with charting the future course a company must take."[14] The president of the Pepsi-Cola Company said, "Our business is the business of marketing."

How well the many companies have actually implemented the concept, however, is still a moot question. We know that there are many forms and degrees of market orientation. Probably in many cases a company, while using the appropriately fashionable titles and other external trappings, is still paying little more than lip service to the concept. Management may believe in the concept and have adopted a marketing attitude, but may not have established a marketing structure and a formal marketing program. In a revealing study conducted among members of the New York Sales Executives Club—and this group includes many of the nation's largest companies—the findings indicated that most of the firms had failed (1) to place all marketing functions under a single marketing executive and (2) to coordinate these activities to reach long- and short-range goals.[15] (Marketing functions as identified in this study were advertising, sales, product planning, marketing research, customer credit, inventory planning, and transportation.) Unfortunately, in too many cases the misunderstanding endures that "marketing" is just a fancy name for selling.

As one might expect, the full implementation of the marketing concept will not be accomplished overnight. The inflexibilities and conservatism of business plus human opposition to change will create some time spread between management's adoption of the concept and the fulfillment of all the consequent necessary organizational adjustments. General Electric executives have estimated that it took over five years to realign that corporation, once the decision was made to adopt the marketing concept.

The key to implementing the marketing concept successfully is a favorable attitude on the part of top management. As an executive of the Chase Manhattan Bank stated, "Marketing begins with top management. Only top management can provide the climate, the discipline, and the leadership required for a successful marketing program. Top management must know the customers and the prospects; it must set the objectives, establish the policies, develop the plans, and create the organization."[16]

In summarizing the organizational implications in the concept, a top marketing executive at the International Minerals and Chemical Corporation warned.[17]

But a company cannot become customer conscious by edict. Since all organizations tend to emulate their leader, it is most important that the head of the business be thoroughly customer conscious. There can only be one marketing head in any business and that must be the president. He can develop a mood, an atmosphere,

---

[14]Alfred C. Veibranz, "Marketing's Role in Company Growth," *MSU Business Topics,* Autumn, 1967, p. 49.

[15]Robert F. Vizza, Thomas F. Chambers, and Edward J. Cook, *Adoption of the Marketing Concept—Fact or Fiction?* Sales Executives Club of New York, New York, 1967. Also see B. Charles Ames, "Trappings vs. Substance in Industrial Marketing," *Harvard Business Review,* July–August, 1970. pp. 93–102.

[16]"The Marketing Executive: Industry's New Crown Prince," *News Front,* August, 1963, p. 30.

[17]Anthony E. Cascino, "Organizational Implications of the Marketing Concept," in Eugene J. Kelley and William Lazer (eds.), *Managerial Marketing Perspectives and Viewpoints,* 3d ed., Richard D. Irwin, Inc., Homewood, Ill., 1967, p. 346.

and an *esprit de corps* reflecting the pre-eminence of the customer that permeates every nook and corner of the company.

Let it be clearly understood that we are *not* saying that marketing executives should hold the supreme position in a firm. In saying that marketing should be the foundation stone for company planning, we mean only that marketing must be fully integrated into a company's management. The marketing concept does *not* imply that the president of a firm must come up through the marketing department, but only that he must be marketing-oriented.

Consumerism and the social responsibility stage. Social and economic conditions in the 1970s have led to the fourth stage in the evolution of marketing management—a period characterized by its societal orientation. It is becoming increasingly obvious that marketing executives must act in a socially responsible manner if they wish to succeed, or even survive, in this era. External pressures —consumer discontent rising from unfulfilled expectations, a concern for environmental and ecological problems, and political-legal forces—are influencing the marketing programs in countless firms.

Profit making will continue as a key goal in marketing management. However, in this fourth stage we can expect to see executives more concerned with long-run, rather than short-run, profit goals. Also, the concepts of social profit and social auditing will influence marketing managers.

Perhaps this fourth stage may be viewed more broadly as a human-orientation period—a time in which there will be a growing concern for the management of human resources in marketing. We sense a change in emphasis from materialism to humanism in our society. One mark of an affluent, economically well-developed society is a shift in consumption from products to services, and a shift in cultural emphasis from "things" to "people." In this fourth stage, marketing management must be concerned with creating and delivering a standard (a better quality) of *life,* rather than only a material standard of *living.*[18]

BROADENING THE MARKETING CONCEPT

The wave of consumer protests starting in the late 1960s—the rise of consumerism—is an indication to some people that there has been a failure to implement the marketing concept.[19] Others go so far as to suggest that the traditional marketing concept is an operational philosophy which conflicts with a firm's social responsiblity.[20]

---

[18]See Leslie M. Dawson, "The Human Concept: New Philosophy for Business," *Business Horizons,* December, 1969, pp. 29–38; Leonard L. Berry, "Marketing Challenges in the Age of People,"*MSU Business Topics,* Winter, 1972, pp. 7–13; and George Schwartz, "Marketing: The Societal Concept," *University of Washington Business Review,* Autumn, 1971, pp. 31–38.

[19]See Hiram C. Barksdale and Bill Darden, "Marketers' Attitudes toward the Marketing Concept," *Journal of Marketing,* October, 1971, pp. 29–36. Peter Drucker (a professor, management consultant, and certainly not unfriendly toward business) referred to consumerism as "the shame of the total marketing concept."

[20]See Martin L. Bell and William Emory, "The Faltering Marketing Concept," *Journal of Marketing,* October, 1971, pp. 37–42; and Laurence P. Feldman, "Societal Adaptation: A New Challenge for Marketing," *Journal of Marketing,* July, 1971, pp. 54–60.

From one point of view, these charges are true. A firm may totally satisfy its customers (in line with the marketing concept), while at the same time be adversely affecting society. To illustrate, a steel company in Ohio can be satisfying its customers in Colorado with the right product, reasonably priced, while at the same time this firm is polluting air and water in Ohio. Automobile manufacturers can satisfy consumers' short-run demand for cars, yet in the long run be creating urban traffic congestion and air pollution.

In the author's opinion, the marketing concept and a company's social responsibility can be quite compatible; they need not conflict. The key to this compatibility lies in extending the *breadth* and *time* dimensions in the definition of the marketing concept.

Regarding *breadth*—if a company's customers which are to be satisfied include not only the buyers of the firm's products, but also the consumers of any elements created by the firm, then the marketing concept and social responsibility in this firm can be compatible. Thus, in the preceding example, the Ohio steel mill has several consumer groups to satisfy—(1) the Colorado customers of the steel shipments, (2) the consumers of the impure air elements given off by the mill, (3) the recreational users of the local river affected by the mill waste matter, and (4) the community affected by employee traffic driving to and from work.

This broadening of the marketing concept is consistent with our previously developed broader, societal definition of marketing. There we recognized that a given marketer may have several different target markets.

Regarding the extended *time* dimension—we must view consumer satisfaction and profitable business as goals in the marketing concept to be achieved *over the long run.* If a company prospers in the long run, it must be doing a reasonably good job of satisfying its customers' current social and economic demands.

In conclusion, if the marketing concept and social responsibility are to be realistically compatible, management must strive for a balance over the long run among (1) satisfying the wants of product-buying customers, (2) satisfying the societal wants which are affected by the firm's activities, and (3) meeting the company's profit goals.

A more detailed discussion of consumers' protests and marketing's social responsibility is postponed until the final two chapters in this book. We can better evaluate these societal issues after we have an understanding of the marketing system and its institutions.

QUESTIONS AND PROBLEMS

1. "From one point of view marketing may be defined as the revenue-generating activity in a company. Production men use these revenues and financial executives manage them. However, the main job of the marketing man is to generate a satisfactory revenue over a long period of time." Discuss the meaning and implications of this quotation.
2. Marketing has been defined as the creation of time, place, and possession utilities. Explain the ideas involved in this definition.
3. What is the difference between marketing and selling?
4. For each of the following organizations, describe: (1) what is being marketed and (2) who is their target market.

    a. Miami Dolphins professional football team.
    b. United Automobile Workers labor union.
    c. Professor teaching a freshman sociology course.
    d. Resort hotel in Catskill Mountains (New York).
    e. Police department in your city.
    f. Denver Symphony Orchestra.

5. In line with the broader, societal concept of marketing, describe some of the ways in which nonbusiness organizations to which you belong are engaged in marketing activities.

6. One way of explaining the importance of marketing in our economy is to consider how we would live if there were no marketing facilities. Describe some of the ways in which your daily activities would be affected under such circumstances.

7. One writer has stated that any business has only two functions—marketing and innovation. How would you explain this statement to a student majoring in production management, accounting, finance, or personnel management?

8. How do you account for the fact that the number of workers engaged in wholesaling and retailing increased twelvefold between 1870 and 1950, as contrasted with only a threefold increase in the number of production workers during the same period?

9. Using a marketing approach (benefits provided or wants satisfied) for each of the following companies, answer the question: What business are you in?
    a. Polaroid (cameras)
    b. Playboy magazine
    c. First National Bank of _____.
    d. Texaco
    e. United Air Lines

10. Distinguish between the sales era and the marketing era in the development of marketing management.

11. Name some companies which you believe are still in the production or sales stage.

12. A 65-year-old vice president of a large midcontinental railroad was quoted as saying that in the railroad business, "marketing is just a new-fashioned idea of calling rates something different; really, marketing is nothing but determining rates." How would you answer him?

13. "The marketing concept does not imply that marketing executives will run the firm. The concept requires only that whoever is in top management be marketing-oriented." Give examples of how a production manager, company treasurer, or personnel manager can be marketing-oriented.

14. Name some companies or industries whose market position has declined considerably because of shifts in consumers' wants or behavioral patterns. What might these organizations have done to prevent their decline?

MARKETING SYSTEMS AND THE ROLE OF MANAGEMENT

In Chapter 1 we observed that the socioeconomic structure in the United States has evolved from an agrarian economy in a rural setting, through a production-oriented, subsistence-level economy in an urban society, and then through a sales-oriented economy into today's customer-oriented economy featuring an affluent society with discretionary purchasing power. In the current stage of this evolution, the marketing concept has emerged as a leading business philosophy. Marketing management, then, is the vehicle which business uses to activate the marketing concept. At the operational level the marketing concept—through marketing management—espouses the notion that an integrated, coordinated organization is essential as an efficient, profitable means of achieving the goal of customer want satisfaction.

This notion is consistent with our definition of marketing—it is a total *system* of business action, and not the fragmented assortment of institutions and activities which has passed as marketing in years gone by.

In this chapter we shall look a little more carefully at this systems concept of marketing. We shall observe that a firm operates its marketing systems within environmental constraints which are largely uncontrollable by it. It is management's role to develop, execute, and evaluate these systems. Finally, because management's responsibilities invariably involve problem solving and decision making, we shall briefly examine an orderly procedure in these activities.

SYSTEMS APPROACH TO MARKETING

An increasing number of companies are adopting the marketing concept and then implementing it with (1) a rational, fact-based approach to solving their marketing problems and (2) a coordinated effort in the management of their marketing programs. In effect, these companies are applying systems theory and analysis to their marketing activities.

WHAT IS A SYSTEM?

Webster's Seventh New Collegiate Dictionary defines a *system* as a "regularly interacting or interdependent group of items forming a unified whole." The concept of a system may be viewed in many contexts. The human body, for example, is a total organic system with digestive, circulatory, and muscular subsystems. We speak of a capitalistic or socialistic politico-economic system. In our natural environment we recognize the river systems and the solar system. While systems theory and analysis is a relatively new approach in the hands of marketing executives, the concept has been applied for many years by military men and engineers.

In the case of a marketing system, the "group of items" in the above definition includes such objects as products, price structures, channels of distribution, and promotional activities. The *systems approach* in marketing, then, is an orderly method of dealing with complex marketing problems under conditions of risk or uncertainty. Typically in these problems, multiple goals and alternative courses of action do exist.

SYNERGISM AND MARKETING SYSTEMS

Synergism is a related concept, useful in helping us to understand the systems approach in marketing. *Webster's* defines *synergism* as the "cooperative action of discrete agencies such that the total effect is greater than the sum of the effects taken independently." In other words, the effectiveness of managerial action in one area of a marketing program depends to a great extent upon decisions made with respect to related variables elsewhere in the program. Thus management cannot establish a price structure without considering the company's promotional program, and still expect to have optimum results in either area. The manufacturer's price of a product should be influenced by the nature of his advertising program, the extent to which retailers will be expected to promote the product, etc. The effectiveness of packaging and labeling is enhanced if a manufacturer's salesmen can persuade retailers to give the product a good display location. The degree to which a company achieves a synergistic result either in the firm as a whole or within its marketing program depends to a great extent upon the executives' ability to manage.

APPLICATIONS OF SYSTEMS CONCEPT OF MARKETING[1]

The systems approach is being applied, in both quantitative and qualitative ways, by companies in many parts of their marketing programs. Symbolic models have been built to describe, quantify, and qualitatively evaluate alternative marketing

---

[1]The remaining part of this section on the systems approach is adapted from Lee Adler,

strategies and programs. When a textile manufacturer color-harmonizes its linens, bedspreads, and towels, it is dealing with a product system. Customers buy need satisfaction through product benefits; that is, they buy beauty, not cosmetics, or the removal and polishing of metal, not a grinding wheel. By understanding this, a company can use the systems approach in product management to plan, develop, and market a related assortment of benefits rather than merely some products. In a later chapter we shall see that companies are using the systems approach in managing their marketing information, thus replacing the traditional notions of marketing research.

One of the first applications of systems theory in marketing was in the area of physical distribution management. Activities such as transportation, warehousing, order filling, inventory control, and materials handling were traditionally managed as separate activities. In many companies they were high-cost functions. However, they were nicely adaptive to quantitative analysis, and innovative features (container ships, forklift trucks, interstate highway systems, etc.) began to appear. These factors led beautifully to the development of computer-based systems which coordinated these formerly fragmented activities in a very effective manner. Also in distribution management, companies are using the systems approach to better integrate the activities of all business units—manufacturer, wholesalers, retailers—in their distribution channels. The above few examples and several other subsystems in marketing will be examined in more detail throughout this book.

BENEFITS AND PROBLEMS IN USE OF SYSTEMS APPROACH

Adler identified several benefits stemming from the use of the systems concept in marketing. It is a methodical orientation to problem solving, encompassing all aspects of a problem. The approach coordinates all appropriate marketing tools, and it offers greater efficiency and economy in marketing operations. Impending problems can be identified more quickly because management can better understand the complex interplay of all pertinent variables. Finally, the results can be evaluated quantitatively. Many elements in the systems approach lend themselves nicely to a computer-based analysis, thus enabling management to process quickly the complex data involving many variables.

These features, in turn, should enable a company to broaden and deepen its market penetration by extending its product lines and being better able to cope with competition. The tourist industry, for example, attracted new customers by creating packaged tours (really product-service systems), which are more convenient and economical than what the consumer could assemble himself.

The systems approach is sufficiently new in marketing, on the other hand, so that it is still beset with some problems. First, the approach can take considerable time and money to implement. One company, for instance, took over a year to develop the mathematical model of its physical distribution system, which was necessary before management could even begin to solve its problems. There are no standardized approaches; each company tailor-makes its own systems. Second, in marketing we must deal with social and psychological considerations in the

---

"Systems Approach to Marketing," *Harvard Business Review,* May–June, 1967, pp. 105–118. See also Stanley F. Stasch, "Systems Analysis for Controlling and Improving Marketing Performance," *Journal of Marketing,* April, 1969, pp. 12–19.

behavior of people. In our study of consumer behavior, however, it is only in relatively recent years that we have been using mathematical models and other quantitative methods of analysis to any significant extent. Even then, this analysis often involves so many assumptions that it is of little practical value. Finally, and perhaps most troublesome of all, is the idea that the psychological nature of many marketing men is such that they are more like artists than scientists. They prefer to "fly by the seat of their pants," resisting the fact-based research, written plans, and other rigidities which are of necessity so much a part of the systems approach.

CONCLUSION

The notion of a systems approach to marketing should be useful as we continue through this book. This approach, however, should also be kept in proper perspective. We must not confuse the tool and its user, nor should we confuse the relative importance of the two. Systems analysis is only an *aid* to executive judgment and decision making; in no way is it a *substitute*. While the computer and quantitative analysis can help management to do a more effective job, we must remember that the output of this analysis is no better than the input. And the numerical input is usually a matter of executive judgment. But perhaps here we have the real key to the value of the systems approach—that is, it forces management to think formally about the right aspects of a problem.

EXTERNAL ENVIRONMENT OF MARKETING SYSTEMS

A company plans and operates its marketing system within a framework of forces which constitute the system's environment. Some of these forces are *external* variables generally *not* controllable by the executives in a firm. Other forces are *internal* to a company and thus are essentially controllable by management. An executive might paraphrase the words of one organization: "Grant me the strength to change the things I can change, the serenity to accept those I cannot, and the wisdom to know the difference." The ability of a decision-making executive may be measured by the skill with which he can (1) adjust to the external elements in his changing environment, (2) forecast the direction and intensity of these changes, and (3) use the controllable variables at his command in adapting to this external environment. Figure 2-1 illustrates the framework of major external, uncontrollable variables which influence a company's marketing system.

MARKET DEMAND: ECONOMIC AND BEHAVIORAL

The environmental factor of the market itself, as was stressed in Chapter 1, is the most significant external influence on the marketing decisions of a firm. This tremendously important force is the subject of Part 2 (Chapter 3 to 7) and is pointed up frequently throughout the text. Both economic and behavioral aspects of consumers affect a firm's marketing system.

In an economic sense, the key market influence is consumer income, along with the number and location of people with this buying power. Management needs to be aware of expenditure patterns of consumers at various income levels. A corollary influence is the general condition of the national economy. Macroeconomic

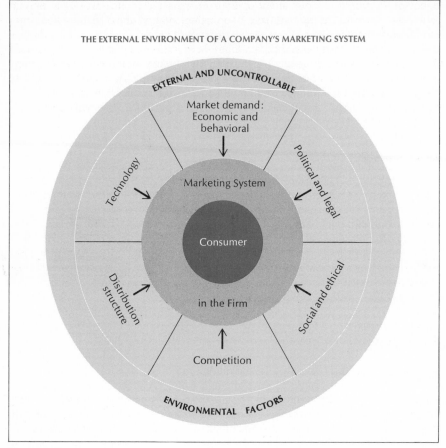

Figure 2-1

influences such as higher interest rates, inflationary pressures, national tax policy, etc., can play major roles in determining the success of a company's marketing system.

The behavioral aspects of a market—sociological, psychological, and anthropological—become important environmental forces particularly as consumer's income increases. As a person's buying power allows him to rise above a subsistence level, he has increasing personal discretion as to how he spends this money. Consequently, marketing executives need to learn as much as they can regarding cultural traditions, consumer motivation, demographic patterns, group sociological behavior, and similar influences.

POLITICAL AND LEGAL FORCES

To an increasing extent a company's existence and conduct are being influenced by the political-legal framework and processes in our society. Legislation at the federal, state, and local levels exercises more influence on the *marketing* activities of a firm than on any other major areas of its operations. Antitrust laws, pricing legislation, and regulatory measures affecting advertising and distribution systems are just a few examples of these governmental forces which set legal guidelines and limits for business operations. Generally over the past half century, United States citizens, through their duly elected representatives, have opted for *more* government planning and controls over society and the economy. Obviously this trend affects marketing management. Moreover, within this general trend, management must be alert to changes in the political attitudes or "climate," depending upon the philosophies of the administration in power at the time.

SOCIAL AND ETHICAL INFLUENCES

Somewhat related to the environmental forces discussed above are the social and ethical influences on a company's marketing program. In fact, the failure of business to meet society's ethical expectations often leads to restrictive legal measures. The increasing political attention devoted to the consumer since the 1960s is expected to continue, and probably at a quickening pace.

Marketing executives are responding to social influences. Management realizes the value of a good company image. Public disapproval of misleading advertising, poor product performance, hidden finance charges, and inadequate product information can indelibly hurt a business. In general, management knows that it must pay attention to its social responsibilities and that its decision making must be done within the framework of acceptable social practices if the company is to benefit in the long run.

COMPETITION

A firm usually faces competition from other firms within the same industry or from companies in other industries offering substitute products or services. Consequently, a marketing executive should understand a great deal about the economics of these industries. Regarding his own industry, he should understand its cost structure, pricing policies, general promotional practices, and any other competitive aspect which may influence his own planning and operation. For instance, in an industry where fixed costs are a large percentage of total costs, management may be willing to adopt flexible pricing practices so that it can cut its price below an announced level in order to make a sale. This willingness stems from the fact that in the short run management needs to cover only variable or out-of-pocket costs; any return above that level will help cover the huge fixed expense.

Management must also be alert constantly to the potential threat of industries marketing substitutable products or services. Steel manufacturers are feeling inroads from aluminum and plastics producers. Interindustry competition between companies making aluminum foil, plastic wrap, tin cans, and other types of containers has been heightened by the revolution in packaging.

DISTRIBUTION STRUCTURE

Several features of the distribution structure—the system by which goods flow physically and title is moved from producer to ultimate user—are beyond the control of executives who must use the structure. Facilities for handling and transporting the goods are largely external factors, for instance, as are the distribution institutions such as retailers and wholesalers.

TECHNOLOGY

In our zeal to have a customer orientation replace a production orientation in business management, we must not overlook the considerable impact which the work of scientists, engineers, and other technically oriented people has on a company's marketing system. The "knowledge explosion" which we have experienced in technology during the past several decades will undoubtedly continue, and probably at an accelerated pace. These advances have occurred not only in disciplines which we think of as being technical fields (the physical and biological sciences, for instance) but also in countless other areas of human endeavor.

Technology is a major environmental influence on marketing because it has such an effect on consumers' life-styles and consumption patterns. Advances in medicine have lengthened the life-span and changed the activities within that span. Developments in transportation and communication have altered our way of living.

The relationship between technology and marketing is a two-way street, however, in that marketing has been (and should be) a major influence on technology. Technology must be marketed; it must be adjusted to consumers' wants. Just building a better mousetrap is not enough, as can be proved by reviewing the fantastic numbers of products which were engineering successes but market failures. Very early in a product's development—in the idea stage—we need to determine its potential market in terms of size, composition, customers' wants, etc.

CONTROLLABLE VARIABLES IN MARKETING SYSTEMS

A firm operates its marketing system within the constraints of the environment we just discussed. The goal of the system is to reach preselected market targets and to satisfy the consumers' needs in a manner profitable to the company. To reach these goals, management has at its disposal two sets of internal, controllable forces: (1) the company's resources in nonmarketing areas and (2) the components of the marketing mix—the product, the price structure, the promotional activities, and some features of the distribution system. Figure 2-2 illustrates this internal framework, and Fig. 2-3 reflects the marketing system as a combination framework of environmental and internal forces.

NONMARKETING RESOURCES

A company's marketing system is influenced by its production, financial, and personnel capability. If management is considering adding a new product to its present assortment, can existing facilities and expertise be used? If the new product requires a new plant or machinery, financial capability enters the picture. Some firms cannot enter new markets or market new products because of inadequate personnel.

Other nonmarketing forces which management must consider are the company's location, its engineering research and development strength as evidenced by its patents, and the overall image the firm projects to its public. Plant

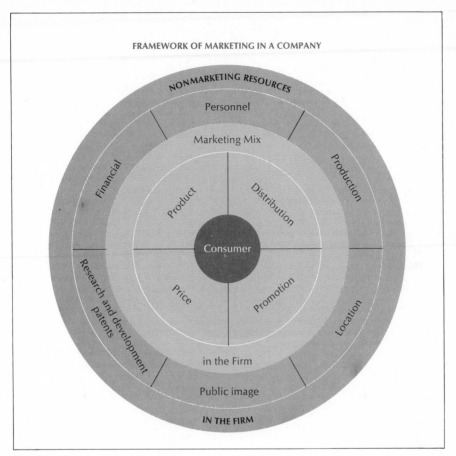

FRAMEWORK OF MARKETING IN A COMPANY

NONMARKETING RESOURCES
Personnel
Marketing Mix
Financial
Production
Product
Distribution
Consumer
Research and development patents
Price
Promotion
Location
in the Firm
Public image
IN THE FIRM

Figure 2–2

location often determines the geographic limits of a company's market, particularly if high transportation costs or perishable products are involved. The R & D factor may determine whether a company will lead or follow in the industry's technology and marketing.

THE MARKETING MIX

A marketing mix, effectively blended and properly attuned to customers' wants, competition, and the other environmental forces, can result in a successful marketing system. *Marketing mix* is the term used to describe the combination of the four inputs which constitute the core of a company's marketing system: the product, the price structure, the promotional activities, and the distribution system.

The four "ingredients" in the mix are interrelated. Again we see the *systems* concept, as decisions in one area usually affect action in the others. Also, each of the four contains countless variables. A company may market one product or several—related or unrelated; they may be distributed through wholesalers or directly to retailers; etc. Ultimately, from the myriad of variables, management must

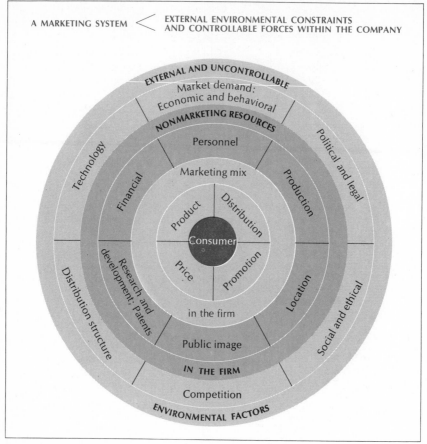

A MARKETING SYSTEM < **EXTERNAL ENVIRONMENTAL CONSTRAINTS AND CONTROLLABLE FORCES WITHIN THE COMPANY**

EXTERNAL AND UNCONTROLLABLE

Market demand:
Economic and behavioral

NONMARKETING RESOURCES

Personnel

Marketing mix

Technology

Financial

Product

Distribution

Production

Political and legal

Consumer

Price

Promotion

Research and development; patents

Distribution structure

in the firm

Location

Social and ethical

Public image

IN THE FIRM

Competition

ENVIRONMENTAL FACTORS

Figure 2-3

select the combination which will be the most effective in profitably adapting to the environment. Relating to an earlier section in this chapter, management is seeking the mix which will lead to the optimum *synergistic* results.

The product. Managing the product component includes planning and developing the right products and/or services to be marketed by the company. Policy and strategy guidelines are needed for changing existing products, adding new ones, and taking other actions which affect the assortment of products carried. Decisions are also needed regarding branding, packaging, color, and other product features.

Price. In pricing, management must determine the right base price of its products and then establish policies for dealing with discounts, freight payments, and many other price-related situations.

Promotion. This is the component used to inform and persuade the market regarding a company's products. Advertising, personal selling, and sales promotion are the major promotional activities.

Distribution. Even though the distribution structure was noted earlier as a non-controllable environmental factor, a marketing executive has considerable working latitude within that framework. He has a choice of channels through which he will distribute his products, and the wisdom he uses in this selection may make the difference between a strong and a weak market position.

Management's responsibility is to select and manage the trade channels through which the products will reach the right market at the right time and to develop a distribution system for physically handling and transporting the products through these channels. Part of the distribution task is to select useful intermediaries (middlemen) in the channel and to develop effective working relationships with them.

In conclusion, a company's marketing effort should start and end with the customers. Management should select its market targets, analyze them carefully, and then develop a program to reach those markets. Permeating the planning and operation of this model is marketing research—a key activity intended to aid management in its decision making. See Fig. 2-4.

MANAGING THE MARKETING SYSTEM

If an effective marketing mix is influential in a firm's well-being, who determines the composition of this mix? The answer is the firm's *management.* The fundamental determinant of a company's success is the caliber of its management.

The "marketing" part of the term, "marketing management" was defined in Chapter 1, but what about the "management" part? *Management* or *administration* (the terms are used synonymously here) may be defined as the process of planning, organizing, directing, and evaluating the efforts of a group of people toward a common goal. As a result of management, the combined group output surpasses the sum of individual outputs. Here again is involved the important concept of synergism.

Management is a separate and distinct skill; it is an art in and of itself. As such, it should not be confused with technical operating skills. Managerial skills and operational abilities are not automatically interchangeable. A good salesman is not necessarily a good sales manager. Conversely, an outstanding administrator may have had only modest success as a technical operator in his field.

Because administrative ability is a distinct skill, it is adaptable to various jobs. The ability to plan, direct, organize, and evaluate human efforts is equally usable whether the executive is working for an automobile manufacturer or an appliance maker. Military leaders have become business executives; business executives have moved into college presidencies; college presidents have moved into administrative positions in other fields.

The management process, as applied to marketing, consists basically of the following activities: (1) developing a plan or program, (2) executing it, and (3) evaluating its results. The development stage includes setting the goals and planning how to reach them. Execution of the plan includes organizing, staffing the organization, and directing the actual operation of the plan. The evaluation stage is a good example of the interrelated, continuing nature of the management process in that evaluation is both a look back and a look ahead. Management looks back to analyze performance results in light of the goals. The findings from this evaluation of past performance then often influence the goals and plans for future periods.

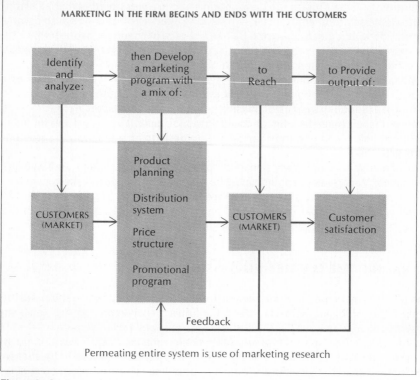

MARKETING IN THE FIRM BEGINS AND ENDS WITH THE CUSTOMERS

Identify and analyze: → then Develop a marketing program with a mix of: → to Reach → to Provide output of:

CUSTOMERS (MARKET) → Product planning / Distribution system / Price structure / Promotional program → CUSTOMERS (MARKET) → Customer satisfaction

Feedback

Permeating entire system is use of marketing research

Figure 2-4

See Fig. 2-5. Now let us look briefly at some applications of these managerial activities in a marketing system.

DETERMINING OBJECTIVES

A firm's activity must be goal-directed to be effective. Since a firm's marketing objectives form the foundation of its marketing management, the first task of the marketing administrators is to determine their goals. These goals are an interpretation by management of its particular needs at a given time and place, and they guide the company's progress along the path to wherever management wishes the firm to be in the future.

Marketing goals should be set forth clearly in writing and then communicated downward in the organization. Otherwise, management runs the real risk that any subsequent planning and operating will be done virtually in a vacuum. The firm is likely to experience misdirected marketing effort, inefficient use of resources, and low morale among the personnel.

Ordinarily a firm has different levels of marketing objectives, ranging from its ultimate long-range goals to its specific short-run operational ones. The broad objective may be to market a volume of goods at a level of profit over the long run that will satisfy the interests of the stockholders, consumers, and labor unions and still meet all governmental regulations. Broadly stated goals, however, such as "maximize profits" or "capture the tape-recorder market," are too vague to guide

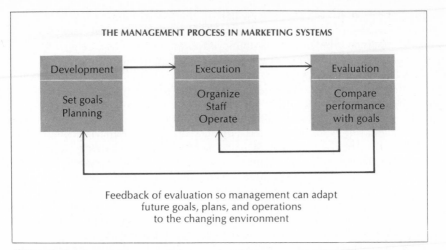

Figure 2-5

management effectively. A specific objective, such as "sign up 300 new dealers next year" or "increase the sales of product C by 20 percent," is a more useful tool for guiding executives in their activities. Viewed from another perspective, the levels of marketing goals range from total program objectives, down through goals for each marketing activity, to separate goals for each salesman, or middleman.

In marketing as in other types of group effort, the goals should be realistic and relevant. Moreover, the planning and operating decisions must be in line with the goals set up by management. For example, if the objective is to reach a mass market with a consumer product, the company must attempt to get distribution through the maximum number of retail outlets. A decision to use only one retail outlet in each city would not be consistent with the goal.

PLANNING

Once management has established its objectives, the next step in the administrative process is to determine the manner in which these goals will be reached. This managerial activity is called *planning*. Without planning, a company's operations have no meaning and no direction; there can be no orderly procedure in management's pursuit of its goals.

Planning may be classified according to the length of time for which it is done and the relative breadth of the activities planned. Short-term planning usually covers a year or less; long-term planning, one to five or ten years. Plans may cover many areas of activity or one area.

The general-management concept of planning has broad and countless applications in the field of marketing. Marketing executives are engaged in long-range and short-range planning regarding their markets, products, distribution systems, and promotional programs. The planning process may include laying plans for the introduction of a new car model or making sales forecasts. Marketing plans may be concerned with major programs, such as deciding when a large department store will open a new suburban branch, or with a specific situation, such as determining ways and means of promoting fresh produce in a supermarket on weekends.

"Strategy" and "tactics" are essentially military terms, but they have achieved wide application in nonmilitary activities. In marketing terms, a *strategy* is the overall plan of action to reach a predetermined marketing objective; *tactics* are the detailed methods and techniques employed to implement the strategy. Assume that a garment manufacturer's goal is to enter the prestige, high-income market for clothes. His strategy regarding channels of distribution would be to sell his product through one high-quality clothing store in each market. The tactics of the situation would involve selecting the specific store, such as I. Magnin, Marshall Field and Company, or Saks Fifth Avenue. As promotional strategy, this manufacturer might plan an advertising campaign around a prestige appeal and nonprice competition. Promotional tactics would include using such media as *The New Yorker* and *Esquire* magazines and never mentioning price in the advertisements.

Unless the objective in a given situation is specifically stated, there may be some confusion about what constitutes objectives, strategies, and tactics. In the above example of the garment manufacturer, some people might reason that the company's objective is to broaden its market. Then its strategy might be to capture the high-income market, and its tactics would consist of distribution in high-quality stores and a prestige-appeal promotional campaign. The issue here concerns the *level* of the objectives; the concepts of marketing strategies and tactics are meaningful only after the level of objectives is established.

ORGANIZING AND COORDINATING

Organizing is another major phase of the management process, and coordinating is a significant part of organizing. *Organizing* is the process of arranging activities and the people engaged in them in such a way as to achieve the maximum output with the highest possible degree of efficiency and coordination. The end structure of the process is an organization. In a good organization, the people involved produce more effectively as a group than they could individually.

Within the marketing department, activities in sales, advertising, marketing research, new-product development, customer service, and sales statistics all require careful coordination. Salesmen can help the advertising division, and the advertising men can be of direct benefit to the sales force. According to a top marketing executive at the Beatrice Foods Company, his company's biggest challenge was to achieve "more effective coordination of the marketing efforts of our scattered and diverse operating divisions, tying these more closely to the overall corporate program."[2]

There are countless possible examples of *interdepartmental coordination.* Marketing can furnish sales estimates so that the production department can better plan its work, or it can push items which are overstocked. Production can help marketing by manufacturing the proper quantity and quality of products at the right time. Production can also provide product information for sales training and advertising programs.

Marketing executives must coordinate their activities with advertising agencies, transportation companies, and other *outside companies* which are helping the seller in his marketing program. Advertising agencies must plan their campaigns to coincide with the introduction of a new model. Transportation companies must have carrier facilities available when and where the product is to be loaded. The manufacturer can help by furnishing information regarding new products. Mid-

---

[2]"What's New in Marketing," *Sales Management,* Nov. 10, 1964, p. 159.

dlemen can help by giving the product adequate promotion and good display space.

The marketing concept implies the coordination of all company activities which impinge on the consumer.[3] Yet the organizational proposals and changes made to achieve this coordination can result in organizational conflicts between the marketing department and other departments. Conflict occurs (1) because each department wishes to stress the importance of its own tasks (just as marketing stresses the consumer point of view) and (2) because each department defines its goals narrowly and in its own self-interest. Thus engineering emphasizes functional features and few models with standard parts; marketing emphasizes sales features and many models with custom components. Finance wants set budgets and prices to cover costs; marketing wants flexible budgets and pricing to further market development. These conflicts will continue as long as each department is judged by the efficient performance of its own tasks, and not by its overall company contribution. In this light, top management should reduce any narrow interest in departmental efficiency and, instead, work toward interdepartmental policies designed to advance total company interest.

STAFFING

The most important function of management is staffing the organization —assembling the human resources. If management is the key to successful business operations, then staffing is the key to successful management. Many will prefer to nominate planning, motivating, or some other activity as the critical function of management. However, proper personnel selection—both executive and nonexecutive—will eliminate or substantially reduce many management problems. A marketing manager's job is made easier if he hires an excellent advertising manager or sales-force manager. The sales-force manager, in turn, has fewer problems with training and compensation if excellent salespeople are hired.

OPERATING

After the goals have been set, the planning accomplished, and the organization established and staffed, the program must be placed in operation. In the final analysis no plan is worth much unless it is carried out effectively. This is particularly important in marketing because success depends upon the way the business is operated. Management may develop excellent plans, but unless the sales force carries out its end of the task, success cannot be achieved. Here again we see the importance of personnel selection. Good people may bring about successful results even if the original planning was mediocre. The management function of operating and directing includes operating a sales force, directing an advertising campaign, and working with middlemen.

EVALUATING

The final stage of the management process consists of analyzing and evaluting the results of the company's operations to determine whether they met expectations.

---

[3]This paragraph is adapted from Philip Kotler, "Diagnosing the Marketing Takeover," *Harvard Business Review*, November–December, 1965, pp. 70–72.

There are at least four major areas of application of this managerial function in the marketing program of a firm. First, the executive may analyze marketing costs by territories, products, or customer groups. In many firms the bulk of the sales volume and net profits comes from a small percentage of the customers, products, or territories. Management is often unaware of this situation. Consequently, it misdirects its marketing efforts by spreading them evenly over all territories or products even though these units do not produce equal returns to the company. Second, the performance of the individual salesmen may be evaluated. Third, both manufacturers and middlemen may evaluate the effectiveness of their advertising programs. Fourth, individual manufacturers may want to evaluate the performance of a middleman's volume in the light of his quota and customers' reactions.

THE ESTABLISHMENT OF MARKETING POLICIES

In order to guide executives in their decision making on recurring marketing problems, management should establish marketing policies covering every phase of its program. A *marketing policy* is a statement of a course of action followed under given circumstances. For example, after careful consideration the marketing executives in a manufacturing company may decide to pay half the cost of any retailer's advertisement which features the manufacturer's product. A retailer may decide to stay open until 9 P.M. on Monday, Wednesday, and Friday nights. Some policies are major ones, such as a manufacturer's decision to sell to only one retailer in a market or a retailer's decision to sell everything in the store at one price; others are less important. But they all serve the same essential purpose: They afford uniform executive action and uniform treatment of customers, and they save valuable executive time.

A policy is only as good as the research upon which it is based. Also, policies should be stable; if they are changed frequently, they cease to serve as guides. At the same time, a policy should be flexible; it should be reviewed periodically and revised when necessary. A flexible policy allows for some leeway in executive judgment and action. It is adaptable to a reasonable range of variations surrounding a given business situation.

PROBLEM SOLVING AND DECISION MAKING IN MARKETING SYSTEMS

Marketing management consists of a never-ending process of recognizing marketing problems, analyzing them, and making decisions. In fact, relative abilities in the combined art of problem solving and decision making are the features which differentiate high-caliber executives from the less able ones. One reason marketing executives generally receive higher-than-average earnings is that problem solving is more difficult in marketing than in many other fields. It is difficult because much of it involves abstract reasoning and subjective analysis.

One hallmark of a good executive is his ability to make decisions and to make them promptly. Some managers evade the responsibility of making decisions by enveloping themselves in a cloak of anonymity called a "committee." Some pass the buck to other executives. Many people find it difficult to make decisions. A student may ask his girl where she would like to go for the evening, rationalizing that he is being considerate. Actually he is refusing to make a decision.

Some decision-evading executives issue progress reports, but never a final decision, saying that they need more information. This is often not a legitimate excuse. Ordinarily nobody has all the information needed or wanted, and yet the situation will not wait; a decision must be made. This is as true in other walks of life as it is in business. The quarterback must call a play and execute it in less than twenty-five seconds, even though he would like more information—for example, what defense is being set up against him. Often all information needed will not be available until after the decision is made. After the team runs the play, the quarterback finds out what kind of defense was set up against him. After a company locates a branch on a given corner, the executives find out whether a sufficient number of customers are attracted.

Management ordinarily will never know whether it made the best possible decision, even after it has been executed and the results are in. No matter how great the results are, an alternative decision might have turned out better. For example, if a quarterback with a ball on his own 15-yard line called a pass play and gained 60 yards, the move would be loudly acclaimed. But was that play the best one to call? No one knows; possibly an end run would have been good for a touchdown.

PROBLEM-SOLVING PROCESSES

The problem-solving responsibilities of today's marketing executives can be assisted considerably by the use of technological and other scientific advances in two general fields. The first is in the area of quantitative analytical tools where such aids as computers, mathematical models, and other quantitative methods are providing problem-solving capabilities of a speed, precision, and magnitude previously unimaginable. Market analysis, warehousing, evaluating middlemen's performance, forecasting sales, setting quotas and territories, and many other marketing tasks can be performed more easily and decisions are apt to be more sound if quantitative analytical tools are used.

The behavioral sciences are the other general area which can aid in marketing decision making. Management should capitalize on the potential contributions of psychology, sociology, and anthropology. These behavioral sciences can help in solving problems related to marketing organizational structures, branding and packaging, consumer behavior, and so on.

One procedure for solving marketing problems will be explained briefly. No single approach is better than any other; basically, all are variations of a scientific method applied to marketing management.

Five steps are involved in this approach. (It is assumed that the executives already have a thorough understanding of their industry, product, and market and of the other environmental forces which will influence their decision.)

1. Carefully and specifically define the problem.
2. Determine reasonable courses of action.
3. Identify the major issues, factors, or subproblems bearing on the main problem.
4. Analyze each major issue and come to a decision on each in light of the alternative courses of action.
5. Make a decision; that is, select the best alternative.

Before an executive can solve a marketing problem, he must recognize that one exists, and then he must be able to identify it clearly. This is no easy task. Sometimes symptoms of a problem are mistaken for the problem itself. An analogy drawn from the medical field may sharpen this point. A person goes to a physician complaining of recurring headaches. Basically the headaches are only symptoms. The real problem may be emotional tension, eyestrain, or any one of several other factors. In any event, the physician must identify and clearly define the problem before he can hope to remedy it.

In a marketing situation a symptom is often diagnosed as the basic problem. A marketing executive may say that his big problem is that his sales have declined steadily for two years. Actually declining sales are only a symptom. The real problem may be noncompetitive pricing, poor service to consumers, poorly packaged products, poor advertising, or a combination of several weaknesses. Truly it may take some careful investigating to pinpoint the real problem. Often a physician or a marketing executive will treat a symptom for some time before realizing that he has not yet found the real source of the trouble.

After an executive has decided what the main problem is, he should carefully define it in the form of a question. A question requires an answer. Instead of stating that the company's problem is its product packaging, the executive will ask: "From a marketing standpoint, what are the weaknesses in the product's packaging?" or "What packaging changes should be made to improve our product's marketability?" Questions should be specific. Broad questions, such as "What can the company do to increase its sales?" do not lend themselves to a good analysis.

The second step in the problem-solving process is to decide upon the alternative courses of action which seem reasonable under the circumstances. Normally this is not a difficult thing to do. Assume that a luggage manufacturer's problem is what channels of distribution he should use for his new line of airplane luggage. On the basis of his understanding of the product, company, market, and other environmental factors, he may decide that the following channels might be used:

Manufacturer—retailers (department stores, large luggage stores, discount houses)—consumers
Manufacturer—leather goods wholesalers—retailers—consumers
Manufacturer—manufacturers' agents—retailers—consumers

Other *possible* alternatives, such as door-to-door selling, are not always *reasonable* ones.

In some problems there may be only two reasonable alternatives. Assume that a manufacturer of business machines such as Burroughs is trying to decide whether to add electric razors to its groups of products. About the only major alternative courses of action are to add or not to add.

The third, fourth, and fifth stages in problem solving are to identify the major issues which bear on the main problem, to analyze these issues, and finally to reach a decision on each one. The conclusions reached will have determining influences on the main decision. In the case of the business machine manufacturer who is trying to decide whether to add a line of electric razors, the major issues bearing on the problems are as follows:

1. Is there an adequate market demand for the proposed product?
2. From a marketing standpoint, can the proposed product be handled through the company's existing channels of distribution, middlemen, sales organization, and advertising program?

3. Does the product fit into the company's present production structure with respect to necessary labor skills, sources of materials, and product facilities?
4. What are the profit possibilities for the proposed product?
5. Does the new product pose any legal problems with respect to patent and antitrust regulations?
6. Is the product in keeping with the company's overall image, self-concept, and objectives?

Thus, before it can make a sound decision on whether to add electric razors, management must first carefully analyze in great detail each of the above issues, or subproblems, and come to a decision on each one. Failure to recognize all the important issues may result in a very poor decision.

Management must consider the effect the subproblem decisions have on one another. Also, the major issues are not always equally important. An administrator cannot count up the number of "yes" and "no" decisions on the subproblems and from this make his final decision. In the above case, the decisions on issues 2 to 6 may have favored adding the product to the line, but the decision on issue 1 may have been negative. This one negative decision—that there is not an adequate market demand—should override all the others, and the firm should not add the product. On the other hand, if there were a substantial demand and the profit possibilities looked encouraging, the manufacturer might add the product even though it did not fit well into the existing marketing or production structure.

The final step is to make the decision regarding the main problem. This involves selecting the best alternative course of action in light of the analysis of the major issues or subproblems.

QUESTIONS AND PROBLEMS

1. How does the systems approach to marketing differ from the more traditional approaches?
2. Explain how the concept of synergism is related to the systems approach to marketing.
3. How can the systems approach benefit a company's marketing effort?
4. Explain, giving examples, how a firm's marketing system can be influenced by the environmental variable of technology. By political and legal forces.
5. If administrative ability is a distinct skill and is transferable among various jobs, why do so many more top marketing executives come up through the ranks of the sales force than through other divisions in marketing such as advertising or marketing research?
6. "The targets assigned to departmental operating executives should be consistent with company goals." Give some examples of sales department goals which might be in conflict with the goals assigned to production executives. To financial executives.
7. On the basis of your knowledge of their recent advertisements, what do you think are the current marketing objectives of the following companies?
   a. The Ford Motor Company
   b. The manufacturer of Crest toothpaste (Procter & Gamble)
   c. A leading department store in your college city or in the nearest large city
   d. The telephone company

e. An office machines manufacturer such as IBM, Burroughs, or National Cash Register

8. Interview a few small, local retailers (barbershop or beauty shop, restaurant, shoe repair shop, hardware store, clothing store, etc.) located near your campus to determine what, if any, specific marketing objectives they have consciously established.

9. Suggest some strategies and tactics which might reasonably be employed to reach the following marketing goals:
    a. A furniture manufacturer wishes to market patio furniture as an addition to his present group of products.
    b. A wholesaler of building materials wants to increase the average size of his sales; that is, he hopes to reduce the number of small orders.
    c. The cigar manufacturers' trade association wants to increase the market for cigars among college students.

10. How do you suggest that effective coordination might be secured between the department which includes the salesmen and each of the following departments?
    a. Advertising   *c.* Finance
    b. Production   *d.* Engineering

11. A manufacturer of small hand tools (hammers, saws, screwdrivers, etc.) frequently runs out of stock on some items, while holding a five-year supply of other articles. Who is at fault for this badly balanced inventory situation?

12. Suggest some specific ways that the salesmen and the advertising division within a marketing department can help each other.

13. "The evaluation stage may be considered both the final and also the first stage of the management process; that is, this stage involves both a look backward and a look forward in managing a company." Explain.

14. Give some examples from your everyday life which show the need for making decisions and the difficulty of doing so.

CASE FOR PART

CASE 1. LAVOISIER PIPELINE COMPANY*

The vice president in charge of de-marketing

Lavoisier Pipeline Company (LPC) was a major transporter of natural gas for residential, commercial, agricultural, and industrial uses. The firm owned and operated a 2,000-mile system of high-volume pipelines extending from gas fields in southwestern U.S. to LPC's service area in six northwestern states. LPC also was a major producer of natural gas, explored for gas, operated drilling rigs, wells, processing plants and related equipment. LPC also produced and sold "bottled" gas and certain other packaged gas products for suburban and rural residential consumers, agriculture, and industry.

LPC did not sell gas to the ultimate users. Its customers were local utility companies called "gas retailers," who operated distribution systems serving homes, businesses, industrial plants, and institutions. Some gas retailers also sold gas appliances, such as stoves, water heaters, refrigerators, air conditioners, outdoor grills, ornamental lighting, and camping items. Gas retailers included both privately owned and municipal firms.

*Case prepared by Prof. Phillip McVey, University of Nebraska–Lincoln. Reproduced with permission.

Demand for gas in LPC's service area was growing. But there were several constraints on the firm's business. Rates, pipeline routes, service areas, construction and operating practices, competition and issuance of securities were closely regulated by several government agencies at the federal and state levels, the most comprehensive being the Federal Power Commission. There was competition from other fuels (electricity, oil, and coal). Also the gas industry had been attacked by environmentalists and consumerists who had protested at various times about the potential for air and water pollution or noise from gas industry operations, dangers of gas explosions or fires, or the threat of degrading the land during the construction and operation of pipelines. Important results of such protests included delays and limitations imposed on the building of a new pipeline from northern Alaska to the U.S. and a slowing down in the leasing of federal lands, offshore, that could have excellent gas resource potentials.

LPC officials believed the protesters were overlooking the real problem facing them, which was a potential long-run, continuing shortage of natural gas.

LPC had never before experienced serious gas shortages either locally or throughout its service area. The company had regularly delivered the quantities contracted by the gas retailers. Its seasonal peaks in gas demand had always occurred in the winter because of the requirements to supply space heating users. During the winter period, however, it could not always supply its gas retailers the entire requirements of contract quantities plus business, industrial, and institutional users who were equipped to use alternate fuels and who bought gas on an "interruptible" basis. When cold temperatures were experienced, gas retailers telephoned interruptible users telling them to "get off gas" until further notice. These users, of course, paid a lower price for gas than other customers because of the lower value of the service they received. Residential consumers were not affected.

Late in 1972, LPC was concerned about the threat of a general "energy crisis" involving long-term shortages, not only of natural gas but also of oil, gasoline, and electricity. As a result of some news stories, which LPC officials said were partly untrue, the bad publicity formerly aimed at LPC by protesters was supplanted by public alarm over a possible gas shortfall. Questions came from home owners, builders, industrial users, and from regulatory agencies. There was a decline in sales of gas appliances.

To meet the energy crisis, LPC began a general study of all its operations, including a search for new gas supplies, more efficient ways of producing, storing, and transporting gas, and better ways to forecast demand from various kinds of users.

As a part of this effort the LPC president asked his executive staff to call a meeting of all gas retailers served by LPC. The meeting would be a review of the whole gas supply situation and of the marketing operations of both LPC and the gas retailers. Each gas retailer would be told that he could expect to receive the same contracted volumes as he had in the preceding 12 months. This meant there would be no increases to supply any new housing and commercial developments or other high-priority users. In addition, the interruptible consumers could receive perhaps as little as 75% of the gas that had been sold the preceding year. The president also wanted to present a marketing plan for LPC for the year beginning July 1, 1973, plus a model tie-in plan for gas retailers to use in the same period.

The president told his marketing executive, "Maybe we should change your title to Vice-President in Charge of *De*-Marketing. We face the strange challenge of asking our customers not to use so much of our product. The wrong users of gas, or the inefficient uses of it, cannot be supplied anymore."

"We are opening up to our competitors the market comprised of all the new housing and commercial growth in our service area. We've got to plan what to do in the event commercial, industrial, and institutional interruptible users are cut back below previous supply levels and must turn to alternate fuels which are equally short in supply—or worse. And what about our profit? How do we recoup the revenue losses resulting from a smaller sales volume?"

"We are going to have to help the gas retailers fix priorities, and tell them how to allocate available gas. At the same time we've got to reassure high-priority users, and prevent panic. And we'll have to help the gas retailers tell the story to *their* customers!"

The marketing executive replied, "My staff and I have already been talking about such a plan. I'm glad you don't view this crisis as a time to throw marketing out of the window, as some industries have done when they faced product shortages. But shouldn't we also use this occasion to think hard about what kind of business LPC is *really* in?"

The president looked at him, startled. "What do you mean by that?" he asked.

QUESTIONS

1. Answer the president's question at the end of the case.
2. What questions will the gas retailers probably ask at the forthcoming meeting? What, if anything, should the LPC marketing department be prepared to do in their behalf?
3. What new tasks should be assigned to the LPC sales force? To the advertising personnel? To marketing research? Other marketing groups?

PART TWO

THE MARKET

MARKETS:
PEOPLE AND MONEY

A sound marketing program should start with a careful quantitative and qualitative analysis of the market demand for the product or service. Adam Smith and other economists and philosophers both before and after him stated the fundamental importance of consumption—it is the only social and economic justification for production. Yet, because of the scarcity of goods, the difficulty of understanding the consumer, and the ease of measuring machine output, most American economists devoted their attention to production rather than to consumption prior to the 1920s. This concentration on the study of production went on even longer in other countries.

In the United States, however, the output of the production system has been so great since the end of World War I that surpluses have developed. In this economy of abundance, the social and economic emphasis has shifted from production to consumption. For several years now it has been considered axiomatic that "the consumer is king." The consumer is the basic determinant of what goods and services will be produced and of where, when, and at what price they will be sold. Up to the limits of his income, the consumer today is free to choose the amount and kind of want-satisfying goods and services which he buys.

From a realistic standpoint there are considerable limitations to consumer sovereignty. Possibly the principal ones are the consumer's lack of organization, his lack of a voice to make his edicts known, and his general apathy. If he is king, he maintains a strange palace court in which the subjects have to spend huge sums to try to find out what the vacillating, disorganized, fickle king desires and to proclaim loudly that they, over all other courtiers, have just what he wants.

Import restrictions also limit the consumer. In many instances they keep him from getting fine foreign products at reasonable prices. Interstate trade barriers reduce the free flow of some products from one state to another. Efforts of farm, labor, and business interests take price control out of the hands of the consumers. Determination of product quality by the consumer is often difficult, if not impossible.

WHAT IS A MARKET?

The concept of a market is sometimes confusing. There is a stock market and an automobile market, a retail and a wholesale market for furniture, and a local and a national market for building materials. One person may be going to the market; another may plan to market his product. Really, what is a market? Clearly, there are many usages of the term in economic theory, in business in general, and in marketing in particular. A market may be defined as a place where buyers and sellers meet and function, goods or services are offered for sale, and transfers of ownership of title occur. A market may also be defined as an aggregate demand by potential buyers of a product or service. For example, there is a farm market for petroleum products. In economic theory a market implies a set of conditions and forces which determine prices. That is, the meeting of buyers and sellers, price determination, and transfer of title are activities essential to the existence of a market. The concept of a market also implies a *demand* for a product or service. In fact, the terms "market" and "demand" are often used interchangeably, and they may also be used jointly as "market demand."

The above definitions of a market still may not be sufficiently usable by a marketing executive in an individual firm. Consequently, in this book a *market* will be defined as people with needs to satisfy, the money to spend, and the willingness to spend it. Thus in the market demand for any given product or service, there are three factors to consider—people with needs, their purchasing power, and their buying behavior. We shall employ the dictionary definition of *needs*: A need is the lack of anything that is required, desired, or useful. We do not limit needs to the narrow physiological requirements of food, clothing, and shelter essential for survival. The potentially limitless number of needs offers unbounded opportunities for market growth. Satisfying wants may be interpreted as the first step toward satisfying needs. We want something that will answer our needs.

MARKET SEGMENTATION

A company that is production-oriented is likely to treat its entire market as a single undifferentiated homogeneous unit. Under this concept—known as *market aggregation*—management will develop one product and one marketing program designed to reach as many customers as possible. Market aggregation enables a company to maximize its economies of scale in production, physical distribution, and promotion. Producing and marketing one product means longer production runs at lower unit costs. Inventory costs are minimized when there is no (or a very limited) variety of colors, styles, and sizes. Warehousing and transportation efforts are more efficient. Advertising costs per unit presumably are lower for one product than when several are being promoted.

When competition becomes severe and management is forced to cut prices with the resultant drop in profits, a firm may try to differentiate its product from those of its competitors. Under this concept of *product differentiation*, a company will introduce some new feature—a package change (butter in a plastic squeeze tube), a new size (little cigars), a new flavor (cinnamon-flavored toothpaste), or a new color. The new feature often is accompanied by heavy promotional expenditures in an effort to convey to the aggregate market that there are some actual or psychological differential benefits in the new product. But please note we still are dealing with the production-oriented philosophy of one market (market aggregation).

The total market for most types of products is too heterogeneous for market management to derive maximum value from an analysis of it as a whole. To speak of the market for vitamin pills, electric razors, or tractors is to ignore the fact that within the total market for each of these products there exist submarkets which differ significantly from one another. This lack of homogeneity may be traced to differences in buying habits, ways in which the product is used, motives for buying, or other factors.

WHAT IS MARKET SEGMENTATION?

Market segmentation is the process of taking the total, heterogeneous market for a product and dividing it into several submarkets or segments, each of which tends to be homogeneous in all significant aspects. In terms familiar to an economist, we are developing several demand schedules—a separate one for each market segment—where only one schedule representing the total market existed previously. Thus, instead of speaking of a market for Bermuda shorts, we now segment this market into several submarkets—those for college men, college women, businessmen, housewives, and retired people. Still further segmentation might be based on geographic location; for example, we might speak of the Eastern college men's market.

Market segmentation is a customer-oriented philosophy. We first identify customers' needs in a submarket and then design a product and/or a marketing program to reach that submarket (segment) and satisfy those needs. Thus, in effect, each market segment calls for a separate marketing program which is different in some respect from the programs designed to reach other submarkets. Stated another way, in market segmentation we are employing a "rifle" approach (separate programs, pinpointed targets) in our marketing activities, as contrasted with the "shotgun" approach (one program, broad target) used in market aggregation.

As part of the strategy of segmenting its markets, a company frequently will develop for each segment a different variety of the basic product. Thus, auto producers and ski manufacturers, for example, have developed different models, each intended for a different market segment. On the other hand, market segmentation can be accomplished with no change in the product, but only with separate marketing programs each tailor-made for a given market segment. A producer of vitamin pills, for instance, can market the identical product to the youth market and also to the over sixty-five market, but in each case the promotional programs and probably the channels of distribution will be different. The same portable electric typewriters or the same airline or telephone service can be marketed effectively to different market segments by using different marketing programs. The promotional appeals, for instance, would stress different user benefits in each case.

BENEFITS OF MARKET SEGMENTATION

As suggested at the start of this chapter and also in the preceding chapter, a successful marketing program starts with a quantitative identification of the present and potential customers plus an understanding of their buying behavior and decision-making processes. A careful job of market segmentation supports this idea, and also can serve as a foundation stone for developing effective marketing strategies. By tailoring marketing programs to pinpointed market segments, management can do a better marketing job and make more efficient use of marketing resources. A small firm with limited resources might compete more effectively in one or two market niches, whereas the same firm would be buried if it tried to take on the total market.

More specifically, market segmentation can aid management in such ways as:[1]

1. Channeling money and effort to the potentially most profitable markets
2. Designing products that really match market demands
3. Determining what promotional appeals will be most effective for the company
4. Choosing advertising media more intelligently and determining how to allocate better the budget among the various media
5. Setting the timing of the promotional efforts so that they are heaviest during those times when response is likely to be at its peak

CONDITIONS FOR EFFECTIVE SEGMENTATION

Ideally, management's goal should be to segment its markets in such a way that each segment will respond in a homogeneous fashion to a given marketing program. Three conditions will help management move toward this goal. First, the bases for segmenting—the characteristics used for categorizing customers—must be *measurable and data must be accessible*. To illustrate, fear of social disapproval or a desire for ecologically compatible products may be characteristics identifying a given segment of the market for a product, but data for these factors are neither readily accessible nor easily quantified.[2]

As a second condition, the market segment itself must be *accessible* through existing channels of distribution, advertising media, salesmen, etc.—all with a minimum of cost and waste. To aid in this matter, some national magazines such as *Time, Newsweek,* and *Sports Illustrated* publish separate geographical editions. In

---

[1]Daniel Yankelovich, "New Criteria for Market Segmentation," *Harvard Business Review,* March–April, 1964, pp. 83–84.

[2]See Barnett A. Greenberg and Roy A. Herberger, "Is There an Ecology-Conscious Market Segment?" *Atlanta Economic Review,* March–April, 1973, pp. 42–44. For the contention that markets can be segmented on the basis of consumers' social consciousness, see W. Thomas Anderson, Jr., and William H. Cunningham, "The Socially Conscious Consumer," *Journal of Marketing,* July, 1972, pp. 22–31; and Thomas C. Kinnear, James R. Taylor, and Sahrudin A. Ahmed, "Ecologically Concerned Consumers: Who Are They?" *Journal of Marketing,* April, 1974, pp. 20–24.

this way an advertiser can run an ad aimed at a Western segment of his market and not incur the waste of having the ad exposed to other nonmarket areas.

The third condition is that each segment should be *large enough* so as to be profitable. Conceptually, management could treat each single customer as a separate segment. Actually this situation may occur in the industrial market as, for example, when Boeing markets passenger airplanes to commercial airlines, or when a firm like Westinghouse Electric markets huge generators to the government for a hydroelectric power dam. In the process of segmenting a consumer market, a firm conceivably could go to the extreme of developing a wide variety of styles, colors, sizes, and prices. Obviously the diseconomies of scale in productions and inventory ordinarily will put reasonable limits on this type of expansion and multiplicity.

BASES FOR MARKET SEGMENTATION

There are many different ways by which a company can segment its market. And the methods will vary from one product to another. Moreover, the segmentation process should be an ongoing activity for two reasons. First, markets are dynamic, not static. They change continually as our attitudes, life-style, family situation, income, geographic patterns, etc., change. Second, the markets for a product change as it goes through its life cycle (from its introduction, through its growth stage, to the period of sales decline).

Ultimate consumers and industrial users. One very important way of segmenting the entire American market is to divide it into ultimate consumers and industrial users, the sole criterion being the reason for buying. *Ultimate consumers* buy and/or use products or services for their own personal or household use. They are satisfying strictly nonbusiness wants, and they constitute what is called the "consumer market." A mother who buys food and clothing and the family members who eat the food and wear the clothes are all ultimate consumers.

Industrial users are business, industrial, or institutional organizations who buy products or services to use in their own businesses or make other products. A manufacturer who buys chemicals with which to make fertilizer is an industrial user of these chemicals. The farmer who buys the fertilizer to use in commercial farming is an industrial user of the fertilizer. (If a homeowner buys fertilizer to use on his yard, he is an ultimate consumer because he buys it for household use.) A supermarket, hospital, bank, or paper manufacturer that buys accounting machines, pencils, and floor wax is an industrial user of these products because it uses them in a business or institution. Industrial users in total constitute the "industrial market."

The segmentation of all markets into two groups—consumer and industrial—is extremely significant from a marketing point of view because the two markets buy differently. Consequently, a seller's marketing program—his products, distribution, pricing, and promotion—will differ depending upon whether he is selling to the consumer or to the industrial market.

Bases for segmenting consumer markets. Simply dividing the total market into consumer and industrial segments, while a worthwhile start, still leaves too broad and heterogeneous a grouping for most products. Consequently, we shall identify some of the widely used bases for further segmenting the consumer market.

The model we will use is related to the three components of a market as defined early in this chapter, and is a topical outline of Chapters 3 through 6. Thus, markets are:

A. People. (Chapter 3.) So we might segment on demographic bases such as:
    1. Regional population distribution
    2. Urban-suburban-rural population
    3. Age
    4. Sex
    5. Family life cycle
    6. Others—race, religion, nationality, education, occupation
B. With money to spend. (Chapter 3.)
    1. Distribution of disposable income
C. And the willingness to spend it. (Chapters 4, 5, and 6.) This topic gets us into consumer buying behavior where the prime determinants are:
    1. Psychological (psychographic) factors such as:
        a. Personality
        b. Attitudes
        c. Product benefits desired
    2. Sociological groupings
        a. Cultural groups
        b. Large social classes
        c. Small groups, including the family

When using the above bases to segment markets, it is helpful to keep in mind two points. First, buying behavior is rarely traceable to only one segmentation factor. Useful segmentation typically is developed by including variables from several of the above bases. Even looking at the demographic variables above, rarely is a useful market segment identified by a single market factor. To illustrate, rarely does the market for a product consist of all women, or all the people living in Pacific Coast states, or all people over sixty-five. Instead the segment is more likely to be narrowed down by combining several of these variables. Thus a market segment might be women, living in Pacific Coast states, married, with young children, and above a certain income level.

The other point to observe is the interrelationship at least among the demographic factors. For instance, the age factor and life cycle stage typically are related. Income is tied to some degree with age, life cycle stage, education, and occupation. Education and occupation can be interrelated.

Bases for segmenting industrial markets. As with consumer markets, the broad, diverse industrial market usually must be further segmented in order for companies to develop effective marketing programs to reach industrial users. The industrial market is discussed in Chapter 7.

POPULATION—ITS DISTRIBUTION AND COMPOSITION

According to our definition, population is one of the main components of a market. Therefore, a marketing person should study the geographic distribution and demographic composition of the population. In the following sections we shall consider only those population factors which affect the consumer market. The industrial market is discussed in Chapter 7. In analyzing population, a marketing executive should first find out which characteristics of the population—such as age, education, or family size—substantially affect the composition of the market for his product. Then he should get the current quantitative measurement of each of these characteristics. Finally, he should determine the trends in these data and understand the significance of these trends in terms of his marketing program.

TOTAL POPULATION

A logical place to start is with an analysis of total population, and here the existence of a "population explosion" becomes evident. The population of the United States did not reach 100 million until 1915. However, it took only another 52 years (until 1967) to reach the 200 million mark. By the year 2000 we can expect to have over 250 million people living in the United States, even though the birthrate has been declining since the 1950s and is expected to stay at its present low level. This lower birthrate is expected to result in a higher standard of living, greater labor productivity, and increased savings leading to increased capital formation.[3] Truly, in numbers the total population is tremendous, and the marketing implications in this situation are staggering. But the market is so large and so heterogeneous that it must be analyzed in segments.

REGIONAL DISTRIBUTION

Figure 3-1 shows the distribution of the U.S. population in 1973 and the projected growth from 1970 to 1980 by census regions. The biggest markets are still in the East and Midwest. The Middle Atlantic states represent about 18 percent of the population, and the East North Central region accounts for 20 percent. The greatest percentage increases in the 1970s, however, are expected in the Pacific and Mountain regions. This westward movement of population is expected to rise by 20 percent in the Pacific region and 16 percent in the Mountain states, as contrasted with a 12 percent increase for the country as a whole.

The regional distribution of population is important to marketing people because sectional differences exist in the demand for many products. These differences are traceable to climate, religion, social customs, and other factors. Bright, warm colors are preferred in Florida and the Southwest, while grays and cooler colors predominate in New England and the Midwest. Per capita consumption of soft drinks and cosmetics varies substantially among the regions of the country. People in the West are less formal than Easterners, and they spend more time outdoors. Consequently, as the Western population increases, there will be a larger market for such products as patio furniture, sports clothes, and barbecue equipment. To a marketing man, the fact that southern California, Florida, and Arizona are growing so rapidly means that there will be an increased demand for suntan

---

[3]See "The Burgeoning Benefits of a Lower Birth Rate," *Business Week,* December 15, 1973, p. 41. Also see James D. Foust and Al D. Southwood, "The Population Fizzle," *Business Horizons,* February, 1973, pp. 5–20; and George H. Brown, "'1984'—Plus One," *Conference Board Record,* December, 1970, pp. 20–24.

REGIONAL DISTRIBUTION OF POPULATION, 1973, AND PROJECTED GROWTH, 1970-1980

New England
A = 6
B = 12

Middle
Atlantic
A = 18
B = 8

South
Atlantic
A = 15
B = 14

East
South Central
A = 6
B = 5

East
North Central
A = 20
B = 11

West
North Central
A = 8
B = 7

West
South Central
A = 10
B = 12

Mountain
A = 4
B = 16

Pacific
A = 13
B = 20

A = 1973 % distribution
B = 1970-1980 % growth
projection

Figure 3–1. Although the East North Central and Middle Atlantic census regions account for the largest part of our total population, the Western regions have a more rapid growth rate. The Pacific area is growing at the fastest rate. Movement of the population center of the United State is still generally west-ward. *Source:* U.S. Bureau of the Census.

lotion, swimsuits, backyard swimming pools, air conditioners for homes and automobiles, and other warm-weather products.

URBAN, RURAL, SUBURBAN, AND INTERURBAN DISTRIBUTION

For many years in the U.S. there has been a relative and absolute decline in the farm population, and this decline is expected to continue. In 1940 about one out of four people lived on a farm; in 1950 it was about one out of six; and in 1970, one out of twenty. The declining farm population has led some marketing people to underrate the rural market. Both as an industrial market for farm equipment and supplies and as a consumer market with increased buying power and a more urbanlike sophistication, the farm market is still a big one. Sociological patterns (family size and customs) among rural people differ significantly from those of city dwellers, and these patterns have considerable influence on buying behavior. Per capita consumption of cosmetics and other beauty aids, for example, is much lower in farm markets than in city markets.

In recognition of the growing urbanization of the American market plus the inadequacies of market data based only on political boundaries, some years ago the federal government established the concept of a Standard Metropolitan Statistical Area (SMSA) as a geographic market-data-measurement unit. An SMSA is defined as a county or group of contiguous counties with a total population of at least 100,000 and a central city with a minimum population of 50,000 (or two closely located cities with a combined population of 50,000). The boundaries of SMSAs may cross state lines, but the counties must constitute a socially and economically integrated unit. Virtually all employment must be nonagricultural.

The government has identified 264 SMSAs, and in 1974 they accounted for about 70 percent of the nation's population. The ten largest alone represented about one-quarter of the total population (Table 3-1). Obviously these areas present attractive, geographically concentrated market targets with considerable sales potential.

While it is true that the farm population has been declining and the metropolitan areas growing, something else is also going on *within* the metropolitan areas. The central cities are growing very slowly, and in some cases the older established parts of the cities are actually losing population. The real growth is occurring in the fringe areas of the central cities or in the suburbs outside these cities. For the past 30 years, one of the most significant social and economic trends in the United States has been the shift of population to the suburbs. As middle-income families have moved to the suburbs, the economic, racial, and ethnic composition of many central cities (especially the core areas) has changed considerably, thus changing the nature of the markets in these areas.

The growth of the suburban populations has some striking marketing implications. Since a great percentage of suburban people live in single-family residences, there is a vastly expanded market for lawn mowers, lawn furniture, home furnishings, and home repair supplies and equipment. The suburbanite is more likely to want two cars than is the city dweller. He is inclined to spend more of his leisure time at home, so there is a bigger market for items used for home entertainment and recreation.

Marketing people are watching a possible modest countertrend—that is, the movement back to the central cities on the part of older people whoe children are grown. Rather than contend with commuting, home maintenance, and other sub-

Table 3-1. Ten largest standard metropolitan statistical areas in 1974.
Together these ten areas represented close to one-quarter of the nation's population. What companies might want to market only in these 10 areas? Suggest
some products for which the best markets might lie outside of any metropolitan
area.

Rank	SMSA	Population 1/1/1974 (millions)
1	New York	9.9
2	Chicago	7.1
3	Los Angeles–Long Beach	6.9
4	Philadelphia (Pennsylvania–New Jersey)	4.8
5	Detroit	4.5
6	Boston	3.4
7	San Francisco–Oakland	3.2
8	Washington, D.C. (Maryland-Virginia)	3.1
9	Nassau-Suffolk (Long Island)	2.6
10	Dallas–Fort Worth	2.5

Source: "Survey of Buying Power," *Sales Management,* July 8, 1974, p. B-12. © 1974, Sales Management
Survey of Buying Power; further reproduction is forbidden.

urban challenges, they are moving to new high-rise apartments located near the
downtown facilities.

In several places in the United States the metropolitan areas have expanded to
the point where there is no rural space between them. This joining of metropolitan
areas has been called "interurbia." Where two or more city markets once existed,
there is today a single market. For example, there is virtually no space along the
Atlantic coastline between Boston and Virginia which is not part of the SMSA. This
is a 600-mile-long single market. The areas along the shores of the Great Lakes
from Buffalo to Detroit, then across the lower part of Michigan to Gary, Chicago,
and Milwaukee, constitute another series of interurban areas. Soon the coastal
region from north of San Francisco to the Mexican border in California will be one
great interurban market.

AGE GROUPS

The size of various age groups has a substantial effect on the market for certain
products. In the 1970s, as an illustration, nearly 60 percent of the growth in total
population will come in the young adult 20 to 34 age group. See Fig. 3-2. And it is
while they are in this age bracket that people usually begin their careers, get
married, start families, and spend money in a big way.

The youth market (roughly grade school ages five to thirteen) carries a three-way
marketing impact. First, these children can influence parental purchases; second,
billions of dollars are spent on this group by their parents; and third, these children
themselves make purchases of goods and services for their own personal use and
satisfaction.[4] Promotional programs are often geared to this segment of the mar-

[4]See James U. McNeal, "The Child Consumer: A New Market," *Journal of Retailing,* Summer,
1969, pp. 15–22ff.

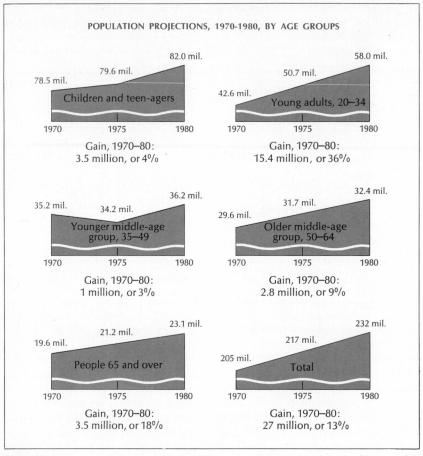

POPULATION PROJECTIONS, 1970-1980, BY AGE GROUPS

Children and teen-agers
78.5 mil. — 79.6 mil. — 82.0 mil.
1970 — 1975 — 1980
Gain, 1970–80:
3.5 million, or 4%

Young adults, 20–34
42.6 mil. — 50.7 mil. — 58.0 mil.
1970 — 1975 — 1980
Gain, 1970–80:
15.4 million, or 36%

Younger middle-age group, 35–49
35.2 mil. — 34.2 mil. — 36.2 mil.
1970 — 1975 — 1980
Gain, 1970–80:
1 million, or 3%

Older middle-age group, 50–64
29.6 mil. — 31.7 mil. — 32.4 mil.
1970 — 1975 — 1980
Gain, 1970–80:
2.8 million, or 9%

People 65 and over
19.6 mil. — 21.2 mil. — 23.1 mil.
1970 — 1975 — 1980
Gain, 1970–80:
3.5 million, or 18%

Total
205 mil. — 217 mil. — 232 mil.
1970 — 1975 — 1980
Gain, 1970–80:
27 million, or 13%

Figure 3-2. Young adults will be the fastest-growing group in this decade. If your market target was the 35 to 49 age group, what impact would this forecast have on your planning? *Source: U.S. News and World Report,* Jan. 12, 1970, p. 33, based on U.S. Census Bureau data.

ket. Children's television shows, for instance, are sponsored by cereal manufacturers and other advertisers in an effort to develop brand preferences at an early age.

The teen-age market is recognized as an important one, and yet it has proved to be difficult to reach in some cases. While some companies (American Airlines, TWA, J. C. Penney, and Yardley, for example) have had notable successes, other well-known firms have "bombed out" in their attempts to reach the older end of the youth market. Possibly the mistake is trying to lump all teen agers into one group. thus ignoring the many subgroups segmented by income, race, political bent, geographic location, etc. Certainly the 13 to 16 age group is different from the 17 to 20 bracket.[5]

[5]See Paul Gilkison, "Teen-Agers' Perceptions of Buying Frames of Reference: A Decade in Retrospect," *Journal of Retailing,* Summer, 1973, pp. 25–37. Repeating a study he had made 10 years earlier (*Journal of Retailing,* Fall, 1965, p. 33), the author discovered significant changes over a 10-year period in the buying frames of reference used by teen-agers.

Yet understand the teen-age bracket a manufacturer must, not only because of the size of this market, but also because its members have an increasing amount of money to spend. They are good customers for records, automobiles, cosmetics, clothes, jewelry, and other products. In order to tap this market, many manufacturers are adopting new product and distribution policies. For instance, some clothing manufacturers are now designing junior ready-to-wear dresses which reflect the age and not merely the size of the teen-age girl. Bobbie Brooks, Inc, is also altering the distribution systems for its junior wardrobes. Many department stores have conventional ready-to-wear departments labeled "college," "junior," or "miss," which handle similar styles but different sizes. Furthermore, items such as skirts, sweaters, and blouses are sold in separate departments. The Bobbie Brooks firm feels this is "splintering" the market and consequently urges retailers to develop one "young adult" department which will carry all sizes and all items necessary for the complete wardrobe of girls from 15 to 24 years old.

At the other end of the age spectrum are two market segments which should not be overlooked. One is the group of people in their 50's and early 60's. This mature market is large and financially well-off. They are at the peak of their earning power and typically no longer have financial responsibilities for their children. Thus this market segment is a good target for marketers of high-priced, high-quality products and services.

The other older age group are people over 65—a segment which is increasing both absolutely and as a percentage of the total population. Manufacturers and middlemen alike are beginning to recognize that people in this age group are logical prospects for small, low-cost housing units (trailers, as well as more conventional types of housing), cruises and foreign tours, health products, and cosmetics developed especially for older people. Many firms are also developing promotional programs to appeal to the buying motives of this group and to cater to their buying habits.[6]

The life-styles of the 1970s have had an interesting influence on the traditional segmentation by age groups. Marketers are finding that the youth market is not what it used to be. The youth market is no longer confined to the young in age, but should be redefined as the young in heart. "When blue-jeaned youths troop through Cartier's (New York City) on a Saturday afternoon, what is an exclusive jeweler to think? How does a volume fashion store such as Alexander's (New York City) react when mothers poke around its Experiment I, a free-standing boutique set up for hippie types?"[7] The youth market needs to be treated as a state of mind, because it overflows all age boundaries. In a promotional program, for example, *youth directed* advertising (advertising targeted at the under-25 market) will be different from *youth-oriented* advertising which will be aimed at the entire 14 to 65 age market.

SEX

Sex is probably an obvious basis for consumer market segmentation. In many product categories—autos, for example—women typically look for different product benefits than men do. Market segmentation by sex is also useful because many

---

[6]See "The Power of the Aging in the Marketplace," *Business Week,* Nov. 20, 1971, p. 52.

[7]"Why 'Youth' Needs a New Definition," *Business Week,* Dec. 12, 1970, p. 34; also see "Youth Appeal . . . A Creative Booby Trap," *Grey Matter,* January, 1971.

products have traditionally been purchased by one sex or another. However, some of these traditional buying patterns are breaking down, and marketers certainly should be alert to changes involving their products. Not too many years ago, for example, the wife did practically all the grocery shopping for her family, and the husband bought the products and services needed for the automobile. Today men are frequent food shoppers and women buy the gas. Marketing people also must be aware of product categories where women typically buy the products, but the goods are used by others in the family.

The changing role of women in the 1970s also has tremendous marketing implications. The increasing number of working women (married or single) has greatly expanded the markets for frozen foods, household appliances, and other laborsaving products and services. Products and activities considered limited to the male market not many years ago are today readily accepted by the women. Successful attempts to remove barriers of discrimination against women have generated many market opportunities. Interestingly enough, however, it has *not* been nearly so easy to get males to accept products traditionally considered feminine.[8]

FAMILY LIFE CYCLE

The demographic factors of sex or age alone often do not adequately explain consumer buying behavior. Even when age and sex are combined into market segments such as young adult women or middle-aged men, we will find different buying behavior within the same segment. Frequently the factor accounting for the difference in consumption patterns between two people is that each—while of the same age and sex—is in a different life cycle situation. The concept of a family life cycle refers to the important stages in the life of an ordinary family. A six-way classification of these stages is as follows:

1. Bachelor stage: young, single people
2. Young married couples with no children
3. Full nest I: young married couples with children
4. Full nest II: older married couples still with dependent children
5. Empty nest: older married couples with no children living with them
6. Older single people, still working or retired

Segmenting a market by life cycle stage recognizes the fact that life cycle position is a major determinant of buying behavior. A young couple with two children (the full-nest stage) have quite different product and service needs than does a couple in their mid-fifties with children no longer living at home (the empty-nest stage). Typical buying patterns found in each of the various stages are discussed in more detail in Chapter 5 in connection with family buying behavior.

A segmentation factor related to the life cycle is the *rate* of household and family formation. A *household* is defined as one or more persons living in the same dwelling unit; a *family* is a group of two or more related persons living together. Every new household or family is potentially a market for a dwelling place, furniture,

---

[8]See John R. Stuteville, "Sexually Polarized Products and Advertising Strategy," *Journal of Retailing,* Summer, 1971, pp. 3–13-

appliances, and other home furnishings. For manufacturers of appliances and furniture, the number of families is often more important than the size of the family. A refrigerator manufacturer, for example, may hope to sell three refrigerators to three couples, whereas he would probably sell only one to a family with six people in it.

Two rapidly growing markets—reflecting the changing life-styles of the 1970s—are called *singles* and *mingles*.[9] In the early 1970s the census showed that households of people living alone were increasing three times as fast as family units. "Mingles" — people living with nonrelatives without benefit of clergy or even city hall—increased over 800 percent in the decade 1965–1974. Granted that the members of mingles are still relatively small, the marketing implications in this trend are far reaching.

Compared with the population as a whole, the singles segment is (1) more affluent, (2) more mobile, (3) oriented to immediate pleasures rather than long-term concerns, (4) fashion and appearance conscious, and (5) active in leisure pursuits.

The impact which singles of both sexes have on the market is demonstrated by such things as apartments for singles, social clubs for singles, special tours and cruises, and eating places seeking the patronage of singles. Truly, it is an interesting marketing challenge to isolate, reach, and then persuade the singles and mingles market segments.

OTHER DEMOGRAPHIC BASES FOR SEGMENTATION

The market for some consumer products is influenced by such factors as education, occupation, race, national origin, and religion. With an increasing number of people attaining higher levels of education, for example, we can expect to see changes in product preferences and buyers with more discriminating taste and higher incomes. To identify and analyze some segments, occupation may be a more meaningful criterion than income. Truck drivers, carpenters, or auto mechanics may earn as much as young retailing executives, college professors, or lawyers. But the buying patterns of the first three occupations are different from the second trio because of the influence of attitudes, interests, and other lifestyle factors.

Geographically mobile consumers constitute a sizable and perhaps unique market segment which is just beginning to receive attention. In view of the fact that some 20 percent of the American people move each year, it is surprising that studies of the socioeconomic characteristics, life-styles, and buying behavior of this group have been relatively neglected until recently. Yet this segment of consumers presents a rather attractive market in that many of them have good incomes. Moreover, their moves force them to develop new shopping habits, seek new sources of products and services, and possibly develop new brand preferences.[10]

---

[9]See "Singles and Mingles—A Meaningful Marketing Explosion," *Grey Matter,* January, 1974.

[10]See James E. Bell, Jr., "Mobiles—A Possible Segment for Retailer Cultivation," *Journal of Retailing,* Fall, 1970, pp. 3–15; John R. Thompson, "Perceived Risks and Learning Systems of Geographic Mobiles," *Southern Journal of Business,* July, 1968, pp. 74–78; and Alan R. Andreasen, "Geographic Mobility and Market Segmentation," *Journal of Marketing Research,* November, 1966, pp. 341–349.

For some products it is quite useful to analyze the population on the basis of race, religion, or national origin. People of Mexican descent in the Southwest (Chicanos) have some product preferences that are quite different, say, from those consumers of Oriental descent living on the West Coast. Religious mores in Utah affect the market for tobacco, liquor, and coffee. There is a large market for Polish sausage in some Midwestern areas.

One ethnic group which is receiving increasing attention because of its large and growing potential is the black American market—containing an estimated 25 million consumers with a combined buying power of about $40 *billion* in 1974. "Controversy and emotionalism notwithstanding, there is a Negro market—a *big* market, with plenty of buying brawn, and some individualistic traits that demand the attention of every marketer!"[11] That statement, made early in the 1960s, is even more true in the 1970s. There are distinct differences between black and white American markets—not only in color, but also in socioeconomic charac-teristics (income, family structure, education, occupation, expenditure patterns, and consumption patterns). To market successfully to black consumers, a com-pany must understand something about their buying behavior and their motiva-tion. Furthermore, the problems of understanding the Negro market are in-tensified because the market is not a homogeneous unit any more than any other population segment consisting of 25 million people is. The Negro market contains subsegments based on income, occupation, geographic location, etc.[12]

For some products, another ethnic market well worth studying is the Spanish-speaking market segment, about half the size of the black American market and geographically concentrated in New York City, Miami, southern California, and the Southwest. This is a relatively accessible market segment because of its common language, geographic concentration, and relative homogeneity in income, that is, low income. Promotional accessibility is improved by an advertiser's use of Spanish-speaking radio stations, TV programs, movies, newspapers, and mag-azines.

CONSUMER INCOME AND ITS DISTRIBUTION

People alone do not make a market; they must have money to spend. Conse-quently, a detailed study of income, its distribution, and how it is spent is essential in any quantitative market analysis which an individual firm may make.

---

[11]"Marketing to the Negro Consumer," *Sales Management*, Mar. 11, 1960, p. 36.

[12]For some insights into the black American market, see D. Parke Gibson, *The $30 Billion Negro Market*, The Macmillan Company, New York, 1969; also see Douglas J. Dalrymple, Thomas S. Robertson, and Michael Y. Yoshino, "Consumption Behavior across Ethnic Categories (Blacks and Japanese-Americans)," *California Management Review*, Fall, 1971, pp. 65–70; Carl M. Larson and Hugh G. Wales, "Brand Preferences of Chicago Blacks," *Journal of Advertising Research*, August, 1973, pp. 15–21; John P. Maggard, "Negro Market—Fact or Fiction?" *California Management Review*, Fall, 1971, pp. 71–80; Keith K. Cox, James E. Stafford, and James B. Higgenbotham, "Negro Retail Shopping and Credit Behavior," *Journal of Retailing*, Spring, 1972, pp. 54–66; John W. Gould, Norman B. Sigband, and Cyril E. Zoerner, Jr., "Black Consumer Reactions to 'Integrated' Advertising: An Exploratory Study," *Journal of Marketing*, July, 1970, pp. 20–26 and John J. Wheatley, "The Use of Black Models in Adver-tising," *Journal of Marketing Research*, August, 1971, pp. 390–392.

NATURE AND SCOPE OF INCOME

What is income? There are so many different concepts of income that it is well to review some definitions. The following outline is actually a mathematical equation:

National income: The total income from all sources including employee compensation, corporate profits, and other income

> Less corporate profits and social security contributions
> Plus dividends, government transfer payments to persons, and net interest paid by government, *equals*

Personal income: The income from wages, salaries, dividends, rent, interest, business and professions, social security, and farming

> Less all personal federal, state, and local taxes and nontax payments, *equals*

Disposable personal income: The amount available for personal consumption, expenditures, and savings

> Less (1) essential expenditures for food, clothing, household utilities, and local transportation and (2) fixed expenditures for rent, house mortgage payments, insurance, and installment debt payments, *equals*

Discretionary purchasing power: The amount of disposable personal income over and above fixed commitments (debt repayments, homeowner taxes, tenant rent) and above that required for essential household needs. Consequently, as compared with personal income data, discretionary purchasing power is a better or more sensitive indicator of the consumer's ability to spend for nonessentials. (The definition and measurement of discretionary purchasing power are the works of The Conference Board.)

In addition, we shall hear the terms "money income," "real income," and "psychic income." *Money income* is the amount a person receives in actual cash or checks for wages, salaries, rents, interest, and dividends. *Real income* is what the money income will buy in goods and services; it is purchasing power. If a person's money income rises 5 percent in one year but the cost of what he buys increases 8 percent on the average, then his real income decreases about 3 percent. *Psychic income* is an intangible but highly important income factor imputed to climate, a satisfying neighborhood, enjoyment of one's job, etc. Some people prefer to take less real income in order to live in a pleasant suburb or in a part of the country which features a fine climate and recreation opportunities.

On the basis of income, the American market has grown fantastically since the end of World War II. Disposable personal income rose from $210 billion in 1950 to $936 billion in 1972, an increase of over 300 percent in a little more than twenty years. Discretionary purchasing power also quadrupled during the same period of time. (See Table 3-2.)

Even after allowing for the rise in price level and the increase in total population, the advances in income are still very substantial. Some of these figures may be more meaningful when expressed on a per capita basis. Figure 3-3, for instance, shows per capita disposable income from 1950 to 1972. (These income figures are

Table 3-2. Personal, disposable, and discretionary income in the United States, in billions of dollars.

Briefly, personal income is gross income before taxes; disposable personal income is the money remaining after taxes; disposable personal income less expenditures to maintain a reasonable standard of living equals discretionary income—the amount which can be spent on nonessentials. See text for more precise definitions.

	1950	1960	1972	Percentage increase in 1972 Over 1950	Over 1960
Total personal income	$228	$401	$936	311	136
Disposable personal income	210	350	795	280	127
Discretionary purchasing power	91	144	364	300	153

Sources: Personal and disposable income: *Survey of Current Business.* Discretionary purchasing power: The Conference Board.

expressed both in 1972 dollars and in dollars which reflect the price levels of each specific year.) Thus, in terms of 1972 dollars, per capita disposable income increased 68 percent between 1950 and 1972 (from about $2,300 to almost $3,800).

INCOME DISTRIBUTION

To get full value from an analysis of income, a marketing executive should carefully study the variations and trends in the distribution of income among regions and among population groups. Regional income data are particularly helpful in pinpointing the particular market to which a firm wishes to appeal. Income data on cities and even sections within cities may indicate the best locations for shopping centers and suburban branches of downtown stores.

The income revolution which has been going on in the United States in recent decades may be seen in the changing profile of family income distribution, as pictorialized in Fig. 3-4. (These relationships are all expressed in constant purchasing power—1971 dollars—so the inflationary effects of rising prices are eliminated.) We are seeing the changes in *real* income. In 1960 the income distribution formed an inverted pyramid, with almost one-third of the families under the level of $5,000, and only 11 percent over $15,000. A major income development has been the tremendous growth of the middle-income market and a shrinking of low-income groups. By the end of the 1980s the distribution should look like a pyramid. By 1985 over half of the families are expected to be earning over $15,000, and the percentage in the lowest brackets should be quite small. We shall still have low-income families. However, far fewer will be below the poverty level, even though that level (by definition) is moving up in recognition of the inflationary factor and our more abundant society.

MARKETING SIGNIFICANCE OF INCOME DATA

The declining percentage of families in the poverty bracket, coupled with the sharp increases in the upper-income groups, presages an explosive growth in discretionary purchasing power. The level of discretionary income is of particular importance

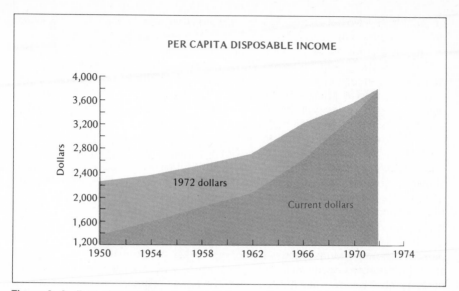

Figure 3–3. Even after adjusting for the inflationary effects of a rising price level, per capita disposable income has increased substantially over the past several years. Stated in constant (1972) dollars, per capita disposable income increased 69 percent between 1950 and 1972. *Source:* U.S. Department of Commerce data.

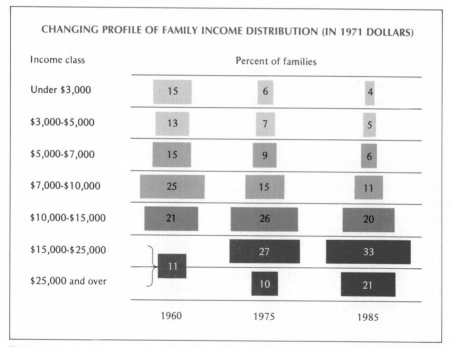

Figure 3–4. The income pyramid will be turned upside down in a 25-year period. Families in the under $3,000 class should decline from about 15 to 4 percent of the total. What are the marketing implications in the dramatic increase in the $15,000-and-over categories? *Source:* The Conference Board projections using U.S. Department of Commerce data.

because as this type of income increases, so too does the demand for items which once were considered luxuries.

The middle-income market is a big market and a growing market, and it has forced many changes in marketing strategy. Manufacturers are seeking the widest possible distribution system which will appeal to the middle-income and not the low-income market. Many stores which once appealed to low-income groups are now "trading up" to the huge middle-income market by upgrading the quality of the products they carry and by offering additional services.

In spite of the considerable increase in disposable income and purchasing power in the past 25 years, many households are still in the low-income bracket or find their higher incomes inadequate to fulfill all their wants. Consequently, consumers give certain wants priority, and the sellers of many different products must compete for every consumer dollar. Furthermore, many customers are willing to forgo services in order to get lower prices. One consequence of this market feature has been the development of self-service retail outlets and discount houses.

The existence of a vast middle-income market should not blind a marketing person to the importance of the high-income market. Although the "luxury market" is small, its purchasing power is impressive. The highest income groups spend four times as much on food, five times as much on housing, and about eleven times as much on transportation and clothing as the lowest income groups. The high-income market is an excellent one for good jewelry, furs, better housing, automobiles, and boats.

EXPENDITURE PATTERNS

For most of the major categories of consumer products, there is a surprisingly high degree of similarity in the expenditure patterns of the nation's nonfarm families. This point was ably developed from the information collected in a survey conducted by the Bureau of Labor Statistics of the U.S. Department of Labor. The Conference Board later processed the survey data and published them in a form more useful to marketing researchers.[13]

RELATION TO POPULATION DISTRIBUTION

In Table 3-3, the nonfarm family expenditure patterns for nine categories of goods and services are tabulated in percentage form for (1) the four major geographic regions of the nation and (2) the metropolitan and nonmetropolitan area markets. In all families, regardless of region or urban-rural classification, 10 to 11 percent of total expenditures went for clothing and accessories, 9 to 10 percent was devoted to medical and personal care, and 5 to 6 percent was spent on house furnishings and equipment. The greatest variations were found in the transportation and the housing-household operations categories. Central-city families, for instance, devoted only 13 percent of total spending to transportation, as contrasted with nonfarm rural families, where the figure was 17 percent.

---

[13]See U.S. Department of Labor, Bureau of Labor Statistics, *Consumer Expenditures and Income: Total United States, Urban and Rural, 1960-61*, BLS Report no. 237–93, 1965; *Expenditure Patterns of the American Family*, The Conference Board, New York, 1965; and *Market Profiles of Consumer Products*, The Conference Board, New York, 1967.

Table 3-3. Annual family expenditure patterns by geographic location.

The regional differences in expenditures for food and transportation are significant. Families in large cities spent 25 percent of their income on housing and household operations, while rural nonfarm families spent only 21 percent on this class of products and services. Note the similarity in expenditure patterns in each of the other product categories. If so much similarity exists, why should we study population characteristics? The text cites four reasons.

Item	Total	Geographic region					Market location				
							Metropolitan areas			Outside metropolitan areas	
		North-east	North-central	South	West	Total	Central cities	Urban fringe	Other areas	Urban	Rural
Percent distribution of:											
All families*	100	26.5	27	29	17.5	100	33	29	6.5	15.5	16
Total expenditures*	100	29	25.5	25	20.5	100	32	34	7	13	13.5
Total expenditures†	$5,152	$5,761	$5,028	$4,410	$5,677		$5,132	$6,303	$5,665	$4,482	$3,813
Percent of total expenditures†	100	100	100	100	100		100	100	100	100	100
Food, beverages, and tobacco	29	29	28	27	27		29	27	27	28	30
Housing and household operations	24	25	24	23	23		25	24	22	24	21
House furnishings and equipment	5	5	5	6	5		5	5	6	5	6
Clothing and accessories	10	11	10	10	10		10	10	10	10	9
Transportation	14	13	16	16	16		13	16	16	15	17
Medical and personal care	10	9	9	10	10		10	9	10	10	10
Recreation and equipment	4	4	4	4	5		4	4	4	4	4
Reading and education	2	2	2	2	2		2	2	2	2	1
Other goods and services	2	2	2	2	2		2	3	3	2	2

* 1966 data from *Market Profiles of Consumer Products*, The Conference Board, New York, 1967, pp. 20–21.
† 1960–1961 data from *Expenditure Patterns of the American Family*, The Conference Board, New York, 1965, pp. 20–21.

Other tables in The Conference Board report support this impression of conformity in overall spending habits. In most of the broad categories, the expenditure patterns for the professional and managerial occupations do not differ substantially from the spending behavior of families where the head is employed in clerical, sales, craftsman, or operative work. The findings are quite the same for families of different educational attainments and ages, and even for those in various stages of the life cycle.

The key question at this point is: Why should a marketing person study the population in such detail if there is considerable homogeneity among the various segments? Our answer has four parts. First, there is not complete homogeneity. Even among the broad categories in Table 3-3, for example, there are substantial regional differences in the food and transportation classifications. Second, the simple percentages shown in Table 3-3 may be misleading. Although a range of 5 to 6 percent (as in house furnishing and equipment) is only one percentage point, this is, from another perspective, a variation of 20 percent. Thus, for each product group in Table 3-3, the variation is considerable if the variation in percentage points between the areas with the highest and the lowest figures is expressed as a percentage of the lowest region's figure. To illustrate, families in central-city parts of the metropolitan areas devote 19 percent *more* of their total expenditures to housing and household operations than rural families. Third, similarity exists only when we speak of the broad categories. A detailed breakdown of the product and service groups shows that often there are large internal variations. Finally, differences exist among population segments with respect to buying motives and habits. Separate regional groups or age groups may each spend the same share of their income on clothing, but they react favorably to entirely different selling appeals. Basically the same vitamin pills may be bought for consumers under ten or over sixty-five, but different appeals are used for the different age groups. It is essential, therefore, to study all aspects of population in detail and not be lulled by the superficial similarities.

RELATION TO STAGE OF FAMILY LIFE CYCLE

Family expenditure patterns will vary—and in substantial portions for some products—according to the life cycle stage a family is in (Table 3-4). Young married couples with no children typically devote large shares of their income to clothing, autos, and recreation. When children start arriving, expenditure patterns shift as the young family buys and furnishes a home. Families with teen-agers find larger portions of the budget going for food, clothing, and educational needs. Families in the "empty-nest" stage, especially when the head is between fifty and sixty-five, are attractive to marketers because typically they have more discretionary purchasing power. The children are grown and on their own, and the house is paid for; yet the family earning power is typically at its peak.

RELATION TO INCOME DISTRIBUTION

Marketing men can glean considerable information from an analysis of expenditure patterns of families in various income groups. For each income, group, Table 3-5 shows the percentage distribution of family expenditures among nine major categories of goods and services. Despite the general similarity of ex-

Table 3-4. Annual family expenditure patterns by stage in life cycle.

Expenditure patterns differ depending upon which life cycle stage the family is in. Families with older children spend relatively large amounts on food and clothing. Young families must devote large shares to buying and furnishing a house.

Item	Total	Families with child under 6		6 or over		No children	
		Some under 6	All under 6	All 6 to 11	Any 12 or over	Husband-wife	Other
Percent distribution of:							
All families*	100	13.5	11.5	4.0	26.5	24.5	20.0
Total expenditures*	100	15.5	12.0	4.5	34.0	21.5	12.5
Total expenditures†	$5,152	$6,070	$5,406	$6,045	$6,710	$4,549	$2,664
Percent of total expenditures†	100	100	100	100	100	100	100
Food, beverages, and tobacco	29	30	26	28	28	27	28
Housing and household operations	24	24	27	24	21	25	30
House furnishings and equipment	5	5	6	5	5	5	4
Clothing and accessories	10	11	9	11	12	9	9
Transportation	14	13	17	15	15	16	12
Medical and personal care	10	9	9	9	9	11	10
Recreation and equipment	4	4	4	4	4	4	3
Reading and education	2	2	1	2	3	1	1
Other goods and services	2	2	1	2	3	2	2

Stage in life cycle

* 1966 data from *Market Profiles at Consumer Products*, The Conference Board, New York, 1967, p. 17.
† 1960–1961 data from *Expenditure Patterns of the American Family*, The Conference Board, New York, 1965, p. 17.

Table 3-5. Annual family expenditures by income groups.

There is a marked similarity in the expenditure patterns of middle-income families ($5,000 to $15,000) except in the food and housing categories. But note the sharp differences in expenditure patterns that exist between the high-income and low-income families. How do you explain the fact that families in the $7,500-to-$10,000 bracket spend a lesser percentage of their incomes on food than families with lower incomes?

Item	Total	Family income (before taxes)					
		Under $3,000	$3,000– $4,999	$5,000– $7,499	$7,500– $9,999	$10,000– $14,999	$15,000 and over
Percent distribution of:							
All families*	100	16	15	21	19	29	
Total expenditures*	100	5	9	17.5	21	47.5	
Total expenditures†	$5,152	$2,043	$3,859	$5,315	$6,788	$8,679	$12,687
Percent of total expenditures†	100	100	100	100	100	100	100
Food, beverages, and tobacco	29	33	30	28	27	26	23
Housing and household operations	24	31	25	24	23	22	24
House furnishings and equipment	5	4	5	5	6	5	5
Clothing and accessories	10	7	9	10	11	11	12
Transportation	14	9	14	16	16	17	15
Medical and personal care	10	11	10	9	9	9	9
Recreation and equipment	4	2	4	4	4	6	5
Reading and education	2	1	1	2	2	2	3
Other goods and services	2	2	2	2	2	2	4

* 1966 data from *Market Profiles of Consumer Products,* The Conference Board, New York, 1967, p. 18.
† 1960–1961 data from *Expenditure Patterns of the American Family,* The Conference Board, New York, 1965, p. 18.

penditure patterns, significant differences are observable in some categories, and we can safely conclude that income distribution is a major determinant of these differences.

Some of the findings from the Department of Labor study are summarized below to suggest the type of information that an analysis of expenditure patterns by income groups might yield:

1. There was a high degree of uniformity in expenditure patterns of *middle-income* spending units. As we shall learn in Chapter 5, however, social-class structure is a much more meaningful criterion for determining expenditure patterns.
2. For each of the product categories shown in Table 3-5, there was a considerable

absolute increase in dollars spent as income rose (or, more correctly, as we compared one income group with a higher income group). In other words, people in a given income bracket spent significantly more *dollars* in each product category than their less well-off neighbors, even though the lower-income households devoted a larger *percentage* of their total expenditures to the given product class. A marketing person is probably more concerned with the total dollars available from each income group than with the percentage share of total expenditures.

3. In each successively higher income group, the amount spent for food declined as a percentage of total expenditures.
4. The percentage of expenditures devoted to the total of housing, utilities, and home operation remained reasonably stable in the middle- and high-income brackets.
5. Amounts spent for medical and personal care remained a reasonably constant percentage of total expenditures, regardless of income.
6. The share of expenditures going for automotive products and services tended to increase as incomes increased in the low- and through middle-income groups. The proportion leveled off or dropped a bit in the higher-income brackets.
7. Regarding clothing, in each successively higher income group (with one exception), a greater share of total family expenditures went for clothing.

It is interesting to compare these generalizations on expenditure patterns with "Engel's laws." In 1857, Ernst Engel, a German statistician, published the results of his studies of spending patterns of workingmen's families. Later students of consumer spending behavior expanded on Engel's work, and the net result is a series of four statements regarding spending patterns in relation to various income levels. Engel's laws state that as family income increases:

1. A smaller percentage of expenditures goes for food.
2. Approximately the same percentage is devoted to clothing.
3. The proportion of total spending allotted to housing and house operation remains the same.
4. The share of total expenditures apportioned to other items (recreation, education, medical care, etc.) increases.

On the basis of what we have learned from recent empirical studies on spending patterns, we would have to restate Engel's laws somewhat to fit current conditions. The first and third generalizations (regarding food and housing-household operations) still hold true. The fourth is also still correct, with the exception of medical and personal-care items, which seem either to decline or to remain a constant share of total expenditures as income rises. The second generalization, regarding clothing, is *not* operative today. In successively higher income levels, the percentage of income now allocated to clothing increases.

Generalizations such as these provide a broad background against which a marketing executive can analyze the market for his particular product or service. People with needs to satisfy and money to spend, however, must be *willing* to spend before we can say a market exists. Consequently in the next three chapters we shall look into consumer motivation and buying patterns—the "willingness-to-buy" factor in our definition of a market.

QUESTIONS AND PROBLEMS

1. Distinguish between market aggregation and market segmentation.
2. What are some benefits a company can expect from segmenting its market?
3. For each of the following population factors, give several examples of products whose market demand would be particularly affected by the individual population factor:

   a. Regional distribution
   b. Marital status
   c. Sex

   d. Age
   e. Urban, rural, and suburban distribution

4. Cite some sectional differences in product preferences caused by factors other than climate.
5. The average level of formal education attained by people in the United States has risen substantially over the past few decades. What influence does this factor have on buying habits? In what ways might this trend affect the demand for particular products and services?
6. How is the marketing mix for automobiles likely to differ when marketing to each of the following market segments?

   a. High school students
   b. Husbands
   c. Bluecollar workers

   d. Housewives
   e. Young single adults

7. What users' benefits would you stress when advertising each of the following three products to each of the three markets?

   Products

   a. Stereo record player
   b. Toothpaste
   c. 10-day Caribbean cruise

   Markets

   a. School teachers
   b. Retired people
   c. Working women

8. Using the demographic and income segmentation bases discussed in this chapter, describe the segment which is likely to be the best market for:

   a. Snow skis
   b. Good French wines
   c. Power hand tools

   d. Birthday cards
   e. Outdoor barbecue grills

9. List four of the major trends in population noted in this chapter—for instance, a growing segment of the population is over sixty-five years of age. Then carefully explain how each of the following types of retail stores might be influenced by each of the trends:

   a. Supermarket
   b. Sporting goods store

   c. Drugstore
   d. Restaurant

10. Roger Carson, aged thirty-two, is married and has two children. The family income is $750 a month. If the family expenditures are average, approximately how much will the Carson family spend on the following items?

    a. Food
    b. Clothing

    c. Automobile and its upkeep
    d. Recreation

11. How will the expenditures in the Carson family compare with those of Paul Foster and his family? The families are the same size, but Paul's income is $425 a month.

12. In what ways has the rise in disposable personal income since 1950 influenced the marketing programs of a department store? A supermarket?

13. Is psychic income a concept applicable to groups or only to an individual? Can psychic income be measured in a quantitative manner?

14. Give examples of products for which the demand is substantially influenced by fluctuations in discretionary purchasing power.

MARKETS: PSYCHOLOGICAL DETERMINANTS OF BUYER BEHAVIOR

In the course of doing her weekly family grocery shopping Friday afternoon at a local supermarket, a housewife selected a 1-pound can of Maxwell House drip-grind coffee. To the casual observer—and perhaps even to the housewife herself, by now—this may have been a simple, routine purchase. Yet this seemingly simple buying action was the result of decision making on several issues. Why did she buy Maxwell House instead of another brand? Why did she buy a 1-pound can instead of some other size? Why did she buy coffee instead of tea or some other drink? Why was drip-grind selected instead of the freeze-dried or regular instant coffee? Why did she shop at that particular supermarket, and why did she pick Friday instead of some other day?

IMPORTANCE AND DIFFICULTY OF UNDERSTANDING CONSUMER BEHAVIOR

We have reasonably good quantitative data on how many people live in each geographic region, how many are high school graduates, and so forth. We also have reasonably adequate market information about income and its distribution. For some products (snow shovel, oil filter), demographic and economic factors alone may explain why a consumer bought the product. Most consumer purchases, however, are also likely to be influenced by psychological or sociological factors. Differences in demographic and economic factors alone do not satisfactorily explain some variations in personal behavior. These factors alone cannot account for the differences between the woman who loves to cook and the one who does not, or for the differences in brand preferences for soft drinks or cigarettes, when in blindfold tests consumers cannot tell one brand from another.

Consequently, to develop a successful marketing program, typically a company should learn as much as possible about its customers' motives, attitudes, beliefs, interests, values, personality, self-image, and other psychological variables.[1]

We also need to study families and other groups—their internal relationships, their attitudes, and the diffusion of information among them—because these groups also influence buying behavior.

An understanding of the reasons *why* people buy a given product or shop at a certain store is critical. If the seller does not appeal to the right motive, he will probably lose the sale. Attempting to sell decorative outdoor lighting to a buyer in an industrial plant who wants lighting solely for security purposes will probably get a salesman nowhere. An understanding of the buying behavior of various market segments helps a seller to select the most effective product design, price, advertising appeals, channels of distribution, and the many other aspects of his marketing program.

However, we know very little about what goes on in a buyer's mind leading up to a purchase and following the purchasing action. In fact, that infinitely complex mechanism—the human mind—has frequently been referred to as a "black box" because we know so little about how it works.

Sometimes the explanation for his behavior is not even discernible to the buyer himself. To illustrate, buying motives may be grouped on different levels depending upon the consumer's awareness of them and his willingness to divulge them. In the first group, the buyer recognizes, and is quite willing to talk about, his motives for buying certain products. In the second, he is aware of his reasons for buying, but will not admit them to others. A man may buy a backyard swimming pool because he feels it adds to his social position in the neighborhood, or a woman may buy cosmetics to increase her attractiveness to men. But when questioned about their motives, they offer other reasons which they think will be more socially acceptable. The most difficult motives to uncover are those in the third group, where even the buyers themselves do not know the real factors motivating their buying actions. A purchase is rarely the result of a single motive. Furthermore, various motives may conflict with one another. In buying a new dress, a woman may want to please her husband, be admired (or possibly envied) as a fashion leader by other women in her social circle, and strive for economy. To do all this in one purchase is truly a difficult assignment. Buyer behavior also changes over a period of time because of changes in income, changes in life cycle stage, and other factors.

If we add to this complexity the countless variations occurring because each consumer is a separate individual with a unique personality, then our task of

---

[1]The term "psychographics" is currently being used by many marketing researchers as a collective synonym for these psychological variables, although as yet no universally agreeable definition has been developed for the term. See Ruth Ziff, "Psychographics for Market Segmentation," *Journal of Advertising Research*, April, 1971, pp. 3–9; and Fred D. Reynolds, *Psychographics: a Conceptual Orientation*, University of Georgia, College of Business Administration, Athens, Research Monograph No. 6, 1973.

understanding consumer behavior may seem an impossible dream. Yet try we must, because an understanding of buyer behavior is critical to the success of a marketing program. In the face of all the individuality and complexity, a seller must search for reasonably similar behavioral threads permeating a market segment so that he can appeal to a wide group with one marketing program. Fortunately marketing men, working with behavioral scientists, have enjoyed some success in developing generalizations about individual and group factors as they influence consumer buying behavior.

THEORIES OF BUYER BEHAVIOR

Perhaps because we know relatively little about how the human mind works, there is still no comprehensive body of knowledge which is generally accepted as the "theory of buyer behavior." Instead, over the years several different theoretical models have been developed to explain buyer behavior. Each makes some interpretive contribution, and some are more useful than others in explaining the purchase behavior toward a given product. The economic model, for example, might best explain the purchase of expensive industrial equipment, while psychoanalytic theory might be used to explain the demand for cosmetics.[2]

We shall review briefly some of these theories, not only because they have some current validity and realism, but also because they are a part of the evolutionary development of present-day thinking. The first of these constructs was developed by economists. Later models emerged from the behavioral science fields of psychology and sociology.

MICROECONOMIC THEORY

One of the earlier theories of consumer behavior (which in modified form still has some usefulness today) was developed by classical economists in the course of their formulating a comprehensive theory of the individual firm (microeconomics). This behavioral theory, first posed by Adam Smith and others, is based on the notion that man is an economic, rational being and that at all times he is acting in his self-interest. Later this theory was refined by the neoclassical economists, primarily Alfred Marshall of England.

The resultant concept—the marginal-utility theory of value—holds that a consumer will continue to buy units of a given product as long as the satisfaction he receives from the last unit consumed (marginal utility) equals or exceeds the marginal utility derived from the same expenditure for any other product.

This theory is based on some strong assumptions: (1) that the consumer is always trying to maximize his satisfactions (utilities) within the limits of his financial resources, (2) that he has complete knowledge of alternative sources for satisfying his wants, and (3) that he is always acting in a rational manner.

Some of the limitations in such a model should be obvious. First, it does not include the psychological and sociological factors which influence behavior. Totally rational behavior is not typical among consumers. Nor is the theory sound

---

[2]For a review of five models of the buyer's "black box," along with their respective marketing applications, see Philip Kotler, "Behavioral Models for Analyzing Buyers," *Journal of Marketing*, October, 1965, pp. 37–45.

when it implies that impulsive behavior is irrational. Finally, it is difficult to quantify the satisfactions received from a product. Research efforts over the years by scholars in such organizations as the Survey Research Center at the University of Michigan have done much to realistically modify the basic theory.[3]

While it is granted that the economic model cannot fully explain buyer behavior, nevertheless it does have some usefulness. Industrial buyers quite frequently base all or a good part of their buying decisions on the marginal-utility concept. Household consumers, when buying autos or other infrequently purchased, high-priced items, essentially act out the economic model as one significantly determining factor in their purchasing decision. Also, the theory can be particularly useful when it is treated as a *normative* rather than an *absolute* or *descriptive* model of behavior.[4] For instance, from the model we might hypothesize that the sales of a product will increase as its price decreases. For the model to be realistically useful, we must treat this sample hypothesis as a generalization. That is, sales will *usually* increase, or the hypothesis is applicable for most (not *all*) consumers. The fact that some consumers refrain from buying when the price goes down does not invalidate the hypothesis-generalization.

PSYCHOLOGICAL THEORIES

Psychologists are far from agreement about which of their constructs provides the best insights into the consumer's mind. Consequently, we shall summarize briefly some of the dominant theories as formulated by different schools of psychological thought.

Learning theories. Interpreting and predicting the consumer's learning process is a real key to understanding his buying behavior. Therefore, it is unfortunate that no simple learning theory has emerged as universally workable and acceptable. The three principle learning theories described here are (1) stimulus-response theories, (2) cognitive theories, and (3) gestalt and field theories.[5]

Stimulus-response theories. These were first formulated by psychologists such as Pavlov, Skinner, and Hull on the basis of their laboratory experiments with animals. This school of theorists hold that learning occurs as a person (or animal) responds to some stimulus and is rewarded (reinforced) with need satisfaction for a correct response or penalized for an incorrect one. When the same response is repeated in reaction to a given stimulus, habit-behavioral patterns are established.

An application of the S-R model is the *behaviorism* approach, expounded by Watson and still applied in advertising today.[6] He postulated the idea of repeating

---

[3]See, for example, George Katona, *The Powerful Consumer,* McGraw-Hill Book Company, New York, 1960; G. Katona, "Rational Behavior and Economic Behavior," *Psychological Review,* September, 1953, pp. 307–318; G. Katona and Eva Mueller, "A Study of Purchase Decisions," in Lincoln H. Clark (ed.), *Consumer Behavior,* New York University Press, New York, 1954, pp. 30–87.

[4]Kotler, *op. cit.,* p. 39.

[5]See Ernest R. Hilgard and George H. Bower, *Theories of Learning,* Appleton-Century-Crofts, Inc., New York, 1966.

[6]See John B. Watson, *Behaviorism,* The People's Institute Publishing Co., New York, 1925.

the same stimuli over and over in order to solidify the response patterns. Out of this came the idea of constantly repeating an advertisement to firmly reinforce a given purchasing response. Applying this idea, for many years the advertising for Marlboro cigarettes has featured the theme of masculinity (the cowboy) and "Marlboro Country" (the rugged Western outdoors atmosphere). The concept of behaviorism is probably too simplistic an approach, however, because today we realize that perceptions, attitudes, and other cognitive factors (not just the mechanistic S-R concept) also can influence a consumer's response to repetitive advertising.

Cognitive theories. This set of learning theories rejects the S-R model as being too mechanistic. In S-R theory, behavior is the result of *only* the positive or negative reinforcement stemming from a response to some stimuli, and no other influencing variables are recognized as intervening in the S-R channel. Proponents of cognitive theory insist that learning is influenced by factors such as attitudes and beliefs, past experiences, and an insightful understanding of how to use the current situation to achieve a goal. Habitual behavioral patterns, then, are the result of perceptive thinking and goal orientation. In summary, cognitive theorists postulate that a person's brain processes and nervous system are significant in forming his behavioral patterns, while S-R theorists pay little attention to these intervening variables.

Gestalt and field theories. "Gestalt" is a German word for which there is no exact English counterpart. Roughly, the word means "configuration," "pattern," or "form." Gestalt psychologists are concerned with the "whole" of a thing—the total scene—rather than its component parts. They maintain that learning and behavior should be viewed as a total process, in contrast to the individual-element approach in the S-R model.[7]

In this behavioral theory, perception, past experiences, and goal orientation are key elements. (Note the similarity to the cognitive learning model.) Perception, which is discussed later, may be defined as the meaning we attach, on the basis of our past experiences, to stimuli as received through our five senses. According to gestalt theory, a person perceives and reacts to stimuli in light of his experiences. Furthermore, it is assumed that people behave in goal-oriented patterns. That is, some inner drive (tension) arises which demands satisfaction (the goal). Then in a more or less conscious, rational manner the person strives for this goal, solving problems and coping with his environment en route.

Field theory, as formulated by Kurt Lewin, is a useful refinement of gestalt psychology.[8] This theory holds that the only determining force accounting for a person's behavior at any given time is his psychological "field" as it exists at that time. The concept of a person's *field* or *life space,* which is a key element in the theory, may be defined as the totality of existing facts pertaining to the individual and his environment at the time of the behavior. Thus, to understand a consumer's goal-oriented behavior, we must understand him and his perception of his

---

[7]See K. Koffka, *Principles of Gestalt Psychology,* Harcourt, Brace, & World, Inc., New York, 1935; Wolfgang Kohler, *Gestalt Psychology,* Liveright Publishing Corporation, New York, 1947; and Willis D. Ellis (ed.), *Source Book of Gestalt Psychology,* Harcourt, Brace & World, Inc., New York, 1938.

[8]See Kurt Lewin, *A Dynamic Theory of Personality* (1935) and *Principles of Topological Psychology* (1936), both McGraw-Hill Book Company, New York.

environment—all the complex forces, barriers, conflicts, etc., which influence him as he strives to satisfy the drive which initiated the goal-seeking process.

Gestalt psychologists are concerned with man's perception and understanding of his total environment. They believe that man perceives the whole rather than its parts. They further postulate that a person's perception of the whole is quite different from what we might expect if each part were considered separately. Thus, looking at the following configuration, most people will perceive four sets of tracks, four pairs of lines, or four columns, but rarely do they perceive eight vertical lines.

‖   ‖   ‖   ‖

Moreover, rather than perceiving the separate parts—the individual stimuli—a person will organize them (in his perception) into a whole which is meaningful to him in light of his past experiences. That is, it is the properties of the *total field* which influence his perceptions of the stimuli in that field. To illustrate, a distinguished-looking man in a white coat can speak in a serious tone in a TV commercial advertising a pain reliever or a brand of toothpaste. Many viewers will perceive him as a doctor and his message as a medical endorsement because that is how they interpret that total scene in light of their past experiences.

Several "field" principles which have applications in marketing have been developed by gestalt pscyhologists reflecting ways in which field properties of stimuli affect our perception of them.[9] The principle of *closure* postulates that we tend to produce a complete figure in a meaningful way. Thus "13 0" will be "closed" by the viewer to get the letters "B O." A change in spacing (illustrating the principle of *proximity*) can give different results—the number "130" rather than two letters. When the Kellogg Company (cereal manufacturers) ran billboard ads with the name so far to the right that the final "g" was cut off, viewers tended to add that final "g" to produce a complete figure. Incidentally, the attention-getting value of the ad is also increased. Of course, there is the danger that the reader will not take the time to close the gap or that the ad is so subtle that the closure point is missed.

Messages must be placed in a reasonable *context* (a smartly dressed debutante should not be shown painting her house). Also the ads should be *simple* in both structure and content. Because of locational properties, some items will *stand out* in a sea of similar-looking products. This principle places a premium on eye-level shelf position in a supermarket, for example. All parts of a marketing program —price, type of ads, product quality, retailers handling the product, etc.— must be in *harmony,* i.e., consistent with consumers' expectations. And each product marketed by a firm must fit in with the consumer's perception of the total field, i.e., the company and all its other products.

Psychoanalytic theories. The psychoanalytic school of thought, as founded by Sigmund Freud and later modified by his followers and critics, has had a tremendous impact on the study of human personality and behavior. Freud contended that there are three parts to our mind—the id, the ego, and the superego.

---

[9]Adapted from James H. Myers and William H. Reynolds, *Consumer Behavior and Marketing Management,* Houghton Mifflin Company, Boston, 1967, pp. 21–34.

The id houses the basic instinctive drives, many of which are antisocial. The superego is our conscience, accepting moral standards and directing the instinctive drives into acceptable channels, thus avoiding feelings of guilt or shame. The id and the superego are sometimes in conflict. The ego is the conscious, rational control center which maintains a balance between the uninhibited instincts of the id and the socially oriented, constraining superego.

Freud's behavioral thesis was that a person enters this world with certain instinctive biological desires which cannot be satisfied in a socially acceptable fashion. As a person learns that he cannot gratify these needs in a direct manner, he develops other, more subtle means of seeking satisfaction. As the basic urges are being repressed, tensions and frustrations are developing. Also, feelings of guilt or shame about these drives cause a person to suppress and even sublimate them to the point where they become subconscious. Instead, he substitutes rationalizations and socially acceptable behavior. Yet the basic urges are always there. The net result is very complex behavior. Sometimes even the person himself does not understand why he feels or acts as he does.

Some of Freud's followers made refinements in his model when they introduced a cultural perspective to behavior, instead of adhering completely to the biologically determined foundation. Adler believed that man's basic drive is for power and superiority. Fromm felt that man is lonely; instead of freedom, he wants security and human companionship. Horney contended that man's behavioral patterns are influenced by his efforts to cope with his anxieties.[10]

One significant marketing implication in psychoanalytic theory is that a person's real motive for buying a given product, shopping at a certain store, or performing any other consumer buying act may well be hidden. The usual research techniques which are feasible for determining demographic and economic data normally will prove fruitless in uncovering the real reasons for a person's buying behavior. This situation has given rise to marketing's use of motivation research, a series of techniques originally developed for use in psychology. It is through motivation research that marketers concluded, for example, that a housewife who uses instant coffee is perceived as a lazy person who does a poor job caring for her husband and children, and that using household appliances gives a woman the guilt feeling that she is lazy. Manufacturers then promoted the idea that using such products would allow her to spend more time with her family. Motivation research is discussed later in more detail.

In summary, it is out of psychoanalytic theory that marketers realized they must provide a buyer with socially.acceptable rationalizations for his purchasing. Yet they also can appeal subconsciously to his dreams, hopes, and fears.

SOCIOLOGICAL THEORIES

The psychological theories which we have reviewed tend to concentrate on the individual, treating his social environment as a secondary consideration. In the behavioral theories developed by sociologists and cultural anthropologists, the

---

[10]Alfred Adler, *The Science of Living,* Greenberg, Inc., New York, 1929; Erich Fromm, *Escape from Freedom,* Holt, Rinehart and Winston, Inc., New York, 1941; Karen Horney, *The Neurotic Personality of Our Time* (1937) and *Our Inner Conflicts* (1945), both by W. W. Norton & Company, Inc., New York.

primary focus is on interpersonal relations and influences. In the next chapter we shall examine some of these social influences as they relate to buyer behavior.

SUMMARY OF THEORIES

We still have not developed a cohesive, comprehensive theory of buying behavior. We do, however, have some insights into the consumer's "black box" by virtue of contributions from various theoretical models. We see how the consumer balances prices and satisfactions within the limits of his income, although it is granted that the theory is weakened by some unrealistic assumptions. We see how repeated responses to given stimuli lead to habitual behavior. Cognitive theorists introduced the elements of thought, perception, and past experiences into the process. Gestalt and field theorists provided insight into human behavior in light of the total scene rather than the perception of individual elements in that psychological field. From Freudian thought we understand that behavior is influenced by re-pressed desires and hidden motives. Finally, sociologists and anthropologists have explained the interpersonal social influences on behavior.

The differences—sometimes quite wide—in possible interpretations of the same behavior should remind us that the consumer's total psychological field is quite complex and that many forces—past and present, hidden and apparent, instinctive and learned, individual and environmental—all do influence behavior.[11]

PSYCHOLOGICAL DETERMINANTS OF BUYER BEHAVIOR

In discussing the psychological forces in the consumer's behavioral field, our model is as follows: one or more motives within a person will trigger behavior toward a goal which will bring satisfaction. This goal-oriented behavior is influenced by the person's perceptions. His perceptions, in turn, are influenced by his learning experiences, attitudes and beliefs, personality, and self-concept. See Fig. 4-1.

MOTIVATION

We are trying to understand why consumers act (behave) as they do. But first we might ask why a person acts at all. The answer is, "because he is motivated"; that is, all behavior starts with motivation. A *motive* (or drive) is a stimulated need which a goal-oriented individual seeks to satisfy (i.e., he seeks to reduce tension). Thus hunger, a need for security, and a desire for prestige are examples of motives.

It is important to note that a need must be aroused or stimulated before it can serve as a motive. It is possible and usual to have needs which are latent and thus do

---

[11]For an examination of four additional contemporary theories of behavior, set in the context of marketing, see Charles D. Schewe, "Selected Social Psychological Models for Analyzing Buyers," *Journal of Marketing,* July, 1973, pp. 31–39. The four are: (1) the McClelland model, stressing the theory of achievement motivation, (2) the Goffman model of role theory, (3) the Festinger model of cognitive dissonance theory, and (4) the Riesman model of the inner-versus other-directed individual.

Figure 4-1.

not serve as the instigator of behavior until they become sufficiently intense, that is, stimulated. The sources of this arousal may be internal (the person gets hungry) or environmental (he sees an ad for food); or just thinking about food may make him hungry.

There is no single generally acceptable classification of motives, simply because we do not know enough about human motivation. However, psychologists generally do agree that motives can be grouped into two broad categories— *biogenic* needs (such as the needs for food, drink, sex, and bodily comfort), which arise from physiological states of tension, and *psychogenic* needs, which arise from psychological states of tension. Through the years marketers have used such dichotomous classifications of motives as instinctive-learned, product-patronage (why the consumer bought this *product* versus why she shopped at this *store*), and primary-selective (reasons for buying a *type* of product versus reasons for buying a certain *brand* of that product).

A. H. Maslow has formulated a useful theory of motivation. He calls it a "holistic-dynamic" theory in that is fuses the points of view of different schools of psychological thought and also conforms to known clinical, observational, and experimental facts.[12] Maslow identified a hierarchy of five levels of needs, arrayed in the order in which a person seeks to gratify them:

1. Physiological needs—for food, drink, sex, and shelter
2. Safety needs—for security, order, protection, and family stability
3. Belongingness and love needs—for affection, belonging to a group, and acceptance

---

[12]A. H. Maslow, *Motivation and Personality,* Harper & Row, Publishers, Inc., New York, 1954, pp. 80–106.

4. Esteem needs—for self-respect, reputation, prestige, and status
5. Self-actualization needs—for self-fulfillment, for doing what one is best fitted for

For the relatively few people who move through the full array, even to fulfilling a need for self-actualization, Maslow identified two additional classes of cognitive needs:

1. The need to know and understand
2. The need for aesthetic satisfaction (beauty)

Maslow contended that a person theoretically remains at one level until all his needs at that level are satisfied. Then new needs emerge on the next higher level. To illustrate, as long as a person is hungry, thirsty, etc., the physiological (biogenic) needs dominate. Once they are satisfied, the psychogenic needs in the safety category become important. When safety needs are largely gratified, new (and higher-level) needs arise, and so on.

In real life Maslow recognized that there is more flexibility than the rigid hierarchical model seems to imply. Actually a normal person is most likely to be working toward need satisfaction on several levels at the same time. And rarely are all needs on a given level ever fully satisfied.

While the Maslow construct has much to offer us, there are still some unanswered questions and disagreements. For one thing, there is no consideration of multiple motives for the same behavior. A teacher takes a ship's cruise to better her knowledge of foreign countries, to meet new people, and to rest her frazzled nerves. Other problems not fitting our model are (1) identical behavior by several people resulting from quite different motives and (2) quite different behavior resulting from identical motives.

PERCEPTION

Once a person is motivated, his goal-oriented behavior path will be influenced by his perceptions. Earlier we defined perception as the meaning we attribute, on the basis of past experiences, to stimuli as received through our five senses. A person's perceptions are shaped by three sets of influences: (1) the physical characteristics of the stimuli, (2) the relation of the stimuli to their surroundings (the gestalt field idea), and (3) conditions within the individual.

Our senses perceive the shape, color, sound, feel, and taste of stimuli, and our behavior is then influenced by these physical perceptions. Marketers must recognize that we are exposed to a tremendously large number of stimuli. Thus to gain a consumer's attention, a marketer must do something special. This is the principle behind the use of large ads, a novelty approach in advertising, and the use of color in a sea of black-and-white ads (or just the opposite—the use of a black-and-white ad in the midst of colored ads).

Each individual perceives a given stimulus within his own frame of reference. Factors within a person which influence his frame of reference include his learning experiences, attitudes, and personality and the way in which he views himself.

A continuous process of selectivity is going on as far as our perceptions are concerned. First, we are exposed only to a selective number of stimuli. We cannot read every magazine, visit all stores, or watch all TV programs. Then we perceive only part of what we are exposed to. We can read a newspaper and not notice a given ad, or we can watch a TV program and screen out the commercials. Then only part of what we selectively perceive do we retain. Finally, only part of what we selectively retain do we act upon.

There are many marketing implications in these selective processes.[13] From a marketing point of view a product or service does not exist by itself, nor does it have any intrinsic meaning. A product exists in marketing only if a consumer perceives that it will satisfy his wants. Moreover, a given product will be perceived quite differently by different consumers. A child perceives a color TV set as a source of pleasurable entertainment; Mother views it as a baby-sitter, a source of information, and a teacher for her child; Father may view it as an overpriced luxury which prevented him from buying a new outboard motor (the old black-and-white set was perfectly OK as he perceived it); and to the retailer it is just another product carrying a lower gross margin than he thinks is reasonable. Then for countless other consumers this product simply does not exist; it has never entered their field of selective perception.

Marketers cannot afford unlimited advertising exposure, so they strive for the selective exposure which will fall within the target market range of selective perception. Then the message must be sufficiently meaningful and strong to survive the consumers' selective retention processes.

Learning experiences. As a factor influencing a person's perceptions, learning may be defined as changes in behavior resulting from previous experiences. However, also by definition, learning does *not* include behavior changes attributable to instinctive responses, growth, or temporary states of the organism such as hunger, fatigue, sleep, etc.[14]

The stimulus-response model, including reinforcement as an essential element, is an explanation of the learning process which is useful in marketing. Four factors—drive, cue, response, and reinforcement—are fundamental to the process.[15] A *drive* (or motive) is a strong stimulus for response action because it (the drive) requires satisfaction. A drive requires a response, but the *cues*—weaker stimuli—determine the pattern of this response—the "when," "where," and "how" of the behavior. For instance, a TV commercial, store hours, and a change in price are cues which might well shape a consumer's behavior as he seeks to satisfy an aroused need for some food item. Sometimes the cue itself serves to arouse a drive, as when a person passes an ice-cream parlor and realizes he is thirsty or wants something sweet. His *response* is simply his behavioral reaction to the cues and the drive. *Reinforcement* is the result of a rewarding response-action.

If the response is gratifying, a connection between cue and response will be established; that is, a behavioral pattern will be learned. Learning, then, emerges from reinforcement. Continually rewarding responses lead to habit. Once a habitual pattern of behavior is established, it replaces conscious cognitive learning. The stronger the habit, i.e., the more set the reinforcement, the more difficult it is for a competitive product to enter a consumer's learning field. On the other hand,

---

[13]Adapted in part from Harold H. Kassarjian and Thomas S. Robertson (eds.), *Perspectives in Consumer Behavior,* Scott, Foresman and Company, Glenview, Ill., 1968, pp. 58–59.

[14]For a discussion of other definitions of learning, see John F. Hall, *Psychology of Learning,* J. B. Lippincott Company, Philadelphia, 1966, pp. 3–6.

[15]John Dollard and Neal E. Miller, *Personality and Psychotherapy,* McGraw-Hill Book Company, New York, 1950, chap. 3.

if the response-action is not appropriate (not rewarding), the consumer's mind is open to another set of cues leading to another response. For example, she will buy a substitute product type or switch to another brand.[16]

As we observed earlier, no general agreement exists regarding one basic learning process. Cognitive theorists would inject attitudes and beliefs into the learning model. They particularly would give weight to something other than past experience. They believe a person can use his insight or thinking abilities to understand a current problem situation even if there are no historical precedents.

Another approach holds that learning is a probabilistic process, under the assumption that the best predictor of future buying behavior is the sequence, rhythm, and frequency of past buying behavior.[17]

An interesting aspect of learning which has significant marketing implications is the question of whether learning can occur without awareness.[18] That is, can a person learn a new pattern of behavior without being aware that this behavior was influenced or changed? (Awareness is defined here as the conscious recognition of a behavioral stimulus. That is, a person consciously hears a TV commercial or is conscious of seeing a magazine ad. We should note that psychologists identify different levels of conscious and subconscious awareness of external stimuli.)

When awareness is defined in this manner, psychological theories and experimental findings both suggest that an individual may learn and behave without awareness. In other words, consumers perceive stimuli without being aware of them, and these unconsciously received stimuli might influence purchasing decisions. To illustrate, a person may buy a product, unaware that the real stimuli were some ads which he saw some time ago and which in his conscious mind he had forgotten about. Or during a TV commercial, he may engage in conversation, ignoring the commercial. Yet the message stimulus can make a subconscious impression which may lead to a purchase at some future time.

Attitudes and beliefs. Attitudes and beliefs are strong and direct forces affecting consumers' perceptions and buying behavior. They significantly influence a person's perceptions by selectively screening out any exposure of stimuli which conflict with his attitudes. Attitudes also can distort the perception of messages and affect the degree of their retention.

Beliefs may be categorized as knowledge, opinion, or faith, depending upon their verifiability.[19] To illustrate, if we believe that drinking milk is good for a growing child and we know on the basis of evidence that milk is beneficial, our belief has been verified. A belief is defined as knowledge if it can be, or has been, verified by personal experience or by outside-source research. An opinion is a

---

[16]See Norman Kangun, "How Advertisers Can Use Learning Theory," *Business Horizons,* April, 1968, pp. 29–40; see also Sadaomi Oshikawa and John Wheatley, "Learning Theory, Attitudes, and Advertising," *University of Washington Business Review,* Summer, 1968, pp. 24–33.

[17]Kassarjian and Robertson, *op. cit.,* p. 60; for a discussion and application of this approach, see Alfred A. Kuehn, "Consumer Brand Choice as a Learning Process," *Journal of Advertising Research,* December, 1962, pp. 10–17.

[18]This discussion is adapted from Sadaomi Oshikawa, "Learning and Behavior without Awareness: Their Implications to Consumer Behavior and Sovereignty," *California Management Review,* Summer, 1970, pp. 61–69.

[19]This paragraph is adapted from Kassarjian and Robertson, *op.cit.,* pp. 60–61.

belief which has not yet been verified. Faith is a belief which is unverifiable, and yet adhered to.

Attitudes may be defined as a person's enduring favorable or unfavorable cognitive evaluations, emotional feelings, or action tendencies toward some object or idea.[20] Attitudes thus involve thought processes as well as emotional feelings, and they vary in intensity. Attitudes influence beliefs, and beliefs influence attitudes. In fact, for the purposes of our generalized, introductory-level discussion of buying behavior, we shall use the two concepts interchangeably. They both reflect value judgments and positive or negative feelings toward a product, service, or brand.

Various studies uniformly report a very close relationship between consumers' attitudes and their buying decisions, as concerns both the type of product and the brand selections. For many years the Survey Research Center at the University of Michigan has conducted studies of consumer buying intentions regarding *product types.* Consistently the results show that both buying intentions and actual purchases are influenced by consumers' attitudes; also, changes in buying are related to attitude change.[21] Studies of attitudinal influence on *brand selection* show similar patterns, One study, for example, covering low-unit-price products (mostly food items), showed an extremely close relation between consumers' preferences (attitudes) and the brands they actually purchased.

Surely, then it is in a marketer's best interests to understand how attitudes are formed, measured, and changed. They are formed, generally speaking, by the information a person acquires through (1) his past learning experiences with the product or idea, or (2) his relations with his reference groups (family, social and work groups, etc.). The perception of this information is influenced also by his personality traits.[22]

Attitude measurement is far from easy. In limited instances a researcher may simply employ the direct-question, survey research technique. Other studies lend themselves more to the projective technique, to be mentioned later in connection with motivation research. The most widely used techniques, however, have been some form of attitude scaling. Respondents may be asked, for instance, to rank their preferences when shown several models, designs, or materials. In another test the person might be shown several pairs of items, one at a time, and be asked to select which of the two she prefers (the paired-comparisons technique). Another technique is a rating scale where the respondent states her evaluation at some point, ranging from one extreme to another (extremely modern and extremely old-fashioned, for example).[23]

---

[20]See David Krech, Richard S. Crutchfield, and Egerton L. Ballachey, *Individual in Society,* McGraw-Hill Book Company, New York,1962, chap. 5; and Daniel Katz, "The Functional Approach to the Study of Attitudes," *Public Opinion Quarterly,* Summer, 1960, pp. 163–204.

[21]George Katona, *The Powerful Consumer,* McGraw-Hill Book Company, New York, 1960, especially pp. 52–53. For the suggestion that out of many possible attitudes, only a few really determine buying behavior, see James H. Myers and Mark I. Alpert, "Determinant Buying Attitudes: Meaning and Measurement," *Journal of Marketing,* October, 1968, pp. 13–20.

[22]See Krech, Crutchfield, and Ballachey, *op. cit.,* chap. 6.

[23]For a discussion of some widely used scaling techniques, along with excellent footnote references, see James F. Engel, David T. Kollat, and Roger D. Blackwell, *Consumer Behavior,* 2d ed., Holt, Rinehart and Winston, Inc., New York, 1973, pp. 274–283; see also Myers and Reynolds, *op. cit.,* pp. 150–157, for a good discussion of attitude measurement.

Given the hypothesis that attitudes strongly influence buying behavior, then the problem arises: how can a company bring its products and consumers' attitudes into a consonant state, that is, into a situation where a consumer perceives his need to be best satisfied by the given product or brand? A marketer has two choices —either he can change consumers' attitudes to be consonant with his product, or he can determine what consumers' attitudes are and then change his product to match those attitudes. Obviously, it is easier to change his product than to change consumers' attitudes. Nevertheless, attitudes sometimes can be modified, particularly in cases where this may be the only reasonable choice (as when a firm is introducing a truly new product or a quite unusual new use for an existing one).

Marketers should face the fact that it is *extremely* difficult to change consumers' attitudes, regardless of marketing critics' opinions to the contrary.[24] If there is to be a change, it is most likely to occur when a person is open-minded in his beliefs or when existing attitude is of weak intensity, that is, when there is little information to support the attitude or very little ego-involvement on the part of the individual. The stronger a person's brand loyalty is to a certain product, for example, the tougher it is to change that attitude.

Highly persuasive communication is ordinarily needed if a seller is to have any hope of changing a buyer's attitude. The communication (advertisement, personal sales talk, etc.) should attempt to change one or more of the three dimensions in our definition of an attitude. By providing effective information about his brand, for example, a marketer might change the consumer's *cognitive evaluations* of that brand. With a strong, emotionally appealing ad, the seller might change the buyer's *emotional feelings.* The buyer's *action tendencies* toward a brand might be changed by getting him to do something which contradicts his current preferences. For instance, the use of coupons, free samples, or "cents-off" sales might induce the buyer to change his action patterns and try a new brand. Even then the buyer must be open-minded and willing to let his present brand preferences be challenged—no easy assignment for the seller.

Fear appeals. To induce a favorable consumer response (attitude change, decision to buy, etc.) typically a company will use a set of positive promotional appeals. These are appeals which stress the beneficial or desirable results from using the advertised item. However, management should recognize that negative, fear, anxiety-inducing appeals may very well be quite effective.[25] Negative or fear appeals warn the consumer about the bad consequences which will result from using (or *not* using, as the case may be) the advertised product or service. Thus the American Cancer Society advertises the harm that can come from smoking. Insurance companies picture the terrible straits a family is left in when tragedy strikes and there is no insurance protection. People are warned about the dangers of combining drinking and driving. A person is pictured as a social outcast for not using the advertised brand of toothpaste, mouthwash, or deodorant.

Just how effective are these fear appeals in shaping consumers' attitudes and

---

[24]This and the following paragraph are based on Engel, Kollat, and Blackwell, *op. cit.,* chaps. 10–11. These authors caution that much of the attitude-change theory and research so far does not have a lot of practical marketing applicability.

[25]See Michael L. Ray and William L. Wilkie, "Fear: The Potential of an Appeal Neglected by Marketing," *Journal of Marketing,* January, 1970, pp. 54–62.

responses? One landmark study involving dental hygiene reported that a strong fear appeal was less effective than a mild or moderate fear appeal—that is, the stronger the fear appeal the less effective it was.[26] Other studies have concluded that fear appeals are likely to be more effective among nonusers and nonowners of a product than among users or owners.[27] Thus the scare-advertising tactics of the American Cancer Society, regarding the harm from smoking, has been more effective among nonsmokers or low-rate-of-use smokers than among heavy smokers. Possibly heavy users of a product become defensive and thus resist any appeal which suggests they are doing something wrong. One marketing implication in this situation is that fear motivation may be more effective in developing new markets than in selling to, or changing, entrenched ones.

To reach users of a product, fear appeals may be effective in producing behavioral changes if "what is feared is damage to the *social image* of the self rather than to the physical self." Thus, in promoting safe driving, the appeal to "Watch out for that child" is more effective than "Watch out, or you'll be killed."[28]

On balance, the effectiveness of fear appeals seems limited. They have not resulted in any appreciable decrease in smoking, for instance. And traffic deaths did not decrease prior to the gas-shortage-induced lower speeds. But within its limits, fear appeals can be quite useful. It does seem unfortunate, however, that the ones who should respond the most to fear appeals (the heavy smokers or bad drivers) are likely to largely ignore or resist these appeals. And the people who need the admonition the least are the very ones likely to respond the strongest.

What are the ethical implications in the use of fear appeals? Is it a socially responsible approach? Again the answers are mixed, depending upon people's attitudes. Most all people probably would agree that it is socially desirable to use fear appeals (or anything else) to discourage bad driving or the use of drugs. The nonsmoker market segment would agree it is okay to use fear appeals to discourage smoking. But when you get to the area of ads using fear appeals to sell personal grooming products, that is when the real arguments arise concerning the ethics of fear appeals.

Personality. The study of human personality has interested many (and sometimes widely divergent) schools of psychological thought for generations. Yet (and perhaps because of this multifaceted attention) we still lack even a consensus definition of the term. Attempts to inventory and classify personality traits have understandably produced many different structures. In this discussion *personality* is defined as an individual's pattern of inner and outer traits which are a determinant of his behavioral responses.

It is quite generally agreed that a consumer's personality traits will influence

---

[26]Irving L. Janis and Seymour Feshbach, "Effects of Fear-Arousing Communications," *Journal of Abnormal and Social Psychology,* January, 1953, pp. 78–92.

[27]For a report on the relative effectiveness of fear advertising on owners versus nonowners of life insurance, see John J. Wheatley, "Marketing and the Use of Fear- or Anxiety-Arousing Appeals," *Journal of Marketing,* April, 1971, pp. 62–64; also see John J. Wheatley and Sadaomi Oshikawa, "The Relationship between Anxiety and Positive and Negative Advertising Appeals," *Journal of Marketing Research,* February, 1970, pp. 85–89.

[28]John R. Stuteville, "Psychic Defenses against High Fear Appeals: A Key Marketing Variable," *Journal of Marketing,* April, 1970, pp. 39–45, quote at p. 41.

his perceptions and buying behavior. Unfortunately, however, in the present state of the art there is no agreement as to the nature of this relationship, i.e. *how* personality influences behavior. Two points of view prevail. One holds that personality traits are the dominant force in determining behavior, overpowering any external influences. The opposite contention, as advocated by many sociologists and social psychologists, is that the situational environment is the key determining factor; the individual (through his personality, perhaps) *adapts* to various external situations.

The empirical research support for each of these positions suggests they both have merit. Perhaps the answer lies in an approach which represents the *interaction* of the two, i.e., a blend of (1) the past-experience, individual-difference factor with (2) the external situational characteristics.[29]

Several research studies have been made in which the intent was to explain and predict buying behavior on the basis of personality traits as measured by standard personality testing systems. One group of these studies sought marketing applications for Riesman's social groupings of people. Riesman divided people into three groups: tradition-directed (oriented toward the past and resistant to change), inner-directed (guided by internal personal values), and other-directed (dependent upon other people for guidance).[30] Riesman hypothesized that other-directed people are susceptible to external social influences, and subsequent research supports this point. At this writing, however, the research is not sufficiently conclusive for marketers to apply Riesman's ideas in promotional or new-product marketing programs.

Another group of research studies tried to relate a person's personality traits and the ease with which he can be persuaded. Again the results were inconclusive. There is particularly an abundance of published research attempting to predict product, brand, and store choice on the basis of personality traits. Unfortunately, there are sufficient differences of opinions among the various results so as to make them inconclusive.

In summary, the situation regarding personality and buying behavior seems to be this—we are convinced that personality influences buying behavior, but we are not sure how. Current theory suggests that personality and environment interact to shape behavior. For each different environmental scene, a given set of personality traits will result in different behavior. Obviously, however, much additional research is needed.[31]

The self-concept. Another behavior determinant is a person's self-concept, or self-image. The self-image is the way a person sees himself, and at the same time it is the picture which he thinks other have of him. Some psychologists distinguish between a person's *actual* self-concept (the way a person really sees himself) and his *ideal* self-concept (the way a person wants to be or would like to

---

[29]Much of this discussion on personality is adapted from Engel, Kollat, and Blackwell, *op. cit.,* chap. 12.

[30]David Riesman et al., *The Lonely Crowd,* Yale University Press, New Haven, Conn., 1950.

[31]For a review of the state of the art in which we try to relate personality to buying behavior and other aspects of marketing, see Harold H. Kassarjian, "Personality and Consumer Behavior: A Review," *Journal of Marketing Research,* November, 1971, pp. 409–418. The author concludes that most studies show a weak relationship, or none at all, and then he suggests some reasons for these poor results.

see himself). To some extent, the self-image theory is a reflection of other psychological and sociological concepts already discussed. A person's self-image is influenced, for instance, by innate and learned physiological and psychological needs. It is conditioned also by economic factors, demographic factors, and social-group influences.

Studies of actual purchases show that people generally prefer brands and products which are more, rather than less, like their own self-concept.[32] There are mixed reports concerning the role of actual and ideal self-concept as an influence on brand and product preferences. Some psychologists contend that consumption preferences correspond to a person's actual self-image. Others hold that the ideal self-image is dominant in consumers' choices. Studies of prepurchase intentions report essentially the same results as in actual postpurchase reports. That is, when referring to intended future purchases, people still selected products and brands which matched either their actual or ideal self-concept.[33]

Consumers' self-images are not easy to identify, nor do they fall into sharply defined categories. A person's self-image is a complex thing and often consists of conflicting elements. A secretary may see herself as a cooly efficient, highly effective, and valuable asset in a business organization, while at the same time considering herself a good mother, homemaker, and wife.

As marketing people, we want to be able to identify consumers' goals because they influence buying behavior. In many situations, we can determine those goals if we know what a person's self-image is. We must note, however, that a person's self-image tells us only what his goals are. This does not tell us *why* his self-image is as it is, nor does it explain why different people have different self-images. It is helpful just to understand that people do have different pictures of themselves. Our job is to determine what a person's self-image is. Then we can predict what his goals are and what his behavior is apt to be in the marketplace.

SUMMARY

Our model for discussing the determinants of buying behavior in the preceding sections is based on the assumption that this behavior is goal-oriented. The behavior is initiated when aroused needs (motives) create tensions which lead to activity designed to satisfy the needs and thus reduce the tensions. This goal-seeking behavior is influenced by the individual's perceptions of the alternatives open to him. He is quite selective in the stimuli (ad, products, brands, stores) which he exposes himself to, retains, and acts upon. His perceptions, in turn, are influenced by his learning experiences, attitudes and beliefs, personality traits, and self-image and by environmental and social factors. These environmental and social forces are discussed in the following chapter.

---

[32]See Ivan Ross, "Self-Concept and Brand Preference," *Journal of Business*, January, 1971, pp. 38–50. Also see Al E. Birdwell, "A Study of the Influence of Image Congruence on Consumer Choice," *Journal of Business*, January, 1968, pp. 76–88; Edward L. Grubb and Gregg Hupp, "Perception of Self, Generalized Stereotypes, and Brand Selection," *Journal of Marketing Research*, February, 1968, pp. 58–63; and Ira J. Dolich, "Congruence Relationships between Self Images and Brands," *Journal of Marketing Research*, February, 1969, pp. 80–84.

[33]See E. Laird Landon, Jr., "The Differential Role of Self-Concept and Ideal Self-Concept in Consumer Purchase Behavior," *Journal of Consumer Research*, Sept., 1974, pp. 44–51.

QUESTIONS AND PROBLEMS

1. Have your buying motives changed toward any products over a period of years? Name some products and trace the motivation changes, identifying the motives and explaining the reasons for the changes.
2. Explain how a company might apply the theory of marginal utility in the advertising of:
   a. Children's blue jeans
   b. Automatic lawn-sprinkler systems for the home
   c. Vacation trip to Hawaii
3. Does the psychoanalytic theory of buyer behavior have any practical application in the marketing of:
   a. Eye shadow
   b. Electric dishwashers
   c. Outboard motor boats
   d. Portable, 9-inch-screen TV sets
   Explain your reasoning in each case.
4. Explain some of the "field" principles developed in gestalt psychology and describe some marketing applications of each of these principles.
5. Carefully distinguish between biogenic and psychogenic needs, and give examples of each.
6. Which needs in Maslow's hierarchy might be satisfied by each of the following products or services?
   a. Marlboro cigarettes
   b. Travel agency located in your bank building
   c. *Webster's Intercollegiate Dictionary*
   d. Suntan lotion
   e. 1950 model Jaguar convertible selling for $100
   f. Services of a securities broker
   g. Portable cassette tape recorder
7. The following statements were taken from ads in magazines. Which, if any, of Maslow's needs are these products or services (as advertised) trying to satisfy?
   a. "That Maytag washer came to live with us over 14 years ago and its only seen the repairman four times." (Clothes washing machine.)
   b. "Come to where the flavor is. Come to Marlboro country." (Cigarettes and cowboy country.)
   c. "Guaranteed to take from 1 to 3 inches off your waistline in just 3 days or your money refunded." (Sauna belt waistline reducer.)
   d. "How sweet it isn't." (Squirt—the semi-soft drink.)
   e. "Explore the marvelous mechanism that is THE BODY." (*Life* magazine's science library; book is entitled *The Body*.)
   f. "A diamond is forever." (DeBeers diamond mines; the company name is very obscure in this ad.)
8. Explain what is meant by the selectivity factors in perception.
9. Distinguish between *drives* and *cues* in the learning process.
10. Explain the relationship between consumers' attitudes and the brands they purchase.
11. What marketing strategies and tactics might be employed to change consumers' attitudes toward a product or a brand?

12. Is it ethical to use fear appeals in advertising?

13. Describe the differences you would expect to find in the self-images of an insurance salesman and a man working on the assembly line in an automobile plant. Give some examples of resultant buying behavior. Assume that each has the same income.

14. Explain some practical marketing applications of the self-image theory.

MARKETS: CULTURAL AND SOCIAL-GROUP DETERMINANTS OF BUYER BEHAVIOR

The perceptual influences on behavior considered up to this point have focused primarily on the psychology of the individual. However, man is not an island unto himself. How he perceives things—how he thinks, believes, acts, etc.—is determined to a great extent by his cultural surroundings and by the various groups of people with whom he interrelates. In scope and numbers these social influences range from an entire culture down to the family or a close friend. See Fig. 5-1. For help in understanding these influences, marketing has drawn heavily from the fields of sociology and cultural anthropology.

CULTURE

Marketing practitioners and researchers have been predisposed to explain and predict buyer behavior generally on the bases of economic, psychological, and sociological influences. Unfortunately, we have made very little use of concepts in cultural anthropology, even though that field is concerned with man in his society.[1]

---

[1]For a fine discussion of cultural value systems and their implications for marketing, see J. Allison Barnhill, "Marketing and Cultural Anthropology: A Conceptual Relationship," *University*

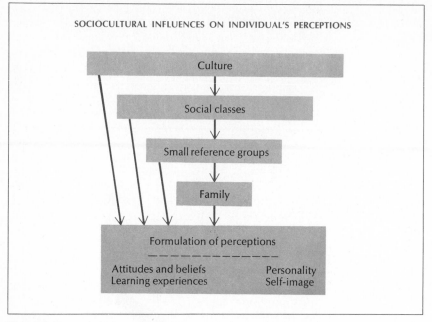

Figure 5-1.

DEFINITION AND CULTURAL INFLUENCE

Culture may be defined as the complex of symbols and artifacts created by man and handed down from generation to generation as determinants and regulators of human behavior in a given society. The symbols may be intangible (attitudes, ideas, beliefs, values, language, religion) or tangible (tools, housing, products, works of art). Culture is a totally learned and "handed-down" way of life. It does not include instinctive acts, although standards for performing instinctive biological acts (eating, bodily eliminations, sexual relationships) may be culturally established. Thus everybody gets hungry, but what we eat and how we act to satisfy the hunger drive will vary among cultures.

Actually much of our behavior is culturally determined. Our sociocultural institutions (family, schools, church, language, etc.) provide behavioral guidelines. Kluckhohn observed: "Culture . . . regulates our lives at every turn. From the moment we are born until we die there is constant conscious and unconscious pressure upon us to follow certain types of behavior that other men have created for us."[2]

of Washington Business Review, Autumn, 1967, pp. 73–84; see also Joseph F. Hair, Jr., and Rolph E. Anderson, "Culture, Acculturation and Consumer Behavior: An Empirical Study," in B. W. Becker and H. Becker (eds.), 1972 *Combined Proceedings,* American Marketing Association, Chicago, Series No. 34, 1973, pp. 423–428.

[2]Clyde Kluckhohn, "The Concept of Culture," in Richard Kluckhohn (ed.), *Culture and Behavior,* The Free Press, New York, 1962, p. 26, as quoted in Barnhill, *op. cit.,* p. 84.

Recall for a moment how some of the foundation stones of American culture have influenced our behavior and consider some of the marketing implications in these cultural influences. American society was developed on the Puritan ethic —work hard to better yourself; idle hands are the devil's helpers; leisure is akin to laziness; save your money; pay cash for what you buy; credit is evil. Hard work paid off in material well-being and the accumulation of wealth. Out of this came an affluent society living in an economy of abundance. We enjoy a relatively high level of political, economic, and social freedom. Social-class barriers have not impeded interclass movement—a poor boy can become President, make a lot of money, etc. At the same time, where racial class barriers have existed, that cultural fact has had serious behavioral repercussions.

Marketing has responded to these cultural influences. Promotional appeals have been geared to improving a person's material standard of living. When labor-saving appliances are marketed, the ads stress that Mother can spend more time with her family, thus providing a reasonable excuse for running counter to the cultural tradition of working hard all day.

CULTURAL CHANGE

Contrary to what some young people may think, cultural influences do change over time as old patterns gradually give way to the new. Today, leisure time and the use of credit, for example, are increasingly accepted as cultural mores. Certainly the articulate younger generations in the 1970s are fostering cultural change. The 1970s has also seen the growth of the first mass market of affluent, educated adults in the United States. This cultural factor is influencing consumer behavior and life-styles in many ways.[3] Marketing excutives must be alert to these changing patterns so that they can adjust their programs to be in step, or even a little ahead of the times.[4] We shall note a few of the changes which have significant marketing implications.

Changing role of women. One of the most dramatic occurrences in our society in recent years has been the changing role of women. The marketing impact of the growing number of working women was noted in Chapter 3. What is even more significant, however, are women's attempts to break from the traditional, and sometimes discriminatory, patterns which have stereotyped the male-female roles in families, jobs, recreation, social clubs, product use, and many other areas. Truly the "women's liberation movement" presents some real challenges to marketing in particular, as well as to business and society in general.[5]

Equally interesting and significant is the impact which the women's liberation movement has had on the blue-collar, working-class wives—a group which in general has been critical of women's liberation. A study conducted by the marketing research organization, Social Research, reported some dramatically changing

---

[3]See E. B. Weiss, "New Life Styles of 1975–1980 Will Throw Switch on Admen," *Advertising Age,* September 18, 1972, p. 61.

[4]See Lee Adler, "Cashing-in on the Cop-out: Cultural Change and Marketing Potential," *Business Horizons,* February, 1970, pp. 19–30.

[5]See Andrew J. DuBrin and Eugene H. Fram, "Coping with Women's Lib," *Sales Management,* June 15, 1971, p. 20.

attitudes among these women.[6] The traditional triangle of husband-children-home has limited the blue-collar wives, but today these women are rejecting these limitations. Almost one-third of the women said they would not choose homemaking as a career if they could go back to being 15 years old. The survey revealed a desire among the women for independence, fewer children, for a new interest in themselves as individuals, and a new interest in jobs and the community. It will be interesting to see how marketers react to the challenge and opportunities presented by the changing role of women in our society.

Impulse buying. In recent years there has been a significant increase in impulse buying, that is, purchases made without much advance planning. A housewife may go to the grocery store with a mental note to buy meat and fruit. In the store she selects some fresh peaches because they look more appealing or are priced more attractively than the other kinds of fruit on display. She sees some cleansing tissue on the shelf and is reminded that she is running low on this item, so she buys two boxes. These are impulse purchases.

In contrast to the patterns of many years ago, substantially more people embark on supermarket shopping trips today without a shopping list of specific items. Many items of clothing, drugs, cosmetics, toys, records, sports equipment, and other products are also bought on impulse.

Increases in disposable income and discretionary income have been major contributing factors to this trend. The self-service method of retailing has been both a cause and an effect of this behavior pattern.

A key point to understand is that impulse buying is often done on a very rational basis.[7] Self-service, open-display selling has brought about a marketing situation wherein planning may be postponed until the buyer reaches the retail outlet.

Because of the trend toward impulse buying, greater emphasis must be placed on promotional programs to get people into a store. Displays must be more appealing because the manufacturer's package must serve as a silent salesman. Manufacturers prefer distribution outlets which offer a consumer an opportunity to buy on impulse.[8]

Desire for conformity. Slowly but surely over the past century we have evolved from a nation of "rugged individualists" to one of conformists. This trend has been accelerated by the tremendous growth in suburban living, with its many look-alike housing developments. Another factor has been the rise of a managerial class working in lower and middle management for large corporations. These executives often strive to follow the prescribed pattern of the "organization

---

[6]As reported in Rob Cuscaden, "Working-Class Wife Is 'Awakened Giant,'" *Denver Post,* Oct. 14, 1973, p. 35.

[7]See Ronald P. Willett and David T. Kollat, "Customer Impulse Purchasing Behavior," *Journal of Marketing Research,* February, 1967, pp. 21–31.

[8]For a discussion of the definitional and other problems which limit the practical usefulness of the concept of impulse buying, plus some recommendations to make the concept more useful in marketing decision making, see David T. Kollat and Ronald P. Willett, "Is Impulse Purchasing Really a Useful Concept for Marketing Decisions?" *Journal of Marketing,* January, 1969, pp. 79–83; also see Joseph S. D'Antoni, Jr., and Howard L. Shenson, "Impulse Buying Revisited: A Behavioral Typology," *Journal of Retailing,* Spring, 1973, pp. 63–76.

man." The fact that most families can afford national mass-communication media such as television and magazines is still another impetus toward conformity. Later in this chapter we shall consider some aspects of group influences on consumer buying behavior. In short, there is a strong drive to be accepted by the group and to be like others.

Importance of time. A frequently heard complaint in our society today is that "I don't have time" to do this or that. In our fast-paced way of living, time is becoming an increasingly precious commodity. This passion for time is coupled with an increasing consumer affluence which is taking some of the glitter from forms of ownership directed more to status than to use. The net result of this combination is a change in shopping patterns and the opening of vast new markets for personal services, disposable goods, and rented products. That is, the trend is to rent a product or buy a disposable one, rather than to own an article which requires our time for maintenance. The consumer's acceptance of time-oriented value systems is bound to have implications for many aspects of a company's marketing program.[9]

Increased leisure time. American families are acquiring an increasing amount of leisure time from a shorter workweek, paid vacations, and laborsaving devices in the home. This trend has created a large market for goods and services such as travel, boating, photography, home swimming pools, musical instruments, outdoor furniture, commercial entertainment, and radio, television, and phonograph sets.

Leisure-market spending shows no sign of abating. One note of alarm in this connection, however: In the American economy it is not possible to continue increasing leisure time unless we have a corresponding increase in productivity. Otherwise there will be a decrease in disposable income and discretionary income.

Leisure time is an influence on how, when, and where people buy. Some years ago the chairman of the board of one of the largest advertising agencies observed that leisure "is a dynamic influence in the character of today's living. It is not simply an attribute of modern life—it is a pervasive force in shaping it. Leisure is a cause." A five-day workweek, for example, permitted Americans to move to the suburbs, and we have already noted some of the influence of this population shift. Now a developing trend toward a four-day workweek can also be expected to have considerable impact on consumer life-styles and buying behavior. As a consequence of the increased leisure-time market, many companies have added greatly to the number and variety of their products. Product design and styling have been influenced by the "do-it-yourself" enthusiasts and by the expanded participation of amateurs in sports activities.[10]

---

[9]For a conceptual consideration of how time enters into consumers' product choices, see Philip B. Schary, "Consumption and the Problem of Time," *Journal of Marketing*, April, 1971, pp. 50–55.

[10]See A. H. Kizilbash and James E. Bell, "Workers' Life Styles and the Four Day Workweek: A Case Study," *Akron Business and Economic Review,* Spring, 1974, pp. 52–57; also see Milton Leontiades, "The Concept of Leisure," *Conference Board Record,* June, 1973, pp. 25–28.

Desire for convenience. As an outgrowth of the increase in discretionary purchasing power and the importance of time, there has been a substantial increase in the consumer's desire for convenience.[11] Several years ago, Charles G. Mortimer (then president and later chairman of the board of directors of the General Foods Corporation) pointed out the following ten kinds of convenience to be reckoned with in marketing.[12]

1. Form. Products must be available in a wide variety of forms. Thus drug products, for example, come in liquid, paste, syrup, powder, pill, or inhalant form.
2. Quantity or units. Goods must be offered in all sizes, quantities, or units desired by the consumer.
3. Time. Products must be available at any time the consumer wants them. This factor has stimulated the success of convenience stores (7-Eleven, Li'l General, Circle K, and others) which carry household necessities and which do most of their business when the supermarket is closed.
4. Place. Sellers must offer opportunities for consumers to shop in the most convenient locations possible. Historically, cities and other trading centers rose, in part at least, to satisfy this demand for convenience. Today the retail structure of cities is intertwined with consumer convenience. One student of the subject perceptibly sharpened the focus on place convenience by pointing out that when consumers make shopping decisions, they do so by balancing commodity costs and convenience costs.[13] *Commodity costs* are defined as the amount of money paid to the seller for the goods or services purchased. *Convenience costs* include expenditures of time, physical and nervous energy, and money (gasoline, parking, phone calls) necessary to obtain the goods or services. Furthermore, convenience costs are becoming an increasingly significant factor in determining where people will shop.
5. Packaging. Packages must be easy to find, open, use, and store.
6. Combination. Combination, or "packaging," convenience is also found in service industries. Insurance firms offer homeowners' combination policies, and the travel industry sells "packaged" tours.
7. Automation. Many consumers dream of a push-button home.
8. Credit. One of the most significant marketing developments in the past 30 years has been the tremendous increase in consumer credit. Years ago our Puritan heritage and the vivid memories of the Great Depression tended to place considerable emphasis on thrift. In recent years, during which incomes have risen and jobs have increased, a new psychology has enveloped the consumer. He wants to buy all kinds of products and services *now* and pay for them out of future income.
9. Selection. A seller must offer his products at convenient prices and in an assortment of colors, materials, or flavors.
10. Readiness. Virtually everything we buy today must be ready and easy to use.

---

[11]See W. Thomas Anderson, Jr., "Identifying the Convenience-Oriented Consumer," *Journal of Marketing Research,* May, 1971, pp. 179–183; and same author, "Convenience Orientation and Consumption Behavior," *Journal of Retailing,* Fall, 1972, pp. 49–70.

[12]Charles G. Mortimer, *The Creative Factor in Marketing,* General Foods Corporation, White Plains, N.Y., 1959, pp. 10–16. This is a reprint of the 1959 Parlin Memorial Lecture, an annual event sponsored by the Philadelphia chapter of the American Marketing Association.

[13]Eugene J. Kelley, "The Importance of Convenience in Consumer Purchasing," *Journal of Marketing,* July, 1958, pp. 34–38.

Every major phase of a company's marketing program is affected by this craving for convenience. Product planning is influenced by the need for convenience in packaging, quantity, readiness, and selection. Pricing policies must be established in conformity with the demand for credit and with the costs of providing the various kinds of convenience. Advertising, display, and personal selling play a role in practically every phase.

Upgraded tastes and desire for elegance. For some years we have been in the midst of a cultural upgrading which is having a significant influence on marketing. This upgrading of living habits is being fostered by both economic forces (increased incomes) and social forces (improved education, extensive travel, and the influence of the mass-communications media). This new age of elegance, improved tastes, and gracious living is reflected in changing patterns of consumption and behavior on the part of consumers. There is a growing appreciation of art, music, literature, and drama; demand is increasing for gourmet foods, vintage wines, two homes, month-long vacations, period furniture, and art collections.

Concern for the environment. Our growing concern for our natural environment is a cultural factor significantly influencing business and marketing today. It seems that once a society acquires a reasonably high material standard of *living* they then turn to improving their standard of *life*. Consequently, our discontent with pollution and resource waste, coupled with resource shortages, has led to some significant changes in our life-styles. And, when our life-styles change, of course marketing is affected. Consumption patterns by both business and consumers changed rather abruptly when we encountered shortages in oil and some other commodities.

SUBCULTURES

Marketers should understand the concept of subcultures and analyze them as potentially profitable market segments. Any time there is a culture as heterogeneous as the one in the United States, there are bound to be significant subcultures based upon factors of race, nationality, religion, geographic location, age, urban-rural distribution, etc. Some of these were recognized in Chapter 3 when we analyzed the demographic market factors. Religion, for example, is a cultural factor which has significant marketing implications. Concentrations of Chinese or Japanese people in West Coast cities provide a market for some products which would go unnoticed in German or Polish sections of Milwaukee or Chicago. In the 1970s increasing attention is being paid to behavioral influences stemming from racial subcultures—black, Mexican-American, American Indian, etc.

The blacks constitute a major racial subculture in the United States.[14] However, we need to recognize that this so-called black market is in reality a series of separate market segments based on demographic, economic, psychological, and sociological factors, just as is true of white markets. The fact that blacks have

---

[14]For a discussion of black cultural influences on consumption, along with a wealth of footnote references, see James F. Engel, David T. Kollat, and Roger D. Blackwell, *Consumer Behavior,* 2d ed., Holt, Rinehart and Winston, Inc., New York, 1973, pp. 178–188.

experienced social constraints and cultural resistance from whites in areas of housing, jobs, and education has influenced the blacks' buying behavior and consumption patterns. A major problem in marketing to blacks as separate market segments is to learn more about their motivations, perceptions, attitudes, etc. In many instances blacks seem torn between accepting or rejecting the consumption values of whites. On balance, it seems that the blacks would like to adopt middle-class white values, but they (the blacks) are at a disadvantage in reaching their goals.[15]

SOCIAL CLASS

Another sociocultural determinant of a consumer's perceptions and buying behavior is the social class to which he belongs. Social classes do exist in the United States, and a person's buying behavior is more strongly influenced by the class to which he belongs, or to which he aspires, than by his income alone. The idea of a social-class structure and the terms "upper," "middle," and "lower" class may be repugnant to many Americans, but the sociologists who identified the class structure and the marketers who use it do not impute value judgments to it. We do not claim that the so-called upper class is superior to, or happier and better off than, the middle class.

Some years ago W. Lloyd Warner and Paul Lunt directed a study which identified a six-class system within the social structure of a small town.[16] A person's placement in the structure was based on his type, not amount, of income and on his occupation, type of house, and area of residence within the community. Descriptions of the six classes and the percentage of population in each group are given below. The percentages are only approximations because they vary according to the city studied. The first three classes constitute the "quality market," and yet they include only about 12 percent of the population. Although we speak of America as a middle-class society, the real mass market (almost 75 percent) is comprised of the lower-middle and upper-lower groups.

1. The upper-upper class, about 0.5 percent, includes the "old families" in the community—the aristocracy of birth and inherited wealth. Usually they are second-or third-generation families, living graciously in large old homes in the best neighborhoods and displaying a sense of social responsibility.
2. The lower-upper class, about 1.5 percent, includes the "new rich," who are wealthy but who have not been accepted socially by the upper-upper families. See Fig. 5-2. This class includes the top executives, well-to-do doctors and lawyers, and owners of large businesses.

---

[15]Raymond A. Bauer and Scott M. Cunningham, "The Negro Market," *Journal of Advertising Research,* April, 1970, pp. 3–13. Also see Dorothy Cohen, "Advertising and the Black Community," *Journal of Marketing,* October, 1970, pp. 3–11; Donald E. Sexton, Jr., "Black Buyer Behavior," *Journal of Marketing,* October, 1972, pp. 36–39; Dennis H. Gensch and Richard Staelin, "The Appeal of Buying Black," *Journal of Marketing Research,* May, 1972, pp. 141–148; and Montrose S. Sommers, "Some Negro-White Differences in Product Symbolism," *Southern Journal of Business,* July, 1968, pp. 163–176. See also footnotes in Chap. 3 in section entitled "Other Demographic Bases for Segmentation."

[16]W. Lloyd Warner and Paul Lunt, *The Social Life of a Modern Community,* Yale University

THE OLD RICH AND THE NEW RICH: SOME BEHAVIORAL DIFFERENCES

The new rich will carry a credit card; the old rich will use check or cash. The new rich will put their initials on their license plate; the old rich won't. The new rich—for example a lady on a trip down to the hair stylist—will sit in the back seat alone; the old rich will sit up front and chat with the chauffeur. The new rich will call the butler by his last name; the old rich by his first. The new rich will hole out all putts when golfing; the old rich will take anything under five feet. The new rich will wear wigs that look natural; the old rich, ones that are frankly false.

Figure 5-2. *Source:* Coleman McCarthy, "The Hard-core Rich," *The New Republic*, March 15, 1969, p. 14. Reprinted by permission of The New Republic, © 1969, Harrison-Blaine of New Jersey, Inc.

3. The upper-middle class, about 10 percent, is composed of the moderately successful business and professional men and owners of medium-sized companies. They are well educated and live well. Their strong drive for success is reflected in the husband's career, the wife's social participation, and their broad range of interests.
4. The lower-middle class, about 33 percent, is made up of the white-collar class of office workers, most salesmen, and owners of small businesses. This is the group striving for "respectability"—doing a good job, living in modest but well-cared-for homes, and saving for the children's college education. This class is the source of America's moral code and aspirational system and is the most conforming, churchgoing part of the society.
5. The upper-lower class, about 40 percent, consists of the blue-collar class of factory workers, semiskilled workers, and the politicians and union leaders who would lose their power if they moved out of this class. Many earn good incomes, but they are oriented toward enjoying life on a day-to-day basis. They want to enjoy the comforts of life, but they are not striving to "keep up with the Joneses."
6. The lower-lower class, about 15 percent, includes unskilled workers, the chronically unemployed, unassimilated racial immigrants from other parts of the country, those frequently on welfare, and many inhabitants of slums. Classes above this one consider this group to be lazy, when often their only sin is being poor and uneducated.

The research division of the *Chicago Tribune* has conducted several studies of the relationships between social class, buying behavior, and consumers' perceptions of various products and types of stores. One of the *Tribune* studies in particular was a giant stride forward in this area. Done under Warner's guidance, the study was made in Chicago to determine whether his own analysis of social-class structure—developed from studies of small towns—also applied to a large metropolitan center.[17]

Press, New Haven, Conn., 1941; and W. Lloyd Warner, Marchia Meeker, and Kenneth Eells, *Social Class in America,* Science Research Associates, Inc., Chicago, 1949.

[17]See Pierre D. Martineau, "Social Classes and Spending Behavior," *Journal of Marketing,* October, 1958, pp. 121–130.

Three basic conclusions, highly significant for marketing, came out of the *Chicago Tribune* study. First, a social-class system is operative in large metropolitan markets and can be delineated. Substantial differences exist between classes with respect to their spending-saving behavior, the stores they patronize, the products they buy, and the brands they prefer. Furthermore, there is relatively little interclass movement. Although our history is replete with examples of people rising to the heights from humble beginnings, and although hard-and-fast barriers between classes do not exist, the vast majority of people always remain within the boundaries of their own class tastes.

The second conclusion is that there are far-reaching psychological differences between classes. Some of the contrasting characteristics of middle and lower groups are listed in Fig. 5-3. The classes do not think in the same way. Thus they respond differently to a seller's marketing program, particularly his advertising. The supersophisticated, clever advertising in *The New Yorker* is almost meaningless to lower-status people. This does not mean that they lack intelligence or wit, but only that they have different symbols of humor or art. Advertising must be believable by the class at which it is aimed. The reader must be able to identify himself with the people and the setting in the advertisement.

The third conclusion is that consumption patterns are symbols of class membership, and class membership is a more significant determinant of buyer behavior than is the amount of income. Traditionally, marketing people have relied on income as an index to buying behavior. With what we now know about social class, however, we question the accuracy of this index. Today the bulk of the population falls in the middle-income group. This group comprises not only white-collar workers—traditional members of the middle class—but also skilled and semiskilled blue-collar workers. These people are poles apart in their behavior, tastes, spending patterns, and aspirations. There is an old saying that a rich man is just a poor man with money, and that given the same amount of money, a poor man would behave exactly like a rich man. Studies of social-class structure have proved that this statement is just not true.[18]

A word of caution, however—buying behavior may very well be different at the various income levels within each social class or occupational group. A carpenter's family with an income of $8,000 a year has consumption patterns different from another carpenter's family where the annual income is $17,000. In this area of social class and income perhaps a more useful basis for market segmentation is some index which combines the two factors of occupation and income.[19]

Some of the points in the preceding paragraphs were illustrated by Coleman's example of typical behavior in three families, each earning about $10,000 a year (in

---

[18]For the contention that ability to buy (income) is a better determinant of buyer behavior than is social class (occupation), see James H. Myers, Roger R. Stanton, and Arne F. Haug, "Correlates of Buying Behavior: Social Class vs. Income," *Journal of Marketing,* October, 1971, pp. 8–15; and James H. Myers and John F. Mount, "More on Social Class vs. Income as Correlates of Buying Behavior," *Journal of Marketing,* April, 1973, pp. 71–73; also see John W. Slocum, Jr., and H. Lee Mathews, "Social Class and Income as Indicators of Consumer Credit Behavior," *Journal of Marketing,* April, 1970, pp. 69–74.

[19]See William H. Peters, "Income and Occupation as Explanatory Variables: Their Power Combined vs. Separate," *Journal of Business Research,* Summer, 1973, pp. 81–89.

PSYCHOLOGICAL DIFFERENCES BETWEEN TWO SOCIAL CLASSES

Middle class	Lower class
1. Pointed to the future	1. Pointed to the present and past
2. Viewpoint embraces a long expanse in time	2. Lives and thinks in a short expanse of time
3. More urban in identification	3. More rural in identification
4. Stresses rationality	4. Nonrational essentially
5. Has a well-structured sense of the universe	5. Has vague, unclear, and unstructured sense of the world
6. Horizons vastly extended or not limited	6. Horizons sharply defined and limited
7. Greater sense of choice making	7. Limited sense of choice making
8. Self-confident, willing to take risks	8. Very much concerned with security
9. Immaterial and abstract in his thinking	9. Concrete and perceptive in his thinking
10. Sees himself tied to national happenings	10. World revolves around family and self

---

Figure 5-3. There are many exceptions to this picture of class attitudes. For instance, can you think of a lower-class person (in terms of income and social status) who has middle-class attitudes? Are there enough exceptions to these patterns to render them invalid in planning marketing campaigns? Source: Pierre D. Martineau, "Social Classes and Spending Behavior," *Journal of Marketing,* October, 1958, p. 129.

1970 dollars), but each from a different social class.[20] There are quite significant marketing implications in their differential behavior. An upper-middle-class family in this income bracket—possibly a lawyer or college professor and his wife—is likely to spend a relatively large share of its resources on a home in a prestige neighborhood, expensive furniture, clothing from quality stores, and club memberships or cultural amusements. In comparison, a lower-middle-class family—that of a salesman or diesel engineer, for example—probably has a better house, but not in so fancy a neighborhood; more furniture and clothes, but not from name stores or by top designers; and a much bigger savings account. Finally, the upper-lower working-class family of a welder or truck driver has a smaller house in a less desirable neighborhood. However, this family will have a bigger, later-model car, more kitchen appliances, and a bigger TV set. The man spends more on sports (ball games, hunting, bowling, fishing).

The wives in these three families each have quite different goals, so there will be differences in the stores they patronize, the magazines they read, the ads

---

[20]Richard P. Coleman, "The Significance of Social Stratification in Selling," in Martin L. Bell (ed.), *Marketing: A Maturing Discipline,* American Marketing Association, Chicago, 1961, pp. 171–184.

they notice, and the clothing and furniture they select. The upper-middle-class wife wants to (1) shop in the "best" stores and (2) furnish her home as a testament to her fine taste, paying attention to the dictates of the "best" magazines, interior decorators in town, and the homes of other women in her class. The lower-middle-class wife relies on medium-level shelter and service magazines and stores to furnish her home so that it is "pretty" enough to suit her and win praise from friends and neighbors. The upper-lower-class housewife first wants a kitchen full of appliances before she worries about any other room. In the coming years it will be interesting to see how much the changing role of women (as noted earlier in this chapter) will alter the behavior patterns briefed in this paragraph.

The concept of social class is most useful in interpreting buying behavior only when the concept is applied in a sophisticated, realistic, and sometimes subtle fashion. There is a risk that the concept may be misunderstood or oversimplified, and thus misused. It does not possess universal applicability. Consequently, a marketing executive needs to understand when and in what ways a social-class stratification is significant in marketing and, conversely, what its limitations of application are. Some products—air conditioners and children's playclothes, for instance—are classless. That is, social class is relevant only to the extent that it is correlated with income.

SMALL REFERENCE GROUPS

Small-group influence on buyer behavior introduces to marketing the concept of reference-group theory, which we borrowed from sociology. A *reference group* may be defined as a group of people who influence a person's attitudes, opinions, and values. A reference group's standards of behavior serve as guides or "frames of reference" for the individual. The reference-group concept may be applied to the full range of social influences from the total culture down to the family. However, the concept was originally developed in connection with small groups.

Reference-group theory is also related to the psychology of imitation.[21] Much of a person's learning is imitative learning, especially at early ages. A child, for example, learns by imitation the different vocational and occupational roles when he is given toy models which imitate the work done by his mother or father. As children grow up, they adopt by imitation certain models of behavior. How many of us have listened to parents saying, "Johnny, why can't you do this or that like the other kids do?" Or, Johnny wails, "All the other kids can do that, why can't I?"

When children observe the behavior in a model, the degree to which the model's behavior is imitated depends upon the response consequences to the model. That is, does the model's behavior meet with reward or punishment? If the children observe reward, they are more likely to imitate than is the case when the model is punished.

A consumer's behavior is influenced by the variety of small groups to which he belongs, or aspires to belong. These groups may include family, fraternal organizations, labor unions, church groups, athletic teams, or a circle of close friends or neighbors. Each group develops its own set of attitudes and beliefs which serve as norms for members' behavior. The members

---

[21]See Albert Bandura and Richard H. Walters, "The Role of Imitation," *Social Learning and Personality Development,* Holt, Rinehart and Winston, Inc., New York, 1963, chap. 2.

share these values and are expected to conform to the group's normative behavioral patterns.

A person may agree with all the standards set by the group or only part of them. A moderate Republican or Democrat may not agree with all the political views of his local party unit. Also, a person does not have to belong to a group to be influenced by it. Youths frequently pattern their dress and other behavior after that of an older-aged group which the younger ones aspire to join. Another point is that some reference groups serve as negative influences on a person. He relates to them by doing the opposite of what they recommend. Banning a book in Boston or X-rating a movie will often increase the book's sales or the movie's attendance.

The behavioral norms set by a reference group may or may not be enforced with penalties for nonconformity. In some instances the norms serve simply as informational guidelines, telling a consumer what is going on, but he can still "do his own thing." A person visits a ski slope and observes what kind of equipment and clothing is being used, but he may or may not buy what seem to be the popular styles. In other cases, failure to follow the norms can result in a penalty—a ticket for speeding or expulsion from the group, for example. In general, however, small groups do tend to exert pressure on their members to conform to the particular group's standards and behavioral patterns.

The type of social group which has the most direct influence on a consumer's buying behavior is the small group in which each member normally can interact with every other member on a face-to-face basis—a family, a circle of friends, a local fraternity chapter, neighbors, an athletic team, or a small garden club, for example. Studies have shown that informal personal advice in face-to-face groups is much more effective as a behavioral determinant than advertising in newspapers, TV, or other mass media. That is, when it comes to selecting some products or changing brands, prospective buyers are more likely to be influenced by word-of-mouth advertising from satisfied customers in the group. This is true especially when the speaker is respected as an opinion leader regarding the particular product.[22]

Another useful finding pertained to the flow of information between and within groups. For years marketing men have operated in conformity with the "snob appeal" theory—the idea that if they could get social leaders and high-income groups to use their products, the mass market would also buy them. The assumption has been that influence follows a vertical path, starting at levels of high status or prestige and moving downward through successive levels of groups. Contrary to this popular assumption, studies by Katz and Lazarsfeld, and by others, have pointed up the *horizontal* nature of opinion leadership. Influence emerges on each level of the socioeconomic scale and permeates a given area wherein the opinion leader is dealing with his peers.[23]

---

[22]See John R. Stuteville, "The Buyer as a Salesman," *Journal of Marketing,* July, 1968, pp. 14–18; Ernest Dichter, "How Word-of-mouth Advertising Works," *Harvard Business Review,* November–December, 1966, pp. 147–166; and William H. Whyte, Jr., "The Web of Word of Mouth," *Fortune,* November, 1954, p. 140.

[23]See Elihu Katz and Paul Lazarsfeld, *Personal Influence,* Free Press, New York, 1955, especially p. 325; see also Elihu Katz, "The Two-step Flow of Communications: An Up-to-date Report on an Hypothesis," *Public Opinion Quarterly,* Spring, 1957, pp. 61–78. For later empirical data supporting the horizontal-flow hypothesis ("trickle across"), see Charles W. King,

The proved role of face-to-face groups as behavior determinants for some products, plus the concept of horizontal information flow, suggests that a marketing person is faced with two key problems: (1) that of identifying the relevant reference group likely to be used by consumers in a given buying situation and (2) that of measuring the extent of the group's influence on these consumers. Then the marketing strategy should focus on identifying and communicating with two key people in the group—the innovator (early buyer) and the influential person (opinion leader). (The adoption and diffusion of new products are discussed in the next section.) Each group has a leader—a tastemaker, or opinion leader—who influences the decision making of others in the group. The key here is for the seller to convince that person of the value of his product or service. The opinion leader in one group may be an opinion follower in another. The mother of a family may be influential in matters concerning food, whereas unmarried women are more apt to influence fashions in clothing and makeup.[24]

The effectiveness of small reference groups as behavioral influences will vary depending upon the product and the availability of information for the consumer. The less information or experience a person has concerning a given product, the stronger the reference-group influence will be for this product. As far as the product itself is concerned, reference-group influence is the strongest when the product is most conspicuous. There are two aspects of conspicuousness in this context: First, the product must be such that it can be seen and identified by others, and second, it must stand out and be noticed. If many people own the product, even though it can be seen and identified, it is not conspicuous in the second sense of the term.[25]

The possible susceptibility of products and brands to reference-group influence is illustrated in Fig. 5-4. According to this model, a particular item might be susceptible to group influence in three different ways, corresponding to three of the four cells. In the upper right-hand cell (product plus, brand plus) the reference-group influence is felt in both the product and the brand. Cars are socially conspicuous as to both product and brand. Cigarette brands cannot easily be differentiated, but advertising has created certain images with reference-group appeal.

In the lower right-hand cell (product plus, brand minus) the use of the product is socially conspicuous, but the particular brand is not important from a reference-group standpoint. In the upper left-hand cell (product minus, brand plus) we find that the product is not significant, but the brand is. That is, most people own

"Fashion Adoption: A Rebuttal to the 'Trickle Down' Theory," in Stephen A. Greyser (ed.), *Toward Scientific Marketing*, American Marketing Association, Chicago, 1964, pp. 108–125.

[24]See Charles W. King and John O. Summers, "Overlap of Opinion Leadership across Consumer Product Categories," *Journal of Marketing Research*, February, 1970, pp. 43–50; John O. Summers, "The Identify of Women's Clothing Fashion Opinion Leaders," *Journal of Marketing Research*, May, 1970, pp. 178–185; William R. Darden and Fred D. Reynolds, "Predicting Opinion Leadership for Men's Apparel Fashions," *Journal of Marketing Research*, August, 1972, pp. 324–328; and Reynolds and Darden, "Predicting Opinion Leadership for Women's Clothing Fashions," in B. W. Becker and H. Becker (eds.), 1972 *Combined Proceedings*, American Marketing Association, Chicago, Series No. 34, 1973, pp. 434–438.

[25]This paragraph and the remainder of the discussion on small groups is based on Francis S. Bourne, "Group Influence in Marketing and Public Relations," in Rensis Likert and Samuel P. Hayes, Jr., (eds.), *Some Applications of Behavioral Research*, UNESCO, Paris, 1957, chap. 6; or see the same report originally published by Foundation for Research on Human Behavior, Ann Arbor, Mich., 1956.

REFERENCE-GROUP INFLUENCE ON BUYING DECISIONS

Weak −   Reference group influence relatively: Strong +

Strong +	Clothing Furniture Magazines	Cars* Cigarettes* Beer (premium vs. regular)	+
Reference group	Refrigerator (type) Toilet soap	Drugs*	Brand or
influence relatively:	Soap Canned peaches Laundry soap Refrigerator (brand)	Air conditioners* Instant coffee* TV (black & white)	Type
Weak −	Radios		−
	−	Product	+

*Based on experimental evidence; other classifications are researchers' opinions.

Figure 5-4. Products and brands are classified by the extent to which reference groups influence their purchases. Reference groups influence the decision to buy an air conditioner, but the choice of brand is left up to the consumer. *Source: Group Influences in Marketing and Public Relations,* Foundation for Research on Human Behavior, Ann Arbor, Mich., 1956, p. 8, citing a research study by the Bureau of Applied Social Research, Columbia University.

the products (clothing, furniture, etc.), so they are not socially conspicuous. However, the styles, brands, and types of clothing or furniture are visible and quite susceptible to social influence. Purchasing behavior for items in the lower left-hand cell (product minus, brand minus) is influenced by produce attributes, and usually not by any reference group.

Assuming that a product or brand can be placed in its proper cell, Bourne cites some practical marketing implications. When neither the product nor the brand seems subject to reference-group influence, the seller's advertising should stress product attributes, price, quality, and competitive differential advantages. On the other hand, if reference-group influence does exist, the advertising should stress the kinds of people who buy and use the product or brand. Here it becomes important first to identify the appropriate reference group, and then to reinforce any existing stereotype of users in that group.

NEW-PRODUCT ADOPTION PROCESS AND THE DIFFUSION OF INNOVATION

The process by which a new product is adopted, and the diffusion of that innovation through a group of people, is a logical extension or application of reference-group theory. (By definition, an *innovation* is anything—product, service, idea—which is perceived by a person as being new; the *adoption process* is the decision-making activity of an *individual* involving his acceptance of an innovation; the *diffusion* of innovation is the process by which the innovation is communicated within social systems over time.)

An extensive bibliography exists on these processes, indicating something of the interest in the field.[26] Research activity in adoption and diffusion has extended through many academic disciplines—rural and medical sociology, economics, anthropology, education, and communication, to name just a few. Today the research is emerging in the fields of marketing and consumer behavior. A preponderance of diffusion research has been conducted by rural sociologists dealing with new farming practices and products. This is a reflection of (1) the financial support of the U.S. Department of Agriculture, (2) the ease of identifying and isolating the farmer as a market segment for controlled study, and (3) the socioeconomic importance of farming. Many of the findings and concepts developed in rural sociology research, however, are often applicable to other products and disciplines.[27]

STAGES IN DECISION-MAKING PROCESS

We can identify six separate mental stages which a prospective user goes through in the process of deciding whether or not to adopt something new. First is the *awareness* stage, in which the individual is exposed to the innovation, but knows very little about it. Next is the *interest-information* stage, in which the prospect becomes interested enough to actively seek considerable specific information about the new concept.

In the third stage—*evaluation*—the prospect mentally measures the relative merits of the innovation; this is sort of a mental "test market." Then in the next step—the *trial* stage—the person actually adopts the innovation on a limited basis. Thus a consumer buys a small sample of a product, or a farmer tries a small can of weed killer in his garden before using it broadcast in a large field. If for some reason (cost or physical size, for example) an innovation cannot be sampled, the likelihood of its being adopted will decline.

The fifth stage is the *adoption* stage, in which the individual decides whether or not to use the innovation on a full-scale basis. If the innovation is adopted, the user goes through still another stage, that of *postadoption confirmation,* in which he continues to seek assurance that he made the right decision.

ADOPTER CATEGORIES

Some people will adopt an innovation quickly after it is introduced. Others will delay for some time before accepting the new product, while still others may never adopt it. Drawing from a number of studies in the diffusion of innovation, researchers have identified five categories of individuals, based on the relative time when they adopted a given innovation. Figure 5-5 illustrates the distribution of adopters.

---

[26]For some foundations of diffusion theory, a review of landmark studies on diffusion of innovation, and extensive bibliographical references, see Everett M. Rogers and F. Floyd Shoemaker, *Communication of Innovations,* 2d ed., The Free Press, New York, 1971.

[27]For some insights into the adoption and diffusion processes for industrial products, see Frederick E. Webster, Jr., "New Product Adoption in Industrial Markets: A Framework for Analysis," *Journal of Marketing,* July, 1969, pp. 35–39; Urban B. Ozanne and Gilbert A. Churchill, Jr., "Five Dimensions of the Industrial Adoption Process," *Journal of Marketing Research,* August, 1971, pp. 322–328; and John A. Martilla, "Word-of-Mouth Communications in the Industrial Adoption Process," *Journal of Marketing Research,* May, 1971, pp. 173–178.

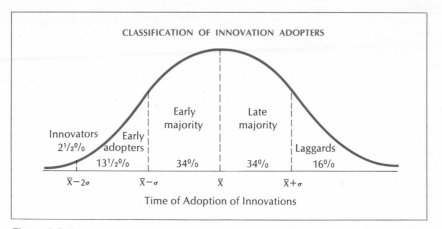

Figure 5-5. Studies show that the distribution of adopters (based on when they adopted the innovation) generally follows the normal curve. Thus, the area lying to the left of the arithmetic mean ($\overline{X}$) minus one standard deviation (σ) includes 16 percent of the people adopting an innovation—the "innovators" and the "early adopters." *Source:* Everett M. Rogers and F. Floyd Shoemaker, *Communication of Innovations,* 2d ed., The Free Press, New York, 1971, p. 182.

The categories are rather arbitrarily partitioned to represent unit standard deviations from the average time of adoption.[28]

Some of the key differences between the early and late half of the adopters are summarized in Fig. 5-6. Understanding these differences can be useful to marketing people when they are planning the advertising and personal selling programs for a new product.

Innovators. This *venturesome* group, which includes about 3 percent of the market, is the first to adopt an innovation and is most willing to accept the attendant risks. In relation to later adopters, the innovators are likely to be younger, have a higher social status, and be in a better financial position. Innovators also tend to have broader, more cosmopolitan social relationships. An innovator is likely to rely more on impersonal sources of information, including those external to his own social system, rather than using personal salesmen or other word-of-mouth sources.[29]

Early adopters. This group—about 13 percent of the market—tends to be a more integrated part of a local social system; that is, whereas innovators are cosmopolites, early adopters are localites. Thus the early-adopter category includes more opinion leaders than any other adopter group. Early adopters are much *respected* in their social system. The "agents of change" who are seeking to speed up the diffusion of a given innovation will often try to work through the early adopters

---

[28]Rogers and Shoemaker, *op. cit.,* chap. 5. Unfortunately, there are no generally accepted standard criteria for classifying adopters into categories. Nor have researchers agreed upon one set of category titles. Also, nonadopters are excluded in our categorization.

[29]See Roman R. Andrus, John Knutsen, and Kenneth Uhl, "The Shopping Behavior of 'Innovators,'" *University of Washington Business Review,* Summer, 1971, pp. 71–75; and Louis E. Boone, "The Search for the Consumer Innovator," *Journal of Business,* April, 1970, pp. 135–140.

DIFFERENCES IN CHARACTERISTICS OF EARLY- AND LATE-ADOPTER CATEGORIES		
	Adopters	
Categories with key feature	Early	Late
	Innovators: venturesome Early adopters: respected Early majority: deliberate	Late majority: skeptical Laggards: tradition-bound
Other characteristics		
Age	Younger	Older
Education	Well educated	Less educated
Income	Higher	Lower
Social relationships: Within or outside community	Innovators: cosmopolites Others: more localites	Totally local
Social status	Higher	Lower
Their information sources	Wider variety; many media	Limited media exposure; limited reliance on outside media; rely on local peer groups

Figure 5-6.

because they are not too far ahead of others in their peer group. Personal salesmen are probably used more by the early adopters than by any other category.

Early adopters, in contrast to later adopters, tend to be younger, better educated, more creative, and more mobile. They are involved in a range of community activities and tend to hold elected positions of leadership.

Business firms in both the innovator and the early-adopter categories are usually large and specialized in their operations.[30]

Early majority. This more *deliberate* group, representing about 34 percent of the market, tends to accept an innovation just before the "average" adopter in a social system. This group is a bit above average in social and economic measures. The members rely quite a bit on advertisements, salesmen, and contact with early adopters. Business firms in this category are average-sized operations.

Late majority. Representing about another 34 percent of the market, the late majority is a *skeptical* group. Usually they adopt an innovation in response to an economic necessity or to social pressure from their peers. They rely on their peers—late or early majority—for sources of information; advertising and personal selling are less effective.

---

[30]See David W. Cravens, James C. Cotham III, and James R. Felix, "Identifying Innovator and Non-Innovator Retail Firms," *Southern Journal of Business,* April, 1971, pp. 45–50; and Lyman C. Ostlund, "Identifying Early Buyers," *Journal of Advertising Research,* April, 1972, pp. 25–30.

This group is older, less well educated, and below average in social and economic status; it does not contain many opinion leaders. Business firms in this category tend to be small and nonspecialized.

Laggards. This *tradition-bound* group—16 percent of the market—includes those who are the last to adopt an innovation. Their point of reference is what was done in the past, and they tend to interact with those holding similar values. Laggards are suspicious of innovations and innovators. Much time elapses between the awareness stage and the final adoption of an idea. By the time laggards adopt something new, it may already have been discarded by the innovator group in favor of a newer idea. Laggards are older and are at the low end of the social and economic scales. Businesses in this group tend to be the smallest and have the lowest degree of specialization.[31]

CHARACTERISTICS OF INNOVATIONS AFFECTING ADOPTION RATE

The rate of adoption for a given innovation may range from a few weeks to several decades. There are five characteristics of an innovation, as perceived by individuals, which seem to influence the adoption rate.[32] One is *relative advantage*—the degree to which an innovation is superior to preceding ideas. Relative advantage may be reflected in lower costs, higher profitability, or some other measure. Another characteristic is *compatibility*—the degree to which an innovation is consistent with the cultural values and experiences of the adopters. Some electric appliances would find little market acceptance in some South American countries, not only because of widespread lack of electric power, but also because in terms of the value systems of the people, they would be rejected as an extravagance.

The degree of *complexity* of an innovation will affect its adoption rate. The fourth characteristic—*trialability*—is the degree to which the new idea may be sampled on some limited basis. On this point, a central home air-conditioning system is likely to have a slower adoption rate than some new seed or fertilizer, which may be tried on a small plot of ground. Finally, the *observability* of the innovation affects its adoption rate. A weed killer which works on existing weeds will be accepted sooner than a preemergent weed killer because in the latter case—even though it may be a superior product—there are no dead weeds to show to prospective adopters.

MARKETING IMPLICATIONS

From an understanding of diffusion theory an executive can develop many useful guidelines for his company's marketing effort. In its promotional program, for instance, it is important (while admittedly difficult) that a company be able to identify, and then communicate with, the early-adopter category of consumers. This market segment includes the greatest share of opinion leaders. Other consumers, in their respect for early adopters, look to them for information, advice, and assurance. Management probably should devote little, if any, promotional or other marketing effort to the laggard market segment because of the socioeconomic nature of the group and the fact that it looks to other laggards for information.

---

[31]See Kenneth Uhl, Roman Andrus, and Lance Poulsen, "How Are Laggards Different? An Empirical Inquiry," *Journal of Marketing Research,* February, 1970, pp. 51–54.

[32]Rogers and Shoemaker, *op. cit.,* chap. 4.

Looking at the product characteristics which affect the adoption rate, the product should be designed in divisible form so that it can be evaluated on a sample basis. If this is physically impossible, as with an automobile or an air conditioner, then the consumer should be able to use the product on a trial basis before having to make an adoption decision. Management should design products which minimize the complexity factor or which make obvious the product's compatibility or relative advantage. Then the advertising and personal selling effort should stress these features. Or if the product really is complex, the promotional program and product-servicing facilities must counteract this limitation.

FAMILY BUYING BEHAVIOR

Of all the small groups an individual belongs to through the years, ordinarily his family is the one which has the strongest and most enduring influence on his perceptions and behavior. For many products the family, or at least the husband and wife, operates as a buying unit.

WHO DOES THE FAMILY BUYING?

A marketer should treat this question as four separate ones because each one may affect different segments of his marketing program and require different strategies and tactics: (1) Who influences the buying decision (this may be a member of the family, or the influence may come from an outside reference group)? (2) Who makes the buying decision? (3) Who makes the physical purchase? (4) Who uses the product? Four different people may be involved, only one member may do all four, or some other combination may be the case. Also, a user today may be the influencer, decider, and/or purchaser when the present product is used up.

For many years women have done most of the family buying. They still exert substantial influence in buying decisions and do a considerable amount of the actual purchasing, but men have increasingly entered the family buying picture. Self-service stores are especially appealing to men. Night and Sunday openings in suburban shopping centers also encourage men to play a bigger role in family purchasing.

In recent years teen-agers and young children have become decision makers in family buying as well as actual purchasers. The amount of money teen-agers now have is substantial enough to be considered in the marketing plans of many manufacturers and middlemen. Even very young children are an influence in buying decisions today because they watch television programs or shop with their parents.

Purchasing decisions are often made jointly by husband and wife (sometimes even the children are included).[33] Young married people are much more apt to

---

[33]See Robert F. Kelly and Michael B. Egan, "Husband and Wife Interaction in a Consumer Decision Process," in Philip R. McDonald (ed.), *Marketing Involvement in Society and the Economy,* American Marketing Association, Chicago, 1970, pp. 250–258; and William D. Perreault, Jr., and Frederick A. Russ, "Student Influence on Family Purchase Decisions," in Fred C. Allvine (ed.), *Combined Proceedings: 1971 Conferences,* American Marketing Association, Chicago, Series No. 33, 1972, pp. 386–389.

make buying decisions on a joint basis than older couples. Apparently the longer a husband and wife live together, the more they feel they can trust each other to act unilaterally. In many cases, decisions regarding savings, life insurance, vacations, housing, food, and the handling of money and bills are made jointly.

Who buys a product will influence a firm's marketing policies regarding its product, channels of distribution, and promotion. If children are the key decision makers, as is often the case in cereals, for instance, then a manufacturer may include some type of cutout toy or other premium with the product. In a department store—traditionally considered a woman's store—the men's furnishings department is often located on the street floor near a door. Then the man can enter, shop, and leave the store without having to wade through crowds of women shoppers. The entire advertising campaign—media, appeals, copy, radio and television programming, and so forth—is affected by whether the target is men, women, or children.

INFLUENCE OF FAMILY LIFE CYCLE

In Chapter 3 we observed that consumer expenditure patterns are influenced considerably by the stage of the life cycle the family is in at any given time. The life cycle concept can also serve as (1) an explanation for family buying behavior and (2) a guide to marketers in planning marketing programs which are consistent with that behavior. Figure 5-7 summarizes the behavioral influences and buying patterns for families in each stage of the cycle. (This figure expands from six to nine the number of stages as classified in Chapter 3.) Marketing people surely need to be aware of the striking contrasts in buyer behavior between, say, people in the full-nest stage with the youngest child under six and those in the empty-nest stages. Even significant differences exist between empty-nest stages I and II (depending upon whether the head of the house is working or retired).

OVERT BUYING PATTERNS AND THEIR MARKETING SIGNIFICANCE

In addition to understanding *why* consumers buy, manufacturers and middlemen must also understand *when, where,* and *how* they buy. We are talking now about consumers' buying habits, or, as they are often called, patterns of overt buying behavior.

When consumers buy. A marketing executive should be able to answer at least three questions about *when* people buy his products or service: During what season do they buy? On what day of the week do they buy? At what time of day do they buy? If seasonal buying patterns exist, he should try to extend the buying season. He may find that a change in his product or in his promotional program will smooth out seasonal fluctuations. There is obviously little opportunity for extending the season on Easter bunnies or Christmas tree ornaments, but the season for vacations has been shifted to such an extent that winter or other "off-season" vacations are now quite popular.

When people buy may influence the product-planning, pricing, or promotional phases of a firm's marketing program. After-shave lotion, cigarettes, and alcoholic beverages are distinctively packaged at Christmastime because they are pur-

BEHAVIORAL INFLUENCES AND BUYING PATTERNS, BY LIFE-CYCLE STAGE

Bachelor stage: young single people not living at home	Newly married couples; young, no children	Full nest I, youngest child under six	Full nest II, youngest child six or over	Full nest III, older married couples with dependent children	Empty nest I, older married couples, no children living with them, head in labor force	Empty nest II, older married couples, no children living at home, head retired	Solitary survivor, in labor force	Solitary survivor, retired
Few financial burdens. Fashion opinion leaders. Recreation oriented. Buy: Basic kitchen equipment, basic furniture, cars, equipment for the mating game, vacations.	Better off financially than they will be in near future. Highest purchase rate and highest average purchase of durables. Buy: Cars, refrigerators, stoves, sensible and durable furniture, vacations.	Home purchasing at peak. Liquid assets low. Dissatisfied with financial position and amount of money saved. Interested in new products. Like advertised products. Buy: Washers, dryers, TV, baby food, chest rubs and cough medicine, vitamins, dolls, wagons, sleds, skates.	Financial position better. Some wives work. Less influenced by advertising. Buy larger sized packages, multiple-unit deals. Buy: Many foods, cleaning materials, bicycles, music lessons, pianos.	Financial position still better. More wives work. Some children get jobs. Hard to influence with advertising. High average purchase of durables. Buy: New, more tasteful furniture, auto travel, nonnecessary appliances, boats, dental services, magazines.	Home ownership at peak. Most satisfied with financial position and money saved. Interested in travel, recreation, self-education. Make gifts and contributions. Not interested in new products. Buy: Vacations, luxuries, home improvements.	Drastic cut in income. Keep home. Buy: Medical appliances, medical care, products which aid health, sleep, and digestion.	Income still good but likely to sell home.	Same medical and product needs as other retired group; drastic cut in income. Special need for attention, affection, and security.

Figure 5-7. *Source:* William D. Wells and George Gubar, "Life Cycle Concept in Marketing Research," *Journal of Marketing Research,* November, 1966, p. 362.

chased for gifts. In order to smooth the seasonal peaks and valleys in his production schedule, a doll manufacturer may want retailers to buy well in advance of the Christmas season, the season when the majority of dolls are sold. To get the retailers to do this, the manufacturer may offer them "seasonal datings," a pricing policy whereby retailers take delivery in September but do not have to pay until December.

Where consumers buy. A firm should consider two factors with respect to *where* people buy—where the buying decision is made and where the actual purchase occurs. For many products and services the decision to buy is made at home. On the other hand, the decision is often made in whole or in part right at the point of purchase. A person may be shopping in a sporting goods store for golf clubs when he sees some tennis balls on sale, knows he needs some, and decides on the spot to buy them. A husband may decide at home that he wants to buy a birthday gift for his wife, but he waits until he gets to the store before deciding whether it will be jewelry, candy, or lingerie.

A company's entire promotional program, and in many cases its product planning, must be geared to carry the greatest impact at the place where the buying decision is made. If the decision to buy is made in the store, then attention must be devoted to packaging and other point-of-purchase display materials, particularly if the store is operating on a self-service basis. A shopper may decide at home to buy some cold cereal, but the key decision regarding which type and which brand may be made at the store. Of course, some advertising effort must be directed to the consumer in his house because a totally unknown brand, no matter how attractively packaged, will usually be rejected in favor of a known brand.

How consumers buy. The *how* part of consumers' buying habits encompasses several areas of behavior, and it affects product and pricing policies, promotional programs, and other management decisions.

Long ago, for example, many firms found that consumers preferred to buy such products as pickles, cookies, and butter already packaged. The advantages of cleanliness and ease of handling offset the higher unit price. If consumers buy a manufacturer's product primarily in self-service stores, increased importance is placed on developing an attractive package and label. When deciding to use packages, manufacturers and middlemen should be aware of consumer preferences with respect to quantity. If a soap manufacturer packages all his soap in lots of three bars in an attempt to stimulate buying, much business will be lost if customers typically buy only one bar at a time.

The trend toward one-stop shopping has encouraged retailers to add related and even unrelated lines of merchandise to their basic groups of products. Self-service stores have found, however, that the addition of certain products to their lines does not materially increase sales. Many people prefer to buy groceries and drug items on a serve-yourself basis, but they will not buy clothing, carpets, or furniture this way.

Some people always pay cash, whereas others prefer to buy on credit. A firm may have to abandon its cash-and-carry policy if there is considerable demand for credit buying. Services such as delivery, installation, and even credit may be priced separately and offered on an optional basis.

QUESTIONS AND PROBLEMS

1. How is the women's liberation movement likely to influence consumer buying patterns and consumption?
2. How do you account for the increase in impulse buying?
3. What effect is the four-day workweek likely to have on family consumption patterns?
4. Give some examples of specific companies whose marketing programs reflect an attempt to satisfy consumers' desires for the following kinds of convenience:
   - a. Form
   - b. Time
   - c. Readiness
   - d. Quantity
   - e. Automation
5. What criteria did Lloyd Warner use as the bases for placing a person in Warner's social-class structure? Why is the *amount* of income not given more weight as an indicator of social class?
6. What were the major conclusions drawn from the *Chicago Tribune's* study of social-class structure in a large industrial city?
7. Which of the six social classes do you identify with each of the following products or activities? In some cases more than one class may be listed, but try to associate each item with only one of the six classes.
   - a. Debutante parties
   - b. A cocktail before dinner
   - c. Wine and liqueurs with dinner
   - d. Beer with dinner
   - e. A Cadillac
   - f. *The New Yorker* magazine
   - g. Boats
   - h. Sitting on the front porch in warm weather in an undershirt
   - i. Shopping at a credit jeweler
   - j. Borrowing at a bank
   - k. Borrowing from a pawnbroker
8. Discuss the concept of a reference group, explaining:
   - a. The meaning of the concept
   - b. Its use in marketing
   - c. The relationship between reference groups and attitude formation (from Chapter 4)
9. "Reference groups stifle initiative, foster robotlike conformity among the members, and inflict severe penalties for failure to meet the group's standards of behavior." Discuss.
10. Using the product and brand, plus (+) and minus (−), system as modeled in Figure 5-4 for measuring susceptibility to reference-group influence, rate each of the following products or brands. Explain your reasoning in each instance.
    - a. Color television set, console model
    - b. Perfume
    - c. Electric kitchen range
    - d. Fresh hamburger meat
    - e. Wall-to-wall carpeting
    - f. 35 mm. camera priced at $100
11. In the "trial" stage of deciding whether to adopt some innovation, the likelihood of adoption is reduced if the product cannot be sampled because of its cost or size. What are some products which might have these drawbacks? How might these drawbacks be overcome?
12. Describe the people likely to be found in the innovator category of adopters. In the late-majority category.
13. Give some examples of innovations which meet the "compatibility" characteristic in new-product adoption and some which possess the "relative advantage" feature.

14. Cite examples of manufacturers or retailers who are recognizing the emergence of teen-agers as decision makers in family buying and as actual purchasers.

15. Cite a few examples of products where the same person normally makes the buying decisions and the physical purchase and also uses the product. Then give some examples in which two or three different people are involved in these processes. Explain how a firm's marketing program may be affected by the number of people involved in the deciding, buying, and using processes.

16. Families in which stage of the life cycle are likely to be the best prospects for each of the following products or services?
   - a. Braces on teeth
   - b. Suntan lotion
   - c. Second car in the family
   - d. Vitamin pills
   - e. Refrigerators
   - f. Life insurance
   - g. Snow skis
   - h. 46-day Mediterranean cruise

17. Explain how the factors of *when* and *where* people buy might affect the marketing program for each of the following products:
   - a. Water skis
   - b. House paint
   - c. High-quality sunglasses
   - d. Outboard motors
   - e. Room air conditioners

BUYING DECISION PROCESS AND CLASSIFICATION OF CONSUMER GOODS

In this concluding chapter on consumer buying behavior, we incorporate some of the material covered in the preceding three chapters. First we study the decision-making process in buying. Then there is a brief description of current significant efforts toward the statement of a comprehensive theory of buyer behavior. Next comes a consideration of what we call motivation research. In the final section we segment consumer goods, classifying them on the basis of buyer behavior and then considering the marketing implications of this classification.

DECISION-MAKING PROCESS IN BUYING

It is time now to tie together some of the points discussed in the preceding two chapters and to describe the process a consumer goes through when making a purchasing decision. The process is a problem-solving approach consisting of the following five steps (Fig. 6-1):

1. Recognition of an unsatisfied need
2. Identification of alternative ways of reducing tensions, i.e., achieving satisfaction
3. Evaluation of alternatives
4. Purchase decision
5. Postpurchase behavior

Figure 6-1.

Once the process is started, a potential buyer can withdraw at any stage prior to the actual purchase. A total-stage approach is likely to be used only in certain buying situations—a first-time purchase of a product, for instance, or when buying high-priced, long-lived, infrequently purchased articles. For many products the purchasing behavior is a routine affair in which the aroused need is satisfied in a habitual manner by repurchasing the same brand. That is, past reinforcement in learning experiences leads directly to the buying response-act, and thus the second and third stages are bypassed. However, if something changes appreciably (price, product, services), the buyer may reopen the full decision process and consider alternative brands.

RECOGNITION OF UNSATISFIED NEED

The process starts when an unsatisfied need (motive) creates tension. It may be a biogenic need aroused internally (the person feels hungry), or the need may have been dormant until it was aroused by an external stimulus, such as an ad or the sight of the product. Perhaps dissatisfaction with the present product or brand created the tension.

Once the need is recognized, quite frequently the consumer or his family immediately becomes aware of conflicting motives or competive uses for their scarce resources of time, manpower, or money. Let us say that a husband has a desire to install a swimming pool in his backyard at a cost of $2,000. His wife reminds him that she needs some new furniture for the living room or that the $2,000 would help Junior get started in college next year. Or the man may fear that one of his key reference groups would not approve, or that the weather would be too cool for him to get enough use out of the pool to warrant the cost.

A person must resolve these conflicts before he can proceed. Otherwise, the buying process for the given product stops at this point.

IDENTIFICATION OF ALTERNATIVES

Once a need is recognized, then both product and brand alternatives must be identified. Let us say that a housewife wants to make her hands softer. Some alternative solutions include buying a new dishwasher, rubber gloves, a different detergent, or a new hand cream, or getting the kids to wash dishes and scrub floors. If one of the product alternatives is selected, there are several brands to choose from.

The search for alternatives, and the methods used in the search, are influenced by such factors as (1) what the time and money costs are (not much time is spent buying hamburger, as compared with buying a new winter coat), (2) how much information the consumer already has from past experiences and other sources, and (3) the amount of the perceived risk if a wrong selection is made.

For his sources of information the consumer may rely on his reference groups. He may also pay attention to advertisements, or make several shopping trips to various stores, seeking product demonstrations or help from salesclerks.[1]

EVALUATION OF ALTERNATIVES

Once all the reasonable alternatives are identified, the consumer must then evaluate each one preparatory to making the purchasing decision. Many of the same factors influence buyer activity in both the search and the evaluation stages. If the aroused need is urgent, less time is likely to be devoted to either of these stages. A buyer who likes to shop will spend more time evaluating than a person who does not have this propensity. People with more education and higher incomes are more likely to do a thorough evaluation job. The criteria a consumer uses in his evaluations should seem familiar by now. They include his past experiences and his attitudes toward various brands. He also uses the opinions of members of his family and other reference groups as guidelines in selection.

PURCHASE DECISION

After much searching and evaluating, the consumer at some point has to decide whether he is going to satisfy his aroused need or not, i.e., whether he is going to buy. Assuming that the answer is "yes," he is faced with a series of decisions as to the product type, brand, price, store, possibly quantity and color, etc.

Anything a marketer can do to simplify decision making will be attractive to a buyer because most people find it very hard to make a decision. Perhaps in his advertising the seller can suggest what color is best for a given product use. Sometimes several decision situations can be combined and marketed as one package. A travel agency simplifies a traveler's decisions on transportation routes, hotels, local transportation, and which tours to take, by selling a packaged tour.

To do a better marketing job in this stage of the buying process, a seller needs to know answers to many questions regarding consumers' shopping behavior. For instance, how much effort is the consumer willing to spend in shopping for the product? What factors influence where a consumer will shop; i.e., what are her *patronage*-buying motives? Do stores each have an image? If so, is this important to a shopper when selecting a store? What factors determine the image of a given store? How does a retailer determine what is the image of his store? What are the differentiating characteristics, if any, of impulse buyers? What influences do store layout and other physcial store characteristics have on buyer behavior?[2]

---

[1]See Terrence V. O'Brien, "Information Use in Consumer Decisions," paper presented at American Psychological Association, September, 1972; and "An Empirically Validated Model of Consumer Information Processing," Institute of Management Sciences, April, 1972.

[2]For some research findings on several of these questions, see James F. Engel, David T. Kollat, and Roger D. Blackwell, *Consumer Behavior,* 2nd ed., Holt, Rinehart and Winston, Inc., New York, 1973, chaps. 19–21. See also Ben M. Enis and Gordon W. Paul, "'Store Loyalty' as a

Manufacturers and retailers, alike, are interested in knowing what motivates consumers to buy at certain stores. A producer who appeals to prestige and status motives in the sale of his product ordinarily would not want it distributed to retail stores which feature low-priced merchandise and no services. A consumer, of course, prefers to patronize stores where she perceives she is maximizing money, service, and product benefits while minimizing her risks as perceived in terms of product price, acceptability of product offerings, and required expenditure of time and effort.

Patronage motives, like product motives, are multiple and sometimes conflicting. Obviously a retailer cannot be all things to all people. He should not stress his many services and luxurious furnishings while trying to build up a low-priced economy-appeal image.

Some of the more important consumer patronage motives are as follows:

1. Convenience of location, rapidity of service, ease of locating merchandise, and uncrowded conditions
2. Price
3. Assortment of merchandise
4. Services offered
5. Attractive store appearance
6. Caliber of sales personnel

The several motives to which a store appeals can be used to describe the store's image or personality. Truly every store has an image, and the store's advertising is largely responsible for creating it. Women shoppers are acutely sensitive to cues in store advertising. They can accurately identify the characteristics of a store from its advertising alone. The findings from one study of a leading store in Kansas City illustrate this point (Fig. 6-2). Women in two cities, Kansas City and Atlanta, were asked to evaluate the store's newspaper ads. The evaluations made by women who did not know the store's identity and who were judging solely by the physical appearance of the advertisements almost perfectly matched those made by shoppers who knew the store personally.

The marketing implications in this advertising-store image relationship make it imperative, from the beginning, that management plan its advertising program so as to accomplish the store's intended purposes. The store's image preselects its customers and thus determines the composition of its market. It is possible to change a store's image, but this can be done only gradually over a period of time.[3]

Patronage motives and choice of stores are related to the concept of social-class structure described in Chapter 5. The *Chicago Tribune* study of social class in Chicago showed definitely that people match their own values and expectations

---

Basis for Market Segmentation," *Journal of Retailing,* Fall, 1970, pp. 42–56; and Edward M. Tauber, "Why Do People Shop?" *Journal of Marketing,* October, 1972, pp. 46–59.

[3]For a report on how downtown and suburban department stores differ in their respective images, see Stuart U. Rich and Bernard D. Portis, "The 'Imageries' of Department Stores," *Journal of Marketing,* April, 1964, pp. 10–15. See also John H. Kunkel and Leonard L. Berry, "A Behavioral Conception of Retail Image," *Journal of Marketing,* October, 1968, pp. 21–27; Joseph Barry Mason and Morris L. Mayer, "Insights into the Image Determinants of Fashion Specialty Outlets," *Journal of Business Research,* Summer, 1973, pp. 73–80; and Dale L. Varble and Jim L. Grimm, "Image Assessment Can Be Administered by a Small Retailer," *Business Ideas and Facts,* Summer, 1972, pp. 15–21.

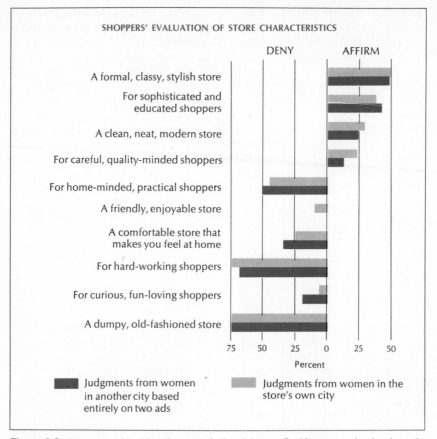

SHOPPERS' EVALUATION OF STORE CHARACTERISTICS

DENY   AFFIRM

A formal, classy, stylish store
For sophisticated and
educated shoppers
A clean, neat, modern store
For careful, quality-minded shoppers
For home-minded, practical shoppers
A friendly, enjoyable store
A comfortable store that
makes you feel at home
For hard-working shoppers
For curious, fun-loving shoppers
A dumpy, old-fashioned store

75   50   25   0   25   50
Percent

Judgments from women   Judgments from women in the
in another city based   store's own city
entirely on two ads

Figure 6-2. Shoppers often identify a store's "social status" without ever having been in the store, by reading its advertisements. The judgments of women who read a store's advertising but had never been inside it were almost identical to those of people who knew the store. For instance, nearly 50 percent of both groups agreed that the store in this study was for "sophisticated and educated shoppers." Almost everyone in both groups denied that the store was for "hardworking shoppers." *Source:* Pierre Martineau, *Motivation in Advertising*, McGraw-Hill Book Company, New York, 1957.

with the status of the store. Not all people want to shop at glamorous, high-status stores. A lower-status woman knows that she will be punished in subtle ways by the clerks and other customers if she goes into an exclusive department store. "The clerks treat you like a crumb," is one response. Because social-class membership and choice of store are closely related, an important function of retail advertising today is to help a shopper make the necessary social-class identification. The shopper does not want to go to a store where she does not fit, and if she has any doubts she is apt to stay away from a store whose advertising appeal is not clear-cut. Usually a retailer must select his desired niche in the social structure and then set up his marketing and advertising accordingly. Normally, a store—even a large department store with a bargain basement as well as exclusive salon departments—cannot appeal strongly to all classes.[4] As mundane a store as a supermarket may project a certain image. The *Chicago Tribune* study showed that two grocery chains offering essentially the same products, services, and prices in the same neighborhood still appealed to two different social classes.

POSTPURCHASE BEHAVIOR

All the behavior determinants and the steps in the buying process up to this point are operative *before* or *during* the time a purchase is made. However, a buyer's feelings and evaluations *after* the sale are also significant for a marketer because they can influence repeat sales and also influence what the buyer tells others about the product or brand.

Typically a buyer experiences some postpurchase anxieties in all but routine purchases. Leon Festinger refers to this state of anxiety as *cognitive dissonance*.[5] Festinger theorizes that a person strives for internal harmony, consistency, or congruity among his "cognitions" (knowledge, attitudes, beliefs, values). Any inconsistency in these cognitions is called "dissonance."

Postpurchase cognitive dissonance occurs because each of the alternatives considered by the consumer usually has both advantages and limitations. Thus, when the purchase decision is finally made, the selected alternative has some drawbacks, while the rejected alternatives each possess some attractive features. That is, the negative aspects of the item selected and the positive qualities of the rejected products create cognitive dissonance in the consumer.

In the above explanation the consumer was aware of the dissonant elements before he made the purchase decision. Cognitive dissonance can also be aroused if disturbing information is received *after* the purchase is made. Currently we have some classic examples—consumers learn that the cholesterol in animal fats may lead to heart trouble; cigarette smokers learn that smoking apparently can lead to lung cancer; women are learning that the contraceptive pill can have bad side effects.

Festinger developed some hypotheses about the intensity of cognitive dissonance. Dissonance increases (1) as the dollar value of the purchase increases, (2) as the relative attractiveness of unselected alternatives increases, and (3) as the relative importance of the decision increases (buying a house or car potentially creates more dissonance than buying a candy bar).

To restore his internal harmony and minimize his discomfort, a person will try to reduce his postpurchase anxieties. Thus he is likely to avoid information (such as ads for the rejected products) which is likely to increase his dissonance. He may even change his behavior (cutting down on animal fats or quitting smoking, for example). He may change his opinions, or he may seek increased amounts of consonant information. Prior to making the purchase, he may shop around quite a bit, especially for a high-priced, infrequently purchased article. He is seeking to

---

[4]See William Lazer and Robert G. Wyckham, "Perceptual Segmentation of Department Store Markets," *Journal of Retailing,* Summer, 1969, pp. 3–14; and John V. Petrof, "Race as a Factor of Store Preference," *Southern Journal of Business,* July, 1968, pp. 177–183.

[5]Leon Festinger, *A Theory of Cognitive Dissonance,* Stanford University Press, Stanford, Calif., 1957; see also Jack W. Brehm and Arthur R. Cohen, *Explorations in Cognitive Dissonance,* John Wiley & Sons, Inc., New York, 1962.

avoid or minimize postdecision dissonance by spending more time in predecision evaluations. As was the case with personality theory, cognitive dissonance is a potentially useful concept. The marketing studies to date, however, have been somewhat conflicting or inconclusive.[6]

At the same time, some useful generalizations can be developed from the theory. For example, in his advertising or personal selling, anything a seller can do to reassure a buyer by stressing desirable features of a product can do much to reduce dissonance. This reduction will reinforce the consumer and increase his likelihood of repeat purchases. When the product in question is expensive and infrequently purchased, the seller's postsale service program can be a significant factor in reducing dissonance.

TOWARD A COMPREHENSIVE THEORY OF BUYER BEHAVIOR

The traditional approach to the study of buyer behavior has typically been a fragmented one. That is, research is done on attitudes or personality or social-group influence. This is perhaps a necessary approach when a new field is being developed. Certainly many of the theories and research findings on separate parts of buyer behavior have shed some light on the mental processes in the consumer's "black box." Also, many of the findings have been applied in a profitable manner by marketing practitioners.

In recent years, however, some notable attempts have been made to formulate a comprehensive theory of buyer behavior. Two of these models are described here in a *very* brief manner. Any more complete explanation is outside the scope of this book. Typically, any of the comprehensive models pose some problems. First, they are complicated and very difficult to explain, but then, consumer behavior is a complex activity. Second, the validity of the models still needs further empirical testing. Third, it is still difficult for a businessman to translate the theoretical abstractions into practical company research.

THE HOWARD-SHETH THEORY

One broad theory was developed by Howard and Sheth over a period of time which included a three-year validation test.[7] The model is based on the assumptions that (1) buying is a rational exercise in problem solving and (2) buyer behavior is systematic (not random) and thus is caused by inputs (stimuli) and results in outputs (buying behavior). The theory then attempts to describe what occurs between the inputs and outputs. This is reminiscent of the learning and cognitive theories discussed in Chapter 4.

The Howard-Sheth theoretical model is based on the idea that four sets of variables determine buyer behavior: (1) stimulus-input variables from the marketing program and social environment; (2) internal variables which together show

---

[6]See Sadaomi Oshikawa, "Can Cognitive Dissonance Theory Explain Consumer Behavior?" *Journal of Marketing,* October, 1969, pp. 44–49.

[7]Adapted from John A. Howard and Jagdish N. Sheth, "A Theory of Buyer Behavior," in Harold H. Kassarjian and Thomas S. Robertson (eds.), *Perspectives in Consumer Behavior,* Scott, Foresman and Company, Glenview, Ill., 1968, pp. 467–487. See also Howard and Sheth, *A Theory of Buyer Behavior,* John Wiley & Sons, Inc., New York, 1969.

the state of the buyer (his motives, attitudes, experiences, perceptions); (3) seven variables which affect the internal state of the buyer (these are called "exogenous" variables and include social class, culture, time pressure, and financial status); and (4) response-output variables (the buyer's behavior based on interactions of the first three sets of variables).

Summary of the theory. Much buying behavior is usually repetitive. When confronted with repetitive brand-choice decisions, a consumer tends to simplify his task by storing relevant information and establishing a routine in his decision process. The elements in this brand-choice decision are (1) a set of motives, (2) alternative choices of products and brands (called his *evoked set*), and (3) decision mediators.

Decision mediators are a set of rules which the buyer uses to match his motive and the alternatives for satisfying these motives. These mediators rank-order the motives and then rank-order the brands on the basis of their potential for satisfying these motives. The rank ordering of the brands is based on learning experiences or outside information (ads, reference-group advice, etc.). From these influences a person develops his attitudes (H-S theory calls them "predispositions"). Inhibitors (price, availability, buyer's financial status) may interfere in the buying process.

When a buyer is considering a type of product which is new to him, he has no set of decision mediators, so he actively seeks information from his environment and will try to draw from experiences with similar types of products. It is important that a marketing executive try to determine the intensity of this information-seeking effort. If the buyer's brand choice is satisfactory, he tends to repeat that choice in future purchases. He is striving to develop a routine, thus reducing the complexity of buying. This is called the *psychology of simplification.* On the other hand, sometimes the same routine and the same brand become boring. When the buyer is satiated even with his preferred brand, he will complicate the situation by starting the search process all over again. This is called the *psychology of complication.*

The theory also explains how a given stimulus may result in different responses among buyers, depending on the person's "level of motivation." In the case of response to the stimulus of an advertisement, for example, one person may buy the brand, one may read the ad and store the information, and a third may ignore the ad. The concept of "predisposition toward a brand" is used to explain how two buyers may both need a product but why they buy two different brands.

THE ENGEL-KOLLAT-BLACKWELL THEORY

These three men have developed a comprehensive theoretical model which conceives of a person as being a system with outputs (behavior) which respond to inputs.[8] The model recognizes the existence of "intervening variables" between the initial inputs and ultimate outputs. We then try to understand how these variables affect the processes going on in the consumer's mind (called his *central control unit*). This theory holds that an individual's psychological makeup (personality, attitudes, stored information from learning experiences) affects the mental processes in his central control unit.

Inputs in the form of physical and social stimuli hit a person's sensory receptors

---

[8]Engel, Kollat, and Blackwell, *op. cit.* The model serves as the conceptual framework for the book, but see pp. 49–67 for a brief description including two examples of using the model.

and arouse some needs. How these stimuli are received and interpreted depends on the person's selective perceptions. These perceptions determine whether action will result. If so, problem recognition occurs, and the decision process goes into operation. This involves the search for, and evaluation of, alternatives; the purchasing act; and postpurchase evaluations.[9]

MOTIVATION RESEARCH

For many years various forms of marketing research have been used to interpret and predict buyer behavior. Observational techniques have measured the patterns of overt buying behavior. Survey techniques with structured questionnaires have been used to ask people why they bought a certain brand or why they patronized a certain store. In some cases these techniques have been valuable in explaining why consumers behave as they do. However, often a buyer's real motives and other behavioral influences are too unknown, hidden, or complex to be determined by direct questioning. Consequently, we have borrowed some *indirect* research techniques from behavioral science fields, especially psychology and psychiatry, to help us better understand why people respond as they do to various products, advertisements, and other marketing situations.

The term "motivation research" is used to describe these indirect techniques as applied to marketing. Actually the term is misleading in that these techniques are used to study attitudes, personality traits, reference-group influences, and other behavioral variables, as well as motivation. Motivation research attempts to explain the "why" of buying behavior, especially in situations where the buyer himself does not know the real reasons or, if he does, is not willing to state them openly.

INDIRECT MOTIVATION RESEARCH TECHNIQUES

Three useful research techniques borrowed from other fields are attitude scaling (which we alluded to briefly in Chapter 4), the depth interview, and projective techniques.

Depth interview. This technique involves a long unstructured interview during which the interviewer gets the respondent to talk freely about the subject without inhibitions or fear of disapproval. The interviewer is primarily a listener and a recorder, interrupting only to keep the interview from rambling. A few probing questions may be necessary to bring out important comments from the respondent. This technique requires highly skilled interviewers and analysts.

Projective techniques. The various types of projective techniques used in motivation research have essentially the same purpose. The idea is to get a respondent to project his thoughts into a completely innocuous situation or to place

---

[9]For two other comprehensive models, see Francesco M. Nicosia, *Consumer Decision Processes: Marketing and Advertising Implications,* Prentice-Hall, Inc., Englewood Cliffs, N.J., 1966; and Alan R. Andreasen, "Attitudes and Customer Behavior: A Decision Model," in Lee Preston (ed.), *New Research in Marketing,* University of California, Institute of Business and Economic Research, Berkeley, 1965, pp. 1–16.

himself in another person's position and express what he thinks the other person is doing or saying. In this way it is expected that the respondent will reveal his own true motives and beliefs. One such technique is the *word-association* test, in which the researcher mentions a word and the respondent tells the first word or first few words that come to his mind when he hears the test words. A variation of the word-association technique is the *incomplete-sentence* test. The respondent is asked to complete with the first thought that comes into his mind a sentence such as, "I use brand A because . . ." or "I think the average person would prefer brand A because. . . ." Another extensively used projective technique is the *Thematic Apperception Test (TAT).* Respondents are shown one or more vague or ambiguous pictures and are asked to tell a story about the pictures or to tell what is happening in them. Again the intent is that the respondent will reveal his own feelings by projecting himself into the situation. The *cartoon* test is a variation of the TAT. A respondent is shown a cartoon and alternative captions and is asked to select the caption he feels best suits the situation. In another type of cartoon test, two people are pictured, and the comment made by one of them is shown. The respondent is supposed to fill in the remark that he thinks the second person is making.

CONTROVERSY IN MOTIVATION RESEARCH

Motivation research has generated much controversy in marketing The major argument has been over the validity and reliability of the samples used in the research. Typically in such a study the researchers work with very small samples, sometimes with only 50 respondents and often with only 100 to 200. Opponents of motivation research object to the broad market generalizations drawn from the small sample and the uses to which the findings are put. It is questionable whether results based on psychological clinical procedures can be quantified and projected to represent mass market motivations. These studies can, however, develop generalizations which in turn should lead to further quantitative marketing studies. Opponents point out that to be effective, the type of research done in motivation research should be conducted by trained scientists.

On the other hand, applying motivation research techniques to a small sample of people permits a *complete* response from a few individuals rather than *superficial* answers from many.

CLASSIFICATION OF PRODUCTS

Just as it is necessary to segment *markets* for meaningful programming in marketing, so also is it helpful to separate *products* into homogeneous classifications. First we shall divide all products into two groups—consumer goods and industrial goods—a classification that parallels our segmentation of the market. Then later we shall divide each of the major product categories still further.

CONSUMER GOODS AND INDUSTRIAL GOODS

Consumer goods include all products which are "destined for use by ultimate consumers or households and in such form that they can be used without (further) commercial processing." *Industrial goods* are those which are "destined to be sold primarily for use in producing other goods or rendering services as contrasted with goods destined to be sold primarily to the ultimate consumer."[10]

The fundamental basis for distinguishing between the two groups is the *ultimate* use for which the product is intended in its present form. A cash register purchased by a retailer for use in his store (the product renders a service in a business), a pair of overalls bought by a farmer to be worn while working (farming is his business), and materials or parts bought by a manufacturer for use in making his product—all are industrial goods.

A particular stage in a product's distribution has no effect upon its classification. Cornflakes or children's shoes would be classed as consumer products whether they were in the manufacturer's warehouse or on retailers' shelves because ultimately they will be used in their present form by household consumers. Cornflakes sold to restaurants and other institutions, however, are classed as industrial goods.

Often it is not possible to place a product definitely in one class or the other. A portable typewriter may be considered a consumer good if it is purchased by a student or a housewife for nonbusiness use. But if the typewriter is bought by a traveling salesman for use in his business, it is classed with industrial goods. The manufacturer of such a product recognizes that his product falls in both categories and therefore develops separate marketing programs for the different markets.

MARKETING SIGNIFICANCE OF PRODUCT CLASSIFICATION

The two-way product classification is a useful framework for programming marketing operations because each major class of products ultimately goes to a different market and requires different marketing methods. In the field of product planning, for example, branding, packaging, and fashion are generally far more significant for a consumer product than for an industrial good. Since the channels of distribution for consumer products are typically longer and involve more middlemen than those for industrial goods, distribution policies would vary. Advertising policies, too, would be affected. Manufacturers of consumer goods ordinarily use much more advertising than do manufacturers of industrial products.

CLASSIFICATION OF CONSUMER PRODUCTS

Although the marketing differences between consumer and industrial goods make a two-part classification of products valuable, the category of consumer goods is still too broad for a marketing manager. Consequently, consumer products are further classified as convenience goods, shopping goods, and specialty goods (see Table 6-I). This is the traditional classification, and while it raises objections in some quarters, it is still better understood and more generally followed by businessmen than any of the alternatives yet suggested. It is important to note that this three-way subdivision is based on consumer *buying habits* rather than on consumer *products.* Specifically the two criteria used as bases for classifying consumer products are (1) the degree to which the consumer is aware of the exact nature of the product *before* he starts on his shopping trip and (2) the satisfaction received from searching for and comparing products, weighed against the time and effort required for this task.

---

[10]Committee on Definitions, *Marketing Definitions: A Glossary of Marketing Terms,* American Marketing Association, Chicago, 1960, pp. 11, 14.

Table 6-1. Characteristics of classes of consumer goods and some marketing considerations.

Characteristics and marketing considerations	Type of product		
	Convenience	Shopping	Specialty
Characteristics:			
1. Time and effort devoted by consumer to shopping	Very little	Considerable	Cannot generalize. May go to nearby store and exert minimum effort, or may have to go to distant store and spend much time
2. Time spent planning the purchase	Very little	Considerable	Considerable
3. How soon want is satisfied after it arises	Immediately	Relatively long time	Relatively long time
4. Are price and quality compared?	No	Yes	No
5. Price	Low	High	High
6. Frequency of purchase	Usually frequent	Infrequent	Infrequent
7. Importance	Unimportant	Often very important	Cannot generalize
Marketing considerations:			
1. Length of channel	Long	Short	Short to very short
2. Importance of retailer	Any single store is relatively unimportant	Important	Very important
3. Number of outlets	As many as possible	Few	Few; often only one in a market
4. Stock turnover	High	Lower	Lower
5. Gross margin	Low	High	High
6. Responsibility for advertising	Manufacturer's	Retailer's	Joint responsibility
7. Importance of point-of-purchase display	Very important	Less important	Less important
8. Advertising used	Manufacturer's	Retailer's	Both
9. Brand or store name important	Brand name	Store name	Both
10. Importance of packaging	Very important	Less important	Less important

Convenience goods. The significant characteristics of convenience goods are that the consumer has complete knowledge of the particular product (or its substitutes) which he wants *before* going out to buy it and that it is purchased with a minimum of effort on his part. Normally the gain resulting from shopping around to compare price and quality is not considered worth the extra time and effort required. The consumer is willing to accept any of several substitutes, and thus he will buy the one which is most accessible. For most buyers this subclass of goods includes groceries, tobacco products, inexpensive candy, drug sundries such as toothpaste and shaving accessories, and staple hardware items such as light bulbs and flashlight batteries. When the need for this type of goods arises, the consumer wants to make his purchase as rapidly and as easily as possible. Consequently, this type of product must be readily accessible in any shopping area.

Convenience goods typically have a low unit price, are not bulky, and are not greatly affected by fad and fashion. Among the well-known brands, one is not usually *strongly* preferred over another. Convenience goods are purchased frequently, although this is not a differentiating characteristic. Items such as Christmas tree lights or birthday cards are convenience goods for most people, even though they may be bought only once a year.

Marketing considerations. Since a product must be readily accessible when the consumer's demand arises, a manufacturer must secure wide distribution. But since most retail stores sell only a small volume of a manufacturer's output, it is not economical for him to sell directly to all retail outlets. Instead, he relies on wholesalers to reach part of the retail market.

The promotional policies of both the manufacturers and the middlemen, especially the retailing middlemen, are involved here. A retailer typically carries several brands of a convenience item, so he is not able to promote any single brand. He is not interested in doing much advertising of these articles because many other stores carry them, and any advertising he does may help a competitor. Furthermore, quality and price of competitive products are reasonably similar, the product requires little or no explanation, and the retailer normally has no incentive to push one brand over another. Therefore, many retailers of convenience goods have adopted a self-service marketing technique. As a result, virtually the entire promotional burden is shifted to the manufacturer. He must advertise extensively to develop a recognition of, and a preference for, his brand. Self-service in retailing places great importance on point-of-purchase displays and packaging because these tools have considerable influence on impulse buying.

Shopping goods. Shopping goods are products for which a customer usually wishes to compare quality, price, and style in several stores before purchasing. A key identifying characteristic, and the one which separates shopping goods from convenience goods, is that for shopping goods the consumer lacks full knowledge of pertinent product features before embarking upon the shopping trip. Thus, on the trip not only does he purchase the article, but he first must assess the relative suitability of alternative products. This search will continue only as long as the customer believes that the gain from comparing product features offsets the additional time and effort required. Examples of shopping goods typically include women's apparel, furniture and other durable goods, jewelry, piece goods, and, to some extent, men's ready-to-wear and shoes. In general, shopping goods are larger in unit value and are purchased less frequently than convenience goods.

Marketing considerations. The buying habits associated with shopping goods affect the distribution and promotional strategy of both manufacturers and middlemen. A manufacturer of a shopping good requires fewer retail outlets because the consumer is willing to look around a little for what he wants, purchases are usually made infrequently, and the need does not require immediate satisfaction. In order to increase the convenience of comparison shopping, a manufacturer tries to place his product in a store located near other stores carrying competing items. Similarly, department stores and other retailers who carry primarily shopping goods want to be bunched together.

Manufacturers usually work closely with retailers in the marketing of shopping goods. Since a manufacturer uses fewer retail outlets, he is more dependent upon those he selects. Retail stores typically buy shopping goods in large quantities. Thus there is less use of wholesalers than there is with convenience goods; distribution direct from manufacturer to retailer is common. Finally, the store name is often more important to the buyer of a shopping good than the manufacturer's name.

This last point carries significant promotional implications. The retailer is quite willing to assume a good part of the advertising, display, and selling costs, particularly for items such as wearing apparel, where the average customer does not know or care who made the product.

Some socioeconomic trends may be decreasing the scope and importance of the shopping goods category. Increased incomes, higher values placed on leisure time, and widespread exposure to mass-media advertising are forces which lessen a consumer's propensity to search and compare. Any significant decline in the search-shopping activity may influence future distribution policies, store locations, and retailing techniques.[11]

Specialty goods. Specialty goods have been defined as those with "unique characteristics and/or brand identification for which a significant group of buyers are habitually willing to make a special purchasing effort."[12] In the case of specialty goods, as with convenience goods but unlike shopping goods, the buyer has complete knowledge of the particular product he wants before going on his buying trip. The distinctive feature of specialty goods is that the buyer will accept only one brand. He is willing to forgo more accessible substitutes in order to procure the wanted brand, even though this may require a significant expenditure of time and effort. Examples of products usually classified as specialty goods include expensive men's ready-to-wear, fancy groceries, health foods, hi-fi components, photographic equipment, and, for many people, automobiles and certain home appliances. Ordinarily, only certain *brands* of these products fall into the specialty goods classification. For many men, a Kuppenheimer suit would be considered a specialty good—they insist on the brand and will accept no other——but men's suits in general would not be so classified.

---

[11]William P. Dommermuth and Edward W. Cundiff, "Shopping Goods, Shopping Centers, and Selling Strategies," *Journal of Marketing,* October, 1967, pp. 32–36.

[12]Committee on Definitions, *Marketing Definitions: A Glossary of Marketing Terms,* American Marketing Association, Chicago, 1960, p. 22.

The consumer's *insistence* on a certain brand is the key characteristic of specialty goods. Since the consumer insists on a certain brand, he is willing to expend considerable effort to find it. Consequently, manufacturers can afford to use fewer outlets. With the insistence on a given brand and with few outlets, the consumer *must* make a special effort. Thus the *willingness* to exert extra effort becomes a *need* to do so.

Marketing considerations. Usually only one outlet is used in a given area or market. Ordinarily, the manufacturer deals directly with his chosen retailers. The retailers are extremely important, particularly if the manufacturer is using only one in each area. Where the franchise to handle the product is a valuable one, the retailer may become quite dependent upon the producer. Actually they are interdependent; the success of one is closely tied to the success of the other.

Because brand is important and because only a few outlets are used, both the manufacturer and the retailer advertise the product extensively. Often the manufacturer pays some portion of the retailer's advertising costs, and the retailer's name frequently appears in the manufacturer's advertisements.

Criticism of product classification. Although we continue to use the convenience-shopping-specialty categorization, we cannot ignore its shortcomings. One of the quarrels with the traditional classification is that we really are not classifying consumer products at all. Instead, we are grouping consumer buying patterns. We are talking about convenience buying habits, not convenience products. The critics point out, and with justification, that buying habits may be categorized in this manner but that products cannot. When we attempt to establish the three-way classification, we find that given products shift in and out of one or more of the groups. Automobiles furnish a good illustration. When a person first buys a car, he may shop extensively. He finally buys a Ford and is quite satisfied. When he needs a replacement, he goes straight to a Ford agency without any shopping around. To him a car has shifted from a shopping to a specialty good. Later, for one reason or another, he becomes disenchanted with his Ford. Then when car-buying time comes around a third time, he will revert to shopping.

An adjunct to this first basic criticism is that the attempt to classify products by systems that were really designed to sort out buying habits results in considerable overlapping of the product groups. Not all consumers react in the same way to a given product. In fact, some items may fall in all three classes, depending upon the consumers.

A second objection to the classification is that it suggests sharp, rigid demarcations, when in fact none exist. Actually this criticism should not worry a marketing man. He should have long since realized that marketing does not lend itself to sharply demarcated categorizations. Instead, he deals constantly with gray areas and twilight zones where imperceptible shadings often occur. In reality, the classification of goods is better depicted as a continuum representing degrees of effort expended, with convenience goods clustered at one end and specialty products occupying positions near the other end.

Another criticism concerns the confusion surrounding the concept of specialty goods. The term "specialty" itself is used in conjunction with several other aspects of marketing—specialty salesmen and specialty stores, for example—and these have no connection with specialty products. In fact, many specialty stores carry shopping goods, and many specialty salesmen sell convenience products.[13]

Classification extended to retail stores. [14] Bucklin proposes that the system for classifying consumer goods can be extended to retailing, with a resultant classification of consumer patronage motives and retail stores. That is, we have convenience stores, shopping stores, and specialty stores. The category in which a given store is placed depends upon whether consumers shop there because it is accessible or because they prefer that store regardless of its accessibility.

By cross-classifying product and patronage motives we get a nine-cell matrix as follows:

	Stores:		
Goods:	Convenience	Shopping	Specialty
Convenience			
Shopping			
Specialty			

The nine possible types of buying behavior represented by this matrix are as follows.[15]

1. Convenience Store—Convenience Good: The consumer, represented by this category, prefers to buy the most readily available brand of product at the most accessible store.
2. Convenience Store—Shopping Good: The consumer selects his purchase from among the assortment carried by the most accessible store.
3. Convenience Store—Specialty Good: The consumer purchases his favored brand from the most accessible store which has the item in stock.
4. Shopping Store—Convenience Good: The consumer is indifferent to the brand of product he buys, but shops among different stores in order to secure better retail service and/or lower retail price.
5. Shopping Store—Shopping Good: The consumer makes comparisons among both retailer controlled factors and factors associated with the product (brand).

---

[13]For a proposal that we draw from the theory of cognitive dissonance to develop a fresh set of behavioral criteria for classifying consumer goods, see Stanley Kaish, "Cognitive Dissonance and the Classification of Consumer Goods," *Journal of Marketing,* October, 1967, pp. 28–31. See also John E. Mertes, "Taste, Variety, and Change: Yesterday and Today," *Business Perspectives,* Fall, 1968, pp. 4–11, for the suggestion that we incorporate the concept of fashion goods into the classification.

[14]This section is adapted from Louis P. Bucklin, "Retail Strategy and the Classification of Consumer Goods," *Journal of Marketing,* January, 1963, pp. 50–55. For a conceptual extension of Bucklin's classification, adding the dimension of retail strategies, see Morris L. Mayer, Joseph Barry Mason, and Morris Gee, "A Reconceptualization of Store Classification as Related to Retail Strategy Formulation," *Journal of Retailing,* Fall, 1971, pp. 27–36.

[15]Bucklin, *op. cit.,* pp. 53–54.

6. Shopping Store—Specialty Good: The consumer has a strong preference with respect to the brand of the product, but shops among a number of stores in order to secure the best retail service and/or price for this brand.
7. Specialty Store—Convenience Good: The consumer prefers to trade at a specific store, but is indifferent to the brand of product purchased.
8. Specialty Store—Shopping Good: The consumer prefers to trade at a certain store, but is uncertain as to which product he wishes to buy, and examines the store's assortment for the best purchase.
9. Specialty Store—Specialty Good: The consumer has both a preference for a particular store and a specific brand.

This matrix is a realistic representation of how people buy. Supermarkets (convenience stores) do carry some exotic specialty foods, and we can buy common brands of after-shave lotion (convenience goods) in exclusive men's shops. Normally, however, consumer behavior toward a given product can be represented by only three or four of the categories. With this cross-classification system to guide him, a retailer can first select his market targets and then develop appropriate strategies to reach those segments. To illustrate, to appeal to the convenience store-specialty good segment, two important elements in the retailer's marketing mix would be (1) a highly accessible location, and (2) a good selection of widely accepted brands. Depth of assortment, price, and personal selling are less important. Store promotion and facilities probably are also of little importance.

QUESTIONS AND PROBLEMS

1. What patronage motives influence your choice of the following?
   a. Restaurant
   b. Movie theater
   c. Department store
   d. Sporting goods store
   e. Shoe store
2. Following is a series of headlines or slogans taken from advertisements of various retailers. To what patronage motive does each appeal?
   a. "Factory trained mechanics at your service."
   b. "We never close."
   c. "Nobody but nobody undersells Gimbels."
   d. "Where Denver shops with confidence."
   e. "We never have missed paying a semiannual dividend since we opened." (Savings and loan association.)
   f. "One dollar down, no payments until the steel strike is over."
   g. "Most complete department store west of the Mississippi."
3. In what ways can retail stores make profitable use of the findings on social-class structure? If possible, use specific stores to illustrate your points.
4. Explain the concept of cognitive dissonance as it operates in the buying decision process.
5. What causes cognitive dissonance to increase in a buying situation? What can a seller do to decrease the level of dissonance in a given purchase of the seller's brand?
6. Describe some of the techniques used in motivation research to determine hidden, but real, buying motives.

7. Give some examples of products, other than those cited in this chapter, which are both consumer and industrial goods. What determines the category in which a product will be placed?

8. What are some brands or types of products which are specialty goods so far as your personal buying patterns are concerned? In each instance do you believe that most consumers would classify the article as a specialty product? If not, how do you explain your own rating?

9. "As brand preferences are established by women with regard to women's shoes and ready-to-wear, these items, which traditionally have been considered shopping goods, will move into the specialty goods category. At the same time, women's clothing is moving into supermarkets and variety stores, thus indicating that some articles are convenience goods." Explain the reasoning involved here. Do you agree that women's clothing is shifting away from the shopping goods classification? Explain.

10. In what way is the responsibility for advertising a convenience good distributed between the manufacturer and the retailers? A shopping good? A specialty good?

11. Compare a manufacturer's marketing mix for a convenience good with the mix for a specialty good.

12. To what extent is the marketing mix for a shopping good similar to the mix for a specialty good?

THE INDUSTRIAL MARKET

Besides the consumer market there is another market—a big, rich, and widely diversified one, requiring the efforts of millions of workers in thousands of different jobs. This market is not criticized for extreme claims in selling or advertising; it is not accused of costing too much, of offering duplicate brands, or of paying middlemen exorbitant profits. It is not a target for widespread complaint because it is largely unknown to the public. The market of which we speak is the industrial market.

NATURE AND IMPORTANCE OF THE INDUSTRIAL MARKET

In Chapter 3 *industrial users* were defined as business or institutional organizations that buy products and services either to use in making other goods and services or to use in their own business. *Industrial goods* were differentiated from consumer goods on the basis of their ultimate use. Industrial goods are those intended for use in making other products or for rendering a service in the operation of a business or institutional enterprise. *Industrial marketing,* then, is the marketing of industrial goods and services to industrial users.

Because the industrial market is largely an unknown quantity to the average consumer, he is apt to underrate its significance. Actually this market is a huge one in terms of its total sales volume and the number of firms involved in it. It is estimated that about 50 percent of all manufactured goods are sold to the industrial market. In 1973, this volume of manufactured industrial goods was about $433 billion.

As large as these figures are, they by no means give the complete picture of the industrial market. They are for *manufactured* products only. In addition to manufactured products, about 80 percent of all farm products and virtually all minerals and forest and sea products are industrial goods. They are sold to firms for further processing. Industrial farm products and minerals alone would add another $80 billion to the volume of industrial goods marketed.[1]

The magnitude and complexity of the industrial market may also be shown by the many transactions required in producing and marketing a product. Consider the number of industrial marketing transactions and the total sales volume involved in getting a pair of cowhide work shoes to a consumer. First, the cattle must go through one or two middlemen before reaching a meatpacker. Then the hides are sold to a tanner, who in turn sells the leather to a shoe manufacturer: The shoe manufacturer may sell to a shoe wholesaler, who will market his products to factories which supply shoes for their workers. Each time the cow, leather, and shoes are sold, it is an industrial marketing transaction.

In addition to the leather, the manufacturer must buy metal eyelets, laces, thread, steel safety toe plates, rubber or composition heels and/or soles, and shoe polish. He does not make any of these products himself. Although he may buy shoestring material in large quantities, cut it to the desired length, and add the metal tips, other industrial firms must first buy the raw cotton and then spin, weave, dye, and cut it so that it becomes shoestring material. All the manufacturers involved have plants and offices with furniture, machinery, and other equipment —industrial goods which have their own marketing patterns and problems. The factories themselves are industrial products, as are the heating and maintenance equipment and supplies. In short, a myriad of industrial products and industrial marketing situations come into play before almost any product, whether it is a consumer or industrial good, reaches its final destination.

Another indication of the scope and importance of the industrial market may be seen in the following industry classifcations which make up this market:

1. Agriculture, forestry, and fishing
2. Mining and quarrying
3. Contract construction
4. Manufacturing
5. Transportation, communication, and other public utilities
6. Wholesale trade
7. Retail trade
8. Finance, insurance, and real estate
9. Services
10. Government—federal, state, and local

---

[1]Total sales volume of manufactured goods from *Survey of Current Business,* February, 1974, back cover. Sales volume of minerals produced in the United States in 1972 was about $32 billion according to *Statistical Abstract of the United States: 1973,* p. 646. Cash farm income in 1972 was estimated at about $60 billion; 80 percent of this (industrial farm products) is about $48 billion.

Every retail store and wholesaling establishment is an industrial user. Every bus company, airline, and railroad is part of this market, as is every hotel, restaurant, bank, insurance company, hospital, theater, garage, and so on. In total there are close to 12 million industrial users in the United States. While this is far short of the approximately 220 million consumers, the total sales volume in the industrial market far surpasses total sales to consumers. This differential occurs because so very many industrial marketing transactions are involved before a final product is sold to its ultimate user.

THE FARM MARKET AND THE GOVERNMENT MARKET

Two large segments of the industrial market—the agricultural market and the government market—deserve an expanded discussion at this point because they often are underrated and overlooked, as so much attention is typically devoted to the manufacturing segment. The high level of cash receipts—$60 billion in 1973 —from the sales of farm products gives farmers as a group a level of purchasing power which makes them a highly attractive market. Moreover, the world population forecasts and the continued existence of diet deficiencies in many countries undoubtedly will keep pressure on farmers to increase their output. Manufacturers and middlemen hoping to sell to this farm market must analyze it carefully and be aware of significant trends. Both the farmers' share of total population and the number of farms have been decreasing and probably will continue to decline. Counterbalancing this has been the increase in large corporate farms, and even the surviving "family farms" are tending to increase in size. Farming is becoming more automated and mechanized. This means, of course, that capital investment in farming is increasing. Truly, agribusiness is becoming big business in every sense of the word. As a buyer, the farmer is becoming increasingly sophisticated and well informed. As farm customers become fewer and larger, manufacturers must change the distribution and promotional strategies to reach this market effectively.

The fantastically large government market includes thousands of federal, state, and local units buying for countless government institutions such as schools, offices, hospitals, and military bases. Spending by the federal government alone accounts for about 20 percent of our gross national product, and spending at the state and local levels accounts for another 10 percent. The government as a buyer is so big, however, that it is difficult to comprehend and difficult to reach key buying influences. Certainly government procurement processes are different from those found in the private sector of the industrial market.

A unique feature of government buying is the bidding system. Much government procurement, by law, must be done on a bid basis. That is, the government advertises for bids, stating the product specifications. Then it must accept the lowest bid which meets these specifications. In other buying situations the government negotiates a purchase contract with an individual supplier. This marketing practice might occur when the Department of Defense wants someone to develop and build a new weapons system, and there are no existing comparable products for effective bidding purposes.

Many companies make no real effort to sell to the government, preferring not to contend with the red tape. Yet government business can be quite profitable. To deal with the government to any significant extent, however, usually requires specialized marketing skills, techniques, and information.

CLASSIFICATION OF INDUSTRIAL PRODUCTS

Separating all products into consumer and industrial goods is a valuable aid to marketing executives. The general category of industrial products is still too broad however, because marketing practices for various products are different. Consequently, some subdivision is necessary. The classification used here separates industrial goods into five categories: raw materials, fabricating materials and parts, installations, accessory equipment, and operating supplies. This classification is based on the broad *uses* of the product, in contrast to the classification of consumer products on the basis of buying habits. (See Table 7-1.)

Parenthetically, it may be noted that the consumer goods classification of convenience-shopping-specialty products is also applicable in part to industrial goods. Items such as scratch pads, light bulbs, and dust mops are the "convenience goods" of the industrial market. They are purchased with a minimum of effort and searching time. For other products, such as office machines or replacement motors for production machines, a purchasing agent for a manufacturer will shop carefully. He will compare price, quality, product features, and service given by the sellers, thus placing these products in the shopping goods category. Industrial products fall into the specialty goods category when, for example, a coal mining firm insists on Goodyear conveyor belts or a steel mill insists on safety goggles made by the American Optical Company.

RAW MATERIALS

Raw materials are industrial goods which will become a part of another physical product and which have received no processing at all other than that necessary for economy or protection in physical handling. Raw materials include (1) goods found in their natural state, such as minerals, land, and products of the forests and the seas, and (2) agricultural products, such as wheat, corn, cotton, tobacco, fruits, vegetables, livestock, and animal products—eggs and raw milk. These two groups of raw materials are marketed quite differently.

Marketing considerations. The marketing of raw materials found in their natural state is influenced by several factors. The supply of these products is limited and cannot be substantially increased. Usually only a few large producers are involved. The product must be carefully graded and, consequently, is highly standardized. Because of their great bulk, their low unit value, and the long distance between producer and industrial user, transportation is an important consideration.

These factors necessitate short channels of distribution and a minimum of physical handling. Frequently marketing is direct from producer to industrial user; at most, one middleman may be used. The limited supply forces users to assure themselves of adequate quantities. Often this is done either by contracting in advance to buy a season's supply of the product or by vertical integration. Advertising and other forms of demand stimulation are used very little. Because there is little brand or other product differentiation, competition is built around price and the assurance that a producer can deliver the prescribed quality of the product in the exact quantity specified.

Agricultural products used as industrial raw materials are supplied by many

Table 7-1. Classes of industrial products—some characteristics and marketing considerations.

Characteristics and marketing considerations	Type of Product				
	Raw materials	Fabricating parts and materials	Installations	Accessory equipment	Operating supplies
Characteristics:					
1. Unit price	Very low	Low	Very high	Medium	Low
2. Length of life	Very short	Depends on final product	Very long	Long	Short
3. Quantities purchased	Large	Large	Very small	Small	Small
4. Frequency of purchase	Frequent delivery; long-term purchase contract	Infrequent purchase, but frequent delivery	Very infrequently	Medium	Frequent
5. Standardization of competitive products	Very high; grading is important	Very high	Very low; custom-made	Low	High
6. Limits on supply	Limited; cannot be increased quickly or at all	Usually no problem	No problem	Usually no problem	Usually no problem
Marketing considerations:					
1. Nature of channel	Short; no middlemen	Short; middlemen only for small buyers	Short; no middlemen	Middlemen used	Middlemen used
2. Negotiation period	Hard to generalize	Medium	Long	Medium	Short
3. Price competition	Important	Important	Not important	Not main factor	Important
4. Presale/postsale service	Not important	Not important	Very important	Important	Very little
5. Demand stimulation	Very little	Moderate	Salesmen very important	Important	Not too important
6. Brand preference	None	Generally unimportant, but some sellers try	High	High	Low
7. Advance buying contract	Important; use of long-term contracts	Important; use of long-term contracts	Not usually	Not usually	Not usually

small producers located some distance from the markets. The supply is largely controllable by man, but it cannot be increased or decreased rapidly. The product is perishable and is not produced at a uniform rate throughout the year. Close attention must be given to transportation and warehousing. Transportation costs are high relative to unit value, and standardization and grading are very important.

Because producers are small and numerous, many middlemen and long channels of distribution are needed. Very little promotional or demand-creation activity is involved, and branding is unimportant.

FABRICATING MATERIALS AND PARTS

Fabricating materials and parts are industrial goods which become an actual part of the finished product. They have already been processed to some extent (in contrast to raw materials). Fabricating *materials* will undergo further processing. Examples include pig iron going into steel, gray goods becoming a part of finished printed cloth, yarn being woven into cloth, and flour becoming a part of bread. Fabricating *parts* will be assembled with no further change in form. They include such products as spark plugs and fan belts in an automobile, the barrel and stock of a rifle, and the buttons on a dress.

Marketing considerations. Fabricating materials and parts are usually purchased in large quantities. To ensure an adequate, timely supply, a buyer may place his order a year or more in advance, with the guarantee that he will be given the advantage of price reductions. Because of these buying habits, most fabricating products are marketed on a direct-sale basis between producer and user. Individual industries, such as textiles, may provide exceptions to this rule.

Middlemen are used most often where the buyers are small or are placing small fill-in orders on a rapid-delivery basis. Normally, buying decisions are based on price and service provided by the seller. Branding is generally unimportant, although some firms have made successful attempts to pull their products out of obscurity by identifying them with a brand. Botany Woolen Mills, Timken Roller Bearing Company, and Burlington Mills are notable examples.

INSTALLATIONS

Installations are manufactured industrial products—the long-lived, expensive, major equipment of an industrial user. Examples would include large generators in a dam, a factory building, diesel engines for a railroad, coke ovens and blast furnaces for a steel mill, computers for a missile manufacturer, and jet airplanes for an airline. The differentiating characteristic of installations is that they set the scale of operation in a firm. Adding twelve new typewriters will not affect the scale of operation at Eastern Airlines, but adding twelve new jet airplanes certainly will.

Marketing considerations. Marketing of installations presents a real challenge to management because every single sale is important. Usually no middlemen are involved; the channel is direct from producer to industrial user. Typically the unit sale is large, and often the product is made to detailed specifications. There may be a long negotiation period before the transaction is consummated. Much presale and postsale servicing is needed. High-caliber salesmen are needed to market installations, and often sales engineers are used. Promotional emphasis is on personal selling rather than advertising, although some advertising is used.

While direct sale is most common, middlemen agents or wholesalers are often used to sell less expensive, standardized installations. Middlemen are also relied upon to reach small buyers, and to sell supplies and replacement parts used with large installations.

ACCESSORY EQUIPMENT

Accessory equipment is a class of industrial products used to aid and implement the production operations of an industrial user, but it does not have a significant influence on the scale of operations in a firm. Accessory equipment does not become an actual part of the finished product. The life of accessory equipment is shorter than that of installations and longer than that of operating supplies. Examples would include office equipment, cash registers in a retail store, small power tools, and forklift trucks.

Marketing considerations. It is difficult to generalize on the distribution policies of firms marketing accessory equipment. In some cases direct sale is used, particularly where the order is for several units of the product or where the product is of relatively high unit value. A firm like the Hyster Company in Portland, Oregon, manufacturing forklift trucks, may sell directly because the price of a single unit is large enough to make this distribution policy profitable. In the main, however, manufacturers of accessory equipment use middlemen because the market is geographically dispersed, there are many different types of potential users, and individual orders may be relatively small.

Accessory equipment is not generally made to specification, so the products of a given manufacturer are ordinarily standardized. Also, the goods are not highly technical. For these reasons, manufacturers can use advertising effectively in a promotional program.

OPERATING SUPPLIES

Operating supplies are the "convenience goods" of the industrial field; they are short-lived, low-priced items usually purchased with a minimum of effort. They aid in a firm's operations, but do not become a part of the finished product. Illustrations are floor wax, lubricating oils, pencils and stationery, registration supplies in a university, heating fuel, and washroom supplies.

Marketing considerations. As with consumer convenience products, industrial operating supplies necessitate broad distribution. A firm will make extensive use of wholesaling middlemen because the product is low in unit value, is bought in small quantities, and goes to many users. Price competition is heavy because competitive products are quite standardized and brand insistence is low.

CHARACTERISTICS OF INDUSTRIAL MARKET DEMAND

Four general demand characteristics help to differentiate the industrial market from the consumer market.

DEMAND IS DERIVED

Since industry has no purpose except to supply the wants of the consumer market, the amount of goods which can be sold to an industrial user is dependent upon the behavior of the ultimate consumer. That is, the demand for industrial goods is derived from the demand for consumer products which the industrial items play a part in making. The demand for steel is partially dependent upon the consumer demand for automobiles and refrigerators, for example. The demand for steel is also dependent upon the demand for butter, baseball gloves, and bongo drums because the tools, machines, and other equipment involved in making these items are made of steel. Thus as the demand for baseball gloves increases, the glove manufacturers may buy more steel sewing machines, steel filing cabinets, or adding machines.

We should note, however, that the factor of derived demand is often operative only over the long run. In the short run, the derived demand is most noticeable in those products which are used directly in the production of consumer goods, for instance, steel used to make automobiles. This would exclude the large number of goods (often called "producers' durables") whose demand is so indirectly dependent on consumer demand that it is hardly amenable to treatment as derived demand at all. Their demand is dependent largely on other variables, such as changes in the cost of labor, in technology, and in the availability of capital.

There are several important marketing implications in the fact that industrial market demand is a derived demand. The producer of an industrial product may direct a considerable share of his promotional program to the ultimate consumer. Thus steel manufacturers, through consumer media such as television and magazines, have urged consumers to have a "white Christmas" by buying new refrigerators and stoves or by furnishing their kitchens with all-steel cabinets. The Du Pont Company has advertised to the consumer the advantages of clothing made of Dacron (a Du Pont–branded fiber).

Accurate long-range market planning and forecasting of consumers' needs are of vital importance to producers of industrial goods. Telephone, gas, and electric companies must forecast consumer population movements years in advance so that pipelines, cables, and other equipment can be installed underground.

DEMAND IS INELASTIC

Another significant characteristic of the industrial market, and one related to the derived-demand feature, is that the demand for many industrial products is inelastic. That is, the demand for the product will respond very little to changes in its price. If the price of buttons for men's shirts and jackets should suddenly rise or fall considerably, there would probably be no appreciable change in demand. If there were a radical increase in price, manufacturers might put fewer buttons on coat sleeves; or if prices were to drop substantially, some firms might stockpile a supply. On balance, however, there would be very little shift in demand.

A basic reason for the general inelasticity of demand for industrial goods is that the cost of a single part or material is ordinarily an inconsequential portion of the total cost of the finished product. The cost of the chemicals in paint is a small part of the price that a consumer pays for a gallon of enamel; the cost of enamel on a refrigerator is a small part of the price of the product to the consumer. Even the cost of expensive capital equipment (installations), when distributed over thousands of units of a product, becomes a very small part of the total unit cost. As a result, when the price of the industrial product shifts, there is very little change in demand for the ultimate consumer product, even when the effect of the price shift is passed on to the consumer. If there is no appreciable shift in the demand for the consumer good, then by virtue of the derived-demand feature, there is no change in the demand for the industrial product going into the consumer good.

From a marketing point of view, there are three factors to consider regarding the inelasticity of industrial market demand. The first is the position of an entire industry as contrasted with that of an individual firm. An industry-wide cut in the price of steel belts used in tires will have a negligible effect on the demand for automobile tires, and consequently there will be a negligible change in the total demand for steel belts. The pricing policy of an individual firm, however, can substantially alter the demand schedule facing this firm. If one supplier significantly cuts the price of steel belts, he may draw a great deal of business away from his competitors. His advantage, of course, will be temporary because his competitors will undoubtedly retaliate in some way in order to recapture their lost business. Nevertheless, in the short run, the demand curve facing a single firm is much more elastic than the industry's curve.

Another marketing factor involved here is time. Much of what has been said refers to short-run situations. Over the long run, the demand for a given industrial product is more elastic. If the price of cloth for men's suits is raised, there probably will be no immediate shift in the price of the finished garment or in the demand for it. The increase in cost of materials may be reflected in a $10 rise in suit prices for next year and may influence the demand for suits, and thus for cloth, over a period of a year or more.

One further aspect of this point is the relative importance of a specific industrial product in the cost structure of a finished good. We may generalize to this extent: The more significant the cost of an industrial product as a percentage of the total price of the finished good, the greater the elasticity of demand for this industrial item.

DEMAND IS WIDELY FLUCTUATING

The market demand for most classes of industrial goods fluctuates considerably more than the demand for consumer products. Fluctuations in the demand for installations—major plant equipment, factories, large generators, etc.—are especially great. Substantial fluctuations also exist in the market for accessory equipment—office furniture and machinery, minor plant equipment, delivery trucks, and similar products. These are reflected in, and tend to accentuate the swings in, the demand for industrial raw materials, such as metals and other minerals. One exception to this generalization is found in agricultural products intended for processing. There is a reasonably consistent demand for animals intended for meat products, for fruits and vegetables which will be canned or frozen, and for grains and dairy products.

Fluctuations in market demand for industrial products can influence all aspects of a firm's marketing program. In product planning, they may stimulate a firm to diversify—to go into other product lines, even into consumer products—in order to ease production and marketing problems. Distribution policies may be affected.

Rather than use a sales force, which must be either trimmed back or maintained at full strength (but at a loss) when demand declines, a seller may decide to make greater use of manufacturers' agents or wholesalers to reach his market. Pricing policies and practices may be involved; management may attempt to stem a decline in sales by cutting prices and thus attracting the business of competing firms. Marketing management is hard pressed to know how to budget for its advertising program. When demand declines, the inclination is to cut back in advertising. Yet at the same time, a firm wants to keep its name before its potential market and also be in there promoting when the market starts to pick up again.

MARKET IS KNOWLEDGEABLE

Unlike the ultimate consumer, the typical industrial buyer is usually well informed about what he is buying. He knows the relative merits of alternative sources of supply and of competitive products. A purchasing agent's advancement in the firm, often his very job, depends upon how well he performs. Naturally he will do all he can to ensure that what he orders is a combination of the lowest cost, best quality, and most service from the seller.

In marketing its product, an industrial goods firm places greater importance on its personal selling program than a firm selling consumer goods. Industrial salesmen must be carefully selected, properly trained, and adequately compensated. They must give the most effective sales presentation possible and furnish satisfactory service both before and after the sale is made.

DETERMINANTS OF INDUSTRIAL MARKET DEMAND

To make a detailed analysis of market demand, a firm selling to *consumer* markets would make a quantitative analysis of the distribution and composition of population and income and a qualitative analysis of consumer motivation and buying patterns. Essentially the same basis of analysis can be used by a firm selling to the *industrial* market. The factors affecting the market for industrial products are the number of potential industrial users and their purchasing power, buying motives, and buying habits. Since the quantitative and qualitative aspects of the industrial market are examined from the point of view of an individual seller, it will be possible to bring out additional differentiating characteristics of this market and to observe specific differences between consumers and industrial users.

NUMBER AND TYPES OF INDUSTRIAL USERS

Total market. Analysis of the industrial market shows that it contains relatively few buying units when compared with the consumer market—approximately 12 million industrial users, in contrast to 220 million consumers divided into more than 70 million households. The industrial market will seem particularly limited to most companies because they sell to only a segment of the total. A firm selling to manufacturers of metal cans in 1967, for example, had only 241 customer plants with twenty or more employees. In that same employment-size class, the Bureau of the Census listed only 239 establishments manufacturing textile machinery and 955 meat-packing plants.[2] Consequently, marketing executives should try to pinpoint their market carefully by type of industry and geographic location. A firm marketing hard-rock mining equipment is not interested in the total industrial market or even in all 30,000 firms engaged in mining and quarrying. This seller is interested in information which will help him identify the market for his particular products.

One very useful information source developed by the federal government is the Standard Industrial Classification system (S.I.C.), which enables a company to identify relatively small segments of its industrial market.[3] All types of businesses in the United States are divided into ten groups, and a range of two-digit classification code numbers is assigned to each group as follows:

01–09   Agriculture, forestry, fishing
10–14   Mining
15–19   Contract construction
20–39   Manufacturing
40–49   Transportation and other public utilities
50–59   Wholesale and retail trade
60–67   Finance, insurance, and real estate
70–89   Services
90–93   Government—federal, state, local, and international
99   Others

A separate two-digit number is assigned to each major industry within each of the above groups; then, three- and four-digit classification numbers are used to subdivide each major industry into finer segments. To illustrate, within the broad category of manufacturing, "apparel and related products" carries S.I.C. #23. Some of the subclassifications are as follows:

S.I.C. code	Industrial group
231	Men's and boys' suits and coats
232	Men's and boys' furnishings
2321	Men's dress shirts and nightwear
2322	Men's, youths', and boys' underwear

Size of industrial users.   While the market may be limited in the total number of buyers, it is large in purchasing power. As one might expect, industrial users range in size from very small companies with fewer than 5 employees to firms with over 2,500 workers. A relatively small percentage of firms account for the greatest share of the value added by a given industry. As an example from the 1967 Census of Manufactures, 2 percent of the firms—those with 500 or more employees—accounted for about 51 percent of the total dollar value added by

[2]U.S. Census of Manufactures: 1967, vol 1.

[3]For a description of the Standard Industrial Classification system and a complete listing of all S.I.C. numbers and classifications, see *Standard Industrial Classification Manual*, U.S. Government Printing Office, Washington, D.C., 1972. For some suggestions on how to use the S.I.C. system as an aid in making marketing decisions, see Joel J. Barr, "SIC: A Basic Tool for the Marketer," *Industrial Marketing*, August, 1969, p. 52.

manufacturing and for 46 percent of the total employment in manufacturing. The firms with fewer than 50 employees accounted for 81 percent of all manufacturing establishments, but produced only 12 percent of the value added by manufacturing (Table 7-2).

The marketing significance in these facts is that the buying power in the industrial market is highly concentrated in a relatively few firms. This market concentration has considerable influence on a seller's policies regarding his channels of distribution. He has greater opportunity to deal directly with the industrial users. Middlemen are not so essential as in the consumer market.

Regional concentration of industrial users.   There is a substantial regional concentration in many of the major industries and among industrial users as a whole. A firm selling products usable in oil fields will find the bulk of its market in Texas, Oklahoma, Louisiana, and southern California; another segment is found in parts of North Dakota and Montana and in the "four corners" region, where the states of Colorado, New Mexico, Arizona, and Utah are joined. Hat manufacturers are located mostly in New England, shoes are produced chiefly in New England and St. Louis, and a substantial share of the nation's garment manufacturers are located in Chicago, New York, and southern California. There is a similar regional concentration in the farm market.

The eight states comprising the Middle Atlantic and East North Central census regions accounted for a little over 50 percent of the total value added by manufacturing in 1967, according to the Census of Manufactures. Just ten counties alone (out of the more than three thousand in the United States) contained 25 percent of all manufacturing establishments and accounted for about 20 percent of both the manufacturing employment and the total value added by manufacturing.

While a large part of a firm's market may be concentrated in limited geographic areas, a good portion may lie outside these areas. Consequently, a distribution policy must be developed which will enable a firm to deal directly with the concentrated market and also to employ middlemen (or a company sales force at great expense) to reach the outlying markets.

Vertical and horizontal industrial markets.   A marketing executive who is analyzing his industrial market should determine whether this market is vertical or horizontal. If his product is usable by virtually all firms in only one or two industries, he has a *vertical* market. Some precision instruments are intended only for the marine market, but every boatbuilder or shipbuilder is a potential customer. Many types of agricultural equipment may have no market outside the farm market, but every operating farm is a potential user. If his product is usable by many industries, his market is said to be broad, or *horizontal*. Industrial supplies, such as lubricating oils and greases, small tools, small motors, and some paper products, may be sold to a wide variety of industries.

This analysis of the market will influence a firm's marketing policies. In a vertical market a product can be tailor-made to meet the specific needs of one industry. In a horizontal market the product must be developed as an all-purpose item. Middlemen are more apt to be used in the marketing program for horizontal markets, although some vertical markets do employ middlemen simply because the orders are too small to warrant the cost of using company salesmen. Advertising and personal selling programs can be more pinpointed in vertical marketing situations, and trade journals in specific fields can be used as an advertising medium.

Table 7-2. Size distribution of manufacturing establishments in the United States, 1967, by number of employees.

This table shows that buying power in the industrial market is highly concentrated among relatively few firms. Four percent of the companies—those with 250 or more employees—accounted for 65 percent of the value added by manufacturing. How might this market concentration influence a seller's marketing program.

Number of employees	Number of establishments	Percentage of firms	Percentage of value added	Percentage of employees
1–4	117,514	38.5	1.1	1.1
5–9	39,349	12.9	1.3	1.4
10–19	41,678	13.6	2.7	3.1
20–49	48,942	16.0	7.0	8.3
50–99	24,923	8.2	8.0	9.4
100–249	19,762	6.5	14.9	16.6
250–499	7,749	2.5	13.8	14.5
500–999	3,450	1.1	13.3	12.8
1,000–2,499	1,639	0.5	15.0	13.2
2,500 or more	674	0.2	23.1	19.6
Total	305,680	100.0	100.0	100.0

Source: 1967 *Census of Manufactures*, vol. 1, part 2.

BUYING POWER OF INDUSTRIAL USERS

Another determinant of industrial market demand is the purchasing power of industrial users. This can be measured either by the expenditures of industrial users or by their sales volume. Many times, however, expenditures or sales volume data are not available or are very difficult to estimate. In such cases it is more feasible to use an activity indicator, or market factor, which is related to income generation and expenditure. Sometimes an activity indicator is a combined indicator of purchasing power and the number of industrial users. Following are examples of activity indicators which might be used to estimate the purchasing power of industrial users.

Measured by manufacturing activity. Firms selling to manufacturers might use as market indicators such factors as the number of employees, the number of plants, and the dollar value added by manufacturing. A firm selling work gloves used the number of employees in manufacturing establishments to determine the relative values of various geographic markets. A company which sold a product to control stream pollution used two indicators—the number of firms processing wood products (paper mills, wood pulp processors, plywood mills, and so forth) and the manufacturing value added by these firms.

Measured by mining activity. The number of mines operating, the volume of their output, and the dollar value of the product as it leaves the mine all may indicate purchasing power of mines and thus may be used by any firm marketing industrial products to mine operators.

Measured by agricultural activity. A company marketing fertilizer, feed, or agricultural equipment can estimate the buying power of its market by studying such indicators as cash farm income, acreage plants, or crop estimates and yields. The chemical producer who sells to a fertilizer manufacturer might study the same indices because the demand for chemicals in this case is derived from the demand for fertilizer.

Measured by construction activity. If an enterprise is marketing building materials, such as lumber, plywood, brick, gypsum products, or builders' hardware, its market is dependent upon construction activity. This may be indicated by the number and value of building permits issued or by the number of construction starts by type of housing (single-family residence, apartment, commercial). A seller must select the appropriate indicator. A firm producing residential builders' hardware (door locks, window catches, and kitchen cabinet hardware) should not use an index which includes industrial and commercial construction.

BUYING MOTIVES OF INDUSTRIAL USERS

Industrial buying behavior, like consumer buying behavior, is initiated when an aroused need (a motive) is recognized. This leads to goal-oriented activity designed to satisfy the need. Once again marketing practitioners must try to determine what motivates the buyer.

Industrial buying motives, for the most part, are presumed to be rational, and an industrial purchase normally is a methodical, objective undertaking. The industrial buyer is motivated primarily by a desire to maximize his firm's profit. More specifically, his buying goal is to get the optimum combination of price, quality, and service in the products he buys. On the other hand, salesmen would maintain that some industrial buyers seem to be motivated more toward personal goals (moving up in the firm, or even lining their own pockets) which are in conflict with their employers' goals.

Actually, the industrial buyer does have two goals—to improve his position in the firm (personal self-interest) and to further his company's position (in profits, competition, acceptance by society, etc.). Sometimes these goals are mutually consistent, and sometimes they are in conflict. Obviously, the greater the degree of similarity, the better for both the organization and the individual. That is, he sees the mutuality of his and the company's goals, and he is more susceptible to rational promotional appeals from sellers. When very little mutuality of goals prevails, the situation is poor. Probably the more usual situation is to find some overlap of interests, but also to find a significant area where the buyer's goals do not coincide with those of the firm. In these cases a seller might appeal to the buyer on a rational, "what's-good-for-the-firm" basis and also on an ego-building basis. Promotional efforts attuned to the buyer's ego are particularly useful when two or more competing sellers are offering essentially the same products, prices, and services.[4]

---

[4]For the notion that industrial buying behavior often is motivated by noneconomic influences such as buyers' personality, personal needs, and emotions, see David T. Wilson, "Industrial Buyers' Decision-Making Styles," *Journal of Marketing Research,* November, 1971, pp. 433–436; Jack Schiff, "Why Pros Buy Like Amateurs," *Sales Management,* October 15, 1970, p. 50; Ernest Dichter, "Industrial Buying Is Based on Same 'Only Human' Emotional Factors that Motivate Consumer Market's Housewife," *Industrial Marketing,* February, 1973, p. 14; and

INDUSTRIAL BUYING PROCESS

Competition and the complexity of industrial marketing are encouraging companies to focus attention on the *total* buying process and to treat it as an ongoing relationship of mutual interest to both buyer and seller. As one example of this approach, researchers in a Marketing Science Institute study developed a framework to explain different types of industrial buying situations.[5] The grid-type model for this framework is illustrated in Fig. 7-1. The model reflects two major aspects of the industrial buying process—(1) the classes of typical buying situations and (2) the sequential steps in the buying process.

Three typical buying situations (called *buy classes*) were identified as follows: new tasks, modified rebuys, and straight rebuys. The *new task* is the most difficult and complex of the three, and it usually involves more buying influences than the other two. The problem is new, information needs are high, and evaluation of alternatives is critical. The seller has his greatest opportunity to be heard and to display his creative salesmanship in identifying and satisfying the buyer's needs.

Straight rebuys—a routine purchase with minimal information needs and no real consideration of alternatives—is at the other extreme. Buying decisions are made in the purchasing department, usually working from a list of acceptable suppliers. Suppliers, especially those from new firms not on the "list," have difficulty getting an audience with the buyer. *Modified rebuys* are somewhere between the other two in terms of time required, information needed, alternatives considered, etc.

The other major element in the buy grid reflects the idea that the industrial buying process is a sequence of eight stages, called *buy phases.* The process starts with the recognition of a problem; ranges through the determination and description of product specifications, the search for and evaluation of alternatives, and the buying act; and ends with postpurchase performance feedback and evaluation. (This surely is reminiscent of the consumer's buying decision process outlined in the preceding chapter.)

BUYING PATTERNS OF INDUSTRIAL USERS

Overt patterns of buyer behavior in the industrial market differ significantly from consumer behavior patterns on several points.

Length of negotiation period. The period of negotiation in an industrial sale is usually much longer than that in a consumer market sale. Some of the usual reasons for the extended negotiations are (1) several executives are involved in the buying decision; (2) the size of the sale is often large; (3) the industrial product is made to order, and considerable discussion is involved in establishing the

---

Wallace Feldman and Richard Cardozo, "The Industrial Revolution and Models of Buyer Behavior," *Journal of Purchasing,* November, 1969, pp. 77–88.

[5]Patrick J. Robinson, Charles W. Faris, and Yoram Wind, *Industrial Buying and Creative Marketing,* Allyn and Bacon, Inc., Boston, 1967; in the same vein, see Frederick E. Webster, Jr., and Yoram Wind, "A General Model for Understanding Organizational Buying Behavior," *Journal of Marketing,* April, 1972, pp. 12–19. For a more complete conceptual study of the topic, see Webster and Wind, *Organizational Buying Behavior,* Prentice-Hall, Inc., Englewood Cliffs, N.J., 1972.

THE BUY-GRID FRAMEWORK

		BUY CLASSES		
		New task	Modified rebuy	Straight rebuy
B U Y P H A S E S	1. Anticipation or recognition of a problem (need) and a general solution			
	2. Determination of characteristics and quantity of needed item			
	3. Description of characteristics and quantity of needed item			
	4. Search for and qualification of potential sources			
	5. Acquisition and analysis of proposals			
	6. Evaluation of proposals and selection of supplier(s)			
	7. Selection of an order routine			
	8. Performance of feedback and evaluation			

Figure 7-1. The most complex buying situations occur in the upper left-hand portion of the "buy grid" framework when the largest number of decision makers and buying influences are involved. The initial phases of a new task generally represent the greatest difficulty for management. *Source:* Patrick J. Robinson, Charles W. Faris, and Yoram Wind, *Industrial Buying and Creative Marketing*, Allyn and Bacon, Inc., Boston, 1967, p. 14.

exact specifications; and (4) bids are often involved (as in construction work), and the seller needs time to prepare careful estimates.

Frequency of purchase. In the industrial market, firms buy certain products very infrequently. Large installations are purchased only once in many years. Smaller parts and materials to be used in the manufacture of a product may be ordered on long-term contracts, so that an actual selling opportunity exists only once every year. Even standardized operating supplies, such as office supplies or cleaning products, may be bought only once a month.

Because of this buying pattern, a great burden is placed on the advertising and personal selling programs of industrial sellers. Their advertising must keep the company's name constantly before the market so that when a buyer is in the market, he will be acquainted with the selling firm. The salesmen must call on potential customers often enough to know when a customer is considering a purchase. In this instance, patterns of infrequent sales and lengthy negotiation periods are closely related. A salesman for the National Cash Register Company may find out, through a regular call, that a hospital is considering the installation of a machine accounting system. The sale may not be consummated for a year or more. Nevertheless, the seller would have lost all opportunity for the sale if his representative had not called when the prospective customer was first contemplating the changeover.

Size of order. The average industrial order is considerably larger than its counterpart in the consumer market. This fact, coupled with the infrequency of purchase, means that an industrial seller cannot afford to lose sales because of weaknesses such as poor salesmanship, noncompetitive pricing, uncertain delivery, or imperfect products.

Many sellers in the industrial market are plagued by firms that buy in small, hand-to-mouth quantities. A small order is unprofitable for most sellers, who are constantly combating this problem through buyer education and changes in their pricing and distribution policies.

Direct purchase. Direct sale from the producer to the ultimate consumer is rare. In the industrial market, however, direct marketing from the producer to the industrial user is quite common, especially when the order is large and much technical assistance is needed by the buyer both before and after the sale is made. From a seller's point of view, also, direct marketing is reasonable because there are relatively few potential buyers, these are big buyers, and they are geographically concentrated. Nevertheless, some products, such as hand tools, office supplies, and many manufacturing supplies, are marketed through middlemen, as are most industrial agricultural products.

When a seller deals directly with industrial users, he must organize and operate a high-caliber sales force. If a firm cannot build up a topnotch sales force, middlemen may have to be used in spite of the advantages of direct selling.

Multiple influences on purchases. In the industrial market, the purchasing decision is frequently influenced by more than one person, particularly in medium-sized and large firms. Even in small firms where the owner-manager makes all major decisions, he will probably consult with someone in the office or factory before making certain purchases. In firms large enough to have a separate purchasing department, a seller may be misled into thinking that the real purchasing power in the firm lies in one man or one department. We must distinguish between (1) initiating a purchasing project, (2) determining product specifications, and (3) selecting a supplier. Typically, the purchasing department places the orders. In many instances the purchasing agent also selects the individual supplier, but he must select one who carries the item or brand agreed upon by others in the firm.[6]

This buying pattern tends to lengthen the negotiation period, and it requires salesmen who are capable of determining who influences the buying decisions. Very often a salesman will call on the wrong executive. Even after he finds out who the decision makers are in the buying firm, it may be very difficult to reach them.

Reciprocity arrangements. A highly controversial industrial buying habit is the practice of reciprocity, the policy of "I'll buy from you if you'll buy from me." Traditionally, reciprocity has been common among firms marketing homogene-

---

[6]For a comprehensive study of purchasing procedures, indicating which departmental executives are involved in each stage of the process, see *How Industry Buys: 1970,* Research Department of *Scientific American,* New York, 1970. This study reported on the purchase of materials, component parts, and equipment by industry as a whole and by separate major industries. Also see, Steve Blickstein, "How to Find the Key Buying Influence," *Sales Management,* Sept. 20, 1971, p. 51.

ous basic industrial products (oil, steel, rubber, paper products, chemicals) where price competition generally does not exist and one of the firms is a major supplier to the other. Today, however, reciprocal selling is found in a wide range of industries. Several companies have established a "trade relations" department. This unit, aided by the computer, can quickly collect the sales records and purchasing data needed to make the most effective use of this powerful selling tool.[7]

Some reasons are suggested for the increased use of reciprocity arrangements. First, a tightening in economic conditions may stimulate some firms to adopt reciprocity as a countermeasure to declining sales volume. Then after these conditions improve, the companies are hesitant to give up their new policy. Second, the trend toward product diversification opens additional avenues and opportunities for reciprocity dealings. Also, increased competition encourages sellers to try to control markets through reciprocity. Finally, many products today are of such acceptable quality that a given item made by any one of several manufacturers normally will satisfy a buyer's need for that type of product.

On the other hand, reciprocity has several built-in "powder kegs." Its use in a systematic, formalized manner, particularly in large and diversified companies, is forbidden by both the Federal Trade Commission and the Justice Department's antitrust division. Under pressure from these agencies, several firms have abolished their trade relations departments, and have stopped generating information relating to a supplier's status as a customer. A firm engaging in reciprocity runs the risk of serious loss of morale in its sales force. Similarly, unless a clear policy statement is written regarding the practice, the morale and efficiency of the purchasing department may suffer. Under any circumstances it is difficult to justify purchasing from customers unless the purchases are voluntary acts and unless the buyer is getting competitive prices, quality, and service from the reciprocating seller.[8]

Catalogue buying and selling. Catalogue buying is quite prevalent among industrial users, particularly in connection with standardized, short-lived, and relatively low-priced products. Many wholesalers depend heavily upon their catalogue when selling to retailers.

From a marketing standpoint, catalogue buying relieves a sales force of some pressure but adds considerable importance to the preparation of the printed sales messages. In some cases, printed aids do virtually the entire selling job; salesmen call infrequently or not at all. In other instances, a salesman always calls but depends heavily on his catalogue. A firm selling to catalogue buyers has two general choices regarding the distribution of its printed materials: It may send its own catalogue to each buyer, or it may contribute its printed information to a

---

[7]For a discussion of the trade relations director—his rise, his responsibilities, and the typical services he performs—see Velma A. Adams, "The Rise of the Trade Relations Directors," *Dun's Review,* December, 1964, p. 35; Edward McCreary, Jr., and Walter Guzzardi, Jr., "A Customer Is a Company's Best Friend," *Fortune,* June, 1965, p. 180; and "Trade Relations Men Walk Shaky Tightrope," *Business Week,* Oct. 5, 1968, p. 96.

[8]For a report on reciprocity and the conditions of market structure and corporate organization which may draw government censure of reciprocal selling arrangements, see F. Robert Finney, *We Like to Do Business with Our Friends,* Marketing Science Institute, Cambridge, Mass., 1969. See also Reed Moyer, "Reciprocity: Retrospect and Prospect," *Journal of Marketing,* October, 1970, pp. 47–54; and "Reciprocity Is Dead," *Sales Management,* Oct. 15, 1970, p. 27.

common catalogue which will include material furnished by competitive firms and firms selling related products. *Thomas's Register of Manufacturers* is an example of a widely used common catalogue.

Demand for product servicing. The user's desire for excellent service is a strong industrial buying motive and may determine buying patterns. Consequently, sellers appeal for sales on the basis that they furnish better service than competitors. Frequently a firm's only attraction is its service, because the product itself is so standardized that it can be purchased from any number of companies.

Sellers must stand ready to furnish services both in advance and after the sale. A manufacturer of office machines may study a firm's accounting operation and suggest a more effective, lower-cost system which, incidentally, involves using the seller's machines. He will also arrange to retrain the present office staff. He may even assume the responsibility of selecting and training additional machine operators. After the machines are installed, other services, such as repairs, may be necessary; buyers want to know that the seller will handle these matters promptly.

Quality and supply requirements. Another industrial buying motive which is reflected in buying patterns is the industrial user's insistence upon an adequate quantity of uniform-quality products. Variations in the quality of materials going into his finished product can cause considerable trouble for a manufacturer. He may be faced with costly disruptions in his production processes if the imperfections exceed quality-control limits. Adequate quantities are as important as good quality. A work stoppage caused by an insufficient quantity of material is just as costly as one caused by an inferior quality of material.

Meeting these supply requirements is in large part the responsibility of the seller's production department. But the marketing people are not completely absolved of responsibility, because they must furnish forecasts of what quantity and quality will be needed and when it must be available.

Adequacy of supply is an especially big problem for sellers and users of industrial raw materials such as agricultural products, metal ores, or forest products. Climatic conditions may disrupt the normal flow of goods, for example, when logging camps or mining operations become snowbound or when agricultural products fluctuate in quality and quantity from one growing season to another. These "acts of God" create additional managerial problems for both buyers and sellers with respect to their warehousing, standardization, and grading activities.

Leasing instead of buying. A growing behavioral pattern among firms in the industrial market is that of leasing industrial products instead of buying them outright. In the past, this practice was limited to large equipment, such as shoe manufacturing equipment (The United Shoe Machinery Company), data-processing machines (IBM), packaging equipment (American Can Company), postage meters, heavy construction equipment, and textile machinery. Even some freight cars and locomotives are owned by life insurance companies and leased to railroads. Today, industrial suppliers and users are expanding leasing arrangements to include delivery trucks, salesmen's automobiles, machine tools, agricultural feed mills, storage bins, and other items generally less expensive than big installations.[9]

---

[9]See Leonard L. Berry and Kenneth E. Maricle, "Consumption without Ownership: Marketing Opportunity for Today and Tomorrow," *MSU Business Topics,* Spring, 1973, pp. 33–41.

Leasing has several merits. For the firm leasing out its equipment, total net income, after charging off pertinent repair and maintenance expenses, is often higher than it would be if the unit were sold outright. Also, the market may be expanded to include users who could not afford to buy the product, especially if it is large installation type of equipment, such as that leased by IBM and the can manufacturers. Leasing offers an effective method of getting distribution for a new product. Potential users may be more willing to rent a product than to buy it. If they are not satisfied, their expenditures are limited to a few monthly payments. Another advantage to the lessor is that he may be able to sell supplies for use with the machine (although he can no longer *require* the renter to buy his supplies).

From the lessee's point of view, some of the benefits may be summarized as follows:

1. Leasing allows the user to keep his investment capital free for other purposes.
2. There may be significant tax advantages; rental payments are totally tax-deductible, and they are usually larger than corresponding depreciation charges on owned products.
3. The advantages of using the equipment can be enjoyed sooner, and the disadvantages of major capital expenses avoided, if the equipment is rented rather than purchased.
4. New firms can enter a business with less capital outlay than would be necessary if they had to buy the equipment outright. This may not be an unmixed blessing, however. While ease of entry increases competition, it can also lead to an overcrowding of the field.
5. The user has available to him the newest products developed by the lessor.
6. Rented products are usually serviced by the lessor; this eliminates one headache associated with ownership.
7. Leasing is particularly attractive to users who need the equipment seasonally or sporadically, as in food canning or construction.

On the foundation of a careful market analysis an industrial goods manufacturer or middleman can develop strategies with respect to various parts of his marketing mix. In the following three chapters we shall consider some of the programming done in connection with one ingredient in the marketing mix—the product.

QUESTIONS AND PROBLEMS

1. "About 80 percent of all farm products are industrial goods." Give some examples of farm products which are *consumer* goods.
2. In which of the five subclassifications of industrial goods should each of the following be included? Which products may belong in more than one category?

   a. Typewriters
   b. Central air conditioners
   c. Nuts and bolts
   d. Dental chairs
   e. Automobile wax
   f. Land
   g. Cotton cloth
   h. Printing presses
   i. Copper wire
   j. Trucks
3. Give some examples of industrial products where the factor of derived demand is operative mainly in the long run. In the short run. From a marketing standpoint,

what difference does it make whether the derived-demand characteristic is effective in the long run or the short run?

4. If the demand for most industrial goods is inelastic, why is it that sellers do not raise their prices to maximize their revenues?

5. Why do industrial goods usually fluctuate more widely in demand than consumer goods?

6. What are some marketing implications in the fact that the demand for industrial goods:
   a. Fluctuates widely.　　　　　　　　c. Is derived
   b. Is inelastic

7. "Economic recessions decrease the market demand for industrial goods more than for consumer goods." Do you agree? Explain.

8. What are the marketing implications for a seller in the fact that his customers are geographically concentrated and limited in number?

9. What differences would you expect to find between the marketing program of a company selling to horizontal industrial markets and that of a company selling to vertical industrial markets?

10. In the industrial buying process we identified eight stages, called "buy phases." Yet the consumer buying decision process had only five steps, according to our discussion in Chapter 6. How do you account for this difference? Are some of the required steps in the industrial buying process not necessary when a household consumer is making a buying decision?

11. Select four of the "buy phases" in the industrial buying process and explain how the relative importance of each one changes depending upon whether the buying situation is a new task or a straight rebuy.

12. Select three advertisements of industrial products and identify the buying motives stressed in the ads.

13. National Cash Register, IBM, Burroughs, and other manufacturers of office machines make a substantial proportion of their sales directly to industrial users. At the same time, wholesalers of office equipment are thriving. Are these two market situations inconsistent? Explain.

14. What suggestions do you have for industrial sellers to help them determine who influences the buying decision among industrial users?

15. What are the marketing implications for both buyers and sellers in the fact that a multiple purchasing influence often exists in industrial marketing?

CASES FOR PART

CASE 2. MIDGET MOTORS COMPANY*

Analysis of a market

On June 1 of last year, Mr. Vernon Eads assumed responsibility for the operation of the Midget Motors Company, located in Athens, Ohio. This company produced the King Midget auto. The King Midget was a small, rugged, lightweight, 9¼-horsepower, 2-passenger auto that could attain a top speed of 40 miles per hour on a level highway, and could go 50 miles on a gallon of regular gasoline. (See illustration on page 158.)

Mr. Eads had agreed to increase production from 1.4 autos per working day to at least 4 per day within the next three months. The company had produced 320 autos during the previous twelve months. Mr. Eads realized that he would need to design a new, complete marketing program to market this increased output. He believed that the first step in developing such a program should be to find out all he could about the present and potential market for the King Midget auto.

*Adapted from case prepared by Prof. Robert S. Raymond, Ohio University. Reproduced with permission.

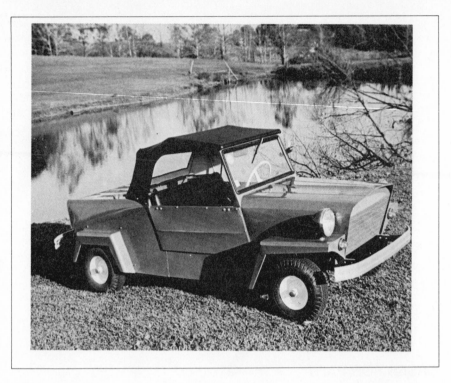

The Midget Motors Co. was founded in 1947 in a garage in Athens, Ohio, by two mechanics, Claud Dry and Dale Orcutt, as an extension of their hobby, building small lightweight automobiles. They were not businessmen, or financiers, or engineers, or production experts. Hence, although they had eventually expanded their operation into a 20,000-square-foot factory building and produced between one and two cars each working day, they had not really been interested in selling more than enough cars to maintain a modest standard of living. Most of the inquiries they received, even those with checks enclosed, had gone unanswered. Most of their sales had come from word-of-mouth advertising and publicity. Several feature articles had appeared in national magazines. They sold direct to their customers and had no dealers.

Dry and Orcutt did not have the knowledge, the time, or the money necessary to study consumer needs and characteristics and build a car for a particular market segment. For example, when they had needed an engine, they had had to choose one already built and available. It was a one-cylinder, 4-cycle, air-cooled, 8-horsepower, Kohler engine which they had mounted in the rear of the car so that it could drive the right rear wheel with a chain. The car was in effect a 4-wheel motorcycle. The items which they could not buy already made they had made themselves and sometimes patented, e.g., a suspension system for the front end and a transmission with a centrifugal clutch arrangement which gave the car an automatic shift.

The 8-horsepower engine, operating at its normal speed, could move 750 pounds about 35–40 miles per hour on the highway. This limited the car to one passenger. However, they had found that most of their customers wanted a

2-passenger car. Therefore, in 1949 they had begun to install a 9¼-horsepower engine which pushed the 670 pound car along a level highway at 40 miles per hour with two passengers. Most of their customers were able to do the maintenance and minor repairs themselves, e.g., change the spark plug and keep the drive chain clean and lubricated. For other engine repairs they had been advised to see one of the 1,200 Kohler dealers scattered throughout the U.S. Dry and Orcutt had eventually made it a rule not to sell their cars within 50 miles of Athens. This had eliminated requests for service at the factory. There had been no annual model changes, and technical improvements had been added as they were discovered. Cars were offered in just one color, white. Since galvanized steel was used in making the body, the car was suitable for seaside communities and islands because it would resist the corrosive salt air.

The auto was sold direct to customers for $895 ($1,115 with all optional extras such as doors, side curtains, speedometer, etc.). The car was promoted by word-of-mouth advertising, as well as by small ads (one column inch) in several magazines such as *Popular Mechanics, Popular Science,* and *Mechanix Illustrated.*

There also were seven dealers widely scattered in Louisiana, New York, Illinois, Nebraska, Indiana and Wisconsin, who received a discount of 21 percent off the $895 price and sold 40% of the output. The dealers were initially required to buy six cars and $400 worth of parts. The initial six-car order was required because: (1) dealers were easy to attract, (2) the company did not make as much on each car sold through a dealer as on a direct sale and wanted to hold down its costs, and (3) the auto trailer used to deliver the cars held six King Midgets.

Whether the sale was direct, or through a dealer, the customer sent in $100 with his order. The car was then scheduled for production. As soon as it was finished, the customer had to pay the balance due. The car was then stored in the yard outside the plant or in a warehouse until a trailer load of six cars going to the same general area could be accumulated. The average time between the initial deposit and delivery was about six months.

A small group of businessmen in New York purchased the Midget Motors Co. a year ago last March for $500,000 from its founder-owners. The former owners were then put in charge of research and development. The new owners were counting on the backlog of orders and hundreds of inquiries from all over the U.S. and many foreign countries, which Dry and Orcutt had never bothered to answer. The new owners intended to operate the company for several years and then sell its stock to the public to recover their investment and make a profit.

The new president and general manager was Mr. Joseph Starkey. He had been a navigator in the Strategic Air Command for 10 years and had spent another decade working, at the dealer level, for Ford, Chrysler, and most recently, for Rootes Motors, Ltd., of Great Britain as general manager in the U.S. for Sunbeam imported cars. During Mr. Starkey's first year as president, the company experienced poor sales performance, a build-up in inventory of unsold cars, and financial losses. By May of last year, the working capital was depleted and payments to suppliers were far in arrears.

On June 1 of last year Mr. Eads arrived on the scene, and by late in July he had reached his first goal—the plant was producing 4 cars per working day. By that time, however, there were 72 unsold cars on hand and the financial situation continued to be very poor. The real problems now were in sales and finance, not in production.

At that point the Board of Directors promptly relieved Mr. Starkey of all his presidential duties at the plant so that he could concentrate on selling the increased production. He was provided with an airplane and departed for Florida and the Bahama Islands. It was believed that the biggest market for the King Midget was in a warmer climate, because the car had a convertible top which was not weather tight, and because it did not travel well on snow or ice because of the chain drive to the right rear wheel. It was ideal for the Florida coastal and island areas because the galvanized steel body resisted corrosion better than Detroit cars. Moreover, Mr. Starkey wanted to sell to fleet users such as motels, factories, golf courses, and auto rental companies, because it was as easy to sell six cars to a business as to sell them one at a time to individual buyers.

During the next month no sales were made. Therefore, with 120 cars in the warehouse, Mr. Eads finally shut down the plant and arranged to meet with the Board of Directors in New York at the end of August. He explained to them the present condition of the company and found that they were unwilling to invest further in it. Because all of them were wealthy and connected with large companies, they had no solution for this small business except to liquidate it and use it as a tax loss. However, Mr. Eads had become personally interested in the little auto company, so he agreed to stay on to see whether it could be salvaged. Another result of the meeting was that all the investors (directors) agreed to appoint Mr. Eads as the chief executive of Midget Motors in place of Mr. Starkey.

When Mr. Eads returned to Athens, he was faced with two problems. First, he had to sell the 120-car inventory in order to get money to operate the plant. Second, he had to appease the suppliers (creditors) in order to prevent them from throwing the company into bankruptcy, and then persuade them to continue selling him materials and parts.

He had never sold automobiles before, but because there was no one else available, he set about doing it. He did not know where to go or whom to sell to. First, he obtained a map of the United States and, with the help of a secretary, put map pins, about 700 of them, in all the locations where cars had been sold during the past two years. The pattern which emerged was that King Midget had been sold not in Florida or the South but in the largest cities of Indiana, Ohio, Pennsylvania, New York, and New Jersey.

Next he obtained another map and more map pins and located all the inquiries received during the past two years from individuals and companies who wanted to be King Midget dealers. Fewer pins were used, but the same pattern emerged.

The advertisements in *Popular Mechanics* and *Mechanix Illustrated* had made two offers. If the reader sent in 25¢ he would receive information about the car. If he sent in $1.00, he would receive an illustrated brochure giving more information about the car and how it was produced. About 7,000 with $1.00 enclosed had been received during the past two years. Mr. Eads plotted these 7,000 inquiries on another map and found that they reinforced the same pattern shown on the first two maps. This convinced him that he had found out where the cars could be sold.

Mr. Eads decided to use the most recent inquiries from the last group as a mailing list. However, he realized that if he was going to keep his work force together and his creditors at bay, there wasn't time to undertake a direct-mail sales campaign. Therefore, he traded in the company car for a half-ton panel truck and loaded it with a King Midget. Then, with the shop foreman, who knew the car thoroughly, he set out to call on his list of prospects literally door to door. During the next three months he sold 80 cars.

QUESTION

1. Using the information in the case plus any outside information, analyze and describe in some detail the market for the King Midget auto.

CASE 3. MARTIN BROTHERS, INC.*

Analysis of consumer market

The Martin brothers, John and Frank, were troubled because the sales in the paint department in their new retail hardware store were substantially below the levels—both in dollar volume and as a share of total store sales—which had been attained in the store which they had owned a few years ago. Because the paint department had constituted a major part of their business in earlier years, the two brothers were determined to identify and rectify the reasons for the currently poor performance.

In 1969 John and Frank were the owner-managers of a chain of three full-line retail hardware stores in a midwestern city of 750,000 people. The stores had a combined annual sales volume of about $800,000. At that point in time, the brothers sold the stores, and John returned to school to work for a master's degree in business administration.

In 1972 the brothers decided to reenter the hardware business, so they purchased a store located in a suburban shopping center in an area called Forest View. This store also happened to be one of the units which they had previously owned and operated. John had received his M.B.A. degree and was teaching accounting at a university nearby. Frank worked at the store full time.

The Forest View store had 2,500 square feet of floor space, and the total store offering was classified for control purposes into the following nine departments:

1. Toys
2. Sporting goods
3. Lawn and garden
4. Tools
5. Builders' hardware
6. Fasteners (screws, bolts, etc.)
7. Plumbing and electrical supplies
8. Paint and paint sundries
9. Housewares

As this was the same departmental breakdown which they had used previously, the Martins were able to compare present performance with past results. When the

*Adapted from case prepared by Michael D. Hutt and Roger W. Hutt, Michigan State University. Reproduced with permission.

Forest View store was re-acquired, it was not a continuing business. The store had been closed because of bankruptcy in 1971. Initially, the Martins were concerned about this situation, but by 1973 they realized that most of the departments were falling back into line. By 1974, all of the departments had reached or exceeded previous sales levels with the exception of the paint department. This troubled the Martins because paint had constituted a major part of their business in 1969 and earlier years. (See Table 1.)

During the last half of 1974, the Martins purchased two additional hardware stores in the local area and hence had little time to devote to the paint problem at the Forest View store. Early in 1975, however, John again began to concentrate his efforts on the paint department problem and reflect on the past. "Before we sold out in 1969, we were doing $800,000 in sales for the three stores. The paint department contributed $160,000 of this total." This volume had enabled Martins to sell their own private brand of paint. The private label paint was made by a local manufacturer and sold under the label Martin Brothers. The private label paint accounted for 13 percent of the paint sales volume in the three stores in 1968. The bulk of the remainder came from Glidden interior house paint. Custom-mixed paint had accounted for a very small portion of sales in 1968. John had liked the private label because it "got the Martin name into homes and tied people to our brand of paint." The Martins however, felt they did *not* have the sales volume in 1974 to justify having a private label. Private brand paint had to be purchased in truck load lots at a cost of $5,000 per load.

When the Martins sold out in 1969, the nearest competition was Fairfax paint store, located in the same shopping center. When the Forest View store was re-acquired in 1972, there was new competition—Bargain Paint Center and Plaza Discount Store. Bargain Paint Center carried several national brands such as Dutch Boy and Du Pont in addition to their own private label. John described Bargain Paint Center's strategy in this manner: "They advertise national brands but they don't have much depth in them. Just a sampling. Also, they emphasize price and then try to switch you to their own brand." Plaza carried Moore paint and the Martins were not sure of the effect of their competition.

John could not pinpoint the exact cause of the decline, but he believed at least three factors contributed to it. First, wall paneling became more important and there was a re-birth of interest in wallpaper. Since interior paint constituted the major portion of total paint sales, this would naturally have an impact on the paint sales. Second, from discussions with salesmen, John thought that mixed colors were possibly more important in 1974 than they had been in 1969. Martins had used a mixing system before they sold out. However, because custom-mixed paint accounted for only a very small portion of sales, they had not used it since re-acquiring the Forest View store. Moreover, the equipment needed for the mixing system cost $1,200 and it required some experience and time on the part of the employees. Martins had no one that specialized in paint because they had a low overhead operation with no more than one full-time and one part-time employee working in the store.

Third, John was not convinced that potential paint customers were brand conscious. He did, however, believe that Bargain Paint Center had been successful in attracting customers by advertising national brands and then selling their private label at discount prices. Since the re-opening of the Forest View store, the Martins had been selling Glidden paint at discount prices. They also had been carrying specialty paint (spray paint and touch-up paint) and also paint supplies.

Table 1. Forest View Store

Year	Total sales	Paint dept. sales	Paint dept. sales as % total sales
1968	$100,000	$19,000	19
1969	100,000	20,000	20
1973	107,000	5,350	5
1974	145,000	7,250	5

In the way of corrective measures, John believed that there were at least three alternative courses of action worthy of consideration: (1) purchase a paint-mixing system and train the employees to use it; (2) sell a private label paint; (3) follow Bargain Paint Center's strategy and offer two or three national brands in addition to a private brand.

Before making any decisions involving product or promotional policies, John thought they ought to find out more about the buying motives and habits of their present and potential paint customers. To gather this information that would aid in their decision making, the Martins retained the services of Mr. Paul Carillo, a marketing instructor at a nearby university. Mr. Carillo discussed the problem with the Martins and personally evaluated the competition. He then developed a questionnaire that was passed out to customers in the store by Martins employees. Of the 600 questionnaires distributed, 430 were returned and the findings were tabulated for analysis. The highlights of these results are shown in the Appendix.

QUESTIONS

1. Analyze Martin's market for its paint products, and describe the characteristics of this market.
2. What course of action should the Martins take to improve the sales performance of their paint department?

APPENDIX: HIGHLIGHTS OF MARTIN BROTHERS' PAINT QUESTIONNAIRE
(Based on 430 Respondents)

1. Have you purchased any paint within the past year?

Yes	No	Total
79%	21%	100%

2. Factors which are most important, somewhat important, and unimportant when making a paint purchase.

	Most important	Somewhat important	Unimportant	Total
Famous brand name	24%	50%	26%	100%
Number of famous brands available	11%	50%	39%	100%
Number of colors available	74%	26%	0	100%

Discount prices	42%	55%	3%	100%
Assistance of experienced salesperson	72%	25%	5%	100%
Availability of credit terms	5%	6%	89%	100%

3. Name the store (or stores) that provides the best combination of those factors which are most important to you when making a paint purchase.

Percentage of Responses

Bargain Paint Center	38%
Martins	19%
Sears, Roebuck	19%
Fairfax Paint Store	16%
Plaza discount store	3%
Midtown department store	3%
Any paint store	2%
Total	100%

4. Who purchases most of the paint for your home?

Percentage of Responses

Wife only	21%
Husband only	63%
Husband and wife	11%
Painting contractor	5%
Total	100%

5. Who performs the major painting jobs in your home?

Percentage of Responses

Wife only	8%
Husband only	55%
Husband and wife	32%
Painting contractor	5%
Total	100%

CASE 4. **PARK MANOR CONDOMINIUM***

Analysis of social and psychological market factors

Park Manor is a condominium apartment community located twenty-five minutes from downtown Milwaukee, Wisconsin. (A condominium is a building in which individuals own separate apartments, but share the ownership and maintenance of

*Case written by Prof. John M. Hess, University of Colorado.

common facilities such as halls, roofs, heating systems, and outdoor area.) Park Manor was developed especially for individuals who have passed their forty-eighth birthday. In the first five years of its development, the 200-acre development has sold nearly four hundred apartments priced from $22,000 to $35,000, with an aggregate value of some $9 million.

Park Manor differs from the retirement communities which have been so successful on the West Coast and in Florida in that it tries to attract both retired and working individuals. It has succeeded in this attempt, and over two-thirds of the residents are regularly employed. Further, Park Manor has been designed to serve and draw from a local, rather than a national, market. It also differs from the "family" condominiums which have sprouted in most large cities and which abound with children. No one with children under sixteen may live at Park Manor. In other respects, however, Park Manor is similar to the other types of condominium communities. It is attractive, well built, and located on spacious grounds with rapid access to the central city. Numerous recreational and personal-achievement activity opportunities are available. The chief rationale for Park Manor is that it provides "elegant but economical living in a maintenance-free, parklike atmosphere."

Troubled by a significant decline in sales in recent months, the developers, Herbert Klein, Hilton Howard, and Lloyd Franklin, have debated whether they have curtailed the market too severely by their age and no-children barriers. Mr. Howard believes they have already exhausted the "over-forty-eight" market and should lower the minimum age limit. Most present residents, however, view the peaceful, childless atmosphere as a major advantage and would fight such a change. Mr. Franklin contends that the market is hardly touched but that they have drawn too heavily on retired individuals and have not spent enough of their energies attracting working people whose children have left home and who no longer desire a large house with its attendant maintenance problems. Mr. Klein thinks that they have taken the wrong tack entirely in terms of their geographic market. Rather than limiting their efforts to the local area, he suggests that Park Manor should attempt to draw retirees from a regional, or even a national, market. He points out that the Chicago area alone has some 200,000 eligible retirees, with an additional 20,000 persons retiring each year: "Just give me 1 percent of the Chicago retirement market, and I'll be happy."

A recent market study conducted for Park Manor has revealed some public misconceptions and prejudices. There has been a tendency to shift promotional emphasis entirely each time one of the three partners perceives a new market segment which might be approached. This, in turn, has contributed to the public's confusion. A summary statement from the market study report reads as follows:

In review, the chief objections to Park Manor are:

1. Age. Most respondents view Park Manor as an old-people's home. It is clearly identified with the retirement, perhaps even the nursing-home market. Most people, regardless of their age, just do not think they are old enough to move there yet.
2. Income. The majority of the respondents identify Park Manor as an expensive, high-income, high-cost place to live. They frequently parroted words from Park Manor's advertising such as "exclusive," "luxurious," and "country-club atmosphere." Another group has taken the economy advertising seriously and sees Park Manor as low-cost housing.
3. Institutionalization. People feel that they would lose their freedom if they moved

to Park Manor. They associate the many activities and facilities with regimentation and institutionalism.

4. **Not quite respectable.** Many respondents perceive Park Manor as being not quite respectable. They suggested that the residents were probably rather shiftless and hedonistic. Words such as "playgroud," "leisure living," "pleasure," and "fun" were apparently drawn directly from advertising copy by such respondents.

5. **Apartment living.** Homeowners do not like the idea of living in an apartment, and apartment dwellers do not wish to invest or tie up funds in their residence.

It appears that each segment of the market reads or hears only that portion of the advertising which confirms his feelings that Park Manor is for someone else.

The development company has learned that buying a home and moving are emotion-laden activities, and that each segment of the market has substantially different motives for changing residences. Unfortunately, it also appears that the motives of various segments are often at cross-purposes, so appeals to one segment may well alienate other segments. Park Manor, however, can no longer prosper by appealing to one segment of the market, so it must identify and select those market elements which are most compatible.

QUESTIONS

1. Which market should be the prime target for Park Manor?
2. Identify other logical submarkets for Park Manor and indicate which might be approached without alienating other submarkets.
3. What psychological or sociological factors are at work in limiting the market for Park Manor condominium apartments?

PART THREE

THE PRODUCT

PRODUCT PLANNING AND DEVELOPMENT

After carefully analyzing his market, a marketing manager is in a position to develop a total marketing program designed to capture his desired share of that market. He has the four components of the marketing mix with which to work: his product, the price structure, the distribution system, and promotional activities. Each of Parts 3 to 6 is devoted to one of these components.

MEANING OF THE "PRODUCT"

In a very *narrow* sense, a product is simply a set of tangible physical and chemical attributes assembled in an identifiable form. Each different product category carries a commonly understood descriptive name, such as apples, steel, shoes, or baseball bats. Product attributes appealing to consumer motivation or buying patterns play no part in the definition. A Sunbeam Shavemaster and a Schick Flexamatic are one and the same product—an electric shaver.

A *broader* interpretation recognizes each brand as a separate product. In this sense a Kuppenheimer man's suit and a Hickey-Freeman man's suit are two different products. So too, Squibb's aspirin and Bayer aspirin are separate products, even though the only tangible difference may be the imprint of the brand name on the aspirin tablet. The brand name suggests a product difference to the consumer. Thus the concept of consumer want satisfaction begins to enter the picture.

Any change in a physical feature (design, color, size, packaging, etc.), however minor it may be, creates, in effect, another product. The seller has an opportunity to use a new set of appeals to reach what may be essentially a new market. When the manufacturer of Marlboro cigarettes came out with a flip-top box, this packaging change created a new product. Mennen's shave cream, Rise, became three products when ingredients in the basic item were modified to create Rise with Lanolin, Rise with Menthol, and Rise Regular.

Carrying the analysis further, we can see that an RCA television set bought in a discount house on a cash-and-carry basis is a different product from the identical model purchased in a department store, where the customer buys the set for a higher price but gets it on credit, has it delivered free of extra charge, and avails himself of other store services. Again the interpretation of "product" is broadened, and we come nearer to a definition valuable to marketing people.

Our definition is as follows: A *product* is a complex of tangible and intangible attributes, including packaging, color, price, manufacturer's prestige, retailer's prestige, and manufacturer's and retailer's services, which the buyer may accept as offering satisfaction of wants or needs.

The key idea in this definition is that the consumer is buying more than a set of chemical and physical attributes. Fundamentally he is buying want satisfaction. A wise firm sells product *benefits* rather than just the product. As Elmer Wheeler, an author and well-known sales training consultant, said, "Don't sell the steak, sell the sizzle." A travel agency should not sell a two-week Caribbean cruise; rather, it should sell romance, glamour, rest, a chance to meet people, and the opportunity for education.

Manufacturers sell symbols as well as products. "People buy things not only for what they can do, but also for what they mean."[1] Goods are psychological symbols of personal attributes, goals, and social patterns. As was suggested in Chapter 4, we buy products which reinforce our self-image or self-concept, and people are shrewd judges of symbols.

WHAT IS A "NEW" PRODUCT?

We have been talking about the importance of *new*-product planning and development. But just what is a new product? Are the new models that auto manufacturers introduce each autumn new products? If a firm adds men's after-shave cologne to its product mix of toiletries and drug sundries, is this a new product? Or must an item be a totally new concept before we can class it as a *new* product?

Probably it is not important to seek a very limited definition; instead we may recognize several possible categories of new products. What is important for marketing executives to understand, however, is that each separate category may very well require quite different marketing programs to ensure a reasonable probability of market success.

Three recognizable categories of new products are as follows:

1. Products which are *really* innovative—truly unique. These are items such as a hair restorer or a cancer cure—products for which there is a real need but for which there are no existing substitutes generally considered satisfactory. In this first category we can also include those products which are quite different

---

[1]Sidney J. Levy, "Symbols for Sale," *Harvard Business Review,* July–August, 1959, p. 118.

replacements for existing goods serving existing markets. Thus television to a great extent replaced radio and movies, plastics compete with wood and metals, and atomic power competes with other energy sources.

2. Adaptive replacements of existing products involving a *significant* differentiation in the existing article. Instant coffee replaced ground coffee and coffee beans in many markets; then freeze-dried instant replaced older-style instant coffee. Soup and dry cereal manufacturers introduce new types of these products and often discontinue existing ones which no longer fulfill company sales and profit expectations. Annual model changes in autos and new fashions in clothing also belong in this second category.

3. Imitative products which are new to your company but not new to the market. Your firm simply wants to enter that existing market with essentially a "me-too" product.

Perhaps the key criterion as to whether a given product is new is how the intended market perceives it. If buyers perceive that a given item is significantly different (from competitive goods being replaced) in some characteristic (appearance, performance, construction, etc.), then this is a new product.

RELATED TERMS

In addition to "product" and "product policies," you will hear such terms as "product planning," "product development," and "merchandising" and may wonder what they mean and how they are related.

Product planning and product development. *Product planning* embraces all activities which enable producers and middlemen to determine what should constitute a company's line of products. Ideally, product planning will ensure that the full complement of a firm's products is designed to strengthen the company's profit position. *Product development,* a more limited term, encompasses the technical activities of product research, engineering, and design. Here we are concerned with product innovation or improvement and are working with production, research, and engineering departments.

More specifically, the scope of product-planning and product-development activities includes decision making in the following areas:

1. Which products should the firm make and which should it buy?
2. Should the company expand or simplify its line?
3. What new uses are there for each item?
4. What brand, package, and label should be used for each product?
5. How should the product be styled and designed, and in what sizes, colors, and materials should it be produced?
6. In what quantities should each item be produced?
7. How should the product be priced? (Part 4 is devoted entirely to pricing.)

Merchandising. "Merchandising" is probably one of the two most loosely used terms in the marketing vocabulary. (The other, "sales promotion," is discussed in Part 6.) Merchandising means many things to many people. To some it is synonymous with marketing. To others it is the all-inclusive term, and marketing is only part of merchandising. Retailers make particularly heavy use of the word as a verb, noun, or adjective. A clothing buyer may be complimented for have "merchandised" a new sports shirt very well this season. Another executive may claim that sound "merchandising" is the foundation of a store's success. A third may note that the "merchandising" plans for next season are completed. One of the high-level executives in a department store is merchandising manager, and normally retail stores have no one with the title "marketing manager" or "sales manager."

In this book, *merchandising* is synonymous with product planning. That is, merchandising includes all planning activities of manufacturers and middlemen designed to adjust their products to the market demand.

Merchandising by manufacturers versus merchandising by middlemen. While it is true that most manufacturers are concerned with what to *make* and most middlemen are concerned with what to *buy,* one thing that is even more fundamental is that both groups are concerned with what to *sell.* The goals of product planning by manufacturers and middlemen are similar. Both want their merchandising to be market-oriented—to please a consumer by satisfying his wants. In fact, manufacturers and middlemen often work jointly to reach this goal. For instance, some high-quality furniture stores take a customer's order for a sofa covered with individually selected fabrics and then relay the order to a prearranged manufacturer. Very often retailers or wholesalers provide ideas which result in new mass-produced articles or refinements of established products.

IMPORTANCE OF PRODUCT INNOVATION

Most new products are marketing failures! Even large, usually successful companies have had products which did not meet their marketing goals and which were dropped. Ford had its Edsel, and Du Pont lost on Corfam (its plastic product designed to replace leather in shoes). Some other big-name brands which failed in recent years were Campbell's Red Kettle soups, Hunt's flavored ketchups, Gillette's Nine Flags men's cologne, Post cereals with freeze-dried fruit, Colgate's Cue toothpaste, and Rheingold's Gablinger's beer. Estimates of product failure rates have run as high as 80 percent. Even among a group of prominent, well-managed companies, the success rate for products which reached the market was still only two out of three.[2] These sobering facts should point up the importance of a good program for planning and developing new products.

JUSTIFICATION OF A FIRM'S EXISTENCE

Fundamentally, the social and economic justification for the existence of a business is its ability to satisfy its customers, whether they are industrial users or ultimate household consumers. A company meets its basic responsibility to society through the medium of its product (using the terms broadly here to include

---

[2]*Management of New Products,* Booz, Allen & Hamilton, Inc., New York, 1968, pp. 2, 11–12. Failure-rate estimates vary because of different definitions of what constitutes failure in the market.

nontangible "goods," usually called "services"). Unless it fulfills this mission, a firm should not exist, and normally the competitive forces in our socioeconomic system do not permit its continuation, at least not for long.

Here an implicit and corollary social responsibility of business is to make effective use of its resources—particularly to minimize the waste of scarce human resources such as scientific and technical talent. Yet even in leading industrial firms, it is estimated that about 70 percent of new-product expenditures are for products that never become commercial successes. Of the money spent in the scientific and engineering development stage, 80 percent goes into the development of products that fail.[3]

In an even broader context, business management has the responsibility for interpreting correctly the emerging environment so as to identify new needs of various consumer groups. Then business must manage our increasingly sophisticated scientific technology so as to make available the goods and services to fulfill these new needs. As Professor Pessemier observed: "Perhaps the real challenge of product development will be to bridge the gap between the emerging and the fully developed societies. *We need suitable products to improve the present life style of all men, giving the citizens of less-developed nations the means and incentives to join rapidly the more advanced technical societies.*"[4]

MARKETING PROGRAMMING STARTS WITH THE PRODUCT

It has been said that nothing happens until somebody sells something. This is not entirely true. First, there must be something to sell—a product, a service, or an idea. From inside or outside the firm must come the germ of a product idea. In the latter case, an express demand may come from the market. That is, the question may be asked: Why don't they make a _____? The next step is to get the firm's marketing department to determine whether there is an adequate market for the product and to decide how the product should be planned.

PRODUCT IS BASIC PROFIT DETERMINANT

Good executive judgment elsewhere cannot offset weaknesses in product planning. A company cannot successfully sell a poor product over the long run. Often it is easy to create a demand for initial sales, but a company needs a good product to get repeat sales, and repeat sales are needed to stay in business. Problems with channels of distribution are magnified by a poor product.

New-product planning is essential for sustaining a company's expected rate of profit. Figure 8-1 illustrates a typical relationship between the sales volume curve and the profit margin curve through the life cycle of new products. While similar in shape, the two curves have different timing. The profit curve starts to decline while the volume sales curve is still ascending. Often the sales curve has been the basis for marketing planning. The action of the profit curve, however, suggests that management should gear its product strategy to this curve rather than to the sales curve.

---

[3]*Ibid.,* pp. 10–11, 24.
[4]Edgar A. Pessemier, "New-Product Ventures," *Business Horizons,* August, 1968, p. 19.

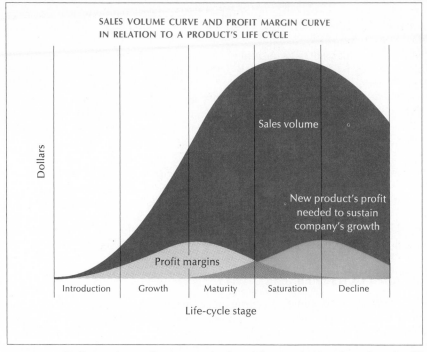

SALES VOLUME CURVE AND PROFIT MARGIN CURVE
IN RELATION TO A PRODUCT'S LIFE CYCLE

Figure 8-1. Profit margin usually starts to decline while a product's sales volume is still increasing. How does the relationship between these curves influence the time at which additional new products should be introduced? *Source*: Booz, Allen & Hamilton, Inc.

HIGH COST OF PRODUCT FAILURES

New complexities in the business environment have increased both the risks and penalties for product failure.[5] Investment requirements for new products continue to climb, thus generating higher break-even points. The net result here is to increase the time period required for a company to pay back its new-product costs. Government environmental controls affecting pollution, product safety, warranties, etc., are new cost factors to contend with. A consequence of these risk factors is to increase the lead time between product idea and market entry. On balance, the pace of innovation may well be slowed down, but the cost of each individual innovation will increase.

NEW PRODUCTS ARE ESSENTIAL TO GROWTH

The watchword for management must often be "innovate or die," and this innovating attitude can become a philosophy almost paralleling that of the marketing concept. Peter Drucker recognized the coimportance of the two concepts

---

[5]Adapted from Thomas A. Staudt, "Higher Management Risks in Product Strategy," *Journal of Marketing*, January, 1973, pp. 4–9.

when he said, "Because it is its purpose to create a customer, any business enterprise has two—and only these two—basic functions: marketing and innovation."[6]

Many companies will get a substantial percentage of their sales volume and net profits this year from products which did not exist five to ten years ago, and this situation undoubtedly will continue. Figure 8-2 shows the dollar sales increase estimated (in 1964) for the period 1963–1967 in 11 industries and the share of this growth which was expected from new products. From 46 percent (for paper products) to 100 percent (for rubber goods) of the sales increase was anticipated from new products; the 11-industry average was 75 percent.[7]

Using historical perspective, the Booz, Allen & Hamilton studies note the fact that growth industries are new-product-oriented. Figure 8-3 shows a comparison between (1) research and development expenditures and (2) growth rates in selected industries. Expenditures for research and development are assumed to be a reasonable indication of new-product effort. Figure 8-3 shows generally that the industries spending the most on new-product development have enjoyed the greatest rates of growth.

INCREASED CONSUMER SELECTIVITY

As the years go by, consumers become more selective in their choice of products. As disposable income in the hands of consumers has increased since World War II and as an abundance of products have become available, consumers have fulfilled many of their wants. The big middle-income market is reasonably well fed, clothed, housed, transported, and equipped. In our economy today, one of Thorstein Veblen's theories may be found in practice. His theory was that as members of a social class attain means to accumulate wealth, they pass through a period of conspicuous consumption, during which they acquire worldly goods to impress their neighbors. When they have proved to themselves that they can pay for a large house or a second car, these people switch to a practice of conspicuous *underconsumption.* They buy small foreign cars or compact American cars. They need not continue to buy additional mountains of goods to impress people because people are already impressed.

If market satiation—in terms of quantity—does exist to some extent, it follows that the consumer may be more critical in his appraisal of a product, more aware of quality differentials, and more responsive to improved labeling. While the consumer is being increasingly selective, the market is being surfeited with products which are imitations or which offer only marginal competitive advantages. This situation in the economy may be leading to "product indigestion," the cure for which is to develop *really* new products and to create *really* new markets. A company's product-planning efforts should be designed to *innovate* and not just *imitate;* these efforts should place emphasis on *leading,* not just *meeting,* competition.[8]

---

[6]Peter Drucker, *The Practice of Management,* Harper & Row, Publishers, Inc., New York, 1954, p. 37.

[7]*Management of New Products, op. cit.,* p. 6.

[8]*Grey Matter,* March, 1968, p. 4.

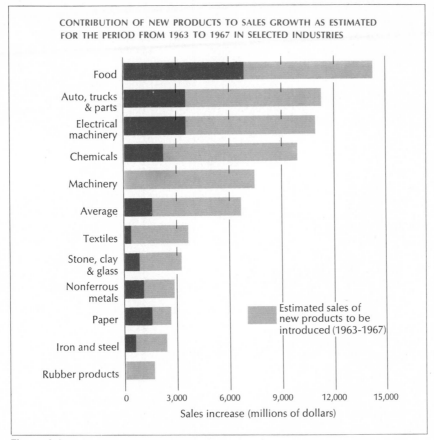

CONTRIBUTION OF NEW PRODUCTS TO SALES GROWTH AS ESTIMATED
FOR THE PERIOD FROM 1963 TO 1967 IN SELECTED INDUSTRIES

Estimated sales of new products to be introduced (1963-1967)

Sales increase (millions of dollars)

Figure 8-2. In an expanding economy, new products contribute substantially to sales growth. For instance, an estimate shows that 70 percent of the sales increase in the electrical machinery industry in the period 1963–1967 came from products first introduced during that same period. *Source*: Booz, Allen & Hamilton, Inc., from Federal Trade Commission and McGraw-Hill data.

DEVELOPMENT OF NEW PRODUCTS

THE DECISION TO MAKE OR BUY

One of the first product problems calling for a decision is whether to make a product or buy it. All manufacturers must wrestle with this problem, while most retailers and wholesalers automatically think in terms of buying. Some large retail food chains, variety chains, and department stores, however, do make their own bakery goods and candy. Other firms, such as Sears, Roebuck and Company, establish such rigid product specifications, work so closely with the product department of a manufacturer, and take such a large percentage of the firm's output that for all practical purposes they are making rather than buying.

A firm may solve its make-or-buy problem at some in-between point. For example, it may decide simply to assemble a series of premanufactured parts. Other

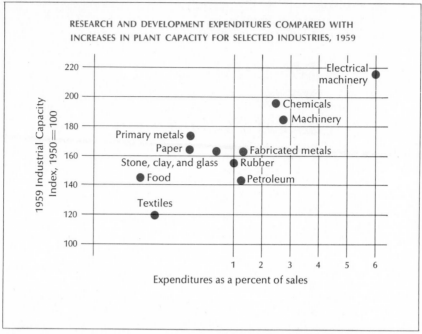

Figure 8-3. There is usually a close relationship between the amount of research and development expenditures and the increases in plant capacity in a given industry. Growth industries are typically new-product-oriented and spend a great deal on research and development. Compare the electrical machinery and textiles industries. *Source: Booz, Allen & Hamilton, Inc.*

firms may decide to make some parts and buy others and then assemble them. Furniture manufacturers usually follow this approach. In still another situation, an enterprise may assemble premanufactured parts and then paint or otherwise finish the end product. Automobiles, generally, are a case in point. Often many of the final parts, such as engines, call for make-or-buy decisions with respect to the components of the part. That is, an automobile manufacturer must decide whether to make or buy spark plugs, gaskets, valves, engine blocks, and other units making up the completed engines.

There are no pat solutions. As in so many other phases of marketing, the answer is: "It depends." Whether to make or buy a product depends upon the outcome of management's analysis of several issues, such as the following:

1. Relative costs of making or buying.
2. Extent to which specialized machinery, techniques, and production resources are needed.
3. Availability of production capacity.
4. Managerial time and talents required—the amount of production supervision needed.
5. Secrecy of design, style, and materials—the extent to which the company wants its processing methods kept secret. Because of a patent situation, what the firm wants may be available only through buying.

6. Attractiveness of the investment necessary to make a product.
7. Willingness to accept seasonal and other market risks. If a company decides to buy, the supplier can still shift some of these risks to the purchaser by requiring a contract guaranteeing acceptance of a certain quantity.
8. Risk of depending upon outside sources—will they raise the price, cut off relationships, etc.?
9. Extent of reciprocity present—is the supplier of the item also a customer for the buyer's other products?

STEPS IN DEVELOPMENT PROCESS

As a new product is developed, it progresses from the idea stage to the production and marketing stage. Although there may seem to be no particular pattern, we can say that in general, it follows the steps outlined below. In each stage management must decide whether (1) to move on to the next stage, (2) to abandon the product, or (3) to seek additional information.

1. Generation of new-product ideas. New-product development starts with an idea. Excellent ideas may come from salesmen or servicemen, nonmarketing employees, consumers or industrial users, middlemen, governmental agencies, competitive products, trade associations, private research organizations, and inventors. The particular source of ideas is not nearly so important as the company's system for stimulating new ideas and then acknowledging and reviewing them promptly.
2. Screening of ideas to determine which ones warrant further study. This is only the first of several screening reviews the product will receive.
3. Business analysis. The idea is expanded into a concrete business proposal in which management (1) identifies product features, (2) estimates market demand and the product's profitability, (3) establishes a program to develop the product, and (4) assigns responsibility for further study of the product's feasibility. The second and third stages embody what is referred to as "concept testing," that is, pretesting the product *idea*, as contrasted to the later pretesting of the product itself and its market.[9]
4. Product development. The idea-on-paper is converted into a physical product. Pilot models or small quantities are manufactured to designated specifications, and laboratory tests and other technical evaluations necessary to determine the production feasibility of the article are made.
5. Test marketing. Market tests, in-use tests, and other commercial experiments in limited geographic areas are conducted in order to ascertain the feasibility of the full marketing program. In this stage, design and production factors may have to be adjusted as a result of test findings. At this point management must make a final decision regarding whether to market the product commercially. Two major problems often encountered in this stage result because (a) competitors can devise ways of disrupting or countering the research and (b) they may take

---

[9]To avoid overestimating a new product's potential during concept testing, management should recognize that consumers may be favorably disposed toward the new product, yet have no need for it, according to Edward M. Tauber, "Reduce New Product Failures: Measure Needs as Well as Purchase Interest," *Journal of Marketing,* July, 1973, pp. 61–64.

advantage of the time lag caused by test marketing and introduce their own version of the new product without pretesting it.

6. Commercialization. Full-scale production and marketing programs are planned, and then the product is launched. Up to this point in the development process, management has virtually complete control over the product. Once the product is "born," however, and enters its life cycle (as discussed later), the external competitive environment becomes a major determinant of its destiny.

In reviewing the six-step evolution, the first three stages—the idea or concept stages—are the critical ones. Not only are they less expensive—each stage becomes progressively more expensive in dollars and scarce manpower—but, more importantly, experience indicates that most products fail because either the idea or the timing was wrong, and not because the company lacked the production or marketing know-how. Studies also indicate, fortunately, that companies in general are doing a better job of eliminating product ideas of limited potential before they reach the more expensive stages of development.[10]

It is encouraging to note that manufacturers of *industrial* products are giving more attention to the development and marketing of new products and to the mortality rates of these products. These firms are seeking ways to minimize the risks of new-product marketing by improving their programs for new-product planning and development.[11] Often in the past these activities seemed to be almost entirely the concern of marketers of *consumer* goods.

Companies are increasingly using mathematical models and other quantitative techniques in various stages of new-product development, and also as evaluative follow-up once the product is being commercially marketed. To illustrate, PERT (Program Evaluation and Review Technique) and CPM (Critical Path Method) are two similar managerial tools used to aid in planning and controlling programs. It is claimed that the successful application of PERT, which was introduced originally for use in the aerospace industry, enabled the Navy to launch the Polaris missile two years ahead of schedule. The use of PERT can aid tremendously in coordinating, timing, and scheduling the many activities in the new-product-development process.[12]

---

[10] For a survey of 203 manufacturing and service firms having active programs of product and service development, describing their methods of judging the merits of proposed new products and services, see The Conference Board, *Evaluating New-Product Proposals,* Report no. 604, New York, 1973.

[11] See *Appraising the Market for New Industrial Products,* National Industrial Conference Board, Studies in Business Policy, no. 123, New York, 1967.

[12] See Edgar A. Pessemier and H. Paul Root, "The Dimensions of New Product Planning," *Journal of Marketing,* January, 1973, pp. 10–18; Warren Dusenberry, "CPM for New Product Introductions," *Harvard Business Review,* July–August, 1967, pp. 124–139; H. B. Sullivan, "Using PERT/CPM to Manage the Introduction of New Products," *Marketing Forum,* July–August, 1967, pp. 31–35; Morris Hamburg and Robert J. Atkins, "Computer Model for New Product Demand," *Harvard Business Review,* March–April 1967, pp. 107–115; A. Charnes, W. W. Cooper, J. K. Devoe, and D. B. Learner, "DEMON (Decision Mapping via Optimum Go-no Networks): A Management Model for Marketing New Products," *California Management Review,* Fall, 1968, pp. 31–46, and Donald S. Tull, "The Relationship of Actual and Predicted Sales and Profits in New-product Introduction," *Journal of Business,* July, 1967, pp. 233–250.

MANUFACTURER'S CRITERIA FOR NEW PRODUCTS

Insofar as possible, a manufacturer should establish objective benchmarks against which he can measure a prospective addition to his product line.

1. There should be an adequate *market demand*. This is the first and by far the most important criterion to apply to a proposed product. Too often management begins with a question such as, "Can we use our present sales force?" or "Will the new item fit into our production system?" The basic question is: Do enough people really want our product? Administrators should try to get quantitative measures of the size and location of the potential market.

2. A company must consider the factor of *social and environmental compatibility* when evaluating a new product.[13] Do the manufacturing processes heavily pollute air or water? (Steel or paper mills.) Will the use of the finished product be harmful to the user or the environment? (Automobiles.) After being used, is the product harmful to the environment? (DDT and some detergents.) Does the product have recycling potential? Early in the developmental process (idea stage, for example) admittedly it may be difficult to assess the socioenvironmental consequences of the new product.

3. The product should fit into the company's present *marketing* structure. The general marketing experience of the company is important here. The Sunbeam Corporation would probably find it easy to add another kitchen appliance to its line, whereas a paint manufacturer would find it quite difficult to add margarine to his. Sometimes the general marketing relationship may not be apparent at first. Many people questioned the wisdom of Procter & Gamble's move in adding Gleem toothpaste to its list of products. On closer observation, however, it can be seen that the marketing of Gleem is similar in many respects to the marketing of Tide, Ivory, and other Procter & Gamble soap products. Gleem is a consumer convenience product which will be distributed, priced, and promoted in much the same manner as consumer soaps and detergents.

   More specific questions may also be asked regarding the marketing fit of new products: Can the existing sales force be used? Do the salesmen have the time and ability to sell the new product? Can the present channels of distribution be used? If the company has a service organization, can it handle the new product?

4. A new-product idea will be more favorably received if the item fits in with existing *production* facilities, manpower, and management.

5. The product should fit from a *financial* standpoint. At least three questions should be asked: Is adequate financing available? Will the new item increase seasonal and cyclical stability in the firm? Are the profit possibilities worthwhile? Here again some objective criteria are needed to decide what a "worthwhile" profit is. Some products must cover their total costs, while others may be considered satisfactory if they cover only their variable costs and contribute something to overhead. The latter type may be acceptable when they are added only to satisfy middlemen who want a full line from a manufacturer.

---

[13]Dale L. Varble, "Social and Environmental Considerations in New Product Development," *Journal of Marketing,* October, 1972, pp. 11–15.

6. Before accepting a new product, management should make certain that there are no *legal* objections. Patents must be registered or applied for, labeling and packaging must observe all pertinent regulations, and so on.
7. *Management* of adequate ability should be available. It is important that the executives in the company have the necessary time and ability to handle the proposed new product.
8. The product should be in keeping with the *company's image,* self-concept, and objectives. The proposed product should not run counter to the company's goals. A firm stressing low-priced, high-turnover products normally should not add an item which shouts prestige or status.

MIDDLEMAN'S CRITERIA FOR NEW PRODUCTS

A middleman who is trying to determine whether to add a new product to his line must consider all the criteria that a manufacturer would, except those related to production. He has, in addition, two further points to consider:

1. Relations with the manufacturer. A middleman in wholesaling or retailing should consider the reputation of the manufacturer. A middleman should examine the possibility of acquiring exclusive sales rights in a given geographic territory. He must be sure that he can get an adequate supply. In the ready-to-wear fields, a retailer often will not place an original order unless he is guaranteed delivery of reorders within a certain number of days after placing them. A retailer should also consider the nature and amount of promotional help given by the manufacturer.
2. In-store policies and practices. A retailer has to study the type of selling effort a new product will require. He must consider how the proposed product fits with in-store policies and practices regarding mechanical service, clothing alteration, credit, and delivery. Stores using self-service ordinarily do not want to add items requiring extensive demonstration and personal selling. For this reason, supermarkets tend to carry very little in the way of clothing and appliances.

IMPORTANCE OF TIMING

An analysis of case histories will show that new-product development is considerably more time-consuming than many marketing executives realize. As a result of underestimating the time needed for orderly development, management may take shortcuts in some of the developmental stages, the result frequently being product failure. In many cases, 10 or more years (television took 55 years, and Talon zippers took 30 years) have elapsed between the time the new-product development was started, and the date the product was introduced in test markets. This means that a company should have several new products in the development hopper at any given time.

Proper timing is of the utmost importance in every stage leading to the introduction of a new product. Managerial decisions involving time generally start with a determination of when to offer the product for sale. If the product has an annual model change or if it is intended primarily for a special season, the decision is reasonably easy. If the product is to be sold to the industrial market or if it affects the use of other products now in the hands of retailers and wholesalers, timing can create many problems for management.

After deciding when the product will be offered for sale to the ultimate consumer or industrial user, the producer must determine when the product will be sold to the wholesalers and retailers. Arrangements must be made to reduce inventories of the old product and build up stocks of the new. The physical distribution of the product must be dovetailed with the promotional program so that supplies will be on hand when advertising is released and the personal salesmen start selling.

ORGANIZING FOR PRODUCT INNOVATION

Product innovation should be a responsibility of top management. Moreover, the extent of the top executives' active involvement in new-product programs is a vital determinant of a company's success with new products. These conclusions have been reached in several studies of programs for product planning and development. To be effectively managed, these programs must be effectively organized and controlled. In one study of major problems encountered in new-product programs, more than four out of five (81 percent) of the companies—and these were experienced, well-managed firms with relative success in new products —identified some kind of problem relating to organization. Organizational problems constituted over one-half (55 percent) of all those mentioned by reporting firms.[14]

NEED FOR CONSTRUCTIVE, INNOVATING ATTITUDE

While it is helpful to have a well-designed organizational framework, a more important key to success is the *attitude* which the entire company has toward planning and developing products. The right attitude must permeate all levels of managerial thinking. This "right" attitude is one that constructively encourages —in fact, thrives on—innovation.

Management should have a critical attitude, but its criticism must be constructive. When management reacts to new-product ideas with the philosophy, "We have been doing it this way for twenty years, why do you want to change it?" management is an impediment to growth. Some managers can test a new product to death. They are forever wanting to run another product or market test, with the result that the item never does reach the stage of a full-scale marketing program.

POTENTIAL PROBLEMS IN ORGANIZATION

In some organizations—the Jell-O division of General Foods, for example—the responsibility for new-product development is separated from product-planning activities (such as finding new uses for a product or making package changes) which are related to the modification of established products. This kind of situation, where the division of responsibility is not always sharply demarcated, can create

---

[14]*Management of New Products, op. cit.,* pp. 16–17; see also Philip R. McDonald and Joseph O. Eastlack, Jr., "Top Management Involvement with New Products," *Business Horizons,* December, 1971, pp. 23–31.

real managerial problems, and careful administrative coordination is an absolute requirement. Effectiveness is greatly reduced if the two separate organizational units disagree over whether a given item is a brand-new product, and thus should be developed by department A, or whether it is an improvement on an already existing product and thus should be assigned to department B.

Regardless of the organizational setup, there may be a shift in responsibility as the product moves through the various stages from the inception of the idea to a full-scale marketing program. A new-product-development manager may be responsible for the initial development and market testing. Then at an appropriate time, responsibility may be handed over to a product manager, who carries the product to its fulfillment as a nationally marketed item. If the product manager is already satisfied with the growth rate and profit results in his department, however, he may not want to take on a new, untried product which may cause a disruption in his scheduled routine.

TYPES OF ORGANIZATION

At the outset, it should be emphasized that there is no "one best type" of organizational structure for new-product planning and development, nor does any one type seem to be selected by a large majority of manufacturers. The type which is most effective for any given firm will depend upon the company's size, products, managerial abilities, and other circumstances.

As one criterion, an organizational structure should enable management to implement effectively the processes of specialization and coordination. While these are basic processes in any organization, they are especially key ingredients in a company's organizational mix pertaining to new-product planning and development. As specialists in the research, production, and sales area all work on product innovation, they typically develop different viewpoints and work better in separate organizational structures. While these specializations and differences may improve the innovative research and development, they may also contribute to disagreements which can impede product innovation. At this point in the innovative process, a company must depend upon its organizational structure to provide a counterbalancing provision for coordination so that the executives with diverse points of view can resolve their differences of opinion, and progress with a unity of effort.[15]

In large and medium-sized companies which have enjoyed relative success in new-product marketing, apparently the popular trend is to locate the organizational responsibility for product planning and development in one of the following: (1) a product-planning committee, (2) a new-product department, (3) product managers, or (4) a venture team. Another alternative is that of using outside new-product-specialist firms alone or in some combination with any of the other types of structures.

Product-planning committee. Today the most widely used organizational structure for new-product planning and development is probably the committee, with heavy representation from top management. The firm's president and men from

---

[15]Jay W. Lorsch and Paul R. Lawrence, "Organizing for Product Innovation," *Harvard Business Review,* January–February, 1965, pp. 109–122.

the marketing, production, engineering, research, and finance departments usually are involved.

In a committee, the ideas and wisdom of several executives can be pooled. Any new product which results is likely to win the approval of the administrators who took part in its development. On the other hand, committee activity takes much valuable executive time and slows the decision-making process. Also, the committee structure makes it difficult to place responsibility for managerial actions and may even serve as a "buck-passing" device.

Many companies which use a new-product-development committee also have a product manager who is responsible for marketing the item after it has successfully passed through the necessary testing and other introductory stages of development. In other instances, a new-product department has evolved as the next step beyond a product-planning committee, but the company will still retain the committee as an advisory group to evaluate new-product ideas and development plans.

New-product department. In recent years a separate department devoted to new-product planning and development has been created in an increasing number of America's best-known manufacturing firms. As suggested earlier, these departments have often evolved as the next logical step beyond a product-planning committee. Although there are some exceptions, generally the departments are relatively small, containing no more than four or five people, and frequently these are one-man departments. Usually the head of this department reports to the president, or the department may be one part of a staff unit directly serving the president. Typically these departments have administrative responsibility for such new-product tasks as determining objectives and programs, recommending new projects, planning the activities, generating and screening ideas, guiding the new products through the various developmental stages, and coordinating the new-product activities involving other departments. When a product is ready for full-scale commercial marketing, it is turned over to the appropriate operating department.

This organizational pattern has the advantage of making new-product development a full-time activity, so there is less risk that it will become a stepchild in a department which is more concerned with day-to-day operating problems. The Booz, Allen & Hamilton studies identify two operating weaknesses sometimes found in new-product departments. One is the failure to plan thoroughly just how the department will operate. The other is the failure to staff the department with a person who has the prestige to gain from other executives the support necessary for success.

Product manager. The structure which activates the concept of the product manager is another widely used form of organization for product planning and development. Normally, however, a product manager's responsibility is *not* limited to new products. This executive—sometimes called a "brand manager" or a "merchandise manager"—is ordinarily an administrator in the marketing department, reporting to a top marketing executive. In business and professional journals the wealth of discussion regarding the product-manager system is some indication of management's interest.[16]

---

[16]See, for example, B. Charles Ames, "Payoff from Product Management," *Harvard Business*

The scope of a product manager's responsibilities varies widely among different companies, thus reflecting differences in their product and market requirements. In companies at one end of the spectrum, the product manager's activities may be limited essentially to selling and sales-promotional work.

Other firms—the National Biscuit Company, Pillsbury, Kimberly-Clark (Kleenex), Colgate-Palmolive, and Procter & Gamble, for example—view the product manager's job as involving a much broader group of activities. In such cases, this executive is responsible for planning the complete marketing program for his brand or group of products. Thus he may be concerned with new-product development as well as the improvement of existing goods. His responsibilities encompass such activities as setting marketing goals and planning marketing strategies, pricing, developing advertising and sales-promotional plans, preparing budgets, and helping field salesmen to do a more effective selling job. However, this executive has no line authority over the field sales force; he can only advise them.

As an organizational concept, the product-manager system is not new. It has been used for years in retailing, especially in department stores, where the department buyer system exists and each merchandise manager has complete product-planning responsibilities for a limited line of goods. In manufacturing, Procter & Gamble and the Johnson and Johnson Company have used the brand-manager system successfully for half a century. For most firms, however, the product manager is a relatively new specialist in marketing organizations; yet his value is being questioned less and less. He brings the benefits of specialization and organizational decentralization to each product line.

Probably the biggest single problem most companies face in the use of a product manager is that they saddle him with great responsibility and yet refuse to give him the corresponding authority. Outside his own department, the product manager has no line authority in the classical organizational sense. He cannot, for example, order the salesmen to do something. Even though advertising may be critical to the success of his plans, the product manager does not select the advertising agency. Perhaps the most burdensome aspect of the product manager's responsibility is that he is made accountable for the profitability of his brand and yet is often denied any control over product costs, the setting of prices, or the determination of advertising budgets.[17]

Review, November–December, 1963, pp. 141–152; B. Charles Ames, "Dilemma of Product/Market Management," *Harvard Business Review,* March–April, 1971, pp. 66–74; Robert M. Fulmer, "Product Management: Panacea or Pandora's Box?" *California Management Review,* Summer, 1965, pp. 63–74; *The Product Manager System,* National Industrial Conference Board, Experiences in Marketing Management, no. 8, New York, 1965; and "The Brand Manager: No Longer King," *Business Week,* June 9, 1973, p. 58.

[17]For suggestions to improve the effectiveness of this type of organization, see Stephens Dietz, "Get More Out of Your Brand Management," *Harvard Business Review,* July–August, 1973, pp. 127–136; and David J. Luck and Theodore Nowak, "Product Management: Vision Unfulfilled," *Harvard Business Review,* May–June, 1965, pp. 143–154.

For illustrations of how various forms of interpersonal influence are exerted by product managers in the absence of formal authority, see Gary R. Gemmill and David L. Wilemon, "The Product Manager as an Influence Agent," *Journal of Marketing,* January, 1972, pp. 26–30. Also see David J. Luck, "Interfaces of a Product Manager," *Journal of Marketing,* October, 1969, pp. 32–36.

Venture team. The venture team is a relatively new, rapidly growing organizational concept for managing product innovation from idea stage to full-scale marketing.[18] A venture team is a small, multidisciplinary group, organizationally segregated from the rest of the firm. It is comprised of representatives from engineering-production, finance, and marketing research. A team operates in an entrepreneurial environment, in effect being a separate small business. Typically the group reports directly to top management and has one goal—to enter a new market profitably.

Once the new product reaches the stage of being commercially viable, typically it is turned over to another division—an existing unit, a new division, or even a new subsidiary company. The given venture team is then disbanded. However, in some cases it may continue on as the management nucleus when a new company is established.

A venture team is designed to avoid the product-development problems found in traditional organizational structures—problems of bureaucratic operation, reluctance to change, a "don't-rock-the-boat" attitude, inability to get decisions made quickly, and lack of authority to move a product through the developmental stages.

Use of outside new-product specialists. To speed up the innovation process and *to sell off their unused new products and technology,* several major manufacturers are relying on a combination of (1) a special type of new-product department plus (2) outside firms which specialize in finding or developing new products. In this rather radical organizational departure from tradition, management is bypassing its research and development department for two reasons. First, R & D's traditional approach to new-product development is too slow for today's competitive environment, and second, often the products are dictated by the technical abilities of the R & D people, rather than reflecting consumer market demands.

An innovative variation of a new-product department has developed in some firms—the General Electric Company and the National Cash Register Company, for example. This department is responsible for generating new products *quickly* by such means as (1) reviving old patents, (2) contracting with outside product brokers who can match other companies' products with the firm's needs, or (3) farming out ideas to firms specializing in new-product development. This new-style department has another unusual job—that of selling off products, inventions, and technology which the manufacturer has developed but which he cannot market right now for one reason or another. Rather than "sit on" the product for several years, management gets some immediate payoff for its research and development investment.

Two types of outside new-product specialists are being used to varying degrees by many major manufacturers—for example, General Foods, Gillette, American Can Company, Dow Chemical, and B.F. Goodrich. One type is a firm which will completely develop a new product—from the idea stage to the commercial marketing stage. In effect, this type of specialist enables a manufacturer to buy, rather than make, a new product. Using an outside firm gives a manufacturer considerable

---

[18]Adapted from Richard M. Hill and James D. Hlavacek, "The Venture Team: A New Concept in Marketing Organization," *Journal of Marketing,* July, 1972, pp. 44–50. Also see Mack Hanan, "Corporate Growth through Venture Management," *Harvard Business Review,* January–February, 1969, pp. 43–61.

flexibility and objectivity. The manufacturer is not limited by its own company attitudes or executives' ego. The outsider brings the benefits of experience and expertise. His use also enables a manufacturer to better control product-development costs.[19]

The other specialist is a product broker who will find a seller of products wanted by a manufacturer, or will help the manufacturer sell off his unused products or technology.

WHY NEW PRODUCTS FAIL: A SUMMARY

As a conclusion to this chapter, we shall summarize the results of one study on why new products fail and then consider some final points for corrective action. The Conference Board surveyed 125 companies which were considered successful product innovators. Even these firms experienced a failure rate of slightly more than 20 percent among products which had been introduced to the market during the preceeding five years.[20] The major reasons given for the failure of the new products or services, in order of frequency of mention, are as follows:

1. Inadequate market analysis This includes overestimating potential sales of the new product, inability to determine buying motives and habits, and misjudgments on what products the market wanted.
2. Product deficiencies. Poor quality and performance, too complicated, and especially the product did not offer any significant advantage over competitive products already on the market.
3. Lack of effective marketing effort. Failure to provide sufficient follow-through effort after introductory program, and failure to train marketing personnel for new products and new markets.
4. Higher costs than anticipated. This led to higher prices which in turn led to lower sales volume than anticipated.
5. Competitive strength or reaction. Speed and ease of copying an innovation soon overcrowded the market.
6. Poor timing of introduction. Usual mistake here was to introduce a product too late, although in a few cases the problem was premature market entry.
7. Technical or production problems. Could not produce sufficient quantities to meet demand, so competition gained an unanticipated share of market.

After analyzing the above factors, two points became quite clear. First, as executives were frank to admit, the factors which led to product failures typically were within the control of the company itself. Second, close to three-quarters of the causes of failure were marketing-related shortcomings, while all other functions of

---

[19]For an analysis of this "outside" new-product development specialist—its services, relative merits, and track record, see Edward M. Tauber, "The Emerging New Product Development Industry," *Business Horizons,* April, 1973, pp. 5–10.

[20]David S. Hopkins and Earl L. Bailey, "New-Product Pressures," *Conference Board Record,* June, 1971, pp. 16–24. Here it is important to note that the failure rate represents products which failed in some important respect to meet management's original goals. Only about 5 percent of the new products were actually withdrawn from the market.

the business combined (production, engineering, purchasing, etc.) accounted for the remainder.

As corrective action to remedy these deficiencies, the study concluded that the entire process of developing and marketing new products is becoming more systematized with more stringent controls and built-in decision points (go or no-go) along the way.[21] More specifically the corrective action involves:

1. Organizational changes aimed at strengthening new-product planning.
2. Better marketing research to evaluate market needs and prospects.
3. Improved screening and evaluation of ideas and products.

If the first commandment in marketing is "Know thy customer," then the second is "Know thy product." The products or services sold by a firm are prime determinants of the company's rate of growth, rate of profit, and total marketing program. Policies and strategies with respect to the full complement of a firm's products are considered in the following chapter.

QUESTIONS AND PROBLEMS

1. In what respects are the products different in each of the following cases?
   a. An Arrow shirt sold by a local men's clothing store and a similar shirt sold by Sears under the retailer's brand name. Assume that the same manufacturer makes both shirts.
   b. A Sunbeam Mixmaster sold by a leading department store and the same model sold by a discount house.
2. Explain the various interpretations of the term "new product." Give some examples, other than those stated in this chapter, of products in each new-product category.
3. Bring to class three advertisements which stress product benefits. Bring three which stress some part of the product rather than the benefits to be derived from this product.
4. Compare the product-planning activities of a manufacturer and a retailer.
5. What factors account for the growing importance of product planning?
6. What are some of the questions which management is likely to want answered during the "business-analysis" stage of new-product development?
7. Assume that the following additions to their product lines are being considered by the stated companies. What is your initial recommendation, based upon general information which you may already have relating to the criteria set forth in this chapter?
   a. Automobile manufacturer—outboard motors
   b. Firm such as National Cash Register—office dictating machines

---

[21]For the notion that management should develop a formal statement of strategy guidelines for new-product development, see C. Merle Crawford, "Strategies for New Product Development," *Business Horizons,* December, 1972, pp. 49–58.

For three proposals to help management improve its R & D payoff in new-product development, see William V. Muse and Robert J. Kegerreis, "Technological Innovation and Marketing Management: Implications for Corporate Policy," *Journal of Marketing,* October, 1969, pp. 3–9.

     c. Supermarket—wallpaper

     d. Manufacturer of electronic parts and equipment—automatic garage-door opener

     e. Department store—well-known brand of compact cars

8. List the factors which influence the type of organizational structure selected for new-product development. Explain how each of these factors might affect the choice of structure.

9. Under what conditions might a firm profitably use a separate department for new-product development?

10. What are some of the problems typically connected with the "product-manager" type of organizational structure for new-product development?

11. Why do so many new products turn out to be market failures?

PRODUCT-LINE POLICIES AND STRATEGIES

McGraw-Hill (book and magazine publisher) bought the CBS-affiliated TV station in Denver. General Electric eliminated vacuum cleaners and blenders from its group of appliances. The Ford Motor Company dropped the Edsel and later added the Maverick and Pinto. Besides marketing Listerine and Bromo-Seltzer, the Warner-Lambert Company has diversified into eyeglasses, chewing gum, cosmetics, and Schick razors. A producer of industrial materials-handling and construction equipment has expanded into hydraulic pumps, motors, and valves. Several large American department stores regularly shop for the latest European fashion creations and then adapt these to the mass market. All these cases have one thing in common: They involve managerial strategies and policy making with respect to the firm's line of products and services.

PRODUCT LINE AND PRODUCT MIX

A broad group of products, intended for essentially similar uses and possessing reasonably similar physical characteristics, constitutes a *product line*. Wearing apparel is one example of a product line. But in a different context, say, in a small specialty shop, men's furnishings (shirts, ties, and underwear) and men's ready-to-wear (suits, sport jackets, topcoats, and slacks) would each constitute a line. In another context, men's apparel is one line, as contrasted with women's apparel, furniture, or sporting goods.

The *product mix* is the full list of all products offered for sale by a company. The structure of the product mix has dimensions of both breadth and depth. Its *breadth* is measured by the number of product lines carried; its *depth,* by the assortment of sizes, colors, and models offered within each product line. See Fig. 9-1.

MAJOR PRODUCT-LINE STRATEGIES

Several major product-line strategies are used by manufacturers and middle-men in marketing their products. Most of these strategies involve a change in the product mix. However, some involve an expansion of the market by means of new uses for the existing product, but with no alterations in the mix. A discussion of planned obsolescence as a product strategy, and of fashion as an influence on the product mix, is deferred until later in the chapter.

EXPANSION OF PRODUCT MIX

A firm may elect to expand its present product mix by increasing the number of lines and/or the depth within a line. New lines may be related or unrelated to the present products. The Campbell Soup Company added food items—Chunky soups, Swanson frozen TV dinners and pies, Pepperidge Farm bakery goods. Campbell's also added semirelated products—Recipe brand dog food and two restaurant chains in the Pacific Northwest, Clark's and Herfy's.[1] The makers of Chesterfield and L & M cigarettes also market pet foods, watchbands, popcorn, and alcoholic beverages. RCA acquired Hertz rental cars and Sears now sells mutual funds. The Green Giant Company increased the *depth* of its line by adding a series of frozen vegetables to its highly successful canned peas and corn. A company may expand in both breadth and depth. For example, food chains have added lines of drug sundries and housewares (breadth), while at the same time increasing their assortments of dry cereals and cleaning products (depth).

CONTRACTION OF PRODUCT MIX

A product strategy trend in the 1970s is to thin out product lines, either by eliminating an entire line or by simplifying the assortment within a line. The shift from fat and long lines to thin and short lines is designed to eliminate low-profit products and to get more profit from fewer products. RCA and General Electric both dropped their line of computers. B. F. Goodrich no longer markets rubber footware. Motorola thinned its line by deleting portable radios, record players, and tape players.

This practice of slimming the product mix has long been recognized as an important product-line strategy. However, in the 1970s it has *really* been pushed to the forefront by raw-materials scarcities, price controls, and the energy shortage. A wide variety of industries has been forced to retreat from (1) the full-line product concept with its emphasis on growth and total sales volume to (2) a product

---

[1]"The New Soup King at Campbell," *Business Week,* July 1, 1972, p. 42.

PART OF A SKI RETAILER'S PRODUCT MIX, ILLUSTRATING BREADTH AND DEPTH OF LINE		
Breadth (Different lines)	Depth (Assortment)	
Skis	Slalom, cross-country, GLM (short skis)	
Ski boots	Foam, nonfoam, after-ski	Each in several brands and sizes
Ski pants	Men's and women's, ski and after-ski, under- and over-the-boot styles	

Figure 9-1.

position which emphasizes profits and efficient use of materials and energy. Shell Chemical Company cut its production of synthetic rubber and fertilizers. Philco-Ford eliminated 50 percent of its color-TV screen sizes and 40 percent of its refrigerator models. General Electric dropped blenders, vacuum cleaners, fans, heaters, and humidifiers. Crown Zellerbach and other papermakers have cut their lines by as much as 60 percent.[2]

ALTERATION OF EXISTING PRODUCTS

As an alternative to developing a new product, management should take a fresh look at the company's existing products. Often improving an established product can be more profitable and less risky than developing a new one. This alternative strategy should be followed regardless of the breadth and depth of the product mix and regardless of whether management is committed to a policy of expansion or contraction of the mix.

For industrial goods, especially, *redesigning* is often the key to the product's renaissance.[3] Not only did a redesigned pressure switch cost 52 percent less than the model it replaced, but the new one was also easier to install and performed better. The market for a hospital centrifuge was expanded by redesigning it so that it harmonized architecturally with modern cabinetry. *Packaging* has been a very popular area for product alteration, particularly in consumer products. Even something as mundane as thread, glue, or cheesecloth can be made more attractive by creative packaging and display. The *use of new materials* has also been popular. In place of cotton and wool, clothing manufacturers have substituted materials of synthetic fibers.

Sometimes the alteration is only in the advertising appeal—the product remains unchanged—as when the advertising for Welch's grape juice ceased to be *against* fat and *in favor of* refreshment and energy production. It should also be beneficial if management would analyze the qualities which have contributed to the long-lived, seemingly indestructible success of such products as 20 Mule Team borax, Hershey chocolate, Vaseline petroleum jelly, and Arm & Hammer baking soda.

---

[2]See "The Squeeze on Product Mix," *Business Week,* Jan. 5, 1974, p. 50.

[3]Kenneth Van Dyck, "New Products from Old: Short-cut to Profits," *Industrial Marketing,* November, 1965, pp. 85–87.

DEVELOPMENT OF NEW USES FOR EXISTING PRODUCTS

Another major product strategy is to search for new uses for products. Although a company probably cannot rely on this strategy alone to increase volume and profits, we should not underestimate its effectiveness in tapping new markets. The 3M Company has followed this approach successfully with its product Scotch tape. Several years ago, the manufacturers of the soap product Duz offered a weekly prize to the consumer coming up with the best new use for the product.

POSITIONING THE PRODUCT

Management's ability to position a product appropriately in the market is a major determinant of company profits. A product's *position* is the image which that product projects in relation to images projected (1) by competitive products and (2) by other products marketed by the company in question.[4] Thus, Avis positioned itself as only No. 2 in rental cars and so must try harder. The Pinto and Vega autos are positioned to compete head on with foreign imports. Marlboro cigarettes, through its "Marlboro Man" image, is aimed at the rugged outdoor type (or, incidentally, anyone who aspires to be that type or women who want to be associated with that type). The goal here is to position a new or modified product so as to maximize profits; that is, without "cannibalizing" sales and profits from the company's other products. The operational problem is to position correctly and not make positioning errors.

For some products (American subcompact cars, for example) the best position is a head-on stance against competition. For other companies that is exactly what *not* to do. Avis became successful only after it stopped positioning itself directly against Hertz and readily admitted it was No. 2. General Electric and RCA abandoned their computer lines after years of unsuccessfully positioning themselves directly against IBM, a firm with a strong position in the field.[5]

Sometimes a strong position can be established by moving into a previously unoccupied niche in the market. This is what Ford did with its Mustang. Also, 7-Up moved ahead on its claim as an Un-Cola, rather than continuing to fight Coca-Cola and Pepsi-Cola directly. Typically a weak position is a "me-too" stance where a product really has no differentiating features from its entrenched competitors. In some markets (gasolines, toilet soaps, cigarettes, floor waxes) real differences are virtually impossible to establish. In these cases special attention to positioning is essential because the task is so difficult.

TRADING UP AND TRADING DOWN

As product strategies, trading up and trading down are intentional attempts to reposition a product, and they also involve an expansion of product line. Normally, a firm will trade up or down, but not both.

Trading up means that a manufacturer or middleman adds a higher-priced,

---

[4]John H. Holmes, "Profitable Product Positioning," *MSU Business Topics,* Spring, 1973, pp. 27–32. Unfortunately, the term "product positioning" has no generally accepted definition, so this important concept in product strategy remains loosely used and difficult to measure.

[5]See Jack Trout, "Positioning Revisited: Why Didn't GE and RCA Listen?" *Industrial Marketing,* November, 1971, p. 116.

prestige product to his line in the hope of increasing his sales of an existing lower-priced product. In the automobile industry, Ford Motor Company introduced the Thunderbird, and Chevrolet marketed the Corvette. Both companies expected their lower-priced cars to benefit from the reflected prestige of the new ones.

When a company embarks upon a policy of trading up, at least two avenues are open with respect to promotional emphasis: (1) Usually the seller continues to depend upon the older, lower-priced product for the bulk of the sales volume, or (2) eventually he may shift the promotional emphasis to the new product and expect it to produce the major share of volume. In fact, the lower-priced line may be dropped altogether after a transition period. Many department stores have followed this policy as they have traded up from their former target of the low-income market to a new, larger middle-income market.

A company is said to be *trading down* when it adds a lower-priced item to its line of prestige products in the hope that people who cannot afford the original product will want to buy the new one, because it carries some of the status of the higher-priced good. Several years ago Buick attempted to broaden its market by introducing four series of cars in an attempt to compete at all price levels.

Trading up and trading down are perilous strategies because the intended goal may not materialize. The new product may simply confuse buyers, so that the net gain is negligible. Nor is any useful purpose served if sales in the new line are generated at the expense of the older product. Trading up or trading down cannot be considered successful unless sales increase in total or the company retains business that would otherwise go to competitive products.

When trading down, the new article may permanently hurt the firm's reputation and its established high-quality product. This situation may be avoided by using differentiating brands, channels of distribution, promotional programs, or product design.

When trading up, the seller's major problem is to change his image enough so that the market will accept his new, higher-priced, higher-quality product. To illustrate, many women will never believe that they can buy good-quality, high-fashion clothing in women's ready-to-wear chain stores. Through the years these stores have projected a corporate image or personality which connotes low-priced merchandise. Until that image is changed, attempts at trading up will be unsuccessful, no matter how good the products may really be.

PRODUCT DIFFERENTIATION AND MARKET SEGMENTATION

These two concepts were introduced in Chapter 3 in connection with identifying and analyzing markets. Product differentiation and market segmentation also are two related *product strategies* which may be employed by firms who wish to engage in nonprice competition in markets characterized by imperfect or monopolistic competition.[6] These strategies usually require a considerable amount of advertising and other kinds of promotional effort. Consequently, they are often regarded as both promotional and product-planning strategies.

As a product strategy, *product differentiation* involves developing and promoting an awareness of differences between the advertiser's product and the products

---

[6]Much of this section is based on a penetrating analysis of these strategies by Wendell R. Smith. See his "Product Differentiation and Market Segmentation as Alternative Marketing Strategies," *Journal of Marketing,* July, 1956, pp. 3–8.

of competitors. The strategy is used to enable a business to remove itself from price competition so that it can compete on the nonprice basis that its product is different from, and better than, competitive models. Sometimes a company will differentiate the quality or design of the product, or the only differentiation may be in the brand or packaging. Frequently two products are virtually identical in a physical and chemical sense. The difference between them is trivial and sometimes only psychological. This strategy is frequently used by companies selling reasonably standardized products, such as soaps, cigarettes, and gasoline, to a broad horizontal market which is fairly homogeneous in its wants for the given item.

In terms familiar in economic theory, the seller assumes in a general sense that there is a single demand curve for his product. Any variations in the wants of individual consumers will be minimized by extensive advertising and sales promotion emphasizing the product's broad market appeal. Essentially, as Wendell R. Smith has said, " . . . product *differentiation* is concerned with the bending of demand to the will of supply."

Inexorable market pressures are working against the seller who attempts to expand his market by using the strategy of product differentiation. The broader the market, the more difficult it becomes to fit all consumers' wants to the single product. Competition is felt to an increasing extent. Any one of these alternative products is apt to satisfy more precisely the wants of some group in this broadening range of consumers. Our seller must resort to increased promotional expenditures or reduced prices, or both, in his attempts to offset the variations in consumer preference, that is, in his attempts to fit more consumers in that single demand curve.[7]

In employing the strategy of *market segmentation,* a seller recognizes that his total heterogeneous market is made up of many, smaller homogeneous units. Each of these smaller units has a different set of wants, motivations, and other characteristics. He sees his market as a *series* of demand curves rather than the *single* curve considered above in product differentiation. The seller then attempts to develop different products, each one specifically for one or more of these market units. Tailor-made products are extreme examples of this strategy in action. As one marketing executive said, "Proper market segmentation represents the ultimate extension of the marketing concept. It not only starts with consumers and what they want, but it recognizes the fact that not all people are alike and that one man's *mousse au chocolat* is another man's plain chocolate pudding."[8]

Market segmentation has been employed for years in the field of industrial products, where it is quite common to make products according to buyers' specifications. The strategy is also being used to an increasing extent in the consumer market. Some of the specific benefits derived from market segmentation were discussed in Chapter 3. In that same discussion we recognized the problems of

---

[7]For an analysis of the issue of whether product differentiation in the auto industry, through annual style changes and heavy promotion, has transformed a competitive industry into a noncompetitive oligopoly, see H. Paul Root, "Should Product Differentiation Be Restricted?" *Journal of Marketing,* July, 1972, pp. 3–9.

[8]Russell I. Haley, "The Implications of Market Segmentation," *Conference Board Record,* March, 1969, pp. 43–47; quotation on p. 43.

For a report on how some firms treat a market segment of over twenty million consumers —namely, left-handed people—see "Left-handed Compliment," *Sales Management,* Sept. 1, 1969, pp. 34–36.

(1) identifying measurable market segments, which (2) are large enough to be potentially profitable, and which (3) are accessible within reasonable limits of promotion and distribution selectivity. Some useful bases (demographic, psychological, and sociological) for segmenting a market also were identified in Chapters 3, 4, and 5.

Market segmentation attempts to penetrate a limited market in *depth,* whereas product differentiation seeks *breadth* in a more generalized market. Smith says, "The differentiator seeks to secure a layer of the market cake, whereas one who employs market segmentation strives to secure one or more wedge-shaped pieces."

A firm may first employ the strategy of market segmentation, but soon be forced by competition to combine it with product differentiation. A firm that makes electric razors may divide the market into two groups—men and women—and then develop separate products to meet the specific wants of each group. Eventually the women's market will be recognized as a separate market by many firms, each of which will bring out an electric razor for women. Soon all these sellers will resort to differentiation to maintain a separate identity. Thus any given segmentation of markets is a transitory phenomenon, and competitive conditions force a seller constantly to seek new ways of segmenting his market.[9]

Some of the reasons for the emergence of market segmentation as a formally recognized strategy follow:

1. There has been a decrease in the minimum size of the efficient manufacturing unit for many products; thus production runs of identical items need not be so long as in the past.
2. Self-service and similar cost-cutting techniques require that products be better adjusted to demand.
3. Increases in discretionary purchasing power result in more careful shopping; the customer is willing to pay a little more to get just what he wants.
4. A marketer of multiple products fears that one of his brands may draw sales from another of his products, if they are both aimed at the same market.
5. Market segmentation becomes necessary for growth after promotion on a generalized basis to a broad market reaches a point of diminishing returns; that is, a broad-based promotional appeal to a wide market has a weaker effect than a narrower appeal zeroed in on one market segment.

FACTORS INFLUENCING CHANGES IN PRODUCT MIX

A marketing executive who wishes to use his product mix strategically in the market should understand the main factors underlying a company's desire to expand or simplify its line.

CHANGES IN MARKET DEMAND

Consumer population and industrial users. A major change in a component of population may induce a firm to change its product mix. As birthrates declined in

---

[9]See Walter P. Margulies, "Creative Ways of Segmenting Markets to Divide and Conquer," *Marketing Insights,* Oct. 21, 1968, pp. 20–21.

the 1960s, the Gerber Products Company—producer of baby foods—added a line of other baby products (bibs, crib sheets, socks, shirts, and waterproof pants) for distribution through supermarkets, along with its food lines. The growth in suburban population led furniture manufacturers to expand into patio and lawn furniture and encouraged other businesses to develop residential-sized power lawn mowers.

In the industrial market, the mobility of customers may force a company to drop some lines and add others to take up the slack. Many plants have moved from New England to the South. Industries formerly serving these New England factories cannot continue to do so, in part because excessive transportation rates give Southern suppliers a favorable cost differential. Hence the New England firms must look for new products and new markets.

Buying power. Increases in purchasing power have played a significant role in leading several firms to raise the quality of their merchandise. No doubt this is one reason why Evinrude and other manufacturers of outboard motors have added larger motors to their lines.

Oddly enough, products are sometimes dropped because of an increase in purchasing power. In the past two decades, people have become able to afford better merchandise, and the market for low-priced, low-quality goods has declined considerably.

Customer behavior. Several situations involving customer motivation, attitudes, preferences, and buying habits will encourage a marketing executive to expand or contract his product mix. In the first place, he will add products in order to satisfy ultimate consumers or industrial users who want a more complete line. As household consumers have made it evident that they prefer the convenience of one-stop shopping, supermarkets have broadened their mix by adding magazines, health and beauty aids, small housewares, staple clothing, and many other nonfood lines.

Sometimes the impetus for a change in product mix comes from middlemen who prefer a more complete line, for competitive, cost, or promotional reasons. A Colorado manufacturer of a glass-cleaning compound found that when he added other cleaning and polishing products to his line, wholesalers were much more eager to work with him.

The increase in the leisure-time market was undoubtedly a major factor in prompting the Chrysler Corporation to add a line of small pleasure boats and later to add the Volvo inboard-outboard drive engine. The consumer's demand for convenience helped to spark the market for battery-powered, cordless electric appliances such as razors, carving knives, mixers, and vacuum cleaners.

COMPETITIVE ACTIONS AND REACTIONS

In order to meet competition more effectively, a firm may want to differentiate its product line so that price comparisons will not be possible. In other instances a manufacturer may want to diversify his product line so as to free himself somewhat from a bitterly competitive situation in which his profit margins are dangerously low. The plywood industry is a good example of one in which price competition is prevalent and differentiation of the basic product is difficult. Some of the larger firms—United States Plywood Company, for instance—have added other products to their mix, such as a variety of finished interior paneling and adhesives. In the same industry and for the same reasons, the Weyerhaeuser Company has diversified into many fields including packaging products, paper, and molded fiber doors.

A "follow-the-leader" policy often seems to prevail in industry. It is difficult to know whether this "me-tooism" is based on sound marketing analysis or whether it stems from a belief that "if those other fellows are doing it, maybe we should try it too; they usually know what they are doing." Of course, if one firm enters a market with a new product that holds promise of being successful, other companies are almost forced to meet this competition. After the success enjoyed by early manufacturers of metal skis, many competitive firms felt they had to add this product to their lines. Later, similar experiences were observed with respect to fiberglass skis.

MARKETING INFLUENCES

Two major reasons for adding products are (1) to increase sales by tapping new markets or expanding present ones and (2) to use the firm's marketing capacity more efficiently by a better use of salesmen or warehouses. Adding 10 percent more products usually results in less than a 10 percent increase in salesmen's salaries and traveling expenses, marketing research expenses, and other marketing costs.

Of course, in some cases a firm can increase its marketing effectiveness by simplifying its line. The salesmen may be spreading themselves too thinly over the market, or warehouse space may be taken up by slow-moving items. With the elimination of some products, salesmen can concentrate on fewer items and sell them properly.

PRODUCTION INFLUENCES

A manufacturer often wishes to change his product mix in order to use his manufacturing capacity more effectively and thus lower his net production costs. Here it is assumed that the firm is producing at a level of output such that if there were an increase in output, using the present facilities, the result would be a reduction in unit cost. Product additions also occur when a firm wishes to use an item whose manufacture elsewhere has been discontinued.

Product mix may be expanded in order to put by-products to better use. A classic example is found in the meat-packing industry, where by-products have resulted in the production of fertilizer, glue, soap, leather products, and many other items. Several firms have developed new products by using wood scraps.

FINANCIAL INFLUENCES

There are several financial reasons why a business enterprise may wish to change its product mix. One is to enable the firm to generally diversify its financial risks. Any one of several factors, such as a new competitive product or a change in a component of demand, can obsolete a given product. Hence from a financial standpoint, it is wise to spread risks among several products.

Expanding the product mix can help to increase a firm's profitable sales volume.

Supermarkets, for example, have added several nonfood items to their lines; these items ordinarily bring a significantly higher margin than the 15 to 18 percent gross margin typical for the store as a whole. A full line can also help smooth out the seasonal fluctuations in sales volume. The classic example in days gone by was the iceman who added coal to his product mix in the winter.

A full line of products can make a manufacturer's product-servicing organization financially feasible. It is not economical to maintain a service organization, as many appliance manufacturers do, unless there are several products over which the costs can be spread.

A firm may hope to cushion recessions by product diversification. A company with one major product or market is like a town with one industry. Manufacturers who sell virtually all their output to the government, or to a firm with government contracts, are particularly susceptible to losses caused by unrenewed contracts.

Financial considerations may encourage a company to *simplify* its line. Sometimes a few items require so much capital investment in production or inventory facilities that the value of these products to the company can be questioned. By dropping slow-moving items, such as extremely large or extremely small shoe sizes, a manufacturer or middleman may experience a small decline in sales but a substantial decrease in cost. Such a change might result in longer and thus lower-cost production runs, less chance of mistakes in filling and shipping orders, lower insurance and investment costs on inventory, and curtailed losses from obsolescence.

DESIRE TO CHANGE COMPANY IMAGE

Changing the product mix in an attempt to alter the firm's image is related to the strategy of trading up or trading down. Variety chains have added so many higher-quality, higher-priced, non-variety-store items to their mix that today they often are small department stores, a far cry from the "five-and-ten-cent store." Of course, the desire to upgrade a store's image involves more than the emotional factor of management's own self-concept. There are sound, rational business reasons at play: The low-income market is not so big today as it was twenty-five years ago, but the middle-income group is a prime target.

CONCEPT OF THE PRODUCT LIFE CYCLE

Products, like people, have life cycles. From its birth to its death, a product exists in different stages and in different competitive environments. Its adjustment to these environments determines to a great degree just how successful its life will be. One set of product strategies employed by many firms is built around the understanding and management of the life cycles of their products. To better manage the cycle, it is useful to divide a product's life into six stages—introduction, growth, maturity, saturation, decline, and abandonment.

The length of the life cycle varies among products, ranging from a few weeks or a short season (a fad or an apparel fashion) to several decades (autos, telephones). The shape of the sales and profit curves may vary somewhat among products, although the basic shape and the relationship between the two curves are usually about the same as pictured in Fig. 8-1. Even the duration of each stage may be different among products; some take years to pass through the introductory stage, while others are accepted in a few weeks.[10] Certainly not all companies' products go through all stages. Some may fail in the introductory stage, and other firms may not enter with their brand until the market is in the growth or maturity stage. In virtually all cases, however, decline and possible abandonment are inevitable because (1) the need for the product disappears (as when frozen orange juice generally replaced juice squeezers); (2) a better or less expensive product is developed to fill the same need (plastics are replacing wood, metal, and paper in many products); or (3) a competitor does a superior marketing job.

MARKETING AND ENVIRONMENTAL CHARACTERISTICS OF EACH STAGE

It is quite important that management recognize what part of the life cycle its product is in at any given time because the competitive environment and the resultant marketing programs will ordinarily differ depending upon the stage. A brief summary of the competitive environment and some of the marketing reactions which typify each stage may be useful here.

Introduction. During the first stage of a product's life cycle, it is launched into the market in a full-scale production and marketing program. It has gone through the embryonic stages of idea screening, pilot models, and test marketing. The entire product may be new, as in the case of a machine which cleans clothes electronically without using any water. Or the basic product may be well known, but a new feature or accessory is in the introductory stage—a gas turbine engine in an automobile, for example. In still another situation, a product may be well accepted in some market segments, but be in the pioneering stage in other markets. Introductory promotion was needed (and in many cases still is) to sell automatic dishwashers to housewives, air travel to old folks, and home freezers to consumers long after these products and services were well accepted in some markets.

In many respects, the pioneering stage is the most risky and expensive one, as witness the high percentage of product failures in this period, even among firms with a reasonably successful history of new-product introductions. Operations in the introductory period are characterized by high costs, low sales volume, and limited distribution. For really new products, there is very little direct competition. The promotional program stimulates primary, rather than secondary, demand. That is, the type of product rather than the seller's brand is emphasized.

Growth. In the growth, or market-acceptance, stage, both the sales and the profit curves rise, often at a rapid rate. Competitors enter the market, and in large numbers if the profit outlook is particularly attractive. Sellers shift to "buy-my-brand" rather than "try-my-product" promotional strategy. The number of distribution outlets increases, economies of scale are introduced, and prices may come down a bit.

Maturity and saturation. Sometimes it is difficult to tell whether we are dealing with two separate stages or simply separate parts of one stage. During the first

[10]For the quantitative measurement of product life cycles, see William E. Cox, Jr., "Product Life Cycles as Marketing Models," *Journal of Business,* October, 1967, pp. 375–384; and Rolando Polli and Victor Cook, "Validity of the Product Life Cycle," *Journal of Business,* October, 1969, pp. 385–400.

part of the period, we see sales still increasing but at a decreasing rate. While the sales curve is leveling off, the profits of both the manufacturer and the retailers are starting to decline. Marginal producers are forced to drop out of the market. Price competition becomes increasingly severe, and the producer assumes a greater share of the total promotional effort as he fights to retain his dealers and the shelf space in their stores. New models are introduced as manufacturers broaden their lines, and trade-in sales become significant.

As the market reaches the saturation stage, each of the characteristics described in the preceding paragraph is intensified. Replacement sales become a major factor, and the sales curve will react to changes in economic conditions. Good middlemen become particularly important.

Decline and possible abandonment. For virtually all products, obsolescence sets in inevitably as new products start their own life cycles and replace the old ones. Cost control becomes increasingly important as demand drops. Advertising declines, and a number of competitors withdraw from the market. Whether the product has to be abandoned or the surviving sellers can continue on a profitable basis in a specialized, limited market often depends upon management's abilities.[11]

MANAGEMENT OF THE PRODUCT LIFE CYCLE

The shape of a product's sales and profit curves is not inevitable in a company; to a surprising extent, the shape can be controlled.[12] One key to life cycle management is to forecast the profile of the proposed product's cycle even before it is introduced. Then at each stage management should anticipate the marketing requirements of the following stage. The introductory period, for instance, may be shortened by concentrating on broadening the distribution or by increasing the promotional effort. A product's life can be extended in the maturity and saturation stages by revitalizing it through new packaging, repricing, or product modifications. The makers of nylon, Jell-O, and Scotch tape—as an illustration—all have employed four different strategies to expand sales: (1) increase frequency of the product's use, (2) develop more varied use of the product, (3) attract new users, and (4) find new uses for the product.

Perhaps it is in the sales-decline stage that a company finds its greatest challenges in life cycle management. At some point in the product's life, management may have to consider whether to abandon it. The costs of carrying profitless products go beyond the uncovered direct or indirect expenses which are found on financial statements. The real burdens are the insidious costs accruing from the managerial time and effort which are diverted to sick products instead of

---

[11]For the idea that within the decline stage of some products there is a *product petrification stage* during which sales level off, costs are low, and profits actually increase, see George C. Michael, "Product Petrification: A New Stage in the Life Cycle Theory," *California Management Review,* Fall, 1971, pp. 88–91.

[12]See, for example, Theodore Levitt, "Exploit the Product Life Cycle," *Harvard Business Review,* November–December, 1965, pp. 81–94; also see Harry H. Elwell, Jr., "Exploiting the Product Life Cycle—Revisited," *Southern Journal of Business,* January, 1971, pp. 54–63; and John E. Smallwood, "The Product Life Cycle: A Key to Strategic Marketing Planning," *MSU Business Topics,* Winter, 1973, pp. 29–35.

being applied to the healthy ones. Unfortunately, management often seems reluctant to discard a product, either for emotional and sentimental reasons or because they rationalize that they need the item to round out the product line, or that the decline is temporary and they will soon hit the jackpot.

When sales are declining, management has these alternatives:

1. Improve the product in a functional sense or revitalize it in some manner.
2. Review the marketing and production programs to make sure they are as efficient as possible.
3. Streamline the product assortment by pruning out unprofitable sizes, colors, and models. Frequently, this tactic will *decrease* sales and *increase* profits.
4. "Run out" the product; that is, cut all costs to the bare-minimum level that will optimize profitability over the limited remaining life of the product.
5. Abandon the product.

Knowing when and how to abandon products successfully may be as important as knowing when and how to introduce new ones. Certainly management should develop a systematic procedure for phasing out its weak products.[13]

PLANNED OBSOLESCENCE AND FASHION

As a marketing device, obsolescence has not lost its place in our economy. Apparently the roots of our quest for the "new" are deep: our desire to escape boredom, the psychology of a highly mobile population, our love of the frontier, and our belief in progress. Changes cannot be radical, however. The market wants newness, but still it wants to be moved gently out of its habitual patterns, not shocked out of them. Consequently, many manufacturers have developed the product strategy of planned obsolescence.

NATURE OF PLANNED OBSOLESCENCE

The economic and social aspects of planned obsolescence have been discussed at length and usually with much emotion. Although often there is no clear agreement on what planned obsolescence involves or how it should be defined, there does seem to be general agreement on its object. It is intended to make a product out-of-date and thus to increase the replacement market.

Planned obsolescence has been interpreted in a number of ways:

1. Technological, or functional, obsolescence. Under this interpretation, significant improvements as measured by technical standards have been made. When an automobile manufacturer installed power steering and automatic transmis-

---

[13]For approaches to the pruning-out process, see R. S. Alexander, "The Death and Burial of 'Sick' Products," *Journal of Marketing,* April, 1964, pp. 1–7; Conrad Berenson, "Pruning the Product Line," *Business Horizons,* Summer, 1963, pp. 63–70; and Philip Kotler, "Phasing out Weak Products," *Harvard Business Review,* March–April, 1965, pp. 107–118; also see James T. Rothe, "The Product Elimination Decision," *MSU Business Topics,* Autumn, 1970, pp. 45–52; and Paul W. Hamelman and Edward M. Mazze, "Improving Product Abandonment Decisions," *Journal of Marketing,* April, 1972, pp. 20–26.

sions, these changes created functional, or technological, obsolescence with respect to earlier models.

2. Postponed obsolescence. Technological improvements are not introduced until the market demand for present models decreases, and a new market stimulus is needed.

3. Intentionally designed physical obsolescence. A product is designed to wear out physically within a reasonably short period of time. Obviously this is a dangerous strategy because a firm may acquire a reputation for shoddy merchandise. Durability is still a significant buying motive.

4. Style obsolescence. This is sometimes called "psychological" or "fashion" obsolescence. The intent is to make a person feel out-of-date if he continues to use an old model. Superficial characteristics of the product are altered so that the new model is easily differentiated from last year's model.

When a person criticizes planned obsolescence, he is usually referring to this last interpretation—style obsolescence. In our discussion, planned obsolescence will mean style obsolescence only, unless otherwise stated.

NATURE OF STYLE AND FASHION

Although style and fashion are often used interchangeably with respect to planned obsolescence, there is a clear distinction between the two. *Webster's* defines a *style* as a "distinctive or characteristic mode of presentation, construction, or execution in any art, employment, or product, especially in any fine art; also, distinctive manner or mode of singing, playing, behaving, etc." Thus we can have several styles in many different products. There are styles in automobiles (sedans, convertibles, station wagons) and in bathing suits (one-piece suits, swimming trunks, bikinis). Early American and French Provincial are furniture styles, and Gothic and Italian Renaissance are architectural styles.

A *fashion* is any style which is popularly accepted and purchased by several successive groups of people over a reasonably long period of time. "A fashion is always based on some particular style. But not every style is a fashion. . . . A style does not become a fashion until it gains some popular use, and it remains a fashion only so long as it is so accepted."[14]

A *fad* normally does not remain popular so long as a fashion, and it is based on some novelty feature.

A student of fashion should recognize its separate identity, its importance, and its pervasiveness in all societies. Fashion is really a field by itself. It is not simply a factor affecting buying patterns in the consumer market, and it is not merely a product strategy. Fashion is the pursuit of the "new" for its own sake. While basic styles never change, fashion is always changing. Fashion is the behavioral complex underlying all stylistic innovations, that is, all design changes which are not purely the result of engineering advances. In its broad sense, fashion is the means used by society to innovate, select or reject, and progress.[15]

Style obsolescence is not limited to the fields of women's ready-to-wear and automobiles. It is found in countless commodities, including appliances, motor

---

[14]Paul H. Nystrom, *Fashion Merchandising,* The Ronald Press Company, New York, 1932, p. 33.

[15]John E. Mertes, "Fashion: A Prod toward Progress," *Dimensions,* June, 1970, pp. 12–18.

boats, and bathroom scales. It is also apparent in such different fields as architecture, pedigreed dogs, and music. Fashion is found in all societies, whether they are primitive groups, the great Oriental cultures, or the societies of ancient and medieval Europe.

However, fashions do change more rapidly in our society. The Industrial Revolution and the rise of the common people account for this accelerated rate of change. Industrialization increased the ease with which fashions could be produced and distributed, and the rise of the common people increased the size of the potential market. The power behind fashion shifted from "the aristocracy of rank to the aristocracy of wealth.[16]

ORIGIN OF FASHION

Sapir has said that "fashion is emphatically a historical concept." A fashion must be studied within its historical context and related to prevailing cultures and social norms.

Fashion is also rooted in sociological and psychological factors. Basically, people are conformists. They follow rather strictly the patterns and standards established by the opinion leaders, or tastemakers, in their groups. At the same time, people yearn to look, act, and be a little different from others. They are not in revolt against custom. They simply wish to deviate a bit and still not be accused of bad taste or insensitivity to the code. Fashion discreetly furnishes them the opportunity for self-expression because "fashion is custom in the guise of departure from custom."

Stanley Marcus, president of Neiman-Marcus, the high-fashion women's store in Dallas, Texas, observed[17]

> If, for example, a dictator decreed feminine clothes to be illegal and that all women should wear barrels, it would not result in an era of uniformity, in my opinion. Very shortly, I think you'd find that one ingenious woman would color her barrel with a lipstick, another would pin paper lace doilies on the front of hers, and still another would decorate hers with thumb-tacks. Other women would emulate the examples they liked the best until a bare barrel would be unique. *This is a strange human urge toward conformity, but a dislike for complete uniformity.* [Italics supplied.]

Another socio-psychological factor underlying the growth of fashion in sophisticated societies such as ours is boredom. This is fostered by leisure time and highly specialized forms of activity, and it leads to restlessness and curiosity. In an attempt to break the monotony, people seek change.

Along with the desire to break a little from a regularized conforming existence, there is a corollary factor involving a person's ego. Most people want to add to their personal attractiveness, or to any object of their love or friendship. This ego-building consideration is also expressed in the desire to attract favorable attention and in the desire for prestige or even notoriety.

---

[16]Edward Sapir, "Fashion," *The Encyclopedia of Social Sciences,* The Macmillan Company, New York, 1931, vol. VI, pp. 139–144. Much of the following section on the origin of fashion is drawn from this article.

[17]Stanley Marcus, "Fashion Merchandising," A Tobe ́ lecture on retail distribution delivered at the Harvard Graduate School of Business Administration, Cambridge, Mass., Mar. 10, 1959, pp. 4–5.

WHY YOU WEAR WHAT YOU DO:
UNDERSTANDING THE PSYCHOLOGY OF FASHION

On blue Monday, Linda wore a pale yellow mini dress to work. Tuesday, the 23-year-old management trainee showed up at the departmental meeting in a knee-length, gray, pin-striped shirtwaist with white cuffs and collar. She'd planned to wear another dress on Wednesday, but the rain made her change to a denim smock top and cotton slacks. On the way home, Linda stopped at the dry cleaners to pick up the flowered silk palazzo outfit she planned to wear to the theater on Saturday; and later, she changed into a pair of comfortable jeans, tank top, and floppy suede hat for an informal supper party. Linda doesn't know it, but her clothes are talking — about her.

"Linda obviously has a rich personality and a good self-image," says Jean Rosenbaum, M.D., a Colorado psychiatrist. "She's flexible and has options in her social situations. She takes advantage of the dress options available to her."

Clothes say a lot about Linda — just as they do of everyone. Clothes are a deeply felt, deeply needed, strongly motivated psychological statement — an expression of self. In what people wear and don't wear, in how they wear what they do, in what they do to make their clothes seem unique while still remaining safely part of the group, people are telling the world what they think of themselves.

"We have an image of ourselves, of our bodies. Our clothing is an extension of this image." . . .

The clothes hog — the lady with 60 pairs of shoes in her closet, the man who throws out his old wardrobe and buys everything new when a fashion change is announced — thinks his or her individual personality is worthless, says the doctor. This person has to depend on others for a sense of identity, and could be suffering from hidden depression. "But no matter what this person does, no matter how many hats or purses or suits he or she buys, the bad self-feeling remains." The opposite, on the other hand, is not necessarily the sign of a good self-image. The person who refuses to buy new clothes and continues to wear the noticeably out-of-date, tattered clothing of years back is demonstrating a personal rigidity and inflexibility.

Source: Liz Smith, "Why You Wear What You Do," *Today's Health* (published by the American Medical Association), October, 1973, pp. 36, 38.

FASHION-ADOPTION PROCESS

The concepts of (1) large-group and small-group influences on consumer buying behavior and (2) the diffusion of innovation, as discussed in Chapter 5 may be applied to the fashion-adoption process. We observed that people usually seek to emulate others in the same social or economic stratum, or those on the next higher level. Consequently, in fashion adoption the scene is set for successive waves of purchases, as a given style is popularly accepted throughout a group until it finally falls out of fashion. This wavelike movement, representing the introduction, rise, popular culmination, and decline of the market's acceptance of a style, is referred to as the "fashion cycle."[18] Like an ocean wave, the fashion cycle builds up slowly, but declines rapidly once its crest is reached.

Somewhat conflicting theories exist regarding whether a given fashion cycle flows *vertically* through several socioeconomic strata, or moves *horizontally* and *simultaneously* within several strata. These theories of fashion adoption have been called, respectively, the "trickle-down" and the "trickle-across" processes.

Traditionally, the trickle-down theory has been used as the basic model to explain the fashion-adoption process. For example, designers of women's apparel first introduce a style to the leaders in a group—the tastemakers. Usually these people are social leaders and are in the upper-income brackets. If they accept the style, it will quickly appear in leading fashion stores. Soon the middle-income and then the lower-income markets will want to emulate the leaders, and the product will be mass-marketed. As its popularity wanes, the style will appear in bargain-price stores and finally will no longer be considered fashionable.

To illustrate the trickle-across process, let us again use the example of women's apparel. Within a few days or a few weeks at the most, at the beginning of the fall season, the same style of dresses will appear (1) in small, exclusive dress shops appealing to the upper social class, (2) in large department stores appealing to the middle social class, and (3) in discount houses and low-priced women's ready-to-wear chain stores, where the appeal is to the upper-lower social class. Price, quality, and materials mark the differences in the dresses sold on the three levels—the style is basically the same. *Within each class* the dresses are purchased early in the season by the opinion leaders—the innovators. If the style is accepted, its sales curve will rise as it becomes popular with the early adopters, and then with the late adopters. Eventually the sales decline as the style ceases to be popular. This cycle or flow is a horizontal movement occurring virtually simultaneously within each of several social strata.

Students of fashion marketing are beginning to question whether the trickle-down theory accurately reflects the contemporary adoption process.[19] While granting the existence of some vertical flow, they hypothesize that several market factors today would seem to impede the trickle-down adoption process while at the same time fostering a horizontal flow. Today a much larger segment of the total population can afford to purchase fashion merchandise. By means of modern production processes, communications systems, and transportation methods, we can disseminate style information and products so rapidly that all social strata can be reached at about the same time. In the apparel field, particularly, the fashion industry's manufacturing and marketing programs also tend to foster the horizon-

---

[18]As Nystrom observed, "The popular use of the term [fashion cycle] unfortunately may be both confusing and misleading. Cycle literally means circle and as applied to fashion suggests starting with some style, moving away from it and finally coming back to the same style again. Nothing like this is meant by the term 'fashion cycle' here. . . . The fashion cycle is simply the forward wavelike movement completed and involves no necessary repetition of the style." *Economics of Fashion,* The Ronald Press Company, New York, 1928, p. 18.

[19]See, for example, Charles W. King, "Fashion Adoption: A Rebuttal to the 'Trickle Down' Theory," in Stephen A. Greyser (ed.), *Toward Scientific Marketing,* American Marketing Association, Chicago, 1964, pp. 108–125. The trickle-across theory is also compatible with the small-group research findings of Katz and Lazarsfeld, as noted in Chap. 5, where the *horizontal* nature of opinion leadership was identified.

tal movement of the fashion cycle. Manufacturers produce a wide *variety* of essentially one style. They also produce various *qualities* of the same basic style so as to appeal to different income groups simultaneously. Retailers, in turn, introduce that same basic style simultaneously at different price levels, thus reaching several social strata concurrently. When an entire cycle may last only one short season, a seller cannot afford to wait for the style acceptance to trickle down; he must introduce it into many social levels as soon as possible.

The length of the fashion-adoption cycle may vary considerably from one product to another, although in general the cycle for any given product is shorter today than it was years ago. A style in houses or furniture may remain fashionable for many years, whereas styles in women's hats or shoes may be in fashion for only one season. This does not mean that all parts of the national market accept a style with the same rapidity and eagerness. It may reach a given point in its fashion cycle a year later in Denver than in New York, and it may never be accepted as a fashion in rural communities.

Three basic elements in fashion theory may help to explain why fashions move as they do.[20] First, all styles build up to a point of excess. The overriding responsibility of a fashion designer is the unending provision of novelty. He must keep adding various frills to a basic style in order to give it a continuing semblance of newness so that it will appeal to the market. Thus in the Victorian era so much gingerbread was added to houses and furniture that they became style monstrosities, and the market rebelled. The styles which took over were noted for their stark, functional simplicity. In the 1960s there were indications that some people were preferring a little more decoration and adornment on their furniture and houses. Thus the currently fashionable styles in housing and furniture are already moving from the stage of simplicity toward their inevitable end of complexity and excess.

The second consideration is that the designer must shift the consumers' attention from one feature of a style to another as the style is running its fashion course. Thus as the women's clothing style epitomized by the miniskirt (the "young look") progressed through its fashion cycle, attention was drawn at one time to hemlines, while at other times emphasis shifted to hosiery, shoes, and jewelry.

The third principle of fashion concerns the rapid demise of a given cycle. "A fashion can never retreat gradually and in good order. Like a dictator it must always expand its aggressions—or collapse. Old fashions never just fade away—they die suddenly and arbitrarily."[21] Once a style is sold in large quantities (the economic emulation stage of the fashion cycle), it no longer appeals to fashion leaders who desire distinctiveness. Once the tastemakers begin to seek another style, the emulators rebel against the first, and it collapses as a fashion.

MARKETING CONSIDERATIONS IN FASHION

Management must recognize the stage a fashion cycle is in at any particular time. They must decide at what market they are aiming, at what point they want to get into the cycle, and when they should get out. Ordinarily, a retailer cannot successfully participate in all stages of the fashion cycle at the same time. A high-grade specialty store in women's apparel—whose stocks are displayed discreetly in limited num-

---

[20]Dwight E. Robinson, "Fashion Theory and Product Design," *Harvard Business Review,* November–December, 1958, pp. 121–138.
[21]*Ibid.,* p. 128.

ANOTHER "LAW OF FASHION"

The same dress is indecent 10 years before its time, daring 1 year before its time, chic in its time, dowdy 3 years after its time, hideous 20 years after its time, amusing 30 years after its time, romantic 100 years after its time, and beautiful 150 years after its time.

Source: James Laver, British costume historian, in *Today's Health,* October, 1973, p. 69.

bers without price tags—will want to get in at the start of a fashion trend. A department store appealing to the middle-income market will plan to enter the cycle in time to mass-market the style as it is climbing to its peak of popularity.

A seller—manufacturer or retailer—who typically enters a fashion cycle at its beginning will find that his ability to identify and communicate with the early buyers in any group is one major key to successful fashion marketing. These innovators are often quite influential, serving as opinion leaders, in their social structure. As indicated in Chapter 5, these acceptors of newness do constitute a unique market segment which can be differentiated from other segments.

A manufacturer's product and distribution policies will also be related to the fashion cycle. If he wishes to project an image of distinctiveness, he will produce only a few units of each model. They will be relatively expensive and will be distributed through a limited number of high-grade stores. If he produces low-cost products with inexpensive materials, he must market them through low-quality stores active in the declining stage of the cycle.

To a great extent, success in fashion merchandising lies in the seller's sense of timing. He must not enter the cycle too early or leave it too late. For example, in a mass fashion market, a manufacturer or a middleman who waits until the style reaches its peak of popularity and then produces or stocks it is apt to be left with a large quantity on hand after the downswing starts.

Accurate forecasting is, therefore, of inestimable value in achieving success in fashion merchandising. This is an extremely difficult task, however, because the forecaster is often dealing with complex sociological and psychological factors. Frequently a retailer or a manufacturer operates largely on intuition and inspiration, tempered by considerable experience. Of course, the earlier the stage of the fashion cycle in which a firm participates, the tougher the forecasting job.[22]

FUTURE OF PLANNED OBSOLESCENCE

If someone asks whether obsolescence of any kind is losing its hold on the American market, the answer is a definite "no." Our interest in something new is still strong, and the economy thrives on replacement demand. If the question is whether planned or style obsolescence is diminishing in favor, however, the ans-

---

[22]For the suggestion that fashion trends are easy to detect, see William H. Reynolds, "Cars and Clothing: Understanding Fashion Trends," *Journal of Marketing,* July, 1968, pp. 44–49. For a similar suggestion that a framework built on known aspects of individual and social psychology already exists for predicting the timing and direction of movements in a fashion example, see Chester R. Wasson, "How Predictable Are Fashions and Other Product Life Cycles?" *Journal of Marketing,* July, 1968, pp. 36–43.

wer is a qualified "yes." For instance, planned obsolescence seems to be decreasing in popularity in both the automobile and major appliance industries. On several makes of automobiles, major design changes are no longer introduced every year or even every second or third year.

If planned obsolescence is declining in some fields, then what will take its place? The answer seems to be that technological change will become increasingly important. Increased leisure time, higher discretionary income, and improved communications have opened up new fields to consumers. They still want newness, and they still have the psychological drives that lead to fashion changes. The difference is that they now seek new kinds of products rather than model variations of the same product. They can better satisfy their egoistic demands with a new boat or swimming pool (new product) than with a new car (new model of old product). The consumer is also more discriminating. Finally, people have accumulated considerable quantities of tangible goods, thus socially establishing their ability to buy. As former status symbols lose their prestige, consumers find it fashionable to spend money for travel and other educational and cultural pursuits.

Of course, as technological obsolescence supersedes the emphasis on style and fashion, several marketing problems will arise. Technological obsolescence is expensive and difficult to plan. Product-development costs will increase, and greater burdens will be thrust on marketing research to ensure that the company is making sound marketing decisions. Designers cannot be ordered to "invent on schedule." This means that there may be years when a firm has nothing really new to sell. Technological change may require more advertising than style change does. Technological improvements often are difficult to explain, and they will require new thinking in the advertising and personal selling fields.

EVALUATION OF PLANNED OBSOLESCENCE

Style obsolescence is one of the most controversial aspects of modern marketing. As is true of most social complaints against marketing, much of the criticism of style obsolescence is neither all true nor all false. One criticism is that fashion designers are dictators (especially in women's ready-to-wear) and people voluntarily follow like sheep to buy whatever the designers decree will be fashionable. This is true only in a very superficial sense. The designers themselves obey many masters. First and foremost, the designs must be profitable to the manufacturers. Thus, behind the psychological determinants of fashion, there is the necessity of considering manufacturing processes and the cost of materials. Also, the designer is controlled by established custom; he cannot depart too far from it. Actually, what he tries to do is to anticipate intuitively what the customers want even before they themselves know. That is, rather than impose fashion, the designer seeks to coax people into accepting what they themselves have unconsciously suggested. Furthermore, a designer just cannot combat a fashion trend established by the social psychology factors noted earlier. No matter how aesthetically pleasing a style may be in the abstract, if it does not fit in with a trend it will be a failure.

Professor Sapir, along with other writers, has noted that throughout history there has been both a social and an economic criticism of fashion. Social critics object to fashion—particularly women's ready-to-wear—because it calls attention to the human body. Actually, the criticism is valid. Women's apparel generally is intended to draw attention to the human form. This fits in with human psychology.

People want to be as expressive—even as immodest, perhaps—as society will allow. Fashion helps them to achieve this objective. Regarding the factor of economic waste, whether the criticism is justified or not seems to be somewhat beside the point. "Waste seems to be of no concern where values are to be considered, particularly when these values are both egoistic and unconscious.[23]

Supporters of the strategy of style obsolescence and annual model changes point out that it satisfies the consumers' desire to have something new. It also maintains our economy at a higher level than would be possible if consumers used a product until it wore out physically. Furthermore, people who cannot afford to buy new automobiles or appliances have an opportunity to satisfy their wants for these products by purchasing used models. These would not be available if other consumers had not traded in their older models in order to acquire the latest ones.

Frequently it is difficult to distinguish between technological obsolescence and style obsolescence. Small functional improvements each year may add up to a substantial change over a period of years, but no single change might be said to have created technolgical obsolescence.

Planned obsolescence—both functional and style—is a characteristic of a free and expanding economy. In any economy which is controlled by the state or by cartels, product obsolescence and innovation are apt to take place slowly. In a free economy, in the long run, the consumers' marketplace vote is the controlling factor which determines whether a product stays on the market. As American consumers continue to desire new products and can afford them, and as manufacturers are free to supply them, the result is a flow of new products, which inevitably tends to make obsolete many existing goods.

No matter how marketing people try to answer the social and economic criticisms—and some of the typical answers have been noted above—many people, including businessmen, have a nagging conscience about style obsolescence, and these answers are not sufficiently quieting. Two basic issues seem to keep arising. First, does our prevailing system of style obsolescence make sensible use of our resources and productive capacity? Certainly, antifunctionalism is materialism at its worst. When management is engaged in a policy of style obsolescence, often it has no choice but to make a slight model change in order to make the differentiation apparent to the consumer, even though this is done at the cost of a postponed technological innovation. Frequent model changes increase the manufacturer's production costs and the middlemen's investment in inventory. The second, and related, issue concerns whether the system of planned obsolescence results in an artificially short life for the products which are produced, thus creating some sort of disutility. One cannot help asking why marketing men cannot be just as aggressive with worthwhile appeals and functional innovation as they are with superficial styling and prestige appeals.

After basic decisions have been made concerning the product line and product mix in a company, management may turn its attention to questions of branding, packaging, labeling, color, sizes, and other attributes or characteristics of the products. These topics are covered in the following chapter.

---

[23]Sapir, *op. cit.,* p. 143.

QUESTIONS AND PROBLEMS

1. "It is inconsistent for management to follow concurrently the product-line strategies of *expanding* its product mix and *contracting* its product mix." Discuss.
2. Cite examples of firms that have simplified their product mix in recent years.
3. "Trading up and trading down are product strategies closely related to the business cycle. Firms trade up during periods of prosperity and trade down during depressions or recessions." Do you agree?
4. How might the manufacturers of each of the following articles implement the product strategy of market segmentation? Of product differentiation?
   a. Shoes   *c.* Tape recorders
   b. Paint   *d.* Typewriters
5. Select two of the population trends discussed in Chapter 3 and describe how these two might influence the product mix of consumer goods manufacturers.
6. Name some products which you believe are in the introductory stage of their life cycles. Be sure to identify the market which considers your examples to be new products.
7. Give examples of products which are in the stage of market decline. In each case, point out whether you think the decline is permanent. What recommendations do you have for rejuvenating the demand for the article?
8. How might a company's pricing strategies differ depending upon whether a product is in the pioneering stage or maturity stage of its life cycle?
9. What advertising strategies are apt to be used when a product is in the growth stage?
10. Carefully distinguish between "style" and "fashion," using examples other than the ones (automobiles, swimsuits, furniture, and architecture) cited in this chapter.
11. What products, other than wearing apparel and automobiles, stress fashion and style in marketing? Do styles exist among industrial products?
12. Select a product and trace its marketing as it moves through a complete fashion cycle. Particularly note and explain the changes in the distribution, pricing, and promotion of the product in the various stages of the cycle.
13. What is the relation between fashion and the small-group influence on buying behavior explained in Chapter 5?
14. Is the trickle-across theory applicable in describing the fashion-adoption process in product lines other than women's apparel? Explain, using examples.
15. Planned obsolescence is criticized as a social and economic waste because we are urged to buy things we do not like and do not need. What is your opinion in this matter? If you object to planned obsolescence, what are your recommendations for correcting the situation?

BRANDS, PACKAGING, AND
OTHER PRODUCT FEATURES 10

Have you ever stopped to think why you selected some of the products you are now using? Many industrial plant superintendents insist on Texaco lubricating oils and greases, while others prefer lubricants made by one of the Standard Oil companies. Some women choose Del Monte peaches; others buy Libby's. Yet many people contend that there are no significant differences among the well-known brands of lubricants or canned peaches. The buyer's choice may have been influenced by the guarantee offered or by an attractive package. Frequently the brand, the package, the color and design, and other product characteristics combine to project an image of the product to the prospective consumer.

INFLUENCES OF PRODUCT FEATURES ON BUSINESS FUNCTIONS

Branding, packaging, and the other product features analyzed in this chapter are interrelated with the production and financial functions of a firm as well as with other marketing activities. Production runs will be shorter and thus more costly if goods are manufactured in six colors instead of one. A product made in small units and packaged in an attractive wrapper is ordinarily more costly than one put up in large, bulk-packaged units.

Financial risks increase as the variety of sizes and colors is increased. Packaging products in special Christmas containers exposes a company to a financial loss on merchandise unsold on December 26. A business which offers a generous warranty—double your money back if not entirely satisfied or free servicing for one year—has greater financial risks than a firm which says "all sales are final" and gives no allowances for servicing.

A multitude of interrelationships exist among the various product features and the marketing policies regarding distribution, pricing, and promotion. A few examples will illustrate this point. A firm manufacturing products which will be sold by retailers on a self-service basis must devote special attention to packaging and labeling in order to attract the customer at the point of purchase. Normally, branding increases price rigidity. At the same time, however, well-known brands are most likely to have their prices cut below the usual level to attract customers to the seller's establishment. In some cases a product's label has been redesigned for more effective display on television.

BRANDS

The word "brand" is a comprehensive term, and in one way or another it includes other, more particularized terms. A *brand* is "a name, term, symbol, or design, or a combination of them which is intended to identify the goods or services of one seller or group of sellers and to differentiate them from those of competitors."[1] A brand *name* consists of words, letters, and/or numbers which may be *vocalized.* A brand *mark* is the part of the brand which appears in the form of a symbol, design, or distinctive coloring or lettering. It is recognized by sight but is not expressed when a person pronounces the brand. Tide, Cadillac, and Monsanto are brand names. Brand marks are illustrated by the colonial gentleman on Quaker Oats products and the red star of Texaco petroleum products.

The American Marketing Association defines a *trademark* as a brand which is given legal protection because under the law it has been appropriated exclusively by one seller. Thus "trademark" is essentially a legal term. All trademarks are brands and thus include the words, letters, or numbers which may be pronounced. They may also include a pictorial design (brand mark). Some people erroneously believe that the trademark is only the pictorial part of the brand.

One major method of classifying brands is on the basis of who owns them —producers or middlemen. Chemstrand, Burroughs, Squibb, and Canada Dry are producers' brands, while A & P, Shurfine, Penncrest, Coldspot, and Kenmore are middlemen's brands.

Although the terms "national" and "private" brands have been used to describe producer and middleman ownership, respectively, marketing people prefer the producer-middleman terminology. To say that the brand of a small manufacturer of poultry feed in Birmingham, Alabama, who markets in three states is a national brand, while the brands of A & P or Sears are private brands, seems to be stretching the meaning of the terms "national" and "private."[2]

---

[1]Committee on Definitions, *Marketing Definitions: A Glossary of Marketing Terms,* American Marketing Association, Chicago, 1960, p. 8.

[2]For a proposed new branding language, eliminating the confusion in terminology which has led to communications problems among marketers and to distortion in measurement of trends in manufacturer-owned and distributor-owned brands, see Thomas F. Schutte, "The Semantics of Branding," *Journal of Marketing,* April, 1969, pp. 5–11.

IMPORTANCE TO THE CUSTOMER

Brands are an easy way for a purchaser to identify the product or service he desires. Furthermore, the individual units of a branded item maintain a consistency of quality that buyers can depend upon. A brand also offers some protection to the consumer: it identifies the firm behind the product. A customer may have purchased a fan belt or a few yards of woolen plaid piece goods with which he was greatly pleased. When replacement parts or additional material is needed and the customer wants to get the same product, he can be assured of doing so only if the item is branded. Branding is an insurance of merchandise comparability when the buyer uses more than one source of supply. Westinghouse light bulbs are Westinghouse light bulbs, regardless of where purchased.

Branded products tend to improve in quality over the years. Competition forces this improvement, for brand owners are constantly seeking new ways to differentiate their products in order to secure a stronger market position. In the constant search for more profitable sales volume, product improvements have frequently been the key to success. Improvements may not be perceptible on a year-to-year basis, but a 1975 General Electric flourescent light bulb is noticeably better than one made in 1960.

IMPORTANCE TO THE SELLER

Branding can be used to achieve several of the typical marketing objectives of both manufacturers and middlemen.

To aid in advertising and display programs. Having a brand gives a seller something to advertise—something around which to build a company image. The brand is often of greater help in demand stimulation than the company name or the technical aspects of the product. Not only can brand names or marks denote more to a customer than several lines of advertising copy, but the brand itself can also do it more rapidly. In the case of many manufacturers' brands, the consumer probably does not even know the name of the producer. A firm whose product is sold on a self-service basis ordinarily must rely heavily on brand appeal. The product must be presold through advertising so that it will be recognized and selected by the customer as he walks by the mass of products displayed on shelves.

To help increase control and share of market. A firm which sells unbranded canned tomato juice and advertises and promotes the generic product is helping the whole industry, but is not necessarily increasing its share of the market. By the same token, a retailer who advertises a manufacturer's brand, such as Dutch Boy paints, may stimulate a customer to buy this brand but to buy it in a competitive outlet. Only when a manufacturer or middleman puts his own brand on a product can he be assured of some control over the market. Branding also helps the brand owner to stimulate repeat sales and to protect himself from product substitution. Unless the product has a brand identification, company A has no assurance that a retailer will not substitute a product made by another firm and tell the customer it was made by company A.

To reduce price comparisons and help stabilize prices. A brand in itself differentiates a product and enables the brand owner to establish a price which cannot easily be compared with prices for competing goods. The mere act of branding may create a marketing difference between two items. At the retail level, a store can prevent customers from price-comparison shopping by the expedient of putting its own brand on products instead of using manufacturers' brands. A customer can compare prices on RCA Whirlpool washing machines at several department and appliance stores. Sears, Roebuck and Company avoids this type of competition by placing the Sears' Kenmore brand on its washing machines.

There is little doubt that branding increases a firm's independence in pricing activities. The less desirable alternative for the individual firm is to expose itself to the unrelenting mercies of the market for the determination of its prices. Competition on the basis of price alone may be desirable from a consumer's standpoint, but a seller usually prefers to compete on a nonprice basis. Branding enables the seller to do this to some extent. Price competition is never completely eliminated, of course.

Branding also reduces price flexibility. Several studies have shown that prices of well-known brands tend to fluctuate less than those of nonbranded items or obscure brands. Whether price rigidity is desirable for society in general or for the individual firms involved is open to question.

To facilitate expansion of product mix. If a firm has one or more lines of branded goods, it can add a new item to its product mix much more easily than a company selling unbranded merchandise. If the new item is similar to established products and the same brand can be attached, introduction of the new item is facilitated. Even when a different brand must be affixed, however, it certainly helps to be able to say, "The new product, brand A, is made by the ABC Company, manufacturers of brand Z and other fine products for over fifty years."

REASONS FOR NOT BRANDING

Many firms do not brand their products because they are either unable or unwilling to assume the two major responsibilities inherent in brand ownership: (1) the responsibility for demand stimulation through advertising, personal selling, and other forms of promotion and (2) the responsibility for maintaining an adequate quality of output.

Company considerations. Customer dissatisfaction with the quality of the product purchased will reflect unfavorably on the brand owner. If it is a manufacturer's brand, the customer may seek an immediate remedy from the middleman who sold the item, but the long-run harmful effects are felt by the manufacturer-owner. The customer will hesitate to repurchase not only the item that once proved unsatisfactory but any other product carrying the same brand.

Nature of the product. Some items are not branded because of the difficulty of differentiating the products of one firm from those of another. Clothespins, safety pins, nails, and industrial raw materials (coal, cotton, wheat) are examples of goods for which product differentiation is generally unknown. The physical nature of some items, such as fresh fruits and vegetables, may discourage branding, although now that producers or middlemen are packaging these goods in typically purchased quantities, the brand can be applied to the package.

Producers frequently do not brand that part of their output which is below their regular quality. Products graded as seconds or imperfects are sold at a cut price and are often distributed through channels different from those used for the regular goods.

SELECTING A GOOD BRAND

Selecting a good brand name is one of the most difficult tasks facing marketing management. In spite of the acknowledged importance of a brand, it is surprising how few really good brand names there are. In a study made many years ago, it was found that only 12 percent of the names helped sell the product; 36 percent actually hurt sales, and 52 percent were "nonentities—contributing nothing to the sales appeal of the product."[3] There is no reason to believe that the situation has improved materially since this study was made.

Characteristics of a good brand. Most marketing men would agree that a good brand should possess as many of the characteristics noted below as possible. It is extremely difficult, however, to find a brand which possesses all of them.

In the first place, a brand should suggest something about a product's benefits—its use, characteristics, quality, and action. Furthermore, the name must achieve these objectives without legally being considered descriptive (unfairly appropriating ordinary English words) or deceptive. Examples of names suggesting desirable benefits include Coldspot, Frigidaire (refrigerators and home freezers), Beautyrest, Twindow, and Craftsman (tools). Product action is suggested by Minute Rice, Thermopane, Spic and Span, Duz, Ditto, and Reddi-Wip. The name should be easy to pronouce, spell, and remember. Simple, short, one-syllable names are helpful such as Pard, Tide, Gleem, Mum, and Crest. A brand name should also be distinctive. Many brands with names like National, Star, Ideal, Standard, or Universal fail on this point.

A brand should be sufficiently versatile to be applicable to new products added to the product line. An innocuous name, such as Burroughs, Campbell, or Heinz, may serve the purpose better than a highly distinctive name suggestive of product benefits. Frigidaire is an excellent name for a refrigerator and other cold-image products, but when General Motors expanded its line of home appliances and added Frigidaire kitchen ranges, the name lost some of its sales appeal. Management should select a brand name and a mark which are adaptable to any advertising medium. In recent years many firms—Dutch Cleanser and Citgo (Cities Service Oil Co.), for example—have redesigned their brands in order to meet this requirements more effectively. Finally, the brand selected by a firm should be capable of being registered and protected legally under the Lanham Act and other statutory or common laws.

Generic usage of brand names. Over a period of years some trademarks become so accepted that the brand name is substituted for the generic or descriptive name of the particular product. People associate the name with the product and not with the producer-owner of the brand. Examples of brand names which legally have become generic are linoleum, aspirin, celluloid, cellophane,

---

[3]"Brand Name Bugaboos," *Business Week,* May 14, 1949, p. 67.

kerosene, shredded wheat, and nylon. Originally these were trademarks limited to use by the owner, but they have long since lost their distinctiveness and any firm may use them.

A brand name may become generic in several ways. Sometimes a patent expires and there is no other practicable name available to the public. This happened with shredded wheat, nylon, and cellophane. Sometimes a firm just does too good an advertising and selling job with an outstanding brand name. While not yet legally generic, names such as Band-Aid, Frigidaire, and Kleenex are on the border line. They are outstanding brand names for the original product and have been promoted so well that many people use them generically. Ideally a firm wants its brand to be preferred and even insisted upon by consumers, but it does not want its brand name to become generic. This is a neat tightrope to walk.

There are several strategies which marketing management may adopt to prevent the generic use of its brand. One is to use two names—the brand name in conjunction with the company name, or the the brand name together with the generic name. Eastman Kodak Company advertises, "If it isn't an Eastmen, it isn't a Kodak," thus fighting the tendency of the brand Kodak to become generic. Another alternative is to give actual notice to the public that the brand has been copyrighted. This is accomplished by enclosing the letter R in a circle next to the brand name or by adding the abbreviation Reg. U.S. Pat. Off. (Registered in the United States Patent Office). Additional preventive strategies include displaying the brand in some distinctive typographical fashion or avoiding the use of the trademark in any altered form. Talon (zippers), Sunbeam Corporation, and Sunkist are companies which have adopted the drastic alternative which involves changing the company's name to coincide with that of the brand.

BRAND POLICIES AND STRATEGIES

Manufacturers' strategies. A manufacturer's decision must be based on a recognition of the values of branding and the responsibilities of brand ownership. He must decide whether to brand his product and whether to sell any or all of his output under a middleman's brand.

Market entire output under manufacturer's own brand. Companies which follow this brand policy typically are very large, well financed, and well managed. Polaroid, Maytag, and IBM are some examples. They typically have broad product lines, well-established distribution systems, and large shares of the market. Probably only a small percentage of manufacturers follow this policy, and their number seems to be decreasing.

Many of the reasons for adopting this policy have already been covered in the section on the importance of branding to the seller. In addition, middlemen often prefer to handle manufacturers' brands, especially when the brands have high consumer acceptance. Of course, manufacturers' brands are virtually imperative for middlemen who are unable to establish their own.

Besides the earlier-mentioned responsibilities of brand ownership—the need to promote the brand and stand behind the product's quality—manufacturers face other problems when they use brands. Large retailers who want to use their own brands often will not buy products which carry the producer's brand. Also, many retailers chronically complain that manufacturers' brands provide inadequate gross margins and too little middleman control over the pricing.

Branding of fabricating parts and materials. A corollary to the above strategy is one in which producers of industrial fabricating materials and parts (products used in the further manufacturing of other goods) decide to brand their products. This strategy is used in the case of Botany Woolen Mills, Dan River cottons, Goodyear's Neolite soles and heels, Acrilan fabrics, and many automotive parts—spark plugs, batteries, oil filters, etc.

Underlying this strategy is the seller's desire to develop a market preference for his branded part or material. He wants consumers and industrial users to specify that they want his item in the finished product. For instance, the Du Pont Company wants to build a market situation where customers will insist on a shirt made with Dacron. In addition, the parts manufacturer wants to persuade the producer of the ultimate finished item that using the branded materials will help sell the end product. That is, the Du Pont Company hopes to convince the manufacturers of Manhattan shirts that their sales will increase if their shirts are made with Dacron (the Du Pont Company's branded material).

From the standpoint of a purchaser, this can be an effective strategy for a manufacturer who wishes to capitalize on the reputation of these brands when he is selling his finished product. By building in highly promotable components and materials during the earliest phases of product planning, the seller may be able to keep customer interest alive long after the new-product promotional activities have ceased to be effective.

Certain product characteristics are particularly conducive to the effective employment of this strategy. First, it helps if the product is also a consumer good bought for replacement purposes. If the customer must replace the oil filter or spark plugs in his car, this encourages the branding of Champion spark plugs and Fram oil filters. The seller's situation is improved in a second way if the part is of high unit value and is a major part of the finished product—a television picture tube, for example. In the third place, if the material or part is easily distinguished or frequently replaceable, it is apt to be branded. Here an interesting comparison arises between parts in the hard goods industries and materials in soft goods. Hard goods parts—in automobiles, for example—are not replaced often, but they stand out clearly. In textiles, the material may not be easily distinguished or visibly labeled, but the brand is brought to the fore because the item is replaced more often.

Marketing under a middleman's brand. Manufacturers may elect the strategy of selling part or all of their output under the brands of one or more middlemen. A comprehensive study of brand policy, conducted by the Marketing Science Institute, has contributed much to our understanding of brand management.[4] This study shed light especially on the problems of a manufacturer who sells under a mixed-brand policy, that is, who produces goods under his own label as well as under middlemen's brands. The study indicated that an increasing majority of producers are adopting a mixed-brand policy, and this trend is likely to continue.

Financial considerations are a major reason for this trend. This business generates additional sales volume and profit dollars. Orders typically are large, payment is prompt, and a manufacturer's working-capital position is improved. Also, a manufacturer may utilize his production resources more effectively, including his

---

[4]Victor J. Cook and Thomas F. Schutte, *Brand Policy Determination,* Allyn and Bacon, Inc., Boston, 1967.

plant capacity. Furthermore, refusing to sell under a retailer's brand will not eliminate competition from this source. Many middlemen want to market under their own brands, and if one firm refuses their business, they will go to another. In terms of marketing strategy, a manufacturer can get, from the middlemen whom he is supplying, information regarding consumer behavior, the middlemen's operations, and even competitors' programs. Marketing overhead can be spread over more accounts, and a manufacturer enjoys greater flexibility in his pricing.

Probably the most serious limitation to marketing under a middleman's brand is that the manufacturer is at the mercy of the middleman. This disadvantage increases as the proportion of his output going to the middleman's brand increases. Furthermore, the manufacturer has no assurance of continuity of orders, and often the unit profit is lower on volume sold under the middleman's brand. Another drawback is that the manufacturer's goodwill may suffer if the public becomes aware of his dual role of selling under his own brand and a middleman's brand, particularly if the latter is priced significantly lower than his own.

A declining number of manufacturers market their *entire* output under middlemen's brands. These producers typically are too small, are inadequately financed, or lack the marketing resources and know-how to warrant the use of their own brands.

Middlemen's strategies. The question of whether "to brand or not to brand" must also be answered by middlemen.

Carry only manufacturers' brands. Most retailers and wholesalers follow this policy because they are in no position to take on the dual burdens of promoting a brand and being responsible for maintaining its quality. Manufacturers' products afford a more ready source of supply. Even though they usually carry lower gross margins, manufacturers' brands often have a higher rate of turnover and a better profit possibility.

Carry middlemen's brands in conjunction with manufacturers' brands. Many large retailers and some large wholesalers have their own brands. To establish and market his own brand successfully, a retailer must have earned the confidence of his customers, and he must carefully maintain a high level of quality control over the items which he selects to sell under this brand. He should also have a very large sales volume because no other firm will help him sell this brand.

Large middlemen, retailers particularly, may incur the ill will of manufacturers if they decide to use their own brands in direct competition with strong, established manufacturers' brands. For many reasons, however, a middleman may feel that it is advantageous to market his own brand. In the first place, it increases his control over his market. If a customer prefers a middleman's brand, he can get it only at the middleman's store. By using his own brand a middleman can reap the full benefit of his promotional efforts and any customer goodwill attached to the brand. Salesclerks in the store can even use the sales argument that "our brand is the same as the widely advertised brand A, which is selling for a 20 percent higher price."

If a middleman decides to adopt his own brand, he can usually sell it at a price below that of the manufacturers' brands and still get a higher gross margin. This is possible because he can buy at a lower cost. The cost may be lower because the manufacturer does not include a share of his advertising and selling costs in the price, or because he is anxious to get the extra business in order to keep his plant running in slack seasons.

Middlemen have more freedom and flexibility in pricing products sold under their own labels. Some manufacturers give a retailer no price flexibility, even to meet local competition. At the other extreme, some manufacturers' brands are used as a price football. The price is cut indiscriminately by competing stores to a point where a retailer may lose money on every sale. When a middleman has his own brand, it becomes a differentiated product, and this hinders price comparisons which might be unfavorable to the store.

Middlemen may be able to control their own branded product and its supply more than they can a manufacturer's brand. A middleman who has his own brand need not fear that manufacturers will either withdraw their brand or not sell to him in the first place. Also, a retailer or wholesaler who decides to use his own brand can establish specifications under which it is to be produced.

Strategies common to manufacturers and middlemen. Manufacturers and middlemen alike must adopt some strategy with respect to branding a line of products and also with respect to branding for market saturation.

Branding a line of products. At least four different strategies are widely used by firms which have more than one product: (1) The same "family" or "blanket" brand may be placed on all products. This policy is followed by Heinz, Campbell, Libby, and others in the food field, as well as by Squibb and General Electric. (2) A separate name may be used for each product. This strategy is employed by International Shoe Company, Procter & Gamble, and Lever Brothers. (3) A separate family brand may be applied to each grade of product or to each group of similar products. Sears groups its baby items under the Honeysuckle brand, its women's clothes under Kerrybrook, and its major home installations (furnaces, building materials) under Homart. (4) The company's trade name may be combined with an individual name for the product. Thus there is Johnson's Pride and Johnson's Glo-Coat, and Kellogg's Rice Krispies and Kellogg's Sugar Corn Pops.

When used wisely, a family-brand strategy has considerable merit. It is much simpler and less expensive to introduce new related products to a line. Also, the general prestige of a brand can be spread more easily if it appears on several products rather than on one. A family brand is best suited for a marketing situation where the products are related in quality, in use, or in some other manner. Swift's does not associate its Premium ham brand with Vigoro, its fertilizer.

On the other hand, the use of family brands places a greater burden on the owner to maintain consistent quality among all products. One bad item can reflect unfavorably, and conceivably even disastrously, on all other goods carrying the same brand. Another drawback to family brands is that each individual item under the brand usually gets less aggressive promotional effort than it would if each product were separately distinguished.

Branding for market saturation. Frequently, in order to achieve a greater degree of market saturation, a firm will employ a multiple-brand strategy. Often one type of sales appeal is built around a given brand. To reach another segment of the market, the company must use other appeals. Procter & Gamble's two detergents, Tide and Dreft, illustrate this point. Some people feel that if Tide is strong enough to clean dirty, greasy work clothes, it cannot be used on lingerie and other fine clothing or on dishes because it would be too strong for their hands. For these people, Proctor & Gamble has marketed Dreft, still a detergent, but one whose image is more gentle than that of Tide.

Sometimes a producer wants to expand the number of retail outlets in a given geographic market. Possibly he has granted an exclusive territory to one retailer, and now that the market has enlarged enough to support two or three retailers, the original store does not want to have the brand distributed to its competitors. Rather than antagonize his original dealer, the manufacturer may market the identical product in other outlets but under another brand.

The use of multiple brands on the same or similar products afford the seller some flexibility in his pricing. A competitor may have an attractively priced item, and rather than cut the price on his known brand, a manufacturer may come out with another "fighting brand" priced to beat that of the competitor and still leave the price image of the original brand unscathed.

As a rule, it is a sound strategy to use separate brands on different qualities of the same general type of product. Obviously, to run counter to this policy—that is, to market different qualities under the same brand—is risky. It violates a fundamental thesis in branding, namely, that all units of a given brand should be reasonably consistent in quality. Several manufacturers of sheets, towels, and pillowcases do market various levels of quality under the same general brand, but with additional differentiating labels.

THE BATTLE OF THE BRANDS

Middlemen's brands have proved to be eminently successful in competing with manufacturers' brands. However, neither group has demonstrated a convincing competitive superiority over the other in the marketplace. Consequently, the "battle of the brands," which has been one of the significant marketing developments of the past decade, shows every indication of continuing and becoming more intense. The National Retail Merchants Association estimates that over 60 percent of all department store sales volume is in private brands. More than 90 percent of Sears volume is in its own labels. According to the Marketing Science Institute study, the market impact of middlemen's brands varies considerably among product lines. The share of total industry sales held by middlemen's brands ranged from 7 percent for portable appliances to 52 percent for shoes. In between, the middleman-brand market share was 13 percent in grocery products, 15 percent in gasoline, 33 percent in major appliances, and 36 percent in replacement tires. *Trends* in market share also vary quite a bit. Manufacturers' brands may be declining in importance in some product lines and enjoying increasing market shares in others.

Historically, middlemen's brands emerged generally in the 1920s, became of some significance during the Depression of the 1930s, and with a few exceptions almost disappeared during World War II. Several factors have accounted for the highly successful resurgence of these brands. The thin profit margins on manufacturers' brands in particular, and on total volume in general, have encouraged retailers to establish their own labels. The consumer himself has become more sophisticated in his buying, and his brand loyalty has declined, so he will consider many alternative brands. The improved quality of retailers' brands has boosted their sales. It is quite generally known that middlemen's brands are usually produced by large, well-known manufacturers. Large retailers (Sears and Woolworth, for example) are beginning to make extensive and very effective use of advertising, particularly TV, to promote their own brands.

In this battle, the manufacturers are vocal in their point of view. A few—not many—refuse to produce store-branded merchandise. Manufacturers charge retailers with accepting funds for cooperative advertising of manufacturers' products and then diverting these funds for the advertising of the stores' brands. Furthermore, retailers generally have not contributed much to product innovation. Certainly store brands would be apt to suffer considerably if they did not have manufacturers' advertised brands to use for price and quality comparisons.

Manufacturers do have some effective responses they can use to combat the inroads of retailers' brands.[5] Producers can devote top priority to product innovation and packaging, an area where retailers are not as strong. Manufacturers' research and development capacity enables them to enter the early stages of a product's life cycle, whereas retailer brands typically enter after a product is well established. For example, in recent years retailer brands did not appear in paper diapers until well after several producers' brands had been introduced. Another area where manufacturers are ahead of retailers is in their use of research techniques to position new products, reposition old ones, and generally use shrewd market segmentation. Canada Dry, for instance, improved its market situation considerably when it switched from a mixer-only position to soft-drink status. Manufacturers need to communicate product advantages and a value image more effectively in their advertising. They also must employ increased automation and productivity to reduce the price gap between their brands and store brands. Manufacturers must place more stress on servicing their products so as to compete with large retailers who have achieved a strong market position because of their service capabilities. Finally, when selling to retailers, the manufacturers can stress the strength of well-known brands as "traffic-pullers" for the store.

Court decisions pertaining to the Borden Company's pricing and marketing of its evaporated milk may very well have far-reaching implications for brand marketing. The Borden Company sold evaporated milk under the Borden brand at a price higher than that charged for the identical physical product manufactured under middlemen's labels. Many producers traditionally have followed this practice, justifying it on the grounds that consumers did not consider the manufacturer- and middleman-branded products to be of "like grade and quality." The Supreme Court ruled otherwise, stating that the two brands had to be regarded as being of the same grade and quality and thus were subject to the Robinson-Patman Act, which generally prohibits price discrimination.[6] The case was remanded to the Circuit Court of Appeals, which ruled, in effect, that a manufacturer may sell a middleman's brand at a lower price than the manufacturer's own advertised brand of the identical product, as long as the price difference does not exceed the value of the customers' perceived benefits resulting from the manufacturer's advertising and promotion of his brand.[7] The court decisions left in their wake conflicting interpre-

---

[5] See *Grey Matter,* July, 1973, and December, 1970.

[6] *Federal Trade Commission v. Borden Company,* 86 S. Ct. 1092 (1966).

[7] *Federal Trade Commission v. Borden Company,* 381 F. 2d 175 (1967); see also Thomas F. Schutte, Victor J. Cook, Jr., and Richard Hemsley, "What Management Can Learn from the Borden Case," *Business Horizons,* Winter, 1966, pp. 23–30; and Morris L. Mayer, Joseph B. Mason, and Einar A. Orbeck, "The Borden Case—A Legal Basis for Private Brand Price Discrimination," *MSU Business Topics,* Winter, 1970, pp. 56–63.

tations and unanswered questions—how does a manufacturer measure the consumer's differential preference for his brand, for example? It may be some time before the impact of the Borden case is fully understood.

PACKAGING

Packaging may be defined as the general group of activities in product planning which involve designing and producing the container or wrapper for a product. Packaging obviously is closely related to labeling and branding because the label often appears on the package and the brand is typically on the label.

There are three reasons for packaging:

1. A utilitarian as well as a marketing reason for packaging a product is to protect it on its route from the manufacturer to the consumer or industrial user, and in some cases even during its life with the customer. Compared with bulk items, packaged goods generally are more convenient, cleaner, and less susceptible to losses from evaporation, spilling, and spoilage. Packaging helps to identify a product and thus may prevent substitution of competitive goods.

2. Packaging also may implement a company's marketing program. A package may be the only significant way in which a firm can differentiate its product. In the case of convenience goods or industrial operating supplies, for example, most buyers feel that one well-known brand is about as good as another. Also, changing a package is an inexpensive way to give the impression that the product itself has been changed. Packaging can be used effectively to help introduce a new product or to help increase or maintain the market for existing products.

    In a distribution system, wholesalers derive cost benefits from protective packaging of manufacturers' products. Also, retailers recognize that effective protection and promotion features in a package can cut their costs and increase sales.

    The utilitarian reasons for packaging—protection, identification, and convenience—may in themselves by exploited in selling. Some features of the package may serve as a sales appeal, for example, a no-drip spout, a self-applicator, an aerosal spray dispenser, or a reusable jar. Furthermore, the package advertising copy will last as long as the product is being used in its packaged form. Every time the housewife takes down a jar of peanut butter, she is exposed to the message on the label. At the point of purchase, the package serves as a silent salesman encouraging impulse buying.

3. Management may package its product in such a way as to increase profit possibilities. A package may be so attractive that customers will pay more just to get the special package—even though the increase in price exceeds tha additional cost of the package. Also, an increase in ease of handling or a reduction in damage losses will cut marketing costs.

GROWING IMPORTANCE OF PACKAGING

Packaging is in the socioeconomic forefront today because of its relation to environmental pollution issues. Perhaps the biggest challenge facing packagers is how to dispose of their product after it has done its job of marketing, product protection, and consumer convenience. Used packaging is a major contributor to the solid-waste disposal problem. The consumer's desire for convenience (in the form of throwaway containers) conflicts with his desire for a clean environment. Already one state (Oregon) has banned the sale of nonreturnable containers for beer, soft drinks, etc., and other states may adopt similar legislation. There is here a real challenge to our *technology,* but perhaps even more difficult is the *marketing* challenge to influence consumer attitudes favorably toward recycling waste and the more efficient use of packaging.[8]

Most companies recognize that packaging is important for purposes of protection and convenience. The activity has been production-oriented in most firms, however, and marketing values have been ignored. But this attitude is changing, and the marketing significance of packaging is being recognized.

The increased use of branding and the public's rising standards of health and sanitation have contributed to the growth of packaging. The major factor, however, is the importance of packaging as a real competitive force in today's struggle for markets. The widespread use of self-service, automatic vending, and other self-selection methods of retail selling means that the package must do the selling job at the point of purchase. It is no simple task for a manufacturer even to get his product placed on display in a retail outlet. Shelf space is at a premium, and retailers are inclined to cater to producers who have used effective packaging.

The pace of packaging development has left industry the victim of unplanned obsolescence. These new developments, occurring rapidly and in a seemingly endless flow, require management's constant attention to packaging research and design in order that the marketing opportunities presented by these features can be optimized. We see new packaging materials replacing the traditional ones, exotic new shapes and sizes, new closures (flip-top, pull-tab, rip-cap), and other new features (measured portions, fractional packages, metered flow)—all making for increased convenience for consumers and additional selling points for marketers. In many cases the consumers perceive that the package is part of the product. To illustrate, when shoe polish is sold in a can with an applicator and polishing cloth or when cheese spread comes in an aerosol can, an executive asks, "Which is the product and which is the package? We are selling the combination and it's getting harder to tell the difference."

Because of the growing importance of packaging, the responsibility for this activity should rest with top management. Packaging decisions are being centralized at the vice-presidential and even the presidential level. Major companies—General Foods and the National Biscuit Company, for instance—have established separate corporate packaging staffs, and at Nabisco the head of this division is a vice-president.

POLICIES AND STRATEGIES OF PACKAGING

Changing the package. Whether to change a package and, if so, when to make the change are related problems. The trend today is in favor of change, and this

---

[8]See Tom Alexander, "The Packaging Problem Is a Can of Worms," *Fortune,* June, 1972, p. 105; William N. Gunn, "Packagers and the Environmental Challenge," *Harvard Business Review,* July–August, 1972, pp. 103–111; and William G. Zikmund and William J. Stanton, "Recycling Solid Waste: A Channels-of-Distribution Problem," *Journal of Marketing,* July, 1971, pp. 34–39.

trend is gaining momentum. In general, management has two reasons for considering package innovation: a decrease in sales or a desire to expand a market by attracting new groups of customers.

More specifically, a firm may want to correct a bad feature in the existing container. The box may leak after being opened, or it may not be sufficiently airtight. A company may want to take advantage of new materials. Some companies change their containers to aid in the firm's promotional program. The new package may be used as a major appeal in the advertising copy, or the old containers may not show up well in advertisements.

Packaging the product line. A company must decide whether to develop a family resemblance in the packaging of its several products. *Family packaging* involves making the package identical for all products or using some common feature on all the packages. For example, Heinz and Campbell soups each use virtually identical packaging on their condensed soup products. Management's evaluation of family packaging parallels its evaluation of family branding. When new products are added to a line, promotional values associated with old products extend to the new ones. On the other hand, this strategy should be used only the products are related in use and are of similar quality.

Reuse packaging. Another strategy to be considered is reuse packaging. Should the company design and promote a package which can serve other purposes after the original contents are consumed? Glasses containing cheese can later be used for fruit juices. Peanut butter, jelly, and pickle jars make good containers for leftovers or can be used for home canning purposes. Reuse packaging should stimulate repeat purchases. If a person purchases a certain brand of peanut butter in order to collect a set of drinking glasses and, once he has them, switches to another brand, the dual-use packaging strategy has been of little help to the peanut butter manufacturer.

Multiple packaging. For many years there has been a trend toward *multiple packaging,* or the practice of placing several units in one container. Dehydrated soups, motor oil, beer, golf balls, soap, building hardware, candy bars, towels, and countless other products are packaged in multiple units. Test after test has proved that multiple packaging increases total sales of a product. Multiple packaging can also help introduce new products and win consumer acceptance of a new concept. Although a user may not particularly like the different taste of a new product the first time he tries it, by the time he has finished the third box that came in the multiple package he may be impressed favorably. In other instances, multiple packaging is convenient for special price offers and for the sale of small items. Retailers like this method of packaging because it cuts unit-handling and price-marking costs. On the other hand, if a product is used infrequently or if it lasts a long time, quantity packaging is not advantageous.

LABELING

Labeling is another product feature which requires managerial attention. The *label* is that part of a product which carries verbal information about the product or the seller. A label may be part of a package, or it may be a tag attached directly to the product. Obviously there is a close relationship between labeling and packaging and between labeling and branding.

Labeling also has considerable social significance. Several of the public's criticisms of marketing have centered around charges of false, misleading, or deceptive packaging and labeling. In the textile field, this has led to federal legislation on the labeling of furs, wool products, and other textiles. Historically, inadequate labeling hastened the passage of the federal Food, Drug, and Cosmetic Act. More recently, consumer criticism led to the passage of a "truth in packaging" law—the Fair Packaging and Labeling Act (1966).

Although there has been immeasurable improvement in labeling practices over the past twenty-five years, legislation alone cannot do the job. Further improvement is needed, and it will come as additional firms realize the marketing advantages of good labeling. Nevertheless, it will not be easy to develop a labeling system which will enable consumers to determine quality and compare products. Standards must be developed so that comparisons can be made. Then customers will have to be taught the meaning of the standards and the importance of reading the information on the labels.

TYPES OF LABELS

Typically, labels are classed as brand, grade, descriptive, and informative. A *brand label* is simply the brand alone applied to the product or to the package. Thus some oranges are brand-labeled Sunkist or Blue Goose, and some clothes carry the brand label Sanforized. A *grade label* identifies the quality by a letter, number, or word. Canned peaches are grade-labeled A, B, and C, and corn and wheat are grade-labeled numbers 1 and 2. In this book, *descriptive labels* and *informative labels* are used synonymously. These are labels which give written or illustrative objective information about the use, construction, care, performance, or other features of the product. On a descriptive-informative label for a can of corn there will be statements concerning the type of corn (golden sweet), style (creamed or in niblet kernals), can size, number of servings, and net contents. A descriptive-informative label on a suit, on sheets, or on an electric blanket will give details concerning (1) what the item is made of, (2) how it is made (worsted or flannel, thread count), (3) how it should be cared for (dry cleaning only), (4) how it should be used (AC current only), (5) how it will perform (water-repellent, wrinkle-free), and (6) the name and address of the manufacturer or middleman.

Relative merit. Brand labeling creates very little stir among crititcs. While it is an acceptable form of labeling, its severe limitation is that it does not supply sufficient information to a buyer. The real fight centers around grade versus descriptive labeling, and whether grade labeling should be made mandatory. Historically, consumer organizations have been in favor of grade labeling, and businessmen have advocated descriptive-informative labeling. Some of the arguments on both sides are noted here, but on balance it seems that no one type of labeling is best for all products.

The proponents of grade labeling argue that it is simple, definite, and easy to use. They also point out that if grade labels were used, prices would be more related to quality, although grade labeling would not stifle competition. In fact, they believe that grade labeling might increase competition because consumers would be able to judge products on the basis of both price and known quality. The cost of grade labeling is very low, so it would not place a great burden on the manufacturer. Grade labeling would in no way do away with brand names. Many firms already using grade labeling have tied in the grade with their promotional programs.

Those who object to grade labeling point out that it is not possible to grade differences in flavor and taste, or in style and fashion. A very low score on one grading characteristic can be offset by very high scores on other factors. Companies selling products which score high *within* a given quality bracket would be hurt by grade labeling. It would not be possible for these companies to justify a higher price than that charged for another Grade A product which scored very low in the Grade A quality range. Some people feel that grades are an inaccurate guide for consumer buying because the characteristics selected for grading, the weights assigned to them, and the means of measuring them are all established on an arbitrary basis.

STATUTORY LABELING REQUIREMENTS

The importance of labeling and its problems are evidenced to some extent by the large number of federal laws regulating this marketing activity. Several states also have labeling statutes. The Federal Trade Commission Act of 1914 and the Wheeler-Lea Amendment (1938) state that unfair competition is illegal if it may injure a competitor or the consumer. Although the law does not give explicit examples of unfair trade practices, a false, misleading, or deceptive label or package would provide a specific instance of unfair competition.

Consumer discontent with packaging and labeling has continued to mount, however, with charges, for example, that there is a confusing number of sizes and shapes of packages for a given product, that some packages are only partially filled, that some shapes are deceptive, and that contents measured in odd amounts (e.g., 6.25 ounces) make unit price comparisons very difficult.[9]

Congress responded with the Fair Packaging and Labeling Act. This law provides: (1) *mandatory* labeling requirements, (2) an opportunity for industry to *voluntarily* adopt packaging standards which will limit proliferation of weights and measures, and (3) administrative agencies (the Food and Drug Administration and the Federal Trade Commission) with the *discretionary* power to set packaging regulations where deemed necessary.[10]

In the past, the labeling of clothing, furs, and piece goods was often confusing and misleading to the consumer, and existing laws were apparently inadequate. As a result, three important labeling laws have been passed. The Wool Products Labeling Act (1941) provides that a clothing product which contains any wool must be labeled to explain clearly what kind of wool is used (virgin, reused, reprocessed, etc.) and what percentage (by weight) of each type is included in the product. Label legislation was expanded in 1952 with the passage of the Fur Products Labeling Act. This law provides that in identifying a fur garment, the label must state the usual or natural name of the fur and its country of origin. The Textile Fiber Products Identification Act (1960) provides that clothing garments and household textiles,

---

[9]For a two-part report on consumers' opinion of the packaging of drugstore products, see "Drugstore Packages as Consumers See Them," *Sales Management,* Sept. 15, 1970, p. 41; Oct. 1, 1970, p. 51.

[10]See Warren A. French and Leila O. Schroeder, "Package Information Legislation: Trends and Viewpoints," *MSU Business Topics,* Summer, 1972, pp. 39–44.

including rugs, must carry the generic or chemical description of the fiber content. It is insufficient to give only the fiber maker's brand name or to use only such descriptive terms as "wash and wear." Also, the label must state the percentages (by weight) of all fibers present in amounts over 5 percent and the name of the manufacturer of the article.[11]

The Food and Drug Act of 1906 and its 1938 amendment, the Food, Drug, and Cosmetic Act, are administered by the Food and Drug Administration. These laws provide explicit regulations for labeling drugs, foods, cosmetics (except toilet soaps), and therapeutic devices. If artificial coloring or preservatives are used, the label must note this fact. Any conditions for safe use must be included on the label, and items with poisonous content must be so labeled. In 1972 the Food and Drug Administration established a set of nutritional-labeling standards for packaged foods. A label is supposed to indicate the amount of vitamins, minerals, fats, carbohydrates, calories, and proteins contained in the contents of the package. While this program is voluntary, food packagers expect that pressures from consumers and competition will, in effect, make this labeling mandatory.[12]

In an effort to bring safety and quality controls into line with the swift pace and modern methods found in the drug industry, Congress passed in 1962 a bill establishing considerably tighter controls over the manufacture and marketing of ethical pharmaceuticals. One section of the law provides that labels and advertising must display prominently the generic name of the drug in addition to the brand name.

The U.S. Department of Agriculture has established standards for A, B, and C grades of canned food products, but a producer is not obliged to have his products so graded. There are mandatory provisions for inspecting and labeling as "U.S. Inspected" any fresh meats sold in interstate commerce.

OTHER IMAGE-BUILDING FEATURES

A company cannot assert that it has a well-rounded program for product planning and development until it has instituted a company policy on several additional product attributes: product design, color, sizes, product quality, and guarantee and servicing.

PRODUCT DESIGN

One way to build an image of a product is through its design. In fact, a distinctive design may be the only significantly differentiating feature of a product. Many firms feel that there is considerable glamour and general promotional appeal in product design and the designer's name. It is not at all unusual to see in an advertisement that a product or package was designed by Raymond Loewy, Henry Dreyfuss, or Walter Teague. In the field of industrial products, engineering design has long been recognized as extremely important, but today there is a realization of the marketing value of appearance design as well. Office machines and office furniture are

---

[11]See Marshall C. Howard, "Textile and Fur Labeling Legislation: Names, Competition, and the Consumer," *California Management Review,* Winter, 1971, pp. 69–80.

[12]See "Del Monte Living with New Labeling Rules," *Business Week,* Feb. 3, 1973, p. 42; and Edward H. Asam and Louis P. Bucklin, "Nutritional Labeling for Canned Goods: A Study of Consumer Response," *Journal of Marketing,* April, 1973, pp. 32–37.

examples of industrial products where conscious attention has been given to product design, and often with good sales results. The marketing significance of design has been recognized for years in the field of consumer products, whether they are big items like automobiles and refrigerators or small products like fountain pens and apparel.

Product materials and performance are related to design. New developments in plastics, synthetic fibers, lightweight metals, and other materials have broadened the designer's horizon considerably. Of course, the marketing opportunities presented by new materials must not obscure production and financial considerations. Regarding product performance, the designer must know the answers to the following questions: What will the product be used for? What does the buyer expect? What is the cost of building in the various levels of performance?

Good design can improve the marketability of a product in many ways. It can make the product easier to operate; it can upgrade the product's quality or durability; it can improve product appearance and lower manufacturing costs. Good design can also generate new uses for a product or make it adaptable for initial use by new customers.

COLOR

People seem to be more conscious of color today than in the past. It is often the determining factor in a customer's acceptance or rejection of a product, whether it is a dress, a table, or an automobile. Even in industrial products, color is an important aspect of design.

Color by itself, however, is no selling advantage because many competing firms offer color products. The marketing advantage comes in knowing the right color, how many colors to use, and when to change colors. If a garment manufacturer or a retail store's fashion coordinator guesses wrong on what will be the fashionable color in women's clothing, it can be disastrous. There is an increasing need for thorough research and expert help on the subject. Many firms employ the services of color stylists today.

Marketers must reckon with color as both a psychological and a sociological force. Its careful use can increase sales, increase worker productivity, reduce eyestrain, and generally affect emotional reactions. Some colors have different meanings to various ethnic groups, and there are geographic preferences in colors.

SIZES

The assortment of sizes in which goods are produced by a manufacturer or stocked by middlemen can have a substantial bearing on the marketing success of a firm. It is simply lost business when an industrial distributor does not have a desired size of valve or rubber belting in stock, or when a clothing store does not have the right shirt or blouse size.

Manufacturers and middlemen alike are pressured to increase the number of sizes they market and to carry something for everybody. On the other hand, middlemen know that their shelf space is at a premium and that the little-called-for sizes often end up being sold at a considerable markdown. Manufacturers may fight the pressure because they too fear economic losses inherent in slow-moving sizes.

It is difficult to detect whether there is a trend toward larger or smaller package sizes. Possibly there is significant movement in both directions. Coca-Cola added a 12-ounce bottle to the traditional 6-ounce size. Jell-O added a larger package size, and several brewers have come out with 16-ounce containers for beer. On the other hand, Coors now markets some of its beer in 7-ounce aluminum cans, and some brands of coffee appear in 1/2-pound tins. Large packages offer economy, and small ones offer convenience.

PRODUCT QUALITY

The quality of a product is extremely important, but probably the most difficult of all the image-building features to define. Users frequently disagree on what constitutes quality in an item, whether it is a cut of meat, a piece of music, or an article of clothing. Personal tastes are deeply involved. Nevertheless, a marketing executive must make several decisions about product quality. First, the product should reach only a level of quality compatible with the intended use of the item; it need not be any better. In fact, "good" and "poor" are misleading terms. "Correct" and "incorrect" would be much more appropriate. If a housewife is making a peach cobbler, Grade B or C peaches are the correct quality. They are not necessarily the best quality, but they are right for the intended use. It is not necessary to pay Grade A prices for large, well-formed peaches when these features will not be seen in the cobbler.

Next, units of output must maintain as consistent a degree of quality as is reasonably possible. Furthermore, all the components of a given product should be similar in quality. Like the parts of the "one-hoss shay," ideally all parts will perform equally well and cease performing simultaneously.

PRODUCT WARRANTY

The general purpose of a warranty is to give the buyer some assurance that he will be compensated in case the product is not up to reasonable expectations. In years past, courts seemed generally to recognize only *express* warranties—those stated in written or spoken words. Usually these were quite limited in what they covered and seemed intended only to protect the seller from buyers' claims.

But times have changed! Consumer complaints have led to a governmental campaign to protect the consumer in many areas, one of which is product liability. Today, courts and government agencies are broadening the scope of warranty coverage by recognizing the concept of *implied* warranty—that is, the idea that warranty was intended by the seller, although not actually stated. Manufacturers are being held responsible, even when the sales contract is between the retailer and the consumer. Warranties are considered to "run with the product." Manufacturers are held liable for product-caused injury, whether or not they are to blame for negligence in manufacturing. It all adds up to "let the seller beware."[13]

Manufacturers are responding by broadening and simplifying their warranties,

---

[13]See Lynn J. Loudenback and John W. Goebel, "Marketing in the Age of Strict Liability," *Journal of Marketing,* January, 1974, pp. 62–66; Conrad Berenson, "The Product Liability Revolution," *Business Horizons,* October, 1972, pp. 71–80; John S. Berens, "Consumer Costs in Product Failure," *MSU Business Topics,* Spring, 1971, pp. 27–30; David L. Rados, "Product Liability: Tougher Ground Rules," *Harvard Business Review,* July–August, 1969, pp. 144–152; and Alfred A. Cox, "Product Liability," *Southern Journal of Business,* April, 1969, pp. 80–86.

and they are using them as a promotional device to stimulate purchases by reducing the consumer's risks. As a dimension of competitive strategy, a promotional warranty policy will probably be most effective when:

1. The unit price of the product is high.
2. The product is purchased infrequently.
3. The product is perceived by consumers as being complex.
4. The buyer does not have much knowledge of the product; he cannot judge the product's quality by inspecting it; or, as in mail-order selling, the purchasing decision (and maybe the payment) must be made in advance of seeing the product.
5. The seller's share of market is small or the product is not well known.[14]

The Consumer Product Safety Act (1972) epitomizes how the ground rules have changed regarding product liability and injurious products. This act potentially could be the most powerful consumer-oriented law ever passed. The act created the Consumer Product Safety Commission (CPSC) which, in turn, could well be the most powerful business regulatory agency ever established by our government. The commission has authority to establish mandatory safety standards for practically all consumer products. It can publish information—naming brands and manufacturers—regarding injurious products. It can ban the distribution of these products without a court hearing. The top management of offending companies may face criminal, not just civil, charges. There is further discussion of this law and its regulatory commission in Chapter 29.

PRODUCT SERVICING

A related problem is that of adequately providing the services guaranteed by the warranty. One writer has proposed the following four guidelines to help management meet its social responsibilities in these areas, as well as to ensure customer satisfaction.[15]

1. Ensure the integrity and credibility of the warranty.
2. Institute a meaningful education program regarding use of the product.
3. Strengthen the company program for quality control in manufacturing.
4. Provide high-quality maintenance and repair service.

Product servicing requires management's attention as products become more complex, service facilities seem unable to keep pace, and consumers grow increasingly dissatisfied and vocal. To cope with the problems, management can consider several courses of action. For instance, a producer can establish several geographically dispersed factory service centers, staff them with well-trained company employees, and strive to make servicing a separate profit-generating activity. Or a manufacturer can shift the main burden to his middlemen, compensate them for their efforts, and possibly even train their service

---

[14]Jon G. Udell and Evan E. Anderson, "The Product Warranty as an Element of Competitive Strategy," *Journal of Marketing*, October, 1968, pp. 1–8.

[15]George Fisk, "Guidelines for Warranty Service after Sale," *Journal of Marketing*, January, 1970, pp. 63–67.

employees. As a promotional strategy, management may stress its high-quality service. Conversely, a company can view servicing as a costly penance for the sin of engineering or production mistakes, try to minimize this cost, and then spend money to eradicate the mistakes which brought about the need for repairs.

QUESTIONS AND PROBLEMS

1. What is the difference between a brand and a trademark?
2. List five brand names which you think are good ones and five which are poor. Explain the reasoning behind your choices.
3. Evaluate each of the following brand names in light of the characteristics of a good brand, indicating the strong and weak points of each name:
   a. Xerox (office copier)
   b. IBM (business machines)
   c. Mustang (automobiles)
   d. Hush Puppies (shoes)
   e. A-1 (steak sauce)
   f. Hotpoint (appliances)
4. A Senate committee was investigating pricing practices in the drug industry. Some of the legislators objected to the practice of several manufacturers' producing chemically identical products and then differentiating the products by the use of brand names. One senatorial recommendation was to pass a law requiring that all drug products be identified by their generic names rather than by brand names. What is your opinion? Are there other products which you feel should be sold only under their generic names?
5. Suggest some brands which are on the verge of becoming generic. What course of action should a company take to protect the separate identity of its brand?
6. Under what conditions would you recommend that a manufacturer brand a product which will be used as a part or material in the production of another article?
7. In which of the following cases should the company adopt the strategy of family branding?
   a. A manufacturer of men's electric razors introduces a model for women.
   b. A manufacturer of women's cologne and deodorants adds men's after-shave lotion to the product lines.
   c. An automobile manufacturer adds a line of outboard motors to his product mix.
   d. A producer of mattresses introduces a line of electric blankets.
8. Some camera manufacturers follow a strategy of using the same brand name on all their cameras regardless of price and quality and regardless of the type of camera. Evaluate this branding strategy.
9. Why do some firms sell an identical product under more than one of their own brands?
10. Assume that a large department store chain proposed to the manufacturers of Maytag washing machines that Maytag supply the department store with machines carrying the store's brand. What factors should Maytag's management consider in making a decision? If the product were General Foods' Jell-O, to what extent would the situation be different?
11. Give examples of products that are excellently packaged. Mention some that are very poorly packaged.

12. What changes would you recommend in the typical packaging of:
   a. Cornflakes   c. Pepsi-Cola
   b. Toothpaste   d. Typing paper
13. If grade labeling is adopted, what factors should be used as bases for grading the following products?
   a. Sheets and pillowcases
   b. Suntan lotion
   c. Canned peaches
14. Give examples of products in which the careful use of color has increased sales. Can you cite examples to show that poor use of color may hurt a company's marketing program?
15. Explain the relationship between a product warranty on small electric appliances and the manufacturer's distribution system for these products.
16. How would the warranty policies set by a manufacturer of skis differ from those adopted by an automobile manufacturer?

CASES FOR PART

CASE 5. DEL MAR JEWELRY MANUFACTURING COMPANY, INC. (A)*

Addition of new product to manufacturer's line

Del Mar Jewelry Manufacturing Company, Inc., located in Miami, Florida, produced costume jewelry and distributed it through manufacturers' agents to retailers throughout the country. As there was very little manufacturing of jewelry items in the South, the company held a rather unusual position with its retail accounts, especially in Florida. Del Mar's competitive strength decreased, however, as the distance to its retail accounts increased. Its greatest volume of sales was generated by its agents in Florida and the Gulf States.

Some advantages in the sale of Del Mar products was attributed to a natural preference by retailers for high-quality gift merchandise produced in Florida for sale during the tourist seasons. To exploit this advantage further, all of the manufacturers' agents who represented Del Mar noted the local requirements of their retail accounts, and made considerable effort to point out that Del Mar could offer

Case prepared by Prof. Barry J. Hersker, Florida Atlantic University. Reproduced with permission.

services which were unobtainable from northern suppliers. In accord with this policy, Mr. Phillip Johnson, the Del Mar representative in the lucrative Florida Gold Coast area (Palm Beach to Key West), reported a possible opportunity to add several new items to the line of necklaces, bracelets, and earrings—a product group called "Del Mar Jewels."

Mr. Johnson had called upon Mr. Jim Kay, owner of Kay's Accessories Stores of Ft. Lauderdale, Florida. During their conversation Mr. Kay remarked that he was pleased to see that the new items of Del Mar Jewels included Aurora Borealis crystals. (These were imported, cut crystal beads with an iridescent coating that refracted light in many colors.) Mr. Kay stated further that products made with this type of crystal beads were selling very well in all three of his stores. In fact, Aurora-crystal goods were in short supply, and back-orders from New York suppliers were not uncommon.

Mr. Kay placed sample orders for several of the Aurora crystal items from the Del Mar Jewels line, as well as for several other items which did not contain these crystal beads. Mr. Johnson knew that if these samples items moved well, Mr. Kay would reorder in larger quantities.

When producing necklaces, bracelets, or earrings, one styling technique used by Del Mar was to create products that were different from those available from northern suppliers. Thus, direct price comparisons were difficult to make. While the finished products were distinctive, they did compare favorably with merchandise produced by "middle" or "high-end" manufacturing firms in New York City.

Occasionally a large jewelry manufacturer would obtain an "exclusive" on a certain style of bead by purchasing the entire output of that bead from a European factory. Then the bead itself, being only one of a kind, could provide a distinctive look in a piece of jewelry. Del Mar's output was too limited to obtain such exclusive control of particular beads. Almost all of Del Mar's component parts were purchased through import agents or from American manufacturers.

As he was preparing to leave the Kay's Accessories store, Mr. Johnson noticed a recently-arrived shipment of Aurora crystal merchandise which consisted of single-strand necklaces of six-, eight-, and ten-millimeter, tin-cut Aurora crystal beads of the same high quality used by Del Mar. Mr. Kay commented that these items sold so well that he was frequently out of stock. His northern supplier had been slow filling Kay's reorders, primarily because of shortages in the supply of Aurora crystal beads. Mr. Johnson immediately commented that Del Mar could make these items, since they stocked these millimeter sizes of Aurora crystals to use as components of their other items.

Mr. Kay thought this was a fine idea, and promised to reorder all this merchandise from Del Mar if they would supply it locally at the same price as he was buying out of New York. He gave a sample of each style of the necklace to Mr. Johnson to take back to the Del Mar factory to see if they could copy the items.

On his return trip to Miami, several other retail accounts advised Mr. Johnson that they also would be interested in obtaining these items from Del Mar, since they were selling quite well and delivery was slow from New York. Mr. Johnson informed the Del Mar owners about what he had learned and turned the samples over to them for possible duplication. They promised to "price out" the merchandise to see what they could sell it for. Their analysis of the direct cost (labor and materials) of the single-strand, 12½" necklaces using six-, eight-, and ten-millimeter Aurora crystal beads, was as follows:

6 mm Necklace

63 6 mm Aurora @ .012 ea	$.756
Assorted metal parts	.030
Labor	.200
Total direct costs	$.986

8 mm Necklace

31 8 mm Aurora @ .020	$ .620
6 6 mm Aurora @ .012	.072
1 7 mm Aurora @ .015	.015
30 5 mm Spurs @ .007	.210
Assorted metal parts	.030
Labor	.200
Total direct costs	$1.147

10 mm Necklace

26 10 mm Aurora @ .028	$ .736
1 8 mm Aurora @ .020	.020
6 6 mm Aurora @ .072	.072
25 5 mm Spurs @ .007	.175
Assorted metal parts	.030
Labor	.200
Total direct costs	$1.233

The management of Del Mar advised Mr. Johnson that they would be willing to sell the six-millimeter necklace for $36 per dozen, the eight-millimeter necklace for $42 per dozen, and the ten-millimeter necklace for $48 per dozen. Their usual pricing formula called for a markup of three times direct cost, with the resulting price altered to correspond to the nearest price line. Thus, on the eight-millimeter necklace, three times $1.147 = $3.441 each, times 12 = $41.292 per dozen. The nearest customary price line to this would be $42 per dozen. (In the costume jewelry trade, wholesale price lines per dozen were $6.75, $13.50, $18, $24, $30, $36, $42. $48, etc. Corresponding *unit* retail prices were $1, $2, $3, $4, $5, $6, $7, $8.)

Mr. Johnson pointed out that these prices were totally unacceptable. The necklaces supplied by Mr. Kay had wholesaled for $13.50 per dozen for the six-millimeter, and $18 per dozen for both the eight- and ten-millimeter necklaces. "If a northern supplier is selling at these prices, then these are the competitive prices that we must meet."

A Del Mar executive replied, "Even if we apply our minimum markup formula (two times cost) we would have to get $24 a dozen on the six-millimeter and $30 for both the eight- and ten-millimeter necklaces. And this would require our selling for less than the normal markup that we take on the Del Mar Jewels line." "Look," Mr. Johnson argued, "you can still afford to sell for the competitive price, even if it is way below your average markup. There is no telling how much volume we might do on these items. Mr. Kay and my other accounts report that the six-millimeter, Aurora necklace is a terrific seller at $2 retail; and at $3, the eight- and ten-millimeter sell even faster!"

"You salesmen always want to cut price!" exclaimed one of the members of the Del Mar management team. "Where do you think those prices would leave us after we pay you your 12½ percent commission and give the 3 percent cash discount?" (Common terms of sale extended by manufacturers and jobbers in the costume jewelry trade are 3%, 10 days, End of Month.)

"And what about bad-debt expense? Last year that ran 2 percent. Even though we exceeded our average minimum markup percentage last year on the Del Mar Jewels line, the way I figure it, we didn't even cover our overhead on these items."

"But those expenses you must contend with in any event," replied Mr. Johnson.

"On the other hand," another member of the firm commented, "maybe our prices are restricting our volume. Are we or aren't we competitive?—that's what we should be asking."

"You are competitive," Mr. Johnson replied, "but you are speaking of your current line of high-end goods. I'm not arguing about those prices. I'm talking about this one new series of items, on which you might do real volume."

"But the more we sell, the more we'll lower our average markup for our whole line, Johnson. And I don't think we're making any money on Del Mar Jewels the way things are. The reason we've tried not to design this type of item was to avoid the kind of price competition that is bound to exist on something like this. These less elaborate styles are the ones most likely to get kicked around price-wise. And any time we're undersold, our whole reputation suffers and suddenly our accounts will assume we're overpriced on everything."

Another member of the firm added, "I agree we should give our accounts what they want, but they should pay our prices for these items, or we shouldn't be producing them."

QUESTION

1. Should Del Mar add the Aurora crystal necklaces to its line?

CASE 6. GREELEY GAS COMPANY

Product elimination

The executives in the central office of the Greeley Gas Company were evaluating the data on the company's appliance sales and profits to determine whether to continue to sell appliances in any or all of the company's district offices, or whether to get out of the appliance business and concentrate on the sales of natural gas. The Greeley Gas Company was a small public utility, distributing natural gas in six districts within Colorado, Kansas, and Minnesota. The company was not regulated by the Federal Power Commission, because its distribution systems did not cross state lines.

The primary product sold by the company was natural gas. The gas was purchased at wholesale prices from pipeline transmission companies on a yearly contract basis. The natural gas was delivered by Greeley Gas's pipeline distribution system to the customer's home or business where it was metered as it was used. Sales of natural gas accounted for about 91 percent of the company's total sales volume of $8.5 million in 1969.

The remaining 9 percent of the company's revenues was derived from appliance (merchandising) sales ($626,628 in 1969) and jobbing sales ($161,060 in 1969). (*Merchandising* and *jobbing* are accounting terms used by the utility industry. Merchandising is the retail sale and installation of appliances by the gas company. Jobbing includes the sale and installation of buried gas pipe on the customer's property, and any piping which must be done within buildings to provide the gas service. Jobbing, then, is the sale of pipe, fittings, valves, etc., needed to provide the gas service, and the cost of that material plus the installation is paid by the customer.)

Greeley Gas supplied its products and services to 56 communities in the three states. The company had 42,000 customers (meters) in 1969 compared with about 22,000 just 10 years earlier. This increase was due to acquisitions from other distribution companies plus the natural growth in Greeley's own markets. The number of utility customers in 1969 in each district was as follows:

Greeley, Colorado	14,635	Bonner Springs, Kansas	3,671
Craig, Colorado	2,490	Eureka and Herington, Kansas	10,227
Canon City, Colorado	4,496	Minnesota	6,039
		Total	41,558

In an effort to stimulate the use of their products, gas and electric utility companies often sell appliances. The utility company which sells both gas and electricity is not faced with a difficult problem of deciding what appliances to sell. In contrast, a natural-gas utility is faced with a very difficult decision about the appliances it should carry. If it decides to carry only those appliances which use natural gas as a primary fuel, its product line will not be nearly complete. But if a gas company carries a full line, its sales of electrical appliances will benefit its major competitor, the electric utility.

At its six district offices the Greeley Gas Company sold a limited line of appliances, including ranges, refrigerators, clothes washers and dryers, water heaters, space heaters, furnaces, air conditioners, gas lights, and gas grilles. Natural gas was the fuel used for all the company's appliances, except for electrical refrigerators, clothes washers, and washer-dryer combinations.

Greeley Gas had a monopoly on gas sales in the communities which it served. Of course, all of these communities also were served by electric utilities. There was strong competition to provide the service where the consumer could make a choice about the type of product to use. For example, in the area of cooking ranges, either gas or electricity can provide the heat and the housewife will choose the one she prefers.

Appliance dealers usually carry both gas and electrical appliances, but these dealers ordinarily will not push one type over the other. Consequently, this increases the importance of the advertising done by the manufacturers of natural-gas appliances and their trade associates. Advertising of electrical appliances has been very effective. One reason for this success is the wide use of electricity which facilitates nation-wide advertising. Another factor is the advertising done by large manufacturers such as General Electric and Westinghouse who promote their many electrical appliances.

The American Gas Association provides most of the advertising for natural gas, from contributions by the gas-distribution and -transmission companies. The amount of money available for gas promotion has been much less than the amount spent on electricity advertising. The gas advertising has been unable to effectively combat the claims that flameless electric cooking is cleaner, even though there is no real difference in the two cooking processes.

In addition to its contributions to the AGA, Greeley Gas Company developed its own advertising program, using an advertising agency in Denver, Colorado. This program included the following four types of advertising:

1. Appliance promotion designed to sell merchandise at a specific price, or to point out the benefits of modern gas appliances without reference to any specific brand.
2. Gas-product promotion which was designed to keep the customers aware of the benefits of the natural-gas service—especially in home heating which involved nearly every home in the community.
3. Public relations advertising to emphasize the prompt and efficient service which Greeley Gas Company provided.
4. Institutional messages which spoke out in behalf of improving the community or in support of the higher ideals of American life. This form of advertising appeared regularly on occasions such as Christmas, Independence Day, income tax time, and election day.

Another promotional effort used by the company was their "Blue Flame" rooms. These rooms were made available, free of charge, to club groups and community organizations. Each Blue Flame room was furnished with meeting-room equipment and kitchens featuring the latest in gas appliances. The company also used these service rooms to conduct cooking, laundry, and other home economics demonstrations.

The sales and profit figures for the years from 1966 to 1969 in the company's three product divisions are summarized in Exhibit 1. In trying to decide whether to continue the marketing of appliances, the Greeley Gas executives analyzed the operating statements from 1966 to 1969 for the line of appliance products. See Exhibits 2 through 5. Since appliance sales (merchandising) and gas-pipe installa-

Exhibit 1. Greeley Gas Company.
　　Summary of annual sales and net profits, for three product divisions, 1966–1969.

	1969	1968	1967	1966
Total sales:	$8,564,384	$7,633,440	$6,930,058	$6,692,506
Natural gas	7,758,696	6,945,276	6,338,244	6,076,191
Appliances	626,628	543,972	472,464	471,839
Jobbing	161,060	141,718	119,350	144,476
Total net income after income taxes	256,208	295,612	252,013	269,074
Net profits before taxes:				
Appliances	7,805	20,478	(9,755)*	3,101
Jobbing	38,904	37,320	30,323	35,156

* = Loss

Exhibit 2. Greeley Gas Company—Appliances operating statement, by districts, for 1969.

	Greeley	Craig	Canon City	Bonner Springs	Eureka* & Herington	Minnesota	Total
Gross sales	$178,182	$85,909	$124,488	$89,823	$32,748	$115,478	$626,628
Cost of sales	143,650	66,232	102,248	79,446	27,487	96,090	515,152
Gross profit	34,532	19,677	22,240	10,377	5,261	19,388	111,475
Other expenses:							
Supervision	5,003	3,958	3,860	2,398	1,087	7,949	24,255
Commissions	8,697	5,756	6,299	5,919	1,403	7,311	35,385
Advertising	697	40	40	148	56	92	1,073
Insurance	2,911	738	2,173	562	306	1,747	8,437
Bad debts	618	619	1,436	280		30	2,983
Miscellaneous	4,833	3,120	7,191	792	1,431	1,913	19,280
Rent	3,470	3,018	2,588	944	86	2,151	12,257
Total expenses	26,229	17,249	23,587	11,043	4,369	21,193	103,670
Net profit	$ 8,303	$ 2,428	$ (1,347)	$ (666)	$ 892	$(1,805)	$ 7,805
Gross profit %	19.38%	22.90%	17.87%	11.55%	16.06%	16.79%	17.79%

*Property purchased April 1, 1969.

Exhibit 3. Greeley Gas Company—Appliances operating statement, by districts, for 1968.

	Greeley	Craig	Canon City	Bonner Springs	Eureka & Herington	Minnesota	Total
Gross sales	$148,635	$90,541	$127,494	$47,695	$22,359	$107,248	$543,972
Cost of sales	121,090	68,246	102,238	40,691	17,180	87,655	437,100
Gross profit	27,545	22,295	25,256	7,004	5,179	19,593	106,872
Other expenses:							
Supervision		1,856	3,595		1,178		6,629
Commissions	14,872	6,079	6,388	4,761	989	9,157	42,246
Advertising	536	42		140	83	307	1,108
Insurance	2,703	650	1,997	380	243	1,405	7,378
Bad debts			94		32	1,164	1,290
Miscellaneous	4,514	2,386	4,996	550	948	2,402	15,796
Rent	2,970	3,784	2,063	953	58	2,119	11,947
Total expenses	25,595	14,797	19,133	6,784	3,531	16,554	86,394
Net profit	$ 1,950	$ 7,498	$ 6,123	$ 220	$ 1,648	$ 3,039	$ 20,478
Gross profit %	18.53%	24.62%	19.81%	14.68%	23.16%	18.27%	19.65%

Exhibit 4. Greeley Gas Company—Appliances operating statement, by districts, for 1967.

	Greeley	Craig	Canon City	Bonner Springs	Eureka & Herington	Minnesota	Total
Gross sales	$131,610	$108,272	$63,864	$40,312	$26,671	$101,735	$472,464
Cost of sales	109,775	91,532	52,181	33,581	23,237	86,862	397,168
Gross profit	21,835	16,740	11,683	6,731	3,434	14,873	75,296
Other expenses:							
Supervision		1,185	3,772		1,842		6,799
Commissions	14,943	5,619	3,091	4,210	1,437	8,455	37,755
Advertising	609	10	15	188	34	302	1,158
Insurance	2,527	589	1,242	458	422	1,367	6,605
Bad debts	3,369	1,753	661		163		5,946
Miscellaneous	7,429	6,340	6,414	1,556	997	4,052	26,788
Total expenses	28,877	15,496	15,195	6,412	4,895	14,176	85,051
Net profit	$ (7,042)	$ 1,244	$ (3,512)	$ 319	$ (1,461)	$ 697	$ (9,755)
Gross profit%	16.59%	15.46%	18.29%	16.70%	12.88%	14.62%	15.94%

Exhibit 5. Greeley Gas Company—Appliances operating statement, by districts, for 1966.

	Greeley	Craig	Canon City	Bonner Springs	Eureka & Herington	Minnesota	Total
Gross sales	$140,785	$86,680	$81,565	$49,603	$16,522	$96,684	$471,839
Cost of sales	119,360	65,010	66,658	43,025	13,657	82,278	389,988
Gross profit	21,425	21,670	14,907	6,578	2,865	14,406	81,851
Other expenses:							
Supervision		57	3,840	.	1,200		5,097
Commissions	14,848	5,975	4,671	6,507	924	8,347	41,272
Advertising	702	87	165	164	160	249	1,527
Insurance	2,294	478	1,290	500	198	1,637	6,397
Bad debts	652		670		64		1,386
Miscellaneous	3,204	1,922	3,376	645	741	3,314	13,202
Rent	2,615	3,178	2,435	1,034	56	551	9,869
Total expenses	24,315	11,697	16,447	8,850	3,343	14,098	78,750
Net profit	$(2,890)	$9,973	$(1,540)	$(2,272)	$(478)	$308	$3,101
Gross profit %	15.22%	25.00%	18.28%	13.26%	17.34%	14.90%	17.35%

tion services (jobbing) were separate from the gas sales, the company was required to keep separate accounts and charge all applicable expenses to the merchandising and the jobbing accounts.

The company's president would like to get out of the appliance end of the business immediately because the profits had been so low. Some of the other executives pointed out, however, that the supervisor's salary and the rent charged to merchandising were fixed expenses which would have to be absorbed by the jobbing and gas divisions, if appliances were eliminated. It was also observed that some districts were consistently earning much higher profits than others on appliance sales.

Each district purchased its appliances from a wholesaler within the district, which accounted for part of the variances in the cost of sales and gross margins among the districts. The cost (to Greeley Gas) of different brands and models of appliances also varied widely because the manufacturers built their products to compete in different sectors of the market. For example, the cost of a deluxe model of Tappan range was $315, but a low-priced, competition-model Modern Maid range cost $85. Even if the percentage markup on the two units were the same, the dollar profit potential of the Tappan range was much higher. The percentage markup was set by the sales manager of each district, and it was based on his costs and the allowances from the distributor. Competitive appliance prices were maintained, but Greeley Gas did not attempt to undercut the local competitors.

Exhibit 6 is a summary of appliance sales for each type of appliance in each district in 1969, a representative year. The unit sales and gross-margin percentages are shown. The gross-margin percentages for each product varied among the districts, thus reflecting the sales managers' pricing policies, the brand mix, the wholesale distributors' pricing, and the competitive situation in the area.

Exhibit 6. Summary of appliance sales in units, and gross-margin percentages, by product, by district, 1969.

		Total	Greeley	Craig	Canon City	Bonner Springs	Eureka & Herington	Minnesota
Ranges	Sales	288	65	53	46	25	18	81
	G.M.	22.5%	31.6%	18.7%	25.5%	6.8%	24.9%	17.1%
Refrigerators	Sales	22	2	18			1	1
	G.M.	15.0%	4.3%	17.3%			0.0%	13.4%
Clothes washers	Sales	80	21	27	8	5		19
	G.M.	20.2%	16.5%	35.7%	17.5%	23.8%		15.2%
Clothes dryers	Sales	173	32	38	25	8	3	67
	G.M.	21.0%	24.5%	22.3%	20.3%	21.3%	18.1%	18.4%
Washer-dryer combination	Sales	4				4		
	G.M.	27.9%				27.9%		
Water heaters	Sales	530	210	96	79	30	9	106
	G.M.	26.3%	21.6%	30.8%	30.9%	31.7%	29.9%	28.6%

Exhibit 6 (continued).

		Total	Greeley	Craig	Canon City	Bonner Springs	Eureka & Her-ington	Minne-sota
Space heaters (Home type to replace the free-standing coal heating stove)	Sales	249	85	56	35	16		57
	G.M.	31.6%	34.3%	32.1%	31.6%	30.1%		24.3%
Unit heaters (store and garage type)	Sales	41	14	16	2	3	2	7
	G.M.	26.9%	26.1%	28.8%	24.8%	27.2%	33.7%	19.2%
Furnaces	Sales	205	33	27	81	26	5	33
	G.M.	25.3%	24.3%	26.5%	30.3%	20.9%	32.7%	15.9%
Air conditioners	Sales	107	13		23	37	8	26
	G.M.	.9%	9.2%		4.8%	.7%	(6.5%)	(6.4%)
Incinerators	Sales	18	11	1	4	1		1
	G.M.	38.0%	43.6%	25.4%	32.9%	9.0%		16.7%
Gas lights	Sales	620	205	17	124	113	127	34
	G.M.	21.3%	17.0%	11.4%	19.4%	31.8%	22.3%	22.2%
Gas grille	Sales	662	298	24	100	72	98	70
	G.M.	26.2%	27.5%	16.1%	20.0%	32.8%	30.5%	29.0%

One product (air conditioners) had a very low gross margin in all districts. Gas air conditioners were more expensive than the equivalent capacity electric models, hence it was necessary to cut the profit margin and in some cases losses had been incurred. The primary reason for the high cost of gas air conditioners was that the sales volume on a national basis had not been high enough to allow a reduction in production costs. Greeley Gas expected that the cost of air conditioners would be reduced in the future, so the product should be more competitive with electric units and the sales should become more profitable.

QUESTION

1. Should Greeley Gas Company discontinue selling appliances in any of its district offices?

CASE 7. STARLING CORPORATION

Addition of a new product to the line

In answer to a market demand, the Starling Corporation developed a plastic attaché-type carrying case for its line of toy building blocks. The annual sales volume forecasted for this carrying case, however, was too low to cover production costs, plus returning the rate of gross profit established as a company standard. Consequently, Mr. Arnold Ferris, the vice-president of sales in the toy division, proposed that this new carrying case also be added to the line of attaché cases now sold by the company's luggage division. He hoped that this would generate the additional sales volume necessary to make the new product a profitable venture.

Founded in 1910 in the East, the Starling Corporation's headquarters and sales offices were located in a large Midwestern city, while manufacturing facilities were in New England and Illinois. Currently, Starling marketed only in the United States and Canada. Management was planning, however, to enter further into international markets and to establish production facilities overseas.

Generally since its beginning the firm enjoyed a profitable growth rate. Sales in 1970 totaled $90 million, divided among three seemingly unrelated product lines —luggage, small home appliances, and toys. The luggage division accounted for about 75 percent of the annual volume, appliances generated 18 percent, and toys 5 percent. Starling was one of the nation's largest producers of carrying cases, especially men's and women's nonleather luggage. Most of the products were vinyl-covered, over aluminum or magnesium frames. However, some of the units are constructed of injection-molded plastic, and in recent years the company had added a line of fiber glass cases. Shortly before World War II Starling acquired an appliance company in Chicago, producing toasters, irons, mixers, and other small electric appliances. In 1960 a line of plastic snap-together toys was added under the brand name of "Plato" (plastic-toy or play-toy).

Starling conducted an effective advertising, sales promotion, and publicity program. Television and full-color magazine advertising was used extensively. A public relations and publicity program was operated continuously. Starling also "merchandised" its national advertising and publicity programs by making available to retailers complete local advertising, point-of-sale, and other promotional materials. Dealers were encouraged to promote and display Starling's products and to coordinate with Starling's national promotional program.

In the corporate organizational structure there were three vice-presidents of sales and a vice-president of marketing, all reporting to one of the two executive vice-presidents. The marketing executive was responsible for advertising, sales promotion, marketing research, marketing planning, and other marketing services. Each of the sales vice-presidents was responsible for sales of one of the three major product lines, and separate sales forces were used for each line.

It had come to the attention of Mr. Ferris that there was a definite need to improve the packaging of Starling's main toy product—Plato building blocks. These blocks were a system of precision-made, snap-together, colorful plastic units which originated in Denmark and were already one of the largest-selling toy items in Europe. With Starling's capabilities in the precision molding of plastic luggage, management recognized the potential of these building blocks in capturing a share of the $25-billion annual toy market in the United States.

Starling began manufacturing Plato blocks in 1961 under a licensing agreement with the Danish inventor. On the basis of successful results in ten test markets, Plato blocks were launched nationally at the 1962 New York Toy Fair and also in the Canadian market. Growth was rapid, and volume well exceeded the anticipated results. The company became one of the largest in the construction-building-block area of the toy market. Its main competition came from Samsonite Corporation's LEGO blocks, American Toy Company, and Mattel Company.

The toy products were sold to more than one hundred factory-franchised distributors and also directly to large specialty toy retailers. Retail prices ranged from $1.50 for a simple town plan of building blocks, through $4.95 to $9.95 for wheel toys, to $25 for an elaborate town plan. Retailer gross margins were typically 40 percent.

The need for improved packaging was indicated by an increasing number of letters from customers requesting a carrying case that would last for the life of the Plato blocks and would hold two or more sets of blocks. The original cardboard box wore out quickly and held only the set of blocks that came with it. These letters indicated some willingness to pay an additional price for a better case, but the amount was uncertain.

In response to this demand, Starling developed a plastic attaché-type carrying case, about 15 by 12 by 3 inches in size. The case was produced by the injection molding of polypropolene; thus the company could capitalize on its experience in manufacturing plastic luggage.

Upon the recommendation of a sample of toy dealers, a retail price of $9.95 was set for the new case. The wholesale selling price to Starling then would be $6. However, production costs at the expected sales volume would be $5.50, thus yielding a substantially lower gross margin than the 30 percent typically desired by Starling. Moreover, according to a limited survey, only 2 percent of the toy consumers would be willing to pay the $9.95 price. Expected sales at this price would be only about one-third to one-half of the dollar volume necessary to recover the fixed investment (molds, dyes, fixtures) and to meet established profit criteria within the next five years.

Mr. Ferris then conceived the idea that the additionally needed volume of sales might be generated if the toy carrying case were to be added as a low-priced unit to round out the line of attaché cases marketed by the luggage division. Mr. Ferris made this proposal to Mr. Richard Morris, the vice-president of sales in the luggage division. The two men agreed to forward the proposal to the company's executive committee.

The luggage division marketed a wide assortment of carrying cases, including men's and women's luggage, attaché cases, and specialized cases for carrying almost anything, from musical instruments to sensitive electronic equipment. The luggage and attaché cases were sold under the Travelite brand, which enjoyed a fine reputation as a high-quality product. These products were distributed by the luggage division sales force directly to leading department stores and luggage stores on a highly selective basis and to trading-stamp firms, who offered the products as premiums in their redemption catalogues. Fair-trade pricing was used where legal; in other locations a system of strongly suggested retail prices was used. A few retailers who sought to cut these prices soon lost their franchise on the grounds that they did not properly handle, display, or sell the product.

Starling held about a 35 percent share of the total attaché-case market. This product contributed $17 million of the luggage division's total sales of $68 million in 1970. The company's attaché products consisted of two lines: the Travelite *Executive* attaché cases, produced in three sizes and retailing for $25.95 to $29.95 and wholesaling for $14.25 to $16.50, and the Travelite *Signature* cases, manufactured in two sizes and retailing for $16.95 to $19.95 and wholesaling for $9.30 and $10.95.

In the total attaché-case market the price range was from $2.75 to $110. Travelite was a major influence in the middle to high price range. The main competitors were

Samonsite, American Tourister, and Hartman. Investigation of the market made in response to the new-product proposal showed a total market of approximately $14 million for attaché cases in the retail price range of $2.75 to $12.74. Further delineation had shown a $9.5-million market for cases in the $7.75-to-$12.74 price range. The proposed attaché case was described as the third best case for the money in comparison testing with the six other cases expected to offer the strongest competition. Its disadvantages were that it looked cheaper and was less functional.

Management felt that Starling could capture a large share of the market potential for the low-priced case. The executive committee was worried, however, by other considerations involved in adding this case to the existing line in the luggage division.

The case could be made in blue and red for the toy market and in more masculine colors such as brown, black, and olive green with an additional metal stripping for the attaché market per se. However, the case would still look cheap, especially as compared with the more expensive Travelite *Executive* and *Signature* lines.

If marketed as a Travelite case, management recognized that the weight of the brand name would enable Starling to distribute the proposed case through the existing selected outlets. This might preclude direct competition in these outlets from other cases in this price range. However, the Travelite quality image might be endangered. If another brand name were adopted, discount stores could be used in the channels of distribution. However, the proposed case then would not benefit from the presold Travelite name. Also, the consumer had more opportunity for comparison shopping in discount stores, so the product might not fare so well.

Mr. Ferris observed that while the attaché case might not be accepted by the consumer on its own merits as an adjunct to the luggage line, its importance to the toy department in fulfilling the demand for a carrying case might be reason for accepting the proposal as a whole.

QUESTIONS

1. Should the luggage division add the proposed product to its line of attaché cases?
2. If so, should this case carry the Travelite brand?
3. If not, what should the toy division do about a carrying case for its building blocks?

PART FOUR

THE PRICE
SYSTEM

PRICING OBJECTIVES AND PRICE DETERMINATION

11

How much do you think we ought to sell it for?" This is a question frequently asked by executives who have the responsibility for pricing the products or services they are marketing. The question would be more accurately worded if they asked, "How much do you think we can get for this item?" or "How much should we ask for it?" The question would then be in accord with the generalization that *prices are always on trial*. A price is simply an offer or an experiment to test the pulse of the market. If the customers accept the offer, this is fine. If they reject it, the price usually will be changed quickly, or the product may even be withdrawn from the market. Before being concerned with actual price determination, however, an executive should understand the meaning and importance of price, and he should decide on his pricing goals.

IMPORTANCE OF PRICE

IN THE ECONOMY

Pricing is considered by many to be the key activity within the capitalistic system of free enterprise. Price becomes a hub around which the system revolves. It is the balance wheel which keeps the system operating on an even keel. Imperfections in pricing are an indication of imperfections in the system.

The market price of a product influences wages, rent, interest, and profits. That is, the price of a product influences the price paid for the factors of production——labor, land, capital, and entrepreneurship. In this way, price becomes a basic regulator of the entire economic system because it influences the allocation of these resources. High wages attract labor, high interest rates attract capital, and so on. Conversely, low wages, low rent, or low profits reduce the availability of labor, land, and risk takers.

Criticism of the American system of reasonably free enterprise and the public's demand for further restraints on the system are often triggered by a reaction to price, or pricing policies.

IN THE INDIVIDUAL FIRM

A company's pricing structure, more than any other segment of its marketing program, is influenced by state and federal legislation. We have restraining laws affecting packaging, labeling, distribution policies, and promotional activities, but the key legislative regulations in marketing apply to pricing. Because of these legal considerations, executives are hesitant to disclose information about their companies' pricing practices. This hesitancy adds to the difficulty of acquiring the empirical data so badly needed if businessmen are to learn more about pricing.

The price of a product or service is a major determinant of the market demand for the item. Price will affect the firm's competitive position and its share of the market. As a result, price has a considerable bearing on the company's revenue and net profit. The revenue is equal to unit price times the volume of units sold. The profit is equal to revenue minus costs. To some extent, costs are a function of volume, and costs themselves are measured by their price. Price also affects the market segment that will be reached by a firm.

The price of a product also affects the firm's marketing program. In product planning, for example, if management wants to improve the quality of its product or add differentiating features, this decision can be implemented only if the market will accept a price high enough to cover the costs of these changes. The pricing structure will determine whether the manufacturer or his retailers will be expected to finance the bulk of the promotional program.

At the same time, there usually are countervailing forces limiting the importance of pricing in a company's marketing program. Differentiated product features or a persuasive advertising campaign may be more important to a consumer than price. Thus, these forces may engender rigidities or a "stickiness" in the pricing mechanism, so that it does not respond so quickly to changes in demand or supply. Thus, the traditional, theoretical role of price as an allocator of scarce resources is modified somewhat in today's economic system.

To put the role of pricing in a company's marketing program in its proper perspective, then, let us say this—price is important, but not all-important, in explaining marketing success. One study among manufacturing companies, for example, identified product-related activities and sales effort as the most important factors contributing to marketing success in a firm. One-half of the respondents did not even list price as one of the top five factors.[1] Three situations may account for this relatively low ranking of pricing: (1) Because supply generally exceeds de-

---

[1]Jon G. Udell, "How Important Is Pricing in Competitive Strategy?" *Journal of Marketing,* January, 1964, pp. 44–48.

mand, most sellers must be highly competitive (or collusive) in their pricing; (2) today's relatively affluent consumer is interested in more than just price; and (3) a seller may achieve some pricing freedom through successful product differentiation.

PRICE AND PRODUCT-QUALITY RELATIONSHIP

Some of the psychological aspects of pricing should also be understood by a marketing executive. For instance, consumers rely heavily on price as an indicator of a product's quality, especially when they must make purchase decisions with incomplete information. Studies have consistently shown that consumers' perceptions of product quality vary directly with price.[2] Thus, the higher the price, the better the quality is perceived to be. Consumers make this judgment particularly when no other clues as to product quality are available, or when they are judging the quality of products sold by the same retailer or made by the same manufacturer. Consumers' quality perceptions can, of course, also be influenced by store reputation, advertising, and other variables.

MEANING OF PRICE

Undoubtedly many of the difficulties associated with pricing start with the rather simple fact that often we do not really know what we are talking about. That is, we do not know the meaning of the word "price," even though it is true that the concept is quite easy to define in familiar terms.

In economic theory, we learn that price, value, and utility are related concepts. *Utility* is the attribute of an item that makes it capable of want satisfaction. *Value* is the quantitative expression of the power a product has to attract other products in exchange. We may say the value of a certain hat is three baseball bats, a box of red Delicious apples, or 30 gallons of gasoline. Because our economy is not geared to a slow, ponderous barter system, we use money as a common denominator of value and use the term "price" to describe the money value of an item. *Price* is value expressed in terms of dollars and cents, or whatever the monetary medium may be in the country where the exchange occurs.

---

[2]For a summary of several of these studies, see Kent B. Monroe, "Buyers' Subjective Perceptions of Price," *Journal of Marketing Research,* February, 1973, pp. 70–80; Arthur G. Bedeian, "Consumer Perception of Price as an Indicator of Product Quality," *MSU Business Topics,* Summer, 1971, pp. 59–65; and Benson P. Shapiro, "The Psychology of Pricing," *Harvard Business Review,* July–August, 1968, pp. 14–16ff. Also see David M. Gardner, "Is There a Generalized Price-Quality Relationship?" *Journal of Marketing Research,* May, 1971, pp. 241–243; Robert A. Peterson, "The Price-Perceived Quality Relationship: Experimental Evidence," *Journal of Marketing Research,* November, 1970, pp. 525–528; and Norman D. French, John J. Williams, and William A. Chance, "A Shopping Experiment on Price-Quality Relationships," *Journal of Retailing,* Fall, 1972, pp. 3–16ff.

For the contention that price often is *not* a good indicator of product quality, see Ruby T. Morris and Claire S. Bronson, "The Chaos of Competition Indicated by Consumer Reports," *Journal of Marketing,* July, 1969, pp. 26–34.

Practical problems connected with a definition of price arise, however, when we try to state simply what is the price of a pint of fresh strawberries or an office desk. Harry paid 35 cents for a pint of strawberries, while Bill paid only 10 cents and was allowed to eat all the strawberries he wanted at the seller's location. The 10-cent price was what he paid for the strawberries he took home with him. The price quoted to Harry for an office desk was $325, while Bill paid only $175.

At first glance it looks as if Bill got the better deal in each example. Yet when we get all the facts, we may change our opinion. Harry bought his strawberries at the local supermarket. Bill responded to a strawberry grower's advertisement which stated that if one came out to the farm and picked the berries himself, they would cost 10 cents a box. The grower furnished the pint-sized boxes and allowed Bill to eat all he wanted while he was berry picking. Harry's desk was delivered to his office, he had a year to pay for it, and it was all beautifully finished. Bill bought a partially assembled job with no finish on it. (He was a do-it-yourself fan.) He had to assemble the drawers and legs and then painstakingly stain, varnish, and hand-rub the entire desk. He arranged for the delivery himself, and he paid cash in full at the time of purchase. Now let us ask the question of who paid the higher price in each case. The answer is not as easy as it seemed at first glance.

These examples illustrate how difficult it is to define price in an everyday business situation. Many variables are involved. The definition hinges around the problem of determining exactly what it is that a person is buying. This relates to the problem posed in Chapter 8, that of trying to define a product. In pricing we must consider more than the physical product alone. A seller usually is pricing a combination of the physical product plus several other services and want-satisfying benefits. Sometimes it is difficult even to define the price of the physical product alone. On one model of automobile a stated price may include radio, power steering, and power brakes. For another model of the same make of car these three items may be priced separately. In another situation the price may be defined as that which the buyer pays or the seller nets, with the difference being the freight charges. Some sellers quote a price that includes various services (alterations, installation, credit, delivery), while others price these individual services separately.

In summary, *price* is the amount of money (plus possibly some goods) which is needed to acquire in exchange some combined assortment of a product and its accompanying services. Obviously there are many possible combinations of a product and the various services which may accompany it.

PRICING OBJECTIVES

We have observed that before a company can do a marketing job properly, management needs a goal. Pricing is no exception. Management should decide upon the objectives of pricing before determining the price itself. Very few firms, however, consciously establish pricing objectives or clearly state their specific price policies. Even fewer have written statements of their pricing goals.

In a landmark study, the Brookings Institution reported on the price policies and the methods of price determination used by a group of twenty large firms. Many of the findings are also applicable to smaller firms. We can gain considerable insight into *pricing goals* from this study and a related article by one of the principal investigators. Much of the material in this section is drawn from the original study and the subsequent article.[3] See Table 11-1.

The main goals in pricing may be classified as follows:

1. Achieve target return on investment or on net sales.
2. Stabilize prices.
3. Maintain or improve a share of the market.
4. Meet or prevent competition.
5. Maximize profits.

ACHIEVE TARGET RETURN ON INVESTMENT OR NET SALES

Many firms seek to achieve a certain percentage return on investment or on net sales. This goal was the one most frequently mentioned by the subjects of the Brookings Institution study. Target-return pricing may be defined as building a price structure to provide enough return on capital used for specific products or groups of products so that the sales revenue will yield a predetermined average return for the entire company. Target return may be a short-run (one year) or a long-run goal, but it is mostly the latter. If an estimate is made of return expected over the long run, fluctuations will occur in short-run volume, but they will average out.

Many retailers and wholesalers use target return on net sales as a pricing objective for short-run periods. They set a percentage markup on sales which is large enough to cover anticipated operating costs plus a desired profit for the year. In such cases the *percentage* of profit may remain constant, but the *dollar* profit will vary according to the number of units sold.

Target return on investment was typically selected as a goal only when one or both of two conditions were present. First, ordinarily the firms were leaders in their industry, or they sold in protected markets. For example, target return on investment was a stated goal of General Motors, International Harvester, Aluminum Corporation of America, the Du Pont Company, Johns-Manville Corporation, and Union Carbide Corporation. Second, this goal was typical in connection with new products and low-unit-price, high-volume, standardized items.

Some of the reasons most frequently stated by companies for selecting a particular level of return were as follows:

1. It is a fair or reasonable rate. The concept of "fair and reasonable" is important to these companies because most of them are very much in the public eye. Their pricing structure is of great interest to the Antitrust Division of the Justice Department, the labor unions, and the public in general. To avoid charges of monopoly or restraint of trade, they must set "fair and reasonable" prices.
2. It is traditional in the industry.
3. Management wants to reach or improve a corporation's average return over a recent period.
4. It was what the company felt it could get in the long run.

---

[3]A. D. H. Kaplan, Joel B. Dirlam, and Robert F. Lanzillotti, *Pricing in Big Business,* The Brookings Institution, Washington, D.C., 1958; Robert F. Lanzillotti, "Pricing Objectives in Large Companies," *American Economic Review,* December, 1958, pp. 921-940.

Table 11-1. Pricing goals of twenty large industrial corporations.

Company	Principal pricing goal	Collateral pricing goals
Alcoa	20% on investment (before taxes); higher on new products (about 10% effective rate after taxes)	"Promotive" policy on new products Price stabilization
American Can	Maintaining market share	"Meeting competition" Price stabilization
A & P	Increasing market share	Promotive
Du Pont	Target return on investment—no specific figure given	Charging what traffic will bear over long run Maximum return for new products—"life cycle" pricing
Exxon (Standard Oil of N.J.)	"Fair-return" target—no specific figure given	Maintaining market share Price stabilization
General Electric	20% on investment (after taxes); 7% on sales (after taxes)	Promotive policy on new products Price stabilization on nationally advertised products
General Foods	33⅓% gross margin ("⅓ to make, ⅓ to sell, and ⅓ for profit"); expectation of realizing target only on new products	Maintaining market share
General Motors	20% on investment (after taxes)	Maintaining market share
Goodyear	"Meeting competitors"	Maintaining "position" Price stabilization
Gulf	Following price of most important marketer in each area	Maintaining market share Price stabilization
International Harvester	10% on investment (after taxes)	Market share: ceiling of "less than a dominant share of any market"
Johns-Manville	Return on investment	Market share not greater than 20% Stabilization of prices
Kennecott	Stabilization of prices	
Kroger	Maintaining market share	Target return of 20% on investment before taxes
National Steel	Matching the market—price follower	Increasing market share
Sears	Increasing market share (8–10% regarded as satisfactory share)	Traditional return on investment of 10–15% (after taxes) Promotive (low-margin) policy
Standard Oil (Indiana)	Maintaining market share	Stabilizing prices Target return on investment (nonspecified)
Swift	Maintaining market share in meat-packing	
Union Carbide	Target return on investment	Promotive policy on new products; "life cycle" pricing on chemicals generally
U.S. Steel	8% on investment (after taxes)	Target market share of 30% Stable price and margin

Source: Adapted from Robert F. Lanzillotti, "Pricing Objectives in Large Companies," *American Economic Review,* December, 1958, pp. 924–927.

The Brookings Institution study discovered a trend toward the adoption of some form of target return as a pricing objective either for particular products or for the entire company. Some of the major reasons for this trend are:

1. An increasing awareness of the interrelationship of profit, capital, and investment and a realization of the importance of budgeting for this triumvirate.
2. The desire for a common basis for evaluating performance of products and divisions in the company.
3. The fact that government contracts focus attention on rate of return.
4. The tendency to copy large, successful firms which have been using target return as a pricing goal for some time.

STABILIZE PRICES

The goal of stabilizing prices is often found in industries that have a price leader. In industries where demand can fluctuate frequently and sometimes violently, large companies, especially, will try to maintain stability in their pricing. In the Brookings Institution study, United States Steel and Kennecott Copper were pointed out as two firms which apparently sought this goal, but often with considerably less than total success. American Can, The Aluminum Corporation of America, and some of the chemical companies seemed to have achieved a greater degree of price stability.[4]

Price leadership does not necessarily mean that the goal of stability is reached by having all firms in the industry charge the same price as that set by the leader. Price leadership means only that some regular relationship exists between the leader's prices and those charged by other firms. Some companies may regularly sell at a level above or below that set by the leader. In a given geographic market, "minor" oil companies frequently price their gasoline at 1 or 2 cents a gallon under the level charged by the "majors."

Companies seeking stability in their pricing are very anxious to avert price wars, even when demand is declining. Price leaders tend to take a long-run point of view in achieving stability. Their goal, in a sense, is to "live and let live." The companies are willing to forgo maximizing profits in times of prosperity or short supply if they have the opportunity to earn a reasonable profit during less prosperous periods.

Many retailers and manufacturers of consumer products have attempted to stabilize prices throughout a market by resorting to suggested resale prices or to out-and-out resale price maintenance supported by law.

MAINTAIN OR IMPROVE SHARE OF MARKET

In some companies, both large and small, the major pricing objective is to maintain or increase the share of the market held by the firm. One factor that makes market share a workable goal is that a company can usually determine what share of the market it enjoys. In some respects, market share is a better indicator of corporate health than target return on investment, especially in times of increasing markets. A firm might be earning what management considers a

---

[4]For a challenge to the traditional economic theory that prices in some industries are controlled or "administered" by a few large firms, see Gilbert Burck, "The Myths and Realities of Corporate Pricing," *Fortune,* April, 1972, p. 85.

reasonable return. However, unless management keeps fully abreast of conditions in an expanding market, this "reasonable" profit may be too small. The company may be getting a decreasing share of the market. In the Brookings Institution study, market share seemed to be almost as important as a target return on investment. A & P, for example, constantly reported that it sought to increase its share of the market through continuous low pricing.

Large firms may try to limit their share of the market for some reason. In some cases they fear government intervention or restraint if they get too large. General Motors, with approximately 50 percent of the automobile market, has been in this situation for years. Certainly some adjustments are needed either in a company or in an economic system when companies must consciously hesitate to do the most complete, aggressive, and consumer-satisfying marketing job of which they are capable. Some companies—Johns-Manville, for example—said that they preferred to have a *relatively* small market share, say, 20 percent rather than 50 percent, because they would rather work to *expand* a smaller share than to *defend* a larger share.

MEET OR PREVENT COMPETITION

Countless firms, regardless of size, consciously price their products to meet or sometimes even prevent competition. When a company seeks simply through trial and error to find a price at which its output can be sold, we can almost say that it has no pricing objective. At least it has no control over the goal and the means used to reach it.

Large rubber companies, such as Goodyear Tire and Rubber Company, reported that generally they felt that they could exercise very little influence over the market-determined price. In an industry where there is a price leader and where the product is highly standardized, most firms have a "follow-the-leader" policy. National Steel Corporation and the Kroger Company said they pursued this policy as a rule. Gasoline companies professed that they simply set their prices to meet competition, particularly during a price war. The major firms usually wait until they have proof that the price in a market has broken. Then they cut their prices in order to meet the competition.

Some firms consciously price to prevent competition. Normally this goal or practice is not publicly admitted, but it has been brought to light in court cases involving manufacturers and retailers in the food field. When introducing a new product, a company will frequently set a low price in order to discourage competition. Usually this policy is unsuccessful. If the new item is popular enough, other producers will be attracted into the field regardless of the pricing policy of the innovator.

MAXIMIZE PROFITS

The pricing objective of making as much money as possible is probably followed by a larger total number of companies than any other policy yet mentioned. The trouble with this goal is that the term "profit maximization" has an ugly connotation. It is connected in the public mind with profiteering, high prices, and monopoly. In economic theory or business practice, however, there is nothing wrong with profit maximization. Theoretically, if profits become unduly high because supply is short in relation to demand, new capital will be attracted into a field to better balance demand and supply. In the marketplace, it is difficult to find many situations where a monopolistic situation has existed over an extended period of time. Substitute products are available, purchases are postponable, or competition increases, and prices are thus kept at a reasonable level. Where prices may be unduly high and entry into the field is severely limited, public outrage soon balances the scales. If market conditions and public opinion do not do the job directly, government restraints which represent the feeling of the public will soon bring about moderation.

A profit maximization policy is apt to be far more beneficial to a company and to the public if practiced over the long run. Pricing by companies who cannot see beyond the end of their next month's profit and loss statement often results in repercussions which may be detrimental to the firms. Practiced over the long run, profit maximization should result in a socially desirable allocation of resources. Efficient firms are rewarded and inefficient firms disappear. Profits attract new capital into a field. Prices are kept at a reasonable level, and supply is sufficient to satisfy market demands.

To maximize profits over the long run, firms may have to accept short-run losses. A firm entering a new geographic market or introducing a new product frequently finds it advantageous to use relatively low prices in order to build a large clientele. Such companies often do not expect to show a profit for the first few years, but they are laying a solid foundation for adequate profits over the long run.

The goal should be to maximize profits on total output rather than on each single item. A manufacturer may maximize total profits by practically giving away some articles which will attract the buyer's attention or will stimulate sales of other goods. Through its sponsored broadcasts and telecasts of athletic events, the Gillette Company frequently promotes razors at very low, profitless prices. Management hopes that once a customer acquires a Gillette razor, he will become a long-term profitable customer for Gillette blades. In this way the company maximizes profits in total but not on each product in its line. A retailer often finds that the best way to maximize profits over his entire store is to offer well-known items as "leaders." They are sold at a very small profit or even at a loss, but they attract so many customers to the store—customers who stay to buy other items—that the overall profit picture of the store is enhanced considerably.

PROCEDURE FOR PRICE DETERMINATION

The first step in establishing a price system is consciously to formulate an objective and state it clearly in writing. Once the pricing objective is agreed upon, the executives can move to the heart of price management—the actual determination of the base price of the products or services. No one procedure, generally acceptable by all companies, has yet been developed for determining base prices. One critical reason for the lack of exact pricing models or formulas is the fact that sufficiently detailed information on costs at various volumes and on demand at various prices is not available.

The price-determination procedure used here can be divided into six steps:

1. Estimate the demand for the product.
2. Anticipate the competitive reaction.

3. Establish the expected share of the market.
4. Select the price strategy to be used to reach the market target.
5. Consider company policies regarding products, channels, and promotion.
6. Select the specific price.[5]

At this point we are concerned with determining only the basic or list price of the product or service. Later we shall deal with specific policies regarding discounts, freight allowances, price lines, and other factors which may alter this basic price somewhat. Ordinarily the original price setter is a producer, although sometimes a large middleman sets or strongly influences the original price.

The same general steps are followed in pricing a product, whether it is a new article or an established one. Pricing an established product often offers very little challenge because the exact price or a very narrow range of prices may be dictated by the market. At the same time, some stages in the pricing procedure are particularly important and difficult for a new article. Consequently, any special conditions involved in pricing new products will be woven into the discussion.

ESTIMATE DEMAND FOR PRODUCT

The first stage in pricing a product is to estimate the total demand for it. This is easier to do for an established product than for a new one. The seller is not certain that a new product will have any demand at all. Two practical steps in demand estimation are, first, to determine whether there is a price which the market expects and, second, to estimate the sales volume at different prices.

The "expected" price. The expected price for a product is the price at which customers consciously or unconsciously value it. It is what they think the product is worth. Often, rather than being one specific dollar amount, the expected price can be determined within a range. It might be "between $250 and $300" or "not over $10."

It is sometimes surprising how shrewd customers can be in evaluating a product. In the case of a new product, however, direct competition and price comparison are often slight during its early life, so the manufacturer has considerably more latitude in setting his price than is the case with older products. The seller may set a higher initial price on the product than would be possible if it were an established item subject to comparison. Then, after the market has developed an image of a high-priced article, the seller can lower the price and the market may think it is getting a bargain.

A producer must also think of middlemen's reaction to the price. Middlemen are more likely to give an article favorable treatment in their stores if they approve of its price. Because of their extensive experience, retail or wholesale buyers can frequently examine an item and make an accurate estimate of the selling price that the market will accept.

---

[5]For other procedures, see Alfred R. Oxenfeldt, "A Decision-Making Structure for Price Decisions," *Journal of Marketing,* January, 1973, pp. 48–53; Gerald Albaum, "Price Formulation," in J. Howard Westing and Gerald Albaum (eds.), *Modern Market-Thought,* 2d ed., The Macmillan Company, New York, 1969, pp. 346-359; Bill R. Darden, "An Operational Approach to Product Pricing," *Journal of Marketing,* April, 1968, pp. 29-33.

Research may uncover the fact that the expected price is below the level at which the firm can make or buy the product. Unless adjustments can be made in production costs, the relatively low expected price may preclude the production or purchase of the item. However, a manufacturer should not feel that it is impossible to change the expected price, particularly on a new product. This may be done:

1. By adding product features which increase the apparent value of the article by more than the actual cost of the added features, or
2. By selecting distribution channels which reach customers who will see the article in comparison with more expensive items, or
3. By using an advertising program to increase the value of the product in the customer's eye.

It is possible to set a price too low. If the price is much lower than that which the market expects, often sales will be lost. For example, it would probably be a mistake for a well-known cosmetics manufacturer to put a 19-cent price tag on lipstick or to price its imported perfume at $1.29 an ounce. Either customers will be suspicious of the quality of the product, or their self-concepts will not let them use such low-priced merchandise. More than one seller has raised the price of his product and experienced a considerable increase in sales. In terms of market-demand curves, this situation is referred to as "inverse demand"—the higher the price, the greater the unit sales.[6]

How does a seller determine the expected price? He may submit the article to an experienced retailer or wholesaler for appraisal. Manufacturers of industrial products sometimes approach engineers working for prospective customers. By showing models or blueprints, the manufacturer can solicit informed judgments on what the price "ought to be." Another possibility is to observe prices of comparable competitive products. A third alternative is to survey the potential consumers. They may be shown the article and asked what they would pay for it. This approach can bring misleading answers because there is often a considerable difference between what a person *says* the product is worth and what he will actually pay. A much more effective approach is to market the product in a few limited test areas. By trying different prices under controlled research conditions, the seller can determine at least a reasonable range of prices. When it is not practical to produce a sufficient quantity to test the market, the seller may have to rely on some form of depth interviewing of potential customers.

Estimates of sales at various prices. It is extremely helpful in price determination to estimate what the sales volume will be at several different prices. These estimates involve a consideration of the demand elasticity of the product. A product with an elastic market demand should usually be priced lower than an item with an inelastic demand. By estimating the demand for its product at different prices, management, in effect, is determining the demand curve for the item. These volume estimates at different prices are important also in relation to determining break-even points, which are discussed in the next chapter.

---

[6]See Zarrel V. Lambert, "Product Perception: An Important Variable in Price Strategy," *Journal of Marketing*, October, 1970, pp. 68–71; and by same author, "Price and Choice Behavior," *Journal of Marketing Research*, February, 1972, pp. 35–40.

ANTICIPATE COMPETITIVE REACTION

Present and potential competition is an important influence on price determination. Even with a new product, any possible distinctiveness is limited in that it is ordinarily only a matter of time until some form of competition will be felt strongly. The threat of *potential* competition is greatest when the field is easy to enter and the profit prospects are encouraging.

Competition can come from three *existing* sources. First, from directly similar products: the manufacturer of Wheaties must consider the price set on Kellogg's cornflakes or General Foods' Post Toasties. Second, from available substitutes: for many years United States Steel considered only such competitors as Bethlehem Steel Corporation (directly similar). Now steel producers must be alert to prices on aluminum and plastics because for many end products steel is no longer the only reasonable alternative material. Third, competition may come from unrelated items seeking the same consumer dollar.

ESTABLISH EXPECTED SHARE OF MARKET

The next step in price determination, and one which tends to narrow still further the range of the probable pricing decisions, is to determine what share of the market the company expects. An aggressive firm seeking a larger share of the market ordinarily will price differently from a company which is content with its present share. Sometimes the drive for a certain market share is characterized by advertising and other forms of nonprice competition rather than by price appeals.

The expected share of the market will be influenced by present production capacity, costs of plant expansion, and ease of competitive entry. It would be a mistake for a firm to aim for a larger share of the market than its plant capacity can sustain. If a new product is priced low in an attempt to gain a broad market, and if the market response is extremely favorable, the company may not be able to fill its orders. If management is not interested in expanding its plant because ease of competitive entry undoubtedly will drive down future profits, the initial price should be set relatively high.

SELECT PRICING STRATEGY TO REACH MARKET TARGET

Any one of several pricing strategies might be employed by management to achieve the predetermined share of the market. By focusing attention on two alternatives which are polar extremes, we can highlight many of the pertinent issues. These alternatives are popularly referred to as "skim-the-cream" pricing and "penetration" pricing. They are most appropriate to the pricing of new products.[7]

Skim-the-cream pricing. The cream-skimming strategy involves setting a price which is high in the range of expected prices. The seller may continue with this

---

[7]These opposite strategies are discussed in Joel Dean, *How to Price a New Product,* Small Business Administration, Management Aids for Small Manufacturers, no. 62, Washington, D.C., April, 1955; see also Joel Dean, "Pricing Policies for New Products," *Harvard Business Review,* November, 1950, pp. 45-53. Much of the discussion in this section is adapted from these two sources.

strategy for an indefinite period, or he may later lower the price in order to tap other segments of the market. Cream skimming is probably most effective with a highly distinctive article which is aggressively promoted in the early stages of its life cycle.

There are at least five reasons why skim-the-cream pricing may be particularly suitable for new products. First, demand is likely to be less elastic in the early stages of a product's life cycle. In the early stages, price is less important, competition is at a minimum, and the product's distinctiveness lends itself to real salesmanship. Second, this strategy can effectively segment the market on an income basis. The appeal at first is to that segment of the demand curve which responds to distinctiveness and exclusiveness in a product and is relatively insensitive to price. Later on, the seller can lower his price and appeal to segments of the market which are highly sensitive to price.

A third advantage of cream skimming is that it acts as a strong hedge against a possible mistake in setting the price. If the original price is too high and the market does not respond, management can easily lower it, but it is very difficult to raise a price which proves to be too low to cover costs. Fourth, high initial prices can often generate more revenues and profits than can low prices in the early stages of market development. Finally, high initial prices can be used to keep demand within the limits of a company's productive capacity.

Penetration pricing. In this strategy, a low initial price is set in order to reach the mass market immediately. This strategy can also be employed at a later stage in the product's life cycle. Many a firm has saved its product from a premature old age or death simply by switching to penetration pricing from cream skimming.

Compared with cream skimming, penetration pricing is a more aggressive competitive strategy and is likely to be more satisfactory when the following conditions exist: (1) The quantity sold is highly sensitive to price; that is, the product has a highly elastic demand; (2) substantial reductions in unit production and marketing costs can be achieved through large-scale operations; (3) the product faces very strong competition soon after it is introduced to the market; and (4) there is an inadequate high-income market to sustain a skim-the-cream price.

The nature of potential competition will critically influence management's choice between the two pricing strategies. If competitors can enter a market easily and quickly and if the market potential for the product is very promising, management probably should adopt a policy of penetration pricing. Low initial pricing may do two things. First, it may discourage other firms from entering the field because the investment needed in production and marketing facilities will be too great in light of the anticipated low profit margin. Second, low prices may give the innovator such a strong hold on his share of the market that future competitors cannot cut into it. On the other hand, cream skimming may be more feasible where market potential is not large enough to attract the big competitors. While percentage margins per unit of sale may be attractive, the total dollar profits will be too small to attract large firms.

CONSIDER COMPANY MARKETING POLICIES

Another major stage in the pricing procedure is to consider the company's marketing policies with respect to the product itself, the distribution system, and the promotional program.

Product policies. We have already observed that the price of a product is influenced substantially by whether it is a new item or an older, established one. Other aspects of the product must be considered. For example, product perishability influences a firm's pricing policy. The importance of a product in its end use must also be considered. To illustrate, price competition is largely absent and a stable price structure exists among manufacturers of packaging materials, industrial gases, and aluminum fabrications. These products are only an incidental part of the final product.

Whether the article will be sold under a middleman's brand or under the manufacturer's own brand will affect the price established by the manufacturer. The interdependence of the product mix is another consideration. Where products are related, the price set on any one item affects all others in the line. Thus General Motors cannot establish the price for a Chevrolet without considering the prices of other General Motors cars. On the other hand, a firm such as Union Carbide, which sells both Prestone and industrial oxygen, has greater flexibility in pricing.

Channels of distribution. The channels selected, the types of middlemen used, and the gross-margin requirements of these middlemen will influence a manufacturer's price. A firm selling through wholesalers and also directly to retailers often sets a different factory price for each of these two classes of customers.

Promotional methods. The promotional methods used and the extent to which the job is done by the manufacturer or the middlemen are still another factor to consider in pricing. If the bulk of the promotional responsibility is placed upon retailers, they ordinarily will require a larger margin than if the product is heavily advertised by the manufacturer. Even when a manufacturer promotes heavily, he may want his middlemen to use local advertising, store display, and other types of promotion to tie in with his national advertising. Such a decision must be reflected in the dealer's margin and, consequently, in the manufacturer's price.

QUESTIONS AND PROBLEMS

1. Two students paid 69 cents for identical tubes of toothpaste at a leading department store. Yet one student complained that he paid a much higher price than the other. What might be the basis for this complaint?
2. "Watching television commercials is too high a *price* to pay to see a baseball game." "Having to put up with Mr. ____ [a news analyst with a syndicated column in many newspapers] is part of the high *price* we pay for freedom of the press." Are these correct interpretations of the concept of price?
3. Explain how the chosen pricing objective may influence a firm's promotional program. Which goal will involve the largest, most aggressive promotional campaign?
4. "The goal of price stabilization is marked by nonaggressive marketing strategies and is usually found only in mature companies." Discuss.
5. Are the principal and collateral pricing goals compatible in each of the following companies? (Refer to Table 11-1.)
   a. The American Can Company

    b. The Gulf Oil Company

    c. The National Steel Company

6. Evaluate target return on investment or net sales as a pricing goal for a manufacturer. Consider the merits and limitations from both a business-competitive and a social point of view.

7. What marketing conditions might logically lead a company to set "meeting competition" as a pricing objective?

8. Is profit maximization compatible with each of the other major pricing goals?

9. What marketing conditions have served to reduce the importance of the price-setting function in many companies today?

10. What is the expected price for each of the following articles? How did you arrive at your estimate in each instance?

    a. A new type of carbonated cola beverage which holds its original carbonation long after it has been opened; packaged in 8-ounce and 32-ounce bottles

    b. A nuclear-powered, 21-inch, table-model television set guaranteed to run for ten years without replacement of the original power-generating component; requires no battery or electric wires

    c. An automatic garage-door opener for residential housing

11. Name some products for which you think an inverse demand exists. Within which price range does this demand exist for each product on your list?

12. Give some examples of products which have an elastic demand. An inelastic demand.

13. For each of the following products, do you recommend that the seller adopt a cream-skimming or a penetration pricing strategy? Support your decision in each instance.

    a. Original models of women's dresses styled and manufactured by Dior

    b. A new wonder drug

    c. An exterior house paint which wears twice as long as any competitive brand

    d. A cigarette really totally free of tars and nicotine

    e. Instant beer

    f. An atomic-powered motor boat, family-sized

14. Discuss the following propositions:

    a. Skim-the-cream pricing is feasible only when the seller employs an exclusive or a highly selective distribution policy.

    b. Penetration pricing is practical only when a firm engages in intensive distribution.

BASIC METHODS OF
SETTING PRICE

In the pricing procedure outlined in the preceding chapter, the final step was to narrow the range of expected prices to the point where a specific selling price is established. Over the years many different methods have been used by individual companies to accomplish this task. Most of these approaches to price setting, however, are based on one of the following major methods:

1. Prices may be based on total cost plus a desired profit.
2. Prices may be based on a balance between estimates of market demand and costs of production and marketing.
3. Prices may be set by competitive market conditions.

PRICES BASED ON COSTS

In its simplest form, the cost-plus approach means that the selling price for a unit of a product is equal to the unit's total cost plus an amount to cover the anticipated profit on the unit. As an example, a contractor figures that the labor and materials required to build and sell ten houses will cost $150,000 and that his other expenses (office rent, depreciation on equipment, wages of management, etc.) will equal $50,000. On this total cost of $200,000, he anticipates a profit of 10 percent of cost. Cost plus profit amounts to $220,000. Therefore, each of the ten houses will sell for $22,000.

While this is a very simple, easily understood, and easily applied pricing method, it has one serious limitation. It disregards the fact that there are different types of costs and that not all of them act alike as output increases or decreases. Referring to our housing example, if the contractor sold only eight houses, his total sales would be $176,000. His labor and materials chargeable to eight houses would total $120,000 ($15,000 per house). He would still incur the full $50,000 in overhead expenses, however, so his total cost would be $170,000, leaving a profit of only $6,000, or about $750 per house instead of the anticipated $2,000.

DIFFERENT COST CONCEPTS

A more sophisticated approach to cost-plus pricing takes into consideration the several types of costs and their different reactions to changes in level of output. That is, the total unit cost of a product will change as output expands or contracts. The following classification of cost concepts is important for our purposes:

1. Total fixed costs
2. Total variable costs
3. Total cost
4. Average fixed costs

5. Average variable costs
6. Average total costs
7. Marginal costs

Three of these concepts may require some elaboration. *Total fixed costs* are elements, such as rent, executives' salaries, and property taxes, which remain constant regardless of level of output. Even if production ceases entirely, these costs continue. We shall, however, implicitly assume here that we are dealing with a fixed plant capacity and a short-run period of time. Over the long run, *all* costs tend to be variable.

With respect to *average variable costs,* we shall, under a simplified assumption, keep these constant. In such a case the *total* variable costs will increase with each additional unit of output. The direct labor and material costs *per unit,* however, will remain the same. In a more typical production operation, unit variable costs are relatively high for the first few units of output. Then, as total output increases, the average variable costs come down because of quantity discounts on material, more efficient use of manpower, etc. Beyond some optimum point, average variable costs will increase as expanded output results in overtime pay, overuse and crowding of plant facilities, and generally less efficient use of labor and materials resources.

Marginal cost is the cost of producing and selling one more unit, that is, the cost of the most recent or last unit. If it costs $500 to produce sixty units and $527 to produce sixty-one units, the marginal cost is $27.

These seven cost concepts and their interrelationships may be studied in Table 12-1 and in Figs. 12-1 and 12-2, which are based on the table. Figure 12-1 shows the relationship among the curves representing the *totals* of (1) all costs, (2) fixed costs, and (3) variable costs, respectively. Here we can see that total fixed costs are represented by a straight line because they are constant within a short-run period. As output increases, total costs increase by the amount of variable cost incurred by each unit. Thus the total cost curve is a line which rises to the right. In Fig. 12-1, however, variable costs are not constant per unit. Therefore, the total cost line is curved. If variable costs were constant, the total cost line would be straight.

Figure 12-2 graphically displays the interrelationships among the various

Table 12-1. Costs for individual firm.

Total fixed costs never change, despite increases in quantity. These costs are incurred for land rent, executives' salaries, and other items which remain constant no matter what quantity is being produced. Variable costs represent increasing costs for input of materials, labor, power, etc., as production quantity rises. Total cost is the sum of all fixed and variable costs. The other measures in the table are simply methods of looking at costs per unit and always involve dividing costs by number of units produced according to the formulas at the tops of the columns.

Quantity output, Q	Total fixed costs, TFC	Total variable costs, TVC	Total costs, TC = TFC + TVC	Marginal costs per unit, MC	Average fixed costs, AFC = TFC ÷ Q	Average variable costs, AVC = TVC ÷ Q	Average costs per unit, ATC = TC ÷ Q
0	$256	$ 0	$256		Infinity	$ 0	Infinity
1	256	64	320	$ 64	$256.00	64	$320.00
2	256	84	340	20	128.00	42	170.00
3	256	99	355	15	85.33	33	118.33
4	256	112	368	13	64.00	28	92.00
5	256	125	381	13	51.20	25	76.20
6	256	144	400	19	42.67	24	66.67
7	256	175	431	31	36.57	25	61.57
8	256	224	480	49	32.00	28	60.00
9	256	297	553	73	28.44	33	61.44
10	256	400	656	103	25.60	40	65.60

Source: Adapted from Paul Samuelson, *Economics*, McGraw-Hill Book Company, New York, 1961.

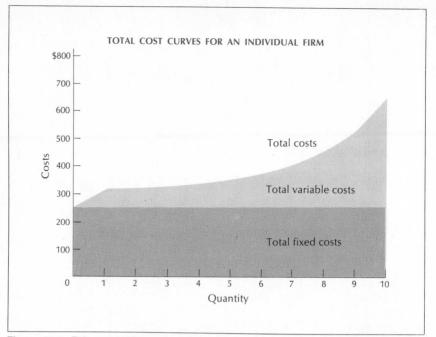

Figure 12-1. This graph shows the relationships among total fixed costs, total variable costs, and total cost so that their significance in pricing can be seen. The effect of total variable costs in this simplified example is to make total cost a slowly ascending curved line.

average unit costs. The average variable cost curve (AVC) would be horizontal if the average variable costs were constant. In our example, it curves downward until the sixth unit is passed, then diminishing returns set in. The average total cost curve (ATC) will slope downward as long as marginal costs are less than average unit costs. Even though the marginal costs are up after the fifth unit, the average cost curve continues to slope downward until after the eighth unit. This is because marginal costs, even though going up, are still less than average costs. The marginal cost (MC) and the average total cost curves intersect at the lowest point of the average total cost curve. Beyond that point (the eighth unit in the example) the cost of producing and selling the last unit is higher than the average of all units. Therefore, from then on the average total cost will rise. The reason for this is that the average variable costs are increasing faster than the average fixed costs are decreasing. Producing the ninth unit reduced average fixed costs from $32 to $28.44, but average variable costs rose $5. The average total cost curve will slope downward as long as average variable costs increase less than average fixed costs decrease.

The marginal cost, as shown by the marginal cost curve in Fig. 12-2 and in column (5) of Table 12-1, is a critical figure to keep in mind. This represents the cost of producing and selling the last unit. Later in the analysis we shall see that to maximize profits, a firm theoretically will continue producing and selling as long as the sales revenue from this last unit (called "marginal revenue") exceeds the cost of the unit.

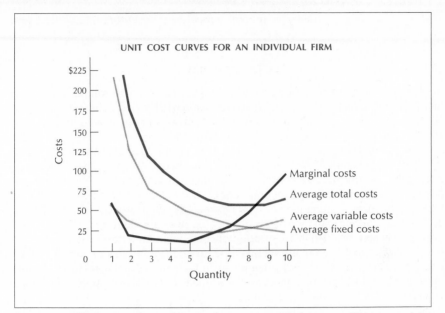

Figure 12-2. Here we see how unit costs change as quantity increases. The average total cost per unit is generally U-shaped. It starts quite high because total fixed cost is spread over so few units. As quantity increases, average fixed cost declines, thus pulling down the average total cost line. But the total cost per unit will start to slope upward when the quantity produced begins to put a strain on the productive capacity of the plant, which shows in increasing average variable costs. The increase in costs is also reflected by the acute U shape of the marginal cost line. The cost of producing one more unit goes up as workers are crowded, machines are overburdened, and other troubles are encountered. What is the most logical solution to this problem for a manufacturer who has a profitable product but encounters rising unit costs as a result of high quantity produced?

REFINEMENTS IN COST-PLUS PRICING

Once management understands that not all costs behave the same as output increases or decreases, refinements are possible in price setting based on the cost-plus approach. If we assume that the desired profit is included either in the fixed costs or in the variable costs schedules, then management can refer to its table or graphs and find the appropriate price, once a decision is made regarding intended output. If the executives decide to produce six units in our above example, the selling price will be $66.67 per unit. A production run of eight units would be priced at $60 per unit.

This pricing method assumes that all the output will be sold. Also, if fewer units are produced, each must sell for a higher price in order to cover all costs and show a profit. Obviously, if business is slack and output is cut, it will not be wise to raise the unit price. The difficulty is that no attention has been paid to market demand in this pricing approach. For this reason the method has limited application by producers. It may be used by a company which enjoys a spatial monopoly because high freight rates will check the number of potential competitors. Cost-plus pricing may also be used by firms in an industry or market where all competitors follow the same approach.

PRICES BASED ON MARGINAL COSTS ONLY

Another approach to cost-plus pricing is to set a price which will cover only the marginal costs, not the total costs. Let us refer again to the cost schedules shown in Table 12-1 and Fig. 12-2 and assume that the firm is operating at an output level of six units. Under marginal cost pricing, the firm will accept an order for one unit at $31 instead of at the full cost of $66.67 because it is trying to cover only its variable or out-of-pocket costs. If the firm can sell for any price over $31, say, $33 or $35, the excess will be considered a contribution to payment of fixed costs. Obviously, not all orders can be priced to cover only variable costs. Marginal cost pricing may be feasible, however, if management wants to keep its labor force employed during a slack season rather than face costly plant shutdowns and start-ups. Marginal cost pricing may also be used in an introductory campaign for a new product or when one product is expected to attract business for another. As an example of the last point, a department store may price meals in its tearoom at a level which covers only the marginal costs, reasoning that this facility will bring shoppers to the store, where they will buy other merchandise.

COST-PLUS PRICING BY MIDDLEMEN

Cost-plus pricing is widely used by retailing and wholesaling middlemen. At least it seems this way upon first glance. A retailer, for example, pays a given amount to buy a product and have it delivered to his store. Then he will add to the acquisition cost an amount (markup) which he estimates is necessary to cover his expenses and still leave a reasonable profit. To simplify his pricing and accounting, he may add the same percentage markup to all his products. This is an average markup which he was determined through experience will be large enough to cover the costs and profit for his entire business. If a clothing store buys a garment for $30, including freight, the item will be priced to sell at 66 2/3 percent over cost, or $50. (Store policy will probably result in this price being set at $49.95; pricing at odd amounts is discussed in Chapter 14.) The price of $50 will give the retailer a markup of 40 percent of his selling price or 66 2/3 percent based on his merchandise cost. Different types of retailers will require different percentage markups because of the nature of the products handled, services offered, etc. A self-service supermarket has lower costs and thus a lower average markup than a full-service delicatessen. Furniture and jewelry stores have higher markups than drugstores. The topic of markups is discussed in more detail in the Appendix.

To what extent is cost-plus pricing truly used by middlemen? At least three significant indications suggest that what seems to be cost-plus pricing is really market-inspired pricing. In the first place, most retail prices which are set by applying average percentage markups are really only price *offers*. If the merchandise does not sell at the original price, that figure will be lowered until it reaches a level at which the merchandise will sell. The second indication of market influences is the fact that many retailers do not use the same markup on all the products they carry. A supermarket will have a markup of 6 to 8 percent on sugar and soap products, 15 to 18 percent on canned fruit and vegetables, and 25 to 30 percent on fresh meats and produce. These different markups for different products definitely reflect competitive considerations and other aspects of the market demand. Some items are slower-moving than others, and some face stiffer competition. In other cases, store location will influence the initial markup. Middlemen find, perhaps through trial and error, what percentage markup will bring in the greatest dollar volume and profit margin from the market. Then this market-reflecting markup is expressed as if it were a cost-plus approach.

The third consideration here is that the middleman usually does not set the basic price. The manufacturer's price is set so as to allow each middleman to add his customary markup and still sell at a retail price circumscribed by the competitive market. That is, the *key* price is set by the manufacturer with an eye on the market.

EVALUATION OF COST-PLUS PRICING

This book has emphasized that a firm must be market-oriented and must cater to consumers' wants. Why, then, are we now considering cost-plus pricing? Actually, it provides a good point of departure in the discussion of price determination. Also, it is spoken of so widely in business that we must understand it. Adherents of cost-plus pricing point to its simplicity and its ease of determination. They say that costs are a known quantity, whereas attempts to estimate demand are fraught with guess work.

This opinion is questionable on two counts. First, it is doubtful whether adequate, accurate cost data are available. We know a fair amount about cost-volume relationships with respect to production costs, but what we know is still insufficient. Furthermore, our information regarding marketing costs is woefully inadequate. Certainly there is a dearth of information about costs of new products because sales volume is still an unknown quantity. Really, when we consider costs in relation to pricing, we are, at best, usually dealing with approximations. The second point concerns the inexactitude of demand estimations. The difficulty of constructing a demand schedule estimating sales volume at various prices is great. Nevertheless, sales forecasting and other research tools can do a surprisingly helpful job in this area.

Critics of cost-plus pricing do not say that costs should be disregarded in pricing. Costs should be a determining influence, they maintain, but not the only one. Costs are a floor under a firm's prices. If prices stay under this floor for a long period of time, the firm will be forced out of business. Ordinarily a company will not sell its products below cost, but it may sell particular items at or below cost if they are needed to round out the line or to generate market acceptance and customer traffic for other profitable items. At the other end of the scale, costs plus a reasonable profit should not act as a ceiling price. The market should set the upper level of prices.

Some students of pricing claim that the cost-plus method is used today to set the price of over one-half of all our products. This conclusion exaggerates the incidence of cost-plus pricing. Many firms say that they use cost-plus as the method of setting their basic prices, but really they are using some form of market-inspired pricing.

Costs furnish a good point from which to start computing price. Management can determine a tentative price on a cost-plus basis but then make adjustments in the cost-plus price when it is able to measure demand factors. When used by itself, cost-plus is a weak and unrealistic method of pricing because it completely ignores the influences of competition and market demand.

BREAK-EVEN ANALYSIS

One way to use market demand as a basis for price determination and still consider costs is to approach pricing through a break-even analysis. A break-even analysis involves developing tables and/or charts which will help a company determine at what level of output the revenues will equal the costs, *assuming a certain selling price.* Sales at levels above the break-even point will result in a profit on each unit, and the further above the break-even point a firm goes, the higher will be the total and unit profit. Output at any stage below the break-even point will result in a loss to the seller. Break-even analysis is also a valuable pricing tool if the company's pricing objective is to maximize profits.

DETERMINATION OF BREAK-EVEN POINT

The method of determining the break-even point is illustrated in Table 12-2 and Figs. 12-3 and 12-4. In our hypothetical situation, the company's fixed costs are $250 and its variable costs are constant at $30 a unit. Thus the total cost of one unit is $280. For five units the total costs are $400 ($30 multiplied by 5, plus $250). In Fig. 12-3 the selling price is $80 a unit. Consequently, every time a unit is sold, $50 is contributed to overhead. That is, the variable costs or the out-of-pocket costs are $30 per unit, and these expenses are incurred in producing each unit. But any revenue over $30 can be used to help cover the fixed costs. At a selling price of $80 the company will break even if five units are sold. Stated another way, the variable costs for five units are $150 and the fixed costs are $250, for a total cost of $400. This is equal to the revenue from five units sold at $80 each. Stated as a formula:

$$\text{Break-even point in units} = \frac{\text{total fixed costs}}{\text{unit contribution to overhead}}$$

Table 12-2.   Computation of break-even point.

At each of several prices, we wish to find out how many units must be sold to cover all variable costs plus total fixed costs. At a unit price of $100, the sale of each unit contributes $70 to cover the overhead expenses. We must sell about 3.6 units to cover the $250 fixed cost. See Figs. 12-3 and 12-4 for a visual portrayal of data in this table.

(1) Unit price	(2) Unit variable costs, AVC	(3) Contribution to overhead, (1) − (2)	(4) Overhead (total fixed costs)	(5) Break-even point (4) ÷ (3)
$ 60	$30	$ 30	$250	8.3 units
80	30	50	250	5.0 units
100	30	70	250	3.6 units
150	30	120	250	2.1 units

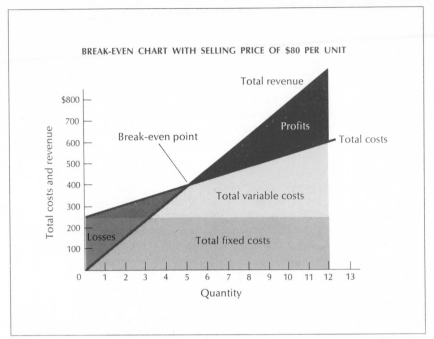

Figure 12-3. Here the break-even point is reached when the company sells five units. Fixed costs, regardless of quantity produced and sold, are $250. The variable cost per unit is $30. If this company sells five units, total costs is five times $30, or $150, plus $250, or $400. At a selling price of $80, the sale of five units will yield $400 revenue, and costs and revenue will equal each other. At the same price, the sale of each unit above five yields profit.

It is important to note the assumptions and limitations underlying the computations in the preceding paragraph and in Fig. 12-3. First, we assume that total fixed costs are constant. This is true only over a short period of time and within a limited range of output. It is reasonably easy, however, to develop a break-even chart wherein the fixed costs, and consequently the total costs, are stepped up at several intervals. This is what happens in actual practice. A good example may be found in the case of the size of the sales force. A static level of fixed costs assumes a given number of salesmen. When demand reaches a higher level, it will be necessary to add one or more salesmen. This involves a sudden increase in fixed marketing costs to cover the additional salaries, expenses, and supervision. A second assumption in our example is that the variable costs remain constant per unit of output. In the earlier discussion of the cost structure of the firm, it was noted that the average variable costs in a firm usually fluctuate. Thus the total costs were shown as a curved line in Fig. 12-1, and the average variable cost line in Fig. 12-2 was curved and sloped rather than straight and horizontal. It is also possible to develop a break-even chart for a company with a fluctuating average variable cost.

Another limitation of Fig. 12-3 is that it shows a break-even point only if the unit price is $80. It is possible and highly desirable to compute the break-even points for several different selling prices. Therefore, in Fig. 12-4 the break-even point is determined for four prices—$60, $80, $100, and $150. Figure 12-4 is also based on Table 12-2. If the price is $60, it will take sales of approximately 8.3 units to break even; at $150, only about 2.1 units. Every different selling price will result in a different break-even point.

BREAK-EVEN ANALYSIS RELATED TO MARKET DEMAND

Up to this point in our discussion of break-even analysis, we have found that its major limitation as a realistic pricing tool is that it ignores the market demand at the various prices. It is still essentially a tool for cost-plus pricing. The revenue curves in Figs. 12-3 and 12-4 show only what the revenue will be at the various prices *if* (and it is a big if) an unlimited amount can be sold at these prices. The curve *presumes* that the company can sell any output at the given price. Actually this presumption smacks considerably of a perfectly competitive market, an unrealistic situation in practice. So far, our break-even charts show only the amount which must be sold at the stated price in order to break even. The chart does not tell us whether we *can* actually sell this amount. The amount which the market will buy at a given price may be below the break-even point. For instance, at a selling price of $80 per unit, the break-even point is five units. If the market will buy only three or four units, the firm will not break even; it will show a loss.

This deficiency in break-even analysis can be remedied by estimating the total demand which actually exists at several different selling prices. Then this market information can be superimposed on the predetermined break-even data. This procedure is illustrated in Table 12-3 and Fig. 12-5. Management first constructs a demand schedule, that is, its estimate of what it can sell at various prices. Columns (1) and (2) of Table 12-3 show this information. From these figures, total revenue at

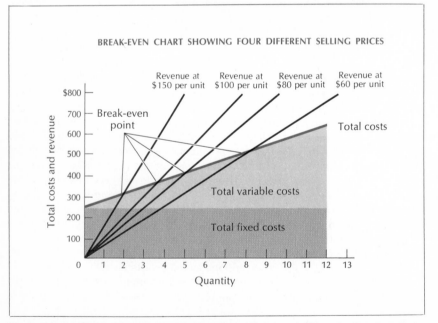

Figure 12-4. Here the company is experimenting with several different prices in order to determine which is the most appropriate. There are four different prices and four break-even points. At a price of $60, the company will start making a profit after it has sold 8.3 units. At the opposite extreme, the break-even point for a price of $150 is about 2.1 units.

Table 12-3. Relations between break-even analysis, total revenue from market demand, and profits.

By comparing market demand and break-even point at each unit price, we find which price will maximize profits. Note that at a $60 price the break-even point is 8.3 units. Yet the market will buy only seven units at the price, so a loss would result. Explain why there is a $50 profit at the $80 price. This is shown graphically in Fig. 12.5.

(1) Unit price	(2) Market demand at the price, in units	(3) Total revenue TR = (1) × (2)	(4) Break-even point	(5) Total cost (TC) of units sold*	(6) Total profits (spread between TR and TC at number of units sold) (3) — (5)
$ 60	7	$420	8.3	$460	$—40
80	6	480	5.0	430	50
100	5	500	3.6	400	100
150	2	300	2.1	310	—10

* Computed from cost data in Table 12-2. (Unit variable costs are $30, and total fixed costs are $250.)

each price is determined—column (3)—and this information is plotted on a graph. The DD curve in Fig. 12-5 is the resulting total demand curve. Students may be more familiar with the traditional demand curves which slope downward to the right. The difference is that the usual demand curve shows *average* revenues, while the DD curve in Fig. 12-5 represents *total* revenues. Basically the curves are developed from the same demand schedule. In fact, a traditional demand curve could be plotted from the figures in columns (1) and (2) of Table 12-3.

After the total DD curve is drawn, it is placed on the break-even chart, which already shows several revenue lines representing different unit selling prices. To maximize profits, management finds the point on the demand curve which is the greatest vertical distance above the total cost curve. The specific selling price selected is the one represented by the revenue line which intersects this point on the DD curve. The optimum level of output is also determined by this intersection. In our example, $100 is the selling price, and five units is the output which will maximize profits at $100. An $80 price will sell six units and bring profits of $50. The other two prices, $60 and $150, however, will result in losses of $40 and $10, respectively, because demand at these prices is less than the output needed to break even.

EVALUATION OF BREAK-EVEN ANALYSIS

Certainly no one should claim that break-even analysis is the perfect pricing tool. Some of its limitations have already been touched upon. For example, many of the underlying assumptions are unrealistic in a practical business operation. It assumes that costs are static, and it requires an empirical determination of the company's cost curve. Break-even analysis has a very limited value as a pricing tool in firms whose costs fluctuate frequently and widely and whose product mixes vary considerably. On the revenue side, break-even analysis often oversimplifies or

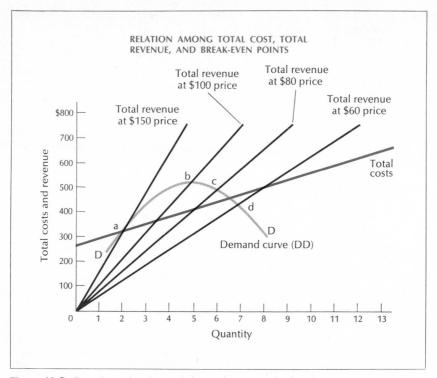

Figure 12-5. Superimposing the total demand curve on the break-even chart graphically shows which price will maximize profits. We seek the point at which the demand curve is the greatest vertical distance above the total cost line (point b in this case). Then we determine which price is represented by the total revenue line intersecting the demand curve at this point. $100 is our price. Note that the lower price of $60 would result in a loss of $40 (point d is below the total cost line).

assumes as static a revenue activity which is really highly volatile. It also assumes that one can accurately estimate demand at different prices.

These limitations should not lead management to dismiss break-even analysis as a pricing tool. While it is not perfect, it is extremely valuable, especially when used in conjunction with an analysis of total demand. Refinements and flexibility can be introduced into a break-even analysis through the use of mathematical models. Even in its simplest form, break-even analysis is very helpful because in the short run many firms are faced with reasonably stable costs and demand structures.

PRICES BASED ON BALANCE BETWEEN SUPPLY AND DEMAND

Another major method of price setting involves balancing unit demand with unit costs in order to determine the best unit price for profit maximization. Firms that do not have profit maximization as their pricing goal should understand this method, and possibly they can use it for setting their basic list prices. This pricing method parallels the marginal analysis of demand and supply which was developed by classical and neoclassical economists. The analytical approach has been updated by the pioneering contributions of Edward H. Chamberlin and Joan Robinson, who developed the theory of monopolistic, or imperfect, competition.

In our discussion of demand, we must be careful to distinguish between the demand curve or schedule facing an individual seller and the one facing the industry as a whole. Theoretically, when a firm operates in a market of perfect competition, its demand curve is horizontal at the market price. That is, the single seller has no control over the price, and he can sell his entire output at the market price. Even in a perfectly competitive market, however, the industry has a downward-sloping curve. That is, for the industry as a whole, more units can be sold at lower prices than at higher prices.

The market situation facing most firms in the United States today is one of monopolistic, or imperfect, competition, characterized by product differentiation and nonprice competition. By differentiating his products, an individual seller has some control over his prices. In effect, each seller becomes a separate "industry"; his product is to some extent unlike any other. An individual seller in monopolistic competition has a downward-sloping demand curve. That is, he will attract some buyers at a high price, but to broaden his market and to sell to more people, he must lower the price.

If the price is to be set by balancing demand and supply, the price setter must understand the concepts of average and marginal revenue in addition to those of average and marginal cost. Marginal revenue is the income derived from the sale of the last unit—the marginal unit. Average revenue is the unit price at a given level of unit sales. It is total revenue divided by the number of units sold. Referring to the hypothetical demand schedule in Table 12-4, we see that the company received an additional $70 (marginal revenue) from the sale of two units instead of one. The fifth unit brought a marginal revenue of $53. After the sixth unit, however, the total revenue declined each time an additional unit was sold. Hence there was a negative marginal revenue.

Table 12-4. Demand schedule for individual firm.
    At each market price, a definite quantity of the product will be demanded at any given time. Thus changing the unit price upward or downward will result in a differing number of units sold and a differing amount of total revenue. Marginal revenue is simply the amount of additional money gained by selling one more unit. In this example, the company no longer gains marginal revenue after it has sold the sixth unit at a price of $60.

Units sold	Unit price (average revenue)	Total revenue	Marginal revenue
1	$80	$ 80	
2	75	150	$70
3	72	216	66
4	68	272	56
5	65	325	53
6	60	360	35
7	50	350	—10
8	40	320	—30

The downward-sloping demand curve which faces most firms is an average revenue curve. It shows how many units will be sold at various unit (average) prices. To make an average revenue curve slope downward, the marginal revenue must always be less than the average revenue. That is, as unit sales increase, the revenue from the last unit becomes progressively smaller (see the revenue curves in Fig. 12-6). The firm's average unit cost curve (average fixed costs plus average variable costs) and its marginal cost curve have been placed in Fig. 12-6, along with the revenue curves, in order to depict graphically the price-setting process.

The firm will continue to sell as long as the revenue from the last unit sold exceeds the cost of producing this last unit. That is, output continues as long as marginal revenue exceeds marginal costs. At the point where they meet, output theoretically should cease. Certainly management will not want to sell a unit at a price less than the out-of-pocket (variable) costs of production. Thus the *point of production* is where marginal costs equal marginal revenue. This is quantity OE in Fig. 12-6. The *price* is determined by locating the point on the average revenue curve which represents OE output. Remember that average revenue represents the unit price. Thus the unit price at OE output is EC. This is the same as OB on the main vertical axis. At price EC the average unit cost is DE. Thus the company enjoys a unit profit of DC. Total profit is OE times DC (quantity times unit profit). This is the area bounded by ABCD.

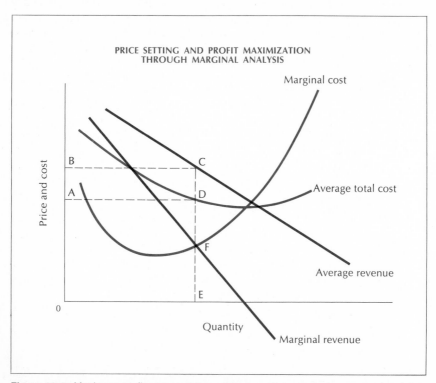

Figure 12-6. Maximum profit occurs at the point where the marginal revenue curve intersects the marginal cost curve. In most situations, the company will not produce one more unit if the revenue derived from selling that unit would be less than the cost of producing and selling it.

Supply and demand analysis as a basis for price setting has enjoyed only limited use. Businessmen usually claim that the analysis does not take into consideration important variables that exist in the dynamic, real-life market situation. They feel that more and better data are needed for plotting the curves exactly. Demand and supply analysis can be used, they feel, to study past price movements, but it cannot serve as a practical basis for setting prices.

Those who are skeptical of the practical values of supply and demand analysis at the present time should take heart: management's knowledge of costs and demand is improving. Better methods of forecasting have been a boon in this area. Data-processing equipment is bringing more complete and detailed information to management's attention all the time. In the preceding chapter it was pointed out that management usually can estimate demand within broad limits, and this is helpful. Also, experienced management in many firms can do a surprisingly accurate job of estimating marginal and average costs and revenue.

PRICES SET IN RELATION TO MARKET ALONE

Cost-plus pricing is one extreme among pricing methods. At the other end of the scale is a method whereby an individual firm's prices are set in relation *only* to the competitive market price. Cost in no way determines the price. In fact, usually it is the other way around—price determines the firm's costs. The seller's price may be set right at the market price level in order to meet competition, or it may be set either above or below the competitive market level, and still be related to this level.

PRICING TO MEET COMPETITION

Management may decide to price a product right at the competitive level when any one of several situations exists. A firm is most likely to use this pricing method when the market is highly competitive and the product is not differentiated significantly from competitive models. To some extent, this method of pricing reflects market conditions which parallel those found under perfect competition. That is, effective product differentiation is absent, buyers and sellers are well informed about the market price and market conditions, and the seller has no discernible control over the selling price. Most producers of agricultural products must set their prices to meet competitive market levels. Even when farmers act as a group, as in an agricultural cooperative, they have very little, if any, real influence over the selling price, at least not in the short run. Manufacturers of gray goods in the textile industry, most manufacturers of automobile tires, and small firms producing well-known, standardized products all ordinarily use the market-based method of pricing.

The market-based method of pricing is also used when a traditional or "customary" price level exists. Candy bars, soft drinks, and chewing gum, for example, were traditionally priced at a nickel or a dime. In the face of rising costs, most sellers, rather than trying to change the price of a candy bar from 10 cents to 12 or 13 cents, accepted the dime price and then tailored their costs to the market price by reducing the quantity or the quality of the bar. (Today in most markets inexorable cost pressures have forced the "customary" price to rise to 20 cents.) The sharp drop in revenue which occurs when the price is raised above the customary level gives an indication that the individual seller faces a kinked demand (see Fig.

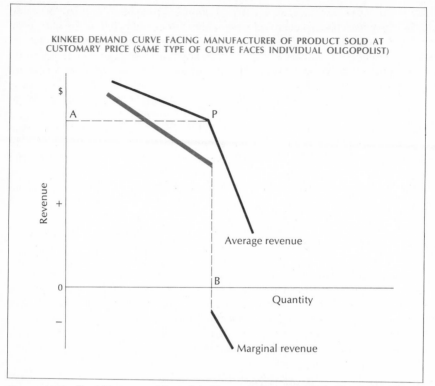

KINKED DEMAND CURVE FACING MANUFACTURER OF PRODUCT SOLD AT CUSTOMARY PRICE (SAME TYPE OF CURVE FACES INDIVIDUAL OLIGOPOLIST)

Figure 12-7. The kink occurs at the point of the customary price (OA). Above OA, demand declines rapidly. A price set below OA will result in very little increase in volume, and consequently the marginal revenue is negative. Which part of the average revenue line reflects an elastic demand, and which segment shows inelastic demand?

12-7). The customary price is at P, the location of the kink in the curve. If the seller tries to go above that level (OA), the demand for the product drops sharply, as indicated by the flat average revenue curve above point P. At any price above OA, the demand is highly elastic. Below price OA, the demand is highly inelastic, as represented by the steeply sloping average revenue curve and the negative marginal revenue curve. That is, the total revenue decreases each time the price is reduced to a level below P. The customary price is so strong that a reduction in price by one firm will not increase the firm's unit sales very much, certainly not enough to offset the loss in average revenue.

Up to this point in our discussion of pricing to meet competition, we have observed market situations which involve many sellers. Oddly enough, the same pricing method is often used when the market is dominated by only a few sellers. This type of market is called an *oligopoly*. The products of all manufacturers are reasonably similar, and the demand is usually inelastic. The demand curve facing an individual seller in an oligopoly is a kinked one, as in Fig. 12-7. An oligopolist must price at the market level in order to maximize profits. Selling above market price will result in a drastic reduction in total revenue because the average revenue curve is so elastic above point P. If an oligopolist cuts below the market price, all other members of the oligopoly must respond immediately. Otherwise the price-cutter will enjoy a substantial increase in business. Therefore, the competitors retaliate with comparable price cuts, and the net result is that a new market price is established at a lower level. Each member of the oligopoly gets about the same share of the market that he had before, but his unit revenue is reduced by the amount of the price cut. Theoretically, an oligopolist gains no advantage by cutting his price. For his own good, he will simply set his price at a competitive level and let it stay there. In reality, price wars are often touched off in an oligopoly because it is not possible to fully control all sellers of the product. Assuming the absence of collusion, every so often some firm will enter the market with a price reduction, and all others usually must follow in order to maintain their respective shares of the market.

The market-equated method of pricing is rather simple to apply. A firm ascertains what the going price is, and after allowing for customary markups for middlemen, it arrives at its own selling price. To illustrate, a manufacturer of men's dress shoes is aware that his retailers want to sell the shoes for $19.95 a pair. He sells directly to the retailers, and they want an average markup of 40 percent of their selling price. Consequently, after allowing $7.98 for the retailers' markup, the manufacturer's top price is about $12. He then decides whether $12 is enough to cover his production and marketing expenses and still leave him a reasonable profit. Sometimes he faces a real squeeze in this matter, particularly when his costs are rising but the market price is holding firm.

PRICING BELOW COMPETITIVE LEVEL

A variation of market-based pricing is to set a price at some point below that which is considered the competitive level. This method of pricing is usually found at the retail level of distribution, although it is not unknown among manufacturers. In recent years, the most talked-about example of this kind of pricing has been discount-house pricing. Discount houses typically price well-known, nationally advertised brands 10 to 30 percent below the suggested retail list price or the price actually being charged by most other retailers. They operate on the principle of low markup and high volume. The manufacturer's reputation for quality merchandise usually offsets customer concern about the reputation of the retailer.

Often firms prefer to operate on the basis of fewer services but lower prices. For years, Macy's New York store advertised that its prices were at least 6 percent below those charged by stores which granted credit. Pricing below competition is also a good way for a company to penetrate a new market. It is a method particularly adaptable to products with an elastic demand. That is, in general, the type of product upon which the discount houses have built such huge volume. At the manufacturing level, pricing below market is a strategy employed by small fringe firms attempting to compete with much larger organizations.

PRICING ABOVE COMPETITIVE LEVEL

Manufacturers or retailers sometimes set their prices above the market level. This may be done by a producer who follows a temporary or even a permanent strategy of cream skimming. Usually above-market pricing can be done only when the product is distinctive or when the seller has acquired prestige in his field. An outstanding women's specialty clothing store is able to price an article above the market level just because the article carries the store's label. Most cities have a prestige clothing, jewelry, or furniture store where price tags are noticeably above the competitive level set by other stores which handle similar types of products.

CONCLUSION

In view of the importance of pricing, it is unfortunate that so much mystery, tradition, and fuzzy thinking seem to pervade businessmen's approach to this marketing activity. Many pricing concepts are based on the models of classical economic theory. In that setting the emphasis was on production (not consumption) and an agrarian-subsistence economy. We assumed the existence of perfect competition and rational buying behavior in the economy. Now we must identify more realistically the type of economy in which business operates, and also understand the socio-psychological aspects of buyers' perceptions of prices.

Figure 12-8 outlines 16 criteria which executives can use as practical guidelines in their price determination. Many of these generalizations were discussed in the past two chapters, so Fig. 12-8 also can serve as a meaningful summary.

SUMMARY OF CRITERIA FOR SETTING PRICES		
Low price when	Pricing criteria	High price when
Little	**1.** Promotion	Much
Commodity	**2.** Product type	Propietary
Mass-produced	**3.** Manufacture	Custom-made
Intensive	**4.** Market coverage	Selective
Long-lived	**5.** Product obsolescence	Short-lived
Slow	**6.** Technological change	Rapid
Capital-intensive	**7.** Production	Labor-intensive
Large	**8.** Market share	Small
Short	**9.** Channels of distribution	Long
Mature	**10.** Stage of market	New
Long-term	**11.** Profit perspective	Short-term
Single-use	**12.** Product versatility	Multiple-use
Much	**13.** Promotional contribution to line	Little
Few or none	**14.** Ancillary services	Many
Short	**15.** Product life in use	Long
Fast	**16.** Turnover	Slow

Figure 12-8. Custom-made products are priced higher than mass-produced ones (No. 3). Long-lived products can be priced lower, because costs can be amortized over a longer period (No. 5). Price low if you want a large market share (No. 8). Prices will be higher for new products (No. 10) with multiple uses (No. 12) and requiring much presale and postsale service (No. 14). *Source*: William J. E. Crissy and Robert Boewadt, "Pricing in Perspective," *Sales Management*, June 15, 1971, p. 44.

QUESTIONS AND PROBLEMS

1. Explain the difference between variable costs and marginal costs.
2. Referring to Fig. 12-2, at what point does the marginal cost curve (MC) intersect the average total cost curve (ATC)? Explain why the ATC curve is declining up to the intersection point and rising beyond it. Explain how the MC curve can be rising while the ATC curve is still declining.
3. In Table 12-1, what is the marginal cost of the seventh unit produced?
4. "Without exception, the marginal cost is always equal to the variable cost of the marginal unit." Do you agree?
5. What are the merits and limitations of the cost-plus method of setting a basic price?
6. In a break-even chart, is the total *fixed* cost line always horizontal? Is the total *variable* cost line always straight? Explain.
7. Referring to Table 12-2 and Fig. 12-4, what are the break-even points at prices of $50 and $90, if the variable costs are $40 a unit and the fixed costs remain at $250?
8. Referring to Table 12-2 and Fig. 12-4, find the break-even point for selling prices of $60 and $100 if the fixed cost totals $400.
9. A small manufacturer of ball-point pens sold his product to retailers at $8.40 per dozen. His manufacturing cost was 50 cents on each pen. His expenses, including all selling and administrative costs except advertising, were $19,200. How many dozen must he sell to cover these expenses and pay for an advertising campaign costing $6,000?
10. "Beyond the break-even point, all revenue from sales is pure profit. Consequently, once the break-even point is achieved, it behooves the seller to increase his advertising and personal selling efforts in order to get more of these profitable, above-break-even-point sales." Discuss.
11. Does supply and demand analysis in relation to pricing have any practical value for the businessman?
12. Referring to Fig. 12-6, why would the firm normally stop producing at quantity OE? Why is the price set at EC (same as OB) and not at EF or ED?
13. Are there any stores in your community which generally price above the competitive level? How are they able to do this?
14. A soft drink manufacturer has been pricing his 10-ounce bottled drink to sell for 15 cents at retail. The product has strong market acceptance in its regional market, competing favorably with Coca-Cola, Pepsi-Cola, 7-Up, and other well-known brands. For some time, production and marketing costs have been increasing, and management must now take some action. Which of the following courses of action should the company follow? Can you propose a better alternative?
    a. Raise the price to 18 cents or two bottles for 35 cents.
    b. Reduce the quality of the beverage.
    c. Reduce the quantity to 8 ounces.
    d. Curtail the advertising.

PRICE POLICIES AND STRATEGIES

After setting the basic or list price for a product, management must examine the many facets of its price structure which require specific policies. What kind of quantity discount schedule will it adopt? Should it fair-trade its products? Will it insist upon f.o.b. pricing, or will it occasionally absorb freight?

In this chapter and the next, we shall discuss eleven problem areas in pricing, listed below, which call for executive policy making. We shall also consider the more important legal aspects of some of the price policies.

1. Discounts and allowances
2. Geographic price policies
3. One price versus variable price
4. Unit pricing
5. Pricing multiple products
6. Price lining
7. Resale price maintenance
8. "Leader" pricing
9. Guarantee against price decline
10. Psychological pricing
11. Price competition versus nonprice competition

DISCOUNTS AND ALLOWANCES

Discounts and allowances result in a deduction from the list price. The deduction may be in the form of cash or some other concession, such as a free case of merchandise. The philosophy underlying discounts and allowances is that the customer will in return perform some marketing activities whose value to the seller will be equivalent to the amount of the discount or allowance. Commonly used forms include quantity, trade, cash, and seasonal discounts and promotional, brokerage, and freight allowances.

QUANTITY DISCOUNTS

Quantity discounts are deductions offered from list prices by a seller in order to encourage a customer to buy in larger amounts or to concentrate his purchases with this seller. The discounts may be based on dollar or unit purchases.

Cumulative and noncumulative quantity discounts. A *noncumulative* discount is based upon an individual order of one or more products. Thus a retailer may sell golf balls at $1 each or at three for $2.50. A manufacturer or a wholesaler may set up a quantity discount schedule such as the following, which was used by a manufacturer of industrial adhesives. Noncumulative quantity discounts are expected to encourage large orders. Many expenses, such as billing, order filling, shipping, and salesmen's salaries, are about the same whether the seller receives an order totaling $10 or $500. Consequently, selling expense as a percentage of sales decreases as the order becomes larger.

Boxes purchased on single order	Percentage discount from list price
1–5	0.0
6–12	2.0
13–25	3.5
Over 25	5.0

A *cumulative* discount is based on the total volume purchased over a period of time. These discounts are an advantage to a seller because they tie customers more closely to him. They are really patronage discounts in that the more total business a buyer gives a seller, the greater is the discount. They are especially applicable to the sale of perishable products. The seller wants to encourage a customer to buy fresh supplies frequently so that the merchandise will not grow stale. Thus the discount is based on total purchases over a month, rather than on each separate order.

Either type of quantity discount can be used nicely by a company producing several related or even nonrelated products which are apt to be purchased by a single buyer. Often the sales of a slow-moving item can be stimulated if it is offered in an attractive discount package with more popular items. Finally quantity discounts can help a manufacturer effect real economies in the production end of the business as well as in selling. Large orders can result in lower-cost production runs. A cumulative discount based on total orders from all units in a retail chain may enable a producer to make much more effective use of his production capacity, even though orders are shipped in small amounts with no savings in marketing costs.

Discount schedules can create ill will between buyers and sellers. The buyer whose purchases are just below the next bracket often pressures the seller to give him the higher discount. A salesman may be tempted to overload his customers by urging them to buy larger quantities than they need in order to get higher discounts. Management faces a real problem in the task of constructing the discount schedule. Cost studies and analyses of customer buying habits are usually necessary in order to set up the proper discount percentages and quantity brackets. A drawback to cumulative discounts is that they are in no way related to the size of individual orders. Hence there is no premium attached to buying in large, economical units.

TRADE DISCOUNTS

Trade discounts, sometimes called "functional" discounts, are a reduction from the list price offered to buyers in payment for marketing functions which they will presumably perform. A manufacturer may quote a retail list price of $400 with trade discounts of 40 percent and 10 percent. The retailer pays $240 ($400 less 40 percent), and the wholesaler pays the manufacturer $216 ($240 less 10 percent). The wholesaler is given the 40 and 10 percent. He is expected to keep the 10 percent to cover the costs of his wholesaling functions and to pass on the 40 percent to the retailers. It should be noted that the 40 and 10 percent do not constitute a total discount of 50 percent off the list price. Each discount percentage in the "chain" is computed on the amount remaining after the preceding percentage has been deducted. Trade discounts vary considerably from one industry to another because of differences in the normal markups required by various types of middlemen and differences in the customary channels used.

In addition to allowing a middleman his usual markup in payment for functions he performs, trade discounts serve other purposes. They are usually high enough to cover high-cost middlemen, who otherwise would not be interested in handling the product. A large discount, however, may offer retailers an opportunity to sell below list. They can show the list price to the customer and make him feel he is getting a bargain. In another situation, many companies publish catalogues with list prices. The net price can be varied simply by changing the amount of the trade discount. Therefore, if prices change, the seller does not have to print a new catalogue. He just changes the trade discount on the particular item.

Trade discounts originated in the traditional channel relationships which existed within each industry. A wholesaler was a wholesaler, and his functions were easy to distinguish from those of a retailer. Today, however, channel structures are far more complex, and price differentials occasioned by trade discounts are much more difficult to justify on a cost basis. Unless management makes a detailed marketing cost analysis by classes of customers, it can hardly prove that the discounts are equivalent to the cost differentials incurred in dealing with these different classes of customers.

CASH DISCOUNTS

A *cash discount* is a deduction granted to the buyer for paying his bill within a specified period of time. The discount is computed on the net amount due after first deducting trade and quantity discounts from the initial price. If a buyer owes $360 after the other discounts have been granted and he is offered terms of say, 2/10, n/30 on an invoice dated November 8, he may deduct a discount of 2 percent ($7.20) if he pays his bill within 10 days after the date of invoice (by November 18). Otherwise he must pay the entire bill of $360 in 30 days (December 8). In a cash discount, two elements are present—the percentage reduction itself and the time period within which the bill must be paid. There are many different terms of sale because practically every industry has its own combination of these two elements. For example, one may see 2/10, n/30; 2/10 e.o.m. (2 percent discount if paid within 10 days after the end of the month); 3/10, n/60 r.o.g. (the ten-day discount period starts upon receipt of the goods).

Most buyers are extremely eager to pay the bills in time to earn the cash discounts. The discount in a 2/10, n/30 situation may not seem like very much. But management must realize that this 2 percent is earned just for paying 20 days in advance of when the entire bill is due. If a buyer fails to take the cash discount in a 2/10, n/30 situation, he is, in effect, borrowing money at a 36 percent annual rate of interest. (Figuring a 360-day year, there are eighteen periods of 20 days each in the year. Eighteen periods at 2 percent each equal 36 percent.)

SEASONAL DISCOUNTS AND FORWARD DATING

If a firm producing an article, such as air conditioners or lawn mowers, which is purchased on a seasonal basis, management may want to consider the strategy of granting a *seasonal discount*. This is a discount of, say, 5, 10, or 20 percent which is given to a customer who places an order during the slack season. Off-season orders enable the manufacturer to make better use of his production facilities.

Forward dating is a variation of both a seasonal discount and a cash discount. A manufacturer of fishing tackle will seek orders from wholesalers and retailers during the winter months. The bill will be dated, say, April 1, and terms of 2/10, n/30 may be offered as of that date. Thus the seller can get orders in December and January which help him to level out his production. The wholesale or retail buyers do not have to pay their bills, however, until after the season starts.

PROMOTIONAL ALLOWANCES

Promotional allowances are price reductions granted by sellers to buyers in payment for promotional services performed by the buyer. These allowances may also be in the form of promotional materials supplied by the seller. To illustrate, a manufacturer of builders' hardware gives a certain quantity of "free goods" to dealers who prominently display his line. A clothing manufacturer pays one-half the space charge of a retailer's advertisement which features the manufacturer's product. A luggage manufacturer provides advertising display materials for his retailers. The use of promotional allowances as a promotional strategy rather than a price strategy is discussed in Chapter 21.

BROKERAGE ALLOWANCES

When the services of a broker as a wholesaling middleman are employed in the producer's channel of distribution, the broker is paid a certain percentage of the sales volume he generates. This payment is called a *brokerage allowance* and is really just another form of trade discount. Because of the legal implications in certain types of brokerage arrangements, these allowances are noted separately instead of being included with trade discounts. Many times in the past, the commission which the seller normally paid a broker was *instead* paid to large-scale buyers who performed the services usually ascribed to brokers. Today, however, the Robinson-Patman Act prohibits a seller from paying a brokerage fee to the buyer or any firm controlled by the buyer.

THE ROBINSON-PATMAN ACT AND PRICE DISCRIMINATION

The discounts and allowances discussed in this section may result in different prices for different customers. Whenever price differentials exist, there is price discrimination. The terms are synonymous. In certain situations, price discrimination is prohibited under the Robinson-Patman Act. This is one of the most important federal laws affecting a company's marketing program. Federal laws apply only to interstate commerce, but the interpretation of what is "interstate" is quite broad.

Background of the act. In 1890, after many years of public discontent with the monopolistic and collusive practices in restraint of trade by large manufacturers, Congress passed the Sherman Antitrust Act. The intent of the law was to declare illegal any monopolies or combinations in restraint of trade in interstate commerce. Less than satisfactory success with the enforcement of this law led Congress to seek other methods of regulating the trade practices of large companies. Consequently, in 1914 Congress passed two laws—the Clayton Antitrust Act, which generally outlawed price discrimination, and the Federal Trade Commission Act, which prohibited unfair competition. It was felt that monopolies were nurtured by price discrimination and unfair competition. Therefore, by declaring these two business practices illegal, Congress presumably had removed the conditions necessary to develop monopolies and other combinations in restraint of trade.

The years following World War I, however, saw the development of large-scale retailing among mail-order houses and chain stores and the subsequent decline in the competitive position of the small store. The Depression of the early 1930s focused attention still further on the plight of the small-scale merchant. Three questionable trade practices involving price discrimination were pinpointed as particular sources of large retailers' competitive advantage. They were unearned quantity discounts, dummy brokerage allowances, and pseudopromotional allowances. The Clayton Antitrust Act proved inadequate to cope with these practices because, in the course of administering the price-discrimination sections of this law, the government found too many loopholes. Consequently, in 1936, during an era of anti-chain-store feeling, the Robinson-Patman Act was passed to amend Section 2—the price-discrimination section—of the Clayton Antitrust Act.

Main provisions of the act. The Robinson-Patman Act was intended to curb the practices of large-scale retailers only, but it was written in such general terms that through the years it has also become applicable to manufacturers.

Price discrimination. Price discrimination is prohibited between different purchasers of products of like grade and quality, if the effect of this discrimination may be to lessen or injure competition substantially with the person who either grants or knowingly receives the benefits of such discrimination or with customers of either of them.[1]

Injury to competition. Not all price differentials are illegal under this law. One exception involves the impact on competition. Price differentials are considered unlawfully discriminatory only when their effect *may be* to substantially lessen competition. This provision is broad but not unlimited. To establish a prima facie case of price discrimination, the government has to prove only that a *reasonable probability* of injury to competition exists. *Actual* injury does not have to be proved by the government.[2] The injury-to-competition section also applies to three levels of trade. It is unlawful for a seller to discriminate in price if this may lead to a substantial lessening of competition (1) with other sellers, (2) among firms buying from the discriminating seller, or (3) among the customers of these buyers. Thus manufacturer A cannot discriminate if this may unduly hurt other manufacturers, Mr. A's wholesalers, or any retail customers of these wholesalers.

Other exceptions and defenses. Price differentials are allowable in response to changing conditions which affect the market for, or the marketability of, goods. For example, differentials are allowed in response to seasonal obsolescence, physical deterioration of products, or going-out-of-business sales.

Price differentials may be granted if they do not exceed differences in the cost of manufacture, sale, or delivery resulting from differences in the quantity sold or from different methods of sale or delivery of the product. These differentials are allowable even though there is a reasonable probability of injury to competition. This "cost proviso" is a main defense available to firms engaging in differential pricing.

The hitch is that the burden of proof rests with the seller and not with the Federal Trade Commission (FTC) or other plaintiffs in a case. Almost of necessity, a firm must show a detailed marketing cost analysis if it hopes to use the cost defense in Robinson-Patman cases. Furthermore, the history of enforcement of the act suggests that the differential prices should be established as a *result of* a marketing cost analysis. Too often, firms have discriminated in price and then, when called to

---

[1]For an analysis of the "like-grade-and-quality" proviso and the inconsistencies and implications in its interpretations, see Jacky Knopp, Jr., "Branding and the Robinson-Patman Act," *Journal of Business,* January, 1966, pp. 24–34. Most frequently, the interpretation problems center around price differentials established by a manufacturer who sells a product under his own brand and also sells a physically identical product under a middleman's brand. This point was discussed in Chap. 10 in connection with in the Borden Company case involving the pricing and marketing of evaporated milk.

[2]*Corn Products Refining Company v. Federal Trade Commission,* 324 U.S. 726 (1945). In this same decision (p. 742) the Supreme Court apparently contradicted itself or was not careful in its choice of words, for it said that there need be only a reasonable *possibility* that the discriminations *may* have harmed competition. This unfortunate choice of words became part of the basis for the Supreme Court's decision against the Morton Salt Company. See *Federal Trade Commission v. Morton Salt Company,* 68 S. Ct. 822 (1948). The Morton Salt case probably marked the peak of the period of strict interpretation of the "injury-to-competition" clause. Later decisions reverted to the idea that a reasonable probability of injury must exist. Also, there must be proof of substantial and continuing injury, not trivial or sporadic injury, before a prima facie case can be established. See *Minneapolis-Honeywell Regulator Company v. Federal Trade Commission,* 191 F. 2d 786 (1951); certiorari dismissed, 344 U.S. 206 (1952).

task by the FTC, have tried to justify their price differentials by after-the-fact cost studies. Usually these companies have lost their cases. "Anyone who has not considered costs when creating price differences should expect a long, difficult, and expensive experience in preparing and attempting to sustain a cost defense."[3]

Another major defense available under the act is the "meeting-competition" defense. A firm may rebut a prima facie case of price discrimination by showing that its lower price was set "in good faith to meet an equally low price of a competitor." Also, a seller may furnish services and facilities to a buyer if this is done in good faith to meet the services or facilities furnished by a competitor. Through the years, this defense has proved to be something less than satisfactory to most defendants. Usually the decision has been that good faith was lacking when this defense was used in support of price differentials. Also, the FTC has maintained that this defense is only procedural, shifting the burden of proof back to the Commission. The Commission does not consider this a substantive defense which absolves or frees the defendant from the charges brought under the law. In spite of the FTC's opinion on this matter, however, the courts in recent years seem to have established that meeting the equally low price of individual competitors is a complete or substantive defense against charges of price discrimination.[4]

Buyer's liability. The Robinson-Patman Act includes an innovation in trade regulation in that the buyer is as guilty as the seller if he (the buyer) knowingly induces or receives an unlawful price discrimination. This provision is intended to restrain large-scale buyers from demanding discriminatory prices. Prior to the Robinson-Patman Act, a seller who succumbed and granted the differential could be found guilty, and the pressuring buyer would go scot-free.

In general, the interpretations of this provision have shown that it is largely ineffectual in restraining buyers. From a practical standpoint, it has been difficult to prove that the buyer "knowingly" received an unlawful price differential. The courts have ruled that it is not the buyer's responsibility to prove that the price differentials were equal to the seller's cost savings. The buyer cannot be expected to acquire access to the seller's accounting records. Rather, it is up to the Federal Trade Commission to prove that sufficient cost savings did not exist. Also, in the Automatic Canteen Company case, the Supreme Court ruled that the FTC must show that (1) the buyer knew he was getting a lower price and (2) the buyer knew this price could not be justified under the act.[5]

In the same decision, however, the Supreme Court suggested that a buyer's knowledge of prevailing trade practices in his industry might be ample evidence that this buyer knew whether or not he was receiving discriminatory price advantages. In subsequent years, decisions in Circuit Courts of Appeals based on the Supreme Court's inferences in the Automatic Canteen case have strengthened the

---

[3]Donald J. Fennelly, "On the Judging of Mince Pies," *Harvard Business Review,* November–December, 1964, p. 79. This article presents an accountant's view of the cost defense, and it offers six proposals for introducing greater clarity and equity into the enforcement of the Robinson-Patman Act. See also B. J. Linder and Allan H. Savage, "Price Discrimination and Cost Defense—Change Ahead?" *MSU Business Topics,* Summer, 1971, pp. 21–26.

[4]*Federal Trade Commission v. Standard Oil Company (Indiana),* 355 U.S. 396 (1958). See also *Standard Oil Company (Indiana) v. Federal Trade Commission,* 340 U.S. 231 (1951).

[5]*Automatic Canteen Company of America v. Federal Trade Commission,* 346 U.S. 61 (1953).

FTC in its administration of the buyer's-liability section of the Robinson-Patman Act.[6]

Brokerage payments. The Robinson-Patman Act tackles the problem of un-earned brokerage payments by declaring that it is unlawful to pay or receive brokerage allowances except for services rendered. Essentially it is illegal for a seller to pay brokerage fees directly to a buyer or to anyone controlled by the buyer.

While interpretations by the FTC and the courts make the meaning of this section clear, its soundness from a marketing viewpoint is highly question-able. For example, the buyer for a chain of grocery stores may approach a food canner and offer to buy a quantity of canned vegetables, or the chain may purchase through a firm acting as its agent. In either case the chain or its agent is performing all the services normally provided by a broker working for the seller. Prior to the passage of the Robinson-Patman Act, it was common practice for a large buyer to seek, and for a seller to grant freely and openly, the usual brokerage commission. The seller was granting a form of discount to his customers in return for their performance of functions which the seller would otherwise have to pro-vide. In outlawing such practices under the Robinson-Patman Act, the courts have said that buyer and seller are at arm's length in a transaction and that it is not possible for a buyer or anyone working for him to render services to a seller. Any services performed by the buyer are for his own benefit and not that of the seller. Consequently, the "except-for-services-rendered" clause is virtually interpreted out of the act when a buyer seeks a rebate or allowance in lieu of the usual brokerage fee.

To strengthen even more the prohibition against a buyer's getting a brokerage allowance from a seller, the courts have ruled in several cases that the brokerage section stands alone in the act; it is not connected with any other section. Thus the cost defense is not permissible under this section, nor is the defense of meeting competition in good faith. Truly the food brokers—the originally intended ben-eficiaries of this section—have a protective umbrella held over them.

Promotional allowances. Various types of promotional services and facilities, or payments to buyers in lieu of these services or facilities, are lawful under the Robinson-Patman Act *only* if they are offered to all competing customers on proportionally equal terms. Furthermore, the cost defense is not admissible, but a firm may use the defense that it discriminated in order to meet competition in good faith.[7] In the interpretation of the sections on promotional allowances, the real problem is to determine what is meant by "proportionally equal terms." This concept and its practical application are examined in Chapter 23, in connection with a firm's promotional program.

---

[6]See Lawrence X. Tarpey, Sr., "Buyer Liability under the Robinson-Patman Act: A Current Appraisal," *Journal of Marketing*, January, 1972, pp. 38–42. Also see *American Motor Special-ties Co., Inc. v. Federal Trade Commission*, 278 F. 2d 225 (1960); certiorari denied, 364 U.S. 884 (1960); and *General Auto Supplies, Inc., v. Federal Trade Commission*, 346 F. 2d 311 (1965); certiorari denied, 382 U.S. 923 (1965).

[7]See *Exquisite Form Brassiere, Inc. v. Federal Trade Commission*, 301 F. 2d 499 (1961); certiorari denied, 82 S. Ct. 1162 (1962).

History of interpretation of the act. The Robinson-Patman Act is probably one of the most ambiguous, controversial laws ever written for the purpose of regulating trade. It is difficult to set forth many helpful generalizations for use by marketing executives. Some sections, such as those covering brokerage payments and buyer's liability, are reasonably clear. In others, as one writer has said, "twenty-three years of enforcement have produced crystal-clear confusion."[8] One respected legal authority who has been involved in Robinson-Patman litigations sums up his opinion regarding the regulatory impact of the act.[9]

> On balance, a quarter century of Robinson-Patman administration has probably restrained more competition than it has preserved. The Act's chartless enforcement became a "numbers game" which largely missed the "big buyer"—the Congressional target—and often boomeranged on the smaller competitor, the Act's intended beneficiary. Overall, although the Act's prohibitions are porous, it has fostered a regulatory climate which inhibits competition and breeds restraint.

Anticipating no congressional revision of the act and doubting any administrative reorientation toward it, Rowe sees the judicial process as the best hope for adapting "this relic of the Great Depression to the economic setting of a more dynamic age."

Legality of quantity discounts. Because quantity discounts result in different prices to different customers, these differential or discriminatory prices are potentially illegal under the Robinson-Patman Act if the necessary injury to competition can be shown. To justify its price differentials stemming from its quantity discount schedule, management must rely on the cost defense provided in the act. In a nutshell, quantity discounts are legal if the resultant price differentials do not exceed the differentials in the cost of manufacturing, selling, or delivering various quantities of the product. The price differentials may be less than the cost savings, but they must not exceed the differences in cost.

A study of the quantity discount cases brought under the Robinson-Patman Act will show that cumulative discounts have virtually no chance of being defended because it is not possible to show that the discounts make due allowance for differences in cost only.

Noncumulative discounts can be based upon corresponding cost differentials, but defendants have used the cost defense successfully in very few cases over the past twenty-five years. There are two main reasons for this poor record. In the first place, very few companies have sufficiently detailed marketing cost information upon which to build a cost defense. The second reason for the lack of success with the cost defense was suggested earlier. Too often a company has made a cost study *after* the discount schedule was set up and *after* the Federal Trade Commission issued a complaint. Thus it was obvious that the company did not base the schedule on cost differentials, for it really did not know what the differentials were until the case came up.

---

[8]W. David Robbins, "A Marketing Appraisal of the Robinson-Patman Act," *Journal of Marketing,* July, 1959, p. 15.

[9]Frederick M. Rowe, *Price Discrimination under the Robinson-Patman Act,* Little, Brown and Company, Boston, 1962, p. 551.

Legality of trade discounts. There is no specific statement about functional discounts in either the Clayton Act or the Robinson-Patman Act. Consequently, the legal status of trade discounts is still a little fuzzy. Three landmark cases brought under the Clayton Act established the point that separate discounts could be given to separate classes of buyers.[10] That is, one discount could be given to wholesalers and another to retailers, as long as all buyers within a given group were offered the same discount. Whether a firm was classified as a retailer or as a wholesaler depended entirely upon the status and motives of the customers, and not upon the nature of the buying operation or the quantity of the purchases. Therefore, a large chain selling to ultimate consumers would be classed as a retailer, even though it purchased in larger quantities than many wholesalers and even though it performed wholesaling functions in its buying.

Presumably, functional or trade discounts are legal under the Robinson-Patman Act if they are genuinely offered to different classes of customers in return for services rendered. It might also be presumed that the legality of a manufacturer's trade discount schedule would be helped if the differentials in the schedule were reasonably related to cost savings resulting from the use of the various classes of middlemen.

Because of lack of specific coverage in the act, and because changes in distribution patterns have upset traditional channel structures, it seems reasonable to assume that functional discounts will be challenged by the Federal Trade Commission in the years to come.

GEOGRAPHIC PRICE POLICIES

In pricing, a seller must consider the factor of freight costs involved in shipping the product to the buyer. This consideration grows in importance as freight becomes a larger part of total variable costs. Pricing policies may be established whereby the buyer pays all the freight, the seller bears the entire costs, or the two parties share the expense. The decision can have an important bearing on the geographic limits of a firm's market, the location of its production facilities, the source of its raw materials, and its competitive strength in various market areas.

F.O.B. POINT-OF-PRODUCTION PRICING

In one widely used geographic pricing system, the seller quotes the selling price at the factory or other point of production and the buyer pays the entire cost of transportation. This is usually referred to as *f.o.b. mill* or *f.o.b. factory* pricing. Of the five systems discussed in this section, this is the only one in which the seller does not pay *any* of the freight costs. The seller pays the costs of loading the shipment aboard the carrier—hence the term "f.o.b.," or "free on board." The title to the merchandise passes to the buyer at that point, and he assumes all costs and responsibilities for shipping. Even though this policy is usually thought of as a manufacturer's pricing policy and therefore is labeled

---

[10]*Mennen Company v. Federal Trade Commission,* 288 Fed. 774 (1923), certiorari denied, 262 U.S. 759 (1923); *Great Atlantic and Pacific Tea Company v. Cream of Wheat Company,* 277 Fed. 46 (1915); *National Biscuit Company v. Federal Trade Commission,* 299 Fed. 733 (1924), certiorari denied, 266 U.S. 613 (1924).

f.o.b. factory or some other point of production, it is used by many middlemen. Cash-and-carry wholesalers price their merchandise f.o.b. warehouse. Many retailers sell on an f.o.b. store basis, and the consumer pays the delivery costs.

Under the f.o.b. factory price policy, the seller nets the same amount on each sale of similar quantities. The delivered price to the buyers varies according to the freight charges. Although the Federal Trade Commission has, in general, considered an f.o.b. mill pricing system nondiscriminatory, this pricing policy has serious economic and marketing implications. In effect, f.o.b. pricing tends to establish a geographic monopoly for a given seller. Freight rates prevent distant competitors from entering his market. He in turn is increasingly priced out of markets that are far from his factory. At the same time, buyers located some distance from the seller pay heavy freight bills. If freight is a significant part of the total cost of the seller's product, it can have considerable influence on the size of his market.

UNIFORM DELIVERED PRICING

Under a uniform delivered pricing system, the same delivered price is quoted to all buyers, regardless of their locations. This policy is sometimes referred to as "postage stamp pricing" because of the similarities of the pricing of mail service. Actually, the seller is pricing f.o.b. at the buyer's location. The seller receives varying factory net prices on each sale depending upon the amount of his shipping costs.

A uniform delivered price is typically used where transportation costs are a minor item in the seller's total cost structure. The policy is also used by many retailers who feel that "free" delivery is an additional service which will strengthen their market position.

It has been generally established by the Supreme Court that a uniform delivered price is legal when it is truly maintained over the seller's entire geographic market.[11] A uniform delivered price does mean, however, that the seller is absorbing freight on shipments to distant customers and overcharging on freight (called "phantom" freight) in sales to buyers located near the shipping point.

Under a uniform delivered price system, buyers located near the seller's factory are paying for some of the costs of shipping to more distant locations. The counterargument is that an f.o.b. *factory* system gives an undue advantage to buyers located near the factory. Critics of f.o.b. factory price are usually in favor of a uniform delivered price. They feel that the freight expense should not be isolated and charged to individual customers any more than any other single marketing or production expense. From a marketing standpoint, a uniform delivered price is a convenient method of quoting a price. It also lends itself to national advertising.

ZONE DELIVERED PRICING

Under a zone price policy, a seller's market is divided into a limited number of broad geographic zones, and a uniform delivered price is set within each zone. Zone delivered pricing is similar to the system used in pricing parcel post serv-

---

[11]*Federal Trade Commission v. A. E. Staley Manufacturing Company,* 324 U.S. 746 (1945); see particularly p. 757.

vices and long-distance telephone service. A firm which quotes a price and then says "slightly higher west of the Rockies" is using a two-zone pricing system.

Whether the company uses a single-zone pricing system (uniform delivered price) or a multizone system, the freight charge built into the delivered price is approximately an average of the charges at all points within a zone area. Therefore, a seller either absorbs some of the freight costs or includes phantom freight in sales to all points, with one exception. This exception is sales made to buyers who are located at the point in the zone where the actual freight costs are equal to the arbitrary freight figure included in the selling price.

When a zone delivered price system is employed, the seller must walk a neat tightrope to avoid charges of illegal price discrimination among buyers or among customers of the buyers. This means that the zone lines must be drawn so that all competing buyers are in the same zone. This condition is almost impossible to meet in the dense market areas of the East and the Midwest.

FREIGHT ABSORPTION PRICING

A freight absorption price policy may be adopted to offset some of the competitive disadvantages of f.o.b. factory pricing. With an f.o.b. factory price, a firm is at a price disadvantage when it tries to sell to buyers located in markets nearer to competitors' plants. In order to penetrate more deeply into these markets, a seller may be willing to absorb some of the freight costs. As a policy, freight absorption usually means that seller A will quote to the customer a delivered price which is equal to A's factory price plus the freight costs which would be charged by the competitive seller located nearest the customer.

Our seller can continue to expand the geographic limits of his market as long as his mill net after freight absorption is larger than the marginal costs on the units sold. Freight absorption is particularly adaptable to a firm whose fixed costs per unit of product are high and whose variable costs are low. In these cases, management must constantly seek ways to cover fixed costs, and freight absorption is one answer.

The legality of freight absorption is reasonably clear. The policy is legal if it is done independently and not in collusion with other firms. Also it must be done only to meet competition. In fact, if practiced properly, freight absorption can have the effect of strengthening competition, because it can break down spatial monopolies and barriers around protected markets. Predatory freight absorption with the intent of destroying competition obviously would be unlawful.

BASING-POINT PRICING

Even though it is not so widely used as it once was, and even though its legality is questioned, the basing-point system still is important. Under this system the delivered price of a product is equal to (1) the price at the point of production plus (2) published freight charges between the basing point nearest the buyer and the buyer's locations. The actual shipping point has no bearing on the computation of the delivered price. A basing point itself is simply an arbitrary location from which delivered prices are computed by all competing sellers in an industry. Usually all basing points used by an industry are also important production points for the commodity, but not all production locations are basing points. Thus there are fewer basing points than production centers, and, as we shall see later, this factor has considerable influence on the legality of basing-point pricing.

To illustrate basing-point pricing, let us assume that a buyer is located in Kansas City and that Chicago is the nearest basing point. The established freight rates between Chicago and Kansas City for the product in question are $15 a unit. Manufacturers are located in Detroit, Chicago, and Kansas City. Freight charges between Detroit and Kansas City are $25 a unit. Let us assume also that all three manufacturers can produce and sell the product for $100 a unit at their factories. The delivered price in this example is $115—the price at point of production plus freight from the basing point closest to the buyer, regardless of the actual shipping point. The Chicago seller would have a mill net of $100; he just breaks even in this transaction. The Detroit manufacturer would have to absorb $10 of freight and would net only $90 at his factory. The Kansas City manufacturer would have a mill net of $115 because he would receive $15 in nonincurred, or phantom, freight.

Sellers may use either a single or a multiple basing-point system (a two-city basing-point system is shown in Fig. 13-1). Probably the best-known single basing-point system was the Pittsburgh-plus system used for years in the steel industry. The delivered price quoted for any steel product was equal to the mill price plus freight from Pittsburgh, regardless of where the sellers were located. This system generally aroused no objections so long as the steel producers were all located in or near Pittsburgh. As the industry expanded into Birmingham, Chicago, Cleveland, and other cities, however, trouble developed. Buyers located in Chicago, for example, objected to paying phantom freight from Pittsburgh when they purchased from Chicago mills. Although mills in or near Chicago might enjoy receiving phantom freight, they also might object to the single basing-point system. Under it, sellers located long distances from the basing point could not take advantage of their locations by offering lower prices to nearby customers.

Eventually a multiple basing-point system developed in the steel industry, and several other cities were designated as official basing points for various classes of steel products. As long as some sellers' locations are not designated at basing points, however, and as long as these sellers are closer to some buyers than the nearest basing point is, phantom freight is inescapable.

Characteristics of industries using basing-point system. In addition to the steel industry, such industries as cement, sugar, gypsum products, plate glass, heavy chemicals, lumber products, and corn products have used the basing-point system. These industries have several common characteristics which are conducive to the use of basing-point pricing. In the first place, the product in each case is a standard, nondifferentiated item. Sugar is sugar, and window glass is window glass. Price is all-important, and brands are not significant. Another point is that freight constitutes a substantial cost element. Further-more, fixed expenses constitute a large part of total costs, and excess capacity typically exists in basing-point industries. Thus, there is a constant thread of price-cutting by firms willing to accept orders at any price above variable costs. Even though total costs are not covered, any return over variable costs is a contribution to overhead. Finally, there are relatively few firms in the in-dustry, and it is rather easy to get agreement on the use of the system and to enforce the agreement.

Evaluation of basing-point system. Several rather strong objections are typi-cally raised against the basing-point pricing system. One is that it is not possible

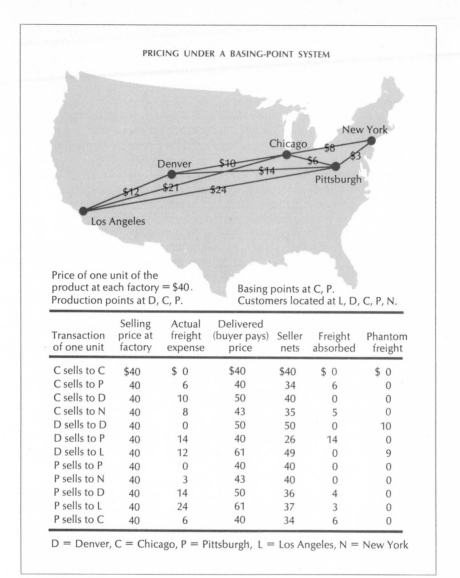

PRICING UNDER A BASING-POINT SYSTEM

Price of one unit of the
product at each factory = $40.
Production points at D, C, P.

Basing points at C, P.
Customers located at L, D, C, P, N.

Transaction of one unit	Selling price at factory	Actual freight expense	Delivered (buyer pays) price	Seller nets	Freight absorbed	Phantom freight
C sells to C	$40	$ 0	$40	$40	$ 0	$ 0
C sells to P	40	6	40	34	6	0
C sells to D	40	10	50	40	0	0
C sells to N	40	8	43	35	5	0
D sells to D	40	0	50	50	0	10
D sells to P	40	14	40	26	14	0
D sells to L	40	12	61	49	0	9
P sells to P	40	0	40	40	0	0
P sells to N	40	3	43	40	0	0
P sells to D	40	14	50	36	4	0
P sells to L	40	24	61	37	3	0
P sells to C	40	6	40	34	6	0

D = Denver, C = Chicago, P = Pittsburgh, L = Los Angeles, N = New York

Figure 13-1. Dollar amounts shown between various locations represent freight rates for shipping one unit of the product between the two given cities. The figures in the table show the prices in this system, which has two basing points.

to justify the phantom freight. This is an unearned element, and it results in price discrimination. Another incriminating objection is that collusion is required to make the basing-point system work. The use of a freight rate book, published by the industry's trade association and rigidly followed when quoting prices, is considered evidence of collusion by many people.

Another criticism of basing-point pricing is that it eliminates price competition and makes for rigidity in the pricing structure. All sellers quote the same delivered price at any one location. Usually any attempt to cut below the "proper" price is met with swift retaliation from competitive sellers. One seller cannot effectively take advantage of the fact that he is located nearer to buyers than other sellers are. Without a basing-point system, new plant development might be encouraged in markets where present demand exceeds supply and where there are good growth prospects. These new sellers could use their locational advantage to serve as the basis of a price advantage. Finally, there is a considerable amount of transportation crosshauling, which results in duplicate use of transportation facilities and resources. Because the delivered price is the same regardless of shipping point, a Birmingham firm, for example, may buy from a Pittsburgh seller, and a Pittsburgh firm may buy from a Birmingham seller.

A number of advantages are stated in support of basing-point pricing, but they have some fundamental weaknesses. A frequently mentioned merit is that basing-point systems prevent the growth of spatial, or geographic, monopolies. Without this system, buyers would be at the mercy of the nearest seller. Consequently, many buyers are said to prefer basing-point pricing. This argument is weak on at least three points. First, if a seller were really prospering in his geographic area because outsiders could not overcome the freight barriers, other sellers would soon build competitive plants in the area. Second, distant sellers could still enter the market by absorbing freight on an independent basis. Finally, the buyers who are located near the sellers and who are paying phantom freight are certainly not in favor of basing-point pricing.

Legality of basing-point pricing. There is no law against the basing-point system per se. In various cases since about 1920, however, the Federal Trade Commission has sought to have the system outlawed, whether it was practiced by one company independently or by members of an entire industry working together. In the 1940s the Commission met with considerable success. Cases were brought separately against two large manufacturers of glucose, a corn syrup used in candy manufacturing. These firms employed a single basing-point system, using Chicago as the basing point, even though some of their plants were located elsewhere. There was no charge of collusion between the two sellers. Nevertheless, the FTC and the Supreme Court ruled in each case that the single basing-point system used by these firms involved phantom freight, was discriminatory, and thus was illegal under the Robinson-Patman Act.[12] A later and possibly even more important case involved the Federal Trade Commission's proceedings against the Cement Institute (a trade association) and its members, who were using a multiple basing-point system.[13] In this case the system was ruled illegal on two major counts. First, it was ruled to be unfair competition, and thus a violation of Section 5 of the Federal Trade Commission Act, because it was proved that collusion and combination in restraint of trade existed in the employment of the pricing system. Second, the multiple basing-point system was ruled unlawfully discriminatory and thus a violation of the Robinson-Patman Act.

In spite of these decisions, the legality of basing-point pricing is still not entirely clear. The Cement Institute case was decided in part by the fact that combination and conspiracy in restraint of trade were shown. The status of basing point pricing

---

[12]*Corn Products Refining Company v. Federal Trade Commission,* 324 U.S. 726 (1945); and *Federal Trade Commission v. A. E. Staley Manufacturing Company,* 324 U.S. 746 (1945).
[13]*Federal Trade Commission v. Cement Institute et al.,* 68 S. Ct. 793 (1948).

where there is no proof of collusion is not entirely clear. Nevertheless, in the Cement Institute decision the Supreme Court referred to the glucose cases, where there was no hint of collusion. From this reference, we can infer that a basing-point system is inherently discriminatory (because of phantom freight) and thus unlawful under the Robinson-Patman Act, whether or not collusion is present.

QUESTIONS AND PROBLEMS

1. Carefully distinguish between cumulative and noncumulative quantity discounts. Which of these two types of quantity discounts has the greater economic and social justification? Explain your position, disregarding the legal considerations for the time being.
2. A manufacturer of appliances quotes a list price of $500 a unit for a certain model of refrigerator. He then grants trade discounts of 35, 20, and 5 percent. What is his selling price? Who might get these various discounts?
3. Interview a few different types of local retailers (restaurant, clothing store, sporting goods store, furniture store, etc.) and determine what terms of sale are customarily applied to their purchases. What accounts for the variations among the different types of retailers?
4. Two families living in the same apartment house each purchased a set of dining-room furniture from the same retailer. One family was charged $25 more than the other family. Is this a violation of the Robinson-Patman Act?
5. The Robinson-Patman Act prohibits price discrimination, and yet manufacturers and wholesalers often charge different customers different prices. Is this illegal?
6. Company A sells to all its customers at the same published price. A sales executive finds that company B is offering to sell to one of A's customers at a lower price. Company A then cuts its price to this customer, but maintains the original price to all other customers. Is this a violation of the Robinson-Patman Act?
7. Explain the provisions of the section of the Robinson-Patman Act which deals with brokerage allowances.
8. Carefully explain the cost-defense provision in the Robinson-Patman Act.
9. Name some products which logically might be sold under a uniform delivered price system.
10. "An f.o.b. point-of-production price system is the only geographic price system which is fair to all buyers." Discuss.
11. Distinguish between a uniform delivered pricing system and a zone delivered system.
12. Explain how the basing-point system of pricing enables a seller to expand his market.
13. "The pricing system based on freight absorption has all the desirable features but none of the undesirable features of the basing-point system." Discuss.
14. If an Eastern manufacturer wants to compete in Western markets, where he is at a significant disadvantage with respect to freight costs, what pricing alternatives are open to this firm to help it overcome the freight differential?
15. "Adopting a multiple basing-point system eliminates the inherent undesirable features of basing-point pricing." Discuss.

PRICE POLICIES AND
STRATEGIES (CONT.)

ONE-PRICE VERSUS VARIABLE-PRICE POLICY

Rather early in its pricing consideration, management should decide whether the company will follow a one-price policy or a variable-price policy. While adopting one will not necessarily preclude the use of the other, normally it is not strategic to waver back and forth.

Under a *one-price* policy the company charges the same price to all similar types of customers who purchase similar quantities of the product under essentially the same terms of sale. Discounts and allowances may be granted under this policy if they are offered on equal terms to all comparable customers.

When a *variable-price* policy is used, the company will sell similar quantities to similar buyers at different prices. Sometimes variable prices are offered when the buyer and seller are friends. In other cases, sellers want the business of certain customers and will offer them favorable differential prices. Usually, however, under this policy the price is set as a result of bargaining.

In the United States, the one-price policy has been used more than variable pricing, particularly at the retail level. This is in contrast to many foreign countries where the final price is customarily determined by bargaining and haggling. A one-price policy is by no means the rule in the United States, however. In the marketing of any product where a trade-in is involved, variable pricing abounds.

Thus a one-price policy is virtually unknown in automobile retailing, even though posted factory list prices may suggest that the same price is offered to all.

A one-price policy builds customer confidence in a seller, whether at the manufacturing, wholesaling, or retailing level. Weak bargainers need not feel they are at a competitive disadvantage. The policy is also a great time-saver. Finally, this policy can be adopted whether personal salesmen are used or not. It lends itself nicely to self-service retailing, mail-order selling, and automatic vending.

A variable-price policy also has some advantages. It offers the seller flexibility in his dealings with different customers. The seller may wish to make price concessions to woo a buyer away from a competitor, or he may want to give a buyer a better deal because the customer shows promise of becoming a large-scale buyer in the future.

On balance, however, a variable-price policy is generally less desirable than a one-price policy. In sales to business firms, not to consumers, variable pricing is likely to be in violation of the Robinson-Patman Act. Variable pricing generates considerable ill will when the word gets around that some buyers acquired the product at lower prices. Variable pricing can trigger a price war and bring strong retaliation in some industries. In most retail stores, variable pricing would result in chaotic selling conditions and a virtual absence of managerial control.

UNIT PRICING

Unit pricing is a retail price-information-reporting policy which to date has been employed largely by supermarket chains, although the same method is adaptable to other types of stores and products. The policy is a business response to consumer protests that the proliferation of packages sizes (especially in grocery stores) has made it virtually impossible to compare prices of similar products. In canned beans, for example, is 15½ avoirdupois ounces for 19 cents a better deal than 1-pound 1-ounce (482 grams) at 2 cans for 45 cents? How does the price of 41 cents for a 1-pound 4-ounce box of Tide detergent compare with 83 cents for the 3-pound 1-ounce box of Cheer brand of detergent?

Under a policy of unit pricing, for each separate product and package size there is a shelf label which states (1) the price of the package and (2) this price expressed in dollars and cents per ounce, pound, pint, or some other standard quantity measure.

Several studies have been conducted on unit pricing to measure the consumers' response, the impact on the retailer, and the possible repercussions on manufacturers.[1] Because unit pricing was generally instituted only recently (1970s), it is a little too early to get complete information on its effect. The hope is that consumers will make more informed purchase decisions. Undoubtedly, there

---

[1] See Lawrence M. Lamont and James T. Rothe, "The Impact of Unit Pricing on Channels Systems," in Fred C. Allvine (ed.), *Combined Proceedings: 1971 Spring and Fall Conferences,* American Marketing Association, series no. 33, Chicago, 1972, pp. 653–658; Kent B. Monroe and Peter J. LaPlaca, "What Are the Benefits of Unit Pricing?" *Journal of Marketing,* July, 1972 pp. 16–22; Michael J. Houston, "The Effect of Unit-Pricing on Choices of Brand and Size in Economic Shopping," *Journal of Marketing,* July, 1972, pp. 51–69; and James M. Carman, "A Summary of Empirical Research on Unit Pricing in Supermarkets," *Journal of Retailing,* Winter, 1973, pp. 63–70.

will be some consumer switching of sizes, brands, and even stores. Installing and maintaining unit pricing is an added retailer cost, hopefully offset by societal benefits. Unit pricing will force manufacturers to change packages and labels. Brand loyalties may decline as price competition increases. Middlemen's brands may become stronger. All in all, unit pricing will pose several challenges to a manufacturer's marketing program.

PRICING MULTIPLE PRODUCTS

Most firms market several lines of products or offer a breadth of products within one line. As the number of products increases, the pricing problems become more complex. No article produced or carried by a company is an island unto itself. It is related to the company's other products through market demand, through cost, or through both. Management must consider these interrelationships when pricing the company's full complement of products.

On the cost side of the pricing equation, it can be seen that some products present joint cost situations. In the product lines of a meat-packer, for example, many items are derived from one beef carcass. In pricing related products, management may decide that each article must recoup its full cost plus a profit or that each must cover only variable costs, with any return above that level considered a contribution to overhead.

On the *demand* side, the products may differ but be related in quality, uses, or sizes. These interrelationships reduce management's flexibility in pricing because the executives must consider the effect which the price of one item will have on the prices of other products. A manufacturer of outboard motors sells a line of products in which one of the relative differences is the size of each model as measured by its horsepower. Thus when pricing a 15-horsepower motor, the executive must consider this price in relation to the ones set for motors of 7.5, 10, and 25 horsepower.

A key consideration in the pricing of multiple products is the degree to which the market for each size, quality level, brand, etc., can be isolated from the market for other sizes, brands, and quality levels. In the above example, if various sizes of outboard motors were sold to separate markets, isolated from one another, then each size could be priced without reference to the others. These markets usually are not isolated, however; they overlap and actually represent a continuum.

Another key consideration in pricing multiple products is that the firm should be trying to achieve a pricing goal on its total output or for a related group of products but not necessarily for each individual item. If a company can increase its total profits by pricing certain articles below total costs, then this is sound marketing strategy.

PRICE LINING

Price lining is found more commonly among retailers than among wholesalers or producers. It consists of selecting a limited number of prices at which the store will sell its merchandise. A shoe store may sell several styles of shoes at $14.95 a pair, another group at $19.95, and a third assortment at $24.95. Price lining is used extensively in the retailing of all types of apparel. Many years ago, Woolworth's and other variety stores got the nickname "five-and-ten-cent-stores" because of their policies of price lining everything at one of these two levels.

For the consumer, the main benefit of price lining is that it simplifies buying decisions. From the retailer's point of view, the policy is advantageous because it helps the store owner to plan his purchases. A dress buyer, for example, can go into a market looking for dresses which may be retailed for $19.95, $29.95, or $39.95.

On the surface, price lining may seem to ease management's pricing decisions because the retail price is already set. Initially, however, the company had to decide how many lines to have and at what level each price line should be. Furthermore, every time the retailer wants to make a purchase, he has fundamentally the same pricing decisions to make that an executive in any non-price-lining company has. The only difference is that in a price-lining company, the cost must fit into the price. The retailer still has the alternative of equating marginal cost and marginal revenue or of using cost-plus pricing in the form of his usual markup. The decision is made with respect to the price paid for the merchandise rather than the price at which it will be sold.

Two big problems in price lining center around the task of setting the initial price lines and the difficulties encountered when the costs are increasing. In determining the price lines, management does not want too many or too few, and care must be taken that they are not too close together or too far apart. If they are too close together, the consumer may not be able to see why one item is x dollars higher than another. If they are too far apart, sales may be lost because some consumers want an article at the price in between the two levels.

Rising costs can put a real squeeze on price lines, because a company hesitates to change its price line every time costs go up. But if costs increase and prices remain stationary, profit margins are compressed, and the retailer may be forced to seek products with lower costs. Where longtime relationships exist between manufacturers and retailers, or where price lines are traditional, as in 5- and 10-cent candy bars, manufacturers may reduce the product's size or quality (and thus its costs) and enable retailers to hold prices at existing levels.

RESALE PRICE MAINTENANCE

Some manufacturers want to control the prices at which retailers will resell their products. They can do this by means of suggested resale prices or by means of a resale-price-maintenance policy supported by law.[2]

For some producers who follow a policy of suggested list prices, the price is just a guide for retailers; it is a list price on which discounts may be computed. For others, the suggested price is so rigidly enforced that a retailer's franchise will be canceled if he does not adhere to the manufacturer's list. Normally, strict enforcement of the suggested list price is possible only when a manufacturer uses a

---

[2]For an analysis of methods used to encourage retail price stability by manufacturers, see Louis W. Stern, "Approaches to Achieving Retail Stability," *Business Horizons,* Fall, 1964, pp. 75–86. This investigation showed that the most effective and legally justifiable methods were those involving restricted distribution, market segmentation, and reductions in discounts and allowances. Methods which seemed inadequate included fair trade, granting promotional allowances, and moral suasion.

selective or exclusive distribution pattern and when the brand is a desirable one from the retailer's point of view.

One of the most controversial of all price policies is that of resale price maintenance established under state and federal laws. The policy is employed by manufacturers, and it governs prices at the retail level. Resale-price-maintenance laws have come to be known as "fair-trade" laws. This is truly a strategic choice of titles: who can argue against fair trade? Opponents use the term "resale price-fixing," claiming there is nothing "fair" about fair-trade laws.

LEGAL ASPECTS OF RESALE PRICE MAINTENANCE

The Depression days of the 1930s spawned the state fair-trade laws. The intent of the laws was to protect the small-scale retailers from the onslaught of large retailers, especially the chain stores. At the peak of their popularity, these laws existed in all states except Vermont, Missouri, and Texas. There also was no such legislation in the District of Columbia.

State legislation. In general, the state laws follow one of two model acts. In one model the manufacturer sets the *exact* price at which the product will be sold at retail. In the other, the producer sets the *minimum* resale price. These laws are voluntary; the manufacturer does not have to fair-trade his products. They apply only to branded, copyrighted, or otherwise identifiable products sold in open competition. Usually under the laws a retailer may cut below the fair-trade price if he is holding a distress sale or discontinuing the product. In such cases, however, several of the laws first give the manufacturer the opportunity to buy back the stock at invoice price.

The key provision of the state fair-trade laws is known as the "nonsigners" clause. It states that when a manufacturer signs a fair-trade contract with one retailer in a state, every other retailer in the state is bound by this contract after due notice of the price has been given.

No state agencies have been set up to enforce these contracts. Enforcement is left up to the individual companies or groups of companies. It is a tremendous task and constitutes one of the greatest weaknesses in the laws.

Federal legislation. There was some concern, however, that resale price maintenance in interstate commerce was price-fixing in violation of the federal antitrust laws, so in 1937 the Miller-Tydings Act was passed as a piece of enabling legislation. It is an amendment to the Sherman Antitrust Act. It is not a federal fair-trade law. It simply enables a firm in one state to fair-trade its products in any other state *which has a fair-trade law* without being in violation of the antitrust laws.

The Miller-Tydings Act and the state fair-trade laws withstood legal attack from many sources until 1951, when the nonsigners clause was held to be invalid in interstate competition.[3] In 1952 this loophole and others were plugged by the passage of the McGuire Act as an amendment to the Federal Trade Commission Act. The right to use the nonsigners clause in interstate commerce was specifically approved, and thus the teeth were restored to the state laws.

---

[3]*Schwegmann Bros. v. Calvert Distillers Corporation,* 341 U.S. 384 (1951).

Current status of fair-trade legislation. Since the 1950s, fair-trade laws have become less and less effective. In a noticeable trend, several state laws have been ruled unconstitutional in whole or in part by the courts. Some state legislatures have repealed the entire law or the nonsigners provision. Furthermore, court decisions are making it increasingly restrictive and costly for a manufacturer to maintain and enforce a fair-trade program.

Realizing that fair-trade legislation on the state level is proving to be largely ineffective, the proponents of legalized resale price maintenance are exerting tremendous pressure to have a federal fair-trade law passed. Such a law, interestingly enough, is strongly opposed by the Federal Trade Commission, the Antitrust Division of the Department of Justice, the Department of Agriculture, the Department of Commerce, and countless business interests.

Prevalence of resale price maintenance. It is estimated that not more than 5 to 10 percent of retail sales have ever been covered by fair-trade contracts. Resale price maintenance was especially prevalent in the drug trade—in toiletries, drug sundries, patent medicines, etc. This pricing practice has also been used by manufacturers of leather goods, photographic equipment, sporting goods, liquor, and small appliances.

Fair trade has virtually never been used on grocery items—a major segment of total retail trade. One reason for this is that grocery prices fluctuate too frequently. The task of notifying all grocery outlets would be unfeasible. Fair trade in food lines is also risky because most of the large grocery retailers have their own highly accepted brands. These middlemen's brands could easily be substituted for fair-traded manufacturers' brands. Fair trade is not at all practical where trade-ins are customary, as in large appliances or automobiles. If refrigerators were fair-traded, for example, a discount seller could cut below fair trade by offering a large trade-in allowance on an old ice cube tray.

EVALUATION OF RESALE PRICE MAINTENANCE

Manufacturer's viewpoint. A manufacturer may want to fair-trade his product in order to advertise its price or to prevent its being used as a loss leader. He may fear that price cuts will damage his product's prestige. If price reductions are permanent, as they would be in the hands of some large retailers, consumers may feel that the regular list price is an inflated indication of the product's value. Also, if the product becomes a price football, dealers who sell at the regular list price may discontinue the product or push substitute brands.

A manufacturer may want to protect his small dealers from the price competition of large-scale retailers, because he feels that he needs small dealers. A price-cutting retailer may not be willing to provide the selling effort and in-store promotion desired.

On the other hand, the competitive limitations of fair trade far outweigh any advantages which this policy may seem to have for manufacturers. It is doubtful that the absence of a fair-trade policy really can hurt the prestige of a product. Consumers are used to paying different prices at different outlets. If the product is a good one and is properly promoted by the manufacturer, many retailers will continue to carry it because of consumer demand.

Also, the factor of substitution is a two-edged sword. Some manufacturers fear that retailers will bury a product which is not fair-traded. At the same time, a product which is fair-traded may not even be carried by many of the large-volume, low-cost retailers. The key words here are "low cost." For example, Sears did not handle Sunbeam appliances while they were fair-traded. After the Sunbeam Corporation discontinued its fair-trade policy, however, some of their appliances were carried in the Sears catalogues and stores. Most large-volume, *high-cost* retailers, such as department stores, did carry Sunbeam and other fair-traded appliances. Manufacturers should also remember that a major reason why some middlemen have instituted their own brands and why these have been so successful is that they have had a price advantage over the higher fixed price of fair-traded manufacturers' brands.

Finally, it may be virtually impossible to enforce fair-trade contracts if any distribution policy except exclusive distribution is followed. Because of enforcement problems, a fair-trade policy has been discontinued by many formerly staunch advocates.

Retailer's viewpoint. Small retailers and high-cost, large retailers have traditionally favored fair trade. Small retailers are unable to match the price cuts offered by large stores. Smaller operators do not have enough sales volume on other items or on the price-cut items to offset the loss from price reduction.

How retailers can afford to cut below list price? Some retailers do it to attract customers to the store. This is called "leader pricing" and is discussed in the next section. Price cuts may also be possible because the retailer buys in such large quantities that he gets substantial discounts or because he offers a minimum of service.

Fair trade has drawbacks for retailers as well as for manufacturers. The economic and moral effects of the nonsigners clause are important. These points have been argued in the courts for many years, and opinion is still substantially divided. This author's opinion is that the clause is undesirable. It seems that one retailer should not be bound by the interests of another. Also, if a retailer buys a product and assumes all risks of ownership, this should be a sufficient basis for letting him determine the price at which he will sell it.

Another disadvantage of fair trade is that it eliminates price competition at the retail level. Fair trade protects the high-cost, inefficient operator who wishes to maintain high unit margins even though he sells only a relatively small number of units. On the other hand, fair trade penalizes the retailer who prefers to earn a small profit per unit of sale and depend upon huge volume to reach his total profit goal. Retail price maintenance also penalizes the low-cost retailer who is not able to use his competitive advantage by passing on to consumers the lower prices resulting from the efficiency of his operation. Fair trade works particularly to the *advantage* of the full-service retailer and to the *disadvantage* of the retailer whose costs are low because he offers few services.

It is difficult to show that fair trade has helped small merchants. In fact, in some respects it has hurt the retail drug industry. Drug products, with their high gross margin protected by resale-price-maintenance laws, have been extremely attractive to other stores, especially supermarkets. As a result, today a substantial volume of drug items are sold through grocery stores. Furthermore, it is difficult to show that independent druggists have been better off through the years than independent retailers in grocery, apparel, or other non-fair-trade fields.

Consumer's viewpoint. From the point of view of the consumer, it is difficult to build a case in support of fair trade. Some people claim that fair-trade laws tend to keep prices on all products at a reasonable level. Without fair trade, it is claimed, prices would be cut on a few items but raised on articles whose prices are not so well known to consumers. Proponents of fair trade state that the policy ensures wide distribution of products and makes it possible for consumers to buy items at conveniently located small stores.

On balance, these arguments are weak. The biggest objection to fair trade from the consumer's viewpoint is that, as various studies have shown, prices are higher on an item when it is fair-traded than when it is not. Also, if consumers are willing to forgo services and instead enjoy lower prices, this alternative is not open to them if the product is fair-traded.

LEADER PRICING AND UNFAIR-PRACTICES ACTS

Many firms, primarily retailers, cut prices temporarily on a few items in order to attract customers. This price and promotional strategy, involving the use of loss leaders, is called *leader pricing.* Leader items should be well-known, heavily advertised articles which are purchased frequently. Actually, the term "loss leaders" is a misnomer. "Profit leaders" would be more descriptive of the goal of the policy. The idea is that customers will come to the store to buy the advertised leader items and then stay to buy other regularly priced merchandise. The net result, the firm hopes, will be an increase in total volume and total profits.

Today about twenty-five states have laws (unfair-sales acts, unfair-practices acts) to regulate leader pricing. Originally passed in some thirty states in the 1930s, these laws were part of the general drive against chain stores and other large-scale retailers. The intent was to prohibit predatory price-cutting and other sales below cost. In contrast to the voluntary fair-trade laws, the unfair-practices acts are mandatory. They apply to all middlemen and to sales of all products, whether or not they are branded or specifically identifiable.

The states have followed one of two model laws. Under one model, a reseller is prohibited from selling an item below invoice cost, including freight, plus a stated markup which is usually 2 percent at wholesale and 6 percent at retail. Under the other model law, the minimum price is set at invoice cost, including freight, plus the retailer's or wholesaler's cost of doing business.[4]

The general intent of these laws is commendable. They eliminate much of the predatory type of price-cutting. However, they permit firms to use loss leaders as a price and promotional strategy. That is, a retailer can offer an article below full cost but still sell above cost plus 6 percent markup. Under the unfair-practices acts, furthermore, low-cost efficient businessmen are not penalized, nor are high-cost operators protected. Differentials in retailers' purchase prices can be reflected in their selling prices, and savings resulting from the absence of services can be passed on to the customers.

On the other hand, the unfair-trade-practices acts have some glaring weak-

---

[4]See Stephen Paranka, "Appraisal of State Unfair Trade Practices Acts," in Donald F. Mulvihill and Stephen Paranka (eds.), *Price Policies and Practices,* John Wiley & Sons, Inc., New York, 1967, pp. 313–317.

nesses. In the first place, the states do not establish agencies for enforcement. It is the responsibility of the injured party to seek satisfaction from the offender in a civil suit. Another limitation is that it is difficult or even impossible to determine the cost of doing business for each individual product. It is on this point that some states have declared their laws unconstitutional. The third weakness is that the laws seem to disregard the fundamental idea that the purpose of a business is to make a profit on the total operation, and not necessarily on each sale of each product.

GUARANTEE AGAINST PRICE DECLINE

A producer must decide whether he will make a refund to his middlemen in case he reduces his price within a stated period of time after filling their orders. Some sellers guarantee the price until orders are delivered or received. Others protect the price well into the season when the merchandise is being sold by the middlemen. If a manufacturer must reduce his price, he simply credits each middleman's account with an amount equal to the unit price cut times the number of units the middleman has on hand.

Wisely used, a price-guarantee policy is especially worthwhile for firms producing goods subject to seasonal fluctuations in demand. This policy should encourage middlemen to place large orders well in advance of the season. Then the manufacturer can keep his plant operating in what would otherwise be a slack season. During periods of falling prices a middleman can order in large amounts and have no fear of taking a loss if prices decline still further.

This policy has some limitations from the standpoint of the manufacturer. If he has sold huge quantities of merchandise and the price drops, he may be faced with a heavy financial loss. The cost of policing the policy is an important factor, especially if the manufacturer guarantees the price until the merchandise is resold. Middlemen might inflate their inventory figures, and bad customer relations might be created, if the manufacturer used his salesmen to check the middlemen's stocks. Price guarantees encourage inventory speculation by middlemen. They take no risk at all. If prices go up, they gain; if prices drop, the guarantee protects them. Also, price guarantees may lead to price rigidity. Even when market conditions call for a price cut, manufacturers may hesitate to reduce their prices because they dislike having to give a rebate.

PSYCHOLOGICAL PRICING—ODD PRICING

Several price policies can be grouped under the general heading of psychological price policies. We have already touched upon three of these: price lining, prestige pricing above competitive market levels, and the use of customary prices at the market level. We also pointed out that if a price is set below the expected level, sales will suffer. Actually, volume can be increased by raising the price.

At the retail level, another psychological pricing policy is commonly used. Prices are set at odd amounts, such as 19 cents, 49 cents, $19.95, etc. Automobiles are priced at $3,995 rather than $4,000, and houses sell for $26,950 instead of $27,000. The practice originally developed as a control measure over theft by retail sales-clerks. Odd pricing usually forces a clerk to make change, and this in turn forces him to ring up the sale on the cash register.

In general, retailers believe that pricing items at odd amounts will result in larger sales. Thus 49 cents or 98 cents will bring greater revenue than 50 cents or $1. Furthermore, retailers believe that buying psychology is such that odd prices will bring more sales volume than the next *lower* even-numbered price. That is, at 49 cents or 98 cents, a firm will sell more units than at 48 cents or 96 cents. In this situation the seller's average revenue curve would have a zigzag shape, as shown in Fig. 14-1.

There is little concrete evidence to support retailers' belief in the value of odd prices. Various studies have reported inconclusive results.[5] Odd pricing is often avoided in prestige stores or on higher-priced items. Thus expensive men's suits are priced at $150, not $149.95.

PRICE COMPETITION VERSUS NONPRICE COMPETITION

In the course of developing its marketing program, management has a choice of emphasizing price competition or nonprice competition. Rarely is one of these strategies employed to the exclusion of the other, but one can be intentionally stressed more than the other.

PRICE COMPETITION

With monopolistic competition and product differentiation so prevalent in the economy today, we may overlook the fact that there is still a considerable amount of price competition. Management may decide to engage in price competition by regularly offering prices which are as low as possible. Often when this is done the seller also offers a minimum of services. In their early years, discount houses and chain stores competed in this way. Two other situations involving price competition which we should examine are (1) price changes made by our company and (2) our reaction to price changes made by a competitor.

Price changes by our firm.   Any one of several situations may prompt a change in price. As costs increase, for instance, management may decide that the best course of action is to raise the price, rather than to cut quality or aggressively promote the product and still maintain the price. If our company's share of the market is declining because of strong competition, we may react initially by reducing our price. We should, of course, try to determine what accounted for the improvement in our competitor's position—an improved product or aggressive advertising, for example. In the long run, our best alternative may be to improve aspects of our own marketing program, rather than to rely on the price cut.

Temporary price adjustments may be necessary to correct an imbalance in inventory. Temporary price cuts may also be used as a promotional tactic when introducing a new product or in an effort to stimulate sales of an existing product. One study of temporary price reductions on three consumer items (regular coffee,

---

[5]For example, see David M. Georgoff, "Price Illusion and the Effect of Odd-Even Retail Pricing," *Southern Journal of Business,* April, 1969, pp. 95–103.

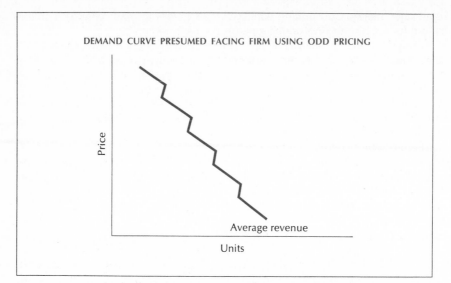

DEMAND CURVE PRESUMED FACING FIRM USING ODD PRICING

Figure 14–1. Some segments of the curve slope negatively. That is, as the price declines, volume also decreases. The zigzag shape reflects the idea that a familiar odd price will bring more sales volume than the prices immediately below these figures. Thus by pricing an article at 49 cents or 98 cents, the company will sell more units than at 48 cents or 96 cents. Do you agree? What types of stores use odd pricing? What products lend themselves to odd pricing?

cleansing tissue, and frozen dinners) established some useful guidelines for management. Professor Hinkle concluded.[6]

1. Off-season reductions are more profitable than equal or even greater reductions during high-volume seasons.
2. Frequent price cuts on the same brand bring successively smaller gains in market share.
3. Temporary price reductions seldom prevent new brands from gaining a foothold in the market.
4. Price cuts on new brands are more effective than price cuts on established products.
5. Price reductions seem to have little power to reverse a declining sales trend.

Before changing a price, management should consider several factors. Price-cutting may be advisable, for example, only when the seller is faced with an elastic demand curve. By reducing its price, management hopes that the volume will be increased sufficiently to increase total revenue. If demand is inelastic, a price cut will serve only to reduce total revenue.[7]

---

[6]*Marketing Science Institute,* July, 1965, p. 1; see also Charles L. Hinkle, "The Strategy of Price Deals," *Harvard Business Review,* July–August, 1965, pp. 75–85; and Alfred Gross, "Cents-off: A Critical Promotion Tactic," *MSU Business Topics,* Spring, 1971, pp. 13–20.

[7]For a new concept of price sensitivity—one which suggests that the pricing decision should rest on a better rationale than elasticity, because often there are identifiable desensitizing factors (such as eccentricities in consumer behavior, unequal ability of salesmen, and difficulty

A seller should also determine what percentage of sales increases will be necessary to offset any given percentage cut in unit price. For example, if unit prices are cut 20 percent, sales must increase 25 percent to give the same dollar sales volume as before the cut. The formula is

$$X = \frac{C}{1 \text{ minus } C}$$

where C is the percentage price cut and X is the percentage by which sales must increase to give the same dollar sales volume as before the cut.

Management should also determine what effect a given price cut will have on *gross margin,* and what sales increase (in units or dollars) will be needed to offset this reduction. To determine the increase in *dollar* sales volume needed to earn the same dollar gross margin as before a price cut, the formula

$$X = \frac{M(1 - C)}{M - C} - 1$$

where C is the percentage price reduction, M is the gross-margin percentage, and X is the percentage increase in *dollar* sales volume needed to earn as many gross-margin dollars as before the cut. This formula assumes that unit production costs remain constant. Thus if a firm has a 30 percent gross margin and cuts prices 10 percent, it needs a 35 percent increase in *dollar* sales volume.[8]

From the seller's standpoint the big threat in price-cutting is that competitors will retaliate, especially in oligopolistic market situations. The net result can be a price war, and the price may even settle permanently at a lower level. Price-cutting is most likely to be found in markets where there are several sellers and the products or services are reasonably similar. In such a situation, a cut below market price will probably bring a large increase in volume.

We should note that an oligopoly is not necessarily found only among large firms. The term "oligopoly" means "a few sellers." Thus, a group of small neighborhood merchants can constitute an oligopoly. For instance, the barbers in a community may try to avoid price competition because if one reduces his price, all must follow.

Reaction to competitors' price changes. We can assume that our competitors will change their prices. We may not know when the change will occur, what its magnitude will be, or whether it will be an increase or a decrease. But change they will. Consequently, we should at least be ready with some policy guidelines or, better yet, have a plan of reaction established. Advance planning is particularly necessary in the case of a competitive price reduction, since time will then be of the essence. If a competitor boosts his prices, a reasonable delay in reacting will probably not be perilous. In fact, it may turn out to be the wise thing to do if his

---

in comparing different products)—see Richard T. Sampson, "Sense and Sensitivity in Pricing," *Harvard Business Review,* November–December, 1964, pp. 99–105.

For a challenge to conventional wisdom when deciding on price changes for *industrial* goods, see Reed Moyer and Robert J. Boewadt, "The Pricing of Industrial Goods," *Business Horizons,* June, 1971, pp. 27–34.

[8]To determine the increase in unit sales volume needed to maintain the same dollar gross margin in face of a price cut, the formula is $X = \frac{M}{M - C} - 1$. In the above example, the unit sales increase needed is 50 percent.

increase was a mistake. Our decision on what to do in the face of a price cut by a competitor will depend upon answers to such questions as: (1) Why did he cut his prices—is it a temporary move, or do we gauge it to be a long-run strategy? (2) *Can* we meet the price cut—that is, do we forecast that our cost-price-volume relationships permit a cut, or should we try to counter in nonprice fashion? (3) *Must* we meet the reduction—how important is this product or market to us, and how sensitive is the market to price competition?

NONPRICE COMPETITION

In nonprice competition, a seller maintains a stable, constant price and attempts to improve his market position by emphasizing his product, distribution system, promotional program, or services. Of course, management still has the task of setting the price, and competitive prices still must be taken into consideration. Furthermore, the price may change over a period of time. Nevertheless, in a nonprice competitive situation the emphasis definitely is on something other than price.

By using terms familiar in economic theory, we can differentiate nonprice competition from price competition. In price competition a seller attempts to move up or down his demand curve by changing the price. In nonprice competition a seller attempts to *shift* his demand curve to the right by means of product differentiation, promotional activities, or some other device. This point is illustrated in Fig. 14-2. At $150 the producer of a given model of metal skis can sell 35,000 pairs a year in the western region of his market. On the basis of price competition alone, he can increase his sales to 55,000 if he is willing to reduce his price to $130. The demand curve facing him is still *DD.* However, he is interested in boosting his sales without any decrease in selling price. Consequently, he embarks upon a promotional program—a form of nonprice competition—and he is able to inform and persuade enough new customers to buy at the original $150 price so that his unit sales increase to 55,000 pairs a year. In effect, his entire demand curve has shifted to position *D'D'.*

There is an increasing use of nonprice competition in marketing. Companies want, at least to some extent, to be the masters of their own destiny. In nonprice competition, a seller's entire advantage is not removed when a competitor undersells him. Furthermore, customer loyalty is fleeting when price competition is relied upon exclusively. Buyers will stick only as long as a seller offers the lowest price. Patronage built upon nonprice factors is less susceptible to a competitor's price appeal. Many sellers dread the price wars which can result from price competition.

When used by a manufacturer, the strategy of nonprice competition is often accompanied by a policy of price control which prevents middlemen from using price as a direct competitive weapon. Producers accomplish this control by (1) circumventing middlemen entirely and selling directly to ultimate consumers or industrial users, (2) leasing or selling on consignment, (3) fair-trading the product, or (4) using suggested resale prices along with a carefully policed exclusive distribution.

Methods of nonprice competition. One of the major forms of nonprice competition is *product differentiation,* a concept inherent in monopolistic, or imperfect, competition. The seller attempts to avoid direct price comparisons with competi-

Figure 14-2. Use of nonprice competition can shift the demand curve for a product. A company selling metal skis in a Western market used a promotional program to sell more skis at the same price, thus shifting *DD* to *D'D'*. Volume increased from 35,000 to 55,000 units at $150 (point *X* to point *Y*). Besides advertising, what other devices might this firm use to shift its demand curve? If price competition were used, at what price could the company sell 55,000 pairs?

tive products, so he makes his product actually or seemingly different from others. This concept was discussed in Chapter 9 in connection with product planning.

Some firms emphasize the *variety and quality of services* they offer to middle-men and final customers. Liberal credit terms, free delivery, unlimited returns, free installations, and product warranties are offered by many firms. Sometimes *convenience of location* can be used as the basis for nonprice competition. Suburban shopping centers stress this factor when competing with downtown shopping districts. At the manufacturing level, a firm may open sales branches in order to serve its market better.

Although *trading stamps* have been used for many years as a method of nonprice competition, it was not until the 1950s and 1960s that they became really popular. At peak use, more than four out of five families were stamp savers. In the 1970s the use of trading stamps declined in *product* marketing. Supermarkets and gasoline service stations (which once accounted for well over one-half of trading stamp volume) have generally dropped trading stamps. Rising food prices and conversion to discount operations triggered the supermarkets' move. A shortage of gasoline was the prime factor behind the service stations' decision to abandon trading stamps. The possible increased use of stamps as a nonprice promotional device in the marketing of services—banks, travel agencies, etc.—may offset the decline to some extent. It is interesting to note, however, that the dominant firm in the trading stamp industry—S & H—is diversifying into other fields.[9]

Several good studies have been made regarding the effects of trading stamps.[10] The net effect of stamps on retail prices, however, is still not entirely clear. As with many marketing problems, the answer is: It depends. In some cases, prices seem to have increased in stamp-giving stores, but in other instances there were no price increases. The net effect is also influenced by whether a customer religiously redeems all his stamps. Stamps cost the retailer 2 to 3 percent of sales. (He pays $2 to $3 for a thousand stamps and then gives one stamp for every 10 cents' worth of purchases.) He can absorb this cost if he can cut some other promotional expense or if he can increase his volume so that the unit fixed costs are reduced enough to offset the 2 or 3 percent increase in unit variable costs.[11]

Possibly the most important method of nonprice competition is *promotion.* In fact, along with product differentiation, promotion is a hallmark of nonprice competition and monopolistic competition. The topic of promotion is treated later, in Part 6.

QUESTIONS AND PROBLEMS

1. Under what marketing conditions is a company likely to use a variable-price policy? Can you name some firms which employ this policy, other than when a trade-in is involved?
2. What effects is unit pricing likely to have on a manufacturer's marketing program?
3. Are retailers ever faced with the problem of pricing multiple products? Explain.
4. Should Congress pass a federal resale-price-maintenance law?
5. Explain how the nonsigners clause works in fair-trade laws.
6. Why is it that, historically, manufacturers frequently fair-traded their small appliances (toasters, electric razors, etc.) but not their large ones (refrigerators, washing machines, etc.)?
7. Traditionally, resale price maintenance has been widespread in the retail drug

[9]"S & H Fights a Slump in Trading Stamps," *Business Week,* August 25, 1973, p. 72. See also Harold W. Fox, "The Trading Stamp Industry in Transition," *Baylor Business Studies,* vol. 3, no. 4 (1972–1973), pp. 7–31.

[10]For example, see Harold W. Fox, *The Economics of Trading Stamps,* Public Affairs Press, Washington, D. C., 1968; Harvey L. Vredenburg, *Trading Stamps,* Indiana University, Bureau of Business Research, Business Report no. 21, Bloomington, 1956; F. E. Brown and Alfred R. Oxenfeldt, "Price and Quality Comparisons between Stamp and Nonstamp Food Stores," *Journal of Retailing,* Fall, 1969, pp. 3–10ff; and Gilbert A. Churchill, Jr., Neil M. Ford, and Urban B. Ozanne, "The Trading Stamp-Price Relationship," *Journal of Marketing Research,* February, 1971, pp. 103–106.

[11]For opposite points of view on the economic merits of trading stamps, see Carolyn S. Bell, "'Liberty and Property, and No Stamps,'" *Journal of Business,* April, 1967, pp. 194–202; and E. Beem and L. Isaacson (executives in S & H Company—green stamps), "Schizophrenia in Trading Stamp Analysis," *Journal of Business,* July, 1968, pp. 340–346.

See also Bernard J. LaLonde and Jerome Herniter, "The Effect of a Trading Stamp Discontinuance on Supermarket Performance: A Panel Approach," *Journal of Marketing Research,* May, 1970, pp. 205–209.

field and virtually nonexistent in the grocery store field. Small, independent grocers, however, have done a pretty good job of competing with the chains through the years, while small, independent drugstores have experienced a high mortality rate. How do you account for this situation?

8. "The real battle over fair trade is between high-cost and low-cost retailers, not between small-scale and large-scale firms." Do you agree?

9. What are the significant differences between fair-trade laws and unfair-trade-practices acts?

10. Distinguish between leader pricing and predatory price-cutting.

11. Explain the reasoning underlying the zigzag shape of the demand curve in Fig. 14-1. Does this demand phenomenon actually exist in real life?

12. "The use of periodic, temporary price cuts to stimulate consumer demand is not a wise marketing strategy." Discuss.

13. How should a manufacturer of prefinished plywood interior wall paneling react if a competitor cuts his price?

14. What factors account for the increased use of nonprice competition?

15. "Trading stamps are socially and economically undesirable." Discuss.

16. On the basis of the topics covered in Chapters 13 and 14, establish a set of price policies for the manufacturer of a new glass cleaner which is sold through a broker to supermarkets. The manufacturer sells the product for $4.90 for a case of a dozen 16-ounce bottles.

CASES FOR PART FOUR

CASE 8. HILLCREST PRODUCTS, INC.

Pricing a new product

The executives of Hillcrest Products, Inc., were trying to decide what the retail price should be for their new product—a glass cleaner—which was ready for marketing on a full-scale basis. Hillcrest Products, Inc., was a new company, and the glass cleaner was its first product to be marketed commercially, although it had developed and market-tested several other cleaning products. Plans called for the introduction of the other products as soon as they could be given adequate attention by management. Since the company was small, the executives wisely did not wish to spread their efforts over too many products at one time.

The new glass cleaner was liquid in form and golden in color. It was competitive with such brands as Windex, Bon-Ami, Glass Wax, and Easy-Off. Windex was easily the leading brand in sales. For example, the *Denver Post* survey of consumer brand preferences had shown that Windex was the brand purchased in about 70 percent of the households using commercial glass cleaners. No other brand reached over 10 percent of this market.

Management in the Hillcrest company felt that its product was demonstrably superior to anything on the market. Market tests had shown that once consumers tried this product, they strongly favored it over anything they had used previously.

The product's main differential advantage was that it did not leave a film. Also, the Hillcrest product was nontoxic, a distinct advantage in households where there were small children.

The product came in two attractively labeled packages—a Duo-Pak and a 16-ounce glass refill bottle. The Duo-Pak consisted of a 16-ounce bottle plus an 8-ounce empty clear plastic bottle with a plunger-type spray dispenser top. The intent was that the consumer would fill the plastic bottle and use it, rather than the glass bottle, for actual cleaning work. The fact that the plastic was unbreakable was another favorable differentiating product feature. Both the Duo-Paks and the refills were packed twelve to a case.

Hillcrest marketed through supermarket chains in much of the Great Plains and Rocky Mountain regions. The company used a separate food broker to reach the chains in each brokerage area, such as Denver, Kansas City, Omaha, Oklahoma City, and Wichita. For example, chain buying offices in the Denver brokerage area represented stores in Colorado, Wyoming, northern New Mexico, and parts of Oklahoma, Kansas, Nebraska, and South Dakota.

Hillcrest had no desire to sell its product under resale-price-maintenance (fair-trade) contracts. In setting its own selling price, however, the company had to have some intended retail price in mind in order to allow for the necessary broker's fee and retailer's margin. The company planned to allow retailers a margin of 25 percent of their selling price, and the brokers a fee of 10 percent of Hillcrest's selling price.

The unit variable costs for Hillcrest's product packed in case lots were 33 cents for the Duo-Pak and 14 cents for the refill. These costs included the glass and plastic packages, the cardboard holder for the Duo-Pak, the liquid cleaner itself, the shipping carton, freight, and direct labor for filling the packages and preparing the cartons for shipment. Actually, the largest single direct costs were the glass and plastic packages. If the company could order these packages in lots of 50,000 or more, the unit cost could be reduced 2 cents.

The company conservatively expected to sell 1 million 16-ounce bottles during the first year in a 1:2 ratio of Duo-Paks to refills. It was difficult to estimate overhead very accurately at this stage. Administrative and office salaries would be about $35,000. Other overhead costs, including travel expense but excluding advertising, were figured at $16,000. Of course, the largest single indirect expense was advertising. The company expected to plow all available funds into advertising and display. If necessary, the company would operate at a loss for a few years rather than skimp on advertising. The advertising budget for the first year was set at $50,000.

The usual retail selling prices of competitive products in supermarkets were as follows:

Brand	Product	Price, in cents
Windex	20-oz bottle	40–45
Windex	14-oz aerosol can	59
Windex	8-oz bottle	24
Windex	Plunger-type spray dispenser	15
Easy-Off	15-oz aerosol can	49
Bon-Ami	15-oz aerosol can	65
Glass Wax	16-oz bottle	59

QUESTIONS

1. What unit retail prices do you recommend for the Duo-Pak and for the refill?
2. What should be Hillcrest's selling prices per case for Duo-Paks and for refills?
3. What is the break-even point in sales volume and in units, assuming that Duo-Paks and refills sell in a 1:2 ratio?

CASE 9. WILSON ELECTRONICS, INC.*

Price determination

The Wilson Electronics Corporation was an industrial supplier of small electronic components used by other manufacturing firms. The company prided itself on the quality of their products and on their ability to manufacture to the precise specifications of industrial customers. The company "salesmen" were greatly respected by Wilson's customers.

One of Wilson's major customers was a producer of a varied line of equipment and appliances. This customer, Magnus Manufacturing, Inc., purchased a wide line of Wilson products. Magnus had contracted with Wilson to purchase an intricate thermostatic switch. To produce the requested item known as "Model K-50," Wilson developed a specialized stamping machine which could not be readily used for any other purpose, at an investment of almost $250,000. At the time the decision was made, Magnus Manufacturing agreed to purchase at least 10,000 units of K-50 yearly at a price not to exceed $16.00 per unit for a minimum of 5 years. Wilson estimated that the cost of production of K-50, including depreciation on the specialized machinery, would approximate this price. That is, Wilson only expected to "break even" on K-50, but the Magnus account was believed to be so important that Wilson undertook to produce this item as a "service" to them. The possibility of selling additional quantities of K-50 to others was considered to be "rather remote," but the physical capacity to increase output existed and such production would not require any additional capital investment.

A problem in quality control developed with K-50 during the third contract year, and to settle a resulting dispute, Wilson agreed to lower the price of K-50 units to $15.50 each. Mr. Maxwell, president of Wilson, stated, "We are determined to maintain the loyal patronage of the Magnus Manufacturing Company. Their volume of purchases is considerable, and we must remember that the machinery and equipment currently used on K-50 cannot readily be used for any other production. It cannot be permitted to remain idle."

The following year, the purchasing director of Rigbee Controls, who was not a previous customer of Wilson, contacted the firm about an unusual requirement for a thermostatic switch. Considerable executive friendships existed between the Magnus and Rigbee corporations. The Wilson engineers discovered that with minor changes in specifications, K-50 would adequately fulfill Rigbee's requirements. Rigbee then asked Wilson to quote a price in quantities of 15,000 units annually, and assured them that they could contract for delivery in these quantities for several years to come.

---

*Case prepared by Prof. Barry J. Hersker, Florida Atlantic University. Reproduced with permission.

Wilson engineers reconfirmed the fact that ample capacity existed to expand production of K-50. Their comptroller, Mr. Fred Shaw, indicated that production costs would be lower at this increased volume. He estimated that these new costs could permit Wilson to receive a profit estimated at $3.68 per K-50 unit, and it was decided to offer it to Rigbee at $15.50 each.

Rigbee responded that they could not use K-50 at any price higher than $11.50 per unit. They said they would be better off to substitute another apparatus entirely if that price could not be met. Rigbee also admitted that they probably never would be a large purchaser of Wilson products other than K-50. The Wilson engineers confirmed the fact that Rigbee could not afford K-50 at more than $11.50 and that they would probably never purchase any other items from Wilson. They also confirmed that Magnus would not use more than 10,000 of the K-50 units annually, no matter how low Wilson set the price. At a later meeting of Wilson's executives, one vice president said that maybe the Rigbee price would be acceptable, since increased volume lowered production costs enough to offset the small loss from the sale of K-50 to Magnus at $15.50.

"You're not suggesting that we sell to Rigbee at $11.50 and to Magnus at $15.50, are you?" exclaimed Mr. Ernest Bennett, the vice president of the sales division. "This line of reasoning is out of the question! Rigbee and Magnus are friends. How would Magnus react if we charge them, our good customer, more than we charge Rigbee? This conduct is highly questionable on both a legal as well as an ethical basis."

Mr. Maxwell interrupted the dispute, and asked the vice president of sales for his specific suggestions on the matter. "Well, let's look at it this way," Mr. Bennett responded. "K-50 has been an apparent loser. The reason—sales were too low! We've got the chance to add 15,000 more units, and believe we could sell still another 25,000 units if we priced realistically! The specifications of K-50 lend themselves to a wider range of industrial applications than we previously assumed. Five more of our current accounts would be willing to buy this item which would push our volume to 50,000 units per year. This is, admittedly, our current productive capacity, but I feel sure we could reach this level within one year."

"Mr. Bennett, your job is to sell our products," Mr. Maxwell interrupted, "but why haven't we exploited this market potential long ago?"

"Well, to hit a capacity volume of 50,000 units, we need to offer K-50 at a competitive price. If we can offer the item for $10.00, I know this volume can be reached," Mr. Bennett replied.

"Pardon the interruption," broke in Mr. Alfred Horn, assistant to the president. "Wouldn't this price be below our cost of production?"

"I have asked the comptroller to bring the detailed cost data with him for capacity volume. While this is admittedly out of my area of responsibility, I do believe that the feasibility of my suggestion deserves your consideration," Mr. Bennett continued.

Fred Shaw, the comptroller, was the next to speak. "Ernest, I'm sorry that I did not have time to go over this with you in greater detail before. Costs are lower toward capacity, but these savings are not as great as you evidently assumed. I prepared a cost schedule to make it easier for us to view the situation at various volumes. (See Exhibit 1.) I calculated unit costs and charges at 10,000, 25,000, and 50,000 unit levels of production. Labor charges per unit are constant, since this is a machine operation and output varies directly with the time of the run. We experience some economies on material by purchasing in larger quantities, and our

Exhibit 1. Unit costs for model K-50 at various production volumes.

Costs	Unit costs at output of:		
	10,000	25,000	50,000
Labor	3.18	3.18	3.18
Material	1.52	1.48	1.44
Plating	.10	.08	.05
Indirect charges[1]	.48	.48	.51
Depreciation allowance[2]	4.00	1.60	.80
Overhead[3]	1.06	1.06	.06
Total factory production cost	10.34	7.88	6.04
Selling and Administration charges[4]	5.17	3.94	3.52
Total costs per unit	15.51	11.82	9.56

[1] Indirect charges include supplies, repairs, and routine maintenance on specialized equipment, electric power, etc., expressed on a per-unit-of-output basis.

[2] Depreciation is straight-line basis over life of Magnus contract, less residual value, computed per unit of output.

[3] Allocation to cover fixed factory overhead costs, charged at the rate of 33.3% of direct labor.

[4] Allocation to cover selling and administrative expenses, charged at the rate of 50% of total factory production costs.

subcontractor will be able to plate the necessary components at half the price if we hit 50,000 units. But, on the other hand, we must remember that capacity volume will require more frequent servicing. We'll lose some ground here—three cents in indirect charges, to be exact, between 25,000 and 50,000 units. But, of course, that is only an added expenditure of $1,500."

"You'll have to slow up, Mr. Shaw. I'm afraid this gray head can't absorb your calculations quite so quickly," Mr. Maxwell interrupted.

"I'm sorry, Mr. Maxwell—perhaps I'd better distribute the data. If we sell and produce K-50 at a capacity output, our costs per unit only fall to $10.56. I've itemized these details for you on the cost sheet I've prepared for each of you." (At this point, Mr. Shaw distributed the cost data presented in Exhibit 1.)

The executives examined the cost data for a few moments. Mr. Horn was the first to speak. "Perhaps I'd better summarize what Mr. Shaw appears reluctant to point out. He is saying that Mr. Bennett would have us lose 56¢ on every item of K-50 we sell at this 50,000 volume! Or, at least we would, in fact, lose 32¢ per item, if we even sell to Rigbee and hit a total of 25,000 units!"

"But not if we average out—I say, sell to Magnus at $15.50 and to Rigbee at $11.50!" added another executive.

"That is out of the question!" exclaimed Mr. Bennett.

"Gentlemen, let's have a little order at this meeting," interjected Mr. Maxwell.

"Mr. Maxwell has the right idea—I say just sell only to Magnus as a favor at $15.50 and let the sleeping dogs lie," added Mr. Horn. "That does it; I'll not preside over a free for all. And, stop putting words in my mouth, Mr. Horn!" angrily exclaimed Mr. Maxwell. "Ernest, we here at Wilson have an obligation to our stockholders as well as to our customers. It appears that perhaps I was the one who made all the decisions on the K-50 from the very beginning. So, I'll make this one, too. But first, I want all of you here in my office tomorrow at 9:00 A.M. sharp. This meeting is adjourned!"

QUESTIONS

1. Analyze the cost data, especially considering the fixed and variable costs and the allocation bases.
2. What action should Mr. Maxwell take regarding the Rigbee offer and the pricing of the K-50 switch?

CASE 10. ANDERSEN STARCH COMPANY*

Pricing policies and strategies

The Andersen Starch Company was one of several manufacturers, importers, and sales agents of starch products and dextrines. The company carried on profitable operations for many years and currently was a leading supplier to the paper industry, textile manufacturers, foundries, bakers, confectioners, corrugated-box manufacturers, carpet mills, manufacturers of pharmaceuticals, soap manufacturers, and furniture manufacturers.

Among the products marketed were corn starch, tapioca flour, potato starch, wheat starch, dextrines (converted from all of the above starches), sago flour, and natural gums. For many years, some of these products have been sold to wholesale and large retail grocers. Included among the Andersen company customers were Alpha Supermarkets, First Union Stores, and Grand National Groceries, Inc. These three concerns were among the most profitable and aggressive food distributors in the country and had large capital investments in the most modern plants and equipment that could be purchased. All of them had extensive laboratory facilities and were well staffed with research and development personnel.

Recently a competitor of these firms had introduced a pudding using a starch base that gained immediate consumer acceptance throughout the country. The techniques of manufacturing this starch base were different from any used by the three firms in making products sold under their private brand labels, and special equipment was required to produce it. As a result, the three firms individually approached the Andersen company and requested assistance in the development of a competitive product that could be sold under their private brands.

Since the research department of Andersen company had been working on problems closely related to the pudding, it was able to develop a base product that, when submitted to slight additional processing and packaging by the grocery firms, produced a superior competitive product. The long experience of the Andersen company in the field of starches and dextrines contributed significantly to the problem. Three important raw materials—potato starch, wheat starch, and tapioca starch—could be used alternately in the manufacture of the base depending upon their price and availability. Successful production of the starch pudding base required an exact knowledge of the markets for these three

---

*Case prepared by Prof. James P. Logan, University of Arizona. Reproduced with permission.

raw materials and skill in purchasing them. Such knowledge and skills were ordinarily available only in firms such as Andersen that dealt to a major extent with starches and dextrines.

The quantities required by Alpha, First Union, and Grand National were far in excess of the available production capacity in the Andersen factory. To meet the demand, a large capital investment in new processing equipment was necessary. The Andersen management committee decided to proceed with an investment in equipment to the limit of the company's current ability to finance the investment. Enough equipment was acquired to process 7 million pounds per year of the starch base, 80 percent of the total pounds that the three concerns desired to purchase during the coming year.

Once the decision to buy the equipment was made, it immediately became necessary for the management committee to make a policy decision on pricing the product.

Should the starch pudding base be classified as a specialty and be priced accordingly, or should it be considered a bulk commodity? As a specialty, a profit margin of 9 cents per pound would be established on top of a cost of manufacturing and selling of $19.50 per 100 pounds. A decision to price as a bulk commodity would mean that an average margin of $1.20 per 100 pounds would be established on a current cost of $19.50 per 100 pounds. Margins of these sizes were consistent with those of other Andersen products. Such prices would be f.o.b. the plant. These prices would enable the company to recapture its capital investment in 8 months in the case of a specialty price and in 5 years in the case of a bulk commodity price.

The new pudding introduced by the competitor of Alpha Supermarkets, First Union Stores, and Grand National Groceries, Inc., had put these firms at a considerable competitive disadvantage, and they were now pressing Andersen for as much output as possible. In an attempt to secure large quantities of the starch pudding base, Alpha offered Andersen a contract to cover output for the next 18 months. The contract, which was typical of those this grocery was willing to offer and sign, called for delivery of a minimum of 2 million pounds and a maximum of 5 million pounds at a firm price. Alpha was to be protected against a decline in the market price by a provision that Andersen would meet any lower price offered by competitive suppliers of the starch product base. Should the estimates of consumer market acceptability prove too high, Alpha could reduce the quantity specified. The other firms were also anxious to sign contracts to obtain a supply of the base and were willing to contract for delivery of 2 to 3 million pounds per year each.

Since demand for the base was currently so large, the Andersen management committee had considered the possibility that the grocery firms would install their own facilities for producing the starch product. It was definitely known that these firms could not get into production for another eighteen months. The management committee was almost certain that Grand National Groceries would continue to purchase from Andersen and would not install its own equipment. The behavior of the other two firms could not be forecast with any degree of certainty. It was known that, in the past, Alpha had purchased new items introduced by others, had watched the sales of such items, and if the sales proved sufficiently interesting, had built its own facilities. This was the limit of the management committee's knowledge.

Other products besides this pudding base were sold to the three grocery firms, and the management committee was anxious to do all it could to maintain good relations with these customers. Goodwill was important to the Andersen company, and the company wanted to protect its reputation for dealing fairly with its customers. However, since the grocery business is highly competitive, maintaining good relations is a very tricky and delicate matter at best. The pudding base was more important in volume than all of the other products sold to the three customers, for the dollar sales of all other items were probably less than 10 percent of the dollar sales of the starch base. If the base should continue to be produced by Andersen over a period of years, it would be a very important member of the total product line and possibly one of the big money-makers.

The Andersen management committee had a practice of considering projects such as the production and sale of the base entirely as individual matters. Installing the equipment and operating it to produce the pudding base was to be justified by the profits from this project only. Other uses for the machinery might be developed with a great deal of effort in an emergency situation, but it was felt that the possibility of such other uses should not enter into the original decision. Similarly, the committee believed this project should bear all the costs that could be charged to it under any reasonable accounting convention; the project should not be considered on an out-of-pocket basis. The management committee felt that the costs cited earlier were established fairly and completely on the basis of this policy.

In considering whether any one of the customers might install its own facilities and then no longer purchase from Andersen, the management committee concluded that the customer might well decide that its costs were less than the bulk-commodity price that Andersen might establish. This might occur because of the method of allocation of overhead expenses used by the customer. The management committee was certain that its costs were complete and that its bulk-commodity price would be less than the production costs of any customer provided that customer's costs were also complete.

The management committee felt that no matter which price of the two Andersen established, the price charged by the grocery firms to their customers would remain the same, since the final starch product had to meet competitive prices of other brands and also the competition of other types of foods.

QUESTIONS

1. What policies should Andersen adopt regarding the pricing of the starch pudding base?

CASE 11. **CENTRAL OPTICAL COMPANY**

Action to meet strong price competition

The two Plachy brothers, Homer and Ted, who owned and managed the Central Optical Company, were trying to determine what would be the most effective pricing strategy for meeting the increasing competition from chain budget opticians who sold their products at a much lower price than did Central Optical.

The Central Optical Company, which sold high-quality eyeglasses, was the largest optician in a Midwestern city with a population of about 125,000. The company had its main store in the downtown area, plus a branch in each of the two nearby military posts. Homer and Ted's father, Mr. Conrad Plachy, started the company in 1937 and turned it over to his sons upon his retirement in 1960. Homer supervised all sales activities in the main store as well as the manufacturing of lenses. Ted managed all other business activities, in addition to supervising sales and service in the two branch stores.

Central Optical did its own lens grinding, using the newest and most efficient grinding equipment available. Other companies the size of Central Optical generally would send their lenses out to be ground rather than doing it themselves. The Plachy brothers believed they were one of the five most automated retail optician firms in the United States.

Since its inception the company has had a steady growth, and financially Central Optical has been quite successful. Management attributed the firm's success to the rapid growth of their city and the somewhat necessary nature of their product, as well as to their high-quality service and eyeglasses.

Last year the company's sales exceeded $400,000. Although this was an increase of $25,000 over the previous year's sales, the net profit last year was $10,000 *under* expectations. The two brothers attributed the lower-than-expected profits to the rising cost of goods sold. Plastic and glass lenses plus the eyeglass frames were continuing to increase in price.

At the same time, Central Optical had not raised the retail price on its finished eyeglasses in more than five years. Homer and Ted were reluctant to raise prices, because already their prices were higher than most other opticians in the city. Central Optical felt it was unethical to advertise, because of the professional nature of the business. Consequently, the company depended upon strong customer loyalty, word-of-mouth advertising, and doctors' recommendations for its continued growth and success. A price increase might jeopardize those promotional stimulants, reasoned Homer and Ted.

While eyeglasses were the company's main product, Central Optical also sold contact lenses, sunglasses, eyeglass cleaner and tissue, and other related products. Of all the products carried by the company, eyeglass frames provided the highest gross margin—40 percent. While the price range was $10 to $20 for men's frames and $10 to $30 on frames for women, the frames most frequently selected sold at retail for about $14. The frames usually amounted to about 65 percent of the total price of the eyeglasses. Most of the completed spectacles (frame and lenses) cost the customer from $20 to $30.

Because Central Optical had a much higher investment in lens-grinding equipment, the company earned a slightly lower net profit on lens sales than do most opticians. The owners felt, however, that the added expense was justified by the fact that they could fill customers' orders within one day. Most other opticians sent lenses away to be ground, and this usually took five to six days. The company purchased all of its glass from nationally known manufacturers such as Shuron, Bausch and Lomb, and Titmus. Moreover, Central Optical bought only the highest quality orthogon glass, which cost about two dollars per blank unground lens. The retail customer's price for these lenses after grinding was usually in the neighborhood of $10 to $12. The company bought lenses in lots as large as $20,000, in an attempt to earn maximum quantity discounts and thus offset some of the high costs involved in the grinding operations.

During the past five years Central Optical's share of market had been reduced significantly by an influx of low-priced, "budget" opticians into the city. Prior to that time Central Optical had the market virtually to itself. Two of the largest new competitors were separate subsidiary divisions of a national chain of jewelry stores.

These two new firms sold eyeglasses for as low as $12. These chain opticians and other similar low-price firms were able to sell at such prices for three reasons. First they had their own central manufacturing plant for making frames and grinding lenses. Second, they often imported frames and unground lenses from Japan. Japanese lenses could be purchased preground for as little as 68 cents each. Japanese frames, which looked to be identical to $18 American frames, cost about one dollar. Third, these companies used a much lower quality of plastic and glass in their frames and lenses. Yet upon looking at these glasses, the normal customer could not tell the difference between the high-quality and lower-quality glasses.

These low-price firms sold a large quantity of eyeglasses, partially because they advertised so heavily. Last year the two chain subsidiaries spent about $40,000 in local advertising in Central Optical's market alone. The Plachy brothers thought this advertising had also helped to increase primary demand, because Central Optical's sales also increased so much ($25,000) last year. The fact still remained, however, that Central Optical's management was convinced that the success of the four low-priced opticians now in town was likely to intensify the competition, and thus further cut into Central's declining share of market.

Central Optical thus was faced with increasing competition from low-price firms at the same time that Central's costs of materials were steadily increasing. Smaller optical companies in a similar position had either raised their prices or been forced to use cheaper materials. Through the years Central Optical had been proud of its reputation for providing the very highest quality of service and eyewear. Now, however, management in Central Optical was very reluctant to raise their already high prices. Yet their alternatives seemed equally unattractive. The brothers realized they could increase their gross margin only by (1) raising prices, (2) maintaining existing price levels and cutting the cost (and thus the quality) of goods sold, or (3) cutting prices and also reducing cost of goods sold, thus appealing to the low-price segment of the market.

QUESTION

1. What action should Central Optical take to improve its profits and competitive position?

CASE 12. OAKLAND DRUG COMPANY*

Pricing problems under resale price maintenance

Early in 1972 the Oakland Drug Company released a new drug product, effective in the treatment of rheumatoid arthritis and certain allergies. Ivastan, as the drug was called, was a compound discovered by Oakland scientists and was considered an outstanding development in the field of medical science.

Marketing this product presented many problems to Oakland's management. Among these was the question of whether to establish a minimum retail price for Ivastan under the state resale-price-maintenance (fair trade) laws. Oakland sales executives knew that Marpak Laboratories and Udart & Company, both much

*Case prepared by Prof. Charles L. Lapp, Washington University. Reproduced with permission.

larger firms than Oakland, also would manufacture and market the same compound within a few months. While Marpak's products were all fair-traded at the retail level, only the "over-the-counter" (nonprescription) products of Udart were fair-traded. Udart was considered one of the most aggressive firms in the industry with a field staff four times the size of Oakland's.

In view of these and other facts presented to management, Oakland decided not to fair-trade Ivastan at the retail level. The product was announced to the wholesale and retail drug trade on March 14:

IVASTAN
(brand of stanoxylone)
10 mg. tablets
bottle of 24—Catalogue Price $6.40

Two weeks after the product was announced to the trade and medical profession, Ivastan appeared to be in much greater demand than anticipated. It was an immediate success.

On April 3, Mr. Harvey Lerner, a regional sales manager for Oakland, received a telegram from Mr. Oscar Schall, a retail pharmacist in Port Loma, a fairly large city, admonishing Oakland for not fair-trading Ivastan. He complained bitterly that one of his retail competitors had mailed announcements to all physicians in Port Loma that Ivastan prescriptions could be filled at his store for $4.90 for 24 tablets. The usual practice in the trade was to price prescription products of Oakland at the catalogue price, which was also generally the retail fair-trade price.

The following day Mr. Lerner drove to Port Loma to see Mr. Schall for the purpose of explaining the company's policy and the reasons for its actions. In addition, Mr. Lerner contacted Mr. Philip Andover, president of the state pharmaceutical association with the intent of quieting down other pharmacists who may be forced to cut the price of Ivastan as a result of what they would term "unfair competition."

Several weeks went by and Lerner heard no more about the Ivastan incident in Port Loma. Consequently he considered the situation resolved. During the next two years, only isolated fair-trade problems relating to Ivastan came to Lerner's attention, and each was handled with little or no difficulty, usually at the division level.

On May 4, 1974, the Oakland Drug Company announced another new product, Palaban, considered to be a major break through in the control of "morning sickness" common among pregnant women. Palaban, the brand name selected for the generic product, paratron, presented many marketing problems similar to those encountered with Ivastan. Oakland had also licensed the McLaughton Pharmacal Company, a small competitor, to manufacture and market paratron. These two companies joined in the scientific and clinical studies so that a single New Drug Application could be filed with the Food and Drug Administration. Both Oakland and McLaughton received F.D.A. approval simultaneously and each announced its new product the same day, May 5.

Oakland did decide to fair trade Palaban, and announced to the wholesale and retail drug trade and to the doctors as follows:

PALABAN
(brand of paratron)
100 mg. capsules
bottle of 50—$5.60*

*Minimum Retail Fair Trade Price

McLaughton announced its product, Balcene, as being available in bottles of 40 capsules for $4.50—the "catalogue price"—and made no mention of retail fair trade.

Harvey Lerner received a communication (see Exhibit 1) from Harold Walton, division manager in Port Loma, on May 18.

Exhibit 1.

OAKLAND DRUG COMPANY	INTER-OFFICE MEMO
TO: Mr. Harvey Lerner	DATE: May 15, 1974
FROM: Harold Walton	COPIES:
SUBJECT: Palaban-Balcene Fair Trade	
REFERENCE:	

A situation has developed in Port Loma which I believe to be of interest and importance.

Last Wednesday Mr. Oscar Schall, proprietor of Schall's Ethical Pharmacy in Port Loma, called all Port Loma obstetricians and general practitioners and quoted them a price of $4.25 to the patient for 50 paratron capsules.

Other pharmacists learned of this and protested to the state board of pharmacy on Thursday. The board believes fair trade to be in effect on prescriptions and therefore called Mr. Schall to a hearing on Friday. My information comes from a pharmacy commissioner who is a friend.

The result of the matter was that Schall was cleared because he dispensed McLaughton's Balcene, not Oakland's Palaban. It seems that all prescriptions in this area are written for quantities of 50 capsules. Our 50's are fair-traded but McLaughton's do not have 50's and their 40's are not fair-traded. Apparently, whether or not Balcene 40's are fair-traded does not matter. Thus, the druggist will continue to capture prescription business on paratron and dispense Balcene. Although all but one major obstetrician in the area are now prescribing Palaban, this will undoubtedly change if the situation remains as it is.

If it is true that McLaughton's Balcene is not fair-traded, I would suggest that we drop our fair trade of Palaban to compete effectively with McLaughton.

Harold Walton

QUESTION

1. What should Oakland do now concerning the pricing of Palaban?

PART FIVE

DISTRIBUTION STRUCTURE

DISTRIBUTION CHANNELS AND THE RETAIL MARKET

15

Our product is now ready for its market. The next general step in the marketing process is to determine what methods and routes will be used to bring the product to the market. This involves establishing distribution strategies, including selecting channels of distribution and providing for physical handling and distribution. First, however, we should make certain that management understands something of the concepts underlying the distribution system.

CHANNELS OF DISTRIBUTION

A *middleman* is an independent business concern standing between the producer and the ultimate household consumer or industrial user. A middleman renders services in connection with the purchase and/or sale of products as they move from producer to consumer. Either he takes title to the merchandise as it flows between producer and consumer or he actively negotiates the transfer of title.

The essence of a middleman's operation is his active and prominent role in negotiations involving the buying and selling of goods. His income arises directly from the proceeds of these transactions. It is his part in the transfer of ownership which differentiates a middleman from other institutions, such as banks, insurance companies, and transportation firms, which help in the marketing process but do not take title and are not actively involved in purchase and sales negotiations. Whether a firm actually handles the products is not relevant to the definition of a middleman. Some middlemen warehouse and transport merchandise, while others do not physically handle it at all.

A common method of classifying middlemen is on the basis of whether they take title to the products involved. *Merchant* middlemen actually take ownership title to the goods they are helping to market. *Agent* middlemen do not take title, but they do actively assist in the transfer of title. Brokers and manufacturers' agents are examples of agent middlemen. The two major groups of merchant middlemen are wholesalers and retailers. It should be noted particularly that retailers are merchant middlemen.

A *channel of distribution* (sometimes called a *trade channel*) for a product is the route taken by the *title* to the goods as they move from the producer to the ultimate consumer or industrial user. A channel always includes both the producer and the final customer for the product, as well as all agent and merchant middlemen involved in the title transfer. The channel does *not* include firms such as railroads, banks and other nonmiddlemen institutions which render a marketing service but play no major role in negotiating purchases and sales. If a consumer buys apples from the grower at his roadside stand, or if a manufacturer sells a shirt by mail direct to a college student, the channel is from producer to consumer. If the shirt manufacturer sold to a department store which in turn sold to the college student, the channel would be producer—retailer—consumer.

The channel for a product extends to the last person who buys it without making any significant change in its form. When its form is altered and another product emerges, a new channel is started. When lumber is milled and made into furniture, there are separate channels for the lumber and the furniture. The channel for lumber may be lumber mill—broker—furniture manufacturer. The channel for the finished furniture might be furniture manufacturer—furniture wholesaler—retail furniture store—consumer.

CONCEPT OF CHANNEL STRUCTURE

To understand a channel of distribution, we should first recognize that it is a structure. A structure is organized and evolves in order to do a job. As related to channels of distribution, a structure may represent a choice among alternative channels, or it may involve a description of the different marketing situations faced by the various firms (retailers, wholesalers, producers) within the structure. It may be considered as a series of functions which must be performed in order to market products effectively. Any structure may be evaluated from a socioeconomic point of view.

The distribution structure is a highly complex organism. Its constantly changing nature makes thoughtful analysis difficult and renders a description of it quickly out of date. Another factor obscuring a careful study of the distribution structure is the oversimplified treatment it receives in marketing literature and Bureau of the Census data. In the Census of Business, each separate establishment is placed in a traditional, single category depending upon which category represented over 50 percent of the firm's annual sales volume. Thus if a company does 60 percent of its business at retail and the rest at wholesale, it is classed as a retailer. This system of classification suggests a more orderly structure than actually exists. It effectively reduces the number of categories into which firms are sorted and avoids hybrid, nondescript classifications. However, hybridity is too common among marketing firms to be ignored.[1]

A CHANNEL AS A TOTAL SYSTEM

To maximize benefits to all groups concerned (producers, middlemen, and consumers), a channel of distribution should be treated as a unit—a total system of action. Within this systems concept, a channel would include the marketing organizational units of a manufacturer as well as the organizations of the middlemen used by this manufacturer. Consequently, there is a real need to coordinate the manufacturer's activities with those of the middlemen used in the distribution of the given product. A distribution system properly operated then becomes a significant competitive differential advantage for a company.

Unfortunately, a trade channel all too often is treated as a fragmented assortment of competing, independently operating organizations. A manufacturer may view his own retailers as his competition, or a middleman may be in conflict with his supplier, rather than recognizing that the real threat is other middlemen or the distribution systems of other manufacturers. That is, the real competition is between distribution systems of different producers, rather than between the organizational units within one producer's system.[2]

It is true that power structures do exist in trade channels simply by virtue of the fact that a distribution system is comprised of separate, independent companies. Power struggles may also exist between groups *within* a company. Two marketing units—the advertising department and the field sales force, for instance—may look upon each other as competitors, which is quite contrary to the philosophy of total marketing underlying the market concept.

A CHANNEL AS AN INVESTMENT

Management should also recognize that a channel represents a financial investment in the same sense that the plant, equipment, or any other asset is an investment. If profit maximization is a company goal, then the selection of a marketing channel should be based on the estimated rate of return to be earned on the capital investment in the channels. Thus "the process of channel selection should be considered as an investment decision by a manufacturing firm."[3]

---

[1]Phillip McVey, "Are Channels of Distribution What the Textbooks Say?" *Journal of Marketing,* January, 1960, p. 61.

[2]For the notion that treating a channel as a system of marketing *functions* rather than as a sequence of *institutions* is more useful in understanding marketing channels, see William P. Dommermuth and R. Clifton Andersen, "Distribution Systems: Firms, Functions, and Efficiencies," *MSU Business Topics,* Spring, 1969, pp. 51–56.

[3]Eugene W. Lambert, Jr., "Financial Considerations in Choosing a Marketing Channel," *Business Topics,* Winter, 1966, p. 25. This author suggests that channel choice is determined primarily by financial considerations rather than what are generally thought of as marketing factors.

IMPORTANCE OF MIDDLEMEN

In any economy except a very primitive one, it is often not economically feasible for a producer to deal directly with an ultimate consumer. Think for a moment how inconvenient our daily existence would be if there were no retail middlemen—no drugstores, newspaper stands, supermarkets, or gasoline stations. If we live in a large city, we might think that we could buy things wholesale, but if there were *no* middlemen, there would be no wholesalers.

Concentration, equalization, dispersion. Frequently the quantity and assortment of goods produced by a firm are out of balance with the variety and amounts wanted by consumers or industrial users. A businessman needs paper, pencils, typewriters, and desks. A homeowner wants grass seed, topsoil, fertilizer, a rake, and a roller, and eventually he hopes to need a lawn mower. No single firm produces all the items either of these users want, and no producer may sell any of them in the small quantity the user desires. Obviously there is a need for someone to perform the function of balancing or equalizing what various producers turn out with what the final customers want. This is part of the task of marketing.

The job to be done involves (1) collecting or concentrating the output of various producers, (2) subdividing these quantities into amounts desired by the customers and gathering the various items together in the assortment wanted, and (3) dispersing this assortment to consumers or industrial buyers. In a few cases, the task of concentrating, equalizing, and dispersing is simple enough to be done by the producer and final customer working closely together. A copper miner may sell directly to the smelter firm; iron-ore producers may sell directly to the steel mill. In most cases, however, the producer and consumer are not able to work out the proper quantity and assortment. A specialist in concentration, equalization, and dispersion is needed, and this is the role of the middleman.

Creation of utility. Middlemen aid in the creation of time, place, and possession utilities. In classical economic theory, production is defined as the creation of utility, and several types of utility are recognized. One is form utility, in which something is added in a chemical or physical manner to a product to make it more valuable. Lumber is made into furniture and flour into bread, thus creating form utility. Other utilities are equally valuable to the final user. Furniture located in Grand Rapids, Michigan, or High Point, North Carolina, in April is of little value to people in Austin, Texas, or Los Angeles, California, who want the furniture to give as Christmas presents. Transporting the furniture from Michigan to Texas increases its value: place utility is added. Storing it from April to December adds another value—time utility. The final value of possession utility is created when the Texas and California families buy the items.

PROBLEMS IN MANAGEMENT OF DISTRIBUTION CHANNELS

To establish the channels of distribution for a firm, a marketing executive must undertake the following tasks:

Managerial tasks	Discussed in Chapter
1. Understand the retail and wholesale markets and the types of middlemen institutions available in each.	15–17
2. Understand the conflicts which typically exist between and within channels.	18
3. Decide what channels to use and what type of middlemen (if any) to use at each stage.	19
4. Determine the number of outlets desired in each stage.	19
5. Select the individual middlemen.	19
6. Establish a system for physical distribution of the product.	20

NATURE OF RETAIL MARKET

If a supermarket sells some floor wax to a gift shop operator who wants to polish the floor tiles in his store, is this a retail sale? Can a wholesaler or a manufacturer engage in retailing? When a gas station runs a big sale on tires and advertises that the products are being sold at the wholesale price, is this retailing? "Retailing," "retail store," "retail sales," and "retailers" are terms that should be defined not only to clarify their legal implications but also to avoid any possible misunderstanding in later discussions.

Retailing includes all activities directly related to the sale of goods or services to the ultimate consumer for personal, nonbusiness use. While most retailing is done through retail stores, it may be done by any institution. A manufacturer selling brushes or cosmetics door-to-door is engaging in retailing, as is a farmer selling strawberries at a roadside stand. Any firm—manufacturer, wholesaler, or retail store—which sells something to the ultimate consumer for his nonbusiness use, regardless of *how* it is sold (by person, telephone, mail, or vending machine) or *where* it is sold (in a store or at the consumer's home), is making a *retail sale*.

A *retailer* or a *retail store* is a business enterprise which sells *primarily* to ultimate consumers for nonbusiness use. A key word in the last definition is "primarily." A retailer may sell items infrequently to industrial users, but these are wholesale transactions, not retail sales. If over one-half of his dollar volume of business comes from sales to ultimate consumers, that is, sales at retail, he is classed as a retailer. The word "dealer" is used frequently in business and generally is synonymous with "retailer." In contrast, a distributor is a wholesaling middleman.

EASE OF ENTRY INTO RETAILING

It is easier to go into retailing than virtually any other trade, profession, or line of business. To practice medicine or law, one must pass state licensing examinations. To start a manufacturing or wholesaling firm, one must have a substantial sum of money to acquire a plant, equipment, and merchandise. To enter a laboring trade in many parts of the country, one must acquire union membership, and some unions have strict apprenticeship provisions. But to operate a retail store there are no examinations, and the necessary business licenses are easy to acquire. Furthermore, many people entering retailing have the idea that no real training or special experience is needed.

There are important economic and social implications in the ease with which people may enter retailing. Often, underfinanced, poorly qualified people come into the field. Soon they fail, thus causing economic waste and inefficient use of human and economic resources. Mortality is higher among retail establishments than in any other classification of business and industry.

On the bright side, ease of entry results in fierce competition and added value for the consumer. Except perhaps in a small town, it is rather difficult to establish an unregulated, monopolistic position in retailing. Certainly, large-scale enterprises exist in retailing, and in some markets there is substantial concentration of business among a relatively small percentage of firms. Yet these giants usually compete with one another, and the consumer benefits.

SIZE OF RETAIL MARKET

There are about 1.7 million retail stores in the United States, and their total annual sales volume in 1973 was over $503 billion (see Table 15-1). In contrast, there are about 280,000 wholesaling establishments (excluding manufacturers' sales branches and offices) and about 300,000 manufacturers. In spite of the population boom and rising consumer incomes over the past three decades, there has been no appreciable change in the number of retail stores. The increase in total sales volume, however, has been tremendous. Total retail sales volume in the mid-1970s is about four times as great as it was in the late 1940s. Even after allowing for the big rise in the price level during the period covered in the table, and the increase in population, the retail sales per capita as measured in 1973 dollars were still considerably higher in 1973 than in 1948. That is, there has simply been a huge increase in the physical volume of merchandise sold at retail.

COSTS AND PROFITS OF RETAILERS

Information regarding the costs of retailing is very meager. By gleaning data from several sources, however, we can make some rough generalizations.

Total costs and profits. As nearly as can be estimated, the total average operating expense for all retailers combined is about 25 to 27 percent of retail sales.

Table 15-1. Total retail trade in the United States, selected years.
Retail sales have almost quadrupled since 1948. Even after allowing for the increase in population and the rise in price levels, we find a huge increase in physical volume of merchandise sold. In contrast, note the remarkable stability in the number of retail establishments since 1948.

	1973	1967	1958	1948
Number of stores (millions)	1.66	1.76	1.80	1.77
Total sales ($ billions)	$503.3	$310.2	$200.4	$130.5
Average sales per store	$303,193	$175,964	$111,700	$73,800

Source: U.S. Census of Business: 1967, 1954, Retail Trade. 1973 sales, Survey of Current Business, May, 1974, p. S-1.

Wholesaling expenses are estimated at about 8 percent of the *retail* dollar or about 10 to 11 percent of *wholesaling* sales. Thus retailing expenses in total are about 2½ times the total of the costs of wholesaling when the expenses are stated as a percentage of sales of the middlemen in question.[4] See Fig. 15-1.

The proportionately higher retailing costs are generally related to the expense of dealing directly with the consumer. In comparison with wholesalers' customers, consumers demand more services. Also, the average retail sale is smaller, the rate of merchandise turnover is lower, buying is done in smaller lots, rent is higher, expenses for furniture and fixtures are greater, and salespeople cannot be used efficiently because the customers do not come in at a steady rate.

Costs and profits by kind of business. Studying the expenses of retailers in total is not nearly so meaningful as studying the expenses of one classification of retailers, because the expense ratios vary from one type of store to another. Table 15-2 shows expenses as a percentage of sales when stores are classified by the nature and extent of product lines handled. Total operating expenses and profit range from 14 percent of net sales for motor vehicle dealers through 21 percent for grocery stores, and 30 percent for drugstores, to 37 percent for apparel stores. Table 15-2 also shows the median net operating profit after federal income taxes for selected kinds of business in 1969-70.

ECONOMIC BASES OF RETAILING

To get into retailing is easy. To be forced out is just as easy. Consequently, the social and economic justification for the retailer's existence must be based upon the services he offers. He exists only because he does a better job than his competitors in his primary responsibility—catering to the consumer—and in his secondary job—serving producers and wholesalers.

[4]See Harold Barger, *Distribution's Place in the American Economy since 1869,* Princeton University Press, Princeton, N.J., 1955, p. 60; and Paul D. Converse, "The Puzzle of Marketing Costs," *Journal of Marketing,* April, 1957, pp. 439–441. Barger found a rather narrow range of fluctuation in the total of wholesaling plus retailing costs in the United States since 1869.

Figure 15-1.

IMPORTANCE TO CONSUMERS

The function of the retailer is to make the consumer's buying job as easy and convenient as possible. Essentially, the retailer acts as the consumer's purchasing agent; this task involves anticipating his wants. Then the retailer has the responsibility of supplying the right kind of goods at a reasonable price. The retailer also performs the service of *bulk breaking,* that is, dividing large quantities into smaller units, such as individual cans or boxes, appropriate for consumer use. The retailers offer a large assortment of merchandise, including appropriate sizes, colors, styles, and seasonal items.

Retailers perform the function of transporting and storing the goods so that they will be readily available when and where the consumer wants them. Thus, time and

Table 15-2. Gross margin and net profit, as percentage of net sales, for selected types of retailers.

Wide differences exist in the operating expenses of various types of retailers. Automobile dealers' gross margin is 14 percent of net sales, while apparel stores need a margin of 37 percent to cover expenses and net profit. How do you account for these differences? Note that net profit percentages are very low.

Line of business	Gross-margin %	Net profit % after income taxes
Automobile and truck dealers	14	1.7
Liquor stores	18	N.A.
Food stores	21	0.9
Building materials, hardware, and farm equipment	24	
Building materials		2.4
Hardware		2.8
Gasoline service stations	24	2.5
Drug stores	30	N.A.
Furniture and home-furnishings stores	35	
Furniture		2.8
Household appliances		2.0
General merchandise stores	37	
Department stores		2.1
Discount stores		1.6
Variety stores		2.1
Apparel and accessory stores	37	
Children's and infants' wear		2.5
Women's ready-to-wear		2.3
Men's and boy's clothing		2.8
Shoe stores		1.7

N.A. = Not available

Source: Gross margins from *Cost of Doing Business: Corporations,* Dun & Bradstreet, Inc., New York, 1973, based on Internal Revenue Service data for 1969-1970. Net profit figures from "The Ratios of Retailing," *Dun's Review,* September, 1973, p. 102.

place utilities are created. Retailers usually assume certain consumer risks in that they guarantee the goods they sell. Often retailers provide an installation and repair service.

Financing is another important function of retailers. They offer consumers open-book charge accounts payable once a month, revolving credit plans, and long-term installment programs. Retailers also add to the convenience and ease of consumer purchasing. They offer convenient shopping locations, considerable market information, personal salesmen, and other services, such as ample parking space, clothing alterations, and lessons on product use.

IMPORTANCE TO PRODUCERS AND WHOLESALERS

For the producers and wholesalers, the retailer acts as a specialist in selling. He offers physical facilities and manpower so that the producers and wholesaling middlemen can have a point of contact with consumers near the consumers' homes. He also uses advertising, display, and personal selling to aid in moving the producers' products. In determining the needs and wants of the consumer, the retailer can act as an interpreter of consumer demand and relay vital information back through the channel of distribution.

By dividing large unit quantities into consumer-sized amounts, the retailer is performing a service to manufacturers as well as to consumers. It would be highly uneconomical for manufacturers to package and ship their goods in the quantities demanded by consumers. Retailers' storage activities also help both producers and consumers. By ordering and accepting delivery in advance of the season, the retailer removes some of the risk burden from the manufacturer.

CLASSIFICATION OF RETAILING MIDDLEMEN

To better understand the role that retailing middlemen play in the channel structure, we shall classify them on the following bases:

1. Size of store
2. Extent of product lines handled
3. Geographic location
4. Form of ownership
5. Method of operation

Any given store may be classed according to any one of the above five bases, as we have done below using Sears and a neighborhood paint store as examples.

Sears	Classification base	Paint store
Large	1. Size of store	Small
General merchandise	2. Product-lines carried	Single line
Variety of locations	3. Geographic location	Variety of possible locations
Corporate chain	4. Form of ownership	Independent
Both in-store and mail order; supermarket method and full service depending on product department.	5. Method of operation	In-store selling; full service

SIZE OF STORE

Classifying retailing institutions according to their sales volume recognizes the fact that stores of different sizes present different management problems. Buying, promotion, financing, personnel relations, and expense control are influenced significantly by the volume size of the store. When we discuss retailing on the basis of store size, we find that a dichotomous situation exists. Retailing is at one and the same time both a small-scale and a large-scale operation.

Quantitative measurement. Most establishments are very small. In 1967, about 68 percent of the stores operating the full year had an annual sales volume of less than $100,000, but these stores accounted for only 13 percent of all retail sales (see Table 15-3). Retailing is probably the best example of small business in the United States, particularly when we include retailers of services such as restaurants, barbershops, and garages.

Although most retailers are small, at the same time there is a high degree of concentration in retailing: a small number of establishments account for a substantial share of retail trade. In Table 15-3, we see that stores with an annual volume of over $1 million accounted for only 3 percent of all establishments but for about 44 percent of the total volume.

As impressive as the figures in Table 15-3 may seem, they still do not tell the full story of large-scale retailing because they represent a tabulation of individual *store* sales and not individual *company* volume. A single company may own many establishments, as in the case of chain stores. When retail sales are analyzed by companies, the high degree of concentration becomes even more evident. Table 15-4 shows the sales of the twenty largest retailers in the country in 1973. (Their net profit as a percentage of sales is also shown. The small size of the average profit—1.8 percent—among these giants may surprise people who feel that retailing is highly profitable.) Sales of these twenty firms alone totaled $73 billion, or approximately one-seventh of the total value of retail trade.

Competitive positions of large and small retailers. The relative competitive positions of large-scale and small-scale retailers may be evaluated in the light of several factors.

Division of labor. The opportunity to enjoy the advantages of division of labor both at the executive level and in the manpower ranks is one of the strongest factors favoring large-scale retailers. Large retailers can afford to hire managerial specialists for each major function, such as buying, promotion, and accounting. The small store usually cannot pay enough money or offer enough future opportunity to attract a high-caliber full-time person to perform these functions. The owner-manager may be a good executive, but he has to divide his time among too many activities to be effective in all of them.[5]

Flexibility of operations. Small stores generally are more flexible in their management practices than large units. Small retailers can stock merchandise to suit specific local needs, and they can adopt a flexible policy regarding services.

---

[5]For a study of the way in which a small retailer's personality can affect the success of his daily operations, see L. X. Tarpey and James L. Gibson, "Dogmatism as a Factor in Small Business Retail Management," *Journal of Retailing,* Winter, 1969–1970, pp. 45–55.

Table 15-3. Retail trade in United States, 1967: by sales size of establishments.
Although most retailers are small, there is a high degree of concentration in retailing. Sixty-eight percent of the stores had an annual sales volume under
$100,000 in 1967, and only 3.0 percent of the stores had annual sales over
$1,000,000. However, these few stores accounted for 44 percent of total retail
sales.

	Establishments			Sales volume		
Annual sales	Number (000)	Percent	Cumulative percent	($000,000)	Percent	Cumulative percent
Total, all stores	1,763			$310,214		
Establishments operated entire year, total:	1,670.6	100.0		$299,430	100.0	
With annual sales of:						
$2,000,000 or more	20.5	1.2	1.2	91,334	30.5	30.5
1,000,000—1,999,000	29.8	1.8	3.0	41,542	13.9	44.4
500,000— 999,000	55.4	3.2	6.2	38,464	12.8	57.2
300,000— 499,000	73.7	4.4	10.6	28,110	9.4	66.6
100,000— 299,000	358.6	21.5	32.1	60,290	20.1	86.7
20,000— 99,000	711.3	42.7	74.8	35,604	11.9	98.6
under $20,000	421.3	25.2	100.0	4,086	1.4	100.0

Source: U.S. Census of Business: 1967, Retail Trade, Sales Size.

Buying power. Large-scale institutions have a buying-power advantage. They
can buy in bigger quantities than small stores and secure higher discounts. They
can achieve additional economies by purchasing from manufacturers. Sometimes this buying power is instrumental in acquiring other benefits, such as
allowances for advertising, preferential treatment in case of shortages, and sole
dealership rights in a given market.

Use of advertising. Large stores can make effective use of advertising. It is not
economically feasible for a corner grocery store to advertise in a metropolitan
daily paper or on television. A large department store or a grocery chain with
several stores blanketing a city can make good use of these media because the
media match the market. There is little waste circulation.

Retailer's own brand. Large retail institutions are in a good position to develop
and promote their own brands. For the small store, the potential sales volume
from its own brand is more than offset by the funds required to promote the brand
and guarantee its quality.

Financial strength. Underlying many of the points noted here is the fact that
large retailers are usually in a better financial position. When they need money,
they can attract investors or borrow from lending institutions much more easily
than small retailers can. A strong financial position enables a store to take
advantage of all cash discounts offered, and these are extremely important in
retailing because of the low net profit margins. A good financial position also
enables a store to attract valuable franchises and attention from leading brand

Table 15-4. Twenty largest retailers in United States, 1973: by sales volume.
The $73 billion total sales of these giant retailers represented one-seventh of all retail sales in the United States, and yet their average profit was only 1.8 percent of net sales. What are some of the marketing implications of this concentration for a maker of department store merchandise?

Company	Sales ($ billions)*	Net profit after taxes, as % of sales
1. Sears, Roebuck	12.3	5.5
2. Safeway Stores	6.8	1.3
3. Great Atlantic & Pacific Tea	6.7	0.2
4. J. C. Penney	6.2	3.0
5. S. S. Kresge	4.7	2.9
6. Kroger	4.2	0.7
7. Marcor (Montgomery Ward)	4.1	2.4
8. F. W. Woolworth	3.7	2.5
9. Federated Department Stores	3.0	3.8
10. Rapid-American	2.3	1.3
11. Lucky Stores	2.3	1.4
12. Jewel Companies	2.2	1.6
13. Winn-Dixie Stores	2.1	2.0
14. Food Fair Stores	2.1	0.1
15. American Stores (formerly Acme Markets)	2.0	0.1
16. W. T. Grant	1.9	0.5
17. City Products	1.6	1.9
18. Allied Stores	1.6	2.1
19. May Department Stores	1.6	3.1
20. Grand Union	1.5	0.2
Total	72.9	1.8

*Net sales, including all operating revenues. For companies not on a calendar year, the 1973 figures are for any fiscal year ending not later than March 2, 1974. Sales of subsidiaries are included when they are consolidated.

Source: Fortune, July, 1974, pp. 120-121.

manufacturers. The financial strength of a retailer is a key point in a manufacturer's selection of individual middlemen.

Integration—horizontal and vertical. Large retailers handle a sufficient volume of merchandise to make it worth their while to take over wholesaling functions and sometimes even manufacturing operations. A large grocery chain may buy or set up a bakery just to supply its own stores.

Cost of operations. There is a lack of precise information regarding the effect which size has on operating expenses. Generally, large stores have higher operating expense ratios than small stores. The expenses in large organizations, however, also include the wholesaling activities conducted by these firms. Certainly, large stores have higher overhead expenses than small ones. Part of the advantage of management and labor specialization is offset by the higher cost attendant upon the division of labor. Large stores also have a greater percentage of total employees in nonselling jobs.

Experimentation, innovation, and marketing research. With their specialized executive manpower and great financial strength, large retailers are in a good position to conduct all kinds of needed marketing research. They can experiment with new ideas. They can afford to risk more on innovative features, such as a daring new style of clothing or a new selling method (self-service in housewares or automatic vending of staple clothing items). A multistore organization can test something in one store before committing all units to the new practice.

Legal considerations. Large-scale retailers have been a major target of legislators. Time and again, laws have been passed to equalize the economic position of large and small retailers. Fair-trade laws, which allow a producer to set the minimum price at which a retailer may sell his products, prevent a large store from substantially underselling a small one. Other legal measures have been aimed at the price which the retailer pays for his goods. The Robinson-Patman Act, for example, attempts to control the buying power of the large retailer. These laws were discussed in greater detail in Chapters 13 and 14.

Improved position of small retailer. The competitive position of some small retailers in many fields has improved over the years by virtue of developments among both the large and the small firms. One such development has been the voluntary association of retailers into a chainlike form of organization which gives the individual members of these associations the features of specialized management, buying power, and other advantages of scale discussed above. A second development has been the expansion of franchising operations in many fields of products and services (Holiday Inn, Howard Johnson, Hertz and Avis, McDonald's hamburgers, for instance). In these stores, small-scale businessmen are able to operate their own small business under the name and guidance of a large company, thus giving these small enterpreneurs sort of the best of both worlds. Franchising and voluntary associations are discussed in more detail in the next chapter.

Changes in the consumer market is another factor working to the advantage of a small retailer. At the same time that huge supermarket-type stores carrying a wide variety of merchandise are catering to consumers' wants, we find also that small boutiques and other specialty shops are growing in number and apparently thriving in response to another facet of consumer buying behavior. A small retailer who takes advantage of his flexibility can adapt not only his merchandise lines to his market, but also he can establish his own store's personality through unusual store layout and design. The relative position of small stores also is improved because large retailers suffer from operating problems seemingly inherent in large-scale operations—retailing or otherwise. High overhead costs, problems of unionized sales forces, difficulty in motivating salesclerks, and organizational inflexibilities all combine to limit the competitive position of the large-scale retailer.

EXTENT OF PRODUCT LINES HANDLED

Retail stores may be classified according to the extent of the product lines they carry. In this classification, stores are grouped as general merchandise stores, single-line stores, and specialty stores. Subdivisions within these three groups are recognized by names which consumers typically use in identifying retail stores. That is, we speak of department stores, hardware stores, gas stations, and so on.

This basis of classification is still useful for some types of stores—apparel, furniture, building materials, for instance. For other types such as food stores and drugstores, however, the store's sales figures are becoming less meaningful as accurate indicators of the relative sales volume of the different commodities. The reason for this is that there has been a pronounced trend toward scrambled merchandising, that is, the practice of adding new, unrelated lines to the products customarily sold in a particular type of store. It is a mistake, for example, to interpret food store sales as being equal to total sales of food products. Supermarkets carry many nonfood lines, and food products, in turn, are sold in drugstores, gas stations, department stores, etc.

General merchandise stores. Institutions which offer a large variety of lines, usually with some depth of assortment in each line, fall into the classification of general merchandise stores. The classification includes department stores, dry goods stores, variety stores, and general stores. As a group, these retailers account for 17 percent of the total retail trade. Department stores—usually considered a major segment of the retailing structure—represent a little over 10 percent of all retail sales, and variety stores contribute less than 2 percent of the total.

Department stores: importance and relative merits. To be considered a department store for the Census of Business classification, an institution must employ at least 25 people; apparel and soft goods must account for at least 20 percent of the total sales volume; and the variety of merchandise carried must also include furniture, home furnishings, appliances, and household linens and dry goods.

Department stores are highly organized business enterprises. Merchandising or product planning, headed by a general merchandising manager, is usually the key to a store's success. Under the merchandising manager are the department buyers. In effect, each department is a business in itself, and the buyer has considerable autonomy.

Another department store feature is the common use of leased departments. The store leases a department to an outside firm which will establish and operate it. To all external appearances, a leased department is operated by the store itself. Beauty shops, restaurants, and departments handling hearing aids, optical goods, millinery, and groceries are frequently leased.

Leased departments offer several advantages to a department store. They help to round out a store's line with no risk to the store. This is especially advantageous in fields where fashion risks are high. Leased departments may bring to the store a highly qualified specialist in a given product field and thus relieve the store's own managerial burden. Stores can also gain financially by leasing out a department whose establishment would require considerable capital outlay.

The lessee is in a favorable position because his rent is often based on a percentage of his sales volume. In such cases, the rent is a variable expense, and the store assumes a significant part of the risk of poor sales. Also, the lessee enjoys the prestige of the store, and he can make use of other store services, such as delivery and credit.

In addition to the general merits of large-scale retail operation (specialized management, buying power, etc.), other advantages accrue to department stores in particular. Department stores offer a wider variety of products and services than any other type of retail institution where the customer comes to the store. (A form of nonstore retailing—the mail-order house—may carry more lines than a department store.) The opportunity for one-stop shopping is almost unlimited.

Department stores suffer from several specific limitations, as well as from those generally associated with large-scale activity. Operating costs are considerably higher than for most other kinds of retail business, running about 35 percent of sales. One of the features of department stores—their many services—also contributes significantly to the high operating expense.

A substantial problem confronting department stores has been their location —typically in the heart of the downtown shopping district. The population exodus to the suburbs and the traffic problems downtown have combined to force many department stores to open branches in the suburbs. The big downtown store, with its large investment, high-tax location, and high-cost operations, must be maintained, but it reaps a decreasing share of the total business in the area. Department stores are running into strong competition on other fronts as well. In the late 1940s and 1950s the high gross margin of department stores gave impetus to the development of discount selling.

Besides building branches in suburban shopping centers, department stores are making other concerted efforts to meet the new competition. Working with other downtown merchants, the stores are spearheading movements to revitalize downtown areas. Stores have been modernized and redecorated, and better municipal transit service and expanded parking facilities are being developed.[6] To meet the competition from discount sellers, perhaps in general the best alternative for department stores is a compromise—that is, to upgrade merchandise lines and stress fashion, while at the same time offering on a limited basis some of the discounters' features.

Today's innovative competitive strategies of department stores reflect an attitude of "Get aggressive or go out of business"—a philosophy stated by Bullock's, a Los Angeles–based department store chain.[7] Stores are building "out-of-store" specialty shops to attract younger shoppers. Bargain basements are being revitalized to counter the lower prices in discount stores. Macy's now honors American Express credit cards in several of its stores. The May Company experimented with new discount stores, extended store hours, and some "shop-at-home" schemes. Several department stores have adopted programs of selling via warehouses, the mail, and catalogue outlets. Stores are marketing services such as travel agencies, income-tax counseling, insurance, and mutual funds. Stores are experimenting with hybrid outlets such as the Penney's store in Winona, Minnesota, which combines the standard department store, a discount unit, and a food store under one roof. Management in many stores is using more marketing research and is trying to upgrade the effectiveness of the salesclerks.

Single-line stores. This category of retailing institutions includes stores which carry a considerable assortment of a related group of products. Thus we find stores identified by the names of the individual line of products featured: grocery

---

[6]For some case examples of what various organizations are doing to revitalize the downtown areas, see "Suburban Malls Go Downtown," *Business Week,* Nov. 10, 1973, p. 90; see also E. B. Weiss, "Reversing the Trend: Downtown Areas, the Original Shopping Centers, To Become New Mecca of Retail," *Marketing Insights,* Feb. 27, 1967, p. 16.

[7]"Department Stores: Selling in All Directions," *Sales Management,* Nov. 27, 1972, p. 27.

stores, appliance stores, furniture stores, building materials stores, hardware stores, and sporting goods stores. In some cases, stores of this type carry two related lines, such as men's and women's clothing.

Specialty stores. Specialty stores constitute that class of retail institution which carries a limited variety of products. Typically they handle only part of a single line of convenience or shopping goods. Examples of this type of store include dairy stores, tobacco shops, bakeries, meat markets, men's shoe stores, millinery shops, and furriers. Specialty stores should not be confused with specialty goods. Actually, specialty shops often do not carry specialty goods. The term "specialty" in relation to the store implies a limited line of merchandise, rather than the well-known, branded products which people are willing to expend considerable effort to purchase. Although there is some chain-store activity in this field, the majority of the business is done by independent small-scale retailers.

Because specialty stores handle a limited line of merchandise, they usually have an excellent assortment. In the apparel field, they often feature the newest fashions. Frequently they are the exclusive dealers for certain brands in a given market. Successful specialty stores usually have highly capable buyers who are expert judges of what will sell. Because they limit their merchandise to a narrow field, these stores can often buy reasonably large quantities and thus secure favorable prices.

GEOGRAPHIC LOCATION

Classifying retail stores according to their geographic location tells us something about consumer buying patterns. It also brings out the general conclusion that retail trade is concentrated in relation to population. In 1972, for instance, the South Atlantic census region accounted for 15.3 percent of population and retail sales. The East North Central states contributed 20 percent of both retail sales and population. Thus an analysis of the geographic location of retail trade can be used to evaluate regional market potentials for many products.

Urban-rural distribution. As we might expect, the great bulk of retail sales and retail stores is concentrated in the very small land mass which constitutes the Standard Metropolitan Areas. *Sales Management* magazine (in its "Survey of Buying Power" published annually in the summer) has identified 295 present and potential metropolitan areas. *Sales Management* estimated that these 295 areas accounted for 78 percent of the nation's retail sales in 1972.[8]

Distribution within urban parts of metropolitan areas. Within the central city and its adjacent cities and suburbs in a metropolitan area, there are several discernible types of shopping districts. Together these constitute a retailing structure which should be recognized by marketers. The hub of the retailing activity traditionally has been the central downtown shopping district—the location of the main units of department stores, major apparel specialty stores, and single-line jewelry and furniture stores. This district is the heart of shopping goods stores, although convenience goods are also readily available. The downtown area draws customers from a wide market, in some cases from over 100 miles.

---

[8]"Survey of Buying Power," *Sales Management,* July 23, 1973, pp. 13–24.

In the older, larger cities in the East and Midwest, we often find a secondary shopping district.[9] This may be located in the main city about 5 to 8 miles from the downtown area. It may also be found in the "downtown" areas of older suburbs, such as Oak Park and Evanston, Illinois. These districts are not planned or controlled for marketing purposes and thus are differentiated from the modern, planned suburban shopping centers. Secondary districts often contain a branch of a downtown department store and branches of specialty or limited-line stores. Shopping goods are available, but not in so wide an assortment as in downtown areas.

A third type of shopping district found in cities is a string-street development or a small cluster of neighborhood stores. Most of the retailers are small, and convenience goods stores predominate, although some small furniture or apparel stores also locate in these districts. The trading area in a neighborhood district is quite small compared with that in a secondary or downtown district.

Since World War II, another significant type of shopping district has arisen in metropolitan areas—the planned, controlled suburban shopping center. Such a center differs from all other shopping districts in that it is planned, developed, and controlled by one organization. The developer may be a major downtown department store or an individual promoter-investor-developer. These planned centers evolved from (1) *neighborhood* centers built around a supermarket, through (2) *community* centers featuring a discount store or junior department store, to (3) the earlier-built *regional* centers anchored by a branch of one or two downtown department stores. In the regional centers, ideally there is at least one specialty or limited-line store to compete with each department in the department store.

In recent years there has been a trend to develop giant-sized regional centers —in effect, they are miniature downtowns.[10] These supercenters have as many as five department stores, plus many small stores and service operations. They also include hotels, banks, office buildings, churches, and theatres. These comprehensive centers integrate retail, cultural, and commercial activities all enclosed under a roof and with a climate-controlled mall featuring fountains, sculptures, and ample floral displays.

The country's 12,000 planned shopping centers accounted for one-third of all retail trade in 1970, and by the mid-1970s close to one-half of all retail sales volume will come from stores in these centers. The success of suburban shopping centers lies essentially in their appeal to, or conformity with, consumer buying patterns. A wide selection of merchandise is available; stores are open evenings; an informal atmosphere encourages mothers to dress informally and bring the children; plenty of free parking space is available. The success of these centers is enchanced by the group effort of the member stores. By coordinating their promotional efforts, all stores benefit; one builds traffic for another. Many stores in these centers are too small to do effective, economical advertising on their own, but they can make good use of major media by tying in with overall shopping center advertising and promotion. They also cash in on the general prestige and reputation of the center.

---

[9]With a few exceptions, such as Seattle or Los Angeles, Western cities do not have secondary shopping districts because most of these cities did not become large enough to support such a district until after World War II. By that time, major retailing developments were taking place in planned suburban shopping centers.

[10]See "Shopping Centers Grow into Shopping Cities," *Business Week,* Sept. 4, 1971, p. 34.

QUESTIONS AND PROBLEMS

1. "You can eliminate the middleman, but you cannot eliminate his functions." Discuss.

2. Which of the following institutions are middlemen? Explain.
   a. Food broker
   b. Stockbroker
   c. Real estate broker
   d. Department store
   e. Railroad
   f. Advertising agency
   g. Chain supermarket
   h. Bank
   i. Grain elevator
   j. Hardware wholesaler
   k. Fuller Brush salesman
   l. Radio station

3. What is a channel of distribution, and how is it related to the physical distribution of the product?

4. Explain how time, place, and possession utility may be created in the marketing of the following products. What business institutions might be involved in creating these utilities?
   a. Sewing machines
   b. Fresh peaches
   c. Hydraulic grease racks used in garages and service stations

5. Define the terms "retailing," a "retail sale," and a "retailer." Explain the three concepts in light of the following situations:
   a. Avon cosmetics saleslady selling door-to-door
   b. Farmer selling his produce door-to-door
   c. Farmer selling his produce at his roadside stand
   d. Sporting goods store selling uniforms to a professional baseball team

6. How do you account for the wide differences in operating expenses between the various types of retail stores shown in Table 15-2?

7. Why is retailing more expensive than wholesaling? Why is retailing inherently less efficient than manufacturing?

8. The mortality rate among retail stores is one of the highest among all types of business institutions. How do you account for this?

9. "Retailing is typically small-scale business." "There is a high degree of concentration in retailing today; the giants control the field." Reconcile these two statements, using facts and figures where appropriate.

10. Referring to the ten criteria given in this chapter for evaluating competitive positions of large-scale and small-scale retailers, on which counts are small stores in a stronger competitive position than large-scale retailers? In light of your final score, how do you account for the numerical preponderance of small retailers?

11. What courses of action might a small retailer follow to improve his competitive position?

12. What can department stores do to offset their competitive disadvantages?

13. What can single-line and specialty stores do to compete effectively with department stores?

14. Identify the various types of shopping districts in a nearby city. Relate this structure to the one described in this chapter.

15. What is the relationship between the growth and successful development of planned suburban shopping centers and the material studied in Chapters 3 to 6 regarding the consumer?

RETAILERS AND
METHODS OF OPERATION

In the preceding chapter, retailing institutions were analyzed on three bases: the size of the store as measured by sales volume, the extent of the product lines handled, and the geographic location. In this chapter, we will discuss forms of ownership and methods of operation.

RETAILERS CLASSIFIED BY FORM OF OWNERSHIP

Classified according to form of ownership, retail institutions fall into two major groups: independent stores and corporate chain stores. A third group, which we shall consider here, consists of voluntary associations of independents who band together in chainlike fashion in order to compete more effectively with the corporate chain-store organization. Other less important ownership categories, such as leased departments, company stores, consumers' cooperatives, and government commissaries, account for a negligible percentage of total retail trade.

CORPORATE CHAIN STORE

A *chain-store system* is an organization consisting of two or more stores centrally owned and managed, and handling generally the same lines of products on the

same level in the distribution structure. Technically, two or more units may constitute a chain, although today many merchants who consider themselves small-scale
independents have two or three units which they have opened in shopping centers
and newly populated areas. These retailers ordinarily do not think of themselves as
a chain. Consequently, it might be more meaningful to consider a larger number of
units to be a reasonable minimum when categorizing a store as a chain. For
instance, eleven or more units (one of several categories used by the Census
of Business) is a good definitional basis for discussing chain stores.

Central ownership is the key factor which differentiates corporate chains from
voluntary associations of independent wholesalers or retailers. The third element in
our definition of a chain-store system is central management. Individual units in a
chain have very little autonomy. Buying is highly centralized with respect to both
the physical purchasing and the determination of what will be bought. Centralized
management also leads to considerable standardization in operating policies
among the units in the chain.

Many chains are also vertically integrated, but this feature is not essential for
definitional purposes. Safeway Stores, the large grocery chain, maintains large
distribution centers where they buy from producers, do their own warehousing,
and then distribute to their own stores in their own trucks. Some chain organizations, such as the A & P Company, actually own and operate manufacturing plants
to supply some of their needs. Another form of vertical integration has resulted in
manufacturer-owned retail chains, such as apparel chains (the Bond Clothing
Company) and gasoline service stations (the Standard Oil Company of California).

Importance. In number of stores and total sales, independent single-unit stores
constitute by far the largest segment of retail trade when institutions are classed
by ownership. In fact, the 1972 Census of Business shows that about 88 percent
of all stores are single-unit stores and that they account for about 60 percent of
all retail sales. Of course, the other side of these statistics suggests the degree
of concentration in retailing. Organizations with 11 or more stores did 31 percent of total retail business with only 7 percent of total stores.

The importance of chains varies considerably from one type of commodity to
another (see Table 16-1). Chains dominate in the department store business, where
companies with eleven or more stores account for close to 90 percent of all
department store sales. In the variety store field chains do 80 percent of the
business, but the chains' share of market in variety stores has not changed
much in some 20 or more years. In the food field there are several giant firms,
yet chains still account for only a little more than one-half of food store sales.

Chain-store companies have increased their share of the total retail market since
1960, but the growth has not been uniform in all fields. In the department store
business the chains' share of market has increased steadily, reflecting the branch-
store expansion in the suburbs and the department stores' ability to use mass
advertising and centralized buying power. The growth of chains in the drugstore
field reflects the way these stores have expanded into a wide variety of products.
Further growth in drug chains is likely as they capitalize on potential Medicare-
related business and the fact that the over-sixty-five market is increasing in size and
buying power.

Competitive advantages. Chain-store organizations are large-scale retailing
institutions and, as such, enjoy the general competitive advantages of large-scale

Table 16-1. Chains' share of total sales volume, by kind of business, 1972.

Chain stores dominate in the department store and variety fields. Since 1958 chains have made their biggest gains in drugstores and department stores. How do you account for the growth of drugstore chains?

Kind of business	Percent of sales*
Total retail sales	31
Department stores	88
Variety stores	80
Food stores	52
Shoe stores	46
Drug stores	36
Tire, battery, accessory stores	30
Women's apparel, accessory stores	26
Men's and boy's wear stores	15
Furniture–appliances–home furnishings stores	9

*Chains with 11 or more units.
Source: Statistical Abstract of the United States: 1973, p. 742.

retailing discussed in Chapter 15. In addition, chain stores per se have some particular merits.

Lower selling prices. Chain stores have traditionally been credited with selling at lower prices than independents. This is an image chains have projected to the public, but the claim of lower prices needs careful scrutiny because it can be misleading. It was probably more justified in the past than it is today. Many independents have improved their operating methods and thus have reduced their costs. They have also pooled their buying power so that in many instances they can buy products at the same prices as the chains.

It is very difficult to compare prices of chains with those of independents. The merchandise is often not exactly comparable because many chains sell items under their own brands. It is difficult to compare the price of Del Monte peaches with A & P peaches. Also, it is not accurate to compare the price of a product sold in a cash-and-carry, no-customer-service store with the price of an identically branded product in a full-service store. The value of services should be included in the comparison.

When the chains do have a price advantage, it is traceable to one or more of three factors. First, chain-store operating costs may be lower than those of independents. Chains usually offer fewer "free" services. They reduce costs by careful buying and careful inventory controls which maximize their rate of turnover and minimize the number of slow-moving items in stock. Chains further reduce operating costs by doing their own wholesaling and, in some instances, their own manufacturing.

The second factor holding prices down is that chains normally are satisfied with a lower percentage of new profit. They depend upon huge sales volume to maximize their dollar profit. Some of the large food chains, for example, show net profits of 1 to 2 percent of net sales, and this is *before* income taxes.

The third factor is the buying ability of the chains. The quantities in which they buy—carloads and even trainloads—and their ability to contract often a year in advance for the output of a farm or factory enable them to secure a favorable price. Chain-store buyers typically are very skilled specialists in their business.

Opportunity to use advertising.   Chain organizations are in a much better position to make effective use of advertising than even large independents. This competitive advantage is more a result of the multitude of chain outlets than of the total volume size of the corporation. That is, a grocery chain may have 25 medium-sized stores blanketing a city, and an independent competitor may have one huge supermarket doing three to four times the business of any single unit of the chain. Yet the chain can use the metropolitan daily newspaper as an advertising medium with much less waste circulation than the independent can. Many chains also make effective use of national advertising media.

Ability to spread risks.   Chain stores do not have all their eggs in one basket or in one store. Even large-scale independent department stores or supermarkets cannot match this advantage of the chain. A multiunit operation automatically has spread its risks among many members. If one store is located in a declining market, that store can be closed and any loss absorbed by other, still healthy outlets.

Flexibility for experimentation.   In many respects a chain is bogged down in administrative inflexibility solely because the multiunit operation requires standardization. This same multiunit operation, however, offers a number of opportunities for flexibility. As a case in point, one outlet's slow-moving merchandise can be moved to another outlet whose customers might view it more favorably. The company can experiment with layouts, different store fronts, or new types of merchandise by introducing any of these features into a few stores before committing itself to a full-scale introduction.

Competitive disadvantages.   Chain stores suffer the limitations of all large-scale retailing institutions, as well as a few additional ones.

Standardization and inflexibility.   The feature of standardization, the hallmark of a chain-store system and a major factor in its success, is a mixed blessing. Chains have not always been able to adjust rapidly to local competition or to take full advantage of local market opportunities because store managers could not act without first getting approval from a central office.

Chains are well aware of these limitations and have instituted several measures designed to give store managers greater freedom and to lessen the rigidities of merchandising policies. Chain-store executives, however, are also aware that in decreasing the amount of standardization, they run the risk of increasing their operating costs. Consequently, the single-unit store undoubtedly will continue to enjoy the advantage of flexibility in competition with a chain.

Personnel problems.   Chain stores are particularly susceptible to the personnel problems associated with large-scale businesses. Store managers are shifted from one store to another, thus making it difficult for them to establish real rapport with other employees or with a particular community.

Poor public image. In the past the chains were generally held in very low regard and high suspicion by a great many American consumers. Some common criticisms were that chains are run by absentee ownership; that they do not pay their fair share of taxes; that they have miserable personnel policies, such as long hours and low pay; and that they are monopolistic and engage in unfair competition. Many of these charges were half-truths, and others were not true at all. Nevertheless, this poor image undoubtedly presented substantial obstacles to chain development. Changing social and economic considerations, along with more enlightened, socially responsible chain-store management, have improved the situation, but chains will probably never enjoy the degree of public sympathy and support that local, independent merchants do.

Anti-chain-store legislation. In the 1930s, popular resentment against corporate chains led to the enactment of several major pieces of anti-chain-store legislation at both the state and the federal level. Although these laws do not apply exclusively to chain retailers (some apply also to manufacturers and other middlemen), they restrict chain stores most, and usually were designed to do so. Today the federal laws are enforced with great vigor because of judicial interpretations through the years, but many state laws have been tempered somewhat.

At the federal level, the Robinson-Patman Act (1936), amending the Clayton Antitrust Act of 1914, is probably the most significant anti-chain-store law. This law affects the chains in three ways: It places restrictions on discounts allowed for quantity buying; it prohibits allowances to chains for performing brokers' services; and it limits the granting of allowances for advertsing and other promotional activities. The Robinson-Patman Act was discussed in greater detail in Chapter 13.

Major state laws affecting chains are resale-price-maintenance laws, unfair-sales-practices acts, and chain-store tax laws. Resale-price-maintenance (fair-trade) laws prevent a retailer from selling a product below the price set by the manufacturer. Thus chains are not able to undersell other stores on fair-traded items, regardless of the chains' lower operating costs, willingness to take lower profit margins, and offer of fewer services. Unfair-practices acts prohibit the sale of merchandise at a price lower than cost plus a small markup. Fair-trade and unfair-practices acts were discussed in Chapter 14. Chain-store tax laws were passed by 29 states and still exist in 12. These laws provide for graduated tax rates. The state tax per store usually depends upon the number of stores the chain has, either within the given state or in the entire nation.

FRANCHISE SYSTEMS INVOLVING SMALL, INDEPENDENT RETAILERS

One of the strongest competitive limitations facing corporate chains in the past 30 years has been the increased effectiveness of independent retailers and wholesalers who have copied chain-store marketing methods. Independents have adopted self-service methods in many types of stores; they have improved store appearance and layout; they have sought better locations, including suburban shopping centers; they have improved their merchandising practices by eliminating some slow-moving items and keeping fresh stock; and they have improved their accounting and inventory control systems.

Probably the most effective measure adopted by small independents has been their practice of voluntarily associating with wholesalers, manufacturers, or other retailers in some form of contractual franchise system. In some instances these associations resemble a corporate chain so closely that about the only significant difference is that the retail stores are not centrally owned. These voluntary affiliations coupled with the limitations of large, corporate chain forms of retailing and the changing nature of the consumer market are resulting in a revitalization of the small, independent retailer.[1]

Nature of franchise systems. The concept of franchising is blurred sometimes by the broad, loose usage of the term and by the many variations in the scope of franchise agreements. Historically in marketing, a franchise was defined narrowly as "a system under which a manufacturer granted to certain dealers the right to sell his product or service, in generally defined areas, in exchange for a promise to promote and merchandise the product in a specific manner."[2]

Perhaps at this point it will be more useful if we broaden our interpretation of franchising to include any contractual arrangement between a franchiser (a supplier, who may be a manufacturer or a wholesaler) and a series of independent franchisees (either wholesalers or retailers). The franchiser grants the right to sell certain goods or services in generally defined markets. He usually provides equipment, the products or services for sale, and managerial services. In return the franchisee agrees to market the product or service in a manner established by the supplier. Within the broader definition we find two main types of franchising systems—one is a voluntary association of retailers and/or wholesalers; the other is a retailer network initiated and sponsored by a manufacturer.[3]

Associations of independent retailers. These associations may take any of several forms, but the two most important are wholesaler-sponsored groups and retailer-sponsored groups, also known, respectively, as voluntary chains and retailer cooperative chains. A *voluntary chain* is an association of independent retailers, initiated and sponsored by a wholesaler for the primary purpose of assuring the wholesaler of a series of profitable retail outlets for his products. The connecting link between the wholesaler and the retailer is a contract. In some instances, the wholesaler who sponsors a group of independent stores also belongs to a federation or association of similar group-sponsoring wholesalers. An example in the food field is the Independent Grocers Alliance (IGA), which grants a franchise to a wholesaler, who in turn licenses his member retailers as IGA stores.

The essence of the contract in a wholesaler-sponsored chain is that the wholesaler will furnish various services to member retailers, who in turn will buy all or almost all their merchandise from this wholesaler. Through the tremendous buying power of the combined retail units, wholesalers are able to buy at prices competitive with those of corporate chain organizations. Wholesalers offer various marketing and management services, such as proposals for store

---

[1]See Alton F. Doody and William R. Davidson, "Growing Strength in Small Retailing," *Harvard Business Review,* July–August, 1964, pp. 69–79.

[2]Charles M. Hewitt, "The Furor over Dealer Franchises," *Business Horizons,* November, 1958, p. 81.

[3]For the point of view that these two systems are sufficiently different that they should be identified as separate concepts and that the term "franchise selling" should be limited to the manufacturer-sponsored system, see Leonard J. Konopa, "What Is meant by Franchise Selling?" *Journal of Marketing,* April, 1963, pp. 35–37.

layout, effective display methods, advertising aids, accounting and stock control systems, reasonable credit, and field supervisors. Sales volumes of voluntary chains, particularly the combined organizations such as IGA, are big enough to enable them to market under their own brand. This practice provides lower-cost buying opportunities, offers promotional advantages, and prevents consumers from making direct price comparisons with merchandise offered by corporate chains.

A *retailer cooperative chain* is an organization instituted and sponsored by a group of independent retailers who jointly buy and operate a wholesale warehouse. The formal tie is stock ownership in the cooperative warehouse. The retailer members usually maintain their separate identities, as in the case of the Associated Grocers and the Certified Grocers—two of the larger retailer cooperative chains in the food field.

Retailer-sponsored chains have the same basic purpose as wholesaler-sponsored chains—to enable independent wholesalers and retailers to meet more effectively the competition from corporate chain stores. These associations of independents differ from each other in the following respects: (1) sponsorship of the association—retailer or wholesaler, (2) ownership of the wholesale house —retailer or wholesaler, (3) the connecting link between wholesaler and retailer —stock ownership or contract, and (4) the nature of services provided by the wholesaler.

Manufacturer-sponsored systems. This type of franchise system follows the narrow definition stated earlier. That is, a manufacturer sets up a network of retail outlets by contracting with new or established independent operators. The contract may cover (1) a single department in a store (Russell Stover candies or Mode O'Day clothes), (2) only one brand within a department (Magnavox or Maytag appliances), or (3) the entire retail outlet (dealerships for autos, farm equipment, or petroleum products; McDonald's or Dairy Queen drive-ins; Holiday Inns and Howard Johnson restaurants; Fred Astaire dance studios; Hertz or Avis auto rentals; Kelly part-time help).

We can distinguish between two concepts in producer-sponsored franchise systems. One features franchising as a form of exclusive distribution. This type has existed for years and often involves a large-scale retailer. The other concept is the rise of entrepreneurship franchising. This practice is relatively new, and it typically has involved small-scale retailers. Enterprise franchising has especially proliferated in (1) the fast-foods industry (Kentucky Fried Chicken, Baskin-Robbins ice cream, McDonald's hamburgers) and in (2) service industries (recreation, auto rentals, motels, auto repairs).[4]

Extent of franchising systems. Wholesaler-sponsored chains (IGA and Super Valu Stores, for example) are more prevalent in the grocery field than in other lines of retailing, although these chains do exist in the fields of hardware (Ace Hardware Co.), variety stores (Ben Franklin stores), auto supplies (Western Auto

---

[4]For a comprehensive study of fast-food franchising, see Urban B. Ozanne and Shelby D. Hunt, *The Economic Effects of Franchising,* U.S. Government Printing Office, Washington, 1971; see also Jack M. Starling, "Franchising," *Business Studies* (North Texas State University), Fall, 1970, pp. 10–16; and *Journal of Retailing,* Winter, 1968–1969, special issue devoted to franchising.

Supply Co.), and drugs (Walgreen Co.).[5] Retailer-sponsored chains are also quite significant in the grocery field, but otherwise they are not very important in the total retailing picture. Group affiliations of independent retailers have been growing rapidly since World War II. In grocery store sales, for instance, it is estimated that voluntary chains and retailer cooperatives together account for a little over one-third of the market. The corporate chains' (eleven or more units) share of this market is a little over one-half. Unaffiliated independents are left with something under 10 percent, representing a substantial decline from the market position they enjoyed three decades ago.

Among manufacturer-sponsored systems, the concept of franchising an entire retail outlet (as contrasted with a single department or one brand within a department) is not new—oil companies and automobile manufacturers have done this for years. What is new, however, is its substantial growth since about 1950 and its spreading into many new fields. In addition to a huge volume in fast-food and refreshment services, today producer-sponsored franchise selling also embraces a variety of other products and services including auto mufflers, putting greens, paint, part-time office help, hearing aids, motels, and dance studios.

Competitive advantages. Franchising has many economic and social factors encouraging its growth. In voluntary groups a manufacturer may reach hundreds of independents simply by contacting one wholesaler. A manufacturer-sponsored system offers a manufacturer an opportunity for greater control and supervision over the pricing, advertising, and selling of his product—a sharp contrast with the situation he faces when distributing through giant retailers. Franchising also provides a supplier with the means for rapid market expansion and a wide distribution system at a relatively low cost. The franchisee typically puts up some of the money. With his own money at stake, a franchisee has more incentive and is apt to be a more dedicated entrepreneur than a store manager hired by the manufacturer.

In both types of franchise systems, retailers are identified as a group. Thus a manufacturer can make effective use of cooperative advertising programs, display materials, and other promotional features. The group buying power enables the independent retailer-members to obtain lower-cost merchandise and a better selection of the latest products. Furthermore, the retailers are able to do a better job of retail store management because of the administrative services furnished by the wholesaler, particularly in voluntary chains. Finally, the opportunity to use group advertising enhances the competitive position of these retailers.

In a manufacturer-sponsored network particularly, franchising enables a person to realize a dream that many people have—the opportunity to own his own business. This goal now can be reached, and with the added security that the business has been tested. Also, the franchisee's investment is relatively small, and it is easier for him to borrow the necessary funds now that a big national firm is behind him. He may be an independent, small-scale retailer, and

---

[5]Walgreen's is an interesting example of a corporate chain. It has almost five hundred retail stores of its own, and through its wholesale division it has franchised almost two thousand "Walgreen Agency Drug Stores." These independent retailers provide additional outlets for Walgreen-branded products, while at the same time benefiting from Walgreen's advertising, protected territories, and managerial guidance. See also "The Wholesaler-Run Retail Drug Voluntaries," *Chain Store Age,* October, 1972, pp. 47–49.

yet he is backed by the buying power, promotional programs, and management know-how of a big company.

Limitations. In the author's opinion, the biggest single competitive weakness of all independent retailers, whether affiliated or not, is their assumption that the sole advantage of the chain is its buying power. In fact, the Robinson-Patman Act was based largely on this premise. Through the years many retailers have come to the conclusion that this assumption is false. But too many still fail to realize that the real strength of a large-scale institution lies in its superior management personnel and specialized management practices.

Ignorance or disregard of this fact today places major limitations on voluntary associations of independents. Too often these retailers reject the management advice given by field supervisors. Many retailers still think of the association as a buying aid only and make little use of advertising, display, accounting, and other association services. In general, the problem is simply that these retailers are independent in every sense of the word. They want to be in business for themselves, and they do not take kindly to outside supervision.

The rapid expansion of producer-sponsored franchising systems during the past 20 years also brought the industry its share of problems.[6] One is the charge that franchising agreements are terribly one-sided—all in favor of the franchisor. To the extent that this charge is true, any imbalance can be minimized if both parties will carefully analyze all appropriate criteria when selecting a franchising partner.[7] The problem of one-sidedness also can be minimized by carefully designing the contract, and by the franchisor's intelligent handling of conflict situations.[8] If all else fails to protect the rights of the franchisee, state and federal legislation has been established to generate fairness and openness in franchising agreements.

Another problem is that franchisors sometimes engage in deceptive practices when selling franchises and negotiating franchise agreements. While unethical techniques do exist, Hunt concluded that there was no widespread, systematic misrepresentation.[9] Nevertheless, the problem seemed serious enough to generate both state and federal protective legislation.

Perhaps the major threat to continued successful expansion of franchising is the practice whereby the producer-sponsor takes over the ownership of successful units in his franchise system. This, in effect, turns the independent units into a corporate chain system. One unfortunate aspect of this trend is to reduce the numbers of successful, small, independent entrepreneurs.[10]

---

[6]For an evaluation of the favorable and unfavorable consequences of franchising, see Shelby D. Hunt, "The Socioeconomic Consequences of the Franchise System of Distribution," *Journal of Marketing,* July, 1972, pp. 32–38.

[7]See Ronald L. Tatham, Ronald F. Bush, and Robert Douglas, "An Analysis of Decision Criteria in Franchisor/Franchisee Selection Process," *Journal of Retailing,* Spring, 1972, pp. 16–21ff.

[8]See P. Ronald Stephenson and Robert G. House, "A Perspective on Franchising," *Business Horizons,* August, 1971, pp. 35–42.

[9]Hunt, *op. cit.,* pp. 37–38. See also Shelby D. Hunt, "Full Disclosure and the Franchise System of Distribution," in Becker and Becker (eds.), 1972 *Combined Proceedings,* American Marketing Association, series no. 34, Chicago, 1973, pp. 301–304.

[10]See Shelby D. Hunt, "The Trend toward Company-Operated Units in Franchise Chains," *Journal of Retailing,* Summer, 1973, pp. 3–12; see also Alfred R. Oxenfeldt and Anthony O. Kelly, "Will Successful Franchise Systems Ultimately Become Wholly-Owned Chains?" *Journal of Retailing,* Winter, 1968–1969, pp. 69–83.

RETAILERS CLASSIFIED BY METHOD OF OPERATION

Manufacturers and wholesalers will find some value in analyzing retail middlemen according to their methods of operation. The two broad categories observed here are in-store retailing and nonstore, or outside-of-the-store, retailing. Major methods of in-store retailing which should be considered are full-service retailing, supermarket retailing, and discount retailing. Major forms of nonstore retailing are mail-order selling, automatic vending, and personal selling on a door-to-door basis.

FULL-SERVICE RETAILING

This is the traditional form of in-store, across-the-counter retailing where the customer comes to the store, is waited on by a salesman, and may avail himself of other store services. It is no secret that this form of retail selling has declined considerably over the past thirty years or so. It is still prevalent, however, and probably will remain so in product lines where high-fashion goods are involved or where a salesman's demonstration, explanation, or fitting is needed.

SUPERMARKET RETAILING

It is somewhat difficult to analyze supermarket retailing because there is no universally accepted definition of the term. To some people it is a *type* of retail institution found in the grocery business. To others, the term describes a *method* of retailing and may be used in connection with stores in any field.

In this discussion, a *supermarket* will be defined as a large-scale, departmentized retailing institution offering a wide variety of merchandise (including groceries, meats, produce, and dairy products), operating largely on a self-service basis with a minimum of customer services, and featuring a price appeal and usually ample parking space. No minimum sales volume is established as a criterion in this definition. It is believed that in selecting a channel of distribution, a manufacturer is more concerned with the marketing methods of a type of retailing institution than with its precise volume.

The major marketing policies and strategies of a supermarket are stated or implied in the above definition. First, these stores operate largely or entirely on a self-service basis, and they characteristically offer very few services, such as credit or delivery. Second, the limited service feature, combined with the large buying power and willingness to take low percentage profit margins, means that supermarkets can sell at low prices. A third marketing characteristic of supermarkets is that they offer a wide variety of merchandise, and it looks as if the trend toward product diversification will continue.

Development of supermarkets. Supermarkets, as we know them today, had their start in the Depression days of the early 1930s. They were owned and operated by *independents* attempting to compete with the chain stores. Those "pine-board" operations were a far cry from the supermarkets of today. As large-scale retailers, supermarkets enjoy the general advantages attributable to scale, and they also may escape one of the serious problems of bigness, namely, the impersonal relations that exist between store and customer. Because most consumers who shop in supermarkets prefer to be left alone, the big store's lack of friendly, sociable salesclerks may be no limitation.

Supermarkets are overwhelmingly the dominant institution in food retailing today. Yet in the 1960s several factors combined to level off the expansion rate of conventional supermarkets. As the market share held by the full-service food stores became very small, there was less of an area to expand into. Thus the demand for large, self-service stores became well saturated.

Consequently, the large retailers resorted to competing fiercely with one another, because a new supermarket had to attract much of its business from existing large stores. At first the struggle was in the form of price competition. When store profits were reduced to dangerously low levels, companies shifted to nonprice competition by offering trading stamps, contests, longer store hours, and other services. These forms of nonprice competition did, of course, increase operating costs and selling prices, but unfortunately not profits.

Discount supermarkets. The inviting vacancy at the bottom of the supermarket pricing structure enticed innovative competitive institutions to fill the voids. A move toward discount selling in food products started when discount department stores established discount-food departments in their stores. The next evolutionary development in food retailing was the establishment of separate, "free-standing" discount supermarkets. Both types of these discount-food retailers operate with fewer services, lower gross margins, no trading stamps, and lower prices compared with conventional supermarkets. In fact, competition from discount food retailers has become so intense that well over one-half of the nation's food chains have converted some or all of their stores to discount operations.[11]

"Convenience stores." Another innovative competitor of conventional supermarkets has been the "convenience stores," which interestingly enough have higher prices and a more limited product assortment and are smaller in size. But they do have longer shopping hours, convenient locations, and the ability to provide fill-in type of purchases when other food stores are closed. In some ways they are a throwback to the corner grocery store of years past. These stores (7-Eleven, Li'l General, Minit Markets, and U-Tote'M, and more) have enjoyed an exceptionally high growth rate. Many conventional supermarkets are meeting convenience-store competition by extending their store hours into nights and Sundays.[12]

The superstore. The newest and possibly the toughest innovative competitor of the supermarket is the superstore—also called a hypermarket or a super-supermarket. By the late 1970s, this new breed of supermarket—a combination grocery and general merchandise store—may well capture over one-half of the food store sales in the U.S. Supermarkets and the newer superstores are alike in that they both are low-cost, high-volume, limited-service operations. The key difference between the supermarket and superstore concepts lies in the breadth

---

[11]"Discounting: A Food Chain Reaction," *Business Week,* Sept. 26, 1970, p. 44; see also Robert J. Minichiello, "The Real Challenge of Food Discounters," *Journal of Marketing,* April, 1967, pp. 37–42.

[12]See "The Threat to Southland's (7-11 stores) Growth," *Business Week,* Oct. 28, 1972, p. 60; and Philip D. Cooper, "Will Success Produce Problems for the Convenience Store?" *MSU Business Topics,* Winter, 1972, pp. 39–43.

of consumer needs to be filled.[13] The supermarket strives mainly to fulfill the consumers' needs for food, laundry, and home cleaning products. The super-store is designed to provide those same products plus filling other routine purchasing needs such as: personal-care products, alcoholic beverages and tobacco products, some apparel, low-priced housewares and hardware items, gasoline, consumable lawn and garden products, stationery and sewing sup-plies, some leisure-time products (books, records, hobby items), and household services (laundry, dry cleaning, shoe repair).

Some quantitative measures were made in a study comparing the super-store with the average supermarket. In the superstore, customer traffic was double; average sale was almost double; total store sales volume was more than triple; the superstore was twice the size and carried four times as many items; gross margin was higher; and net profit before taxes was almost double.[14]

In conclusion, executives in the conventional supermarket chain organizations are faced with substantial competitive challenges designed to meet the heterogeneous demands of the market. How they meet these threats in the late 1970s and 1980s will determine their rate of survival and degree of success.[15]

DISCOUNT RETAILING AND THE DISCOUNT HOUSE

The development of the modern discount house in the decade following World War II is quite significant. This institution or method of selling entered the re-tailing field as a brash innovator and forced a re-examination of traditional pricing structures and operating margins, costs, and methods.

What is a discount house? Is it a retailing *institution* which is separately dis-cernible and which is capable of being defined so as to differentiate it, or are we really talking about a *method* of retail pricing and sales promotion which is applicable to almost any type of store? Actually there is nothing new about discount selling—the practice of selling below the list price or the regular advertised price. There is also nothing new about discount houses. They have existed in some form for many years. If this is the case, one may wonder why suddenly in the late 1940s and early 1950s there was so much excitement about them. The reason is that the earlier discount houses were of a different type. Many were small establishments which displayed no merchandise; instead, customers selected from manufacturers' catalogues and placed orders by model or style number. Generally, access to these stores was restricted in some fashion.

The discount houses which emerged after World War II, however, and which caused so much consternation in the ranks of traditional retailers are different. They are large stores, freely open to the public, advertising widely, carrying a reasonably complete selection of well-known brands of hard goods (appliances,

---

[13]Walter J. Salmon, Robert D. Buzzell, and Stanton G. Cort, *The Super-Store—Strategic Implications for the Seventies,* Marketing Science Institute, Cambridge, Mass., study commis-sioned by *Family Circle* magazine, 1972. This study was later summarized by same authors in "Today the Shopping Center, Tomorrow the Superstore," *Harvard Business Review,* January–February, 1974, pp. 89–98.

[14]"Anatomy of the U.S. Super Store," *Progressive Grocer,* May, 1973, pp. 44–59ff.

[15]See Rom J. Markin, "The Supermarket Today and Tomorrow!" *Atlanta Economic Review,* October, 1972, pp. 20–24; and Fred C. Allvine, "The Supermarket Challenged!" *Business Horizons,* October, 1968, pp. 61–70.

home furnishings, sporting goods, jewelry), consistently selling below nationally advertised list prices, operating in heavily traveled but low-rent districts, and offering a minimum of customer services.

Growth of discount retailing. To understand the early success of the discount house, let us examine the reasons why some retailers were able to sell at low prices, and then analyze the market to see why consumers were so receptive to a low-price-no-service appeal. First, what factors led to the traditional retail markup on appliances and other products that are typically discounted? In the 1930s, electric home appliances were relatively new products and were generally classed as luxuries. Consequently, manufacturers had to offer retailers large markups—30 to 40 percent—to encourage them to stock the products and perform the necessary services. Personal selling was required to demonstrate, explain, and truly *sell* these items. Retailers had to advertise the products in the local market, and the dealers had to service them.

By the end of World War II, product and market considerations had changed substantially. Products were presold to consumers through national advertising by the manufacturers. The products were of better quality, so the manufacturer's guarantee on parts was sufficient for the consumer.

After the war a new consumer market emerged—a vast middle-income market—composed in large part of people who had been in low-income groups. These people were price-conscious. They were the people with whom supermarket methods of selling had been so successful. The supermarkets conditioned these consumers for discount selling—low prices and few services. Also, this market had a pent-up demand from the war years. With so many wants and limited income, people were forced to place importance on price when buying.

The situation was ripe for major changes in retailing. Most retailers, however, either failed to grasp the significance of the situation or paid no heed. Instead, they maintained their traditional markup policies. On the other hand, the discount sellers saw the tremendous possibilities in a low-margin, high-turnover type of operation, with few services but big price reductions. Their operating methods enabled them to limit expenses to 12 to 18 percent of sales, as compared with the 30 to 40 percent found in department and limited-line stores.

Recent developments in discount retailing. Discount selling has led to a revision of traditional retailing margins. Manufacturers have altered their channels of distribution to include discounting retailers. Small-scale retailers have been forced to drop discounted products or else meet the discount-house price by offering fewer services and adopting more efficient methods. Large-scale retailers, such as department stores, have responded in several ways. In selling appliances, some stores conduct almost a continual warehouse sale. Others have realistically lowered their markups on discounted products.

The discount houses themselves are changing. Some are upgrading their image to that of a "promotional department store," and some have opened stores in suburban shopping centers. In general, all discounters are trading up in products and services. In the early 1950s, discount sellers ordinarily did not carry food products or soft goods. Today many have added soft goods, including a line of wearing apparel. In fact, reasonably expensive, high-fashion women's ready-to-wear is carried in a number of large discount houses. We noted earlier that discount-food supermarkets have been established as departments in discount houses. Separate discount department stores are even being established by "conventional" retailers such as Woolworth (Woolco), Kresge (K-Mart), and Grand Union (Grand-Way).

The discount sellers' risks and operating costs are, of course, being increased as they add more expensive merchandise, broaden their assortments, move into fancier buildings and locations, and add more services. Vastly intensified competition is also causing real financial problems for many discounters, and there are signs of a slowdown in the rate of entry into the field.

As discount houses and conventional retailers adopt each other's strong points, we can see discount sellers losing their identity as a distinctive form of retailing institution. Perhaps price will cease to be their principal appeal for consumer patronage. Instead, mature discount houses will have to rely more on the forms of nonprice competition (services, quality products, good location, believable promotion, ethical standards, etc.) used by older types of retailers.

NONSTORE PERSONAL SELLING

One of the oldest retailing methods in history is to have buyer and seller transact their business at the buyer's home or at some other nonstore location. This is called *door-to-door* or *house-to-house* selling. Unfortunately, these terms are a poor description of nonstore personal selling. They suggest a cold canvass, wherein the salesman literally goes from door to door, without advance selection of prospects. Actually, relatively little selling is done in this haphazard way.

Nonstore sales may be made by either producers or retailers selling directly to consumers. Bakery and dairy products are frequently distributed in this fashion. Many manufacturers also use this method, including makers of cosmetics (Avon), brushes (the Fuller Brush Company), costume jewelery (Sarah Coventry), housewares (Stanley Home Products), reference books (World Book Encyclopedia), and vacuum cleaners (Electrolux). At the retailer level, automobile dealers do some door-to-door selling. Also, rugs, draperies, and home heating departments in department stores often have their salesmen call directly on people at home.

The oldest and most common way for a "direct-to-home" salesman to reach his prospects is simply to make a door-to-door canvass of a neighborhood. Another way is "party-plan" selling where one customer acts as the hostess of a party to which she invites several friends. The salesman, who is at the party and actually stages it, has a larger prospective market under more advantageous conditions than if he had approached each of the "guests" individually on a house-to-house basis. Another house-to-house approach is to make the initial contact in a store, by telephone, or by having the prospect mail in a coupon. Then the salesman follows up by calling at the prospect's home.

Door-to-door selling is not a substantial part of the total retailing picture. At the same time, however, there are indications that an increasing number of companies are using this method to sell a widening variety of products.[16] Also, interestingly enough, a number of American firms feel that there is a big, profitable growth market overseas which can be reached by door-to-door selling.

In-house selling is attractive to consumers because it offers the convenience of buying at home, plus personalized service. From the company's point

---

[16]See "The Awesome Potential of In-Home Selling or Look Who's at the Door," *Sales Management,* Apr. 15, 1971, p. 27.

of view, door-to-door selling provides an opportunity for the most aggressive forms of retail selling, plus the chance to demonstrate a product in the customer's home. A sales talk can be prepared in detail, with the assurance that this talk is more apt to reach prospective customers if it is given by a door-to-door salesman than if it is passed through retailers' salesmen.

It is questionable whether the cost and profit factors of door-to-door selling are an advantage or a limitation. By eliminating the middleman, consumers may think they are saving money. Yet products sold door-to-door are probably higher-priced than those sold in stores, although price comparisons are difficult because the products are not identical. Sellers, in turn, are attracted by the seemingly high profit margins. Retail prices are easy to maintain at the producer's suggested level. The biggest single selling expense—salesmen's commissions and expenses—is a variable one because salesmen usually are paid a straight commission on sales and they pay their own expenses out of their commissions. Higher net profits are hardly possible, however, unless the producer can perform all wholesaling and retailing functions at a lower total cost than would be possible if separate middlemen were used. On balance, the presence of higher profits is frequently a mirage.

The problems inherent in door-to-door selling explain why it will probably remain a minor form of modern retailing. First, while offering some conveniences to a consumer, it also runs counter to other buying habits, such as the desire to select from a wide assortment of merchandise or to shop and compare price and quality.[17] This method of selling has acquired a poor reputation because many door-to-door salesmen have been nuisances or even unscrupulous, fraudulent operators. Many communities have passed laws regulating this method of selling. Another limitation is that managing a door-to-door sales force poses tremendous problems. Good salesmen are extremely hard to find, and the turnover rate is high. Often they are poorly selected, inadequately trained, and insufficiently supervised. On top of everything else, door-to-door selling is the most expensive form of retailing. Salesmen's commissions alone run as high as 40 to 50 percent of retail price. When we add to this the costs of managing the sales force, plus freight on the merchandise, we often get total margin requirements which are higher than a corresponding total of wholesalers' and in-store retailers' margins.[18]

NONSTORE, NONPERSONAL SELLING

Two other forms of nonstore retailing that involve no personal contact between buyer and seller are mail-order selling and automatic vending.

Mail-order selling. In mail-order selling, a consumer may (1) buy out of a catalogue, (2) mail in an order form appearing in an advertisement, or (3) use an order form received from the seller directly through the mail. Some of the mail-order houses (Sears, Montgomery Ward, Spiegel, Penney's) are *general merchandise* houses offering an exceptionally wide variety of product lines with much depth of assortment in each line. Other institutions might be termed

[17]See Peter L. Gillett, "A Profile of Urban In-Home Shoppers," *Journal of Marketing,* July, 1970, pp. 40–45; and William H. Peters and Neil M. Ford, "A Profile of Urban In-Home Shoppers: The Other Half," *Journal of Marketing,* January, 1972, pp. 62–64.

[18]See Marvin A. Jolson, "Direct Selling: Consumer vs. Salesman—Is Conflict Inevitable?" *Business Horizons,* October, 1972, pp. 87–95.

specialty houses in that they limit the number of lines they carry—books, records, garden supplies, or food, for example.

Mail-order retailing enjoys some competitive advantages. Operating costs are lower than for in-store retailing. Labor costs per dollar sales are low. Mail-order houses are in low-rent locations, and they do not need elaborate store fixtures. Mail-order retailing also fits in with some consumer buying habits. A wide variety of merchandise is offered by general merchandise houses. Also, the consumer can leisurely shop the catalogue and then place an order without the inconvenience of going to a store. Stated prices seem lower because they usually are quoted f.o.b. warehouse, that is, without the freight charges which the consumer must pay.

Mail-order retailing has some drawbacks both for the consumer and for the seller. Except where items are displayed at catalogue stores, customers must place their orders without actually seeing the merchandise they are buying. This limitation is counteracted to some extent by liberal return privileges, guarantees, and excellent catalogue presentations. Customers must plan their purchases well in advance in order to allow time for delivery. Mail-order houses have attempted to speed delivery by establishing branch warehouses and transmitting orders by teletype. Mail-order houses have little flexibility. Catalogues are costly and must be prepared long in advance of the season. Price changes and new merchandise offerings can be announced only through the issuance of supplementary catalogues, and these are a weak selling tool.

Several of the factors which accounted for the early growth of mail-order retailing no longer exist. Automobiles and good rural roads have made city stores easily accessible to farmers, and rural retailing generally has improved. Far from being in a state of decline, however, catalogue buying by mail and telephone is resurging. The convenience of in-home, "one-stop" shopping appeals to a large group of consumers who are showing signs of revolting against standing in line, getting no help from salesclerks, and fighting the traffic and parking problem.

Automatic vending. Today an amazingly wide variety of products is sold through coin-operated machines which automatically vend merchandise (or services) without the aid or presence of a salesclerk. Usually the machines are owned by a vending machine operating company which rents the space needed for desirable locations. In 1972, according to *Vend* magazine, the total volume of products sold through vending machines was $7 billion (approximately 1.5 percent of total retail trade), with the bulk of this volume coming from cigarettes, soft drinks, candy, and hot beverages. The remainder was spread over a wide field of such diverse goods as hosiery, cosmetics, film, sandwiches, T-shirts, and fishing worms, and such services as laundering and insurance policies.

Vending machines can expand a firm's market by reaching customers where and when it is not feasible for stores to do so. Products sold through vending machines typically have low unit values and low markups, so they are relatively expensive to sell through regular retail stores. Many stores use vending machines as a complementary form of retailing. Some have placed a bank of machines outside the store to get nighttime business. Another major expanding market for automatic vending lies in the field of in-plant feeding, that is, the feeding of employees of factories, offices, and other places where large numbers of workers must be fed in a short period of time. The outlook for "robot retailing" is promising. Even department stores are experimenting with vending machines.

Automatic vending still faces major problems, however. In the first place, operating costs are high, and there is a continual need for machine mainten-ance and repair. New machines make former expensive models obsolete before they are depreciated. The prices of automatically vended products are fre-quently higher than store prices of the same products. A second significant problem is that products which can be sold successfully by machine must be well-known, presold brands with a high rate of turnover. They must be reason-ably low in unit value, small and uniform in size and weight, and generally of a convenience goods nature. Only a limited amount of processing can be accom-plished. A related set of problems concerns the extent to which automatic vend-ing is compatible with consumer buying habits. Normally, consumers like to feel or see a product before buying. Also, the machine offers no opportunity to return unwanted merchandise.

TRENDS AND PROSPECTS

Producers and wholesalers of consumer goods, and marketing men who work with them, must understand the retail market before they can intelligently develop distribution strategies. In this and the preceding chapter we have noted many current developments and trends in particular retailing institutions.

The retailing structure is not static; rather, it is a complex, dynamic organism, with stress particularly on the word "dynamic." Three major forces causing change are (1) the changing consumer markets served by retailers, (2) the retailers' own constant search for more effective and profitable methods, and (3) the manufactur-ers' realization that they need mass-marketing methods to keep up with the mass production of goods. These forces underlie several broad, significant trends in the retailing structure.[19]

One of these trends is the continuing move toward *scrambled merchandis-ing*—the practice of product diversification which results in an intensification of competition among traditionally different types of stores now carrying the same products. In the constant search for higher-margin items, one type of store will add products which traditionally were handled by other types of outlets. Consequently, wholesalers and manufacturers must change their channel sys-tems, and retailers must adjust their marketing programs to meet this challenge of scrambled merchandising.

Out of dangerously low and shrinking profit margins is coming an intensified drive for *better management and increased productivity* in retailing. Through sophisticated applications of computer technology, retailers' information systems—accounting, inventory control, marketing research, etc.—are becoming more effective.[20] Automated materials-handling systems are helping to cut physical distribution costs. Operations research techniques are starting to be used to aid management decision making in areas such as product selection and pricing, store

---

[19]For the trends on some 60 specific issues in retailing as forecasted by a sample of top executives from large retail firms, see Leo Bogart, "The Future in Retailing," *Harvard Business Review*, November–December, 1973, pp. 16–18ff.

[20]See M. S. Moyer, "Market Intelligence for Modern Merchants," *California Management Review*, Summer, 1972, pp. 63–69.

location and layout, and advertising and sales-force activities.[21] Regarding credit plans for consumers, stores are expected to move from their own credit cards (or bank credit cards) to a centralized system which someday will be part of a checkless, cashless society. Even top management in retailing is changing. Traditionally store presidents came up through the merchandising ranks and were "good merchants." Today accountants and lawyers are moving into the top spots.[22]

There is a trend toward *concentration of retail trade* among a relatively small number of large-scale institutions. No matter how we classify retailers, it is obvious that fewer stores are doing a steadily increasing share of the retail business. Concentration has developed through mergers of corporate chains, voluntary associations of independents, and the expansion of chains into new geographic markets. An important by-product of concentration in retailing has been the increasing power of large retailers in the marketing system. No longer are these retailers at the mercy of manufacturers and wholesalers. Some retailers have integrated backward to take over wholesaling and manufacturing activities. Others have established their own brands in effective competition with manufacturers' brands.

An interesting *polarity in store size and merchandise assortment* is developing in retailing. At one pole are the mass-merchandising operations of superstores, discount stores, and department stores with their huge stores and their tremendously wide variety of products. At the other end of the spectrum is the small specialty shop—the boutique-type store. Even large stores (department stores, for example) are setting up separate specialty stores featuring a deep assortment of products, but in one very limited line such as women's sportswear or home furnishings.

We can anticipate a considerable increase in *nonstore retailing* in the coming years, to the point where some executives forecast that as much as one-third of all general merchandise business will be done outside the store by the end of this century.[23] Mail-order sales, in some cases tied in with catalogue showrooms, and telephone sales are expected to increase. On the horizon is buying through television-telephone (phonovision) systems coupled with computer systems. Consumers will be able to do much of their buying at home, using a telephone, seeing the merchandise on a television screen, and ordering through a computerized system which will deliver the products and arrange for automatic payment from the customer's bank account.[24]

In the institutional structure in retailing there is a real *breaking away from the traditional store classifications*. The variations are proliferating. Already we have noted such changes as department stores developing small branches as specialty shops, rather than the usual full-line branch. (A New York City department store opens a home-furnishings branch in Boston.) Warehouse retailing and catalogue showrooms are expected to flourish. "Free-form" corporations are evolving

---

[21]M. S. Moyer, "Management Science in Retailing," *Journal of Marketing*, January, 1972, pp. 3–9.

[22]"The New Breed that Runs the Big Stores," *Business Week*, June 26, 1971, p. 54.

[23]Bogart, *op. cit.*, p. 26.

[24]See William G. Nickels, "Central Distribution Facilities Challenge Traditional Retailers," *Journal of Retailing*, Spring, 1973, pp. 45–50.

from former department stores.[25] In these organizations there is no specialization by channel level or by kind-of-business classification. Penney's, for example, operates urban department stores, auto service centers, Treasure Island discount stores, Thrifty drugstores, a catalogue sales division, a life insurance marketing program, a series of European stores, and a financial subsidiary for its accounts' receivable. Dayton's (Minneapolis) and Hudson's (Detroit), two large department store companies, merged and now operate department stores in Arizona and Oregon, the Target discount chain, a hard-goods mass merchandiser in Boston, specialty book stores, jewelry stores, and a real estate subsidiary.

Through the years, many of the evolutionary changes in retailing have followed a cyclical pattern which we call the *wheel of retailing*. As Professor McNair has so succinctly explained it:[26]

> The cycle frequently begins with the bold new concept, the innovation. The innovator has an idea for a new kind of distributive enterprise. At the outset he is ridiculed, condemned as "illegitimate." Bankers and investors are leery of him. But he attracts the public on the basis of a price appeal made possible by the low operating costs inherent in his innovation. As he goes along he trades up, improves the quality of his merchandise, improves the appearance and standing of his store, attains greater respectability. Then, if he is successful, comes the period of growth, the period when he is taking business away from the established distribution channels that have clung to the old methods. Repeatedly something like this has happened in American distribution. . . .
>
> The maturity phase soon tends to be followed by top-heaviness, too great conservatism, a decline in the rate of return on investment, and eventual vulnerability. Vulnerability to what? Vulnerability to the next revolution of the wheel, to the next fellow who has the bright idea and who starts his business on a low-cost basis, slipping in under the umbrella that the old-line institutions have hoisted.

This familiar cycle can be observed in several instances in the past 100 years. First the department stores supplanted small retailers in the cities during the late 1800s and early 1900s. In the 1920s mail-order houses hit their peak. In that same decade the chain stores grew at the expense of independents, particularly in the grocery store field. In the 1930s the independents retaliated with supermarkets,

---

[25]William R. Davidson, "Changes in Distributive Institutions," *Journal of Marketing*, January, 1970, pp. 7–10. Also see Rollie Tillman, "Rise of the Conglomerchant," *Harvard Business Review*, November–December, 1971, pp. 44–51.

[26]Quoted in *Sales Management*, Nov. 21, 1958, p. 9. See also M. P. McNair, "Significant Trends and Developments in the Postwar Period," in A. B. Smith (ed.), *Competitive Distribution in a Free, High-level Economy and Its Implications for the University*, The University of Pittsburgh Press, Pittsburgh, Pa., 1958, pp. 17–18. For an excellent critical analysis and refinement of McNair's "wheel of retailing" hypothesis, see Stanley C. Hollander, "The Wheel of Retailing," *Journal of Marketing*, July, 1960, pp. 37–42. For an interesting analogy in which (1) channels of distribution are regarded as social and ecological systems, and (2) a retailers's chances for survival and success within this ecological system are explained in terms of the ecological concepts of *requirements, tolerances,* and *adaptation,* see Rom J. Markin, "The Retailer in the Vertical Marketing Network," *University of Washington Business Review*, Autumn, 1971, pp. 39–44.

which proved so successful that the chain stores copied the method. In the 1950s the discount houses—young innovators—placed tremendous pressure on department stores, which had become staid, mature institutions. By the early years of the 1960s the discount houses had passed the youthful stage, and discounters in soft goods and foods were appearing. Now we wait to see what new institution or method will be the innovator in the 1970s and 1980s—perhaps it will be automated retailing. By the same token, manufacturers must keep abreast of the inevitable changes in the retailing institutional scene and be ready to appraise the potential of any retailing innovators. Also, established retailers must be alert to meet the challenge with innovations of their own. Truly, a retailer must be ready, willing, and able to innovate, for the alternative is to die.

QUESTIONS AND PROBLEMS

1. "High-price, high-quality, high-fashion merchandise lines ordinarily do not lend themselves to chain-store operation." Why?
2. Do chains sell at lower prices than independents? Compare prices on several items carried by both chain stores and independents in your community.
3. Carefully distinguish between a retailer cooperative chain and a voluntary chain. Are there examples of either type in your community?
4. In what ways does a corporate chain (Safeway, A & P, or Sears) differ from a voluntary chain such as IGA?
5. With all the advantages attributed to voluntary associations of independents, why do you suppose some retailers are still unaffiliated?
6. "The only significant competitive advantage which chains have over independents is greater buying power. If buying power can be equalized through antichain legislation or by having the independents join some voluntary association, then independents can compete equally with the chains." Discuss.
7. "The supermarket, with its operating expense ratio of 20 percent, is the most efficient institution in retailing today." Do you agree? In what ways might supermarkets reduce their operating expenses?
8. Name some discount houses in your community or in a large nearby city. Is there a distinction between "discount selling" and a "discount house"?
9. How have department stores met the challenge of the discount house?
10. "House-to-house selling is the most efficient form of retail selling because it eliminates both the wholesalers and the retail stores." Discuss.
11. "The factors which accounted for the early growth of mail-order retailing no longer exist, so we may expect a substantial decline in this form of selling." Discuss.
12. Why would a retailer install vending machines to sell products that he already carries in his store?
13. What are the conditions which will limit the growth of in-home buying? Of automatic vending?
14. The ease of entry into retailing undoubtedly contributes to the high mortality rate among retailers, with the resultant economic waste. Should entry into retailing be restricted? If so, how could this be done?
15. What recommendations do you have for reducing the costs of retailing?
16. Looking to the future, what retailing institutions or methods will decline and which ones will increase in importance? Explain.

THE WHOLESALE MARKET AND WHOLESALING MIDDLEMEN

"Let's eliminate the middleman" and "The middleman makes all the profit" are cries which have been echoed by many consumers, businessmen, and legislators through the years. Typically these people are focusing their complaints on the wholesaling segment of the distribution structure. Historically, the wholesaler has been a truly powerful figure in American marketing. During the past 25 to 50 years, however, many manufacturers and retailers have made successful attempts to eliminate the wholesaler from their trade channels. Yet wholesaling middlemen continue to be an important force, and in many cases a dominant figure, in the distribution system.

NATURE AND IMPORTANCE OF WHOLESALING

For several marketing and legal reasons, the wholesaling concepts discussed here should be defined precisely and distinguished carefully from the corresponding retailing terms. For example, when manufacturers are establishing their pricing structures, they often must allow wholesalers and retailers different discounts, because the two groups perform different services and thus have different operating costs to cover. State fair-trade laws, unfair-sales-practices acts, chain-store taxes, and the federal Robinson-Patman Act usually apply to retailers and wholesalers in different ways.

WHOLESALING BROADLY DEFINED

Wholesaling or wholesale trade includes the sale, and all activities directly incident to the sale, of products or services to those who are buying for purposes of resale or for business use. Thus, broadly viewed, sales made by one manufacturer to another are wholesale transactions, and the selling manufacturer is engaged in wholesaling. A retail variety store is engaged in wholesaling if it sells pencils or envelopes to a restaurant. That is, wholesaling includes sales of any firm to any customer except an ultimate consumer who is buying for personal, nonbusiness use. As in defining retailing, the only real criterion in identifying wholesaling and wholesale sales is the purchaser's purpose for buying.

THE NARROWER DEFINITION OF WHOLESALING

While the above general definition of wholesaling is accurate, it is too broad to be of practical value for our purposes of (1) understanding the role of wholesaling middlemen and (2) establishing channels of distribution policies. For analytical convenience, the definition must be limited. Therefore we shall be concerned with companies which are engaged *primarily* in wholesaling. We shall exclude retailers who occasionally make a wholesale sale. We shall also exclude sales of manufacturers and farmers because their major activity is not wholesaling. Primarily, they are engaged in creating form utility rather than time, place, and possession utilities. If a manufacturer operates a physically separate establishment, such as a sales branch where the main function is wholesaling and not manufacturing, however, this establishment will be included as a wholesaling middleman. Thus ownership of the establishment does not determine its classification. It may be owned by a manufacturer (a sales branch), a retailer (a retailer cooperative warehouse), or a farmer (a cooperative grain elevator) and still be considered a wholesaling establishment.

WHOLESALERS AND WHOLESALING MIDDLEMEN

The term "wholesaler" applies only to a *merchant* middleman engaged in wholesaling activities; that is, he takes title to the goods he handles. "Wholesaling middlemen" is the all-inclusive term, covering wholesalers and other wholesaling middlemen, such as agents and brokers, who do not take title to the merchandise. Thus a food broker or a manufacturers' agent is not a wholesaler, but he is a wholesaling middleman. Sometimes one hears the terms "jobber" and "distributor." Although usage varies from trade to trade, in this book these terms are considered synonymous with "wholesaler."

DEVELOPMENT AND ECONOMIC JUSTIFICATION OF WHOLESALING

Up to the end of World War I, the merchant wholesaler remained the kingpin in the channel structure. In general, manufacturers were small and poorly financed. They had no knowledge of the market, and it was not economically feasible for them to establish their own sales forces to go directly to the retailers, or even to deal directly with other manufacturers. At the same time, the retailers were also small, geographically scattered, and financially weak.

Even though large-scale activity in manufacturing developed in the late 1800s and the early 1900s, manufacturers still had to rely largely on wholesalers to reach the retailers. After World War I, however, large-scale retailers, such as corporate chains, began to expand considerably. Thus the existence of large-scale business- es in manufacturing and in retailing set the scene for a shift in the balance of power. While the wholesaler has remained remarkably healthy and has continued to grow over the last 40 years, it is true, however, that he does not enjoy his old-time, almost monopolistic position in most channels of distribution.

Most manufacturing companies in the United States are still small and specialized. They have inadequate capital with which to maintain the sales force necessary to contact many scattered small retailers. Even among manufacturers who have sufficient capital, output is too small to justify the necessary sales force. Conversely, the typical retailer buys in small quantities and has a limited knowledge of the market and sources of supply. Wholesalers can pool the orders of many retailers and so furnish a market for a small manufacturer, and at the same time perform a buying service for retailers.

Looking at wholesaling from a macro point of view, it brings to the total distribu- tion system the economies of skill, scale, and transactions. Wholesaling middle- men are marketing specialists. Wholesaling *skills* can be effectively concentrated in a relatively few hands, thus saving the waste and duplication of effort which would occur if the many producers, now using these middlemen, were to take on the wholesaling functions themselves. Economies of *scale* are effected because, by using existing wholesaling middlemen, rather than duplicating them, there is an effective use of manpower resources. Also, wholesalers, typically can perform the physical handling and other wholesaling functions at an operating expense per- centage lower than that at which most manufacturers can do the job. *Transaction* economies come into play when wholesaling middlemen are introduced between producers and their customers. Assume nine manufacturers want to sell to nine retailers. Without a wholesaling middleman there are 81 transactions. By using one wholesaler the number of transactions is cut to 18—9 occurring when the produc- ers all sell to the wholesaler, and another 9 when the wholesaler sells to all the retailers.

SIZE OF TOTAL WHOLESALE MARKET

In 1972 there were about 350,000 wholesaling establishments in the United States, and they had a total annual sales volume of $680 billion. Table 17-1 shows that in each Census of Business since 1948, the number of establish- ment increased substantially over the preceding census year. The 1972 total wholesale trade represented an increase of 90 percent over 1963 and of 278 percent over 1948. Of course a substantial part of this increase is traceable to the rise in the price level. Even if each year's wholesale trade were expressed in constant dollars, however, we would still see a major increase.

CLASSIFICATION OF WHOLESALING MIDDLEMEN

Any attempt to classify wholesaling middlemen in a meaningful way is a precarious project. It is easy to get lost in a maze of categories, because in real life these middlemen vary all over the place in (1) the products they carry, (2) the markets they sell to, and (3) their methods of operation. In an attempt to minimize students' *(a)*

Table 17-1. Total wholesale trade in United States compared with total retail stores.

Total wholesale sales in 1972 increased 90 percent over 1963 and 138 percent over 1958. How do these figures compare with growth in retail sales?

Year	Number of wholesaling establishments	Wholesale sales (billions)	Retail sales (billions)
1972	350,000	$680.0	$448.4
1967	311,000	459.5	310.2
1963	308,000	358.4	244.2
1958	287,000	285.7	200.4
1948	216,000	180.6	130.5

Sources: U.S. Census of Business: 1972 (Preliminary Estimate), Wholesale Trade, United States Summary, Retail Trade, United States Summary; and U.S. Census of Business: 1954.

yawns about this whole topic and *(b)* complaints that "we gotta memorize a bunch of wholesalers," we will set up a classification based on the KISS (Keep it simple, stupid!) system. See Fig. 17-1.

All wholesaling middlemen are grouped into only three broad categories——merchant wholesalers, manufacturers' sales branches and offices, and agents and brokers. These three groups basically are tied to the classification used in the Census of Business, because the Census is the major source of quantitative data covering wholesaling institutions and markets.

Merchant wholesalers.   These are the firms we usually refer to as wholesalers, jobbers, or industrial distributors. They typically are independently owned and they take title to the merchandise they handle. They are the largest single segment of wholesaling institutions when measured either by sales or number of establishments. Merchant wholesalers accounted for 49 percent of the total wholesale trade in 1967. For our purposes this category also includes petroleum bulk plants operated by independent firms, and assemblers of farm products. (In the Census of Business these two groups are treated as separate categories.)

Manufacturers' sales branches and offices.   These establishments are owned and operated by manufacturers, but they are physically separated from the manufacturing plants. The distinction between a sales branch and a sales office is that a branch carries merchandise stock and an office does not. In 1967 sales branches and offices accounted for 38 percent of the total wholesale trade.

Agents and brokers.   These middlemen do *not* take title to the merchandise they handle, but they do actively negotiate the purchase or sale of products for their principals. The main types of agent middlemen are manufacturers' agents, commission men (in the marketing of agricultural products), brokers, and selling agents. As a group their sales represented 13 percent of total wholesale trade in 1967.

TYPES OF WHOLESALING INSTITUTIONS

Merchant Wholesalers
{ Independently owned
{ Take title to their merchandise
{ May be called jobbers, distributors, mill supply houses
{ Specialization by product line:

Full-service:
    General-line wholesaler (drugs, hardware)
    Specialty wholesaler (frozen foods, product)
Special types:
    Rack jobber
    Petroleum bulk plants
    Assemblers of farm products

Limited service:
    Drop shipper
    Truck jobber

Manufacturers' sales branches (with merchandise) Owned and operated by manufacturer
    offices (without merchandise stocks)

Agents and Brokers:
{ Independently owned
{ Do not take title to merchandise, but actively help in negotiating the transfer of title

Manufacturers' agents
Commission men
Brokers
Selling agents

Figure 17-1.

Some of the subcategories widely used in the wholesaling business are reflected in Fig. 17-1. This model actually cuts across several different classification bases often used in describing the wholesaling structure. For example, it cuts across:

Ownership of products—merchant wholesalers versus agent middlemen
Ownership of establishment—manufacturers' sales branches versus independent merchants and agents
Range of services offered—full-service wholesalers versus limited service firms
Depth and breadth of line carried—general-line wholesalers (drugs, hardware) versus specialty firms (frozen foods, dairy products)

The quantitative measures in Table 17-2 for the three groups of wholesaling middlemen reflect their current status and sales trends. There has been stability among the five groups over the past 20 to 25 years. The only major change since before World War II seems to be that manufacturers' sales offices and branches have gained at the expense of agents and brokers. This is due to the fact that as market potentials have increased in various areas, many manufacturers have established branches in territories once served by agent middlemen.

CUSTOMERS OF WHOLESALING MIDDLEMEN

One might expect that total retail sales would be considerably higher than total wholesale trade, because retail prices on a given product are higher than the wholesale price and because many products sold at retail never pass through a wholesaler's establishment and so are excluded from total wholesale sales. Total sales figures belie this particular line of reasoning (see Table 17-1). In each case, the volume of wholesale trade is about 40 percent higher than total retail sales.

The explanation for this seemingly upside-down situation may be found in an analysis of the customers of wholesaling middlemen (Table 17-3). A substantially smaller percentage (from 59 percent in 1939 down to 39 percent in 1967) of merchant wholesalers' sales are made to retailers for resale today than before World War II. Large quantities of *industrial* products are now sold through merchant wholesalers, and larger quantities of *consumer* products are now sold directly by producers to retailers, thus bypassing the wholesaler.

Furthermore, manufacturers' branches carrying stocks of merchandise do appreciably more of their business with retailers than do the offices which have no inventories. Apparently, retailers prefer to buy from a wholesaling middleman who performs the storage function. On the other hand, the manufacturers' sales offices without stocks find industrial users a good market, possibly because the products bought by industrial users can be shipped directly from the factory.

OPERATING EXPENSES AND PROFITS OF WHOLESALING MIDDLEMEN

The average total operating expenses for all wholesaling middlemen combined has been estimated at about 11 percent of *wholesale* sales. It has also been estimated that operating expenses of retailers average about 27 percent of *retail* sales (omitting bars and restaurants, which do some processing of products).

Table 17-2. Total wholesale trade and percentage of total sales: by type of operation.
Merchant wholesalers have maintained the largest share of the market—consistently close to 50 percent. How do you account for the relative decline of agents and brokers?

Type of operation	Number of establishments (000)	1972 sales (billions)	Percentage of total sales		
			1972	1963	1954
United States, total		$	100	100	100
Merchant wholesalers	238	224	49	48	49
Manufacturers' sales branches & offices	47	175	38	37	34
Agents and brokers	26	61	13	15	17
Manufacturers' agents	2	7	2	3	3
Brokers	12	15	3	4	5
Commission men	4	14	3	3	4
Selling agents	5	14	3	2	2
Others	3	11	2	3	3

Source: Adapted from U.S. Census of Business: 1967, 1963, 1954, Wholesale Trade. Merchant wholesalers category includes "assemblers of farm products" and "petroleum bulk stations" operated by independent companies. Manufacturers' sales branches and offices include petroleum bulk plants operated by refineries.

Therefore, on a broad average, the expenses of wholesaling middlemen take about 8 percent of the consumer's dollar.

Expenses by type of operation. Table 17-4 shows operating expenses as a percentage of net sales for the major categories of wholesaling middlemen. Merchant wholesalers have the highest average operating expenses (14 percent), and agents and brokers the lowest (4 percent). Sales branches of manufacturers have higher expenses than sales offices—11 percent, compared with 4 percent. This is because branches have the extra cost of handling merchandise stocks.

We should be careful when interpreting these figures. For instance, we should not conclude that agents and brokers are highly efficient and merchant wholesalers inefficient because of the disparity in operating expenses. The cost differentials are traceable to the differences in the services provided by these institutions. Also, a more careful analysis is necessary before we hand accolades to manufacturers' sales branches and offices which seem to have lower expenses than service wholesalers. Careful analysis shows that the comparison is often "loaded" in favor of the manufacturers' branch operations. Branches and sales offices are located only in the markets offering the highest potential sales and profits. Thus the manufacturers' operations would get more sales per dollar of effort. Often, too, a branch is not allocated its full share of costs. Many indirect administrative expenses are charged in full to the home office, even though the branches share in the benefit. Finally, costs of manufacturers' sales branches and merchant wholesalers are not always comparable because of differences in services provided.

Table 17-3. Sales of wholesale establishments, selected years: by class of customer.
Since World War II, a declining share (47 percent down to 39 percent) of merchant wholesalers' sales have been made to retailers. How do you account for this? Who are the main customers of agents and brokers?

		Percentage of sales made to:			
Type of operation	Year	Retailers for resale	Industrial or business users	Other wholesale establishments for resale	Others (mainly export market)
Merchant wholesalers*	1967	39	39	15	8
	1958	46	32	15	6
	1948	47	32	14	8
	1939	59	24	11	6
Manufacturers' sales branches and offices	1963	32	44	19	4
Manufacturers' sales branches	1948	41	35	21	3
Manufacturers' sales offices	1948	20	52	26	3
Agents and brokers	1967	18	42	32	8
	1948	16	42	37	6

Source: U.S. Census of Business, Wholesale Trade, for respective years.
*Does not include assemblers of farm products.

Table 17-4. Operating expenses as percentage of net sales of wholesaling middlemen, 1967: by type of operation.
Merchant wholesalers have the highest operating costs (13.8 percent). Are they less efficient as a class than agents and brokers, whose expenses are only 4.0 percent of sales? Why are manufacturers' sales branches a higher-cost operation than manufacturers' sales offices?

Type of operation	Operating expenses, percentage of net sales
Merchant wholesalers, total	13.8
Domestic service wholesalers	14.8
Manufacturers' sales branches (with stocks)	11.3
Manufacturers' sales offices (without stocks)	4.1
Agents and brokers	4.0
Brokers	3.2
Selling agents	4.2
Manufacturers' agents	6.4
Petroleum bulk plants, terminals	0.3
Assemblers of farm products	8.6

Source: U.S. Census of Business: 1967, Wholesale Trade, United States Summary.

Expenses by kinds of goods handled. An executive in a given company is probably interested in more detailed cost data. There are tremendous variations in the wholesaling costs of different products. Product considerations such as perishability, value in relation to bulk, rate of turnover, special storage and handling requirements, and technical selling needs influence the operating cost ratio. According to the 1967 Census of Business, for example, operating expenses of wholesalers of a general line of groceries were 6.4 percent of sales, and tobacco distributors' costs were 5.9 percent of sales. At the other extreme, distributors of office equipment and supplies had average expenses of 31 percent of sales, and wholesalers of professional equipment and supplies, 23 percent.

Net profits. Net operating profits expressed as a percentage of net sales are extremely modest for wholesaling middlemen and are considerably lower than those for retailing middlemen. Only seven groups of wholesalers out of 32 product lines reporting in 1972 showed a median net profit of more than 2 percent of sales, according to a Dun and Bradstreet report on financial ratios in wholesaling.[1] The three highest groups of wholesalers were automotive equipment (2.7 percent), paints and varnishes (2.6 percent), and air-conditioning – refrigeration equipment (2.5 percent). Three other groups (groceries, meats, and tobacco) reported less than 1 percent profit on net sales, after making provisions for federal income taxes.

REGULAR, OR FULL-SERVICE, WHOLESALERS

A regular, or full-service, wholesaler is an independent merchant wholesaling middleman who generally performs a full range of wholesaling functions. This is the firm which fits the layman's image or stereotype of a wholesaler. He may be called simply a "wholesaler," or he may go under the name of "distributor," "mill supply house," "industrial distributor," or "jobber," depending upon the usage in his line of business. He may handle consumer and/or industrial products, and these goods may be manufactured or nonmanufactured, and imported or exported. Most of our discussion in this section, however, revolves around the *full-service* wholesalers of *manufactured* goods in the *domestic* market, because they account for about 85 percent of all merchant wholesalers' sales.

Merchant wholesalers (of manufactured products or farm products) have accounted for close to one-half of total wholesale trade for over 30 years (recall Table 17-2). Thus the regular wholesaler has held his own in the competitive struggles within the distribution system. Maintaining their market-share percentage means, of course, that the regular wholesalers' dollar sales have increased substantially over the years, even in the face of competition from agents and brokers as well as from direct-selling manufacturers and their sales offices and branches, and from direct-buying customers.

This picture of stability in the regular wholesalers' share of market, when viewed in the aggregate of total wholesale trade, may be a bit misleading in that it hides the volatility and shifting competitive positions within various industries. Wholesalers have increased their market share in some industries and have

---

[1] "The Ratios of the Wholesalers," *Dun's Review,* October, 1973, p. 98.

declined in other areas where they once dominated. Certainly the aggregate market-share figures are misleading in industries where wholesalers are, and always have been, used very little.

SERVICES RENDERED TO CUSTOMERS AND SUPPLIERS

Growth among service wholesalers has occurred in the face of strong competition from other wholesaling middlemen and from large manufacturers and retailers who are attempting to bypass the wholesaler. In light of the fact that nobody is subsidizing the wholesaler, the presumption is that his existence is maintained by the socioeconomic services which he renders. This will be clearer if we examine briefly the services that wholesalers render to their customers and to manufacturers.

Buying. Wholesalers act as purchasing agents for their customers whether they are small retailers or industrial users. The wholesaler determines in advance what his customers will want, and then he has the merchandise on hand when the customers are ready for it. Wholesalers have a broad knowledge of sources of supply and are able to assemble in one place the products from these different sources. A good wholesaler has trained buyers constantly in touch with the appropriate markets, who seek out new and better products and acquire other types of market information. Through the use of wholesalers, the retailer can talk to a few salesmen—the wholesalers'— and thus have access to all these manufacturers. Essentially the same situation prevails among industrial users. These users often prefer to buy from industrial distributors rather than from manufacturers, especially when the product is not technical, has a small unit value, and is purchased infrequently and in small quantities.

In serving as the purchasing agent for retailers and industrial users, the wholesaler also indirectly but significantly aids manufacturers. By ordering enough of a given item to take care of the needs of several retailers, the wholesaler is able to submit a larger order than any of his individual customers could place. Many operating costs, such as order filling, billing, and shipping, are therefore lower per dollar of sales.

Selling.   As has been noted before, most manufacturers are small and have limited financial resources. They can build a good product, but they need someone to sell it. The wholesalers perform this service.

The key to an appreciation of the selling activity of wholesalers is a recognition of the nature of the retail market. Of the 1.7 million stores, about 90 percent are independent, single-unit operations. Most of these are small, and many are located in small towns. A wholesaler can afford to sell to these small scattered retailers because he represents many manufacturers and can carry many items. Consequently, he can usually get orders large enough to justify his widespread operations.

The cost of direct selling from manufacturer to retailer would be prohibitive, and even if a manufacturer attempted direct distribution, retailers would often reject it. In many cases the retailers know and trust the wholesaler as a result of past business dealings. The manufacturer is a stranger and would not be accorded the same welcome.

For industrial products, the industrial distributor offers a manufacturer essentially the same selling services as a wholesaler of consumer goods. The distributor provides a manufacturer who has no marketing facilities, or who is manufacturing a narrow line and cannot support a sales force, with an excellent means of reaching the market. He is frequently in a good position to know who influences a customer's buying decisions. The prestige which an established industrial distributor enjoys makes him an excellent middleman for introducing a new product.

A firm using a wholesaler to help distribute its products is faced with certain problems in the selling area. Since the wholesaler is not an employee of the firm, it has little control over his selling methods. The wholesaler represents many firms and can provide only part-time selling effort for the products of any of them.

Dividing, or bulk breaking. One service provided by wholesalers—dividing, or bulk breaking—is probably of equal value to their customers and to manufacturers. The wholesaler buys in carload or truckload lots from a manufacturer and resells in case lots or less. Because of transportation costs alone, manufacturers find it economically unjustifiable to sell in small quantities directly to retailers. When carload or truckload quantities are shipped, the transportation costs are computed at the carload or truckload rate. If the manufacturer had to ship in smaller quantities to the retailer, a much higher freight rate would be charged. Furthermore, many manufacturers refuse to sell in the less-than-carload or less-than-truckload quantities, and many retailers will not buy in the larger quantities.

Transportation. In addition to buying in such quantities that the transportation costs are minimized for both manufacturer and customer, a wholesaler furnishes other transportation services to his customers. Since he usually provides quick and frequent delivery, retailers and industrial users need not carry large inventories. Consequently, their costs are reduced because their investments in inventory, insurance, and storage costs are lower. For the retailer, there is less risk that the merchandise will spoil or become obsolete and require markdowns.

Warehousing. Wholesalers create both place and time utility through their warehousing activities. The customer's opportunity to order frequently and in small quantities implies that the wholesaler has the desired merchandise on hand where and when the retailer wants it. Furthermore, wholesalers ordinarily have better storage facilities and can make more effective use of a given amount of space than their customers.

Manufacturers also benefit from this efficiency of storage, particularly manufacturers of seasonal items. Consider the warehousing problems of two manufacturers, one making snow skis and the other producing baseball equipment. A wholesaler can store these two alternate seasonal items in a single unit of space. As the space is emptied of skis during the fall and winter, it can be filled with baseballs and gloves.

Financing. In general, wholesalers aid their customers financially through open-book credit. They usually offer a cash discount if the customer pays his bill within a given period of time after the date of invoice or the receipt of goods. If the customer does not pay within that cash discount period, however, he still has several weeks or months, depending upon the practices in the trade, before the bill falls due. In many cases wholesalers have carried retailers for extended periods of time when the retailers were unable to collect on their customers' accounts.

The financing activities of a wholesaler tend to reduce a retailer's capital requirements. We have already mentioned the advantage of being able to maintain a low inventory. In addition, on seasonal merchandise, such as fishing tackle or Christmas items, wholesalers often deliver the merchandise in advance of the season but do not require payment until after the season is under way. Thus the retailer actually pays for his goods with the money he receives for selling them. This is very close to consignment selling or grubstaking.

In most cases, manufacturers either could not or would not offer comparable aid. They are too far removed from the retailers and industrial users to risk granting credit, and they are not nearly so able to get current and accurate credit information as the wholesaler is.

By granting credit to retailers, the wholesaler is indirectly providing financial help to manufacturers. In addition, wholesalers often supply a more direct form of financial aid to producers. Wholesalers will buy in advance of a season or will accept and store several shipments, paying for them well in advance of the time they will be resold to retailers. Wholesalers also help by generally paying their bills promptly, thus further reducing a manufactuer's capital requirements.

Risk bearing. Several of the points already mentioned suggest ways in which wholesalers reduce risks for their customers and for manufacturers. In addition, wholesalers usually guarantee the merchandise they sell, and the retailer can thus get immediate satisfaction on claims involving defective merchandise.

Simply by taking title to the merchandise, a wholesaler reduces a manufacturer's risk. If the product deteriorates, goes out of fashion, or for some other reason does not sell, the wholesaler usually bears the burden. Also, a manufacturer's credit loss is reduced by dealing with wholesalers because the wholesaler is absorbing the higher-risk venture of granting credit to retailers.

Management services and advice. By furnishing managerial services and advice, especially to retailer customers, wholesalers have significantly strengthened their own position in the market. The existence of a full-function wholesaler is dependent upon the economic health and well-being of small retailers. Therefore, by helping the retailer the wholesaler really helps himself. Some of the managerial services provided by wholesalers today include training of retail salesclerks; advising on, and helping with, store displays and store layout; and establishing better systems for inventory control and accounting. Wholesalers can supply information regarding new products, competitors' prices, special sales by manufacturers, and other data regarding market conditions.

SPECIAL TYPES OF MERCHANT WHOLESALERS

Within the broad category of merchant wholesalers there are a few subclassifications worth observing because of the special nature of their operations. Their titles reflect either the specialized nature of their job or the limited range of wholesaling services they offer. (Recall Fig. 17-1.)

Rack jobber. The rack jobber, called a "rack merchandiser" in the Census, emerged after World War II as supermarkets added nonfood items. The rack jobber has expanded to serve drugstores, hardware stores, variety stores, and other stores which have instituted the self-service method of retailing. The general-line grocery wholesalers in these nonfood lines could not easily sell to supermarkets for at least three reasons. First, the wholesalers' regular customers, such as drugstores or hardware stores, would complain loudly and probably withdraw their business. Second, too many different wholesalers would have to call on the supermarket to fill all the nonfood lines, and the retailer would object to so many wholesalers. Third, a single supermarket ordinarily would have too small an order in any one nonfood line to make it profitable for the wholesaler in that line.

One rack jobber (or a very few) can furnish all the nonfood items in a supermarket. The rack jobber furnishes the rack or shelves upon which to display the merchandise, and he stocks only the fastest-moving brands on these racks. He is responsible for maintaining fully stocked racks, building attractive displays, and price-marking the merchandise. In essence, the retailer merely furnishes floor or shelf space and then collects the money as the customer goes through the checkout stand.

With the expansion of nonfood items in supermarkets, the position of rack jobbers should become stronger and more attractive. The only significant threat to his position is the possibility that the nonfood business in supermarkets will grow so large that retailers will want to deal directly with the manufacturers.

Petroleum bulk plants and terminals. Basically these fall in the broad category of either (1) merchant wholesalers or (2) manufacturers' sales branches. That is, they are owned by independent wholesalers, or they are owned and operated by petroleum refiners. (Recall the categories in Table 17-2.) In either case, they perform all the usual wholesaling services. They are classified separately in the Census of Business because of their special physical-plant facilities and their somewhat different operations. These middlemen are engaged in the buying, storing, and wholesale selling of gasoline, oil, gases, and other bulk petroleum products. In 1972 there were 30,000 such establishments, accounting for 5 percent of all wholesale trade.

Assemblers of farm products. Another separate Census classification includes various firms engaged in buying raw farm products from agricultural producers, or fish and seafood products from fishermen. In contrast to the other types of wholesaling middlemen, assemblers buy in *small* quantities from *many* producers and sell in *large* quantities to *fewer* customers. After the products are concentrated in large, economical quantities, they are sold to other wholesaling middlemen in central wholesale markets or to industrial users, such as food processors. Assemblers are mentioned separately because their methods of operation, their physical facilities, and the products they handle all pose a different set of problems. However, assemblers are similar to some of the middlemen already mentioned. For instance, assemblers are merchant wholesalers in that they take title to the products and usually perform many marketing services, such as storage, delivery, and dissemination of market information. Although the aggregate sales volume of assemblers has increased, their relative importance in wholesaling has declined over the years (6 percent of total wholesale trade in 1948, down to 2 percent in 1967). Improvements in transportation, storage, and market communications have made it possible for retailers and food processors to deal directly with the producers.

Limited-function wholesalers. A small group of merchant wholesalers who have received attention in marketing literature through the years, possibly more attention than their numerical importance merits, are the limited-function wholesalers. These are merchant middlemen who do not perform all the usual wholesaling functions. The activities of most of these wholesalers are concentrated in a few product lines. In general, operating costs are lower for limited-function wholesalers than for full-service wholesalers, but this is to be expected because of the differential in services performed. The major types of limited-function wholesalers are truck jobbers, drop shippers, and retailer cooperative warehouses. The retailer cooperative warehouse was discussed in the preceding Chapter.

A *truck distributor* or jobber (sometimes still called a "wagon jobber" in memory of the days when he used a horse and wagon) is a specialty wholesaler, chiefly in the food field. He carries nationally advertised, fast-moving, and perishable or semiperishable goods, such as candies, dairy products, potato chips, and tobacco products. The unique feature of his method of operation is that he sells and delivers merchandise during his call. His competitive advantage lies in his ability to furnish fresh products so frequently that the retailer can buy perishable goods in small amounts and have a minimum risk of loss. The major limitation of a truck jobber is his high operating cost ratio, which is caused primarily by the small size of his orders and the inefficient use of delivery equipment. A truck is an expensive warehouse.

The *drop shipper,* sometimes called a "desk jobber," gets his name from the fact that the merchandise he sells is delivered directly from the manufacturer to the customer and is called a "drop shipment." Drop shippers take title to the products, but they do not physically handle the goods. They operate almost entirely in coal and coke and in lumber and building materials. These products are typically sold in carload quantities, and freight is high in comparison with unit value. Thus it is desirable to minimize the physical handling of the product.

AGENT WHOLESALING MIDDLEMEN

Another important group of wholesaling middlemen consists of agents and brokers. These middlemen are distinguished from merchant wholesalers in two important respects: Agent middlemen do *not* take title to the merchandise, and they typically perform fewer services for their clients and principals. (See Table 17-5.) For these reasons, the average operating expenses for agents and brokers in 1967 were only 4 percent, as compared with 15 percent for service wholesalers (see Table 17-4). There were 26,500 establishments of agents and brokers in 1967, and they transacted 13 percent of the total volume of wholesale trade (Table 17-2). Based on sales volume, the major types of agent middlemen are manufacturers' agents, selling agents, brokers, and commission men.

All agent middlemen have some characteristics in common which help to explain the role they play. One such similarity relates to their customers. Industrial users constitute the major customer group, and together with retailer customers the two groups account for over 60 percent of the agents' total sales. (Review Table 17-3.)

Table 17-5. Services provided by agent wholesaling middlemen.

Services	Manufacturers' agents	Selling agents	Brokers	Commission men
Provides buying services	Yes	Yes	Some	Yes
Provides selling services	Yes	Yes	Yes	Yes
Carries inventory stocks	Sometimes	No	No	Yes
Delivers the products	Sometimes	No	No	Yes
Provides market information	Yes	Yes	Yes	Yes
Sets prices and terms of sale	No	Yes	No	No
Grants credit to customers	No	Sometimes	No	Sometimes
Reduces producers' credit risks	No	Yes	No	No
Sells producers' full line	Sometimes	Yes	Sometimes	No
Manufacturer uses his own sales force along with agents	Sometimes	No	No	No
Continuing relationship with producer throughout the year	Yes	Yes	No	No
Manufacturer uses same agent for entire market	No	Yes	No	No

A second common characteristic of agent middlemen is that they are usually compensated by a percentage commission based on the volume of sales or purchases they negotiate. The third point is that agent middlemen generally either act as a substitute for a manufacturer's sales force or serve as an addition to the sales force, thus enabling a manufacturer to sell in markets located beyond the limits of his own salesmen. A final common characteristic, and one which sometimes creates a problem, is that although most agent middlemen ostensibly are working for a seller (they are paid by a seller), they often act in the best interests of the buyer. Apparently their idea is that they can always get another supplier, but customers are hard to find and hold.

The relative importance of agents and brokers in wholesale trade has declined over the past 30 to 40 years. Their market share has dropped from 20 percent in 1939 to 13 percent in 1967. In the wholesaling of agricultural products, agent middlemen are being replaced by merchant wholesalers, or by direct sales to retailers and food processors. In the marketing of manufactured goods, the agent middlemen are being supplanted by manufacturers' sales branches and offices (review Table 17-2). As manufacturers become larger and their markets grow in potential sales, they no longer have to rely on manufacturers' agents or brokers to reach customers in these markets. From a marketing and economic point of view, it is more effective for the manufacturer to establish his own outlets and sales force in these markets.

MANUFACTURERS' AGENTS

A *manufacturers' agent* (frequently called a manufacturers' representative) is an agent commissioned by a manufacturer to sell part or all of the producer's products in a restricted territory. The agent, however, is independent and is in no way an employee of the manufacturer. He has little or no control over the price and terms of a sale; these are established by the manufacturer. Because a manufacturers' agent sells in a restricted territory, a producer typically uses several agents. The size of an agent's territory usually depends upon the density of its potential. One territory may be limited to the Chicago metropolitan area; another may cover Washington, Oregon, Idaho, western Montana, and Alaska. Unlike a broker, a manufacturers' agent has a continuing, year-round relationship with his principal. He usually represents several noncompeting manufacturers of related products and can pool into one profitable sale the small orders which otherwise would go to several individual manufacturers. For this reason, he can operate in markets that none of his principals could individually afford to enter. Besides, buyers may prefer to deal with one representative rather than with direct salesmen from several manufacturers.

Manufacturers' agents are used extensively in the distribution of many types of consumer products and industrial products. The main service offered to manufacturers by this agent middleman is selling. He seeks out and serves markets which the manufacturer himself cannot profitably reach. Furthermore, because a manufacturers' agent does not carry nearly so many lines as a regular wholesaler, the agent can offer a higher-caliber, more aggressive form of selling service. Operating expenses depend upon the product sold and whether the merchandise is stocked. Some representatives operate on a commission as low as 2 percent, while others charge as much as 20 percent. These commissions cover operating expenses and net profit. On an overall basis, the operating expense ratio is about 6 percent for agents.

There are some limitations which a manufacturer may face if he decides to use manufacturers' agents. If the agent does not carry merchandise stocks, the manufacturer may be at a competitive disadvantage because he cannot fill orders quickly. Most agents cannot furnish customers adequate technical advice and repair service, nor are they equipped to install major products. While the agent's commission may be reasonably low, the additional cost of services that the manufacturer must perform himself may result in a total marketing cost which is higher than it would be if another type of middleman were used.

Manufacturers' agents may be used in three characteristic situations:

1. In a small firm, usually a new one, with a limited number of products and no salesmen, manufacturer' agents may do all the selling.
2. In a firm which wants to add a new and possibly unrelated line of products to the existing product mix, where the present salesmen either are not experienced in a new line or cannot reach the new market, the new line may be given to manufacturers' agents. Thus a company may have both salesmen and agents covering the same geographic market.
3. In a firm wishing to enter a new geographic market which is not yet sufficiently developed to warrant sending salesmen, manufacturers' agents familiar with that market may be used. If a company has been selling from the Atlantic Coast to the Rocky Mountains and now wishes to extend into the Pacific Coast states, it can employ agents who know potential customers and may already be calling on them with other products.

SELLING AGENTS

A selling agent is an independent middleman who is used essentially in place of a manufacturer's entire marketing department. This agent typically performs more marketing services than any other type of agent middleman, and he also has more control and authority with respect to the marketing program of his client-principal. A manufacturer will employ one selling agent to market the full output of the firm over its entire market. Selling agents are used most in the marketing of textiles and coal, although they are also found to some extent in the distribution of apparel and of food, lumber, and metal products. Their operating expenses average about 4 percent of sales.

Agents usually have considerable authority in establishing prices and terms of sale, and they frequently supply financial aid to manufacturers. Because of their critical position in a manufacturer's operations, selling agents sometimes really run their clients' companies—a sort of "tail wagging the dog" situation in which manufacturers are pretty much at the agents' mercy.

Despite the apparent similarity between a selling agent and a manufacturers' agent, there are some fundamental differences between the two. First, a manufacturer uses only one selling agent, whereas he would use several manufactuers' representatives if he took this alternative. Manufacturers' agents have restricted territories; selling agents do not. Second, if a selling agent is used, a manufacturer will have no salesmen; if manufacturers' representatives are used, a seller will often have a sales force of his own. Third, selling agents have far more control over prices and terms of sales. Fourth, selling agents always sell the entire output of a firm; manufacturers' agents usually sell only part of the product line in all the market, or all the product line in only part of the market.

BROKERS

Brokers are agent middlemen whose prime responsibility is to bring buyers and sellers together. They furnish considerable market information regarding prices, products, and general market conditions. Brokers do not physically handle the goods. Also, they do not work on a continuing basis with their principals. Most brokers work for sellers, although about 10 percent represent buyers. A broker has no authority to set prices. He simply negotiates a sale and leaves it up to the seller to accept or reject the buyer's offer. Because of the limited services provided, brokers operate on a very low cost ratio—about 3 percent of net sales.

Brokers are most prevalent in the food field. Their operation is typified by a seafood broker handling the pack from a salmon cannery. For possibly three months out of the year, the cannery is in operation. The canner employs a broker (the same one each year if relationships are mutually satisfactory) to find buyers for the salmon pack. The broker provides information regarding market prices and conditions, and the canner then informs him of the price he desires. The broker seeks potential buyers among chain stores, wholesalers, and others. When a transaction is completed, the broker receives his commission—usually 2 percent of the total sale. When the entire pack is sold, the agent-principal relationship is discontinued until possibly the following year.

An evolutionary development in the food brokerage field should be noted. Through the years many brokers have established permanent relationships with some principals and are performing activities which more accurately would classify these middlemen as manufacturers' agents. They still call themselves "food brokers," however, and they are classed as brokers in the Census of Business.

COMMISSION MEN

In the marketing of many agricultural products such as fresh fruits and vegetables, grains, and livestock, a widely used middleman in the large central markets is a *commission merchant,* also called a *commission man* or a *commission house.* (The term "commission merchant" is actually a misnomer. This handler is really an agent middleman. In many transactions today, he does not take title to the commodities he handles.)

The commission method of operation in central markets may be described briefly as follows: An assembler in a local market (possibly a local resident produce buyer or a grain elevator) consigns a shipment to a commission merchant in a central market. These firms usually have established working relationships over a period of years. The commission man meets a train or truck and takes charge of the shipment. It is his responsibility to handle and sell the goods. He arranges for any necessary storage, grading, and other services prior to the sale. He finds a buyer at the best possible price, makes the sale, and arranges for transfer of shipment. He deducts his commission, freight charges, and other marketing expenses and remits the balance as soon as possible to the local market shipper. In some cases, commission men extend credit to local shippers or make advance payments on carloads consigned to them.

During the past thirty years, commission dealings in fresh produce have declined. To an increasing extent, commission men are taking outright title to the goods they handle. Today it is not at all uncommon to find wholesale carlot receivers who act as commission men (agent middlemen) in some transactions and as merchant wholesalers in others. Three reasons underlie the decline in commission selling of fresh fruits and vegetables. First, many shippers lost faith in the system: some commission men abused their trust and shortchanged the shippers, taking advantage of the fact that shippers were far away and knew little about market conditions. Second, facilities for physical handling, storing, and shipping have improved, so that losses from perishability are reduced. Finally, improved dissemination of market information means better data, and thus less risk, on demand and supply in a given market.

Commission selling is still widespread in such commodities as grain and livestock. These products are not so perishable, and there is always a market for them. The key to the continued success of a commission merchant is his ability to sell at prices satisfactory to the shipper, to move the commodities quickly with minimum losses due to perishability, and to manage the commodities properly and in good faith. The organized systems of trading on commodity exchanges and the improved dissemination of information have reduced the likelihood of abuses.

WHOLESALING SERVICES PROVIDED BY NONMIDDLEMEN

There are several types of firms which are not middlemen but which do provide important services for manufacturers and middlemen alike.

FAIRS, TRADE SHOWS, AND EXHIBITIONS

Many industries periodically hold trade shows, fairs, or exhibitions of products. Some hold these affairs annually in one city, while others have three or four shows a year, each in a different city. For example, there are annual furniture shows in Chicago, Grand Rapids, Dallas, and High Point, North Carolina. These are not permanent exhibitions; they last for a few days or a week. They offer an opportunity for a manufacturer to display his wares and make contacts with wholesalers and retailers. Middlemen in turn can contact suppliers and customers.

MERCHANDISE MARTS

Several cities have central market facilities where manufacturers or wholesaling middlemen rent space and exhibit their products on a reasonably permanent basis. The Merchandise Mart and the Furniture Mart in Chicago are good examples of such facilities. Showrooms usually are not open to consumers, but the exhibits offer retailers and wholesalers an opportunity to see what is available and to place orders.

PUBLIC WAREHOUSES

Bonded public warehouses are independently owned storage facilities which provide warehousing and other wholesaling functions. Many specialized types are available, such as cold-storage warehouses and grain elevators. These institutions may be used by manufacturers or wholesaling middlemen in lieu of maintaining their own storage facilities. A manufacturer may rent space in several public warehouses located throughout his market, thus maintaining stocks of merchandise at strategic locations near his wholesalers or other customers. Upon notice from the manufacturer, the warehouseman will fill an order and make arrangements for shipping it. Public warehouses are discussed in more detail in Chapter 20, where we consider the management of phsyical distribution.

FREIGHT FORWARDERS AND TRANSPORTATION COMPANIES

Railroads, truckers, and other common carriers, as well as freight forwarders, which typically provide some wholesaling services, are discussed in Chapter 20.

Our survey of the major types of wholesaling middlemen and of the services they render, their costs, and typical situations in which they might best be used gives some insight into the way a firm establishes a channel structure for its products. Wholesaling middlemen are specialists in marketing. A producer must decide which wholesaling services he needs and then select the right institutional specialist to perform these services. When a manufacturer criticizes the high cost of a given wholesaler, he may be using the wrong type of wholesaler, or he may be paying for services which he is not using

QUESTIONS AND PROBLEMS

1. A large furniture warehouse is located in a major Midwestern city. The following conditions exist with respect to this firm:
   a. All merchandise is purchased directly from manufacturers.
   b. The warehouse is located in the low-rent, wholesaling district.
   c. Merchandise remains in original crates; customers use catalogues and swatch books to see what the articles look like and what fabrics are used.
   d. About 90 percent of the customers are ultimate consumers, and they account for 85 percent of the sales volume.

    e. The firm does quite a bit of advertising, pointing out that consumers are buying at wholesale prices.

    f. Crates are not price-marked. Salesmen bargain with customers.

    g. Some 10 percent of sales volume comes from sales to furniture stores.

    Is this firm a wholesaler? Explain.

2. Which of the following are wholesaling transactions?

    a. A farmer sells fresh produce to a restaurant.

    b. A chemical manufacturer sells chemicals to a fertilizer manufacturer.

    c. A drug wholesaler sells drugs to a hospital; to a drug retailer.

    d. A retail lumberyard sells plywood to a building contractor; to a homeowner for his "do-it-yourself" project.

3. Carefully distinguish between the following: wholesaler, wholesaling, jobber, wholesaling middleman, distributor.

4. Historically, what have been the economic justifications for the existence of wholesaling middlemen? Which of these still exist?

5. What conditions account for the fact that manufacturers' sales offices and branches have maintained a steadily increasing share of total wholesale trade, while the agents' and brokers' share has declined in each census year since 1948?

6. How do you account for the substantial variation in operating expenses among the major types of wholesalers shown in Table 17-4?

7. In comparing the operating expense ratio for retailers and for wholesalers in Tables 15-2 and 17-4, we see that wholesalers typically have lower operating expenses. How do you account for this?

8. What activities could regular wholesalers discontinue in an effort to reduce operating costs?

9. What service does a full-function wholesaler provide for a manufacturer?

10. What types of retailers, other than supermarkets, offer reasonable fields for entry by the rack jobber? Explain.

11. Carefully distinguish between a selling agent and a manufacturers' agent.

12. Why would a manufacturing firm prefer to use manufacturers' agents instead of its own company sales force?

13. Why is it that manufacturers' agents often can penetrate a market faster and at a lower cost than a manufacturer's sales force?

14. What is the economic justification for the existence of the broker, especially in light of the few functions he performs?

15. Which type of agent middleman, if any, is most likely to be used by each of the following? Explain your choice in each instance.

    a. A small manufacturer of a liquid glass cleaner to be sold through supermarkets

    b. A small manufacturer of knives used for hunting, fishing, and camping

    c. A salmon canner in Alaska packing a high-quality, unbranded product

    d. A small-tools manufacturer who has his own sales force selling to the industrial market and who wishes to add backyard barbecue equipment to his line

    e. A North Carolina textile mill producing unbranded towels, sheets, pillowcases and blankets.

16. Looking into the future, which types of wholesaling middlemen do you think will increase in importance, and which ones will decline? Explain.

COMPETITIVE CONFLICTS AND COOPERATION IN DISTRIBUTION CHANNELS

18

In Chapter 15 we set forth the idea that a company's trade channel should be regarded as a total system of distribution, rather than as a fragmented assortment of independent institutions operating in an uncoordinated fashion. Manufacturers and middlemen alike should understand that the middlemen used by a manufacturer are only a logical component of a systematic organization which starts with the manufacturer and is designed to maximize marketing effectiveness in the sale to the final customer. The systems concept of distribution suggests then a need for cooperation and coordination among channel members. Yet power structures do exist in trade channels, and a struggle does go on continuously among channel members.

At the root of this struggle is institutional change, several examples of which were observed in our study of retailing and wholesaling institutions. This change, in turn, is caused first by the shifting nature of market demand and second by the economic growth and competitive activity among the institutions. It is axiomatic that change begets conflict and that, conflict very often results in change.[1]

---

[1]For an approach to anticipating changes in distribution structures before such changes develop into obvious trends, see Bruce Mallen, "Functional Spin-Off: A Key to Anticipating Change in Distribution Structure," *Journal of Marketing,* July, 1973, pp. 18–25.

While pressures for institutional change have mounted over the years, at the same time strong psychological and sociological barriers stand in the path of this change. These barriers often persist in the face of economic analyses showing that the change may result in channels which will offer economic advantages and that resistance to change may extend the life of uneconomic channels.

Several of these noneconomic barriers may be identified.[2] One is the presence of group solidarity and collective action among resellers of common backgrounds—retail druggists, for example. Sometimes entrepreneurial values —particularly those of small retailers—place higher ratings on stability than on growth, and this of course tends to restrict innovation. Even in larger organizations, change may be resisted because it "violates group norms, creates uncertainty, and results in loss of status." Finally, a firm's position in the channel may be correlated to its acceptance of, or resistance to, change. That is, the "insiders" in the dominant channel, the "strivers" who want to become part of that system, and the "complementors" who assist the first two groups are all emotionally and economically committed to the dominant channel. They endeavor to maintain the status quo against the minor intrusions of "transients" and the major threats from "outside innovators" who would realign the existing structure.[3]

NATURE OF THE CONFLICTS

Three separate forms of competitive conflicts within channels of distribution may be identified. Two of these occur on the horizontal level of distribution: the first is competition between middlemen of the same type—hardware store versus hardware store, or industrial distributor versus industrial distributor; the second is competition between different types of middlemen, but still on the same level —hardware store versus paint store, or industrial distributor versus manufacturers' agent. The third type of conflict is vertical in nature, involving instituions on different levels of distribution—manufacturer versus wholesaler, for example.

COMPETITION ON THE SAME LEVEL OF DISTRIBUTION

On the same level of distribution, perhaps the main form of conflict has been the competition engendered by "scrambled merchandising"—that is, the practice whereby a middleman diversifies his product assortment by adding merchandise lines not traditionally carried by that type of institution. This practice, which started before World War II, has spread throughout the fields of retailing and wholesaling. Today it continues to show signs of increasing, rather than decreasing in intensity.

We have seen grocery supermarkets, as an illustration, add toiletries, drugs,

---

[2]Bert C. McCammon, Jr., "Alternative Explanations of Institutional Change and Channel Evolution," in Stephen A. Greyser (ed.), *Toward Scientific Marketing,* American Marketing Association, Chicago, 1964, pp. 477–490.

[3]For a conceptual model of conflict in channels of distribution and its effect on the efficiency of channel performance, see Bert Rosenbloom, "Conflict and Channel Efficiency: Some Conceptual Models for the Decision Maker," *Journal of Marketing,* July, 1973, pp. 26–30; and Larry J. Rosenberg and Louis W. Stern, "Toward the Analysis of Conflict in Distribution Channels: A Descriptive Model," *Journal of Marketing,* October, 1970, pp. 40–46.

clothing, magazines, small appliances, records, alcoholic beverages, and other nonfood lines. The retailers who traditionally sold these lines become irritated both at the grocery stores for diversifying and also at the manufacturers for using these "unorthodox" channels. The stimulus for product proliferation among middlemen and the crossing of traditional channel lines may come from three general sources—the market, the middleman, or the manufacturer.

Market-inspired. Preference for one-stop shopping and the trend toward self-service selling are two changes in consumer buying behavior which have encouraged the development of scrambled merchandising. Consumers want convenience in their shopping. They prefer to go to one store and buy food, toothpaste, and a couple of inexpensive cooking pans, for example, rather than having to visit three different retailers. Also, the consumer acceptance of—even preference for—self-selection of merchandise has acted as an incentive for many stores to add new product lines which lend themselves to self-service selling.

Middleman-inspired. The middleman's constant search for more profitable marketing methods has furnished an impetus to the growth of scrambled merchandising. A retailer, such as a food supermarket, operating on a gross margin of 18 to 20 percent is bound to be attracted to items such as drug sundries or housewares, where the margin may be about 30 percent.

Some retailers seek to increase their store traffic by adding new merchandise lines. Furniture stores have added small appliances, and jewelry stores have added records and gift items for this purpose. In other situations, any really new product is usually very attractive to all types of retailers who consider the item even remotely marketable in their store. Consequently, product innovation will continue as a big factor in the further scrambling of traditional product assortments.

A substantial segment of a middleman's total costs are fixed, and furthermore they are common to all products sold. That is, they cannot be identified directly with any given product, nor do they vary with sales volume in the short run. This cost factor is a real incentive for a retailer or wholesaler to add new product lines to broaden the base over which he can spread his fixed costs. This proliferation intensifies the degree of channel conflict.

Manufacturer-inspired. Sometimes the stimulus for scrambled merchandising comes from the manufacturer. Consider the manufacturers who have taken over the responsibility for repair service on their products. Appliance manufacturers used to be limited in the type and number of retailers they could use because it was essential that the dealer be prepared to service the appliances. Once the manufacturer assumes that responsibility, he can sell through many new types of retailers who formerly were not qualified.

In another situation, a manufacturer may add new products to his line and want new types of outlets so as not to antagonize his existing middlemen. Thus he keeps harmony in his present channels, but creates conflict in the new, nontraditional outlets. Finally, improvements in production technology may change the shape and location of a manufacturer's cost curve. His break-even point may be higher, or he may be in a position to decrease his unit costs considerably by increasing his output. In any event, the marketing department must find new markets (and thus possibly new types of middlemen) for the potential increase in output.

CONFLICT BETWEEN DIFFERENT LEVELS OF COMPETITION

Perhaps the most severe competitive conflicts in distribution systems today are of a vertical nature—that is, between retailer and wholesaler, between manufacturer and retailer, or between manufacturer and wholesaler. Retailers may make some sales to institutions and other industrial users, thus competing with wholesaling middlemen, as when stationery stores sell office supplies to other retail stores, for example. Producers compete with retailers by selling house-to-house, by selling through the manufacturers' own retail stores, or by selling at the point of production—at the factory or farm. Conflicts frequently develop between manufacturers and agent middlemen when manufacturers place their own sales forces in territories which were developed and heretofore covered by the agents. The remainder of this chapter is devoted to the vertical types of conflict.

WHO CONTROLS THE CHANNELS?

In marketing literature, authors have generally taken a manufacturer-oriented approach to channels of distribution. The implication is that the manufacturer is the one who makes the decisions regarding type of outlet, number of outlets, and even the selection of individual outlets. This is a one-sided point of view. Actually, the middleman has considerable freedom to make his own choices in establishing channels. "The selection of a multi-stage channel is not the prerogative of a manufacturer unless his franchise is coveted by the middlemen he seeks, as being more valuable to them than their franchise would be to him."[4] Certainly the name of Macy's, Safeway, Sears, and other strong retailers means more to the consumers than most of the brands sold in these stores. Large retailers today are challenging manufacturers for channel control, just as the manufacturers challenged the wholesaler fifty years ago. Even a small retailer may be influential in a local market, and his prestige may become greater than that of his suppliers. McVey observed: "In some instances his local strength is so great that a manufacturer is virtually unable to tap that market, except through him. In such a case the manufacturer can have no channel policy with respect to that market."

Actually, the questions of who is the channel leader and who *should* be remain largely unsettled.[5] The position supporting leadership by the manufacturer is production-oriented. He creates the new products, and he needs the increasing sales volume to derive the benefits of large-scale operations. A large retailer may use the same arguments, especially if he provides new-product ideas or specifica-

---

[4]Phillip McVey, "Are Channels of Distribution What the Textbooks Say?" *Journal of Marketing,* January, 1960, pp. 61–65; see also Robert W. Little, "The Marketing Channel: Who Should Lead This Extra-corporate Organization?" *Journal of Marketing,* January, 1970, pp. 31–38.

[5]This paragraph is adapted from Bruce Mallen, "Conflict and Cooperation in Marketing Channels," in L. George Smith (ed.), *Reflections on Progress in Marketing,* American Marketing Association, Chicago, 1965, pp. 74–77; see also Louis P. Bucklin, "A Theory of Channel Control," *Journal of Marketing,* January, 1973, pp. 39–47; David L. Wilemon, "Power and Negotiation Strategies in Marketing Channels," *Southern Journal of Business,* February, 1972, pp. 71–82; and Adel I. El-Ansary and Louis W. Stern, "Power Measurement in the Distribution Channel," *Journal of Marketing Research,* February, 1972, pp. 47–52.

tions. Also, one can argue that the retailer is the natural leader under the marketing concept—standing closest to the consumer, knowing his wants, and being his purchasing agent. Perhaps the best answer to the channel-control questions is a compromise—a balance of power should exist rather than a domination by any one level in the distribution channels.

MANUFACTURER VERSUS WHOLESALER

A significant channel conflict during the past half-century has been between the manufacturer and the wholesaler, as manufacturers have tried to bypass wholesalers and deal directly with retailers. Ordinarily, the battle is between the producers and wholesalers of manufactured *consumer* products. As a rule, it does not involve wholesaling middlemen for industrial products. There is a tradition of direct sale in the industrial field, and where middlemen are used, the need for their services has long been recognized. Nor does this conflict involve agent middlemen for consumer goods to any great extent. The relationships between a manufacturer and his agent middlemen are relatively peaceful for two reasons. First, these relationships are established on a temporary basis. Brokers work with a manufacturer only part of the year. Manufacturers' agents know in advance that they may lose their franchises as soon as the territory can support the manufacturer's sales force. Second, agent middlemen offer fewer services than wholesalers. This means that there are fewer areas of possible conflict with manufacturers.

HISTORICAL BACKGROUND OF THE CONFLICT

The clash of interests between wholesalers and manufacturers in the marketing of manufactured consumer products can be best understood by reviewing (1) the position of the wholesaler before 1920, (2) the changing position of the manufacturer over the years, (3) the changing position of the retailer since 1920, and (4) the net effect these changes have had on the wholesalers and manufacturers.

Historically, the wholesaler occupied a position of major importance in distribution systems. Before 1920, he was dominant because both manufacturers and retailers were small and poorly financed. In addition, retailers were widely dispersed over the entire country. In effect, the wholesaler served as the sales force of the manufacturer and as the purchasing agent for the retailer. In so doing, he granted credit to the retailers, an especially important service in the days when our economy was largely agricultural and cash was available only at harvesttime. He carried a wide assortment of products, even from competing manufacturers. Essentially he was an order taker; he did no aggressive selling, nor did he consider this his function.

As a result of the risks he took and the broad scale of his services, the wholesaler had high operating costs. To cover these costs he needed a wide margin of profit. Through the nineteenth century and the early part of the twentieth, wholesaler institutions suffered increasingly from inertia, a low caliber of management, and a lack of flexibility in management. The firms did not adjust to changing economic and social conditions. Thus we see the familiar picture of an organization which reaches a stage of maturity and faces little competition.

During the last half of the nineteenth century and the first part of the twentieth, the position of the manufacturer changed substantially. Manufacturing was becoming more efficient and production management was of a higher caliber. Furthermore, manufacturers were beginning to realize that it was better to make a small profit on the sale of many units than a wide margin on the sale of a few units. Manufacturers were quick to learn that the best means of achieving increased volume was through a change in marketing methods. Aggressive selling effort, lower prices, product identification through branding, and advertising were recognized as keys to mass markets. Once the manufacturer embarked upon these programs, he disliked giving wholesalers the customary wide margin on sales which his policies were stimulating.

After World War I, the position of the retailer changed considerably. Large-scale retailing institutions developed in great numbers, and retail markets became concentrated in geographic areas in and around metropolitan centers. New organizational forms, particularly the corporate chains, were developing. Large-scale operations entailed large buying power, well-financed retailers, and better-managed firms. Large-scale retailers also were economically able to assume many wholesaling functions. All these factors encouraged retailers to go directly to the manufacturers to purchase their merchandise.

Wholesalers were caught between large-scale, integrated retailers on the one hand and large-scale, direct-selling, integrated manufacturers on the other. The wholesaler saw his prestige being reduced, yet he realized that he could not afford to promote aggressively the products of any one manufacturer, and he resented any cut in his discount margin. By refusing to cooperate in the manufacturer's efforts to promote products to retailers and by installing his own brands of merchandise, the wholesaler further increased the conflict between himself and the manufacturer.

MANUFACTURERS' SIDE OF THE CONFLICT

Reasons for bypassing wholesalers. Basically, either because they are dissatisfied with the wholesalers' services or because of market conditions, manufacturers favor direct sale from manufacturer to retailer or to consumer.

Wholesalers' failure to promote products aggressively. Manufacturers charge that the wholesalers ordinarily will not aggressively promote the products of individual producers—that wholesalers are essentially order takers, not salesmen. To really sell a product, manufacturers say, wholesalers demand special incentives, such as larger discounts or exclusive territorial franchises.

Wholesalers agree that these charges leveled by the manufacturers are largely true. Generally speaking, all products are the same to the wholesaler, and he does not feel that it is his responsibility to promote those of one manufacturer over those of another. With the thousands of items typically carried by wholesalers, it is not possible for their salesmen even to *mention* each item to prospective customers, much less try to sell each one.

Wholesalers' failure to perform storage function. In some cases, manufacturers have eliminated wholesalers because they failed to provide the traditional storage services that producers were used to. Manufacturers have been forced to carry larger stocks and to bear a greater share of the market risk. Several factors have encouraged wholesalers to reduce their storage services and to buy on a hand-to-mouth basis. Improved transportation and communication services, for example, make it possible for wholesalers to get necessary merchandise much more quickly today than in years gone by.

Development of wholesalers' own brands. Also adding to manufacturers' desire to bypass the wholesaler is the fact that many middlemen are aggressively promoting their own brands in direct competition with manufacturers' brands.

Manufacturers' desire for close market contact. Manufacturers sometimes bypass wholesalers in an attempt to control their products over a greater proportion of the distance from producer to ultimate consumer or industrial user. This interest on the part of the manufacturer is particularly evident where installing, servicing, and repairing the product play a significant role in the product's sales success. Furthermore, by eliminating the wholesaler, the manufacturer can better learn how his product is moving in the market and what the consumer's reaction to it is.

Need for rapid physical distribution. If products are subject to physical perishability or fashion obsolescence, it may be essential to reduce the channels to the shortest length possible. Where fashion obsolescence is concerned, it is far too slow and risky to distribute through wholesalers. For products such as women's ready-to-wear or millinery, orders are frequently placed by telephone and shipped by airplane.

Cost of wholesalers' services. One of the biggest pitfalls in the marketing process is the assumption that manufacturers can perform the traditional wholesaling functions at a lower cost. Many producers have learned the hard way that bypassing the wholesaler may actually increase the cost of marketing or result in poor market coverage. Eliminating the wholesaler results in economy only if the manufacturer and/or the retailer can perform the wholesaler's functions more effectively. Even when his research shows that costs will be lowered by eliminating wholesalers, the producer should still investigate further to determine whether the wholesaling services will be performed adequately and whether his long-range market and profit position will be improved.

Preference of retailers for buying directly. Many retailers believe that they can get lower prices on merchandise, more advertising allowances, and better service and merchandise selection if they deal directly with manufacturers. Usually the retailers who prefer to buy directly are large-scale enterprises. Consequently, manufacturers seek their business and try to meet their needs.

Courses of action open to manufacturers. If a manufacturer wishes to bypass wholesalers, he has three major alternative channels: He may sell directly to the retailer, he may establish sales offices or branches and sell directly through them to the retailer, or he may bypass the retailer as well as the wholesaler and sell directly to the ultimate consumer. If a manufacturer prefers to use a wholesaler but needs more aggressive selling, he may employ a group of missionary salesmen.

Whatever alternative channel of distribution is used in lieu of wholesalers, direct selling inevitably places a greater financial burden on the manufacturer and adds immeasurably to his management problems. He must operate a sales force, handle the phsyical distribution of the product, and operate a credit system. Direct selling does not normally result in as intensive a market coverage as wholesalers can provide. Manufacturers are also faced with small-order problems. Finally, once a manufacturer embarks upon a program of direct selling, he must be ready to face competition from his former wholesalers who are now pushing competitive products.

Sell directly to retailers. A decision to sell directly to retailers without the use of sales offices or branches should be based on the situation surrounding five factors. The first is the *market.* An ideal retail market for direct selling is one made up of large-scale retailers who are geographically concentrated, who buy in large quantities, and who maintain central buying offices. Thus we find such retail organizations as corporate chains, mail-order houses, and voluntary chains buying directly from manufacturers. In addition, a manufacturer may establish profitable direct-sale arrangements with specialty stores. While the volume of a specialty store may not be so great as that of a department store or supermarket, the specialty store nevertheless presents an attractive volume outlet in its limited product line. Frequently a shoe store, a clothing store, or a retailer of photographic equipment and supplies will have a sales volume greater than that of a corresponding department in a department store.

The *product* considerations which make direct sale possible or in some cases even necessary are (1) physical or fashion perishability, (2) high unit value or high gross margin, (3) demand for custom-made or specially constructed products, (4) importance of mechanical servicing or installation, (5) manufacturer's output consisting of a full line of related products, and (6) large total order.

Adequately qualified marketing executives are usually a prerequisite for a successful direct-selling program. When circumventing a wholesaler, a manufacturer creates countless managerial problems with respect to operating a sales force.

In direct selling, preferably both the manufacturer and the retailer should have *financial strength*. If the manufacturer employs a field selling force, the financial requirements will be especially heavy. Also, someone must take over the credit risks and responsibilities previously assumed by the wholesalers.

Sometimes a manufacturer can eliminate a wholesaler only if there are excellent *physical distribution facilities* for the product. The existence of public warehouses, for instance, may enable a manufacturer to perform the storage function normally handled by wholesalers.

Open sales offices or branches. Salesmen working out of sales offices or branches under decentralized management may be desirable when:

1. There is a concentrated market for the product.
2. The manufacturer has a large sales force and needs to supervise it closely.
3. The company places greater emphasis on personal selling than on advertising in its promotional program.
4. There is a need to install, service, and repair the product.
5. Customers demand rapid, economic delivery, and the company does not want to use public warehouses.

Executives in a manufacturing establishment should recognize that branch organizational structures raise major financial and operating problems. Not only are operating costs higher because of duplication of manpower and effort, but there is also the fixed cost attendant upon the investment in the branch plant and equipment. Operating decisions must be made regarding which functions will be decentralized and which will be handled in the home office. For instance, who is to have the authority and responsibility for hiring, training, promoting, and firing salesmen? Who is to have the authority to grant credit and to change prices?

On balance, the statement made by Professor Tosdal many years ago still seems pertinent. He said, "If there is any general rule to be applied to the establishment of branch organizations, it is to the effect that the burden of proof is upon those who advocate establishment of branches rather than upon those who oppose such extensions.[6]

Sell directly to consumer. Various distribution methods may be used to make this short channel effective (see Chapter 16). The producer may employ personal nonstore selling (house-to-house) or mail-order selling. He may establish retail stores, or he may sell directly to the consumer at the point of production—the factory, farm, boat dock, or some other location.

Use missionary salesmen. When a manufacturer wants to use a wholesaler but also wants to have the advantages of aggressive selling, he may employ missionary salesmen. Also known as promotional salesmen, detail men, or factory representatives, they perform a number of services and may be used under several different conditions. Typically, missionary salesmen call upon a retailer and aggressively promote the product of the manufacturer. If the salesman secures any orders, he passes them on to the jobber, and the jobber receives his normal commission. Missionary salesmen may be used to install point-of-purchase displays in retail stores or to introduce new items to retailers. Sometimes these salesmen are called in to close difficult sales which wholesalers have not been able to handle themselves. These factory representatives may train retail salesmen, particularly when technical product information is necessary. They may also seek new accounts and stand ready to handle complaints. Because using this sales force is a step short of establishing a sales office or branch, it is less expensive and presents fewer management problems.

WHOLESALERS' SIDE OF THE CONFLICT

The wholesaler in his turn is often dissatisfied with the actions of the manufacturer. Marketing administrators should understand the wholesaler's complaints and evaluate the alternatives open to wholesalers who want to meet the competitive threat of being bypassed.

Reasons for wholesalers' dissatisfaction. Some of the reasons wholesalers are unhappy with manufacturers are implicit in our earlier discussion. The sample of grievances stated here should establish the tenor of the wholesalers' objections.

---

[6]Harry R. Tosdal, *Introduction to Sales Management,* 4th ed., McGraw-Hill Book Company, New York, 1957, p. 513.

Manufacturers fail to understand true role of wholesalers. From the wholesaler's point of view, probably the main irritant is the manufacturer's failure to understand or accept the fact that the primary obligation of the wholesaler is to serve his customers. The wholesaler's responsibility as a service agent for the manufacturer is only secondary.

Manufacturers expect too much. Wholesalers often feel that manufacturers' expectations with regard to warehousing and other services are far greater than the wholesalers' discounts justify. As explained earlier, the wholesaler is in no position to promote individual products aggressively, nor can he push point-of-purchase displays and other promotional material.

Manufacturers skim cream off market. Wholesalers note that often they are used only in the early stages of territorial development. Then, when the market is intensively cultivated, the manufacturers bypass them and deal directly. Wholesalers also note that manufacturers often use middlemen only in the least profitable segments of the market. In the concentrated, fertile segments, producers sell directly to retailers or industrial users. While this observation is accurate, the wholesaler should understand that his real worth lies in being able to reach markets which the manufacturer himself cannot penetrate profitably.

Manufacturers sell to retailers who use their own brands. Manufacturers often sell products to retailers who place their private brands on the product. Wholesalers object to this practice because these products compete with the manufacturers' own brands carried by the wholesaler. Here perhaps the wholesalers are tilting at windmills. Retailers who sell under their own brand names are large-scale organizations. If one manufacturer refuses to sell them, they will get the merchandise from another. And in any event, their brands will still be in the market competing with those carried by the wholesaler.

Courses of action open to wholesalers. Wholesalers have taken several measures to improve their competitive position and to meet the threat of being eliminated. All these measures attempt (1) to improve efficiency to such an extent that neither suppliers nor customers can find more desirable means of accomplishing marketing tasks and (2) to tie retailers to the wholesaler in one way or another.

Improve internal management. Many wholesalers have modernized their establishments and upgraded the caliber of their management. These have been refreshing changes. New, functional single-story warehouses have been built outside the congested downtown areas, and mechanized physical-handling equipment has been installed. In the office, computers and machine accounting systems have streamlined the inventory and accounting controls and have thus reduced losses from obsolete, slow-moving items.

Many wholesalers have added limited-function departments and have otherwise increased the flexibility of their operations. Another cost-cutting, efficiency-inducing factor has been the adoption of selective selling. That is, less profitable accounts are visited less frequently, and really low-profit accounts may be solicited only by mail or telephone.

These and other innovations have generally had the effect of lowering operating costs or of giving the retailer far better service for the same money. Much remains to be done, of course. Activities related to managing the sales force, for instance, have not kept pace with improvements in clerical operations and in the physical handling of products.

Provide management assistance for retailers. Wholesalers are coming to realize that their success is totally dependent upon the success of their small, independent retail customers. Therefore, anything the wholesalers do to improve the retailers' operations is really in their own self-interest. Management guidance for retailers may take several forms. Using their own salesmen or other field employees as management advisers, wholesalers can help retailers choose store locations, improve their store layouts, and install better accounting and inventory processes. They can help retail store operators do a better job of selecting, displaying, and promoting their merchandise.

Form voluntary chains. Voluntary chains of retailers formed by wholesalers have proved to be an effective device for meeting the competitive challenges in channels of distribution. This structure was discussed in Chapter 16. In a voluntary chain, a wholesaler enters into a contract with several retailers, agreeing to furnish them with management services and large-volume buying advantages. In turn, the retailers agree to do all or almost all their buying from the wholesaler.

Develop and promote own brands. Many large wholesalers have successfully established their own brands. If a wholesaler is connected with a voluntary chain of retailers, the chain provides the wholesaler's brand with a built-in market. Private brands help the retailers, too, because consumers cannot easily compare private-brand prices with those of manufacturers' brands carried in other stores.

Seek legislative aid. A final method used by wholesalers to meet the competition of other institutions is to seek legislative aid at the state or federal level. While the author does not recommend this method as a long-run salvation of the wholesaler, it seems to be a favorite choice of many wholesalers. Wholesaler organizations were instrumental in getting the Robinson-Patman Act passed, and they also fought vigorously for the passage of state fair-trade and unfair-practices laws. (These laws are discussed in Chapters 13 and 14.) One intent of these laws was to neutralize the large-scale buying power of giant retailers, such as corporate chains and large, independent department stores. As noted in the discussion of retailing institutions, a fundamental error made by many middlemen—wholesalers and retailers alike—is to believe that the only advantage corporate chains have over small independents is large buying power. Even if all stores bought merchandise at the same price, the other advantages of large-scale enterprises would clearly enable them to out-compete the smaller merchants.

In the author's opinion, legislative aid can help the wholesaler only temporarily. It obscures his basic problems and therefore postpones their effective long-range solution. The wholesaler's real salvation and opportunity for growth lie in his ability to improve the internal management of his establishment and to help the small-scale retailer become a more effective institution.

FUTURE OF THE WHOLESALER

In the 1930s, it was frequently forecast that the full-function merchant wholesaler was a dying institution. Statistics in Chapter 17 and elsewhere, however, show that the merchant wholesaler enjoyed a resurgent growth rate during the past 35 years—a growth rate quite comparable to that in the gross national product. While shifts will continue to occur within the wholesaling structure, the full-function wholesaler today holds a strong and significant position in the economy.

There are two basic reasons for the comeback of the merchant wholesaler. One is a fuller realization of the true economic worth of his services. The other is the general improvement of his management methods and operations. The bandwagon to eliminate the wholesaler proved to be a blessing in disguise. Innumerable firms tried to bypass the wholesaler and came to realize that the net result was unsatisfactory. They could not perform some of the wholesaling functions at all, or they found the cost prohibitive. In many cases, it became evident that the wholesaler was able to provide the manufacturers and retailers with better services, and to provide them at a lower cost, than these firms themselves could.

Wholesalers are still the controlling force in the channels used by many firms. We must not conclude, however, that only low-cost wholesalers can survive in the competitive market. Even seemingly high-cost wholesalers are thriving. A high operating cost ratio is not necessarily a result of inefficiency. Instead, it is usually a result of more and better service. Many wholesalers' costs are high only because they offer an established distribution system (granted, it may be nonaggressive) and many other services which ease the producers' marketing and financial burdens.

Growth in the wholesaling sector also reflects the emergence of new industrial and institutional markets where the demand for wholesaling services is high. There also has been a shift in the wholesaler's traditional role as a middleman for standardized products to one who participates in the marketing of complex products requiring extensive inventories and selling effort. At the same time, mass-marketing practices have not proved as applicable in wholesaling as in retailing. Possibly the future for small-scale middlemen lies more in wholesaling than in retailing.[7]

Wholesalers, admittedly slow to adopt modern business methods and attitudes, are striving to catch up in this respect. Moreover, the already evident trends shaping the future of wholesale distribution suggest that (1) the wholesaler is responsive to his environment and (2) he can effectively adapt to pressures from both suppliers and customers for lower-cost distribution. Indications are that wholesalers will continue to interpret and respond to these pressures.[8]

MANUFACTURER VERSUS RETAILER

Today, perhaps even more significant than the conflict between manufacturers and wholesalers is the struggle for channel control which goes on between manufacturers and retailers. A very basic reason for the conflict is this: *"The*

---

[7]This paragraph is adapted from Louis P. Bucklin, "National Income Accounting and Distributive Trade Cost," *Journal of Marketing,* April, 1970, pp. 14–22, especially pp. 21–22.

[8]See Richard S. Lopata, "Faster Pace in Wholesaling," *Harvard Business Review,* July–August, 1969, pp. 130–143.

people who manufacture the goods and the people who move the goods into the hands of the ultimate consumer do not share the same business philosophy and do not talk essentially the same language."[9] In manufacturing corporations, an executive's point of view is typically characterized as a psychology of *growth*. His goals are essentially dynamic and evolving. He is forever climbing to the top and is not content to rest on past accomplishments. In sharp contrast, the psychology of the small and medium-sized retailer is essentially *static* in nature. His goals are well defined and are far more circumscribed than those of the manufacturing corporation executive. At some point the retailer levels off into a continuously satisfying plateau.

DOMINATION VERSUS COOPERATION

In the struggle each group has weapons it can use in its efforts to dominate. A manufacturer can use his promotional program to build a strong consumer preference for his product. Legal weapons are available to him in the form of franchise contracts, consignment selling, or outright ownership of the retail store. As a negative method of dominating, the manufacturer may refuse to sell to uncooperative retailers. Suggestive devices such as premarking the price on products or advertising the resale price are weaker control methods.

Retailers are not necessarily unarmed in this situation. By effective advertising programs or by establishing their own brands, they can develop consumer preferences for their stores. A retailer can either concentrate his purchases with one supplier or spread his buying among many sources, depending upon the number of manufacturers involved and which strategy is most effective for him.

On the other side of the coin, fortunately, channel members seem to realize that the returns from cooperating with one another do outweigh any reasons for conflict. Perhaps manufacturers and retailers alike understand that it is in their own best interests to treat a distribution channel as a total system—to consider a channel an extension (forward or backward, as the case may be) of their own internal organizations.[10] To implement this concept, a manufacturer should do the sort of thing for a retailer that he does for his own marketing organization. That is, the manufacturer can provide advertising aids, training for dealer salesmen, managerial assistance, etc. Retailers can reciprocate by carrying adequate inventories, promoting the product, and building consumer goodwill. (These methods of mutual cooperation are elaborated on in the following chapter.)

Dual distribution. The increased use of one form of dual distribution is another real source of conflict between manufacturers and retailers. Broadly defined, *dual distribution* is the practice whereby a supplier uses more than one type of channel or marketing organization to distribute his product. We are concerned here with the type of dual distribution in which a manufacturer sells the same brand, or two brands of basically the same product, to the same market through *competing* channel networks. A paint manufacturer, for instance, may distribute

---

[9]Warren J. Wittreich, "Misunderstanding the Retailer," *Harvard Business Review*, May–June, 1962, p. 147. The balance of the paragraph is drawn from this article.

[10]For additional insight on this point, see Valentine F. Ridgeway, "Administration of Manufacturer-Dealer Systems," *Administrative Science Quarterly*, March, 1957, pp. 464–483; and Peter Drucker, "The Economy's Dark Continent," *Fortune*, April, 1962, p. 103.

through a series of retail stores which he owns, at the same time using conventional channels of independent paint wholesalers and retailers—all aiming at the same market. The general practice is not new. For years it has been carried on by oil companies, tire manufacturers, and paint companies. But what is new is the surge in its growth and its adoption in industries heretofore generally untouched.[11]

The impetus for this growth is coming from several sources. In many industries, increasing competition has spurred manufacturers to open their own stores in markets where no satisfactory outlet is available. Some manufacturers establish their own stores as testing grounds for new products and marketing techniques. In suburban markets, small retailers often do not have the financial resources to open a store in shopping centers. Consequently, many large manufacturers must open their own stores in these centers if they want suitable outlets.

VERTICAL MARKETING SYSTEMS

The traditional marketing channel structure hardly deserved to be called a system. The channels for many products were dominated by small and medium-sized firms, each operating independently as profit-seeking, short-run–oriented units. Manufacturers, wholesalers, and retailers frequently competed and conflicted with each other. The net result often was an inefficient, effort-duplicating situation.

Institutional changes in distribution during the past 20 to 30 years have led to the development of vertical marketing systems.[12] In contrast with the traditional individualistic structures, the newer vertical marketing systems offer significant economies of scale and increased coordination in distribution. They also eliminate the duplication of marketing services, providing instead for the singular performance of any given marketing activity at the most advantageous position in the system.

Vertical marketing systems are characterized as corporate, administered, or contractual (see Fig. 18-1). In *corporate vertical marketing systems* the production and marketing facilities are owned by the same company. As manufacturers, for example, Hart, Schaffner & Marx and the Sherwin-Williams paint company each operate a number of their own retail stores. Many large food chains own some processing facilities. Sears has ownership interests in manufacturing firms which supply Sears. In these integrated systems, to refer to the corporate owner as a manufacturer or a retailer oversimplifies the realities of the situation.

In *administered vertical marketing systems* the necessary coordination of production and marketing activities is achieved essentially through the domination of one powerful channel member. This type of distribution is exemplified by Magnavox in home entertainment, Samsonite in luggage, Coors beer in its Western regional markets, Scott Company in lawn products, General Electric, and General Foods. The manufacturer's brand and market position are strong enough to get the voluntary administrative cooperation of retailers in matters of advertising, pricing, and store display.

---

[11]See Lee E. Preston and Arthur E. Schramm, Jr., "Dual Distribution and Its Impact on Marketing Organization," *California Management Review,* Winter, 1965, pp. 59–70.

[12]Much in this section is drawn from the works of Prof. Bert C. McCammon, Jr., of the University of Oklahoma.

Type of network	Control maintained by	Examples
Corporate	Ownership	Hart, Schaffner & Marx clothes Sherwin-Williams paints
Administered	Economic power	Coors beer, Scott lawn products, Samsonite luggage, General Electric
Contractual		
{ Wholesaler-sponsored voluntary chain	Contract	IGA, Super Valu (food stores) Ace Hardware
Retailer-owned cooperative	Stock ownership by retailers	Associated Grocers
Franchise systems	Contract	Auto dealers
{ Manufacturer-sponsored retailers		
Manufacturer-sponsored wholesalers		Soft-drink bottlers
Marketers of services		McDonald's, Hertz, Avis, Fred Astaire, Howard Johnson, Holiday Inn

Figure 18-1. Types of vertical marketing systems.

In *contractual vertical marketing systems,* independent institutions—producers, wholesalers, and retailers—are banded together by contracts to achieve the necessary economic size and coordination of effort. Three types of contractual systems can be identified: wholesaler-sponsored voluntary chains, retailers-owned cooperatives, and franchise systems. All three were discussed in Chapter 16.

Among the major types of vertical marketing systems—corporate, administered, and contractual—the most rapid rate of growth during the past 20 to 30 years has been in the contractually integrated networks.

To conclude, in this chapter we have taken a macro point of view as we studied the constantly evolving, dynamic competitive conflict and cooperation occurring in distribution systems. In the next chapter we shall return to our microanalysis and examine the process by which marketing executives select a channel of distribution and establish working relationships with individual middlemen.

QUESTIONS AND PROBLEMS

1. There is an increase in "scrambled merchandising" on the retail level of distribution. What effect will this trend have on wholesaling middlemen?
2. "Large manufacturers always control the channels used to reach local markets." Do you agree? In your college community, are there big manufacturers who are unable to tap the market except through local independent retailers?
3. Explain the role played by each of the following factors in the conflict between manufacturers and wholesalers, particularly in the marketing of consumer products:
   a. Traditional position of the wholesaler before 1920
   b. Changing position of the manufacturer since the late 1800s
   c. Changing position of the retailer since 1920
4. Why is there considerably less friction between manufacturers and wholesalers in the industrial goods field than in the consumer goods field?
5. Explain the reasons why the manufacturer is dissatisfied with the performance of the wholesaler. Do you agree with the manufacturer's point of view?
6. What can a manufacturer do to stimulate wholesalers into performing a more aggressive, effective job of promoting the manufacturer's products?
7. Use examples to explain how bypassing a wholesaler will sometimes *increase* the cost of marketing.
8. Why are regular wholesalers relatively unimportant in the marketing of women's high-fashion wearing apparel, furniture, and large electrical equipment?
9. "The use of missionary salesmen is a compromise between the use of a wholesaler and the elimination of the wholesaler." Discuss this idea, showing how missionary salesmen may offset manufacturers' objections to wholesalers.
10. In the channel conflict, what are the wholesaler's reasons for being dissatisfied with the manufacturer? Assuming you are the manufacturer, what would be your rebuttal to these points?
11. In one region of the country, a general merchandise wholesaler had been supplying small, independent variety stores for years. Recently, two of the national limited-price variety chains entered the area and are giving the inde-

pendents some stiff competition. Should this general merchandise wholesaler establish his own voluntary chain, signing up as members his present independent retail accounts? Would your recommendation be the same if the field were hardware stores? Stores selling low-priced shoes for the entire family?

12. "The future of the wholesaler depends upon his ability to increase his own efficiency and to furnish managerial aids to his retailers." Discuss, pointing out the alternatives if the wholesaler fails to meet this challenge.

13. What marketing conditions might encourage a manufacturer to adopt a policy of dual distribution at the retail level?

14. What are some of the problems a manufacturer is likely to encounter if he decides to set up his own retail stores?

15. What penalties can a manufacturer level at a retailer who is not living up to this manufacturer's expectations?

DESIGNING AND MANAGING CHANNELS OF DISTRIBUTION

Marketing executives frequently find that designing channels for their products and solving the problems connected with channel management are among their most difficult tasks. In part this difficulty is traceable to the dynamic nature of the distribution structure and its propensity for change. Competitive conflicts constantly call for attention and sometimes force channel adjustments. Long channels compound a producer's problem because he is far from his ultimate consumers or users. Also, frequently he has little or no control over his middlemen and cannot get from them necessary market information regarding his markets and products.

Three steps are involved in this decision-making phase of the marketing process. First, a manufacturer must select the general channel to be used, keeping in mind the goals of the company's marketing program and the job to be done by means of the distribution system. Second, assuming he is going to use middlemen, he must make a decision regarding the *number* of middlemen or the intensity of distribution to be used at each level and in each market. Finally, again assuming he will use middlemen, he must select the specific firms which will handle his product, and then manage the day-to-day working relationships with them.

Only infrequently—as when a new company is started or when an established firm introduces a new product or enters a new market—will a marketing manager establish a distribution system from the ground up. The more usual task of channel management involves a continuing evaluation, and possibly a reorganization, of the existing structure.

You may have noted that the task of establishing channels is approached from the manufacturer's or producer's point of view. Middlemen also face channel problems similar to those of a producer. Furthermore, the control of the channels used by manufacturers and the freedom of choice regarding these channels may actually rest with middlemen. Simply as a framework for analysis in this chapter, however, channel policies and strategies will be studied from the vantage point of the producer.

MAJOR CHANNELS OF DISTRIBUTION

Actually there are several alternative channels, and in most industries each alternative is used by at least a few firms. Even to describe the major channels used for consumer products and for industrial goods is risky because it may suggest an orthodoxy which does not exist. Nevertheless, that risk is taken in the following section, which outlines the most frequently used channels for the two major classes of products. These channels are illustrated in Fig. 19-1.

DISTRIBUTION OF CONSUMER GOODS

Five channels are widely used in the marketing of consumer products. In each, the manufacturer also has the alternative of using sales branches or sales offices. Some students will justifiably conclude that consideration of these institutions triples the number of alternatives. Furthermore, whenever wholesalers are used, goods may be distributed from one large wholesaler to several subjobbers and then to retailers, thus placing two wholesaling links in the chain. Obviously, our suggestion that there are only five major channels is an oversimplification, but one which seems necessary if we are going to discuss this unwieldy subject in a few paragraphs.

Producer—consumer. The shortest, simplest channel of distribution for consumer products is from the producer to the consumer, with no middlemen involved. The producer may sell from house to house, as many dairies and some agricultural producers do, or he may sell by mail.

Producer—retailer—consumer. Many large retailers buy directly from manufacturers and agricultural producers. Also, some manufacturers—the Sherwin-Williams Paint Company, the Bond Clothing Company, and the Florsheim division of the International Shoe Company, for example—have established their own retail stores, although this is not a common practice.

Producer—wholesaler—retailer—consumer. If there is a "traditional" channel for consumer goods, this is it. As was noted in preceding chapters, small retailers and small manufacturers by the thousands find this channel the only economically feasible choice.

Producer—agent—retailer—consumer. Instead of using wholesalers, many producers prefer to use a manufacturers' agent, selling agent, broker, or another agent middleman to reach the retail market, especially *large scale* retailers. A manufacturer of a glass cleaner selected a food broker to reach the grocery store

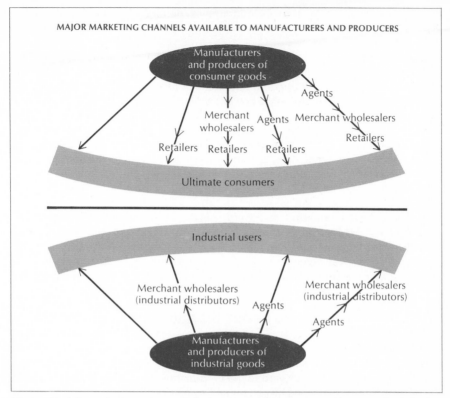

Figure 19–1. In each channel, a manufacturer or producer may use his own sales branches or personnel to reach the next institution. The channel leading directly from producer to consumer at the upper left of the diagram represents door-to-door selling and direct mail. In any channel, two levels of merchant wholesalers may be involved—one wholesaler sells the product to another wholesaler.

market, including the large chains. A manufacturer of a line of fishing lures used manufacturers' agents to reach sporting goods stores, hardware stores, and other retailing institutions.

Producer—agent—wholesaler—retailer—consumer. When trying to reach *small* retailers, the producers mentioned in the preceding paragraph often use agent middlemen, who in turn go to wholesalers who sell to small stores.

DISTRIBUTION OF INDUSTRIAL PRODUCTS

Four types of channels are widely used in reaching industrial users. Again, a manufacturer may use a sales branch or a sales office to reach the next institution in the channel, or two levels of wholesalers may be used in some cases (see Fig. 19–1).

Producer—industrial user. This direct channel accounts for a greater *dollar* volume of industrial products than any other distribution structure. Manufacturers of large installations, such as locomotives, generators, and heating plants, usually sell directly to the users.

Producer—industrial distributor—user. Producers of operating supplies and small accessory equipment frequently use industrial distributors to reach their markets. Manufacturers of building materials, construction equipment, and air-conditioning equipment are only a few examples of firms which make heavy use of the industrial distributor.

Producer—agent—user. Firms without their own marketing departments find this a desirable channel. Also, a company which wants to introduce a new product or enter a new market may prefer to use agents rather than its own sales force.

Producer—agent—industrial distributor—user. This channel is similar to the preceding one, except that for some reason it is not feasible to go through agents directly to the industrial user. Probably the unit sale is too small to sell directly, or perhaps decentralized inventories are needed to supply the users rapidly. In such cases, the storage services of the industrial distributor are required.

SOME GENERALIZATIONS ABOUT DISTRIBUTION CHANNELS

A few broad generalizations may serve as a guide to management in its task of developing channels of distribution. First, channel analysis should begin with the final customer and work backward to the producer because, essentially, channels of distribution are determined by consumer buying habits. This point, of course, is in complete alignment with the philosophy of the marketing concept. Thus if a significant percentage of the potential customers wish to buy on credit or prefer to shop in the evenings, the manufacturer should see to it that the retail section of the channels includes the appropriate outlets.

A second generalization is that the channels finally established must be totally appropriate to the basic objectives of the firm's marketing program. If the company's goal is to render the best possible servicing for its complex industrial product, then a short channel should be used. If management sees as its goal the widest possible distribution of its product line, then obviously an exclusive franchise policy at the retail level is *not* appropriate.

Third, the channels should provide a firm with access to a predetermined share of the market. A manufacturer of golfing equipment seeking as broad a market as possible made a mistake in establishing channels which included only department stores and sporting goods stores at the retail level. The executives should also have considered a channel which would reach discount houses and the professional shops at country clubs, as well as the major trading-stamp companies that included the products in their premium catalogues.

Fourth, the channels must be adequately flexible so that the use of one channel will not permanently close off another. A manufacturer of small appliances (irons, toasters, etc.) distributed only through appliance wholesalers and then to appliance retailers. The company had an offer from a drug chain to buy the products directly from the manufacturer. The appliance retailers threatened to discontinue the line if the manufacturer placed it in drugstores, and the producer decided to turn down the drug chain's offer. Subsequently, a competitive manufacturer accepted a similar offer and profited considerably.

A fifth point to keep in mind is that there is a high degree of interdependence among all firms in the channel for any given product. There can be no weak link in the chain if it is to be successful. In effect, each firm in the channel becomes his brother's keeper. Manufacturers using wholesalers are only as good as the wholesalers. Wholesalers, in turn, are successful only if their retailers do well.

A sixth observation is that evolutionary changes are constantly occurring. Channels of distribution and middlemen are always on trial. Sometimes in the course of categorizing institutional middlemen a person may succumb to the notion that markets are segmented or otherwise protected so that the different types of middlemen do not compete with one another. Actually, there is considerable competition, and this is one of the economic forces making for constant change.

Two other generalizations are corollaries of the preceding one. Middlemen survive only when their existence is economically sound and socially desirable. Nobody subsidizes a middleman if he does not serve well. Furthermore, new middlemen and channels arise to do new jobs or to do those which are not being done well.

FACTORS AFFECTING CHOICE OF CHANNELS OF DISTRIBUTION

In the course of making decisions with respect to its channels of distribution, management should carefully analyze its market, its products, its middlemen, and the company itself.

MARKET CONSIDERATIONS

Because channels of distribution should be determined by customer buying patterns, the nature of the market is the key factor influencing choice of channels.

Consumer or industrial market. The most obvious point to consider is whether the product is intended for the consumer or the industrial market. If it is going to the industrial market, retailers will not be included in the channel. If it is going to both markets, the company will want to use more than one channel.

Number of potential customers. A large potential market is likely to necessitate the use of middlemen. If the market is relatively small in numbers of customers, the company may be able to use its own sales force to sell direct. A related consideration is the number of different industries to which the company sells. A firm selling drilling equipment and supplies only to the oil industry used its own sales force and sold directly to the users. One reason for this channel choice was the relative narrowness of the market. (Incidentally, this company also maintained a few sales branches in order to have the centralized stocks or parts and supplies readily available for its customers.) For a paper products manufacturer, this aspect of the market led to an opposite decision. The company's products were ultimately sold to many different industries and to many firms in each industry. Consequently, the manufacturer made extensive use of industrial distributors.

Geographic concentration of market. Firms selling to the textile or the garment industry will find that a large proportion of the buyers are concentrated in a few geographic areas. Direct sale is more feasible that it would be if the market were spread over the entire nation. Even when a market is truly national, some segments have a higher density rate than others. There are more potential customers for office machines in Chicago than in Chattanooga. In densely populated markets, a seller may establish sales offices or branches, but he will decide to use middlemen in markets where the numbers of potential customers are less heavily concentrated. A company selling hard-rock mining equipment has a geographically concentrated market, and direct sale is feasible. On the other hand, the same company may sell drills, compressors, and other construction equipment to contractors all over the country. Here the lack of a geographically concentrated market, or of market segments with high density rates, forces the company to use industrial distributors.

Order size. The volume of sales to individual firms will influence the channels used to reach these companies. A food products manufacturer will sell directly to large grocery chains because the total volume of business makes this channel economically desirable. The same manufacturer cannot sell to small grocery stores in sufficient quantities to warrant direct sale, so wholesalers will be used because they afford a larger volume potential. One reason industrial operating supplies are typically sold through industrial distributors is that the volume purchased by most individual users is too small to justify direct sales.

Customer buying habits. The buying habits of ultimate consumers and industrial users—the amount of effort the consumer is willing to expend, the desire for credit, the preference for one-stop shopping, and the desire for the services of a personal salesman—all significantly affect channel policies.

PRODUCT CONSIDERATIONS

Unit value. The unit value of a product influences the amount of funds available for distribution. Usually, the lower the unit value, the longer the channels of distribution. In contrast, if the product is of high unit value, more funds are derived from each unit sold, and the company is more apt to use shorter, more costly channels. This is one reason why installation-type industrial products are sold direct, while small accessory equipment usually goes through industrial distributors or agents. However, when products of low unit value are sold in large quantities or are combined with other goods so that the total unit *sale* is large, shorter channels may be feasible.

Bulk and weight. Management must consider the cost of freight and handling in relation to the total value of the product. A producer of a heavy, bulky item, where freight is a significant part of the total value, will seek to minimize the physical handling of the product and will prefer to ship in carload or truckload quantities. This is one reason drop shippers are used in the marketing of coal and building materials. Although the title may go through middlemen, the physical product is shipped directly to the industrial user or retailer.

Perishability. Products subject to physical or fashion perishability must be speeded through their channels. Typically the channels are short. If middlemen are used for physically perishable products, they may be selected because of their special storage facilities. Manufacturers of nonperishables have wider choices in channel selection. They can offer better guarantees to middlemen and normally will find more middlemen willing to carry their goods.

Technical nature of a product and servicing required. An industrial product which is highly technical often will be distributed directly to the industrial user. The manufacturer must have salesmen and servicemen who can explain the product to potential customers and who can provide considerable presale and postsale service. Wholesalers normally cannot do this. Consumer products of a technical nature provide a real distribution challenge for the manufacturer. Ordinarily he cannot sell the goods directly to the consumer. As much as possible, he will try to sell directly to retailers, and even then the servicing of the product often poses problems.

Custom-made versus standardized products. This factor is somewhat related to the preceding one. If a product is custom-made, it will probably be distributed directly from producer to ultimate consumer or industrial user. One important exception is found in tailor-made consumer products, such as home furnishings, where retailers are widely used. In these instances, the retailers do not carry merchandise stock. They have samples and catalogues from which consumers may order.

Extent of product line. A manufacturer's channel choice is influenced appreciably by the *extent* of his product line. In the field of home appliances, for example, a firm is almost required to produce a full line of products if it wishes to secure desirable wholesalers and retailers. In other instances, the broader the line, the shorter may be the channel. The manufacturer with only one item may have to use wholesaling middlemen, whereas he could go directly to retailers if he had several products which could be combined in one large sale. Again using the appliance field as an example, a retailer ordinarily cannot buy a carload of washing machines alone, but he might buy a carload of mixed appliances.

COMPANY CONSIDERATIONS

Probably the one factor which tells most about a company and has the greatest influence on channel policies is its size. The company that has been successful enough to become large is almost certain to have financial strength, capable management, the ability to provide services for middlemen, and a desire to control the channel for its product. Given comparable market and product considerations, a large firm is more apt to have shorter channels than a small enterprise.

Financial resources. A financially strong company needs middlemen less than one which is financially weak. A business with adequate finances can establish its own sales force. It can also grant credit or warehouse its own products, whereas a weak firm would have to use middlemen to obtain these services.

A financially weak firm may deal directly with retailers or industrial users if they can take the entire output of the plant. Some large chains have such working agreements with manufacturers. Usually the product is sold under the retailer's brand. The obvious disadvantage of this arrangement is that the producer is completely at the mercy of its one large customer.

Experience and ability of management. Channel decisions are affected by the marketing experience and ability of the management. Many companies lacking marketing know-how prefer to turn the job over to middlemen. New companies, built upon the engineering and production abilities of management, often rely heavily on middlemen to do the marketing job. An established company planning to sell a new product or enter a new market is likely to use middlemen until it acquires experience in the new field.

Desire for control of channel. A manufacturer may establish a short channel simply because he wants to control the distribution of his product, even though the cost of the more direct channel is higher. The producer may feel that he can give his product more aggressive promotion by controlling the channel. Also, he can better control the freshness of merchandise stocks and the retail prices of the goods.

Services provided by seller. Often a producer's channel decision is influenced by the quantity and quality of marketing services he can provide in relation to those demanded by the middlemen. Frequently manufacturers can sell their products to retail chains only if the goods are presold through heavy advertising. Other middlemen may demand that the.manufacturer build in-store displays or send missionary salesmen to call on retailers and industrial users.

MIDDLEMEN CONSIDERATIONS

Services provided by middlemen. A producer should select middlemen who will provide the marketing services he himself either is unable to provide or cannot economically perform. If a product needs aggressive promotion to enter a new market, a manufacturers' agent can usually provide the service better than a full-function wholesaler. If a product requires special storage facilities, a wholesaler may provide these facilities best. In these examples we can see the relationships between the nature of the product and the services provided by middlemen.

Availability of desired middlemen. The middlemen which a producer desires may not be available. They may be carrying competitive products and may not wish to add another line. In any event, the manufacturer may have to alter his entire channel. One producer of industrial machinery who could not secure desirable distributors in a metropolitan market opened a sales office in that city. It proved so successful that eventually he opened branches or offices in several other markets and discontinued his use of industrial distributors in those cities.

Attitude of middlemen toward manufacturer's policies. Sometimes a manufacturer's choice of channels is limited because his marketing policies are not acceptable to certain types of middlemen. The producer's unwillingness to guarantee the product against a price decline will eliminate many middlemen from consideration. Some types of retailers and wholesaling middlemen are interested in carrying a line only if they can get an exclusive franchise in a territory.

Sales volume possibilities. All other factors being equal, a producer will select a channel offering the greatest potential volume over the long run. There are two problems inherent in that statement, however. The first is the difficulty of forecasting which channel will generate the largest volume. The second is that realistically all other things are not equal. A high-volume channel may also be a high-cost channel, or a firm may secure maximum volume but lose all control over its distribution.

Cost requirements. The final point to consider is the cost of selling through alternative channels. Expenses should be equated with functions performed by the middlemen. As noted in preceding chapters, a high-cost middleman is not to be excluded automatically from consideration. His cost may be high only because he provides so many services. When analyzing these costs, a firm should study the *total* channel expense rather than the expense of *separate* types of middlemen.

Analysis of cost by channels of distribution is a difficult task. (See Chapter 28 for a discussion of this topic.) If such an analysis is not made, however, management has no sound foundation for judging channel expenses. Furthermore, even after a cost analysis shows which is the lowest-cost channel, then the products, the market, or other considerations may indicate that this channel is not the best choice.

SELECTION OF CHANNELS FOR NEW PRODUCTS OR NEW COMPANIES

Special channel problems are faced by an established company adding a new, unrelated product to its line, or by a new company starting out with either a new product or an established product. Three important considerations will influence the decision making in these situations. The first concerns the newness of the product and the extent to which consumers realize they want it. A manufacturer of men's suits who adds shirts to his line faces different channel problems from those of an appliance manufacturer who adds electronic clothes washers which require no water. In the latter case a primary demand must be created, and provisions must be made in the channel to educate consumers regarding the new product.

Second, for any new product or company the promotion requirements are particularly high. Aggressive selling is needed. We have seen that wholesalers do not perform this service. Yet they may be needed to reach retailers or industrial users. The manufacturer, faced with the need to spend huge sums on advertising and to establish a missionary sales force, has some alternatives. Instead of using wholesalers, he may develop his own sales force to call directly on retailers or industrial users. Or he may compromise by employing a manufacturers' agent and giving him a commission large enough to encourage him to sell the product aggressively.

The third point is that the company may find it difficult to establish the channels it wants simply because the middlemen are not eager to take on an unknown company or product. In this case the manufacturer may have to use any channel which will accept the product and hope that in time he can change to more appropriate channels.

USE OF MULTIPLE CHANNELS OF DISTRIBUTION

A manufacturer may use multiple channels either to reach different markets or to sell to the same market.

A firm selling the same products to consumer and industrial markets would usually establish separate channel structures. In like manner, differences in the size of the buyers or the market densities often result in the use of more than one channel. A manufacturer of food products will sell directly to large grocery chains, but to reach smaller stores he will use another channel which includes grocery wholesalers. A producer may establish sales branches in a concentrated market and from these branches send out a sales force to reach wholesalers or retailers. In more sparsely populated markets, the same producer will use manufacturers' agents instead of his own sales force.

Sometimes a producer is reaching different markets, and thus is using multiple channels, because he is selling unrelated products. Firms producing oleomargarine and paint, or rubber products and plastics, illustrate the point. These firms may also have organized their sales forces into separate divisions according to the various customer groups or product lines.

As we noted in the preceding chapter, a significant development in dual distribution (and a source of channel conflict) has been the increased use of *competing* channel systems by manufacturers to sell the same brand to the same market.

DETERMINING INTENSITY OF DISTRIBUTION

After a manufacturer has decided upon the general channels he will use, he then should determine the number of middlemen—the intensity of distribution—to be employed at the wholesaling and retailing levels. In this respect, a manufacturer has three major alternative courses of action. These are not neatly compartmentalized alternatives. Instead, the degrees of intensity of distribution form a continuum, or points on a scale. At one end is *intensive* distribution, in which the manufacturer tries to get maximum exposure for his product by having it sold in every outlet where final customers might possibly look for it. The second alternative is *selective* distribution, in which the producer selects a limited number of wholesalers and/or retailers in a given geographic area. The third possibility is *exclusive* distribution, which involves the use of only one wholesaling middleman or retailer in a specified geographic market.

INTENSIVE DISTRIBUTION

Ordinarily the policy of intensive distribution is adopted by the manufacturers of consumer convenience goods. Consumers demand immediate satisfaction for this class of product and will not defer a purchase in order to get a particular brand. In the field of industrial products, intensive distribution is usually limited to operating supplies or other highly standardized items, such as small tools and some lubricants. Retailers often control the extent to which the policy of intensive distribution can be implemented. For example, a new manufacturer of toothpaste may want distribution in all supermarkets, but these retailers may limit their assortment to the four fastest-selling brands. Intensive distribution also places most of the burden of advertising and promotion on the shoulders of the manufacturer. Retailers are not going to pay to advertise a product which all competitors are selling.

SELECTIVE DISTRIBUTION

Selective distribution covers a wide range of distribution intensity. A business which adopts this policy may have only a few outlets in a particular market, or it may have a large number but still have something short of intensive distribution. The policy of selective distribution lends itself especially well to manufacturers of consumer shopping or specialty goods and industrial accessory equipment, for which most customers have a brand preference. Even makers of convenience goods often limit the number of their outlets to some extent because it simply is not profitable to sell to every existing outlet.

When a firm adopts a selective distribution policy at the retail level, there will normally be a reduction in the number of wholesalers used. Conversely, a firm may limit the number of retail outlets by the simple expedient of first limiting the number of wholesalers to whom it sells. Adopting a selective distribution policy at the retail level may make it possible for the manufacturer to bypass wholesalers.

Many companies have switched to selective distribution in order to achieve higher profit levels. Although they forecast a decline in sales volume, many of them actually increased their volume substantially because they were able to do a more thorough selling job with the smaller number of accounts.

A company may decide to adopt a selective distribution policy after some experience with intensive distribution. The reasons for the change usually hinge upon the high cost of intensive distribution or the unsatisfactory performance of middlemen. Some customers perennially order in small, unprofitable amounts. Others may be poor credit risks. Still others may be chronic complainers, frequently returning goods they ordered or demanding extraordinary services. Some retailers may be eliminated because they are not providing adequate repair and maintenance facilities to service the products.

Once the executives in a firm decide to follow a selective distribution policy, special requirements ordinarily fall upon the chosen outlets. The fewer the number of outlets, the heavier the requirements. For example, if there is a limited number of middlemen, they are expected to display the products more prominently and to promote them more aggressively than if distribution were unlimited.

EXCLUSIVE DISTRIBUTION

Under an exclusive distribution policy the supplier enters into an agreement with a particular wholesaling middleman or retailer whereby the supplier will sell only to that wholesaler or retailer in the given market. Under these exclusive distributorships (with a wholesaler) or exclusive dealerships (with retailers) the middlemen are sometimes prohibited from handling a directly competitive line of product.[1]

When used. A new firm having difficulty establishing a distribution system or an established firm trying to market a new product may attract outlets by offering exclusive franchises. Some risk is involved in using exclusive selling agreements to secure initial distribution because if the manufacturer later wants to terminate the exclusive arrangement, considerable ill will may be engendered. Exclusive dealerships are frequently used in the marketing of consumer specialty products Expensive men's suits, sold under heavily advertised brands, fall into this category. When department stores or very large specialty stores are granted these franchises, a manufacturer often gets a bonus in the form of several outlets in the one market because the retailers open branch stores in suburban shopping centers.

Management often adopts an exclusive distribution policy when it is essential that the retailer carry a large inventory in order to ensure customers an adequate choice. This form of distribution is also desirable when the dealer or distributor must furnish installation and repair service. Manufacturers of farm machinery, large construction equipment, and commercial heating and air-conditioning equipment frequently use exclusive distributorships for this reason.

Evaluation from manufacturer's standpoint. An exclusive distribution policy helps the manufacturer control the retail segment of his channel. He is better able to determine what the retail price of his product will be, and he is in a position to approve advertisements featuring his product. A dealer is more likely to be cooperative and to promote the product aggressively because he realizes that his future is tied to the success of the manufacturer. With fewer accounts, the manufacturer is able to reduce credit losses and marketing costs. His billing, shipping, and order-filling functions are simplified. The dealer will probably carry a complete stock and be more willing to service the products than he would be if there were broader distribution.

On the other hand, there are a few serious competitive limitations to this distribution policy. Probably the most significant is that the manufacturer substantially limits the number of his sales outlets. He may lose the business of some customers who would normally buy his brand if it were available at more convenient locations. Also, the manufacturer will suffer if his exclusive dealer incurs customers ill will. Essentially, the manufacturer has all his eggs in one basket, and

---

[1]In technical language, a contract wherein the middleman agrees not to handle competitive products is known as an "exclusive dealing" agreement. On the other hand, the terms "exclusive selling," "exclusive dealerships," "exclusive distributorships," and "exclusive distribution" refer only to arrangements whereby the seller agrees not to sell to other retailers or wholesalers in the particular market. These arrangements have nothing to do with other products.

Frequently the term "exclusive agency" is used to describe exclusive dealerships, and the retailer is referred to as the "exclusive agent" for the product. No agency relationship exists in a legal sense. The retailer buys the product outright and legally performs in his own interest. He is not the legal agent of a manufacturer-principal. Because he is an independent retailer, the term "exclusive franchise" would more appropriately describe his relationship with the manufacturer.

he is pretty much dependent upon the retailer. Another problem is the difficulty of getting good dealers. Often the best ones in a market are already taken by competitors.

Evaluation from retailer's standpoint. A significant advantage of being an exclusive dealer is that such a retailer reaps all the benefits of the manufacturer's marketing and advertising activities in the particular market and gets all repeat sales. He finds it easier to maintain the margin on the product because he is protected from price-cutting competitors. If he does not carry competitive lines, he may increase his rate of stock turnover in the exclusive product line and also reduce his investment in inventory. Because he is important to the manufacturer, the lone retailer probably gets better treatment from him.

For a retailer, the main drawback to an exclusive dealership is that he becomes wedded to the manufacturer. If the manufacturer does a good job with the product, the dealer prospers. But if the manufacturer fails, the dealer is powerless to do anything but sink with him.

Dealership agreements often require the retailer to invest a considerable sum of money in equipment and facilities. If the agreement is then canceled, he stands to lose a major investment. Having cut himself off from other suppliers, he may have virtually no opportunity to acquire a product line of another firm. Another hazard is that once the volume is built up in a market, the manufacturer may add other dealers. The retailer is often at the mercy of the manufacturer. It is a one-sided arrangement in this respect, particularly if the brand is strong and the franchise is valuable. High quotas and other demands set by the manufacturer may put a heavy strain on the retailer. To keep the valuable franchise, the middleman may have to give up his independence and operate almost as a sales branch.

Legal considerations. Although exclusive distribution is not illegal, federal laws and judicial interpretations have imposed restrictions on three major aspects of its use. One aspect is *exclusive dealing contracts,* the arrangement whereby the franchise holder is prohibited from carrying similar product lines from competing manufacturers. A second involves *tying contracts,* under which the exclusive dealer or distributor is required to carry a manufacturer's full line if this supplier so desires. The third arrangement is the *closed sales territory,* wherein the manufacturer limits each franchise holder to selling only to buyers located within the assigned territory.[2]

None of the three arrangements is automatically illegal. Section 3 of the Clayton Antitrust Act of 1914 specifically states, however, that exclusive sales or lease contracts are unlawful if their effect "may be to substantially lessen competition or

---

[2]For an economic analysis of the impact which these three types of distribution restrictions may have on market competition and of the development of standards for determining whether a company's restrictive distribution arrangements are compatible with governmental policy concerning maintenance of competition, see Lee E. Preston, "Restrictive Distribution Arrangements: Economic Analysis and Public Policy Standards," *Law and Contemporary Problems,* Summer, 1965, pp. 506–529.

For an analysis of a landmark decision (the Schwinn Bicycle Company case) and its implications for restrictions by which manufacturers limit their distributors' choice of customers, see S. Powell Bridges, "The Schwinn Case: A Landmark Decision," *Business Horizons,* August, 1968, pp. 77–85; and *United States v. Arnold Schwinn & Co.,* 338 U.S. 365 (1967).

tend to create a monopoly in any line of commerce." It is under this provision that unreasonably restrictive exclusive dealing contracts and tying contracts have typically been ruled illegal. Questions on the legality of closed sales territories usually involve Section 5 of the Federal Trade Commission Act of 1914, which prohibits unfair competition which may be in restraint of trade.

Exclusive dealing contracts have been declared unlawful rather consistently if the manufacturer's sales volume is a substantial part of the total volume in a market, or if the volume done by the exclusive dealers is a significant percentage of the total business in an area. That is, the law is violated when the competitors of a manufacturer are essentially shut out from a substantial part of the market because of this manufacturer's exclusive dealing contract.

In recent years, probably the key case affirming this position was the one involving the Standard Oil Company of California. The Supreme Court ruled that Standard's exclusive dealing contracts (covering gasoline and other products) with its independently owned Chevron stations were unlawful because they were a substantial threat to competition.[3] About six thousand dealers in seven Western states were involved. Together they represented 16 percent of the service stations and only 6.7 percent of the total sales volume of all these products in the seven-state area.

By inference in some judicial decisions and by outright statement in others, it has been made clear that exclusive dealing is not illegal in all situations. In fact, where the seller is just getting started in a market or where his share of the total market is so small as to be negligible, his negotiation of exclusive dealing agreements may not only improve his competitive position but also strengthen competition in general.

Ordinarily there is no question of legality when a manufacturer agrees to sell to only one retailer or wholesaler in a given territory, provided there are no limitations on competitive products. Also, a manufacturer can sell to dealers who do not carry competitors' products, as long as this is a voluntary decision on the part of the franchise holder.

With regard to tying contracts, apparently a dealer can be required to carry a manufacturer's full line as long as the dealer is not prohibited from carrying competitive products. The arrangement is questionable, however, if a supplier forces a dealer or a distributor to take slow-moving, less attractive items in order to acquire the really desirable products.

Closed sales territories may be illegal because they restrict the franchise holders. They may also tend to create a monopoly for a product in a given territory in that buyers cannot play exclusive dealers in different territories against one another. Perhaps the safest policy is to assign each reseller a geographic area of primary responsibility rather than a closed sales territory.

The situation regarding contractual channel relationships was summed up nicely by Professor Dixon when he observed: "The future importance of contractual integration in marketing will depend in part upon the extent to which the restraints in these contractual arrangements present problems under the antitrust laws."[4]

---

[3] *Standard Oil Company of California v. United States,* 337 U.S. 293 (1949).

[4] Donald F. Dixon, "The Impact of Recent Antitrust Decisions upon Franchise Marketing," *MSU Business Topics,* Spring, 1969, pp. 68–79.

For some managerial guidelines in formulating sales policies in view of pertinent exclusive

SELECTING AND WORKING WITH INDIVIDUAL MIDDLEMEN

When all is said and done, middlemen can often make or break a manufacturer. They are the ones who personally contact the final customer, whether he is an ultimate consumer or an industrial user. Consequently, a manufacturer's entire channel effort is designed to reach one goal—that of maximizing the marketing effectiveness at the point of final sale. This generalization supports the systems concept of a channel of distribution. That is, to maximize the effectiveness of a distribution channel, it must be treated as a complete system and not as a series of independent, competing links. Thus the success of a manufacturer's distribution effort depends ultimately upon how well he selects his individual middlemen and then administers the action system involving these distributors and dealers.

The final step in establishing channels is particularly important at the *wholesaling* level because a manufacturer uses fewer wholesalers than retailers. Furthermore, the choice of wholesaling middlemen preempts to a considerable extent the manufacturer's choice of retailers. At the *retail* level, the choice of individual middlemen is particularly important when the producer has decided upon a policy of selective or exclusive distribution.

FACTORS AFFECTING CHOICE OF MIDDLEMEN

Several factors may contribute to a middleman's success in his business operation. Some, such as business conditions and competition, are external to the firm's operation and generally are not controllable by the wholesaler or retailer. Other points which are controllable by middlemen include the caliber of their executives, their ability to advertise, and the soundness of their product planning.

The manufacturer should establish qualifying standards for each factor so that he will know what he is looking for. Then he must find the available middlemen who meet these predetermined standards. Here we again observe that channel research is one of the most difficult types of marketing research. Getting the desired information regarding potential middlemen will undoubtedly involve some kind of field research. When the manufacturer has a prospective retailer in mind for a selective or exclusive dealership, he probably should talk with the retailer's suppliers and competitors. If possible, the manufacturer should find out what the retailer's customers are like and what they think of his store. It is important to make certain that all information is currently accurate. A store that was doing an outstanding job in promotion last year may have lost the key executive who was the guiding force behind this success.

Access to desired market. In the selection of an individual wholesaler or retailer, by far the most important factor to consider is: Does he sell to the market I want to reach? This really is the *sine qua non* of middleman selection. If he does not now reach the manufacturer's desired market, it is doubtful that the manufacturer's products will induce him to change his customer list substantially.

Location. A good location is particularly important at the retail level, but it must also be considered in selecting wholesaling middlemen because a firm's location is often closely related to its ability to reach a desired market.

---

dealing legislation and its interpretation, see Leonard J. Konopa, "Exclusive Dealing Arrangements in Marketing," *Business Topics,* Summer, 1964, pp. 63–72.

A retailer's location must be considered with respect to competitive outlets and trading areas. A manufacturer who wants to select a specialty store in a shopping center will first want to determine whether the shopping center is the most desirable one in the market. In one case, a shopping center had no leading department store, and therefore a specialty store was not selected in this center. Even the location of the retail store within the shopping center may be an important consideration. Manufacturers of shopping goods will try to select retailers who are located close to competitors and are in an area where there is heavy customer traffic.

Product-planning policies. A manufacturer should carefully consider the product policies of prospective wholesalers or retailers. To illustrate, a manufacturer ordinarily seeks stores where his line will complement rather than compete with the store's other products. If he refuses to sell to middlemen who carry a competing line, then he must seek outlets which have no such line or which are willing to drop their present lines. A garment manufacturer had such a policy, and his products were so attractive to retailers that many stores discontinued their previously handled brands in order to get his line.

The assortment typically carried by a dealer within a product line may influence a manufacturer's choice of outlet. A manufacturer of health and beauty aids produced a wide line of products in several sizes, types of packaging, and colors. Department stores and large drugstores would carry the full assortment, but supermarkets wanted only one or two sizes of a few fast-moving items. This manufacturer could not rely only on supermarkets for his retail distribution. He had to use other stores which were willing to carry a larger proportion of his assortment.

A manufacturer must consider the comparative quality and price of other lines in a store. Even if the retailer were willing, a manufacturer should not be interested in selling his line of dresses which start at $79.95 to stores whose highest-priced lines of other dresses sell for $29.95.

The pricing policies and practices followed by middlemen should influence a manufacturer. A producer who is opposed to resale price maintenance should normally avoid dealers who demand it. By the same token, if the manufacturer wants to maintain a suggested retail price, he must avoid dealers who are well-known price-cutters or who might use the brand as a price football.

Promotion policies. If a manufacturer must rely on middlemen to do the bulk of the promotion, he will select them differently from the way he would if he himself planned to advertise and otherwise promote the product heavily. Some manufacturers have been forced to shun large retailers who were otherwise desirable because these dealers demanded promotional allowances, displays, or product demonstrators. The manufacturers either could not afford these promotional devices or preferred to use other methods.

For producers of many types of goods, the nature of the middleman's personal selling activities is important. A manufacturer of earth-moving equipment made it a point to ascertain the technical abilities of salesmen of industrial distributors before granting a franchise in a territory. If a product does not lend itself to the self-service method of retail selling, then obviously the many stores employing this method are eliminated from further consideration.

Services available to customers. The consumer's acceptance of discount selling, with its limited services but low prices, has changed managerial thinking with regard to the necessity of services. However, this does not mean that manufacturers and middlemen can consider customer service a thing of the past. Where service is important, a manufacturer should judge the potential middlemen on the basis of the services they normally offer to their customers. Manufacturers and wholesalers of big-ticket consumer products, such as furniture and appliances, usually prefer retailers who supply credit and delivery services for their customers. Middlemen for many industrial products must be able to provide their customers with good mechanical service and rapid delivery of parts and supplies.

Financial ability. A manufacturer should investigate a middleman's financial condition and the financing services he provides for his customers and suppliers. Naturally a manufacturer will prefer middlemen who pay their bills regularly and promptly. In some cases a manufacturer will select an individual retailer who is small and financially insecure because he holds great promise for the future.

Quality of management. An overall factor for a manufacturer to consider is the caliber of executives in a middleman's business. Their capacity to manage—that is, their ability to perform all aspects of the management process, such as planning, organizing, and staffing—is crucial to the success of the firm. The quality of management is reflected in all aspects of the middleman's business.

THE WORKING RELATIONSHIP

In the administration of a channel system (as we saw in the preceding chapter), some institutions assume the role of *primary* (controlling) organizations, while others occupy secondary roles.[5] Regardless of whether the manufacturer or the middlemen holds the controlling position, a real interdependence exists between the two groups. Unless the manufacturer is successful, the welfare of the dealer is in jeopardy, and, conversely, the manufacturer has a vital interest in his dealer's success. The greater the share of his total business that a dealer derives from the sale of a given manufacturer's product, the greater is his dependence on that supplier.

There is also a community of interests in what each organization—manufacturer and middleman—expects from the other in terms of support of an effective total marketing program. A series of rewards and penalties may be instituted by either party in order to encourage the other to perform as expected. The major reward for either party is in the form of increased profits. A manufacturer can also use programs of recognition or financial incentives to further reward a dealer. Probably the most powerful penalty which a manufacturer can impose is to terminate his sales agreement with a dealer. A middleman, in turn, can penalize a manufacturer by not promoting his products adequately, by pushing a competitor's products, or ultimately by dropping the manufacturer's line entirely.

---

[5]Ideas in this and the following paragraph are adapted from Valentine F. Ridgeway, "Administration of Manufacturer-Dealer Systems," *Administrative Science Quarterly*, March, 1957, pp. 464–483.

A middleman has a right to expect the manufacturer to provide well-designed properly priced, salable products for which consumer demand has been built by a good advertising program. A manufacturer may also grant territorial protection in the form of an exclusive franchise.

On a day-to-day basis, a manufacturer can furnish promotional and managerial assistance in many forms. Preparing sales manuals and conducting sales training programs for dealer or distributor salesmen are only two examples. A manufacturer's in-store promotional aids may be useful, and his missionary salesmen are often welcomed because they can check stock, build displays, and work with salesclerks. Middlemen should be notified about price changes and stock conditions, and they should be completely informed about new products. Manufacturers can offer managerial assistance in accounting systems, buying activities, and advertising. Managerial advice should be available for a middleman when he selects a location for a new store, arranges a store layout, or modernizes an existing store.

Day-to-day working relationships between manufacturers and their middlemen determine the ultimate success of the arrangement. Friction can develop easily if there is not a real spirit of cooperation. The communication system which provides for information interchange in such categories as physical inventory, promotion, product features, pricing, and market conditions seems essential for the coordination of intrachannel activities. See Fig. 19-2.

In return for the products and services which he supplies, the manufacturer has a right to expect certain assistance from middlemen in day-to-day relationships. Some of these points have been developed at greater length in the preceding chapters on the distribution system. A retailer or wholesaler may be expected to carry adequate stocks of merchandise, undertake some advertising and sales promotion, grant credit to customers, and possibly service the product. The amount of help to be provided in each of these activities depends upon the product itself and the nature of the middleman's franchise. More is expected from holders of exclusive franchises than from middlemen used in intensive distribution.

ANALYSIS AND EVALUATION OF CHANNELS OF DISTRIBUTION

In the face of changing conditions in the market and among middlemen, constant appraisal of channel activity is mandatory. Yet a surprisingly large number of companies assume that the channel job is completed once their channels are established. Executives who regularly sponsor product innovation and who insist on a new advertising campaign twice a year often seem perfectly content with an archaic distribution structure.

Several types of quantitative and qualitative marketing research may be undertaken to aid a business in appraising its channels. In a quantitative sense, a company may analyze the sales volume performance of each of its middlemen to determine whether they are getting an adequate volume from each territory, product line, and customer group. The need for a cost analysis by channels of distribution has already been mentioned. These kinds of quantitative analyses are discussed in more detail in Chapter 28.

To do a proper job of evaluating a middleman's performance, a manufacturer must establish standards and then develop methods for measuring the middleman's performance against three predetermined criteria. A commonly used

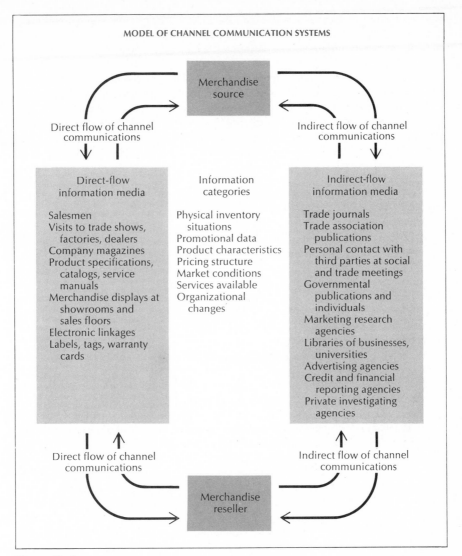

MODEL OF CHANNEL COMMUNICATION SYSTEMS

Merchandise source

Direct flow of channel communications

Indirect flow of channel communications

Direct-flow information media	Information categories	Indirect-flow information media
Salesmen Visits to trade shows, factories, dealers Company magazines Product specifications, catalogs, service manuals Merchandise displays at showrooms and sales floors Electronic linkages Labels, tags, warranty cards	Physical inventory situations Promotional data Product characteristics Pricing structure Market conditions Services available Organizational changes	Trade journals Trade association publications Personal contact with third parties at social and trade meetings Governmental publications and individuals Marketing research agencies Libraries of businesses, universities Advertising agencies Credit and financial reporting agencies Private investigating agencies

Direct flow of channel communications

Indirect flow of channel communications

Merchandise reseller

Figure 19-2.

standard of performance is a sales quota. The manufacturer sets the number of units or the dollar volume of each of his products which a middleman must sell in a given time period. Other bases for appraising performance include the total amount of advertising the middleman devoted to the manufacturer's products, his treatment of competitive lines which he handles, his promptness in paying bills, and the number of complaints which the manufacturer receives from his customers. External factors, such as new competitors and general business conditions in a market, should often be taken into consideration when measuring performance.

Another type of valuable research involves determining the attitudes of middlemen and even final customers toward the manufacturer, his products, and his marketing policies. Essentially, the manufacturer is trying to get some "feedback" from his middlemen and final customers. Middlemen's attitudes may be uncovered by a formal questionnaire survey conducted either by the manufacturer himself or by an outside research agency. A few years ago, a major home appliance manufacturer employed a research firm to determine what the appliance dealers' attitudes were toward the manufacturer's salesmen, distribution system, and advertising program. The main findings were that dealers wanted the products to be presold through advertising and to be of high quality, and they wanted the manufacturer's service facilities close by. Additional findings regarding what the dealers expected from the manufacturer's salesmen were incorporated into the latter's sales training program.

QUESTIONS AND PROBLEMS

1. Which of the channels illustrated in Fig. 19-1 is most apt to be used for each of the following products? Defend your choice in each case.

   a. Life insurance
   b. Single-family residence
   c. Farm tractor
   d. Newspaper printing press
   e. Office furniture
   f. Iron ore
   g. Toothpaste
   h. Women's shoes
   i. Men's shoes
   j. Refrigerators

2. "The great majority of industrial sales are made directly from the producer to the industrial user." Explain the reason for this in terms of the nature of the market. In terms of the nature of the product.

3. A small manufacturer of fishing lures is faced with the problem of selecting his channel of distribution. What reasonable alternatives does he have? Consider particularly the nature of his product and the nature of his market.

4. What special channel problems are involved with new products and new companies? How would you overcome each of the problems?

5. Is a policy of intensive distribution consistent with buying habits for convenience goods? Shopping goods? Is intensive distribution normally used in the marketing of any type of industrial goods?

6. Why would a manufacturer ever want to abandon intensive distribution in favor of selective distribution?

7. Assume that a manufacturer of builders' hardware wanted to move to a selective distribution system. How would he go about determining which accounts to keep and which to eliminate?

8. From the manufacturer's viewpoint, what are the competitive advantages of exclusive distribution?

9. What are the drawbacks to exclusive selling from the retailer's point of view? To what extent are these alleviated if the retailer controls the channel for the particular brand?

10. What is a tying contract? Is it illegal under the Clayton Antitrust Act?

11. Identify a few retailers near your school who have exclusive franchises for particular products. Study these retailers and determine to what extent they meet the standards discussed in this chapter in connection with selecting individual middlemen.

12. How can a manufacturer determine whether an individual retailer or wholesaler sells to the market the manufacturer wants to reach?

13. A manufacturer of a well-known brand of men's clothing has been selling directly to one dealer in a Western city for many years. For some time, the market has been large enough to support two retailers very profitably, and yet the present holder of the franchise objects strongly when the manufacturer suggests adding another outlet. What alternatives does the manufacturer have in this situation? What course of action do you recommend that he take?

14. "A manufacturer should always strive to select the lowest-cost channel of distribution." Do you agree? Should he always try to use the middlemen with the lowest operating costs? Explain.

MANAGEMENT OF
PHYSICAL DISTRIBUTION

After the channels of distribution have been established, a firm can turn its attention to the physical distribution of its product through these channels. *Physical distribution* is the term used to describe the range of activities concerned with the movement of the right amount of the right products to the right place at the right time.

TOTAL SYSTEM CONCEPT OF PHYSICAL DISTRIBUTION

Physical distribution in marketing is essentially a problem in logistics. An army cannot afford to have one of its units in a position where it has guns but no ammunition, or trucks but no gasoline. By the same token, a private business is in a weak position when it has orders but no merchandise to ship, or when it has a good supply of machinery in Atlanta but an urgent customer in New Orleans. These situations indicate the importance of *location* in marketing, whether it is the location of a store, warehouse, or stock of merchandise. The appropriate assortment of products must be in the right place at the right time in order to maximize the opportunity for profitable sales volume.

  Physical distribution, then, is the management of the physical flow of products and the development and operation of efficient flow systems. In its full scope, physical distribution for a manufacturer would involve not only the movement of *finished goods* from the end of the production line to the final customer but also the flow of *raw materials* from their source of supply to the beginning of the production line. Similarly, a middleman would manage the flow of goods *onto* his shelves as well as *from* his shelves to the customer's home or store.

The task of physical distribution may be divided into the five parts listed below. What is done in one area, however, very definitely affects decision making in others. A decision on the location of a warehouse may influence the selection of the transportation carrier. The decision on the carrier influences the optimum size of the shipment. See Fig. 20-1.

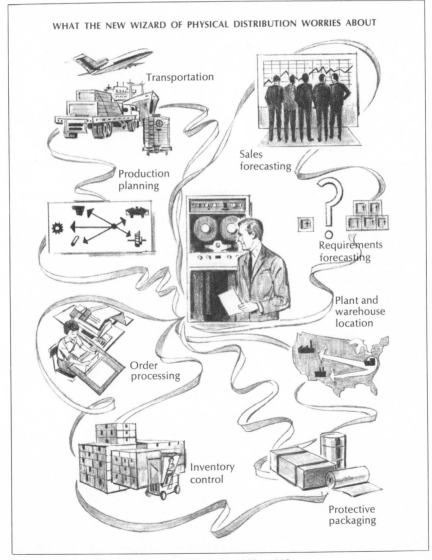

Figure 20-1. *Source: Business Week*, Sept. 24, 1966, p. 113.

1. Determine the inventory locations and establish a warehousing system.
2. Establish a materials-handling system.
3. Maintain an inventory control system.
4. Establish procedures to process the orders.
5. Select a method of transportation.

From time to time in this book, it has been pointed out that marketing is a total system of business action and not a fragmented series of operations. Nowhere is this idea seen more clearly than in the matter of physical distribution. But it has not always been this way. Traditionally—and unfortunately this is still true in too many firms—the activities involved in physical distribution have been fragmented, and managerial responsibility for them has been compartmentalized into units which often have conflicting, and even diametrically opposite, goals. The production department, for instance, sets the production schedule and is interested in long production runs so as to minimize the unit manufacturing costs, even though the result may be abnormally high inventory costs. The traffic department looks at the freight rates rather than at the total cost of physical distribution. Thus carriers with low ton-mile charges are often selected, even though this may mean undue time spent in transit and require larger inventories to fill the long pipelines. The finance department wants to minimize funds tied up in inventories, while the sales department wants to have a wide assortment of products available at locations near the customers. Under managerial conditions such as these, it is not possible to optimize the flow of products. Applying the systems approach to physical distribution, however, should result in more effective linkage and coordination of these various functional activities. See Fig. 20-2.

In physical distribution, management is dealing with a large number of variables which are readily measurable. Problems in this situation lend themselves nicely to solution by statistical and mathematical techniques. For instance, operations research—a technique involving the use of statistical probability theory, mathematical models, and other quantitative methods—has been particularly helpful in such problems as determining the number and location of warehouses, the optimum size of inventories, and transportation routes and methods. Improvements in computers and other electronic data-processing equipment have made it possible to process rapidly the large quantities of data used in these quantitative analyses. In our survey treatment in this chapter, however, we shall be concerned with the fundamentals and the conceptual aspects of physical distribution management rather than with the methods of quantitative analysis used in solving problems in this field.[1]

---

[1]For a more complete textual treatment of physical distribution as an integrated systems concept, see Donald J. Bowersox, Edward W. Smykay, and Bernard J. LaLonde, *Physical Distribution Management,* rev. ed., The Macmillan Company, New York, 1968; J. L. Heskett, Robert M. Ivie, and Nicholas A. Glaskowsky, Jr., *Business Logistics,* 2d ed., The Ronald Press Company, New York, 1973; or James A. Constantin, *Principles of Logistics Management,* Appleton-Century-Crofts, Inc., New York, 1966.

For an appraisal of existing physical distribution planning models and the development of an improved model for long-range planning, see Donald J. Bowersox, "Planning Physical Distribution Operations with Dynamic Simulation," *Journal of Marketing,* January, 1972, pp. 17–25.

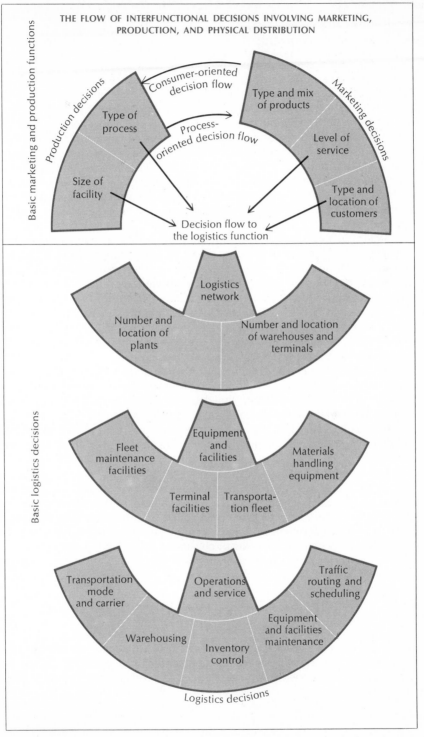

Figure 20-2. *Source:* Alan H. Gepfert, "Business Logistics for Better Profit Performance," *Harvard Business Review*, November–December, 1968, p. 78.

THE TOTAL COST APPROACH

As part of the systems concept, executives should apply the *total cost approach* to the management of physical distribution. A firm has alternative methods of physically handling and distributing its products. The administrators should try to optimize the cost-profit relationship of these various choices after analyzing the total cost of physical distribution, rather than considering separately the costs of shipping, storage, handling, or some other fragmented activity.

Too often an executive looks at the cost of only one aspect of physical distribution—transportation, for example—and tries to minimize this single cost. Possibly he frowns on the high cost of shipment by air freight or shipping in small units. He does not see that efforts to reduce transportation expenses may result in increases in warehousing expenses, which more than offset the saving in freight costs.

The airlines particularly have been conscious of the total-cost concept because unit freight rates are appreciably higher for air transportation than for land or sea shipment. The Armour Pharmaceutical Company (a division of the Armour Company) found that the higher costs of air freight were more than offset by the savings in lower inventory costs, less insurance and interest expense, lower crating costs, and fewer lost sales due to depletion of stock. The company eliminated all except one warehouse, cut inventories by 50 percent, boosted the rate of stock turnover, and found it could supply markets which had previously been inadequately served.

The point made here is *not* that air freight is the best method of transportation. (In fact, Armour later substantially reduced its business with airlines in some parts of the country.) Rather, the idea is that physical distribution should be viewed as a total process and its costs analyzed accordingly. Then management can expect to get a better picture of its operations, better communications with its field activities, and consequently greater control over its distribution system.[2]

Implicit in the total cost concept is the thought that management should strive for an optimum balance between total cost and customer utility. That is, rather than seeking *only* to minimize the total costs of physical distribution, executives should also consider customer want satisfaction in connection with this segment of the firm's marketing program. It may be necessary to incur something above the lowest possible total costs of physical distribution in order to achieve something nearer an optimum level of customer utility.

INCREASING ATTENTION TO PHYSICAL DISTRIBUTION MANAGEMENT

Fortunately, in recent years we have witnessed a significant increase in the emphasis which American business management is placing on physical distribution. Happily, there are no signs at all that this trend is abating. A major rea-

---

[2]For further examples of companies which have improved their performance by treating physical distribution as a total system, see "What You Should Know about Physical Distribution Management," *Sales Management,* Jan. 1, 1971, p. 28. See also Raymond LeKashman and John F. Stolle, "The Total Cost Approach to Distribution," *Business Horizons,* Winter, 1965, pp. 33–46.

son for the increased attention is the fact that physical distribution expenses are a substantial cost factor in many industries. To cite just one study, these costs ranged from about 10 percent of sales in the machinery industry to 30 percent in the food industry.[3] For many products, the largest single operating expenses are those involved in physical distribution. For other products, costs equal to as much as one-half of the wholesale price are incurred in performing transportation and warehousing activities. Not only do these costs already loom large, but they are increasing.

Through the years, management has made substantial progress toward optimizing the costs of production activities. Cost reductions have also been effected in many areas of marketing. This leaves physical distribution as a prime target. It is the new (and perhaps the last) major frontier for cost cutting. By treating this activity as a total system, rather than as a set of fragmented parts, business can take a significant stride toward greater efficiency.

By focusing attention on such a substantial expense item as physical distribution costs, management may recognize the considerable "leverage" effect which cost savings in this area can have on profits. In a supermarket operation, for instance, where the net profit on sales may be 1 percent, every dollar of savings in physical distribution costs has the same effect on profits as does an increase of $100 in sales volume.

In addition to cost considerations, other factors also account for the increased attention being devoted to physical distribution management.[4] Improvements in inventory control and advances in computer capabilities have resulted in a trend toward more frequent ordering of small quantities. Sellers catering to these customers are finding that their existing methods of distributing products do not give the required levels of service. Another factor forcing a review of distribution systems is the dramatic break in recent years from traditional institutional patterns. (These changes were observed earlier in Chapters 15 to 18.) Governmental enforcement of price legislation is encouraging companies to base their discounts and other price differentials on cost differences, so these firms are forced to study their distribution systems carefully to determine their actual costs. Finally, where competitive marketing strategies were at one time centered largely around price and product features, now we are recognizing that effective physical distribution services can constitute a significant competitive differential.

A FIRM'S STRATEGIC USE OF PHYSICAL DISTRIBUTION

The strategic use of business logistics may enable a company to strengthen its market position by providing more customer satisfaction and by reducing total operating costs. The management of this activity can also affect a firm's marketing mix—particularly its product-planning, pricing, and channels of distribution policies.

---

[3]Richard E. Snyder, "Physical Distribution Costs," *Distribution Age,* December, 1963, pp. 35–42; see also Robert P. Neuschel, "Physical Distribution—Forgotten Frontier," *Harvard Business Review,* March–April, 1967, pp. 125–134.

[4]Wendell M. Stewart, "Physical Distribution: Key to Improved Volume and Profits," *Journal of Marketing,* January, 1965, pp. 65–70.

IMPROVE CUSTOMER SERVICE

A sophisticated logistics system can improve the distribution service a firm gives its customers—be they middlemen or ultimate users. The manufacturer of Norge kitchen appliances found that the way to increase profits was to raise its own warehousing costs—this led to more-than-offsetting sales increases as well as allowing the dealers to maintain lower inventories. The level of customer service directly affects demand. So management must strive for the optimum balance between the distribution service given to customers and the cost of this service. In establishing service levels, generally speaking the physical distribution models have stressed spatial considerations (warehouse location, for example). We are beginning to realize that a temporal perspective may be equally useful—that buyers are influenced by service-time differentials among suppliers.[5]

REDUCE DISTRIBUTION COSTS

Many avenues to cost reductions may be opened by the effective management of a company's physical distribution activities. Effectively systematizing these activities may result in a simplification, such as the elimination of warehouses, which will cut costs. Inventories—and their attendant carrying costs and capital investment —may be reduced by consolidating stocks at fewer locations and by shortening the replenishment cycle in warehouses. Sometimes a redesigned package permits more efficient transportation and warehousing.

GENERATE ADDITIONAL SALES VOLUME

A properly designed logistics system can also help to generate additional sales volume. Such a system will minimize out-of-stock conditions, the result being an increase in both sales and customer satisfaction. A responsive system can shorten the order cycle and thus reduce his inventory requirements. Cost savings can be passed on to customers in the form of larger discounts. Increased efficiencies in physical distribution often enable a seller to expand his geographic market.

ADJUST TO RATE, TIME, AND PLACE DIFFERENCES IN PRODUCTION AND CONSUMPTION: CREATION OF TIME AND PLACE UTILITIES

There are several conditions under which management can make profitable use of both transportation and warehousing facilities in adjusting its rate, time, and place of production to meet the market demand for the firm's product. To illustrate, there may be a market situation of year-round consumption but only seasonal production, as in the case of agricultural products. Proper use of warehousing facilities will enable a producer to store the seasonal surplus so that it can be marketed long after the harvest has ended.

In other instances warehousing helps to adjust conditions of seasonal consumption but year-round production, as in the case of skis. A manufacturer likes to produce on a year-round basis in order to operate his plant efficiently. Conse-

---

[5]Ronald P. Willett and P. Ronald Stephenson, "Determinants of Buyers Response to Physical Distribution Service," *Journal of Marketing Research,* August, 1969, pp. 279–283; see also J. L. Heskett, "A Missing Link in Physical Distribution System Design," *Journal of Marketing,* October, 1966, pp. 37–41.

quently, enough surplus stocks are warehoused during the off-season so that the peak-season demand may be met without the need for overtime operation or additional plant capacity. In an economic sense, the main function of the transportation subsystem in physical distribution is to add value to products through the creation of *place utility.* A fine suit hanging on a garment manufacturer's rack in New York City has less value to a retailer or consumer in Baltimore than a similar suit displayed in the retailer's store. Transporting the suit from New York to the retailer in Baltimore creates place utility and adds value to the product. Also, speed in transportation may prevent loss of orders and create place utility more rapidly.

The economic value of storage (as a key part of warehousing) is the fact that it creates *time utility.* A product may be properly located with respect to its market, but the timing may be such that there is no present demand for it. Precious value is added to this item simply by holding and properly preserving it in storage until the demand rises. Time utility is created and value added when bananas are picked green and allowed to ripen in storage, or when meat is aged and tobacco cured in storage. Storage is essential when there is an imbalance in the timing of production and consumption.

In this discussion a careful distinction is made between warehousing and storage. *Storage* is the marketing activity which involves holding and properly preserving products from the time of their production until their final sale. *Warehousing* embraces storage plus a broad range of action-oriented functions, such as assembling, dividing (bulk breaking), and preparing products for reshipping. In' many respects, warehousing is related both to transportation and to storage.

STABILIZE PRICES

Careful management of warehousing and transportation facilities can help to stabilize prices for an individual firm or for an entire industry. If a market is temporarily glutted with a certain product, sellers can warehouse the product until supply and demand conditions are more favorable. This managerial use of warehousing facilities is commonly found in the marketing programs for agricultural products and other seasonally produced goods. The judicious movement of products from one market to another may relieve gluts in one area, enable a seller to avoid a market with depressed prices, or allow a seller to take advantage of a market which has a shorter supply and higher prices.

DETERMINE CHOICE OF CHANNELS AND LOCATION OF MIDDLEMEN

Administrative decisions regarding the management of inventory—its location, handling, transporting, and control—have an important bearing on a manufacturer's selection of his trade channels and the location of his middlemen. Logistics considerations may become paramount, for example, when a company has decided to decentralize its inventory, and now must determine how many sites to establish and whether to use wholesalers, its own branch warehouses, or public warehouses. One manufacturer may select merchant wholesalers who perform storage and other warehousing services, while another may prefer to use a combination of manufacturers' agents and public warehouses. The agents can solicit orders, provide aggressive selling, and do the necessary promotional work, while the orders can be physically distributed through and from the public warehouses.

Logistics facilities may influence a manufacturer's decision on where to locate his branches or in what cities he will seek wholesalers. Sometimes a company wants to locate a branch in a small town or a suburban community, but finds that the additional freight and handling costs from the nearest transportation center are prohibitive. Physical distribution facilities thus force the company to establish its branch in the central city.

A note of caution should be sounded at this point. Rarely are channels selected primarily on the basis of physical distribution considerations. Instead, logistics is only one factor to consider. We can recall from the preceding chapter that the nature of the market and other factors heavily influence channel decisions.

USE TRAFFIC MANAGEMENT TO ENSURE LOWEST COSTS

Effective traffic management can aid a company's total marketing program and improve its profit picture. A good traffic manager will see to it that his company is enjoying the fastest routes and the lowest possible rates on whatever method of transportation the administrator has decided upon. The pricing of transportation services is one of the most complicated parts of the American business scene. To read a rate or tariff schedule properly (this is the carrier's "price list") is a real art and requires considerable practice.

Another service which a traffic manager can render his company is the auditing of freight bills. This job is necessary because carriers sometimes charge a higher rate than the one which should apply. They are not intentionally trying to defraud the shipper. They are simply misinterpreting the complex rate schedule.

A good traffic manager can also negotiate with carriers in order to get his products reclassified or to get a special rate. A company may offer to ship larger quantities on a given carrier if lower rates are granted. The traffic manager should investigate the possibility of having his company operate its own private carriers, especially its own trucking system. If this possibility seems reasonable for a shipper, it can be an effective bargaining tool in getting reduced rates from common carriers.

DETERMINE INVENTORY LOCATIONS (ESTABLISH WAREHOUSING SYSTEM)

The name of the game in logistics is inventory management in the fullest sense of the term. Executive judgment must be exercised regarding the size, location, handling, and transporting of the inventories. Decision making in these four areas is interrelated. Decisions on the number and locations of inventory sites, for example, will influence decisions on inventory size and transportation methods. These interrelationships are often quite complex; they rarely occur in simple, consecutive, straight-line order. The problem of what should be decided first or where management should start in the logistics planning process resembles the "chicken or the egg" proposition.

One place where planning can begin is with a determination of the number and location of inventory sites. Final judgments will depend greatly on the nature of the market (its size, density, and location), the nature of the product, and the seller's financial position. (These considerations were discussed in the preceding two chapters in connection with the selection of channels and the company - branch - versus-the-wholesaler controversy.)

Perhaps basic to the inventory location problem is the company's intended strategy regarding inventory deployment—is it to be heavily concentrated or dispersed throughout the market? Each strategy has its merits and limitations. Centralizing the inventory means that it can be reduced in total size, can be better controlled, and is more responsive to unusual requests. Efficiency in warehousing and materials handling should be increased. On the other hand, centralizing the stocks of products will probably mean higher total transportation charges and slower delivery service to some segments of the market. Dispersing the inventory presents the other side of the coin on any of the points just noted.

To make a decision on the number and location of inventory centers requires consideration of many variables—transportation methods, freight rates, transit times, warehousing costs, customer buying patterns, and production costs and schedules, to mention just a few of the factors involved. Fortunately, with the aid of operations research techniques, a company can simulate the operations and predict the results of several plans of action.[6]

THE DISTRIBUTION-CENTER CONCEPT

Perhaps an effective compromise in the concentration-dispersion inventory deployment controversy is for a company to establish one or more *distribution centers.* Planned around markets rather than transportation facilities, the basic thought behind the distribution-center concept is to develop under one roof an efficient, fully integrated system for the flow of products—taking orders, filling them, and delivering them to customers. The distribution center is a "new look" in warehousing, having achieved prominence only since the 1950s, but the concept is rapidly being adopted by many well-known firms.[7] The Borden Company, for instance, planned to cut from 136 warehouses down to 16 to 18 distribution centers. After a three-year study, Libby, McNeill & Libby eliminated 214 warehouses and in their place established 5 distribution centers. Similar patterns have been followed by the Raytheon Co. (electronics), the Whirlpool Corp. (appliances), the Bigelow-Sanford Co. (carpeting), and many other firms.

Aided by the use of the latest techniques in data processing, materials handling, and inventory control, firms are able to process orders rapidly. This new distribution system has lowered distribution costs by reducing the number of warehouses, cutting excessive inventories, and eliminating out-of-stock conditions. Storage time and delivery time have been cut to a minimum, thus putting into practice the adage that companies are in business to sell goods, not to store them.

OWNERSHIP AND TYPES OF WAREHOUSES

A firm (manufacturer, wholesaler, or retailer) has the option of operating its own private warehouse or using the services of a public warehouse. A private warehouse is more likely to be used if a company moves a large volume of products through it and there is very little, if any, seasonal fluctuation in this materials flow. A

---

[6]See Ronald H. Ballou, "Dynamic Warehouse Location Analysis," *Journal of Marketing Research,* August, 1968, pp. 271–276.

[7]"The New Nerve Centers of Distribution," *Dun's Review,* June, 1963, p. S-104. See also *Chain Store Age,* executive edition, June, 1969, for several articles on the topic "Push-button Warehousing, Automation, Computers Help Run Distribution Centers of Future, Today."

competitive limitation to private warehousing is that it represents a relatively inflexible expense item. Also, it requires an expenditure of managerial time and talent.

Public warehouses offer storage and handling facilities to any interested individual or company. The users pay only for the cubic space occupied by their goods, and they pay only for the time during which this space is occupied. Several types of public warehouses are in wide use today. Probably the most common is the *general merchandise* warehouse, which stores practically any kind of manufactured or nonmanufactured product needing protection from the weather but having no special temperature, humidity, or handling requirements. Various types of *special commodity* warehouses are used for particular agricultural products, such as grains, wool, cotton, and tobacco. Ordinarily each of these warehouses handles one kind of product and offers special services particularly required for that product. Another widely used type of public warehousing facility is the *cold-storage* warehouse.

A particular type of general merchandise warehouse or special commodity warehouse is the *bonded* warehouse. This is used to store products on which a federal tax must be paid before they can be sold. Some imported goods, alcoholic beverages, and tobacco products are typically stored in these facilities. The warehouse is bonded by the U.S. Department of the Treasury. In bonded warehouses the import duty or excise tax need not be paid until the merchandise is sold.

SERVICES OFFERED BY PUBLIC WAREHOUSES

The best-known and most widely used service offered by public warehouses is storage. Products can be stockpiled in appropriate physical condition and in strategic locations until the seller wishes to distribute them to customers. In addition to storage, public warehouses offer other services.

Dividing bulk shipment and reshipping. Public warehouses receive large-quantity shipments, such as carload units, and bulk break, or divide, them into smaller units and then reship the smaller quantities to predetermined customers. In this way a seller can combine several less-than-carload orders into one carload shipment and consign the car to a warehouse located near the several buyers. The shipper enjoys the lower carload rate from his shipping points to the warehouse location. Actually, the warehouseman may be acting as a freight forwarder, since products are not actually stored but simply handled and reassembled for final delivery. Some public warehouses accept products shipped in bulk and then package the goods according to the seller's specifications.

Specialized management and labor. Because they are specialists in the activities which they perform, public warehouses can offer the advantages of specialization in management, labor, and facilities. They can provide management advice with respect to physical distribution. Also, they have the latest equipment required for efficient handling of products.

Financing. Public warehouses can aid the owner of goods financially by issuing a warehouse receipt and providing a field (custodian) warehousing service. A warehouse receipt may be used as collateral to secure a loan from a bank. When the goods are sold, the loan may be paid off and the ownership receipt redeemed so that the merchandise may be released from the warehouse.

Field warehousing (also called custodian warehousing) works in the following manner. Assume that some products are stored in the owner's private warehousing facilities and that he wants to get a bank loan on the merchandise without having the expense of moving it to a public warehouse. The owner calls in a public warehouseman and leases to him a section of the warehouse which contains the merchandise in question. A field warehouse is not limited to a portion of a regular private warehouse. It may be an office cabinet, locked desk drawer, office safe, open yard, grain elevator, or some other storage facility. The products may even be shipped from a manufacturer to his wholesaler's warehouse and then placed under a field warehousing plan. The warehouseman issues a receipt for the goods, and this receipt again serves as collateral for a bank loan. The leased area, in effect, becomes a public warehouse, and the goods cannot be removed until the receipt is redeemed.

Substitute for company branch warehouse or wholesalers. A very significant advantage of public warehouses is that they may be substituted both for a company branch warehouse system and for wholesalers. In addition to the bulk-breaking and reshipping services mentioned above, public warehouses will provide office and display space for sellers. These storage firms will also accept and fill orders for vendors. A manufacturer can ship in carload quantities to a public warehouse, just as he can ship to his own branches or wholesalers. Public warehouses enable him to maintain decentralized stocks of merchandise so that he can satisfy hand-to-mouth buyers and fill orders rapidly. Public warehousing costs are variable expenses requiring no capital investment. A firm does not pay for unused capacity, as it often must with a branch warehouse. Furthermore, public warehouses afford greater flexibility in the location of merchandise stocks. If a seller wishes to change or add inventory locations, he can easily change public warehouses.

Protection and security through government regulations. Legislative action at both the federal and state levels has afforded considerable protection and security to firms using the services of public warehouses. These laws are the guarantee which makes warehouse receipts acceptable as bank collateral, and they also curtail abuses and unethical practices by warehouse operators.

ESTABLISH A MATERIALS-HANDLING SYSTEM

The selection of the proper equipment to handle products is an important aspect of the management of physical distribution. Too often insufficient administrative attention is devoted to this activity. This careless attitude is surprising in light of the fact that the cost of handling products is a substantial part of the total cost of physical distribution.

In this discussion of materials-handling equipment, we include the warehouse building itself. Historically, warehouses have been multistory buildings located in congested, run-down parts of town. Their operation has been characterized by elevators, chutes, and other highly expensive vertical methods of moving products.

Modern warehouses are huge, sprawling, one-story affairs located in outlying parts of town where land is less expensive and loading platforms are easily accessible to motor trucks as well as railroad spurs. Forklift trucks, conveyor belts, motor scooters, and other mechanized equipment are used to move merchandise. In some warehouses the order fillers are even equipped with roller skates.[8]

With respect to materials-handling equipment, many firms have found that "palletization" (the use of pallets to aid in mechanical handling of merchandise) makes physical handling more economical. On the other hand, products which are oddly shaped or are handled in small quantities may not lend themselves to the use of pallets.

"Containerization" is a fledgling cargo-handling system which is gaining increasing acceptance in the physical distribution system. The system involves enclosing a shipment of products in containers of metal, wood, or some other material and then transporting them by rail, truck, and/or ship unopened from the time they leave the shipper until they reach their destination. The bright future of containerization is not without its roadblocks, however. Shippers and carriers are seeking to solve the problems of lack of standardization of containers, labor's unenthusiastic reaction to the system, and the need for revisions in transportation rate schedules.

MAINTAIN INVENTORY CONTROL SYSTEM

A key activity in a firm's physical distribution system is the maintenance of effective control over the size and composition of the inventories. Inventory represents a sizable investment in many companies. The goal of inventory control is to minimize the investment and fluctuations in inventories, while at the same time providing prompt order-filling services for customers.

Perhaps the greatest boon to inventory control in recent years has been the improvements in computer technology. This factor has enabled management to shorten the order-delivery cycle and to reduce substantially the size of inventories. Through use of the computer, a greater variety of more accurate information is more speedily available than was heretofore considered possible.

Inventory size may be determined by balancing the market needs and cost factors. Market demands on inventory can be anticipated by analyzing the sales forecast. Thus, the more accurate the forecast, the greater is the probability of optimizing inventory size. The cost factors to consider are (1) acquisition costs, i.e., the costs of making or buying the products to put in inventory and (2) carrying or holding costs—warehousing expenses, interest on investment, losses due to spoilage and pilferage, inventory taxes, etc.

The inventory's upper limit will also be influenced considerably by the desired level of customer satisfaction, that is, what percentage of orders the company should be able to fill promptly from inventory on hand. Out-of-stock conditions result in lost sales, loss of goodwill, and maybe even a loss of customers. Yet to be able to fill 100 percent of the orders promptly may require an excessively costly

---

[8]See Ronald H. Ballou, "Improving the Physical Layout of Merchandise in Warehouses," *Journal of Marketing*, July, 1967, pp. 60–64.

inventory. One authority estimates that about 80 percent *more* inventory is required to fill 95 percent of the orders than to fill only 80 percent.[9]

Related to the size question is the need to establish the optimum quantity to reorder (make or buy) when it is time to replenish inventory stocks. The determination of this "economic order quantity" (EOQ) for a manufacturer moves us back into the production-scheduling process. Once again we see the total-system aspect of physical distribution. Decisions on the size of the EOQ will be made by balancing acquisition costs, carrying costs, and the desired level of satisfaction in filling customers' orders.

Closely related to the inventory control system and every bit as valuable to management are merchandise planning systems. Two commonly used systems are basic stock lists and model stock plans. Both planning systems are based essentially on an analysis of past sales.

The *basic stock list* is widely used in the distribution of staple goods where identical or closely related items are carried year after year. Under this system, reasonably detailed information is maintained for every item the company keeps in stock. That is, separate records are maintained for each size, color, or other significant feature of a given product. The information includes sales of the item, minimum limits when reordering is necessary, and the quantity to be reordered.

For fashion merchandise the most widely used merchandise planning system is called a *model stock plan.* The same items are not carried year in and year out in product lines subject to fashion changes, so a basic stock list is not feasible. A certain style of women's dress or shoes may be carried for only one fashion season, but there are other factors in the area of fashion merchandise which do remain reasonably constant and thus lend themselves to planning. For example, a dress manufacturer or the dress department in a department store will find that the percentage of total unit dress sales in each size remains about the same over a period of years. Perhaps size 12 dresses account for 16 percent of total sales, size 14 dresses represent 24 percent, etc. Also, the manufacturer or retailer may find that each price line accounts for about the same share of unit sales each year. Consequently, a firm can plan what it considers an ideal, or model, stock on the basis of size, price line, or any other product characteristic which remains reasonably constant for several seasons.

ESTABLISH PROCEDURES TO PROCESS ORDERS

As another step in a physical distribution system, management needs to establish a procedure for handling and filling orders. This should also include provision for credit-granting decisions, invoice preparation, and collections on past-due accounts. A considerable amount of consumer ill will can be generated if a company makes mistakes or is slow in filling orders. From the company's standpoint, the activities connected with handling and filling orders offer opportunities for a substantial reduction in marketing expenses. Processing orders includes activities in two areas—the pertinent office work and the physical task of assembling and shipping.

---

[9]John F. Magee, "The Logistics of Distribution," *Harvard Business Review,* July–August, 1960, p. 92.

SELECT METHOD OF TRANSPORTATION

A major decision involving the logistics system of a company is that of determining which agencies will be used to ship the products from the manufacturer to the middlemen or final customers, or from one middlemen to another. (At this point, we are concerned primarily with *intercity* shipments.) The transportation routes and the freight rate structure are important determinants of the geographic limits of a company's market, the outline of its sales territories, and the location of its inventory stocks. When the decision is made regarding the method of transportation to be used, the company may establish its own facilities, such as its own truck, rail, or barge line, or it may employ common carriers.[10]

Before making the decision, however, management should understand the relative merits, costs, special features, and services of each of the five major forms of transportation: railroads, trucks, water, pipelines, and airplanes. The relative importance of each, along with some trends in its use, is shown in Table 20-1. Note that the figures reflect *intercity* freight traffic only. Ocean coastal traffic between United States ports is not included. Virtually all farm-to-farm and *intracity* freight movements are made by motor truck. Consequently, the figures for water and truck carriers really understate the importance of these methods of transportation by a considerable margin. Nevertheless, Table 20-1 is illuminating. It shows that railroads are still by far the major intercity freight carrier. Although their relative position has declined steadily since 1940, the actual number of ton-miles of freight carried by railroad has increased considerably since that time. Even excluding intracity freight traffic, the use of motor trucks has expanded phenomenally over the past thirty years.

RAILROADS

Railroads are particularly well adapted for long hauls of carload quantities of bulk products which are low in value in relation to their weight and the freight charges Thus these carriers are low-cost agencies for the shipment of items such as autos, coal, sand, gravel, minerals, and agricultural and forest products. On the other hand, railroads are limited by their inflexibility—they can go only where the track is laid. Railroads have been hurt and trucks have been helped by the growth of markets, including suburban markets, not located on rail lines.

In spite of the many services that railroads have instituted, the nature of the market is such that other carriers will probably make further inroads on the railroads. Marketing executives, however, should be aware of the various services offered by railroads because for many products and in many marketing situations, railroads are still the lowest-cost, most efficient method of transportation.

---

[10]Transportation carriers are often divided into three types: common, contract, and private. A *common* carrier is one which is granted operating rights by a government regulatory agency, such as the Interstate Commerce Commission. The carrier operates on announced schedules and rates and is expected to handle merchandise from any shipper. *Contract* carriers operate in a less regulated manner. They enter into contracts with individual shippers and agree to move specified shipments for specified periods of time. *Private* carriers are owned and operated by individual firms for the shipment of their own goods only.

Table 20-1. **Estimated distribution of intercity freight traffic in United States: In millions of ton-miles.**

Railroads are still the major carrier for intercity freight. While the physical volume of rail freight has increased substantially, the railroads share of the market has declined considerably since 1940. Freight shipped by truck or pipeline has increased from 10 percent of the total in 1940 to 22 percent in 1972. If we consider intracity freight, which carrier is most important?

Carrier	Ton-miles 1972	Percent of total 1972	1960	1940
Railroads	785,000	38.9	44.1	61.3
Great Lakes	107,000	5.3	7.6	15.5
Rivers and canals	218,000	10.8	9.2	3.6
Motor trucks	445,000	22.1	21.7	10.0
Oil pipeline	457,000	22.7	17.4	9.6
Air carriers	3,800	.2		
Total	2,015,800	100.0	100.0	100.0

Source: *Yearbook of Railroad Facts,* Association of American Railroads, Washington, D.C., 1973, p. 36.

Carload versus less-than-carload freight rates. Railroads offer substantial savings to firms which can ship in carload (c.l.) quantities as compared with less-than-carload (l.c.l.) shipments. For many items the c.l. freight rate is as much as 50 percent less than the l.c.l. rate. This is a tremendous incentive to shippers of large quantities of products, especially to shippers of minerals, agricultural products, and similar goods where freight expenses are a significant percentage of total value.

Combined shipments. Long ago the railroads realized that they were vulnerable to competition from other types of carriers when it came to handling l.c.l. shipments. Consequently, the railroads have developed several measures designed to reduce the cost of l.c.l. shipments, to speed them up, and generally to make the railroads a more attractive carrier for firms wishing to ship in smaller quantities. These measures provide for combining into a c.l. quantity the freight from one or more companies who are shipping products to customers located in one area. The pooled freight can go at c.l. rates and can be delivered much more rapidly than if its component parts were sent separately in l.c.l. units. Sometimes the initiative in pooled shipments is taken by a group of retailers who arrange to buy a carload of some item, have it loaded at the shipping point, and then provide for the distribution of the individual orders when the car reaches its destination.

In-transit privileges. Two in-transit privileges offered by railroads are (1) diversion in transit and (2) the opportunity to process some products en route.

Diversion in transit allows a seller to start a shipment moving in one general direction and to establish or change destination while the car is en route, just as long as the new destination involves a forward movement of the car and no backtracking. The charges are computed on the basis of the through rate or long-haul rate from the point of origin to the ultimate destination, plus a small charge for diversion. This is a valuable service to shippers of perishable products which are subject to frequent price fluctuations and to variations in price from one city to another on any given day. To illustrate, a Washington cooperative may want to ship Red Delicious apples to Eastern markets. Several carloads will be shipped from Wenatchee, Washington, to Chicago, or they may just be shipped eastward with the specific destination to be determined sometime after the shipment leaves Wenatchee. Before the shipment reaches Chicago, the shipper may receive word that prices in the Chicago market are temporarily depressed but that there is a good market in Memphis. Consequently, at the appropriate "diversion point" (probably Chicago in this case) the cars will be rerouted to Memphis. The freight charges will be based on the through rate from Wenatchee to Memphis. A shipment may be diverted several times before reaching its final destination.

Under the privilege of *processing in transit,* a shipper may have his product unloaded, graded, manufactured, or otherwise processed in some manner while en route, and then have it shipped on to its final destination. As an example, livestock may be shipped from a Western state to Chicago. En route the animals may be unloaded, watered, and fattened in feedlots, but the through rate to Chicago will apply. Wheat may be shipped from Spokane to Minneapolis, where it may be made into flour and the flour shipped to Detroit. Again, the shipper has the privilege of processing in transit. The through rate is usually substantially less than the combined rates from origin to processing point and from processing point to destination.

Piggyback and fishyback services. In recent years the railroads have attempted to meet competition from trucks by offering a "piggyback" service to shippers. Under this arrangement truck trailers are carried on railroad flatcars. The goods can be loaded on trucks at the seller's shipping dock and need not be handled again until they are unloaded at the buyer's receiving station. This combination of truck and rail transportation offers more flexibility than railroads alone can offer. Also, less handling of the goods tends to decrease damage and pilferage.

"Fishyback" service involves transporting loaded trailers on barges or ships. The trailers may be carried piggyback fashion by railroad to the ship's dock, and then at the other end they can be loaded back onto the trains for the completion of the rail haul. In an alternative use of the fishyback service, railroads are not used at all. Merchandise is trucked directly to ports, where the trailer vans are loaded on barges. At the end of the water journey the vans are trucked to the receiving station.

Freight rate structure. A few comments on the railroad rate structure may give some indication of the enormous complexity of transportation rates. Railroads are used as examples because they frequently set standards for rates on other types of carriers. Also, railroad rates are often used as a basis for comparison when analyzing shipping costs on trucks, airlines, or barges. Most products shipped by railroad go under a class rate or a commodity rate, although bargaining and competition from other carriers have led to the establishment of special rates for particular products in certain parts of the country.

Class rates have been established in an attempt to simplify the problem of determining shipping rates for thousands of items shipped between countless points of origin and destination. Many classes have been set up, and each has its own rate per 100 pounds shipped over a given distance. Products which are reasonably similar in size, value, perishability, or some other distinguishing feature are grouped into one class. Several thousand manufactured products are classed in this manner, and their shipping costs are figured accordingly. Within each class, the rates may vary according to distance, but the ton-mile charges are less as the length of the haul increases. Also, there are regional differences in class rates for the same distance. Further complications enter the picture in at least three ways. First, thousands of new rates are filed each year with the Interstate Commerce Commission. Second, attempts are always being made to have products changed to a lower class. Third, a slight change in the description of what is being shipped may move a product from one class to another.

Commodity rates have been established for the shipment of bulky, low-value products, such as sand, gravel, iron ore, lumber, coal, grains, and other agricultural products. A separate rate is set for each product going between two specific points. Thus there is one commodity rate for lumber shipped from Seattle to Boise, Idaho. About 85 percent of railroad freight moves under commodity rates, about 5 percent under class rates, and about 10 percent under some type of special rate.

TRUCKS

The tremendously increased use of highway transportation noted in the discussion of Table 20-1 is traceable largely to three factors: an improved system of highways, new developments in equipment for trucking and materials handling, and the competitive advantages of this method of transportation. Trucks have proved to be a very effective transportation medium for short hauls of high-value merchandise. Highway carriers have the advantages of speed and flexibility of movement. Once the merchandise is loaded at the shipper's dock, it can be sent directly to the buyer without any loading or unloading in between. Truck shipments receive less handling and therefore less careful and expensive packaging than rail shipments.

Another factor favoring highway transportation is its lower total freight cost for many products. This is not because of lower freight rates for trucks. Actually rail and truck freight rates are similar for shipping many products in many parts of the United States. The difference is due largely to the fact that trucks go from the seller's loading dock to the buyer's receiving platform. Railroads go from terminal to terminal, and there are added costs in moving products to and from the teminals.

WATERWAYS

A considerable amount of freight is transported by ships and barges on inland and coastal waterways. These waterways are especially good for shipping bulky, low-value, nonperishable products, such as petroleum, sand, gravel, coal, grain, and metallic ores. Water transportation is the cheapest and also the slowest of all major methods of shipping. Its use is sometimes limited by climatic conditions.

PIPELINES

Pipelines are a rather special method of transportation in that they are limited largely to carrying petroleum products, especially crude oil and natural gas. While pipelines are technically common carriers open to use by any shipper, most of them are used to ship the products of the companies who own the lines. They are obviously limited in use because of their inflexibility. Pipeline shipping of crude oil costs less than rail transportation, but more than water transportation.

AIRLINES

Although the newest of the major methods of transporting products, the airlines have undoubtedly done more than any other type of carrier to spearhead the systems approach and total cost concept in physical distribution. Obviously unable to compete on the basis of rates or ton-mile costs alone, the airlines had to demonstrate that the use of air freight would result in savings in other distribution elements (smaller inventory, faster delivery, fewer warehouses, less expensive packaging, etc.), which would tend to offset the higher air transportation costs. Even though air freight rates have been reduced considerably over the years, and are expected to go still lower as the Boeing 747 (jumbo jet) comes into more general use, these rates are still substantially higher than truck or rail freight rates.

Air express (door-to-door shipment) and air freight (terminal-to-terminal shipment) together account for only a small part of 1 percent of total intercity freight shipments, although the tonnage has increased steadily and appreciably over the past several years. These total figures, however, conceal the wide use of air freight, and the important role it plays, in certain marketing situations. To an increasing extent, the use of air freight as a transportation method is being dictated by management's customer-oriented sales thinking, and not only by its orientation toward total cost savings.

The strongest selling point for air freight is its speed. This factor has enabled many industries and firms to expand their market limits and to open new markets. Products subject to physical deterioration (fresh-cut flowers, biologicals, fresh seafood, radioisotopes) can be delivered to many more markets by air than by any other carrier. Sears, for example, has taken advantage of the speed of air freight to compete with firms which have merchandise stocks much nearer to the market. Montgomery Ward has a warehouse in Denver, and yet one way in which Sears competes effectively in that market is by using daily air freight shipments from its Kansas City warehouse, about 600 miles away.

REA EXPRESS

REA Express is a specialized, small-shipment carrier which has adjusted to changing conditions. Formerly called Railway Express Agency, formerly owned by the major railroads, and formerly a heavy user of passenger trains for shipments, today REA is geared to trucking operations. Air express is just one branch of REA, and rail piggyback transportation is also used. REA offers pickup and delivery service. It will ship orders with freight charges collected on delivery. The rates are higher than those for carload freight shipments, but the service is admirably suited for small shipments of perishables and other products where the freight cost is low in relation to the item's value.[11]

FREIGHT FORWARDERS

The freight forwarder is a specialized marketing institution which has developed through the years to serve firms who ship in l.c.l. quantities. Freight forwarders do not own their own transportation equipment, but they do provide a valuable service in physical distribution. Their main function is to consolidate l.c.l. shipments or less-than-truckload shipments from several shippers into carload and truckload quantities. Their operating margin is generally the spread between c.l. and l.c.l. rates. That is, the shipper pays l.c.l. rates, and the freight forwarder transports the products at c.l. rates. The freight forwarder also picks up the merchandise at the shipper's place of business and arranges for delivery at the buyer's door. In addition to this pick-up and delivery service, an l.c.l. shipper enjoys all the advantages of speed and minimum handling associated with c.l. shipments, even though he pays l.c.l. rates. Also, freight forwarders provide the small shipper with traffic management services. They select the best transportation methods and routes.

ORGANIZATIONAL RESPONSIBILITY FOR PHYSICAL DISTRIBUTION

A significant question which may be asked is: Who is in charge of physical distribution? All too often, the answer is "no one." We observed earlier that activities within the system often are not coordinated and that managerial responsibility is consequently compartmentalized into units which may even have conflicting goals. There are many examples of firms which have developed the ability to analyze their total distribution effort, have identified substantial cost-savings opportunities, and yet have been unable to capture these dollars because they were not organized to do a total physical distribution job.[12]

It is encouraging to note, however, that there is a trend toward the establishment of a separate formal department responsible for the management of all physical distribution activities.[13]

One study suggested that a prospective physical distribution department passes through four stages: (1) shipping—total organizational fragmentation; (2) traffic —a managerial specialist in transportation is used; (3) movement—the dawn of a systems viewpoint; and (4) physical distribution—the activities are planned and operated as a system in the full sense of the word.[14]

---

[11]See "REA Rides Again on a New Track," *Business Week,* Jan. 2, 1971, p. 34.

[12]John F. Stolle, "How to Manage Physical Distribution," *Harvard Business Review,* July –August, 1967, pp. 93–100. See also Robert P. Neuschel, "Physical Distribution: Forgotten Frontier," *Harvard Business Review,* March–April, 1967, pp. 125–134, for a study in which only five out of twenty-six large, profitable companies in a wide variety of industries were ranked "good" (in contrast to "average" or "poor") in all criteria used in this study to evaluate their physical distribution management.

[13]See Donald J. Bowersox, "Emerging Patterns of Physical Distribution Organization," *Transportation and Distribution Management,* May, 1968, pp 53–56.

[14]J. L. Heskett, "Ferment in Marketing's Oldest Area," *Journal of Marketing,* October, 1962, pp. 40–45; see also Robert E. Weigand, "The Management of Physical Distribution: A Dilemma," *Business Topics,* Summer, 1962, pp. 67–72.

Assuming that a company has a physical distribution department, the next organizational question is: To whom should the head of this department report? At the risk of charges of "empire building by the marketing people," current enlightened managerial thinking suggests that physical distribution should be the responsibility of either the chief marketing executive or a separate department whose head reports directly to the president of the company. In any event, logistics management should be viewed by top management as one of its prime responsibilities.[15]

QUESTIONS AND PROBLEMS

1. In some companies, activities such as processing and shipping orders, maintaining an inventory control system, and locating warehouse stocks throughout the market are treated as separate, fragmented tasks. What are some of the administrative and operational problems which are likely to occur in this type of arrangement?
2. "The goal of a modern physical distribution system in a firm should be to operate at the lowest possible *total* costs." Do you agree?
3. Name some products for which the costs of physical distribution constitute at least one-half of the total price of the goods at the wholesale level. Can you suggest ways of decreasing the physical distribution costs of these products?
4. "Storage adds value to products in that it creates time utility. At the same time, the value of a product may be totally destroyed by storing it too long." Explain.
5. Explain how a marketing manager can use transportation and warehousing facilities to stabilize the prices of his products.
6. "Inventory size will be smaller but transportation expenses will be larger if a manufacturer follows an inventory-location strategy of concentration rather than dispersion." Do you agree? Explain.
7. "The use of public warehouse facilities makes it possible for a manufacturer to bypass wholesalers in his channels of distribution." Explain.
8. If a public warehouse can provide so many wholesaling services, why have these warehouses not largely eliminated full-function wholesalers and manufacturers' sales branches?
9. What is the relationship between inventory management and the "economic order quantity" in production scheduling?
10. How are transportation decisions related to packaging policies?
11. Why are l.c.l. shipments so much slower and more costly than c.l. shipments?
12. What alternatives does a manufacturer have if he must ship in l.c.l. quantities, but the competitive price structure for his product is such that he cannot afford to pay the high l.c.l. freight rates?
13. As traffic manager of a large department store in the big city nearest your campus, you are asked to determine the best transportation method and route for the shipment of each of the following items to your store. In each case your store is to pay full freight charges. Unless specifically noted, there is no time urgency involved.

---

[15]For an excellent summary of the "where it has been," "where it is now," and "where it is going" aspects of physical distribution, see Donald J. Bowersox, "Physical Distribution Development, Current Status, and Potential," *Journal of Marketing,* January, 1969, pp. 63–70.

a. Fresh salmon from Seattle, Washington. Total shipment weighs 200 pounds.
b. An assortment of various types of large appliances from Evansville, Indiana. Total weight is 20,000 pounds.
c. A refill order of 200 dresses from New York City. This is a "hot" fashion item, so speed is of the essence.
d. Sheets, pillowcases, and towels from a mill in Alabama. Total weight is 100 pounds.
e. Ten sets of dining-room furniture from Grand Rapids, Michigan.

14. Under what conditions is a company apt to select air freight as its main method of transporting its finished goods?

15. The Belden Wholesale Company has been considering a new ordering system for its salesmen. Under the present system the salesmen write and mail their orders at the end of the day. A new system has been suggested which would have the salesmen phone the home office once a day and dictate the orders into a tape recorder. The clerical staff could then transfer the taped orders onto IBM cards. The main advantages of such a system would be the following:

a. Faster receipt of orders
b. Increased ease and speed of order filling in the stockroom owing to the systematic compilation of orders which the computer would provide.
c. Faster billing.

Following is a comparison of the old and proposed new systems, showing the number of days required from receipt of order to shipment of goods from the warehouse:

	Old	New
Time from order to transmission of order:	½ day	½ day
Time from transmission of order to writing up of order:	3 days	½ day
Time to fill out order:	1 day	½ day
Time to pack, label and move goods to warehouse exit:	½ day	½ day
	5 days	2 days

Customers expect delivery within five days, therefore, Belden has had to stock an almost complete line. Since Belden would have three days' grace and have time to react to stock cuts (under the proposed system), it was estimated that with the reduction in order-processing time, the inventory of $1,500,000 would be reduced by 30 percent. Under the new system it would also be possible to attach the bills to the orders rather than sending out the bills three days after the order as previously. The billings for the year are $50,000,000. You are asked to:

a. Calculate the savings from (1) the smaller inventory and (2) the faster billing, given that the imputed holding cost of inventory is 18 percent and the prime interest rate is 8 percent. Assume 250 billing days per year.
b. Suggest other costs which will decrease and any which will increase.

CASES FOR PART

CASE 13. DEL MAR JEWELRY MANUFACTURING COMPANY, INC. (B)*

Conflict in distribution channels at retail level

The executives of Del Mar Jewelry Manufacturing Company, Inc., were faced with a problem of allocating their merchandise between two highly competitive, but seemingly equally important, retail accounts. These executives decided to let Mr. Phillip Johnson, one of their sales representatives, resolve the problem in view of his excellent record in handling his territory and these two accounts for the past several years.

Located in Miami, Florida, the Del Mar Company had been manufacturing women's costume jewelry for many years. The company used manufacturers' agents to sell to retailers throughout the United States. However, because there was very little manufacturing of jewelry items south of Atlanta, Del Mar held a rather unique position among its local retail accounts, and a considerable portion of the company's sales volume was in the southeastern states.

The Del Mar line of costume jewelry was divided into two categories—one labeled "Enamels by Del Mar" and the other "Del Mar Jewels." The enameled

*Case prepared by Prof. Barry J. Hersker, Florida Atlantic University. Reproduced with permission.

jewelry consisted of tailored, gold costume jewelry items which were hand-enameled with a small brush and which were visibly superior to sprayed and stenciled enameled jewelry. Del Mar's enameled jewelry ranged in wholesale price from $6.75 to approximately $48 per *dozen*. Enameled jewelry was also produced by another Florida firm, Alden Jewelry. Del Mar's line was more extensive than Alden's, and Alden frequently copied Del Mar's styles. Mr. Morris Alden was formerly in partnership with the present owners of Del Mar, and bitterness between the two firms had existed since the dissolution of the partnership.

"Del Mar Jewels" was a line of costume jewelry consisting of necklaces, bracelets, and earrings made from various colors and styles of beads (pearls, ceramic, lucite, crystal, etc.). No other firm south of Atlanta produced similar items, and most manufacturing of this type was done in New York City. Wholesale prices on Del Mar Jewels ranged from $1.50 to $25 per *item*. The retail prices for all the Jewel merchandise, and all but the lowest priced enameled products, carried a 50 percent markup on selling price—the usual markup in retail jewelry stores.

Mr. Johnson believed that Del Mar's success in Florida could be attributed to a variety of factors. The local wholesalers did not carry either enameled or other merchandise of the character or quality of Del Mar products. Northern manufacturers did not produce enameled products comparable to Del Mar Enamels, but they were quite competitive in the other jewelry products. On the other hand, Del Mar, being a local supplier, could offer special services and faster delivery to local retail accounts. Mr. Johnson further believed that "the tourist who buys a gift to take North would naturally prefer locally produced items, especially if they are of high quality. Who wants to purchase a gift in Florida for a friend in New York, only to find that the item could be purchased in every drug store back home?"

Mr. Johnson followed the practice of selecting his retail accounts with great care, and then cultivating them intensively. Although Del Mar had no set policy relating to exclusive franchise agreements, it was Mr. Johnson's policy to select the best retailer in a given area, and then refuse to sell Del Mar merchandise to his competitors. He explained this policy by saying, "Even where two good accounts can be sold in a given area, I believe that if I sell only to one account, who will therefore favor my products, I can sell a greater total volume of goods. One enthusiastic account whom I protect is worth more than two accounts who must compete with each other."

Following this policy had not caused any problems in the past, but when a conflict finally did arise between two accounts in Fort Lauderdale, Florida, the problem proved difficult to solve. Both of these accounts were among Mr. Johnson's best customers, and each of the two had more than one retail store.

One account was owned by Mr. Fred Bier, and consisted of four retail outlets located along the ocean-front route A1A in Fort Lauderdale. The most profitable store owned by Mr. Bier was named the Sea Chest and was located in the shopping area adjacent to some of the finest hotels in Fort Lauderdale. Although the Sea Chest was a small store, its sales volume was quite surprising. Mr. Bier had a policy of handling relatively few individual items in the categories of accessories, jewelry, and handbags, but once having selected fast-moving items, he would reorder heavily. It was not uncommon for Mr. Bier to carry an inventory of several dozen of each item displayed.

Mr. Bier had purchased from Del Mar for many years. His combined volume of purchases from Del Mar had increased to about $8,000 annually. (On this, as on all orders within his territory, Mr. Johnson received a commission of 12½ percent on his sales volume.) Mr. Bier purchased mainly Del Mar Enamels, but Mr. Johnson was hoping to gradually increase Bier's purchases of the Jewel goods.

The second account in question was called Kay's Accessories, owned by Mr. Jim Kay. This firm had two retail outlets, one located in downtown Fort Lauderdale, and the other in a newly-completed shopping center located on a major artery connecting the downtown areas with the northern beach and residential area of Fort Lauderdale. This second store was larger than the downtown branch of Kay's Accessories, was more modern, and carried more expensive merchandise. The two Kay's Accessories stores purchased about $7,500 worth of Del Mar products annually, of which roughly two-thirds were enameled goods and one-third was Del Mar Jewels.

Mr. Johnson received his new lines of Del Mar jewelry in mid-September. He then contacted Mr. Bier to obtain initial reactions and sample orders on this merchandise, only to be advised that both he and Del Mar, in the words of Mr. Bier, had "a very serious choice to make."

Mr. Johnson was then told how Jim Kay was opening a new branch called "Kay's-by-the-Sea," only two stores away from the Sea Chest. Mr. Bier, as Mr. Johnson well knew, was always insistent upon his exclusive right to merchandise in a given area, and so would not tolerate any supplier selling both to his stores and the new Kay's store. In fact, as a result of the new store, considerable personal hostility already existed between Mr. Bier and Jim Kay.

Mr. Bier emphasized, "I'll be glad to buy Del Mar Enamels, but if you sell one item to Kay, you can forget about my business entirely."

"Suppose I get Kay's word that he won't put in his new store the items that you are carrying?"

"You can't trust him—at least I can't and won't. As soon as I place my order, he'll put the goods next door to the Sea Chest. And at that point I've given Del Mar my last order!"

Mr. Bier then commented that he would not even look at the new Del Mar lines until this matter was resolved. He further added that Alden Jewelry was promising to protect him from the "invasion by Kay," and that he intended to increase his volume with that firm if necessary.

Mr. Johnson immediately contacted Mr. Jim Kay. Mr. Kay greeted him warmly saying, "I sure am anxious to see your new line. It looks like a good season. We've added a new branch on the beach, and expect to open in a few weeks."

"Yes, I know," said Mr. Johnson. He then proceeded to explain, as honestly as he could, how Mr. Bier felt about Del Mar and the "invasion" by Kay's stores. He asked Mr. Kay if he would agree *not* to put Del Mar into the new store on the beach.

"Now, you know I can't do that," he replied. "I believe in live and let live. I have no objection to your selling to Bier, so why should he object to your selling to me? I'm sorry, but I can't promise not to sell certain items in my new store. There would be the problem of inventory control, and all that."

"Look, Jim, suppose I divide the line—that is, split it into two lines, and give one to you and one to Bier?"

"If you want to cut your sales to me in half, go ahead. But I can't see any sense in it. Besides, you know that Bier will throw you out if you offer him that deal. He would be afraid that I'd get a good number, and you know how he likes to run a high volume on a few items."

"If I were to give Bier the enamels, and you the jeweled goods, would you agree to that?"

"Maybe—as I said, I am easy to get along with, and this is your problem. But then, I'll have to have to buy enamels from Alden."

"Bier says Alden won't sell to you—that he'll protect Bier at the beach store."

"Well, tell Bier I've already placed a small order with Alden. Somebody is getting kidded on this. My advice to you is, just be fair to yourself. If I don't care whom you sell to, why should Bier care? He'll have your stuff at the Sea Chest and I don't mind. So what if a few items are duplicated at the new Kay's-by-the-Sea? It's live and let live, I say."

Mr. Johnson thanked Mr. Jim Kay, and said he'd be back to show the new line as soon as possible. He discussed the problem with the management of Del Mar and they urged him to exercise extreme caution, since these were the two best accounts in Fort Lauderdale. Further, it was well known that Mr. Bier was prone to hold a grudge for a long, long time, and despite Mr. Kay's protestations of belief in the free enterprise system, he (Kay) probably expected to continue his purchasing from Del Mar rather than to increase his purchasing from Alden.

QUESTION

1. How should Mr. Johnson handle this conflict in Del Mar's retail distribution?

CASE 14. P. M. AUSTIN COMPANY*

Selection of channels of distribution

Mr. Matthew Stagg, an M.B.A. from a western state university, recently was appointed as the marketing manager of the P. M. Austin Company. His first task was to prepare recommendations regarding the future development of the channels of distribution for the company's products. During the rapid growth of the company, little attention had been given to channel selection.

In 1965, 34-year-old David Austin, founder and president of the company, was dissatisfied with the quality and selection of hairpieces available to the male segment of the hair-goods market. He lost most of his hair at a fairly young age and was interested in correcting the fate nature dealt him. However, he was dissatisfied with the quality of the products then available on the market, and he spent a majority of his time experimenting with new methods of manufacturing men's toupees. He developed a product which appeared to be as good as any offered on the market at that time. With the financial backing of a close relative, he began manufacturing men's hairpieces which were distributed through a firm primarily selling women's hair-goods. Although sales were increasing on the local level, no effort was made by the retail firm to sell outside the locality. Problems related to pricing, order time, and quality also developed in the relationship, and after the first year David Austin decided that it would be best to

---

*Case prepared by Professors Gary F. McKinnon, Brigham Young University, and John J. Painter, University of Utah. Copyright by Brigham Young University. Reproduced with permission.

handle both manufacturing and sales through his own firm under the brand name of Manner Way.

Mr. Matthew Stagg had previously been employed as the sales manager of a medium-sized consumer goods company. His appointment as the marketing manager of P. M. Austin was his first introduction to the artificial hair-goods market. Therefore, he spent most of the first month acquainting himself with the organization and the market it served.

Mr. Stagg was most impressed with the growing demand for men's hairpieces. This growth was illustrated by trade estimates which indicated about 375,000 men were wearing some type of hairpiece in 1957, while by 1968, 1,500,000 men were wearing some type of hairpiece. Trade sources estimated that 12 million or more men in the United States were bald or balding. Mr. Stagg contacted several leading dermatologists who indicted that to date there is no known way to prevent or cure what is called "male pattern" baldness, marked by a receding frontal hairline. Most experts believe this to be inherited, related to age, and triggered by male hormones. One dermatologist suggested that three-quarters of the men in the United States over the age of 40 show some signs of this type of baldness.

In contrast to the male segment of the hair-goods market, the market for women's hairpieces is much more extensive as it does not solely consist of bald or balding women. In fact, most wigs are sold to women with an adequate supply of hair. Although Mr. Stagg noted the buying motives affecting the women's segment of the market may be very different from those influencing purchases by males, he wondered if the nature of the male segment of the market could become more similar to the women's market. He noted a growing interest in fashion and hair style among men and that only a limited amount of promotion had been used in selling men's hairpieces in the past.

Hair-goods (hairpieces, mustaches, sideburns, etc.) are more commonly manufactured by hand, or machines, tying hair on a lace or knitted base. The more expensive hairpieces are made from undyed, untreated hair (usually imported from Europe) and manufactured to the wearer's specifications.

Traditionally, the toupee was manufactured to the specifications of a plaster cast which had been applied to the head of the customer. Because of the discomfort of the plaster cast, some firms substituted a paraffin wrap in the measuring process. While continuing his search for technically improved products, David Austin developed a series of six different caps (each with three different adjustments) which could be placed on the head of the customer to acquire the proper size and shape required in the manufacturing process of each custom-made hairpiece. Dealers and customers alike believed this to be a major breakthrough in the hair-goods market as this procedure eliminated the discomfort and mess of the alternative methods.

The price of a quality hairpiece ranged from $300 to $1,000. The less expensive hairpieces, ranging from $50 to $300, were usually made of synthetic hair, Oriental hair, or animal hair. These hairpieces were not usually made to customer specifications, but the customer was sold the hairpiece most closly matching his hair color and size from the retailer's inventory.

Mr. Stagg noted that the competition in the industry serving bald or balding men could not be limited to artificial hairpieces. A growing competitive threat was a process known as hair transplanting. Although hair transplanting had been performed for more than 15 years, it has only recently been considered medically sound. Hair transplanting consists of transplanting small clumps of hair, one clump at a time, from where the client has hair (usually the back of the head) to an area where he wishes hair to grow. Although the process is almost always successful, it is an extremely time-consuming process performed over several months. The process must be performed by a dermatologist or plastic surgeon, and the cost ranges from $1,500 to $3,000. It is fairly painful and there is usually a period of impaired appearance. However, when the treatment is complete, the man can ignore toupee glue and dry cleaning, and he has the satisfaction of having a head of real hair.

Another innovation which has been added to the men's hair business is hair weaving. It is a process by which matched human hair is "woven" on a man's head, using existing hair as an anchor for the new hair. The initial cost runs between $200 and $500, and the weaving must be tightened at least once every four to eight weeks at a cost of $25 to $50. Hairweavers claim the process has many advantages over toupees in that the customer can swim, shower, sleep, and participate in other activities with a full head of hair. However, some customers have complained of shoddy work and the consensus of opinion in the trade is that the toupee looks better than a reweave.

David Austin developed a new method of manufacturing mustaches in 1967, and this patented process was applied to the manufacturing of Manner Way toupees. Hairs are individually implanted on a plastic filament which is almost the texture of skin. Competitive products are usually hand-tied on a fine nylon knit. Both types offer some advantages but, generally speaking, the public as well as dealers prefer the Manner Way products. The Manner Way product is guaranteed against color fade or hair loss for one year.

Mechanized processing enables Manner Way products to compete with those using foreign labor. In addition, superior features such as the filament base and the use of European human hair enable and justify average-to-high pricing on wholesale and retail levels. Manner Way pieces are sold to retailers for $130 and then sold by the retailer for $350. The retailer, usually a barber, must fit the toupee and service it (tapering, cutting, etc.) when sold.

Hairpieces are usually sold by specialty shops, barbers, beauty supply houses, novelty shops, and direct sales people who develop leads from former customers and advertising. Hairpieces have also been sold by department stores. There are no retail chains that dominate the men's hair goods market, either on a regional or national basis. Some manufacturers have also tried mail-order selling through ads in consumer magazines with apparent success.

Matthew Stagg noted that while sales of the company had doubled each year from its founding (1974 sales were $327,000), management had paid little attention to its channels of distribution. The present channel system was made up of some retailers who first were Manner Way mustache dealers, plus a number of barbers who were added to the distribution system when emphasis was placed on men's toupees. These barbers usually contacted the company regarding the possibility of becoming Manner Way dealers. The only communication with these dealers was by telephone or mail. Mr. Stagg found that in eight large cities dealers had been given exclusive rights to sell Manner Way products. These exclusive dealers received the regular markup when selling to the ultimate consumers in their areas, and $50 per hairpiece when other dealers made sales in their exclusive territories. In other areas of the country no such exclusive territories have been granted. An analysis of the sales invoices revealed that Manner Way had a network of 130 dealers, most of them barbers. Only 30 dealers sold as many as five hairpieces per month. Several dealers with exclusive territories sold less than four hairpieces each month.

In the spring of 1972, the P. M. Austin Company opened its first and only retail store in the central shopping district of the metropolitan area (population 580,000) in which the company was located. Although sales through the outlet were modest during the first few months, the breakeven volume was reached within the first year of operation. The store was averaging approximately 30 hairpieces each month. No advertising had been used to promote the Manner Way retail outlet. It appeared that customers became aware of the store through communications with relatives and friends.

The two men employed as salesmen in the store were compensated at a rate of $500 per month plus a commission of $10 on each hairpiece sold. A secretary was employed in the store to keep track of the ordering, bookkeeping, and correspondence. In addition, she helped with the "measuring cap" used in determining specifications for each hairpiece. She received a salary of $400 per month, but no commission. Other fixed expenses for the store's operation amounted to approximately $11,500 per year.

Mr. Stagg felt there were several alternative courses of action which the Austin Company could follow in establishing new channel systems. He was impressed with the potential profitability of the Manner Way retail outlet, but he questioned the feasibility of expanding these stores into new metropolitan areas. Another major alternative was to grant a franchise in specific territories. If this plan was adopted, he wondered whether the franchise holders should consist of *(a)* independent retail store owners, *(b)* wholesale dealers selling to other dealers, *(c)* barbershops, or *(d)* a combination of the above. Although he was puzzled as to what the cost of each franchise should be, he felt this system would simplify the ordering and scheduling problems the firm had encountered in the past. The third alternative was to eliminate the franchise system and sell to any qualified dealers desiring to be part of the channel. Several excellent dealers had been acquired while this policy guided the company's actions in the past.

Just as Matthew Stagg reached the final phase of acquainting himself with the hair-goods industry and Austin Company's growth and position, Mr. David Austin announced that plans had been completed for expanded production facilities. Production would be increased from the present capacity of 250 hairpieces per month to over 1,200 hairpieces. Mr. Stagg realized that the present channel system could never accommodate the additional units.

QUESTION

1. In view of the proposed four-fold increase in its production capacity, what channels of distribution should the Austin Company use?

CASE 15. CROCKETT ELECTRIC COMPANY

Selection of channels of distribution

The vice president in charge of production and engineering at Crockett Electric Company saw an automatic garage-door opener at a home show and became interested in the possibilities of adding a similar article to his company's line. He approached the marketing department executives with the product idea, and they were interested enough to do some preliminary marketing research. Studies showed that a large market potential existed and that only a minute part of this potential had been tapped. Many competitive models existed but none had any degree of market acceptance or success. In brief, here was a product with a terrific potential, but no firm had been able to capitalize on these opportunities.

Crockett's engineers then developed a patentable electronic door opener. The product was fairly simple. It consisted of two units, one of which was to be installed inside the garage. The other was a portable unit which could be mounted in some convenient location within the car or placed in the glove compartment. The user simply pushed a button on the portable unit in the car to open or close the garage door. Once the car was in the garage, the door could also be closed by turning off the garage light. Additional automobile units could be purchased for families with more than one car. The entire product was transistorized. Crockett's model was to retail for about $225, which was well within the range of competitive prices. The product could be installed easily and inexpensively by the homeowner, according to simple and clear instructions.

So far, one important product weakness had been discovered. The unit in one person's car sometimes opened garage doors in other homes having a similar product. This weakness would become increasingly critical as more units of the product were sold. The executives had horrible visions of what might happen in a row of suburban houses, all with garages equipped with Crockett door openers: one person driving down the street and pushing the button in his car unit might open all the garage doors in the block, one by one. The engineers were hard at work on this problem, and had just about perfected a mechanism which would make it possible to set different electronic signals for each door opener produced.

The Crockett Electric Company was a Midwestern manufacturer of industrial and consumer electrical products, including industrial switching and timing equipment, radio and television components, and portable public-address systems. Annual sales were approximately $5 million. The company had a small sales force operating out of three sales offices (the Chicago home office and the New York and Los Angeles offices). Salesmen sold directly to large industrial users, to government agencies, and also to industrial distributors and manufacturers' agents.

The executives were trying to determine what channels to use for the door opener. Part of their indecision stemmed from the fact that they did not know whether they were dealing with an industrial or a consumer market. Mr. Shannon, the marketing vice president, felt that the door opener was a consumer product. He was not, however, certain whether it should be sold through wholesalers and retailers of building materials, whether it should go through channels for home appliances, or whether it should be treated like power lawn mowers and other patio and garden equipment. Mr. Moyer, the sales manager, definitely felt that the door opener was an industrial product. He thought that once a house was built and sold, the resident consumer would not add the door opener, and that Crockett should reach the people who were building the homes. Consequently, he thought that the product should be sold directly to architects and to building contractors engaged in large suburban housing developments. Mr. Moyer also felt that there was a substantial market among all sorts of industrial users, such as manufacturing plants, retail stores, gasoline service stations, automobile repair garages, parking garages, warehouses, and any other type of company with large overhead doors for loading docks.

A related question facing these executives was whether to use the company's present sales force and, if so, to what extent. The product itself presented no problems in this respect. The salesmen were ably qualified to sell it. None of the proposed channels, however, involved middlemen on whom the sales force was presently calling. Thus an entirely new customer list had to be developed. Also, the salesmen would have only one product to sell to these newly added middlemen. It was questionable whether it would be profitable for Crockett's present salesmen to sell the door opener. The executives were considering the feasibility of using manufacturers' agents to reach the appropriate parties.

QUESTIONS

1. Do better market opportunities lie in treating the door opener as a consumer or an industrial product?
2. Which channels should be used to reach your recommended market?
3. Should the company use its present sales force to sell the door opener, should it establish a separate sales force, or should manufacturers' agents be used?
4. Should Crockett select one distributor in each geographic market and offer him an exclusive franchise?

CASE 16. KELSEY MANUFACTURING COMPANY

Getting middlemen to promote manufacturer's products

The Kelsey Manufacturing Company was one of the largest manufacturers of repair materials for automobile tires and tubes in the United States. One of the major objectives set by management was for the company to show a continuous growth in sales and profits at a rate of 10 percent a year. In view of this goal, management was greatly concerned by the fact that Kelsey's annual sales volume had remained at about the same level for eight years. Some executives labeled the sales volume as "stable," while other referred to it as "stagnant." Whatever description was given to this sales situation, management believes it would be improved considerably if the company's wholesalers and retailers could be persuaded to promote Kelsey's products more aggressively. Consequently, management was trying to figure out how to "spread the word"—i.e., disseminate its product and promotional messages—through the company's rather lengthy channels-of-distribution system, so that the ultimate customer—the retail service station operator—effectively received these messages.

The Kelsey Company was founded in the early 1920s as a small, family-owned company to manufacture cold patches for repairing innertubes. Within a few years hot-patch material was introduced, marking the beginning of a period of great growth. Tire repair was a service in much demand during the years of the 1930s depression and World War II. During that war the government took about 90 percent of the production. In 1972 the Kelsey Company was acquired by a large, diversified chemical corporation and was operated as a division of one of that corporation's subsidiary firms.

One key official said, "Once we were just a nice-size family. Now we're really in the mainstream of corporate life. We used to be able to communicate with each other and with our customers on an informal party-line basis. Now we have to pay close attention to the proper channels. As the prison warden said in the movie *Cool Hand Luke,* 'What we've got here is a problem in communication!'"

Kelsey manufactured tire and tube repair materials under three brand names: Lion, which accounted for 54 percent of the sales; Topps, 10 percent of sales; and Air Float, 36 percent. Under the Lion brand the company produced the following products: Chembond patches (a chemical application), rubber cement, liquid buffer and cleaner, Perma Strip patches (outside tire repair), hot vulcanizing patches, clamps, repair gum, cold patches, unitized patches, boot cement, tubeless sealant, tire talc, and rattle stops. In addition, a number of other items were purchased for resale under the Lion name. As a result of the merger with the chemical corporation, Kelsey Manufacturing Company added a new product line consisting of some 280 items in the category of tire valves and accessories.

As the number of products increased, the problem of communicating with the customers was intensified. The sales manager Mr. Ralph Knott summed up the problem by saying, "In the old days our sales representatives could carry the entire line in a small briefcase. Now, we'd be hard pressed to get everything in a station wagon. We just aren't able to let the customers know what we really can do for them."

Top executives in the Kelsey Company believed that the firm held about 15 percent of the total tire and tube repair market. The major competitors were H. B. Egan Company, Bowes Seal Fast Company, Monkey Grip Sales Company, Remaco, Inc., and Kex Products Company. Kelsey, however, marketed the most complete line of products in their field.

Kelsey's annual net sales for the years 1965–1973 were as follows:

1965 —	$ 4,589,000
1966 —	4,136,000
1967 —	4,028,000
1968 —	4,284,000
1969 —	4,208,000
1970 —	4,058,000
1971 —	4,151,000
1972 —	4,205,000
1973 —	3,998,000

During the above period there were no significant fluctuations in the company's gross margin (30-40 percent of sales) or the net profit before taxes (10 percent of sales). While most of Kelsey's sales were to wholesalers who in turn sold to retail service stations, the company also sold in the export market, and under private brands to major oil companies and to chain stores such as Western Auto, Goodrich Tire stores, and Sears.

In recent years there was an increasing demand for the chemical (Chembond) patch at the expense of hot patches. This change in product popularity had enabled competition to make some inroads in the market, since the Kelsey company did not have the advantages productionwise in chemical patches that they had in hot patches.

Looking to the future, Kelsey's management recognized that it faced two problems which were created by technological improvements in other areas: (1) tires are continually being improved, mainly through creation of better rubber and fabric and (2) the highway system is continually being upgraded. These factors tend to produce less tire trouble per mile traveled with less use of repair materials per mile traveled.

However, these points may be offset by the increase in the number of vehicles on the road and the number of miles traveled per vehicle. Also, the two-ply tire, which is standard on most new cars, is more susceptible to punctures than is the four-ply tire. Still another positive factor in this repair-products industry is the large increase in the number of motorbikes, pneumatic industrial tires, and other inflatable rubber and/or plastic items.

The Kelsey Company, like most of its competitors in the industry, distributed its products through manufacturers' representatives (agents) who sold to automotive-parts warehouse distributors. These distributors sold to smaller automotive-parts jobbers who, in turn, sold to service stations. In a sense the service station sells the product to the individual automobile owner, but by the very nature of the tire repair business, the ultimate consumer seldom knows what kind of products have been used to repair his tire or tube.

Because of this lengthy channel of distribution, the Kelsey Company was having trouble getting its product story down to the service station. Obviously, no *real* sale occurred until the service station bought the product. Unless the retailers bought, the jobbers and warehouse distributors, in turn, would not reorder.

In the past, most of Kelsey's manufacturers' agents had handled Kelsey products exclusively. With the increasing difficulty in realizing growth in sales, however, all the representatives now handled other automotive lines, thus dividing their loyalty and decreasing the time available to communicate to the customer about the Kelsey products. Part of the reasoning behind the addition of the new product line of tire valves and accessories was the hope of rebuilding the agents' loyalty to Kelsey.

As Charles Bronson, the Kelsey vice president, said: "Our real problem right now is getting our story told. We've got to have better contacts with the customers. In the past our reps had to tell the story effectively or they didn't eat. Now, they're handling so many other customers that our story gets lost in the shuffle. As we have traveled across the country and talked with service station operators, we find that they have very little knowledge about the benefits or use of our tire repair materials."

On the other hand, Ray Levine, the manufacturers' representative covering Texas, Oklahoma, and Louisiana, saw the problem this way: "The product line is now so large that you can't possibly do justice to the Kelsey products. I'd have to spend a week with each customer to tell him what the company wants told about each product. There just isn't enough time or money to do what they want."

QUESTION

1. What should the Kelsey Company do to get its middlemen to promote the company's products more informatively and aggressively?

CASE 17. FAVORED BLEND COFFEE COMPANY*

Appraising and improving a physical distribution system

In April, 1974, Mr. Clarence Brady, the president of the Favored Blend Coffee Company, called a general management meeting. While the entire group was aware that a physical distribution problem existed, the problem had reached a climax when the Argonaut Foods Company, a large supermarket chain, dropped Favored Blend coffee from its product line. Mr. Brady had been informed by Argonaut Foods' chief executive officer that Argonaut was forced into the decision by alleged poor inventory availability and erratic delivery of orders placed with Favored Blend Coffee. Based upon the apparent inability of Favored Blend's management to correct the adverse situation, Mr. Brady had decided, with the advice of his Board of Directors, to call in an independent consultant to analyze the company's distribution structure.

The Favored Blend Coffee Company was a prominent manufacturer of coffee sold on a nationwide basis to consumer and institutional markets. Sales to the consumer market were made through wholesalers, chain stores, and other grocery product retailers under the brand name "Favored Blend." Sales to the institutional market were made by direct account coverage and by the efforts of brokers under the brand name "Best Blend." With the exception of packaging size and style, the two product lines were identical. Both Favored Blend and Best Blend offered ground and instant coffee in a variety of packages. Both brands were manufactured in the same production plants and were distributed through the same physical distribution system.

In serving its nationwide market, the Favored Blend Company operated processing facilities in Philadelphia, New Orleans, and Los Angeles. Each plant supplied a relatively fixed geographical portion of the United States. Operation at each of these fully integrated plants consisted of receiving shipments of green coffee from overseas, and then blending, roasting, grinding, processing, and packaging the product for customer shipment. As the packaging process was completed, the coffee moved into a shipping and storage area. Here it was consolidated into large order lots for shipment either directly to customers, or to warehouses throughout the territory of distribution.

The production process consisted of running a single-size package until the estimated weekly requirements for that package size were satisfied. Then other-sized packs were processed in a scheduled sequence.

The space devoted to storage and shipping at each plant was small, having been whittled down in recent years by the expansion of space devoted to production facilities for "instant" coffee. A continuing search for additional space in the plants, on plant property, or on property contiguous to the plants had proven fruitless. As an expedient for making space, the distribution services department had come to favor rail shipments principally because the department had discovered that empty railroad boxcars could be used as auxiliary storehouses while being loaded. This added storage space was provided at moderate cost by reason of 48-hour free-time provisions in the demurrage tariff coupled with the fact that switching was per-

---

*Adapted from case prepared by Prof. Donald J. Bowersox, Michigan State University. Reproduced with permission.

formed at 8 A.M. at all plants. As a result, almost three days loading time was provided on free time before demurrage accrued. (*Demurrage* is a rental charge assessed by railroads when their freight cars are detained beyond a free-time limit—usually 48 hours—allowed for loading, unloading, or other purposes.)

Though coffee consumption in general was fairly predictable, orders from customers tended to be sporadic, so that shipments both direct from the plant and from the warehouses were rather irregular. Attempts had been made at predicting orders; however, the results had not be particularly accurate. The distribution services department had utilized warehouses as outlet valves when the storage problem became burdensome at the plant. In total, 30 public warehouses were utilized by the firm for distribution.

Consequently, though there was a planned supply program, some warehouses tended to become greatly overstocked, others considerably understocked. The mixture of Favored Blend and Best Blend products at any single time at any single warehouse often lacked the proper combination of package sizes and grinds. Frequently, crosshauling between warehouses and emergency shipments from plants had been necessary in order to fill customer orders.

The physical pattern of distribution had been a source of friction between the marketing and distribution services departments for a number of years. In general, the physical distribution was accomplished through two principal channels: (1) direct shipments from the plants to the customer in truckload or carload quantities, and with less frequent shipments in l.t.l. (less-than-truckload) quantities and (2) shipments in carload and truckload quantities to public warehouses located in the market area, with l.t.l. shipments from the warehouse to the customer.

Quantity shipments direct from the plant to customers were at one time of considerable significance and were, in general, the lowest cost and most desirable from the distribution services department's standpoint. However, in line with a general trend in business philosophy in recent years toward lower inventory levels, customers have been hesitant to purchase in large enough quantities to warrant delivery in carload or truckload lots. The distribution services department has been confronted with an increasing demand on the part of customers to order in small lots on an immediate delivery basis, with truck delivery requested. The degree to which this trend had progressed is illustrated by tonnage reports for 1973 in comparison to 1968. In 1968, 70 percent of all coffee from all locations combined was shipped to customers by rail and 30 percent by truck. By 1973 these figures had been reversed.

Until 1972 the Favored Blend Coffee Company had prospered and expanded. Sales growth averaged 5 percent annually. Profits, while not increasing in the same proportion as sales, reflected a favorable growth. At the year-end management meeting in 1972, the management group was optimistic about continued growth in both sales and profits. By mid-1974, however, this optimism had given way to a serious situation. While the sales of Favored Blend's two product lines continued to grow, profits dropped sharply in 1973, and for the first quarter of 1974 a loss was experienced for the first time since 1929. Analysis of the operating figures clearly indicated that increased costs in physical distribution constituted the major reason for the profit decline. Transportation cost had increased by 4 percent in 1973 as compared to 1972, and warehousing costs were up by 3 percent. Despite a rigorous cost-control program instituted in the last half of 1973, the cost trend had not been reversed during the first quarter of 1974. Year-end finished goods inventory in 1973 was 8 percent higher than in 1972. By the end of the first quarter of 1974, inventory had been forced in line as the result of a reduced production schedule.

Mr. Brady had spent considerable time with the distribution services and marketing departments in attempting to solve the problem of increasing costs. In general the distribution services department felt that marketing had not instituted realistic price incentives to encourage quantity purchasing and that salesmen allowed customers to unduly dictate terms and routing of shipments. The marketing department, in contrast, pointed to increased competition from private as well as other national branded coffee as the source of the problem. "Competitors provide the service desired by customers and we have little choice but to try to meet this service if we want the business."

At the April general management meeting, Mr. Brady presented his decision to retain the service of Freightway Associates, a firm of physical distribution specialists. The vice president of marketing was in full agreement with the decision. The director of distribution services and the vice president of finance were opposed. In their opinion the problem could be corrected if proper marketing and customer service policies were implemented on a corporatewide basis. They questioned whether a so-called high-powered specialist would in fact have sufficient knowledge of food-product distribution to conduct a meaningful investigation. At one point in the heated discussion, the vice president of manufacturing added to the general argument with the comment that "the last thing we need is some more theory. The last group of so-called experts spent three weeks here and then told us things we already knew and had told them. We need action not research." After about two hours of discussion, Mr. Brady concluded the meeting with the following comment: "Some of you may be right about consultants, but frankly I feel you're defensive, and the figures just don't support standing by while the situation further deteriorates. I am going to call the head of Freightway, give him the facts as I know them, and see what he would do if we give him the job."

In his meeting with Mr. Keith Ralston, the president of Freightway Associates, Mr. Brady reviewed the background of Favored Blend's problem and briefed Mr. Ralston on the points described earlier in this case. Mr. Brady then posed a series of three questions for Mr. Ralston.

QUESTIONS

1. What principles of physical distribution system design will be helpful to guide Freightway Associates in approaching a revamping of Favored Blend's operation if they get the assignment?
2. With 30 warehouses across the nation, why do you feel Favored Blend was constantly faced with the need to crosshaul between warehouses and make emergency shipments to customers from plants? Be as specific as possible regarding current practices that result in poor inventory assortments in individual warehouses.
3. What in your opinion is the total-system impact of the distribution services department's policy of using boxcars as warehouses? Keep in mind that both transportation and warehouse costs have recently increased.

PART SIX

PROMOTIONAL ACTIVITIES

THE PROMOTIONAL
PROGRAM

Having studied the product planning, price structure, and distribution system in a firm, we now examine the final operational area in a company's marketing system—the promotional activities. Chapters 21 to 23 are devoted to the management of the *promotional* mix, that is, the most strategic combination of advertising, personal selling, sales promotion, and other promotional tools that can be devised to reach the goals of the sales program.

When a home handicraft economy exists and a man makes a good product, his neighbors probably know about it. The "better mousetrap" theory is not realistic, however, in our modern economy. The present situation is more accurately described by the statement "Nothing happens until somebody sells something." This statement expresses rather succinctly the place of promotional activities in today's business scene. Promotional activities are probably the most criticized part of the entire marketing program. For this reason, we should remember one thing; not to confuse a tool with its user. Without question, many advertisements are misleading, and many salesmen act in poor taste. This is no fault of the tool of advertising, but simply indicates that it has been used poorly. Yet it is human nature to blame the tool itself: a person will hammer a nail crooked and blame the poor quality of the nail, he will hit his finger and blame the hammer.

NATURE AND IMPORTANCE OF PROMOTION

Many people consider that "selling" and "marketing" are synonymous terms, but actually selling is only one of the many components of marketing. Selling is defined by the American Marketing Association as "the personal or impersonal process of assisting and/or persuading a prospective customer to buy a commodity or a service or to act favorably upon an idea that has commercial significance to the seller."[1]

In this book, "selling" and "promotion" are used synonymously, although "promotion" is the preferred term. This preference is based on the belief of some people that selling suggests only the transfer of title or the use of personal salesmen and does not include advertising or other methods of stimulating demand. We are saying that promotion includes advertising, personal selling, sales promotion, and other selling tools. While the two words may be unfortunately similar, it should be noted particularly that "promotion" and "sales promotion" are different. "Promotion" is the all-inclusive term representing the broad field under discussion here, and "sales promotion" is only one part of it.

In line with the systems approach, a company should treat all its promotional efforts as a complete subsystem within the total marketing system. This means coordinating the sales-force activities, the advertising programs, and other promotional efforts. Unfortunately, today in many firms these activities still are fragmented, and management in the advertising and sales-force areas often conflict and compete with one another.[2]

In economic theory terms, the essential purpose of promotion is to change the location and shape of the demand (revenue) curve for a company's product. (See Fig. 21-1 and recall the discussion of nonprice competition in Chapter 14.) Through the use of promotion, a company hopes to increase a product's sales volume at any given price. It also hopes that promotion will affect the demand elasticity for the product, making the demand inelastic in the face of a price increase and elastic when the price goes down.

Basically, promotion is an exercise in information, persuasion, and influence. These three are related in that to inform is to persuade, and conversely, if a person is persuaded, he is probably also being informed. Many years ago, Prof. Neil Borden, of Harvard University, pointed up the pervasive nature of persuasion and influence in our socioeconomic system when he said that "the use of influence in commercial relations is one of the attributes of a free society, just as persuasion and counterpersuasion are exercised freely in many walks of life in our free society—in the home, in the press, in the classroom, in the pulpit,

---

[1] Committee on Definitions, *Marketing Definitions: A Glossary of Marketing Terms,* American Marketing Association, Chicago, 1960, p. 21.

[2] One helpful countervailing trend is the growing number of books which treat promotion as a total subsystem in marketing. See, for example, James F. Engel, Hugh G. Wales, and Martin R. Warshaw, *Promotional Strategy,* Richard D. Irwin, Inc., Homewood, Ill., 1971; Jerome B. Kernan, William P. Dommermuth, and Montrose S. Sommers, *Promotion: An Introductory Analysis,* McGraw-Hill Book Co., New York, 1970; Rollie Tillman and C. A. Kirkpatrick, *Promotion: Persuasive Communication in Marketing,* Richard D. Irwin, Inc., Homewood, Ill., 1968; and Frederick E. Webster, Jr., *Marketing Communication: Modern Promotional Strategy,* The Ronald Press Company, New York, 1971.

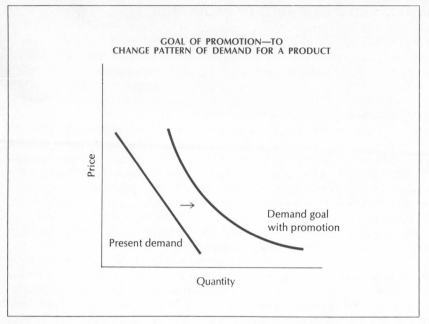

GOAL OF PROMOTION—TO
CHANGE PATTERN OF DEMAND FOR A PRODUCT

Figure 21-1.

in the courts, in the political forum, in legislative halls, and in government agencies for information."[3]

PROMOTIONAL METHODS

The two most widely used methods of promotion are personal selling and advertising. Another is sales promotion, which is designed to supplement and coordinate personal selling and advertising efforts and which includes such activities as setting up store displays, holding trade shows and exhibitions, and using samples or premiums. In addition, there is a group of marketing strategies, discussed in earlier chapters, which are in part promotional. Such strategies as product differentiation, market segmentation, trading up, trading down, and branding belong in this group.

IMPORTANCE OF PROMOTION IN MODERN MARKETING

In the realistic marketplace, perfect competition does not exist. Under conditions of imperfect competition, with product differentiation, nonrational behavior, and less-than-complete market information, promotional activities are essential. Promotion is an adjunct of imperfect competition. In one study of almost five hundred successful products, promotion was perceived by management as being the most important facet of marketing strategy leading to this success.[4]

---

[3]Neil H. Borden, *The Economic Effects of Advertising,* Richard D. Irwin, Inc., Homewood, Ill., 1942, p. 802.

[4]Jon G. Udell, "The Perceived Importance of the Elements of Strategy," *Journal of Marketing,* January, 1968, pp. 34–40.

Several factors point up the need for promotion today. In the first place, as the physical distance between producers and consumers increases, and as the number of potential customers grows, the problem of market communication becomes a significant one. Furthermore, improvements in physical distribution facilities are expanding the geographic limits of markets.

Once middlemen are introduced into a marketing pattern, it is not enough for a producer to communicate only with the ultimate consumers or industrial users. It becomes essential that middlemen be informed about products. Wholesalers, in turn, must promote the products to retailers, and retailers must communicate with consumers.

The intensification of competition between different industries, as well as between individual firms within given industries, has placed tremendous pressures on the promotional programs of individual sellers. In our economy of abundance, want satisfaction has replaced, to a great extent, the mere necessity of fulfilling basic physiological requirements. As consumers engage in the satisfactions of wants rather than needs, they become more selective in their choices of alternative expenditures. To attract customers, a firm must have a good promotional program. Customer demand is largely dormant; it must be awakened and stimulated.

Promotional effort looms important in the overall operations of a business. It is usually the largest part of the total marketing expenses. All promotional expenses together often constitute the largest single cost in a firm—even larger than its total production costs.

Any type of an economic decline quickly points up the importance of selling. During such a period, there are no major problems in product planning. Channels remain essentially the same, and the pricing structure is basically unchanged. The key problem is selling. Promotion is needed to maintain the high material standard of living and the high level of employment which we enjoy in this country.

THE COMMUNICATIONS PROCESS

In any society, the nature of interpersonal relations depends in large measure upon the effectiveness of interpersonal communications. Certainly in business in general, and in marketing in particular, the effectiveness of the system is related to the effectiveness of the communications. To go one step further, within the marketing system the promotional activity is basically an exercise in communications. If an executive understands something of the theory of communications, he should be able to better manage a promotional program in his firm.[5]

The word "communication" is derived from the Latin word *communis*, meaning "common." Thus, when you communicate, you are trying to establish a "commonness" with someone. Through the use of verbal or nonverbal symbols, you as the source send a message through a channel to a receiver in an effort to share an idea, attitude, or some other kind of information. Fundamentally, a communications process requires only three elements—a *message*, a *source* of this message, and a

---

[5]See Jerome B. Kernan and Montrose S. Sommers, "Meaning, Value, and the Theory of Promotion," *Journal of Communications,* June, 1967, pp. 109–135; and Michael L. Ray, "A Decision Sequence Analysis of Developments in Marketing Communication," *Journal of Marketing,* January, 1973, pp. 29–38.

receiver. However, to refine the process into a workable form— one which recognizes environmental practicalities—additional elements come into play. The information which the sending source wants to share must first be *encoded* into transmittable form and then later *decoded* by the receiver at the destination. Another element to be reckoned with is *noise* which may interfere at any stage with the transmission or reception of the message. The final element in the process —feedback—tells the sender whether the message was received and how it was perceived by the destination target. The feedback element is also the basis for planning ahead. The sender learns how he might improve his communications by using different channels, encoding, or messages.

These elements constituting a general communications system may be conceptualized in a model as diagrammed in Fig. 21-2.[6] This same model, as adapted to the promotional activities in a company's marketing program, is illustrated in Fig. 21-3. The information source may be a person with an idea to communicate. He will encode it into a transmittable form by putting it into written or spoken words, or perhaps even into a gesture of some sort (wave his arms, dim his bright lights). The coded message is then carried by print media, sound

---

[6]Adapted from David K. Berlo, *The Process of Communication,* Holt, Rinehart and Winston, Inc., New York, 1960, pp. 30–32. See also the model in Claude E. Shannon and Warren Weaver, *The Mathematical Theory of Communication,* The University of Illinois Press, Urbana, 1949, p. 5.

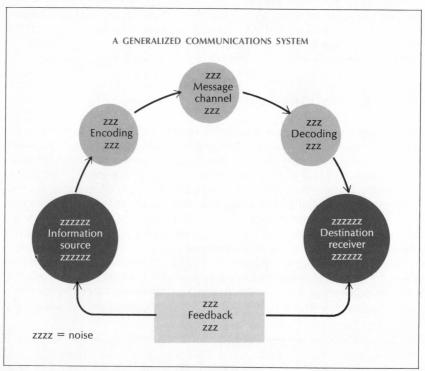

A GENERALIZED COMMUNICATIONS SYSTEM

zzz Message channel zzz

zzz Encoding zzz

zzz Decoding zzz

zzzzzz Information source zzzzzz

zzzzzz Destination receiver zzzzzz

zzz Feedback zzz

zzzz = noise

Figure 21-2.

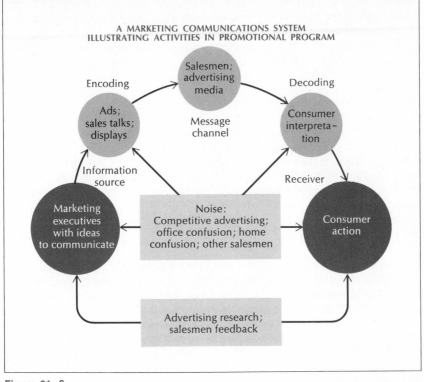

**A MARKETING COMMUNICATIONS SYSTEM
ILLUSTRATING ACTIVITIES IN PROMOTIONAL PROGRAM**

Figure 21–3.

waves, or light waves to the destination—an individual, a church audience, or a university class, for example. Each receiver decodes (interprets) the message in light of his individual experiences or frames of reference. The closer the decoded message is to its encoded form (assuming it was encoded fully and accurately), the more effective the communications is. By the receiver's words or actions (feedback) the sender can judge the extent to which his message got through.

Let us illustrate the process with a marketing example. An executive wants to communicate a selling message to a consumer. The message is encoded into a radio commercial and carried to the consumer via a radio program and a receiving set. The consumer hears the commercial and interprets it. Through marketing research feedback the sender will try to determine how effectively the message came through and how much it moved the consumer to action. At any point in the process, interfering noise may reduce the effectiveness of the system. While the radio commercial is on, the children may be making noise in the house, or someone may ring the doorbell. Competitive advertisements, salesmen, or displays are also forms of noise. The sender can counteract the noise by preparing an especially good commercial or by running it at a time when doorbells and children are apt to be quiet.

In effect, the marketing executive uses his previous analysis of consumer characteristics and behavior to provide him with encoded symbols which can be used to communicate the merits of his product and the reasons for buying it. An analysis of the market for carbonated beverages, for instance, might show that one major market is made up of people who serve soft drinks at parties. The seller can then encode his message in an advertisement which pictures the use of his product in an entertainment setting.

THE CAMPAIGN CONCEPT

When planning the total promotional program in a firm, management must ordinarily make use of the campaign concept. A *campaign* is a planned, coordinated series of promotional efforts built around a single theme or idea and designed to reach a predetermined goal. Although the term "campaign" is probably thought of most often in connection with advertising, it seems more appropriate to apply the concept of a campaign first to the entire promotional program. Then the total promotional campaign can be subdivided into its advertising, personal selling, and sales promotion components, and the subcampaigns can be planned in more detail.

Many types of promotional campaigns may be conducted by a company, and several may be run concurrently. Geographically, a firm may have a local, regional, or national campaign, depending upon the available funds, objectives, and market scope. One campaign may be aimed at consumers, and another at wholesalers and retailers. The stage of a product's life cycle may determine whether a pioneering or a competitive campaign will be conducted. Sometimes a firm is most concerned with building an image of promoting its services through an institutional campaign. A campaign may run for a week, a month, a year, or even longer. Three to six months is quite common.

Perhaps the first step in developing a promotional campaign should be to establish the campaign goals and determine the campaign strategy. One writer has suggested some areas which should be considered in the course of setting this strategy.[7]

1. What is the relative emphasis to be placed on primary versus secondary demand stimulation?
2. What balance is desired between the immediacy of the action-response and the duration of the response?
3. Do we wish to influence everyone a little bit or a few people intensively?
4. At what point are we targeting our emphasis on the spectrum between brand awareness and brand insistence?
5. What issues or product features (both ours and our competitors) shall we stress?

Early in the course of planning the campaign, management should decide what selling appeals will be stressed. This decision will be based to a large extent upon the specific objectives of the campaign and the research findings concerning the buying motives and habits of the customers. If the goal of a promotional campaign put on by an airline is to introduce its new jumbo jet service, the appeals might be to

---

[7]Dodds I. Buchanan, "A New Look at 'Old' Advertising Strategy," *Business Horizons,* Winter, 1965, pp. 85–96.

the customers' desire for speed, a quiet and restful trip, or fine food and courteous service. If the same airline wants to increase its plane loadings of air freight, however, the ads and the personal selling presentation might stress low total cost of air freight, reduction in losses due to spoilage and handling, advantages of savings in packaging, or convenient schedules.

A campaign revolves around a central idea or focal point. This "theme"permeates all promotional efforts and tends to unify the campaign. A theme is simply the appeals dressed up in a distinctive, attention-getting form. As such, it is related to the campaign's objectives and the customers' behavior. It expresses the product's benefits. Frequently the theme takes the form of a slogan, such as Hallmark Card Company's "when you care enough to send the very best" or DeBeers's "a diamond is forever." Some companies use the same theme for several campaigns; others develop a different theme for each new campaign.

In a successfully operated campaign, the efforts of all groups concerned will be meshed effectively. The *advertising program* will consist of a series of related, well-timed, carefully placed ads. The *personal selling effort* can be tied in by having the salesmen explain and demonstrate the product benefits stressed in the ads. Also, the salesmen will be fully informed about the advertising part of the campaign—the theme, media used, schedule of appearance of ads, appeals used, etc. The salesmen, in turn, should carry this information to wholesalers and retailers so that they can become effective participants in the campaign. *Sales-promotional devices* such as point-of-purchase display materials need to be coordinated with the other aspects of the campaign. For each campaign, new display materials must be prepared, reflecting the ads and appeals used in the current campaign, in order to maximize the campaign's impact at the point of sale. Personnel responsible for the *physical distribution activities* must ensure that adequate stocks of the product are available in all outlets prior to the start of the campaign.

DETERMINATION OF PROMOTIONAL MIX

Determining the most effective promotional *mix* is another of the difficult tasks in marketing management. Several different promotional tools or combinations thereof may be used. The underlying difficulty is that management does not know the exact extent to which advertising,personal selling, or any other promotional tool will help achieve the goals of the sales program. The executives do not know how much should be spent on each promotional activity, nor do they know what to expect from the expenditure. Guideposts to aid management in its decision regarding the promotional mix will be examined in the following section.

FACTORS INFLUENCING PROMOTIONAL MIX

Four factors which should influence management's decision making with respect to the promotional mix are (1) the amount of money available for promotion, (2) the nature of the market, (3) the nature of the product, and (4) the stage of the product's life cycle.

Funds available. Regardless of what may be the most desirable promotional mix, the amount of money available for promotion is the real determinant of the mix. Business with ample funds can make more effective use of advertising than enterprises with limited financial resources. Small or financially weak companies are likely to rely on personal selling, dealer displays, or joint manufacturer-retailer advertising. The use of personal salesmen may be inefficient compared with advertising in magazines or newspapers. Either of these advertising media can carry at least part of the promotional message to far more people at a much lower cost per person than personal salesmen can. To do an effective promotional job in advertising, however, may take a considerable sum of money.

Nature of the market. As is true in most problem areas in marketing, management's decision on the promotional mix will be influenced to a great extent by the nature of the company's market. This influence is felt in at least three ways.

Geographic scope of the market. Businesses selling only in local markets will often use promotional ingredients quite different from those used by firms which have national markets. Personal selling may be adequate in a small local market, but as the market broadens geographically, greater reliance must frequently be placed on advertising.

Concentration of the market. Market concentration influences a firm's promotional strategy in three basic ways. First, the total number of prospective customers is a consideration. The fewer potential buyers there are, the more apt a seller is to stress personal selling rather than advertising.

The second consideration is the number of different types of potential customers. A market that is concentrated in one type of customer or industry will call for a different promotional mix from that required when a firm sells to many different customer groups. A firm selling large power saws and other cutting equipment used only by lumber manufacturers may be able to use personal selling effectively, and there will be very little advertising in its mix. In contrast, a company selling hand tools used by thousands of consumers and virtually all types of industrial users probably will include liberal portions of advertising in its mix because personal selling would be prohibitively expensive in reaching the final customers.

Finally, even though a firm sells nationally, it may find its market concentrated in relatively few spots. In this type of market concentration, emphasis on personal selling may be feasible, whereas it would be unrealistic if the potential customers were widely distributed all over the country.

Type of customers. The promotional strategy is influenced by whether the business is aiming its sales campaign at industrial users, household consumers, or middlemen. To illustrate, a promotional campaign aimed at retailers will probably contain a greater percentage of personal selling than will a program designed to attract household consumers. In many situations the middlemen may strongly influence the promotional strategy used by a manufacturer. Often a retail store will not even stock a product unless the manufacturer agrees to do a certain amount of advertising.

Nature of the product. Consumer products and industrial goods frequently require different strategies. Within the category of consumer goods, a promotional mix is influenced by whether the product is generally considered a convenience, shopping, or specialty item. In industrial goods, installations are not promoted in the same way that operating supplies or raw materials are.

Firms marketing convenience goods will normally rely heavily on manufacturers' advertising plus emphasis on dealer displays. Personal selling plays a relatively minor role. This mix is best because a convenience product is widely distributed, needs no special demonstration or explanation, and is competing with many brands that have reasonably equal acceptance. Furthermore, buying decisions are often made at the point of purchase.

In the field of industrial goods, the promotional strategy behind installations usually features heavy emphasis on personal selling. The market for such products is more easily pinpointed than the market for other types of industrial products. Also, the unit sales are typically large, products are often made to specification, and considerable presale and postsale personal service is necessary. Raw-materials sellers also rely on personal selling, often to the total exclusion of advertising. Many raw materials are unbranded, and the products of any one of several firms will fill a buyer's need. Personal services and persuasion from salesmen may be the only differentiating features offered by one seller over another.

Stage of the product's life cycle. In Chapter 9, we observed that products go through a life cycle, starting with the introductory period; then progressing through the stages of growth, maturity, and saturation; and finally ending in decline and possible abandonment. Strategy decisions for promoting a product should be influenced considerably by the phase of its life cycle which it is in at any given time.

In the pioneering, or introductory, stage a seller must stimulate *primary* demand—the demand for a type of product—as contrasted with *selective* demand—the demand for a particular brand. Thus manufacturers first had to sell the consumers on the value of microwave kitchen ovens in general before it was feasible to promote Tappan, Thermador, or some other brand.

When a product is in the pioneering stage (as far as a prospective customer is concerned), the customer does not recognize that he wants the commodity. He does not immediately understand how it will benefit him. Therefore, the promotional strategy is to inform and educate the potential customer. He must be told that the product exists, how it may be used, and what want-satisfying benefits it provides.

Normally, heavy emphasis must be placed on personal selling when a firm is promoting a new product or is pioneering a new market. Trade shows and fairs also may play a major role in the promotional mix, particularly in the case of industrial goods which go directly from producer to customer. Rather than call on each customer or each industrial plant individually, the company can promote its new product at a home show, automobile show, or some other type of trade show where the prospective customers will come to the seller's exhibit. Manufacturers rely heavily on personal selling in attracting middlemen to handle a new product. The middlemen in turn often use more personal selling in their promotional mix than they will after the item gains broader market acceptance.

During the middle stages of a product's life, the promotional mix calls for increased emphasis upon advertising. Customers are aware of the want-satisfying benefits of the product, so advertising can perform whatever informational and educational tasks remain to be done. As a product moves through the middle stages and attracts stiff competition, more and more attention is devoted to advertising as a tool of persuasion rather than of information only. Intense competition forces sellers to devote larger sums to advertising and thus contributes to the declining profits experienced in the maturity and saturation stages.

Most products eventually reach the final stages of their life cycle—decline and possible abandonment. New and better products are taking their place. Manufacturers are discontinuing the production of the older goods, the profit rates are declining, and even promotional effort is substantially cut back.

QUESTIONS OF BASIC PROMOTIONAL STRATEGY

By asking and then analyzing some seven questions regarding promotional strategy, we can set some guidelines to aid management in determining its promotional mix. At the same time, we are relating back to the four basic influencing factors we just discussed.[8]

When should personal selling be main ingredient? Personal selling will ordinarily carry the bulk of the promotional load (1) when the company is small or has insufficient funds with which to carry on an adequate advertising program, (2) when the market is concentrated, or (3) when the personality of the salesman is needed to establish rapport or create confidence. Personal selling will also be emphasized when the product (4) has a higher unit value, (5) requires demonstration, (6) must be fitted to the individual customer's needs, as in the case of securities or insurance, (7) is purchased infrequently, or (8) involves a trade-in.

When should advertising be main ingredient? If the market for the product is widespread, as in the case of a national consumer market, advertising should receive heavy emphasis. Advertising also works best when the seller wishes to inform many people quickly, as in the case of an announcement of new store hours, a special sale, or a new credit policy.

Certainly not every product lends itself to advertising. Many years ago Prof. Neil H. Borden identified five criteria which may serve as guides for management in determining the "advertisability" of its product.[9] If all five of these criteria are met, normally there is an excellent opportunity to advertise. However, this ideal condition rarely exists. Ordinarily a firm has a product which meets some, but not all, of these conditions. Then the decision on whether to advertise becomes more difficult.

The five criteria are as follows:

1. The primary demand trend for the product should be favorable. Advertising works best when the market demand for a product is on the upswing. In spite of the layman's opinion, advertising cannot successfully sell a product that people do not want, nor can advertising reverse a declining primary demand trend.
2. There should be considerable opportunity to differentiate the product. When this condition exists, it is easier to advertise because the company has something to say. For this reason, automobiles or cosmetics are easier to advertise than salt or

---

[8]This question approach to promotional strategy was first noted in the writings of Prof. James D. Scott, University of Michigan.
[9]Borden, *op. cit.,* pp. 424–428.

sugar. Products which are not easy to differentiate by brand may still be advertised by a trade association. Products advertised by the American Dairy Association, the Wool Growers' Association, or the Association of Natural Rubber Producers are cases in point. A retailer who cannot easily differentiate his product lines from those of his competitors may try to differentiate his services, such as credit or location, which are an adjunct to the sale of the product.

3. The product should have hidden qualities. This condition affords the seller grounds for educating the market through advertising. On this point, a sofa or a mechanical device is easier to advertise than greeting cards. Where hidden qualities are important, consumers learn to rely on the dependability of a certain brand. Thus brand preference can be developed.

4. Powerful emotional buying motives should exist for the product. Then buying action can be stimulated by appeal to these motives. It is easier to build an effective advertising campaign for Weight Watchers or some other balanced diet for weight reduction than for an article such as clotheslines, hammers, or sheets. Prestige products or stores have achieved their status largely through advertising which appeals to emotional motives.

5. The company must have sufficient funds to support an advertising program adequately.

When should promotional efforts by retailer be stressed? If the product has important qualities which can be judged at the point of purchase, or if it is a highly standardized item, it lends itself to dealer display. So do products which are purchased on impulse. A product with a limited market, which makes advertising unreasonable, may also be promoted through the dealers. Dealer promotion is particularly important when the retailer is better known in the market than the manufacturer.

When should manufacturer-retailer cooperative advertising be used? There are really three questions involved here. First, when should a manufacturer list his dealers' names and addresses in his advertisements? Second, under what conditions should the manufacturer pay the retailer to mention the manufacturer's product in the retailer's advertisement? Finally, when should a retailer emphasize the manufacturer's product in the store's advertising and display?

In answer to the first of these questions, the retailers' names should be mentioned particularly when the manufacturer employs selective or exclusive distribution policies. It then becomes important to tell the market where the product may be obtained. Concerning the second question, the manufacturer may have to pay the retailer to promote the product in order to get the retailer even to carry the commodity. Also, the retailer may be in a position to demand payment when his name has better selling power than the manufacturer's. In answer to the third question, a retailer should emphasize the manufacturer's products in the store advertising and display when the manufacturer's name is very important.

Is retailer promotion needed when manufacturer emphasizes advertising or personal selling? The answer to this question is "yes." Personal selling, advertising, and merchandise display work done by the retailer can be quite effective. No matter how much advertising the manufacturer does, he can always benefit from high-caliber selling at the retail level. Promotional effort by a well-known, respected store can be the final impetus needed to penetrate a local market and to stimulate consumer buying power. When a retail store operates on a self-service basis, dealer display is almost imperative to move the product, regardless of how good a job the manufacturer has done in his national advertising. Displays serve as an excellent reminder to the customer, reinforcing what he has seen in the national advertising.

If a retailer emphasizes personal selling, does he need to advertise? Under certain conditions the answer to this question is "yes." In the first place, advertising will help to attract the customer to the store. Regardless of the quality of personal selling, it is largely wasted if the retailer cannot first attract an adequate number of potential customers. Furthermore, the advertising can support the efforts of the personal salesmen. If the product is high-price, or is purchased infrequently, again some promotional device is needed to attract the customers to the store. Discretionary purchases are very easy to put off indefinitely.

Should promotional activity be continued when demand is heavy or exceeds capacity? The answer is a definite "yes." It is important that the manufacturer keep his name before the public. Boom conditions may pass, or the seller may acquire new plant capacity. A market is a dynamic institution, and customer loyalty is a "sometime thing;" old customers leave and new customers must be won. If conditions of high demand persist, they are certain to attract competitors. If they are temporary, the seller's heavy advertising may discourage competitors from coming in. In any event, the nature of the advertising message may change. When demand is heavy in relation to supply, the company will probably switch to institutional or indirect-action advertising.

EXAMPLES OF PROMOTIONAL MIX

The business applications of some of the points developed in this section are reflected in Tables 21-1 and 21-2. These tables summarize some of the findings made in a study of marketing expenditures in relation to company sales. Forty-six of the firms sell consumer goods (Table 21-1), and twenty-nine sell industrial products (Table 21-2); some of the firms market both types of commodities. The amount spent for three promotional activities—advertising, sales promotion, and personal selling—is shown as a percentage of net sales. It should be noted particularly that the "—" symbol indicates that data were not reported, not that there were no expenditures for the activity. In this study, sales promotion was defined as those marketing efforts which are neither advertising nor personal selling but which coordinate advertising and personal selling and make them more effective. Expenditures for catalogues, price lists, display materials, and promotional booklets are examples of sales-promotion costs.

One main point which can be gleaned from the tables is the amount of the total promotional appropriation in relation to sales. Among consumer goods firms, the toiletries and cosmetics manufacturers devote as much as 35 to 45 percent of net sales to promotion. At the other extreme, firms producing steel or aluminum spend almost nothing (as a percentage of sales) to promote their consumer products. In general, the proportion of sales revenue expended on the promotion of industrial goods is much smaller than that spent on the promotion of consumer goods.

From the tables it is obvious that several of the firms did not delineate expenditures for the separate marketing activities. Nevertheless, the study does show the differences in the promotional mixes used by the various companies. In the consumer goods fields (Table 21-1), most of the cosmetics and toiletries manufacturers relied much more on advertising than on sales promotion or personal selling. These firms need to develop brand acceptance in a highly competitive national market. The cost of personal selling in these industries probably stems mainly from the heavy use of manufacturer-financed demonstrator salesmen in retail stores. As might be expected, in a mail-order firm (No. 8) the ratio of advertising to all other promotional activities is about 20:1. On the other hand, a tool manufacturer (No. 16), and an automotive parts firm (No. 21) emphasizes personal selling. In these firms, the product requires more explanation, the market is more concentrated as a rule, and manufacturers' brands are not usually important.

Among firms selling industrial products (Table 21-2), more reliance was placed on a sales force than on an advertising program. Some of the firms reported a very high ratio of personal selling to advertising. For example, a textile manufacturer (No.21) stated a 24:1 ratio, and a die-cutting firm (No.15) had a 10:1 ratio.

DETERMINATION OF TOTAL PROMOTIONAL APPROPRIATION

It is extremely difficult to establish promotional appropriations. Management lacks reliable standards for determining how much to spend on advertising or personal selling in total, or how much to spend on specific activities within each area. An even more serious problem is that management normally cannot assess the results of its promotional expenditures. A firm may add ten salesmen or increase its trade-show budget by $20,000 a year, but no one can determine what increase in sales or profits is to be expected, nor can anyone measure the relative values of the two expenditures. The growing number of companies using mathematical methods and a long-range budgeting approach in advertising budgets may be presaging a breakthrough in this problem area.[10] Promotional activities usually are budgeted as current operating expenses, implying that their benefits are used up immediately. Joel Dean and others have proposed that advertising (and presumably other promotional efforts) should perhaps be treated as a capital investment. This change in point of view would have an impact on the evaluation of promotion's effectiveness, on test marketing, and on decision making in other areas.

In determing how much money should be appropriated for the entire promotional program, management should consider promotional costs in light of the influence the program will have on production costs. Here is another instance where it is better to employ the total cost approach instead of basing decisions on a fragmented cost analysis of individual activities. To illustrate, assume that a firm is operating in the declining stage of its cost curve. That is, as output increases the unit costs of production decrease. By increasing its promotional appropriation, the

---

[10]For a review of past, current, and future mathematical approaches to the budgeting of advertising, see Paul E. Green, Patrick J. Robinson, and Peter T. FitzRoy, "Advertising Expenditure Models: State of the Art and Prospects." *Business Horizons,* Summer, 1966, pp. 72–80; see also Robert M. Fulmer, "How Should Advertising and Sales Promotion Funds Be Allocated?" *Journal of Marketing,* October, 1967, pp. 8–11; and Donald C. Marschner, "Theory versus Practice in Allocating Advertising Money," *Journal of Business,* July, 1967, pp. 286–302.

Table 21-1. Promotional costs as percentage of sales of consumer goods: by individual companies.

Note the wide variations in the promotional mixes used by different firms. Compare the cosmetics firm (No. 3) and the insurance company (No. 40). Also note the variations in total promotional appropriations. A paint company (No. 9) devoted 27 percent of sales to promotion, while the promotion budget of an appliance company (No. 28) was only 8 percent of sales. How do you account for these differences?

Number	Type of product	Advertising budget[a]	Advertising	Sales promotion	Sales force
1.	Toiletries and proprietaries	A	30.0	4.0	10.0
2.	Package goods	AA	25.0	8.0	8.0
3.	Cosmetics	AAA	22.0	2.0	10.0
4.	Drug sundries	A	14.0	3.0	5.0
5.	Drugs	A	12.0	8.0	7.0
6.	Books	A	11.0	6.0	5.0
7.	Food	AAA	11.0	6.0	—
8.	Mail order	AAA	10.5	0.2	0.3
9.	Paints	B	10.0	2.0	15.0
10.	Housewares	B	10.0	2.0	6.0
11.	Food	AAA	7.0	5.0	3.0
12.	Appliances	AAA	5.0	1.0	—
13.	Soft drinks	B	5.0	3.0	1.0
14.	Soft goods	C	5.0	6.0	12.0
15.	Salt	C	5.0[b]	—[b]	—
16.	Tool manufacturing	C	4.0[b]	—[b]	10.0
17.	Paper converting	C	4.0	4.0	—
18.	Tires, foam rubber	A	4.0	4.0	—
19.	Pianos	C	4.0	0.3	5.0
20.	Chemicals	D	3.5	1.0	—
21.	Automotive parts	C	3.5	—	10.3
22.	Textiles	B	3.0	0.7	3.6
23.	Marketing cooperative— fresh produce	C	3.0[b]	—[b]	10.0
24.	Baby foods	A	2.7	2.6	6.0

company may be able to increase its total sales to the point where the reduction in unit production costs more than offsets the increased promotional expenditures.

METHODS OF DETERMINING APPROPRIATION

There are four basic methods of determining the budget allocation for promotion. They are frequently discussed in connection with the advertising appropriation alone, but they may also be applied to the total promotional appropriation.

Relation to income. The promotional appropriation may be related in some way to company income. First, the expenditures may be set as a percentage of past

Table 21-1. (Cont.)

Number	Type of product	Advertising budget[a]	Advertising	Sales promotion	Sales force
25.	Hand tools	B	2.5	0.9	7.1
26.	Home furnishings	B	2.5	2.0	6.0
27.	Power tools	C	2.5	—	—
28.	Appliances	A	2.5	1.5	4.0
29.	Airline	AA	2.2	0.7	—
30.	Liquors	A	2.0	—	—
31.	Heating and air conditioning	A	2.0	0.5	4.5
32.	Soft goods	C	2.0	2.5	4.5
33.	Floor coverings	A	2.0[b]	—[b]	—
34.	Shoe manufacturing	D	2.0[b]	—[b]	5.3
35.	Transportation	AA	1.8	0.2	6.0
36.	Building materials	AA	1.5	0.7	8.0
37.	Automotive	D	1.5	—	3.0
38.	Rubber products	C	1.3	1.0	—
39.	Photographic equipment	B	1.3	0.7	3.0
40.	Insurance	A	1.0	0.5	17.5
41.	Textiles	B	1.0	1.0	0.5
42.	Retail food chain	AAA	1.0[b]	—[b]	—
43.	Petroleum	A	0.6	0.3	—
44.	Domestic pumps and water systems	C	0.6	1.0	—
45.	Glass manufacturing	A	0.5	0.2	—
46.	Aluminum	B	0.1	0.1	—

Note: Dash (—) indicates data not given.
[a] AAA—$10,000,000 and over; AA—$5,000,000–9,999,999; A—$1,000,000–4,999,999; B—$500,000–999,999; C—$100,000—499,999; D—under $100,000.
[b] Advertising and sales promotion combined.
Source: Adapted from Dale Houghton, "Marketing Costs: What Ratio to Sales?" *Printers' Ink,* Feb. 1, 1957, pp. 54–55.

or anticipated *sales.* Second, the appropriation may be based on a percentage of net or gross *profit.* Third, some businesses prefer to budget a fixed amount of money per *unit* of past or expected future sales. Manufacturers of products which have a high unit value and a low rate of turnover (automobiles or appliances, for example) frequently use this last method. Fruit growers' cooperative associations assess member growers a certain amount per case of fruit sold through the cooperative.

The percentage-of-sales method is probably the most widely used of all those discussed here. It has achieved broad acceptance because it is simple to calculate. It also sets the cost in relation to sales income and thus tends to act as a variable expense rather than as a noncontrollable fixed expenditure. Actually the method is

Table 21-2. Promotional costs as percentage of sales of industrial goods: by individual companies.

Sales-force expenditures are typically much higher than advertising appropriations. In the promotional mix, marketers of industrial goods usually emphasize personal selling to a much greater degree than firms selling consumer products. Why? Compare this table and Table 21-1. Note that the total promotional budget for industrial products is typically a smaller percentage of sales than that for consumer goods.

Number	Type of product	Advertising budget[a]	Advertising	Sales promotion	Sales force
1.	Paint	D	10.0	—	—
2.	Road construction and agricultural	D	4.0[b]	—[b]	7.0
3.	Office equipment	C	2.5[c]	—[c]	—
4.	Instrument	C	2.0	0.9	9.0
5.	Tool manufacturing	C	2.0[c]	—[c]	10.0
6.	Paper converting	C	2.0	2.0	—
7.	Instruments and controls	C	2.0[b]	—[b]	15.0
8.	Electrical control	C	1.8	3.8	—
9.	Graphic arts	C	1.5	0.5	16.0
10.	Metalworking	C	1.5[c]	—[c]	5.0
11.	Metal-cutting tools	C	1.2	—	5.6
12.	Industrial machinery	D	1.0	2.0	7.0
13.	Automotive parts	C	1.0	0.5	4.5
14.	Nonferrous metals	A	1.0[c]	—[c]	—
15.	Die cutting	D	1.0	—	10.0
16.	Basic metals	AA	1.0	—	—
17.	Aluminum	A	0.8	0.4	—
18.	Chemicals and plastics	A	0.8	—	—
19.	Hand tools	C	0.5	0.2	2.4
20.	Materials handling	B	0.5	0.5	—
21.	Soft goods—textile	C	0.5	—	12.0
22.	Automotive	D	0.5	—	0.5
23.	Plate steel fabrication	D	0.4	0.5	0.5
24.	Foundry	C	0.3	—	—
25.	Rubber products	D	0.3	—	—
26.	Chemicals	B	0.1	—	—
27.	Glass manufacturing	D	0.1	—	—
28.	Oil	C	0.1	—	—
29.	Aircraft	C	0.1	—	—

Note: Dash (—) indicates data not given.
[a] AAA—$10,000,000 and over; AA—$5,000,000–9,999,999; A—$1,000,000–4,999,999; B—$500,000–999,999; C—$100,000–499,999; D—under $100,000.
[b] Advertising, sales promotion, and marketing research combined.
[c] Advertising and sales promotion combined.
Source: Adapted from Dale Houghton, "Marketing Costs: What Ratio to Sales?" *Printers' Ink*, Feb. 1, 1957, p. 24.

unsound and logically inconsistent. By setting promotional expenditures for one year on the basis of sales in the preceding year, management is saying that promotion is a *result* of sales, when, in fact, it is a *cause* of sales. Even when promotion is set as a percentage of future sales, this method is logically indefensible. By forecasting future sales and the setting the promotional appropriation, management is still considering advertising and personal selling to be a result of sales. If sales depend upon promotion, as is truly the case, then they cannot be forecast until the promotional appropriation is determined. Another undesirable result of this method is that promotional expenditures will be reduced just when sales are declining. If the reasons for a sales decline are not clear, management can compound its difficulties by withdrawing promotional support at that time. Experience shows that a better course of action is to maintain the level of promotional activity, even if profits drop temporarily, until the basic causes of the sales decline can be determined and corrected.[11]

Task or objective. A much sounder basis for determining the promotional budget is first to decide what tasks the promotional program is intended to accomplish and then to determine what the cost of promotion must be. Various forms of this method are widely used today.[12] The task method forces management to define realistically and in detail the goals of its promotional program. This method also involves management in long-run, rather than year-to-year, planning. Sometimes this approach is called the "buildup method" because of the way it operates. For example, a company may set as one goal the entry into a new geographic market. The executives decide that this venture will require ten additional salesmen. Compensation and expenses of these salesmen will cost a total of $170,000 per year. Salary for an additional sales supervisor and expenses for extra office and administrative needs will cost $20,000. Thus in the personal selling part of the promotional mix, an extra $190,000 must be appropriated. Similar estimates may be made for the anticipated cost of advertising, sales promotion, and other promotional tools to be used in connection with the goal of entering a new territory.

Use of all funds available. A new company frequently plows all possible available funds into its promotional program. Management may expect to wait one to five years before it will earn a profit and be able to budget for its sales program in a different manner.

Follow competition. A weak method of determining the promotional appropriation, but one which is used enough to be noted here, is to match the promotional expenditures of competitors. Sometimes only one competitor is

---

[11]For some research findings illustrating this point, see A. C. Neilsen, Jr., "Many Measurements Available to Increase Advertising Effectiveness," *Media/scope,* September, 1965, p. 72.

[12]In the study referred to in the preceding footnote, most respondents stated that "the job to be done" was the single most important determinant of their advertising budgets. Yet in practice most of the firms began building their budgets with a set figure—usually either a percentage increase over last year's budget or a percentage of next year's sales forecast. Few companies actually first determined their advertising objectives, then planned the program to reach these goals, and finally calculated the cost of this program.

followed. In other cases management will have access to industry averages through its trade association, and these will become company bench marks. The system is weak on two counts at least. First, a firm's competitors may be just as much in the dark as the firm itself, and second, the firm's needs and goals may be quite different from those of its competition.

SALES PROMOTION

In Chapter 8, "merchandising" and "sales promotion" were called the two most loosely used terms in the marketing vocabulary. In fact, the sales promotion manager of a major oil company once referred to sales promotion as "muddled, misused, and misunderstood."[13] Many businessmen use the terms synonymously with "advertising" or "promotion" in total. Today in the field of marketing, however, we are beginning to get agreement that sales promotion is a separately distinguishable field.[14]

What then is sales promotion? The American Marketing Association says its preferred definition is, "those marketing activities, other than personal selling, advertising, and publicity, that stimulate consumer purchasing and dealer effectiveness, such as displays, shows and expositions, demonstrations, and various nonrecurrent selling efforts not in the ordinary routine."[15]

In what ways are sales promotion and advertising different? First, except for direct mail, advertising deals with media owned and controlled by others, while sales promotion tries to inform and persuade groups through tools and methods controlled by the company itself. Sales promotion deals with nonrecurring and nonroutine matters, in contrast to advertising or personal selling. Finally, while most companies could not exist profitably without advertising or personal selling, they could do without sales promotion. Frey called sales promotion the "plus" ingredient in the marketing mix.

In effect, a major function of sales promotion is to serve as a bridge between advertising and personal selling—to supplement and coordinate efforts in these two areas. Not only are we seeing an increase in the stature of sales promotion, but also the trend is to integrate it as a part of the total marketing strategy. Often, for example, it is being introduced at the inception of a campaign, and not tacked on afterward.

---

[13]See William R. Kelly, "Muddled . . . Misused . . . Misunderstood . . . That's Sales Promotion!" *Sales Management,* Jan. 15, 1954, p. 36. Sixteen years later the same author conducted a comparative survey and found (1) that the role of the sales promotion manager has changed markedly, but (2) that the field of sales promotion as a marketing activity is still vaguely defined and organized. See "Sales Promotion: Super Success Is Still To Come," *Sales Management,* June 1, 1970, p. 25.

[14]For a more detailed treatment of sales promotion, see John F. Luick and William L. Ziegler, *Sales Promotion and Modern Merchandising,* McGraw-Hill Book Company, New York, 1968.

[15]Committee on Definitions, *Marketing Definitions: A Glossary of Marketing Terms,* American Marketing Association, Chicago, 1960, p. 20. In this set of definitions, however, the American Marketing Association also observes that in retailing, sales promotion is interpreted to cover "all methods of stimulating customer purchasing, including personal selling, advertising, and publicity." Thus in retailing, "sales promotion" is used in a broad sense and is virtually synonymous with "promotion," as the term is used in this book and also by most manufacturers.

IMPORTANCE OF SALES PROMOTION

There is a saying in retailing that "it is the final three feet which count." This refers specifically to the distance from the retail salesclerk to the consumer, but the meaning can be broadened to suggest the importance of all activities at the point of purchase, whether it is a purchase by an ultimate consumer, middleman, or industrial user. Firms "have spent millions on determining the most effective techniques and appeals for luring the prospect into the dealer's place of business . . . but they have failed to follow through by studying how to get him to buy—and to buy *their* products—once he is inside the store."[16]

Today much consumer dissatisfaction with respect to retail selling could be alleviated by a good sales-promotional program. The growing use of self-service, automatic vending, and other sales methods where salesmen are not used also points up the need for sales promotion. Sales-promotional devices are often the only promotional materials available at the point of purchase. Advertising media reach potential customers at their homes, at their places of business, or in their travels. When the time for buying arrives, the impact of the advertisements may have worn off (or the prospect may not even have seen the advertisement), but sales-promotional devices at the point of purchase inform, remind, or otherwise stimulate the buyer. People who see the promotional devices are excellent prospects. They are usually in a buying frame of mind, or they would not be there.[17]

SERVICES RENDERED BY SALES PROMOTION

The sales promotion department of a manufacturer may work with many different groups—consumers, dealers and distributors, or other sections of the marketing department. Similarly, retailers engage in sales-promotional activites aimed at consumers. A manufacturer's sales-promotional program which is directed toward the consumer may be divided into two groups—activities intended to *educate* or *inform* the consumer and those intended to *stimulate* him. To inform consumers, companies will prepare booklets, give demonstrations, and offer free consulting services. To stimulate consumers, many firms give away samples and premiums. Others conduct contests, offering prizes for the best statement which tells in 25 words or less why the consumer likes the given product. These various activities are intended to get the consumer to use the product or (as in a contest) to get him to think of all the possible reasons why he likes it.

Services rendered to dealers and distributors include such things as conducting training programs for the middlemen's salesmen, giving managerial advice, and installing displays. In summary, a manufacturer tries to increase the dealers' interest in the product and to enhance their effectiveness as merchants.

Within the manufacturer's marketing department, the sales promotion division can perform services for the personal selling, advertising, and marketing research groups. Sales promotion people can prepare sales manuals, demonstration kits, and other selling aids used by the salesmen. Also, in the field, the sales force can

---

[16]Robert N. McMurry "How to Win or Lose Sales at the Point of Purchase," *Journal of Marketing,* July, 1959, p. 41.

[17]See "A P.O.P. (point-of-purchase) Art Form that Turns Shoppers On," *Business Week,* Jan. 8, 1972, p. 36.

concentrate on product selling while the sales promotion men do all the missionary work with dealers. The marketing research department can get help in field survey work. The sales promotion department can aid the advertising people by preparing displays and other point-of-purchase advertising materials.

In conclusion, a marketing manager should consider the role which sales promotion can play in a marketing mix. This activity should not be submerged in departments which are concerned primarily with advertising or the personal sales force. Once marketing executives become aware of the value of sales promotion work, they will undoubtedly use this tool more effectively to supplement the work of the marketing division. At the present time, unfortunately, much remains to be done to determine the most effective use of sales promotion in a company's marketing program and to measure the results of using these promotional tools.[18]

QUESTIONS AND PROBLEMS

1. What is the difference between selling and marketing?
2. What are the relationships and differences between the following?
   a. Promotion   c. Sales promotion
   b. Advertising   d. Personal selling
3. Explain and illustrate a communications system using the following situations:
   a. A teen-age girl trying to sell her father on the idea that she should get contact lenses instead of glasses
   b. A salesman talking to a prospect about buying a small electric automobile as a second car in the family
4. Identify the central idea—the theme—in some current promotional campaigns.
5. Explain how the *nature of the market* would affect the promotional mix for the following products:
   a. Oil-well drilling equipment   c. Golf clubs
   b. Plywood   d. Cigarettes
6. Explain how the promotional mix is likely to be affected by the life cycle stage in which each of the following products is situated.
   a. Portable electric typewriters   c. Freeze-dried coffee
   b. Telephoto telephones
7. Using Borden's criteria, evaluate the advertisability of each of the following products. Assume that sufficient funds are available in each case.
   a. Car batteries   c. Wall mirrors
   b. Mattresses   d. Small power tools
8. Can you name any products which are advertised heavily but which do not meet the criterion of having hidden qualities?
9. Explain why personal selling is, or is not, likely to be the main ingredient in the promotional mix for each of the following products:

---

[18]For conflicting points of view regarding whether we can quantitatively measure the effect which sales promotion has on sales, see John H. Weber, "Can Results of Sales Promotion Be Predicted?" *Journal of Marketing,* January, 1963, pp. 15–19; Milton J. Margolis, "How to Evaluate Field Sales Promotion," *Journal of Marketing,* July, 1963, pp. 42–46; and Lee Adler, "Sales Promotion Effectiveness *Can* Be Measured," *Journal of Marketing,* October, 1963, pp. 69–70.

    a. Life insurance being considered by a young, newly married couple

    b. Living-room furniture

    c. Burglar alarm system for industrial plant

    d. Metal tennis rackets

10. Explain why retailer promotional efforts should or should not be stressed in the promotional mix for the following:

    a. Expensive men's suits sold through exclusive distribution

    b. Chiquita-brand bananas

    c. A line of expensive cosmetics for women

    d. Steel-belted radial tires

11. If a manufacturer heavily emphasizes advertising to the consumer, is dealer promotion still needed for:

    a. Car batteries   *c.* Alka-Seltzer

    b. Skis   *d.* Expensive men's suits

12. Why is the percentage-of-sales method so widely used to determine the promotional appropriation when, in fact, most authorities recognize the task or objective method as the most desirable one?

13. Visit a supermarket, clothing store, and hardware store, and then make a list of all the sales-promotional tools or devices which you observed in each store. Which of these devices do you feel are particularly effective?

14. Is sales promotion effective for selling expensive consumer products such as houses, automobiles, or backyard swimming pools? Is your answer the same for expensive industrial products?

15. Explain how sales promotion can be used to offset weaknesses in retail salesmanship.

MANAGEMENT OF PERSONAL SELLING

Salesmen have long been featured in song and story; they have been alternately praised and ridiculed. Selling is essential to the health and well-being of our economic system, and it probably offers more job opportunities than any other single vocation today. Yet personal selling is frequently criticized, and it is very hard to attract qualified young people into selling jobs.

NATURE AND IMPORTANCE OF PERSONAL SELLING

The goal of all marketing efforts is to increase profitable sales by offering want satisfaction to the market over the long run. Personal selling is by far the major promotional method used to reach this goal. The number of people employed in advertising is in the thousands. In personal selling, the number is in the millions. In many companies personal selling is the largest single operating expense, often equaling 8 to 15 percent of net sales. Advertising costs average 1 to 3 percent of sales. Expenditures for salespeople's salaries, commissions, and travel expenses; the costs of operating sales branches; and the expenses of managing these salespeople all add up to a tidy sum.

Personal selling is the most important element in the marketing mix, according to a survey among men who manage American industry—the top executives (not the marketing executives) in some four hundred large and successful firms.

These people also reported that the number and importance of sales jobs were increasing in their firms. Most of the companies (63 percent) had increased the share of the marketing budget allocated to personal selling since 1960. Furthermore, about one-half of the companies expected to increase this proportion still more in future years.[1]

RELATIVE MERITS

Personal selling consists of individual, personal communication, in contrast to the mass, impersonal communication of advertising, sales promotion, and the other promotional tools. Consequently, compared with these other tools, personal selling has the advantage of being more flexible in operation. Salespeople can tailor their sales presentations to fit the needs, motives, and behavior of individual customers. Also, salespeople can see the customer's reaction to a particular sales approach and then make the necessary adjustments right on the spot. A second merit of personal selling is that it permits a minimum of wasted effort. In advertising, much of the cost is devoted to sending the message to people who are in no way real prospects. In personal selling, a company has an opportunity to pinpoint its market target far more effectively than can be done with any other promotional device.

In most situations personal selling can be used to make the actual sale. Advertisements can attract attention and arouse desire, but usually they do not get buying action and complete the transfer of title. Finally, salespeople can perform for management many other services which are not strictly selling jobs. They can collect credit information, reflect customer attitudes, and relay complaints to management. Some firms use their sales representatives to handle adjustments, perform major repair services, and act as fieldmen for marketing research projects.

If personal selling has a major limitation, it is its high cost. Even though the use of salesmen enables a business to reach its market with a minimum of wasted effort, the cost of developing and operating a sales force is high. Another disadvantage is that personal selling is often limited by the company's inability to get the caliber of men needed to do the job. At the retail level many firms have abandoned their sales forces and shifted to self-service for this very reason.

NATURE OF THE SALES JOB

The sales job of today is quite different from that of years gone by. The old type of salesman—the cigar-smoking, back-slapping, joke-telling person epitomized by Harold Hill in *The Music Man* and Willy Loman in *Death of a Salesman*—generally has disappeared, and his talents are not especially desired in today's economy.[2]

---

[1]*Penetration,* vol. 5, no. 2, 1966 (publication of Klein Institute for Aptitude Testing, the sponsor of this study, which was conducted by Prof. D. J. Duncan). Findings also were reported in "Top Executives Rank Salesmanship Tops, Study Shows," *Sales Management,* Mar. 18, 1966, p. 120.

[2]See Donald L. Thompson, "Stereotype of the Salesman," *Harvard Business Review,* January–February, 1972, pp. 20 ff; then by way of contrast, see "The New Supersalesman:

True, high-pressure selling still exists and may always have a role in some fields, but it is no longer typical. Instead, as part of the implementation of the marketing concept in a firm, we see a new type of salesperson—a territorial marketing manager. Rather than just pushing whatever the factory has to sell, our new breed of salespeople interpret customers' wants and relay them back to the firm so that appropriate products may be developed. They engage in a *total* selling job—missionary selling, servicing customers, selling the full line of products, being territorial profit managers, and acting as a mirror of the market as they feed back marketing information.

In this new position, the salesman occupies many roles with many divergent role partners, which makes heavy emotional demands on him.[3] Among other roles he is a persuader, serviceman, information gatherer, expediter, coordinator, problem definer, traveler, display arranger, and customer ego builder. His operations are socially, psychologically, and physically independent of the usual worker-boss relationship. In this performance, salesman faces role conflicts of identification and advocacy. He must identify in shifting fashion first with his company and then with the customer. In so doing, there are conflicts regarding whose position—the company's or the customer's—he is advocating. The several groups with whom salesman interacts often have differing and conflicting expectations.

The salesman's job, then, involves a wide range of behaviors, flexibility in behavior, and fluctuating intensity of social contact. The emotional and interactional demands on a salesman are great because of the high level of role conflict and because he must handle the behavioral ambiguities pretty much on his own. If management can determine the temperamental dimensions— that is, the emotional and interactional demands—of a given sales job and then weave these into the existing job requirements and selection devices, the results of the total selection effort certainly should be more successful than in the past.

SALES JOBS ARE DIFFERENT FROM OTHER JOBS

We dwell on the nature of a sales job not only because it is so important to the economic health of a firm, but also because it is quite different from other jobs. Salesmen represent their company to the outside world. Consequently, opinions of a company and its products often are formed from impressions left by the sales force. The public ordinarily will not judge a firm by its office or factory workers. In fact salesmen often are blamed for mistakes made elsewhere in the firm only because these people are so visible and available.

Other employees usually work under close and constant supervisory control, whereas salesmen typically operate with little or no direct supervision of their activities. As another differentiating feature, most nonselling employees

---

Wired for Success," *Business Week*, Jan. 6, 1973, p. 44; Carl Rieser, "The Salesman Isn't Dead—He's Different," *Fortune*, November, 1962, p. 124; and J. N. Bauman, "Rebirth of a Salesman," *Dun's Review*, March, 1968, p. 45.

[3]This paragraph and the following one are adapted from James A. Belasco, "The Salesman's Role Revisited," *Journal of Marketing*, April, 1966, pp. 6–11; see also Richard T. Hise, "Conflict in the Salesman's Role," *University of Washington Business Review*, Winter, 1968, pp. 52–61.

can perform well with relatively less stimulation. To be successful in many selling tasks, however, salesmen must work hard physically and mentally, be creative, persistent, and show great initiative—and all this requires a high degree of motivation.

Salesmen probably need more tact, diplomacy, and social poise than other employees in the organization. Many sales jobs require the person to mix socially with customers, who frequently are people of high rank. The salesman must display considerable social intelligence in dealing with buyers.

Salesmen are among the few employees authorized to spend company funds. They have the responsibility for proper use of money for entertainment, room, food, transportation, and other business expenses. Their effectiveness in discharging this responsibility can have a significant influence on marketing costs and profits.

Sales jobs frequently require a considerable amount of traveling and much time spent away from home and family. Being in the field puts a salesman in enemy territory, where he deals with an apparently endless stream of customers who seem determined not to buy his products. These mental stresses and disappointments, coupled with the physical demands of long hours, much traveling, strange beds and food, and perhaps heavy sample cases, all combine to require a degree of mental toughness and physical stamina rarely demanded in other types of jobs. Selling is hard work!

WIDE VARIETY OF SALES JOBS

No two selling jobs are alike. Even when sales jobs are grouped or classified on some basis, we find that the types of jobs and the requirements needed to fill them cover a very wide spectrum. The job of a soft drink driver salesman who calls in routine fashion on a group of retail stores is in a different world from that of a computer salesman who sells to an automobile manufacturer a system for retrieving and disseminating information. A salesman for a cosmetics manufacturer selling door-to-door has a job only remotely related to that of an airplane manufacturer selling a fleet of executive-type aircraft to large firms.

Perhaps one useful way to classify the many different types of sales jobs is to array them on the basis of the creative skills required in the job, moving from the very simple to the highly complex, as, for example, the following:[4]

1. Positions in which the job is primarily to deliver the product—e.g., driver salesman for soft drinks, milk, or fuel oil. The selling responsibilities are secondary. Good service and a pleasant personality may lead to more sales, but few of these people originate many sales.
2. Positions in which the salesperson is primarily an *inside* order taker—e.g., the retail clerk standing behind a counter. The customer comes to the salesclerk. Most of the customers have already decided to buy; the salesclerk only serves them. She may use suggestion selling, but ordinarily she cannot do much more.

---

[4]Adapted from Robert N. McMurry, "The Mystique of Super-salesmanship," *Harvard Business Review*, March–April, 1961, p. 114.

3. Positions in which the salesperson is primarily an *outside* order taker, going to the customer in the field—e.g., packinghouse, soap, or spice salesperson who calls on retail food stores. In his contacts with chain-store personnel, he actually may be discouraged from doing any hard selling. That task is left to executives higher in the organization. Although good service and a pleasant personality may help him, he does little creative selling.

4. Positions in which the salesperson is not expected or permitted to solicit an order. His job is to build goodwill, perform promotional activities, or provide services for the customers. This is the missionary salesperson for a distiller, for example, or the detail salesperson for an ethical pharmaceutical manufacturer.

5. Positions in which the major emphasis is placed on the salesperson's technical product knowledge—e.g., the sales engineer.

6. Positions that demand creative selling of *tangible* products, such as vacuum cleaners, airplanes, encyclopedias, or oil-well drilling equipment. Here the salesperson's job is often more difficult because the customer may not be aware of his need for the product, or he may not realize how the new product can satisfy his wants better than the product he is now using. When the product is of a technical nature, this category may overlap that of the sales engineer.

7. Positions that require creative selling of *intangibles*, such as insurance, advertising services, consulting services, or communications systems. Intangibles are typically more difficult to sell because they are less readily demonstrated.

DEVELOPMENT AND OPERATION OF A SALES FORCE

SELECTING THE SALES FORCE

As explained in Chapter 2, it is the author's contention that staffing is the most important of all managerial activities. In a promotional program the value of good selection is seen in several ways. First, since it is very difficult to find good salespeople, it is essential that the selection program maximize the opportunity of getting the type of person needed. Second, sales managers are no better than salespeople. No matter how well managed a sales force may be, if it is distinctly inferior in quality to that of a competitor, the competitor will win out. Third, if a sales force is well selected, many other tasks in sales management such as training and superivsion are made easier. Also, selling costs will be reduced because turnover rates will be lower. In addition to its many other advantages, a well-selected sales force should be more productive and should build better customer relations than a poorly chosen group.

Scope of selection task. The three major steps in sales-force selection are:

1. Determine the number and type of people wanted. This step includes the preparation of a written job description. Management must also determine specifically what qualifications are needed to fill the job as it is described.
2. Recruit an adequate number of applicants.
3. Select the qualified persons from among the applicants.

What makes a good salesperson? The key to success in the first step is to establish the proper hiring specifications, just as if the company were purchasing
equipment or supplies instead of manpower. To establish these specifications,
management must first know what the particular sales job entails. This calls
for a detailed job analysis and a written description. It should include specific
statements regarding the title of the job, organizational relationships, job duties,
and applicant qualifications. This written description will later be invaluable in
training, compensation, and supervision.

Determining the qualifications needed to fill the job is the most difficult part
of the selection function. We still really do not know all the characteristics that
make a good salesperson. We do not know to what quantitative degree each
should be possessed, nor to what extent an abundance of one can offset the
lack of another.

Over the years many myths have arisen regarding what traits lead to success
in selling. A good sales representative was supposed to be aggressive, extro-
verted, articulate, well-groomed, and endowed with a great physique. Yet in
actual fact many outstanding salespeople have been mild-mannered and intro-
verted. Other good ones have been somewhat inarticulate and carelessly
dressed. Many good salespeople are of average or even small size.

While the search for what makes a good salesperson may be an impossible
dream, still the quest continues. As one approach to the problem, some companies have analyzed the personal histories of their past sales representatives
to determine traits common to the successful or unsuccessful performers.
Sometimes it helps to interview people when they leave the company to see
whether meaningful patterns can be uncovered.

One psychologist who has worked extensively in sales management concluded that people who are outstanding sales successes inevitably possess
these traits:[5]

1. A high level of energy
2. Abounding self-confidence
3. A chronic hunger for money, status, and the good things in life
4. A well-established habit of industry
5. The habit of perseverance—each objection or resistance is a challenge
6. A natural tendency to be competitive

Moreover, McMurry maintains that the *sine qua non* of sales success is an
intangible, largely intuitive, sensitivity to people. These supersalesmen are,
in effect, constant and habitual "wooers." They have an inherent flair for win-
ning the acceptance of others.

Unfortunately, many of these wooers have what psychologists would call
"infantile" or even "pathological" personalities. Their wooing is a compulsive
need to win and hold the acceptance and affections of others. Often these salesmen are basically passive and dependent persons, craving love and acceptance
and continually battling to prove themselves. They may feel worthless and rejected. Then the hostility in them motivates them to get even by selling. The need
to win love and respect combined with the hostility results in an ambivalent love-

---

[5]*Ibid.,* pp. 117–118. See also Robert N. McMurry and James S. Arnold, *How to Build a
Dynamic Sales Organization,* McGraw-Hill Book Company, New York, 1968, pp. 2–9.

hate attitude toward customers and managerial authority. The salesmen need these other people, but at the same time they resent them. Supersalesmen frequently are difficult to supervise and control.

In another approach to the question of what makes a good salesman, Mayer and Greenberg concluded after some years of research that two personality traits are basic to sales success:[6]

1. Empathy—the ability to identify with the customer and his feelings
2. Ego-drive—the personal need to make a sale, as a measure of self-fulfillment and not just for the money

Recruiting applicants. A planned system for recruiting a sufficient number of applicants is the next step in selection. A good recruiting system has these characteristics:

1. It is operating continuously, not just when there are vacancies on the sales force.
2. It is systematic, reaching and exploiting all appropriate sources of applicants.
3. It provides a continuous flow of qualified applicants in greater numbers than the company can use.
4. It is phased so that mechanical, initial steps can be delegated and will not require a high-level executive's time.

Matching applicants with hiring specifications. The third step involves two tasks. First, management must establish a system of measuring applicants against predetermined standards. Then it must activate the system so as to select the necessary number of people who have the proper qualifications. Sales managers should use all available selection tools in their effort to determine which applicants possess the desired qualifications. These tools include application blanks, interviews, references, credit reports, psychological tests, and physical examinations. Probably all companies use application blanks. They serve as records of personal histories and may be used to implement interviewing. Some companies assign scores to various answers on a blank and total the applicant's score. If this score is below a predetermined level, the applicant will usually be eliminated.

The interview is the other most widely used selection device. Virtually no salesperson is hired without one personal interview, and it is desirable to have several. Ideally these should be conducted in different physical settings and by different people. This should help to reduce the effect of one person's possible bias, to get other people's opinions, and to see how the recruit acts under different conditions. Usually an interview can help an employer to determine how badly the applicant wants the job, whether the company can assure him the success he wants, and whether he will work to his fullest capacity. Patterned or preplanned interviews are usually considered most desirable because they overcome many weaknesses found in the typical interviewing process.

---

[6]David Mayer and Herbert M. Greenberg, "What Makes a Good Salesman?" *Harvard Business Review,* July–August, 1964, pp. 119–125.

ASSIMILATING NEW SALESPEOPLE INTO THE ORGANIZATION

When salespeople are hired, management should pay close attention to the task of integrating them into the company family. Often this step is overlooked entirely. The people are carefully selected and wined and dined to recruit them into the firm. Then as soon as they are hired, the honeymoon is over, and they are left to shift for themselves. In such cases people often become discouraged and may even quit. A wise sales manager will recognize that the new people know very little about the details of the job, their fellow workers, or their status in the firm. A vital need exists to maintain open two-way channels of communication between new sales personnel and management.

TRAINING THE SALES FORCE

Another major aspect of operating a sales force includes developing and conducting a training program. All salespeople, even experienced ones, need some training periodically. Training involves the following problem areas; in each instance, decisions will be based to a considerable extent upon the kind of training program involved—whether it is an indoctrination program, a refresher course, or some other type.

1. What are the goals of the program? In general, the aim of the program is to increase productivity and stimulate the sales force. In addition, executives must determine what specific ends they wish to accomplish. For instance, the goal may be to increase sales of high-margin items, to improve prospecting methods to develop new accounts, or to introduce the new season's line of products.
2. Who should do the training? The training program may be conducted by the line sales executives, by a company staff training department, or by outside training specialists.
3. What should be the content of the program? A well-rounded sales training program should cover three general topics: product knowledge, information about company policies, and selling techniques. Salespeople must know everything possible about their own products and about competitive goods. Usually these subjects are covered in initial training programs, and information regarding new products is included in refresher courses and continuous training programs. The job description will provide an excellent guide to the content of the program.

    A sales force should also know the company history, the executives, and the policies concerning pricing, discounts, returns, delivery, guarantees, minimum orders, etc. Finally, new salesmen especially need to be instructed in whatever selling techniques are required for the particular product.
4. When and where should training be done? Some companies believe in fully training people before they go into the field. Others let people prove that they have some desire and ability to sell and then bring them back into the office for intensive training. Both points of view have merit.

    Firms may employ either centralized or decentralized training programs. A centralized program may involve a periodic meeting which all salespeople attend, or the company may employ an organized school conducted on a continuing or periodic basis. A decentralized program may be held in branch offices, in traveling sales clinics, or during on-the-job training. Decentralized programs generally cost less than centralized programs. They do not take people away from their work for long and do not disrupt home office routine. The trainees can learn right in the environment where they work and where their problems occur. The big problem with decentralized programs is that the quality of instruction is often inferior.

5. What instructional methods should be used? The lecture method can be employed to inform trainees about company history and practices. Demonstrations may be used to impart product knowledge or selling techniques. Round-table discussions are often employed to analyze problems encountered by the sales force in their work. Role playing is an excellent device for training a person in proper selling techniques. On-the-job training can be used in almost any phase of the program.

COMPENSATING SALESPEOPLE

To compensate their sales forces, companies may offer both financial and non-financial rewards. The nonfinancial rewards involve giving people an opportunity for advancement, satisfying their need for recognition of their efforts, and giving them a feeling of belonging. Financial rewards may take the form of direct monetary payment or of indirect monetary payment (paid vacations, pensions, and insurance plans).

Before designing a specific plan, management should understand the broad goals of a sound pay arrangement. It should enable a company to attract, keep, and develop desirable people. It should correlate a person's rewards with his efforts and results, particularly results. A sound plan should enable management to control the activities of the sales force. It should ensure proper treatment of customers. To reach these general goals, the specific plan should (1) provide for a steady income as well as an incentive income, (2) be flexible and yet easy to understand, (3) be economical to administer, and (4) be competitive and still be fair to management and the salespeople. In designing a compensation plan, management should, by referring to the job description, relate the pay plan to the sales job. As much as possible—and this is difficult—the plan should be based upon job elements which are controllable by the salespeople and are also quantitatively measurable.

Establishing a compensation system really involves making decisions on two general problems—the *level* of compensation and the *method* of compensation. The level refers to the total dollar income which a salesperson earns over a period of time. The method of compensation refers to the system or plan by which the salesperson will reach the intended level. The level is influenced by the type of person required for the job and the competitive rate of pay for similar positions.

There are three widely used methods of compensating a sales force: straight salary, straight commission, and a combination plan. Today, well over one-half of the firms in the country use some kind of combination plan.

The straight-salary plan offers a maximum of security and stability of earnings for a salesperson. Management is in a better position to control and direct the activities of the salespeople because they are paid the same amount each month regardless of what tasks they perform. Turnover is usually minimized. Under this arrangement salespeople can consider the customers' best interests.

A commonly stated drawback of the plan is that it does not offer adequate incentive. Also, it is a fixed cost unrelated to sales revenue. Determining the proper salary level is often a problem. Moreover, unless management provides a high quality of supervision and control, the company wastes the advantage of being able to direct people under this plan. Straight-salary systems are typically used for compensating new salespeople and missionary salespeople, when opening new territories, or when the sale involves a technical product and a lengthy period of negotiations.

A straight commission tends to have just the opposite merits and limitations. It provides tremendous incentive for the salespeople, and the commission costs can be related directly to sales or gross margin. Sales representatives have more freedom in their work, and their level of income is determined largely by their own efforts. On the other hand, it is difficult to control the people and to get them to do a fully balanced sales job. It is particularly difficult to get them to perform tasks for which no commission is paid. There is always the danger that they will oversell a customer or otherwise incur his ill will. Straight-commission plans may work well if:

1. Great incentive is needed to get the sales.
2. Very little nonselling missionary work is required.
3. The company is financially weak and must relate its compensation expenses directly to sales or gross margin.
4. The sales force prefers the plan, or it is quite common in the industry.
5. The company is unable to supervise the sales force.

The ideal way to develop a combination plan is to balance the best features of both the straight-salary and the straight-commission plans with as few of their drawbacks as possible.

An important element in a sales force's financial affairs is the reimbursement for business expenses which they incur in traveling or selling. The importance of salesmen's expense control is difficult to overrate. With shrinking profit margins and higher break-even points in a company's operations, many administrators are justly concerned over the expense items incurred by the sales force. It is essential that sales executives develop a plan to control these costs and reimburse the salesmen for them. In principle, a salesman should not make or lose money because of his expense account, nor should he forgo any beneficial sales activities because he will not be adequately reimbursed for the attendant expenses. Most firms pay salesmen for these expenses under an expense account arrangement. Ordinarily, arrangements for reimbursing salesmen for these expenses should be separated from the compensation plan. A substantial number of companies, however, let the salesmen pay all their own expenses from their total salaries or commissions.

SUPERVISING SALESPEOPLE

Another management responsibility involved in operating a sales force is to provide adequate supervision. This activity can serve both as a method of continuation training and as a device to ensure that company policies and practices are being carried out. One of the values of supervision is that it affords a vertical two-way channel of communication between management and the sales force. Executives must determine how much supervision is needed to avoid either over- or under-supervising. There is probably little doubt that personal supervision is most effective. This may be done by field supervisors, branch managers, or home office sales executives. Other methods of supervision include the use of correspondence, reports, and sales meetings.

EVALUATION OF SALESPEOPLE'S PERFORMANCE

Part of the task of managing a field selling force should include the job of establishing and operating an orderly procedure for evaluating the efforts of the salespeople. Until an executive knows what his sales force is doing, he is in no position to make constructive proposals for improvement. By studying salespeople's activities and by establishing standards for what constitutes good performance, management should be able to upgrade the sales force's efforts in general.

By analyzing the characteristic activities of good and poor salespeople, management may be able to identify the factors that lead to sales success. Management may find, for example, that the top ten salespeople average 20 percent more calls per week than the poorest ten. It may find that the successful ones spend more time giving managerial advice to retailers and training retail clerks.

Performance analysis can help the salespeople improve their own efforts. Salespeople with a poor sales record may have known for a long time that they are doing something wrong but be unable to determine what it is because they have no objective standards by which to measure their performances.

Performance evaluation can be an aid in determining what should be included in a training program, and it can help in sales supervision. A supervisor who knows some of the specific strengths and weaknesses of each salesperson can do a better job of directing and training. Performance evaluation can also help management determine salary increases and promotion for the sales force.

BASES FOR EVALUATION

Both quantitative and qualitative factors should be used as the bases for performance evaluation. The quantitative bases generally have the advantage of, or capacity for, being more specific and objective. Qualitative factors, unfortunately, must rely too much on the subjective judgment of the evaluators. For either of the two types of appraisal factors, however, management has the difficult task of setting the standards against which performance can be measured.

Quantitative bases. Sales performance should be evaluated on the basis of both input (or efforts) and output (or results). A person's productive effectiveness is a concept that involves the relationship between the two—output as measured by sales volume, gross margin, etc., and input as indicated by call rate, expenses incurred, nonselling activities, etc.

In a performance evaluation, the importance of output factors is readily recognized. Sometimes, however, the value of input factors is underestimated. Actually, the input factors usually are critical in locating trouble spots. If a person's output performance (average order size, gross margin, etc.) is unsatisfactory, very often the cause lies in the handling of the various input factors over which the salesperson has control.

Some *output* factors which are ordinarily quite useful as evaluation bases are as follows:

1. Sales volume—by products, customer groups, mail, telephone, etc.
2. Sales volume as a percentage of quota or territorial potential
3. Gross margin by product line, customer group, and order size
4. Orders:
    a. Number of orders
    b. Average size (dollar volume) of order
    c. Batting average (orders divided by calls)
5. Accounts:
    a. Percentage of accounts sold
    b. Number of new accounts
    c. Number of lost accounts

Some useful *input* factors to measure are:

1. Calls per day (call rate)
2. Days worked
3. Direct selling expense, in total and as a percentage of sales volume or expense quota
4. Nonselling activities:
    a. Advertising displays set up
    b. Number of service calls made
    c. Number of meetings held with dealers and/or distributors

One key to a successful evaluation program is to appraise a salesperson's performance on as many different bases as possible. Otherwise, management may be misled. A person may have a low ratio of selling expenses to sales volume and be commended for thrifty management of company funds. Yet that low expense ratio may have occurred because the person failed to prospect for new accounts or to cover the territory adequately. A high daily call rate may look good, but it tells us nothing about how many orders per call are being written up. A high batting average (orders divided by calls) may be camouflaging a low average order size or a high sales volume on low-profit items.

Qualitative bases. It would be nice if the entire performance evaluation could be based only on quantitative factors, thus minimizing the subjectivity and personal biases of the evaluators. Unfortunately, this cannot be done. Too many qualitative factors—outlined below—must be considered because they influence a salesman's performance:

1. The salesman's knowledge of the product, company policies, and competition
2. The management of his own time and his preparation for calls
3. Customer relations
4. His personal appearance and health
5. Personality and attitudinal factors, such as:
    a. Cooperativeness
    b. Resourcefulness
    c. Ability to analyze logically and make decisions

The evaluator assumes a key role because the success of a qualitative evaluation depends to a great extent upon the salesperson's ability to be objective and impartial. Merit rating forms are useful at this stage in an evaluation. These forms permit the judgments of the several evaluators to appear in a standardized manner. This uniformity aids in comparing one salesperson with another. Rating forms also provide a written report for company records. What is more important, however, use of rating forms should result in an evaluator's being more thorough in his work, since his appraisals now appear on record for others to see and, perhaps, for him to defend.

THE PERSONAL SELLING PROCESS

If marketing executives understand the fundamentals of salesmanship—that is, the theories underlying the interaction between buyer and seller—they are in a better position to develop an effective selling procedure for their sales force to follow. For the most part these "theories" are based upon research in the behavioral sciences or upon knowledge gained from years of selling experience in practical market settings.[7] The basic concepts explaining buyer-seller interactions were developed in earlier chapters in our discussions of customer motivation and behavior.

Coupling their marketing knowledge with others' research findings in interaction theory, Robertson and Chase derived the following set of predictions relative to the sales process.[8] Salespeople and executives alike should find it useful to incorporate these generalizations into their personal selling programs.

1. The more closely matched the physical, social, and personality characteristics of customer and salesperson are, the more likely a sale is to result.[9]
2. The more believable and trustworthy the customer perceives a salesperson to be, the more likely a sale is to result.
3. The more persuasible a customer is, the more likely it is that a sale will result.
4. The more a salesperson can make prospective buyers view themselves favorably, the more likely it is that a sale will result.
5. The second salesperson to call on a prospect will generally have an advantage over the first one.

---

[7] For a summary of the theoretical aspects of salesmanship with excellent source references, see Richard R. Still and Edward W. Cundiff, *Sales Management,* 2d ed., Prentice-Hall, Inc., Englewood Cliffs, N.J., 1969, pp. 46–56; see also Robert F. Gwinner, "Base Theory in the Formulation of Sales Strategy," *MSU Business Topics,* Autumn, 1968, pp. 37–44; and Harry L. Davis and Alvin J. Silk, *Behavioral Research of Personal Selling: A Review of Some Recent Studies of Interaction and Influence Processes in Sales Situations,* Marketing Science Institute, Cambridge, Mass., 1971.

[8] Thomas S. Robertson and Richard B. Chase, "The Sales Process: An Open Systems Approach," *MSU Business Topics,* Autumn, 1968, pp. 49–50. The systems approach was used to conceptualize the sales process, framing it in an input-output model. That is, inputs (human, technological, and organizational) were transformed by the sales process into the hoped-for output of satisfied customers.

[9] See Franklin B. Evans, "Selling as a Dyadic Relationship: A New Approach," *American Behavioral Scientist,* May, 1963, pp. 76–79.

At this point we shall summarize briefly one procedure which can be used in personal selling.

PRESALE PREPARATION

In the chain of events which it is hoped will lead to a sale, the first step is to make certain that the salesperson is prepared. This means that he must be well acquainted with the product, the market, and the techniques of selling. Before salespeople make their first call, they should know as much as possible about the motivation and behavior of the market segment to which they will sell. They should be informed on the nature of the competition, the business conditions prevailing in their tertitories, etc.

LOCATING OR PROSPECTING FOR POTENTIAL BUYERS

The sales person is now ready to locate customers. This second step toward a sale involves drawing up a profile of the ideal prospect. The salesperson can examine records of past and present customers in his effort to determine the characteristics of such a prospect. From this profile he may develop a list of people or companies who are logical potential buyers of the product.

There are other ways salespersons can acquire a list of prospects. Their sales manager usually prepares a list for them; present customers can suggest new leads; present users may want later or different models of the product. The salesperson might build a list of users of competitors' products. A little thought will often suggest logical prospects. For instance, salespeople of home furnishings, insurance, light fixtures, or telephone equipment find prospects in the regularly published lists of building permits issued. Salespeople of many products find leads among birth or engagement announcements in newspapers.

PREAPPROACH TO INDIVIDUAL PROSPECTS

Before calling on prospects, the salesperson should learn all he can about the person or company to whom he hopes to sell. He might want to know what products or brands the prospect is now using and what the reaction to them is. A salesperson should try to find out the personal habits, likes, dislikes, etc., of the prospect. In general, the salesperson should try to get all the information he can so that he will be able to tailor his presentation to the individual buyer.

SALES PRESENTATION

The actual presentation of the salesperson will start with an attempt to attract the prospect's attention, and then try to hold the customer's interest while building a desire for the product. Then the salesperson will try to close the sale. All through the presentation, the salesperson must be ready to meet any hidden or expressed objections which the prospect may have.[10]

---

[10]*Sales Management* magazine has devoted an entire issue to each of three steps in the sales presentation process. See "Opening the Sale," Oct. 30, 1972; "The Presentation," Oct. 1, 1973; and "Closing the Sale," June 1, 1971.

Attract attention—the approach. Several approaches are frequently used to attract the prospect's attention and start the presentation. The simplest approach is merely to greet the prospect, introduce oneself, and state what one is selling. While this is direct, in many selling situations it is not so effective as other approaches. If the salesperson was referred to the prospect by a customer, the right approach might be to start out with a reference to this common acquaintance. Sometimes this is called the "Joe sent me" approach. The salesperson might suggest the product benefits by making some startling statement. One sales training consultant often greets a prospect with the question, "If I can cut your selling costs in half, and at the same time double your sales volume, are you interested?" This approach parallels the strong, attention-getting headlines often used in advertisements. A fourth approach, which can be effective if the salesperson has a new product, is simply to walk in and hand the product to the prospect. While the prospect looks it over, the salesperson can start the sales presentation.

Hold interest and arouse desire. When the salesperson has attracted the prospect's attention, he can hold his interest and stimulate his desire for the product by means of the sales talk itself. There is no common pattern here. Usually, however, a product demonstration is invaluable. Also, if it has not been possible to determine a prospect's specific needs during the preapproach, certainly this must be done in the course of the presentation. Whatever pattern is followed in the talk, the salesperson must always show the prospect how the product will benefit him.

Many companies insist that their salespeople use a "canned" sales talk. That is, all representatives must give identical presentations verbatim or with very minor changes. Although many people may feel that this is a poor practice, it has been proved time and again that a canned sales talk can be effective. Salespeople can still project their own individual personalities, even though they all say essentially the same thing. These presentations ensure that all points are covered, they employ tested techniques, and they facilitate the sales training job considerably.[11]

Meet objections and close the sale. After explaining the product and its benefits, the salesperson should try to close the sale and write up an order. As part of the presentation, the salesperson may periodically venture a trial close in order to sense the prospect's willingness to buy. By posing some "either-or" questions, a salesperson can start to bring the presentation to a head. That is, he may ask, "Do you prefer the gray or the green model?" "How soon would you want this delivered?" or "Would you plan to charge this or pay cash?"

The trial close is important because it gives the salesperson an indication of how near the prospect is to a decision. A salesperson may lose a sale by talking too much. The prospect may be ready to buy at the beginning and then change

---

[11]For a new look at the different types of canned sales presentations, and the importance of relating the *method* of presentation to the *objective* of the presentation, see Marvin A. Jolson, "Should the Sales Presentation Be 'Fresh' or 'Canned'?" *Business Horizons,* October, 1973, pp. 81–88.

his mind if the salesperson insists on a full presentation. Sometimes sales are lost simply because the representative fails to ask for the order.

The trial close also tends to bring out the buyer's objections. A salesperson should encourage a buyer to state his objections. Then the salesperson has an opportunity to answer them and to bring out additional product benefits or re-emphasize previously stated points.

The toughest objections to answer are those which are unspoken. A salesperson must uncover the real objections before hoping to make a sale. Another difficult situation occurs when the prospect says he wants to "think it over." A generalization on this point is that the salesperson must close the sale then and there, or the chances are that it will be lost.

Textbooks on salesmanship discuss different types of final closing techniques. The assumptive close is probably used as much as any other, and it can be used in a wide variety of selling situations. In this closing technique, the salesperson assumes that the customer is going to buy, so it is just a case of settling the details. He will ask such questions as, "When do you want this delivered?" "Is this a charge sale?" "Do you want this gift-wrapped?" or "What color have you decided upon?"

POSTSALE ACTIVITIES

An effective selling job does not end when the order is written up. Normally, sales success depends upon repeat business. Also, a satisfied customer will furnish leads to other prospects. Consequently, the final stage of our selling process is a series of postsale services which can build customer goodwill and lay the groundwork for many years of profitable business relations. If mechanical installation is necessary, the representative should make certain the job is done properly. It is necessary to make sure that all points in the sales contract and the guarantee are clearly understood. In the case of large industrial products, the salesperson will often spend weeks or months in the customer's establishment, training operators and checking to be sure that the product is working smoothly within the buyer's system.

In general, all these activities by the salesperson serve to reduce the customer's postdecision anxiety—his cognitive dissonance. The theory of cognitive dissonance (as we can recall from Chapter 6) holds that after a person has made a decision, anxiety (dissonance) will usually occur because he knows the alternative he selected has some disagreeable features, as well as advantages. Consequently, the person seeks support and reassurance that he made the correct choice, and conversely he wants to avoid anything which suggests that one of his discarded choices really would have been better. (Sometimes this anxiety will set in before the buying decision is made, and the net result may be no sale because the customer cannot make a decision.)

In this final stage of the selling process, it is the salesperson's job to minimize the customer's dissonance. In addition to other postsale services, the salesperson should reassure the customer that he made the right decision by (1) summarizing the products benefits, (2) repeating why it is better than the discarded alternative choices, and (3) pointing out how satisfied he will be with the product's performance.

REASONS FOR SHORTAGE OF QUALIFIED SALESPEOPLE

In spite of the many job opportunities and the high levels of compensation in selling, there is an acute shortage of qualified people entering this field. Management is often forced to accept submarginal people. For several reasons, talented prospects will consider a selling career only when they cannot qualify for any other job. Selling usually involves considerable traveling, and this is often a deterrent to people with families. The career lacks social prestige and status. Also, many people have a poor image of the salesman owing to the abundance of traveling-salesman jokes and the fact that the only sales activities most people ever see are retail clerking and door-to-door selling. Most sales jobs in no way resemble these two activities. The majority of people are totally unaware of the many really good sales jobs which involve selling to manufacturers, retailers, or wholesalers.

One writer, in analyzing the problem, points out that selling is considered a white-collar job, salespeople receive a relatively high income, and the job offers freedom of action—all three factors being characteristic of high-prestige occupations. At the same time, selling's prestige is lowered because (1) no formalized education and training are required and (2) power and authority are lacking both in the job and in dealing with customers.[12]

Possibly a fundamental reason why people stay away from selling jobs is that they are just not talented enough to become salespeople. Consciously or unconsciously, people may recognize that sales work is one kind of activity that requires grasping the naked sword and coming to grips with reality in a situation stripped of all possibilities for excuse making. It is a virile activity that puts a person's mettle to the test every day. In a sense, sales work reduces the relationship between two people to a very simple test of power: Can I get you to buy? Most other jobs modify this relationship, allowing workers to operate in a protected environment where they may affect sales indirectly and impersonally, without exposing themselves to the possibility of failure and a recognition of their personal inadequacies.

QUESTIONS AND PROBLEMS

1. A double-page, full-color advertisement in one issue of *Playboy* magazine costs much more than the compensation and expenses needed to maintain one salesperson for one full year. A sales-force executive is urging his company to eliminate a few of these ads and instead hire a few more salespeople. This executive believes that one good salesperson working for an entire year can sell more than one ad in one issue of *Playboy*. How would you answer this executive?
2. "The salesman occupies many roles with many divergent role partners, which places heavy emotional demands on him." Explain.

---

[12]John L. Mason, "The Low Prestige of Personal Selling," *Journal of Marketing,* October, 1965, pp. 7–10; see also John L. Mason, "The Salesman's Prestige: A Re-examination," *Business Topics,* Autumn, 1962, pp. 73–77; and Gerhard W. Ditz, "Status Problems of the Salesman," *MSU Business Topics,* Winter, 1967, pp. 68–80.

3. Refer to the seven-way classification of sales jobs found early in this chapter and answer the following questions:
   a. In which types of jobs is the salesperson most free from close supervision?
   b. Which types are likely to be the highest paid?
   c. Which are likely to involve the most traveling?
   d. For which groups is a high degree of motivation necessary?
4. "Salesmen are born, not made" Do you agree? If so, why does a firm need a good training program? If not—that is, if you believe that salesmen are made, not born—why does a firm need a good selection program?
5. "A good selection program is desirable but not essential. Improper selection of salespeople can be counterbalanced by a good training program, by a good compensation system, or by fine supervision." Discuss.
6. What sources should be used for recruiting sales applicants in each of the following firms? Explain your reasoning in each instance.
   a. A company selling executive airplanes to a manufacturer of paper products
   b. A firm selling cosmetics door-to-door
   c. A dress manufacturer selling high-fashion dresses to department stores and exclusive specialty shops
   d. A grocery products wholesaler selling to retailers and institutions in the Pacific Northwest
7. "It is best to hire experienced salesmen because they do not require any training." Discuss.
8. What factors should be considered when determining the level of sales compensation?
9. Compare the merits of a straight-salary plan and a straight-commission plan of sales compensation. Name some types of sales jobs in which each plan might be desirable.
10. What measure might be used to determine whether a salesperson is using high-pressure selling tactics which may injure customer relations?
11. In this chapter, many of the bases for evaluating salespeople's performance seemed to apply more to "outside" salespeople—those who go to the customers. What bases might be used to evaluate the performance of in-store retail salespeople?
12. How can a sales manager evaluate the ability of his salespeople to get new business?
13. What are some of the sources you might use to acquire a list of prospects for the following products?
   a. Automobiles   c. Life insurance
   b. Baby furniture
14. What can a salesperson do when customers object that the price of his product is too high?
15. What can be done to make selling more attractive as a career?

MANAGEMENT OF ADVERTISING

A hunter ordinarily does not use a rifle to hunt ducks. He needs a device which will enable him to hit more ducks with the same amount of effort expended in using a rifle. Thus he will use a shotgun. By the same token, mass communication is needed to reach mass markets at a reasonable cost. Advertising and sales promotion are just the tools for this job. It is too costly and time-consuming to try to do the job with salesmen alone.

NATURE AND IMPORTANCE OF ADVERTISING

Advertising consists of all the activities involved in presenting to a group a non-personal, oral or visual, openly sponsored message regarding a product, service, or idea; this message, called an *advertisement,* is disseminated through one or more media and is paid for by the identified sponsor.

Some important considerations should be noted in connection with this definition. First, there is a significant distinction between advertising and an advertisement. The advertisement is simply the message itself. Advertising is a process—it is a program or a series of activities necessary to prepare the message and get it to the intended market. Another point is that the public knows who is behind the advertising because the sponsor is openly identified in the advertisement itself. Also, payment is made by the sponsor to the media which carry the message. These last two considerations differentiate advertising from propaganda and publicity.

TYPES OF ADVERTISING

Understanding the various ways in which advertising can be classified should be useful to an executive, because different types of advertising will be called for depending upon the company's objectives in its advertising program.

Product and institutional. All advertising may be classed as product or institutional. In product advertising, the advertiser is informing or stimulating the market about his products or services. Product advertising is often further subdivided into direct-action and indirect-action advertising. With *direct-action* advertising, the seller is seeking a quick response to his advertisement. An advertisement with a coupon may urge the reader to send in immediately for a free sample. Thursday-night and Friday-morning advertisements run by supermarkets list products featured in weekend sales. *Indirect-action* advertising is designed to stimulate demand over a longer period of time. Advertisements are intended to inform the customers that the product exists and to point out its benefits so that when they are in the market for the product, they will look favorably upon the seller's brand. Product advertising may also be subclassed as *primary-demand* and *selective-demand* advertising to correspond with the stages of the product's demand or life cycle. (This topic was discussed in Chapter 21.)

Institutional advertising is designed to create a proper attitude toward the seller and to build goodwill, rather than to sell a specific product or service. Institutional advertising may be further subdivided into three areas: patronage, public relations, and public service institutional advertising. In *patronage* institutional advertising, a seller is trying to attract customers by appealing to patronage-buying motives rather than product-buying motives. To illustrate, a retailer may inform his market about new store hours or a change in his delivery policy. A manufacturer may stress new credit and returned-goods policies when advertising in trade journals to attract wholesalers. *Public relations* institutional advertising is used to create a favorable image of the firm among employees, stockholders, or the general public. A manufacturer may run some ads telling what he is doing to reduce stream pollution caused by his plant's operations. *Public service* institutional advertising is illustrated by ads urging the public to support a Red Cross drive or to drive carefully. The New York Life Insurance Company has run a series of ads to help guide young people in their choice of a career.

National and local. National (general) advertising is that sponsored by manufacturers or other producers. Local (retail) advertising is just that—advertising placed by retailers. Although the terms "national" and "local" are used synonymously with "general" and "retail" in the advertising business, this is an unfortunate and inexact comparison. It is true that most manufacturers sell in more than one local market, and it is also true that a retailer's market is usually confined to one locality. As currently used in the trade, however, the term "national" advertising refers only to the level of the advertiser and has no relation at all to geographic coverage. If a manufacturer places a single ad in only one city, this is still referred to as national advertising.

Another purposeful distinction may be drawn between a manufacturer's and a retailer's advertising. A manufacturer's advertising is designed to build a demand for his product. He does not care where the item is purchased, as long as the customer buys his brand. In retailer's advertising, the stress is on the store. A retailer does not care what product or brand you buy, as long as you buy it at his establishment. Therefore, his advertisements often feature appeals to patronage motives, showing you what services he offers and why it is to your advantage to buy at his store.

Nature of market. Several classifications of advertising are based upon subdivisions of the market. Advertising differs depending upon whether the market target is the consumer, middleman, industrial user, or professional man. Consumer advertising is aimed at ultimate consumers who purchase for nonbusiness, personal use. In trade advertising, the target may be retailers, where the appeal is, "Buy this product to resell in your store at a profit." In industrial advertising, an industrial user is urged, "Buy this product to use in your business." The professional market is approached with advertising which says, "Specify this product for use by your patients or clients."

IMPORTANCE OF ADVERTISING

Advertising in one form or another is used by virtually all manufacturers and retailers in the country. The importance of advertising may also be expressed by various quantitative measures.

Advertising expenditures in total and by media. One quantitative indication of the importance of advertising is the total amount spent on the activity in the United States. In 1973, total advertising expenditures were about $25 billion—more than double the amount spent in 1960. Table 23-1 shows the relative importance of the major advertising media. For years, newspapers have been the most widely used medium, based upon total advertising dollars invested. About 85 percent of the expenditures for newspaper advertising go for local rather than national advertising. In recent years, the fastest-growing medium—television—took over second place, a spot held for many years by direct mail.

Advertising expenditures as percentage of company sales. When gauging the importance of advertising, it is often more meaningful to measure expenditures against a bench mark rather than simply to look at the total in an isolated position. Frequently, advertising expenses are expressed as a percentage of a company's sales. Table 23-2 shows the ten companies with the largest dollar expenditures for advertising, and Table 23-3 shows the ten companies with the largest percentage of sales devoted to advertising. It is interesting to note that some of the largest advertisers dollarwise (Sears, GM, Ford, Chrysler) actually devote a *very* small percentage of sales to advertising. Many drug and cosmetic firms, on the other hand, allocate a sizable chunk of their sales revenue for advertising purposes (Table 23-3).

One representative study showed that manufacturers of consumer products spend about 3 percent of sales for advertising purposes, while manufacturers of industrial goods spend less than 1 percent (see Tables 21-1 and 21-2). In a summary report, The Conference Board showed advertising as a percentage

Table 23-1. Volume of advertising expenditures in the United States, in billions of dollars.

Annual volume of advertising expenditures passed the $25 billion mark in 1973, and newspapers maintained their first-place position. Note the rise of television. Do you think that radio and magazines will eventually cease to be important advertising media?

| Medium | 1973 | | 1970 | 1960 | 1950 |
	$ billions	%	%	%	%
Newspapers	$7.6	30	29	31	36
Television	4.5	18	18	13	3
Direct mail	3.7	15	14	15	14
Radio	1.7	7	7	6	11
Magazines, including national farm publications	1.5	6	7	8	9
Business papers	.8	3	4	5	4
Outdoor	.3	1	1	2	3
Miscellaneous*	5.0	20	20	20	20
Total percentage			100	100	100	100
Total $ billion	$25.1		$19.6	$11.9	$5.7

*Includes cost of advertising departments, transportation advertising, weekly newspaper advertising, regional farm publications, point-of-purchase, material not included in direct-mail expenditures, and all other legitimate advertising expenditures not already covered.
Source: 1973 figures from *Advertising Age,* Aug. 12, 1974, p. 53; others from McCann-Erickson, Inc.

Table 23-2. Top ten national advertisers, 1972, based on total expenditures.

P & G's total is still only 7% of its sales and Sears' advertising is 2% of sales. Note the low percentages for auto companies.

| Company | Advertising expenditures | |
	$ millions	As % of sales
1. Procter & Gamble	275	7.0
2. Sears	215	2.2
3. General Foods	170	8.6
4. General Motors	146	0.5
5. Warner-Lambert Pharmaceuticals	134	14.6
6. Ford Motor Company	133	0.7
7. American Home Products	116	9.4
8. Bristol-Myers	115	12.0
9. Colgate-Palmolive	105	12.1
10. Chrysler	94	1.3

Source: Advertising Age, Aug. 27, 1973, p. 28.

Table 23-3. Top ten national advertisers, based on percentage of sales, 1972.

Every one of the top ten, except Johnson's Wax firm, is in the drug and cosmetic field. Why does this industry spend so much on advertising?

Company	Advertising expenditures	
	As % of sales	$ millions
1. Alberto-Culver	33.9	62
2. Carter-Wallace	30.7	40
3. Noxell	29.6	20
4. Block Drug	27.5	25
5. Richardson-Merrell	25.8	66
6. Mennen	21.4	28
7. Miles Laboratories	20.7	48
8. S. C. Johnson	17.9	43
9. Sterling Drug	17.1	84
10. Chesebrough-Pond's	16.8	38

Source: Advertising Age, Aug. 27, 1973, p. 28.

of sales for various types of manufacturers, retailers, and service industries (Fig. 23-1). In the majority of these industries, advertising was less than 2 percent of sales.

Sometimes it may seem as if the public is bombarded on all sides by advertising. However, the total amount spent usually is small in relation to sales volume. For example, large department stores spend quite a bit on advertising, and yet it amounts to only about 2 to 4 percent of sales. Automobile manufacturers spend millions on advertising, and yet the total is about 1 percent of their volume.

Cost of advertising versus cost of personal selling. While we do not have accurate totals for costs of personal selling, we do know they far surpass advertising expenditures. In manufacturing, only a few industries, such as drugs, toiletries, cleaning products, tobacco, and beverages, have advertising expenditures which are higher than those for personal selling. In countless companies, advertising runs 1 to 3 percent of net sales, while in many firms the expenses of managing and operating a sales force run from 8 to 15 percent of sales.

At the wholesaling level, advertising costs are very low. Personal selling costs may run ten to fifteen times as high. Even among retailers in total, and this includes those with self-service operations, the cost of personal selling runs substantially higher than the cost of advertising.

OBJECTIVES OF ADVERTISING

Fundamentally, the only purpose of advertising is to sell something—a product, a service, or an idea. The intent may be to generate a sale immediately or at some time in the future. Nevertheless, the basic objective is to sell. Stated another

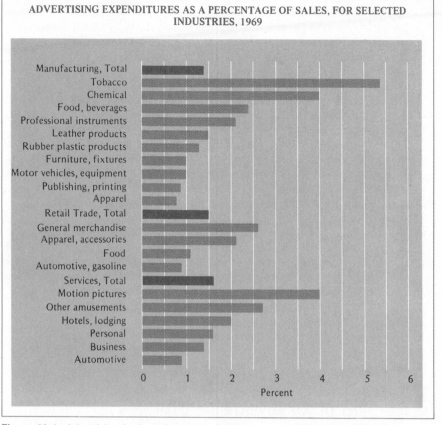

ADVERTISING EXPENDITURES AS A PERCENTAGE OF SALES, FOR SELECTED INDUSTRIES, 1969

Figure 23-1. Advertising budgets in most industries are surprisingly low in relation to total sales. Even though a firm—an automobile manufacturer or a department store, for instance—may spend millions on advertising, this is usually a small percentage of the company's sales volume. *Source: A Guide to Consumer Markets: 1973/74,* The Conference Board, New York, 1973, p. 236; based on data from U.S. Treasury Department.

way, the real goal of advertising is effective communication. That is, the ultimate effect of advertising should be to modify the attitudes and/or behavior of the receiver of the message. Sometimes the public, and even an advertising businessman, overlooks this fact. The businessman is not interested in awarding a prize to his salesman who is best liked by everybody. Instead, he wants to reward the salesman who has the best sales record. At the same time, he may be trying to earn awards for having the best copy or use of color in his advertisements, forgetting that his real aim is, or should be, to build an ad that will sell the most merchandise.

Specific objectives. The general goal of advertising is to increase profitable sales, but this goal is too broad to be implemented effectively in an advertising program. It is necessary to establish more specific objectives which can be worked into the program. A few examples of these more limited aims are listed below:

1. Support personal selling program. Advertising may be used to open customers' doors for salesmen and to acquaint the prospect with the seller's company. Advertising can also reduce selling costs by doing some of the sales prospecting. It permits the salesmen to make fewer calls and enables the company to maintain contact with the customers between salesmen's calls. See Fig. 23-2.
2. Reach people inaccessible to salesmen. A salesman may be unable to reach top business executives and professional men, or he may not be certain who makes the buying decisions in a company. In either case, there is a good chance that all these executives will read a journal which carries the ads.
3. Improve dealer relations. The goal of an advertising campaign may be to attract new dealers by showing them how profitable it is to carry the manufacturer's line. The purpose of other advertisements may be to give the names and addresses of retailers who carry the product.
4. Enter a new geographic market or attract a new group of customers.
5. Introduce a new product.
6. Increase sales of the product. An advertising campaign may be designed to lengthen the season for the product (as has been done in the case of soft drinks), increase the frequency of replacement (as is done in campaigns for spark plugs and light bulbs), increase the variety of product uses, or increase the units of purchase.
7. Expand the industry's sales.
8. Counteract prejudice or substitution.
9. Build good will for the company and improve its reputation by rendering a public service through advertising or by telling of the organization behind the product.

DEVELOPMENT OF AN ADVERTISING CAMPAIGN

Up to this point in our analysis of advertising, it has been tacitly assumed that the firm is going to advertise. Actually, the first decision management must make in this area is whether or not it should advertise its products. Some guideposts to use in answering this question of basic promotional strategy have already been analyzed.

Once the decision is made to advertise, management can get on with the job of developing an advertising campaign. In Chapter 21, a campaign was defined as a planned, coordinated series of promotional efforts built around a central theme and designed to reach a specific goal. The series of ads used in the campaign must be integrated with the sales-promotional efforts and with the activities of the sales force.

INITIAL PLANNING

In the course of planning the total promotional campaign, presumably management has already established its specific goals.[1] It has decided what the central

---

[1]For a report, accompanied by case histories, describing how companies put managementby-objective techniques to work in planning advertising, see *Setting Advertising Objectives*, The Conference Board, Studies in Business Policy, no. 118, New York, 1966.

"*I don't know who you are.*

I don't know your company.

I don't know your company's product.

I don't know what your company stands for.

I don't know your company's customers.

I don't know your company's record.

I don't know your company's reputation.

Now—what was it you wanted to sell me?"

MORAL: Sales start **before** your salesman calls—with business publication advertising.

McGRAW-HILL MAGAZINES
BUSINESS•PROFESSIONAL•TECHNICAL

Figure 23-2. *Source:* McGraw-Hill publications.

theme will be and what appeals will be stressed in light of consumer buying motives and habits. The total promotional appropriation has been determined and has been allocated among the various promotional tools, including advertising. Management can now concern itself with the selection of the advertising media and the creation and production of individual advertisements.

SELECTING THE MEDIA

Three levels of decision making are required in the selection of advertising media. First, management must determine what general types of media to use. Will newspapers, television, or magazines be used? If magazines are to be used, will they be shelter magazines such as *Better Homes and Gardens,* business magazines such as *Business Week,* or some other subtype? If television is selected, will it be local, national network, or spot telecasting? Finally, the specific medium must be chosen. The company which decides first on radio and then on local stations now must decide whether to use station WABC or KXYZ in city A.

Several factors should be considered in making media decisions. Some of these factors affect all three levels of media decision making, whereas others relate more specifically to only one or two levels.

Objective of the advertisement. Media choices are influenced both by the purpose of a specific advertisement and by the goal of an entire campaign. For example, if the goal of the advertising is to make appointments for salesmen who are going to call on industrial users, the advertising company will probably use direct mail. If an advertiser wants to make last-minute changes in an advertisement, or if he wishes to place an ad inducing action within a day or two, he may use newspapers or radio. Magazines are not so good for this purpose because the ad must be placed weeks before the date of publication.

Media circulation. Media circulation must match the distribution patterns of the product. Consequently, the *geographic* scope of the market will influence the choice of media considerably. Furthermore, media should be selected which will reach the desired *type* of market with a minimum of waste circulation. A firm manufacturing shotguns, for example, will advertise in a magazine which appeals primarily to hunters. Media used to reach a teen-age market will be different from those used to reach mothers with young children.

Requirements of the message. Management should consider the media which are most suitable for the presentation of the message to the market. Meat products, floor coverings, and apparel are ordinarily best presented in pictorial form. Thus, radio is not a good medium for these lines. If a product, such as insurance, calls for a lengthy message, outdoor advertising is poor. If the advertiser can use a very brief message, however, as in the case of salt, beer, or sugar, then billboards may be the best choice.

Time and location of buying decision. The advertiser should select the medium which will reach the prospective customer at or near the time he makes his buying decision and the place where he makes it. For this reason, outdoor advertising is often good for gasoline products. Grocery store ads are placed in newspapers on Thursday nights or Friday mornings in anticipation of heavy weekend buying.

Cost of media. The cost of the advertising media should be considered in relation to (1) the amount of funds available and (2) the circulation of the media. In the first instance, the amount of funds available may rule out television as a choice, or possibly the advertiser can afford local television but not a national network. On the second count, the advertiser should try to develop some relationships between the cost of the medium and its circulation.

Cooperation and promotional aids offered by media. A manufacturer may want to tie in his advertising with that of his dealers. Consequently, he will look favorably upon media such as magazines which offer reprints for use in counter or window displays. Another firm may want some research done on local markets. Management may select the individual medium which can provide this service.

Characteristics of major types of media. In the process of selecting the media to use in a campaign, a marketing executive must consider the advertising characteristics of newspapers, magazines, and the other main classes of media. The term "characteristics" is carefully chosen instead of "advantages and disadvantages." To illustrate, one characteristic of radio as an advertising medium is that it makes its impression through the ear. For many products this feature is an advantage. For those which benefit from a colored photograph, this characteristic of radio is a drawback.

Newspapers. As an advertising medium, newspapers are flexible and timely. They can be used to cover one city or several urban centers. Ads can be canceled on a few days' notice or inserted on one day's notice. Newspapers also give an advertiser an intense coverage of a local market because almost everybody reads newspapers. The local feature also helps in that the ads may be adapted to local social and economic conditions. Many newspapers offer promotional assistance, and they are an excellent source of market information. This medium offers an opportunity to use a fair quality of color, and circulation costs per prospect are low. Newspapers are also helpful if the advertiser wishes to present his message to the market frequently. On the other hand, the life of a newspaper advertisement is very short.

Magazines. Magazines are an excellent medium when a high quality of printing and color is desired in an advertisement. Magazines can be used to reach a national market at a relatively low cost per prospect. Through the use of class magazines, an advertiser is able to reach a selective audience with a minimum of waste circulation. Magazines are usually read in a leisurely fashion, in contrast to the haste with which other print media are read. This is a particularly valuable point for the advertiser who must present his message at some length. Some of the less favorable characteristics of magazines are their inflexibility and the infrequency with which they reach the market, as compared with other media.

Direct Mail. Direct mail is probably the most personal and selective of all the media. Because it reaches only the market which the advertiser wishes to contact, there is a minimum of waste circulation. The personal feature and the aspect of selectivity also mean that the copy itself can be extremely flexible. Direct mail is not accompanied by articles or other editorial matter, however, unless the advertiser provides it. As a result, the direct-mail advertisement itself creates its own circulation and attracts its own readership. Direct mail is quite costly in terms of prospects reached when compared with other media, but other media reach many people who are not real prospects. A severe limitation is posed by the difficulty of getting and maintaining good mailing lists.

Television. Television, the newest and fastest growing of all major media, is also probably the most versatile. It makes its appeal through both the eye and the ear; products can be demonstrated as well as explained. It offers considerable flexibility in terms of the geographic market covered and in terms of the time the message is presented. By making its impression through the ear, it can take advantage of the personal, dramatic impact of the spoken word. On the other hand, television is an extremely expensive medium. The message is not permanently recorded. Thus if the prospect is not reached the first time, he is lost forever as far as that particular message is concerned. Television does not lend itself to long advertising copy, nor does it present pictures so clearly as magazines do. As in direct mail and radio, television advertisers must create their own audiences.

Outdoor. Outdoor advertising is a highly flexible, low-cost medium. Because it reaches virtually the entire population, it lends itself nicely to widely used consumer products which require only a brief selling statement. It is excellent for the reminder type of advertising, and it carries the impact of large size and color. There is complete flexibility in geographic coverage and in the intensity of market coverage within the area. These advantageous features, however, carry with them some inherent drawbacks. Unless the product is a widely used consumer good, considerable waste circulation will occur. While the cost is low in terms of reaching an individual prospect, the total cost of a national campaign is quite high. There is no opportunity to present lengthy copy, and it is not possible to show much detail in the pictures.

CREATION OF ADVERTISEMENTS

The advertisements are the heart of the entire advertising program. All the other steps in the campaign are designed to aid in delivering the sales message to the market target in the most effective manner. Obviously, the message itself is of considerable importance, so its creation constitutes a major phase in a campaign.

Before creating the advertisement, the people concerned should remember that the main purpose of advertising is to sell something and that the ad itself is a sales talk. The ad may be a high-pressure sales talk, as in a hard-hitting, direct-action ad. Or it may be a very long-range, low-pressure message, as in an institutional ad. In any case it is trying to sell something. Consequently, it involves the same kind of selling procedure as a sales talk delivered by personal salesmen. That is, the ad must first attract attention and then hold interest long enough to stimulate a desire for the product, service, or idea. Finally, the ad must move the prospect to some kind of action. The desired action may lie anywhere within a virtually unlimited scope of possibilities, ranging from an immediate change in overt behavior to a slowly changing thought process.

Creating an advertisement involves the tasks of writing the copy—including the headline—selecting illustrations which may be used, preparing the layout, and arranging to have the advertisement reproduced for the selected media.

The *copy* in an advertisement is defined as all the written or spoken material in it, including the headline, coupons, and advertiser's name and address, as well as the main body of the message. The *illustration*—whether it is a photograph, drawing, reproduction of a painting, cartoon, or something else—is a powerful feature in an advertisement. Probably the main points to consider with respect to illustrations are (1) whether they are the best alternative use of the space and (2) whether they are appropriate in all respects to the ad itself. The *layout* is the physical arrangement of all the elements in an advertisement. Within the given amount of space or time, the layout man must place the headline, copy, and illustrations. Decisions are made regarding the relative amount of white space and the kinds of type to be used. A good layout can be an interest-holding device as well as an attention getter. It should lead the reader in an orderly fashion throughout the entire advertisement.

EVALUATION OF ADVERTISING PROGRAM

At several stages in the course of the advertising program, management should carefully evaluate the effectiveness of what has been done or what is planned for the future. Executives may wish to evaluate an entire advertising campaign, a single advertisement, or some part of an individual advertisement. They may wish to appraise various aspects of the advertising media.

IMPORTANCE

Advertising typically is one of the most highly criticized segments of our marketing system. While great strides may have been made to improve advertising through the years, much still remains to be done. We need to increase the effectiveness of advertising, and we also must find better ways to evaluate this effectiveness. Management needs to test advertising in order to know not only *which* ads are better than others, but also *why* they are better.

Shrinking profit margins and increasing competition, both foreign and domestic, are forcing management to appraise all its expenditures carefully. Top executives want more proof than they now have that advertising really does pay. They want to know whether dollars spent on advertising are resulting in proportionately as many sales as dollars spent on other activities. Unfortunately, it seems that a very small proportion (educated guesses say less than 1 percent) of total advertising dollars is being spent to measure advertising's effectiveness.[2]

"I know that about half of my advertising is wasted, but I don't know which half."

"I spent $2 million for advertising, and I don't know if that is half enough or twice too much."

—John Wanamaker

---

[2]For a report on interviews with advertisers, agencies, and media to determine why so little is being spent on this measurement task, see "Advertising Really Pays—What's Your Proof?" *Media/Scope,* June, 1969, p. 35.

DIFFICULTY

Many limitations confront a company in its efforts to measure the effectiveness of its advertising. This is one of the least-developed areas of marketing research. One problem is our inability to identify the effectiveness of any given advertisement or even an entire campaign. Except in the case of mail-order advertising, we cannot attribute a given unit of sales to any specific advertisement or campaign. By the very nature of the marketing mix, all elements—including advertising—are so intertwined, and there are so many variables, that measurement of any one by itself is impossible. Many factors besides advertising influence sales success.

Even in evaluating a particular advertisement, management is likely to run into difficulty because one part of an ad may be more easily appraised, and thus given more emphasis, than another.[3] Essentially there are only two parts of an advertisement—*what* is said and *how* it is said. One part deals with product attributes to be explained, and the other comprises the headlines, illustrations, and layouts. Over the years, a great deal has been done to improve the manner of presentation (the "how") because research has been able to establish criteria to measure its effectiveness. Most of the widely used measurement methods have emphasized the use of attention-getting devices in advertisements and the number of people who note, read, and remember the advertisements and the claims in them. Little has been done to aid management in its evaluation of the "what" part of an ad, and at the present time the effectiveness of this part is difficult to judge.

Many individual advertisements, and even entire campaigns, do not aim primarily at immediate sales results. Consequently, it is difficult to measure their effectiveness. Some advertisements simply announce new store hours, new service policies, or a new product. Probably the most difficult type of advertising to evaluate is that which is intended to build good will, create a company image, or influence attitudes. Institutional advertising falls in this category.

Presently used evaluative methods tell us simply which ad is the best among those being appraised. There are no standards for determining what must be included in an ad to ensure success. Furthermore, even though we test several advertisements in advance in order to select the one that is best, we still have no guarantee that sales results will be successful.[4]

METHODS USED TO MEASURE EFFECTIVENESS

When evaluating the effectiveness of its advertising, a company should not rely solely on the opinions of professional advertising men. They have been proved time and again to be poor judges of which ads will elicit favorable consumer response. Often they are too concerned with the manner in which the message

---

[3]Clarence E. Eldridge, "Advertising Effectiveness: How Can It Be Measured?" *Journal of Marketing*, January, 1958, pp. 242–243.

[4]For encouraging reports from some of the companies which are making advances in measuring the effectiveness of their advertising, see Gail Smith, "How GM Measures Ad Effectiveness," *Printers' Ink*, May 14, 1965, p. 19; and "Who Says Ad Impact Can't Be Measured?" (DuPont's story), *Sales Management*, Apr. 19, 1963, p. 37.

is presented—the "how" part of advertising. If possible, management should plan to use some testing technique which will sample customer reaction.

The effectiveness of an advertisement may be tested before the advertisement is presented to the public, while it is being presented or after it has completed its run. The "sales results test" attempts to measure the sales volume stemming directly from the advertisement or series of advertisements being tested.

Most other types of tests are indirect measurements of advertising's effectiveness. One group, called "readership," "recognition," or "recall" tests, involves showing respondents part or all of the previously run advertisement to determine whether it was read, what parts in it were remembered, and whether the respondent knows who sponsored it. The theory underlying these tests is that the greater the number of people who see, read, and remember an advertisement, the greater will be the number who do as the advertisement urges them.[5] Another type of test involves measuring the number of coupons or other forms of inquiries which were received from certain advertisements.

Sometimes marketing people use a consumer panel or consumer jury to appraise a group of advertisements. With respect to radio and television advertising, several techniques are used to measure the quantity and quality of program audiences. The theory is that the number of people who will buy the sponsor's products varies proportionately with the number who watch or hear the program.

Many of these various measurement devices have enjoyed some degree of success. In general, however, there is still a long way to go before really effective evaluation tools and techniques will be developed for advertising. Possibly our hope for the future lies in the more effective use of psychological and sociological testing methods and in the use of mathematical models and operations research.[6]

We should remember, however, that the basic goal of advertising is to sell something—to modify consumer attitudes or behavior. Therefore, when we deal with the evaluation of advertising's effectiveness, we should be more concerned with measuring advertising's ability to influence these attitudes and behavior than with measuring the extent to which consumers recall given advertisements.

ORGANIZING FOR ADVERTISING

There are four widely used organizational arrangements employed to facilitate the work done in an advertising program. Within a company, the job may be done by a separate advertising department, or it may be handled by another department, possibly a general sales department, as only one part of its departmental responsibility. A third arrangement involves turning the entire task over

---

[5]For research findings which refute the idea that a recall of advertised facts about a given product is a significant measure of the effectiveness of these ads, see Jack B. Haskins, "Factual Recall as a Measure of Advertising Effectiveness," *Journal of Advertising Research*, March, 1964, pp. 2–7.

[6]For some of the problems encountered in the use of standard econometric models, see Richard E. Quandt, "Estimating the Effectiveness of Advertising: Some Pitfalls in Econometric Models," *Journal of Marketing Research*, May, 1964, pp. 51–60.

to an advertising agency, and the fourth combines the use of an advertising agency and the company's own department.

ADVERTISING MANAGEMENT WITHIN THE COMPANY

Advertising activities are sometimes administered by the department which operates the sales force. This arrangement is most common when advertising is a relatively unimportant part of the promotional mix or when the firm is small.

In larger businesses or in those where advertising is a substantial part of the promotional mix, advertising activities are usually administered by a separate department. Under these circumstances the head of the department should report to the marketing manager if the company is to implement the marketing concept. In some companies the advertising manager still reports directly to the president. It is considered a better arrangement, however, if all marketing activities are coordinated at an executive level below the president.[7]

Large retailers often have their own advertising departments and do not use an advertising agency. The advertising department performs all the tasks involved in planning and executing the campaign. Many manufacturers have their own departments but also use an advertising agency. The question then arises of why a department is needed if the company has a good agency. In the first place, the department acts as a liaison between the agency and the company. The department approves the agency's plans and advertisements and has the responsibility of preparing and administering the advertising budget. Finally, direct-mail advertisements, dealer displays, and other activities ordinarily not performed by the agency are handled by the company department.

ADVERTISING AGENCY

An advertising agency is an independent company set up to render specialized services in advertising in particular and in marketing in general. Today the term "agency" is a legal misnomer. These firms are not agents in the legal sense, but instead are independent companies. Advertising agencies started as space brokers for handling advertisements placed in newspapers. Through the years, however, the function of the agencies has changed. Their main job today is not to aid media but to serve advertisers.

Services rendered. Many agencies offer a broad range of marketing and advertising services. In the field of advertising alone, they plan and execute entire advertising campaigns. In radio and television, they are responsible for producing the entertainment as well as the commercials. Many of these firms are becoming *marketing* agencies, offering services which heretofore were performed either by another type of outside specialist or by the advertiser himself. A company's decision to involve its advertising agency in performing marketing (but nonadvertising) services for the firm will depend upon the extent to which management perceives that (1) its competitive environment is rapidly changing (as contrasted with a stable environment), (2) the agency is knowledgeable

---

[7]See Lois Stolzman, "The Ad Manager: Where Has He Been? Where Is He Today? Where Is He Going?" *Industrial Marketing*, May, 1970, p. 29.

about the products and the industry, and (3) the costs of agency services are lower than the costs of those provided by alternative sources.[8]

In recent years a series of limited-service, advertising-specialist firms has evolved. These newer institutions provide flexible, cafeteria-style services (media space and time buying, various creative services, for example) in contrast to the traditional full-service agencies. These specialists claim to provide faster service at lower costs, because clients pay only for the services they use.[9]

Reasons for using when a company has own department. Even when a company has a good advertising department, there are several reasons why it may be interested in using an agency. In the first place, the company normally does not have as many types of specialists as a large or medium-sized advertising agency. Because an agency can spread the costs of its staff over many accounts, it can do more for the same amount of money.

The company can also get an objective, outside viewpoint from an agency, assuming that the agency representatives are not acting as "yes-men" in order to keep the advertiser's account. A related point is that the company can benefit from the agency's experiences with its many other products and clients. Another advantage is that an agency feels a greater pressure than the company's own department to produce effective results. Relations between an agency and a client are very easy to terminate, but it is difficult to get rid of an ineffective advertising department. Finally, because of the manner in which agencies are compensated, the use of an agency may not cost the advertiser a single penny.

Agency compensations. There are two major methods of compensating advertising agencies: the commission method and the fee method. Under the typical commission system, an agency receives an amount equal to 15 percent of the cost of the media time or space. The commission is paid by the media, who bill the agencies for the stated rate, less 15 percent. Then the advertiser pays the full rate to the agency. Thus if an agency prepares and places an advertisement in magazine space worth $40,000, the media will bill the agency for $34,000 ($40,000 less 15 percent). The agency in turn bills the client for the full $40,000. It is with this income of $6,000 that the agency performs its services. Most retailers deal directly with the local media and pay lower rates. No agency commission is paid on these rates. If a local advertiser uses an agency, he usually pays a fee.

In the preceding section it was stated that agency services may not cost the advertiser a cent. In the example, the company could have used its own department to prepare and place the advertisement, but the space would still have cost the company $40,000. In addition, the company would have had the expense of preparing the advertisement.

For many years there has been considerable dissatisfaction with the straight-commission system. Profits of the agencies declined because they were forced by competition to perform more and more services without additional compensation. Large advertisers who bought much media time and space felt they were

---

[8]Derek A. Newton, "Advertising Agency Services: Make or Buy?" *Harvard Business Review*, July–August, 1965, pp. 111–118.

[9]See "Advertising that Comes à la Carte," *Business Week*, May 1, 1971, p. 44.

paying too much. Agencies received the same compensation whether they placed the same advertisement in ten different magazines or had the extra expense of creating ten different ads. Furthermore, only accredited agencies were eligible to receive the commission.

The general rigidity of the system bothered many people, including, finally, the government. In the 1950s the Department of Justice sued the American Association of Advertising Agencies and several leading trade associations of publishers. The complaint was that these groups were fixing commission rates and allowing only accredited agencies to receive the commissions, all this in restraint of trade. In 1956 these associations signed a consent decree in which they agreed not to establish fixed commission rates.

Today there is a definite trend toward the use of the fee method or a combination of commission and fee, although the straight-commission method is still probably the most widely used.

REGULATION OF PROMOTIONAL ACTIVITIES

Because the primary objective of promotion is to sell something by means of informing, persuading, or otherwise communicating with a market, promotional activities attract attention. Consequently, abuses of the activities by individual firms are easily and quickly noted by the public. This situation in turn soon leads to public demand for correction of the abuses, assurances that they will not be repeated, and general restraints on promotional activities. To answer this demand, regulations and other safeguards have been established by the federal government and most state governments. In addition, many private business organizations, both profit and nonprofit in nature, have attempted to establish voluntary guideposts for the direction of promotional activities.

For the most part, these regulatory measures have been applied far more to advertising than to personal selling or any other promotional tool. The probable reason for this unbalanced emphasis is that advertising is more centralized and is easier to control. There are far fewer media through which advertising messages may be carried than there are personal salesmen. Also, advertising messages are recorded, whereas usually there is no certain evidence of what a salesman said.

FEDERAL REGULATION

Regulation of promotional activities is authorized in two major pieces of federal legislation: the Federal Trade Commission Act (and its Wheeler-Lea Amendment) and the Robinson-Patman Act. Both of these laws are administered by the Federal Trade Commission.

In recent years the FTC has become more aggressive in its policing of the advertising business—particularly where there may be false or deceptive advertising. For example, the Commission may require a company to submit test results, studies, or other information as documentation to substantiate the company's advertising claims concerning the quality, performance, safety, or comparative prices of its products. Furthermore, this supporting information may later be made public by the FTC.

In another situation the FTC may compel a firm to run "corrective advertising" to counteract allegedly false ads which the company had previously run for a product. Thus ITT Continental Baking Company had to devote 25 percent of its advertising budget for one year to correct any misunderstanding in consumers' minds left as a result of previous ads for Profile bread. Previous ads had claimed that the use of Profile bread was effective for weight reduction, when in fact the only reason a slice of this bread was lower in calories was because the slices were thinner than other breads.

The FTC's current involvement in the regulation of advertising is discussed in more detail as part of Chapter 29 on consumerism.

Federal Trade Commission Act and Wheeler-Lea Amendment. The governmental measure which probably has the broadest influence on regulating the content of promotional messages in interstate commerce is the Federal Trade Commission Act and its Wheeler-Lea Amendment. The main provision of this law bearing on promotional activities is Section 5. This section prohibits unfair methods of competition which have the effect of injuring a competitor. Wisely, no specific examples of unfair competition are spelled out in the law. Instead, it is up to the Federal Trade Commission to determine on a case-by-case basis whether a given act constitutes an unfair competitive act.

Loopholes in the Federal Trade Commission Act led to the enactment of the Wheeler-Lea Amendment in 1938. With respect to promotion, the amendment considerably strengthened the original act in three ways. First, it is a violation of the law if the unfair competitive act injures the public, regardless of the effect this competitive practice may have on a competitor. Under the original Federal Trade Commission Act, false or misleading advertising had to injure a competitor before a violation could be charged.

A second improvement specifically prohibits false, misleading, or deceptive *advertising* of food, drugs, cosmetics, and therapeutic devices.[10] This provision strengthened the Commission's position by specifying four types of products where advertising abuses exist and where the public's health is directly involved. Temporary injunctions may be granted which force the seller to cease the disputed advertising until a decision can be reached. Prohibition of false, misleading, or deceptive advertising under the law is not limited to these four types of products. False advertising of any product may be judged unfair competition and thus be a violation of the Federal Trade Commission Act.

The third significant change concerns enforcement of cease and desist orders issued by the Commission. Such orders automatically become effective in 60 days unless the defendant appeals to the federal courts. Previously, a cease and desist order could be issued, but if there was no compliance, the Commission had the burden of seeking enforcement.

Robinson-Patman Act. The Robinson-Patman Act, which was discussed in connection with price policies, has two sections relating to promotional allowances. One refers to situations where the seller makes payments for promo-

---

[10]The *labeling* of these four groups of products is not included within the scope of the Wheeler-Lea Amendment. Labeling is regulated under the Food, Drug, and Cosmetic Act of 1938, a law which is administered by the Food and Drug Administration. This law was discussed in Chap. 10, along with other laws pertaining to labeling.

tional services and facilities provided by his customers, and the other pertains to situations where the seller himself provides the promotional services and facilities instead of paying the customers for doing the job. The law states that the seller must offer the services, or payments for them, on a proportionally equal basis to all competing customers.

Prior to the Robinson-Patman Act, there were many abuses in the handling of promotional allowances. Large-scale retailers were often favored by manufacturers at the expense of small buyers. Many firms would furnish retail demonstrators to one leading department store in a city, even though many other stores in that city also purchased the firms' products.

Today if a manufacturer wants to furnish demonstrators, window displays, cooperative advertising programs, commissions for salespeople to push his product, or any other type of promotional assistance, this promotional device or a comparable one must be made available on a proportionally equal basis to all firms competing in the resale of the product. "Proportionally equal basis" has sometimes been hard to define. Generally the courts have accepted the amount purchased as a basis for allocation. Thus if store A buys $150,000 worth of merchandise a year from a manufacturer and store B purchases $50,000 worth, store A may be offered promotional allowances valued at three times those offered to store B.

A seller must offer only *similar* promotional allowances, not necessarily *identical* ones. Not all buyers can make equal use of a given promotional aid, and, furthermore, identical allowances are often not economically sound. If a department store buying $100,000 worth of products a year is granted a demonstrator for forty hours a week, it probably makes little sense to furnish one for four hours a week to a store whose purchases total only $10,000. The small store might prefer additional window displays or extra commissions for its salesclerks.

In a 1968 case involving a supermarket chain in Portland, Oregon, the Supreme Court broadened the interpretation of the Robinson-Patman Act with respect to promotional allowances. Prior to this case it was generally understood that promotional allowances must be granted on a proportionally equal basis by a manufacturer to all competing retailers who bought *directly* from this manufacturer. However, the Court has now ruled that when granting cooperative advertising and other forms of promotional allowances, a manufacturer must make certain that retailers who buy his products *indirectly* through wholesalers also get promotional allowances on a proportionally equal basis.[11] This ruling and the subsequent revision of FTC guidelines for promotional allowances have caused uncertainty among manufacturers and have led to alterations in cooperative advertising programs.

STATE AND LOCAL REGULATION

At the state and local levels we can note two types of legislation which regulate promotional activities. The first of these is patterned after the *Printers' Ink*

---

[11]*Federal Trade Commission v. Fred Meyer, Inc., et al.,* 88 S. Ct. 904 (1968). See also Federal Trade Commission, *Guides for Advertising Allowances and Other Merchandising Payments and Services,* Government Printing Office, 1969; and John R. Davidson, "FTC, Robinson-Patman and Cooperative Promotional Activities," *Journal of Marketing,* January, 1968, pp. 14–17.

model statute first developed by *Printers' Ink* magazine in 1911 to establish "truth in advertising" in intrastate commerce. Today almost all states have a *Printers' Ink* statute or one which is quite similar to it. Several states have established a separate state agency to handle various "consumer defense" activities.

A general type of local legislation which affects personal selling goes under the title "Green River" ordinance. This type of legislation is named after the town of Green River, Wyoming, one of the first places to enact such a law. Green River ordinances restrict salesmen who represent firms located outside the affected city and who sell door-to-door or call on business establishments. Ostensibly these laws were passed to protect local citizens from fraudulent operators. Actually the measures also serve to insulate local businesses from outside competition.

REGULATION BY PRIVATE ORGANIZATIONS

Several kinds of private organizations also exert considerable control over promotional practices of businesses. Many magazines, newspapers, and radio and television stations regularly refuse to accept advertisements which they feel are false, misleading, or generally in bad taste. Some trade associations have established a "code of ethics" which includes points pertaining to sales-force and advertising activities. Some trade associations regularly censor advertising appearing in their trade or professional journals. Better Business Bureaus located in major cities all over the country are working to control some very difficult situations.

QUESTIONS AND PROBLEMS

1. How do you account for the variations in advertising expenditures as a percentage of sales among the different types of companies shown in Fig. 23-1?
2. Several specific objectives of advertising were outlined early in this chapter. Bring to class some advertisements which illustrate at least six of these goals, or be prepared to describe a current radio or television advertisement which is attempting to achieve these objectives.
3. In what respects does the advertising of an automobile manufacturer differ from that of a large department store? Consider the objectives, nature, and scope of the advertising as well as the nature of the products and markets of these two firms.
4. Which advertising medium is best for advertising the following products?
   - *a*. Life insurance
   - *b*. Plastic clothespins
   - *c*. Auto seat covers
   - *d*. Suntan lotion
   - *e*. Women's hosiery
   - *f*. Industrial valves and gauges
5. Many grocery products manufacturers and candy producers earmark a good portion of their advertising appropriations for use in magazines. Is this a wise choice of media for these firms?
6. Why do department stores use newspapers so much more than local radio as an advertising medium?
7. Why is it worthwhile to pretest advertisements before they appear in the media? Suggest a procedure for pretesting a magazine ad.

8. What procedures can a firm use to determine how many sales dollars resulted from a given ad or from an entire campaign?

9. Many advertisers on television use program ratings to determine whether to continue the sponsorship of a program. These ratings reflect the number of families who watch the program. Are program ratings a good criterion for evaluating the effectiveness of advertising? Does a high rating indicate that sales volume will also be high? Discuss.

10. If a manufacturer has a good advertising agency, should he discontinue using his own advertising department?

11. Many manufacturers use an advertising agency to help with the company's advertising program, while most retailers do not use an agency. How do you account for this difference?

12. Explain how an advertiser may actually save money by using an agency. In your analysis, consider the factor of agency compensation.

13. How did the Wheeler-Lea Amendment strengthen the Federal Trade Commission Act?

14. Explain the interpretation of "proportionally equal basis" in connection with manufacturers' granting advertising allowances. Consider especially the situations where retailers vary in size.

15. Do you think we need additional legislation to regulate advertising? Personal selling? If so, explain what you would recommend.

CASES FOR PART

CASE 18. GOLD SEAL VINEYARDS, INC.*

Planning a promotional program

In the summer of 1971 the executive committee of the Gold Seal Vineyards, Inc., was developing plans for the company's promotional campaign for 1972. These executives were also discussing what Gold Seal's long-range marketing program should be (in broad outline) for the five-year period of 1972–76.

Gold Seal Vineyards, Inc., founded in 1865, was a winery situated near Hammondsport on the west shore of Lake Keuka, one of the five Finger Lakes in central New York. The company produced a high-quality champagne and other premium wines. (Premium wines are those priced at $1.50 or above for one-fifth of a gallon—four-fifths of a quart.) About one-half of the firm's revenues were derived from sales of champagne. Case sales of Gold Seal wine were as follows for the years 1967–70:

| 1967: 650,000 | 1969: 865,000 |
| 1968: 775,000 | 1970: 955,000 |

Part of the increase in Gold Seal's sales was due to the popularity of the

*Case prepared by Prof. Robert S. Raymond, Ohio University. Reproduced with permission.

company's specialty wines, notably its Pink Catawba and Cold Duck (a blend of Burgundy and champagne).

Five wineries in the Finger Lakes region produced about 70 percent of all New York State wine. The New York wine industry's annual sales were about $100,000,000, compared to California's $800,000,000. However, New York State accounted for almost half of the champagne business in the United States. See Exhibit 1.

The demand for wine currently was one of the fastest-growing of all consumer products. The demand for *premium* wines was increasing at a rate of 13 to 14 percent annually in dollar volume, while the total wine market was growing 9 to 10 percent annually. Wine sales in 1970 were about 8 bottles (1/5-gallon size) per adult, and Gold Seal executives said that this consumption rate was expected to increase to 14 bottles per adult by 1976, according to industry estimates. The effect which this projected increase in demand would have on wine sales is seen in Exhibit 2.

Mr. Arthur Brody, the president of Gold Seal, prepared and distributed the following memo prior to one of the executive committee's planning meetings in August, 1971. The memo reviewed the company's marketing and promotional experiences during the preceding decade.

Briefly, it was like this. In 1962 the company sold about 200,000 cases of wine annually. In 1970 we sold about 900,000 cases. This year we hope to sell about a million cases. Here's how we did it:

Mr. Paul Schlem and I took over the active management of the company in 1962. It had always been modestly profitable, but its annual sales volume had been static at about 200,000 cases for several years. Between 1941 and 1962 the company had five different owners, only one of whom had any real understanding of the wine industry, and therefore it had no long-term planning and no marketing strategy. The company philosophy was "Do business where it is easiest and forget the rest." Hence, distribution in 1962 was in the upstate New York region, in Chicago, and in some parts of Massachusetts. There had been practically no consumer advertising. The company had six or seven salesmen and a few brokers in scattered markets who sold to wholesalers.

Our primary concern in developing a market program for the company was to answer the question: "What business are we in?" In general in the wine industry there are three distinct categories:

A. Small local producers, such as Wente Brothers, Charles Krug, and Louis Martini in California and Dr. Konstantin Frank of Hammondsport, New York, who sell most of their output of high-priced products at or near their wineries.

B. Wineries with national distribution selling premium wines, such as Taylor and Great Western in New York, and Paul Masson, Almaden, and Christian Brothers in California, who sell in all the major markets.

C. Wineries with mass production, selling low-priced wine in mass distribution outlets, such as Gallo (66,000,000 gallons) and United Vintners (52,000,000 gallons). These two accounted for 65 percent of domestic wine gallonage in 1969, most of it in standard wines.

Looking at Gold Seal's strengths and weaknesses, we found that it had a good reputation in the trade; it had a good product, but it lacked a marketing organi-

Exhibit 1. **Sales of wine in United States, in**
cases, 1970.

Sparkling wines	Cases
New York State	3,000,000
California	3,000,000
Other states	700,000
Imported	1,000,000
Total cases	7,700,000

Table wines	Cases
New York State	7,000,000
California	40,000,000
Other states	1,200,000
Imported	1,800,000
Total cases	50,000,000

Flavored and dessert wines	Cases
New York State	5,500,000
California	24,500,000
Other states	1,000,000
Imported	800,000
Total cases	31,800,000

zation; it had no marketing strategy, and its distribution was regional and very spotty. But Gold Seal obviously belonged in Category B, and we set out to put it there. Our marketing plan included consumer advertising, our own sales organization that operated nationwide, and a distributor (wholesaler) network in all of the major metropolitan markets.

We also realized that we would have to gear up production. The wine industry is characterized by unusually long lead times in moving from one level of production to a higher one. It requires five to six years to bring newly planted vines into production. Aging of better wines usually demands two to five years. This means that wineries must plan seven to ten years in advance. If their forecasts of sales are too high, they will be penalized by excess investment in land, cultivation costs, and inventories. If projections are too low, aged inventory is not available, and sales are lost. New York State has an abundance of vineyard acreage, but much of its is planted in Concord grapes and similar varieties which do not

Exhibit 2. **Total wine sales in the United States, based on sales increase**
from present 8 bottles per adult to 14 bottles per adult in 1976,
in millions of gallons.

	Actual 1968	Actual 1970	Forecast 1976
Table wine	98	125	216.2
Sparkling wine	16	20	48.2
Dessert and other wines (includes Vermouth and flavored natural wines)	100	103	129.0

have the attributes necessary for premium wines. Independent growers must be persuaded to plant additional acreage of the improved grape varieties. This long lead time precludes many new entrants in the industry and tends to stabilize the market shares of existing competitors.

Advertising. We decided to keep profits at a minimum and use all the money we could spare for an advertising campaign. We chose Gilbert Advertising, Inc., a small creative agency in New York City, with the thought that, both being small, we could grow with each other. It has paid off very well. Mr. Gilbert handled our account personally and created some very artistic, high-class advertisements for us.

In 1962, our total advertising budget was only $50,000. Because we couldn't reach many consumers with that amount, our initial strategy was to attract distributors (wholesalers) and retailers who would handle the Gold Seal line. Having decided to go first class all the way, we spent it all on twelve full-page color advertisements in the Sunday supplement of the *New York Times* at $4,000 each. That was the whole campaign! Our salesmen showed the advertisements during their calls on prospective distributors, who were very favorably impressed. With these advertisements we looked a lot bigger than we were.

In 1963 and 1964 we increased the advertising budget to $80,000 and continued the full-page color advertisements in the Sunday supplement of the *Times* on the same schedule, plus advertisements in *Life, Esquire,* and the *New Yorker.* In 1965 the budget was $100,000, and we added a few more magazines to the campaign we were using. In 1966 with a budget of $170,000, we cut out most of the national advertising, e.g., using only four advertisements in the Sunday *Times,* and spent the balance in local radio advertising in thirty cities where we wanted to increase our distribution.

In 1967 the advertising budget was $250,000. We continued the radio advertising in the major metropolitan markets and started to advertise on local television with ten-second spots. All our efforts were still basically to impress our distributors and prospective distributors and retailers. In 1968 with an advertising budget of $300,000, we followed the same pattern, a few *New York Times* advertisements, plus local radio, plus ten-second spots on local TV.

In 1969 we started longer (one-minute) spots on network TV. We now had enough distributors to make national TV spots worthwhile. They were aimed at consumers but were used primarily to impress our distributors and retailers. We also had the opportunity to buy some spots on national network shows at bargain prices. For example, we bought one-minute spots on the Don Rickles show along with Buick and Firestone. The show failed, but we profited from the association with other, larger advertisers and a national network show at a small cost. We also picked up some spots on nationally televised professional football and basketball games at bargain prices.

In addition, we commissioned four market studies to find out more about our market. Basically, they told us that our best market was the 25 to 40 age group, college educated, in the upper income bracket (over $13,000–$14,000).

In 1970, with a budget of $500,000, we looked at our top markets for wine and champagne and decided to be more scientific about where we spent our advertising funds. We decided that we needed an eight-week campaign in each market, with a combination of national and local television spots to achieve 125 rating points. (To achieve 125 rating points is to reach 125 percent of the program audience; i.e., on the average each viewer sees the commercial at least 1¼ times each week.) Our advertising agency made three television spot commercials, each of a different length, featuring different products, and for the first time we are trying to pull our products through our distribution network instead of pushing them through.

The budget for 1971 is $600,000. We are covering thirty-five markets with ten-week campaigns, using local television spots only—no national TV spots. Our advertising agency selected the slots when and where our three commercials are shown. In New York City they appeared with the late evening news, on the late talk shows (Dick Cavett), with sports events such as the NCAA football game, and others that would ensure the 125 rating points per week. We felt this was necessary to make an impression on the consumer.

Personal selling. In 1962 we had six or seven of our own salesmen and a few brokers in New York, Massachusetts, and Chicago. We now have a trained and effective sales force of fifty company salesmen (no brokers), who cover the whole United States. The deployment of the salesmen is based on the size of a market, its general potential, and its potential for the sale of Gold Seal products. For example, we have three salesmen in New York City and one that covers Georgia and Tennessee.

The salesmen: first, program and stimulate the distributor and his sales organization; second, open up new accounts and turn these new account orders over to the distributor; and third, merchandise and make sure that our Gold Seal and Henri Marchant products have the best display position and consumer exposure possible.

Two years ago we had a windfall. Gold Seal was chosen as the United States distributor for Tuborg (Danish) beer. Eight of our fifty salesmen are maintained in markets where we would not be represented if they were not selling Tuborg beer.

Distribution. Our distribution problem was to get the best distributor or the best combination of distributors in each market. Distilleries as well as wineries sell through the same wholesalers. Thus, they are the key to distribution, because they alone have access to all the potential accounts at reasonable cost. Some in the New York City area are very large, with eighty to a hundred salesmen and annual sales of $80 to $120 million. In 1962 we had one distributor in New York City, who sold 5,000 cases annually. In 1970 we had eight distributors with a total volume of 65,000 cases. In New Jersey our sales went from 8,000 in 1962 to 40,000 cases in 1970 with only one distributor.

For example, in 1970 our most successful market was Florida. A year and a half ago we suddenly acquired two new distributors there, and sales in 1970 went from 20,000 to 40,000 cases because we persuaded them to handle Gold Seal. All of the advertising and the salesmen had been there before, but it took the combination of all three ingredients—sales manpower, consumer advertising, and the right distributor—to increase sales. Many of the distributors we wanted already carried Taylor or Great Western wines and therefore would not handle a line which was a direct competitor. We had to sell to those distributors who carried the Gallo, or some other low-priced or imported line with which we did not compete.

Obviously it was a combination of our advertising campaigns—e.g., full-page color advertisements in the prestigious *New York Times*—and our own trained sales force that, unlike brokers, could concentrate their full time and attention on Gold Seal products, that enabled us to build by 1971 a national network of about two hundred distributors.

QUESTION

1. Design a total promotional program for Gold Seal in 1972.

CASE 19. CROWN SPECIALTY STEEL COMPANY

Promotional program in expanding industrial market

Mr. Oscar Meade, president of the Crown Specialty Steel Company of Detroit, Michigan, realized that potential sales in the Detroit area far exceeded the area's supply of specialty steel products and services. Moreover, the market was showing signs of expansion. Consequently, Mr. Meade was wondering what kind of a program his firm should develop (1) to take advantage of the growing market opportunities and (2) to minimize the effects of competition, which were sure to intensify.

The Crown Specialty Steel Company's sole line of business was to provide Detroit-area industries with custom-made, alloyed steel products capable of withstanding heavy, excessive abuse in specialized use situations. Basically, Crown was a service organization. The company did not produce any of the products it sold; instead, it acted as a liaison between steel users and steel producers. During regular calls on prospective customers, Crown salesmen would seek to identify problem situations calling for specialty steel products. Or when a user—even a large concern such as Ford Motor Company or General Motors—encountered a problem which might feasibly be solved by the use of high-strength, alloyed steel, that company would initiate the contact with a specialty steel company like Crown. A Crown representative would analyze the problem and recommend the particular type of steel needed in the situation.

An order was then forwarded to a steel manufacturer. There the mill's metallurgists formulated the processes and components which would yield the desired products. Typically some material (tungsten, silicon, manganese, or nickel) was mixed with the molten steel to form an alloy which would give the desired hardness, toughness, tensile strength, or ability to withstand temperature extremes.

Extra-high-strength steel is most useful in heavy-wear areas in a factory or in situations requiring materials which can withstand heavy blows and stresses over long periods of time. Alloyed steel is commonly used in conveyor systems, blast furnaces, and certain machine parts. For example, the conveyor hooks which attach to a car body during automobile assembly must be small, but extremely strong, to provide adequate life while not impairing assembly. These small conveyor hooks are made from a special nickel-alloy, high-strength steel. Conveyors carrying gravel are subject to heavy wear and are also constructed of special steel alloys. Machine parts typically produced with specialty steels include gears, bearings, shafts, connecting rods, blades, springs, pins, and cutting units.

Through the years there have been increasing industrial needs for specialized, high-strength steel products. Two specific reasons, however, explain why the specialty steel suppliers developed to satisfy these needs, rather than the major users' going directly to large steel producers to get these products. First, the major users of special steel found that they did not use this type of product often enough to warrant having a separate facility for its procurement. But when the users *did* need the specialty product, determining its specifications and procuring it were complex tasks. Second, the greatly expanded list of steel alloys available meant that considerable expertise was needed to ensure correct product choice.

The Crown Company's primary market was the heavily industrialized area within a 60-mile radius of Detroit. This included the Windsor, Ontario, and Toledo, Ohio, areas. However, the company did consider that its total market extended out 100 miles from Detroit. The company held 22 percent of the specialty steel market within that 100-mile limit, according to Mr. Meade. Crown faced three competitors in this market. The competitors' market shares and number of salesmen were as follows:

	Market share (percent)	Number of salesmen
Company A	30	11
Company B	28	9
Company C	20	8
Crown	22	8

Competition in the specialty steel industry was usually on a nonprice basis because all the steel-mill suppliers maintained comparable prices. An important part of the product-service mix of a specialty steel firm was the ability of its salesmen to analyze a user's problem and to recommend a steel alloy which would provide the required service at a reasonable cost to the user. However, all Crown's competitors could provide this service. Competition was also affected by the personal relations which salesmen built with their customers and by other promotional efforts designed to strengthen the company image and customer loyalty.

In its relatively short life the Crown Company had experienced some significant ups and downs in its sales history. From its beginning in 1952 until the late 1950s the company showed gradually increasing sales and profits. In the early 1960s, however, Crown's sales leveled off and even declined during four consecutive years. The reason for the decline was Crown's failure to provide fast, reliable delivery on its orders. A steel mill may receive ten to fifty orders a week from specialty steel companies, and often will delay production of a certain order for weeks or even months. Crown's former president, Mr. Michael Latrobe, ordered from several different large steel mills. Consequently, he did not enjoy a favored position with any one mill, nor did he maintain adequate contact with these various mills in order to ensure prompt production of his orders.

In 1965 Mr. Meade took over as president of the Crown Company, and since then sales increased annually to the present level of about $1 million. Net operating profit has increased to 7 percent of net sales. Mr. Meade credited much of this successful turnaround to his methods of working with the steel mills. He selected only one mill supplier—United States Steel Company—and he maintained intensive written and personal contact with that manufacturer. The result was that U.S. Steel filled Crown's orders promptly—sometimes even ahead of orders from other specialty steel firms. Consequently, Mr. Meade was usually able to provide faster service than any of his competitors.

Crown's market position had progressed to the point where Mr. Meade estimated that the four specialty steel companies could handle only 80 percent of the potential business in the Detroit area, and furthermore the market was expanding rapidly. Crown had built a clientele of steady customers in the automotive, cement, and gravel industries. The account list included Ford, Chevrolet, Buick, Pontiac, Oxford Gravel Works, and some smaller cement companies. In addition, new users and new uses of specialty steel offered opportunities for market expansion. Local chemical companies and machine parts makers, for instance, were potential customers.

Crown's main promotional efforts were through the company's eight salesmen. Sometimes Mr. Meade made the initial contact with a customer, but from then on a salesman handled Crown's work with that customer. Further promotion consisted of customer entertainment. No advertising was done at all. In fact, only one of Crown's three competitors used any advertising, and then only in a very small amount.

With demand outrunning supply in the specialty steel market, Crown's market prospects looked good. Mr. Meade was smart enough to realize, however, that the current market situation could very well be a short-run phenomenon. Such a market was bound to attract addition competitors and to draw more aggressive, better-trained selling effort from existing firms. Consequently, he was wondering how he might improve and intensify Crown's promotional efforts in order to capture a satisfactory share of the expanding market.

As one alternative, Mr. Meade considered budgeting $45,000 to $50,000 for an advertising program during the coming year. He consulted a Detroit advertising agency who indicated that a program of direct-mail advertising, plus placing advertisements in selected trade journals and Detroit newspapers, would have several advantages, some of which were:

1. It would make salesmen's efforts more efficient by using advertising to make the initial customer contact.
2. It would establish company identity and image.
3. It would reach customer personnel now inaccessible to the sales force.

Another alternative was to use the same amount of money to hire, train, and compensate three additional salesmen. The total cost per man would be about $16,000, depending on the amount of training they needed—which in turn would depend to some extent upon whether experienced men were hired, thus reducing training costs. Any unallocated funds could be used (1) to further train the present salesmen and (2) to equip the sales force with better sales tools (catalogues, samples, etc.).

An informal market investigation, which Mr. Meade conducted, revealed the following interesting facts about the purchase decision for specialty steel products:

1. The initial purchase idea comes from the first level of management—a foreman or general foreman—which is in closest contact with a company's problems.

2. Buying decisions for specialty steels are made quickly when a need arises, and then the buyer seeks the assistance of a specialty steel company; the purchase is not a long-range, planned affair.

QUESTION

1. What promotional program should the Crown Company use to expand its sales effectively and profitably?

CASE 20. SIMMONS COMPANY

Promotional program for new product

For many years the mattress industry had experienced a low growth rate, static sales, and a low rate of product replacement by consumers. Then in the 1960s the Simmons Company actively promoted queen- and king-size mattresses as a replacement for the traditional 54-inch-wide mattresses. Named the "super-size revolution," this innovation was considered by Simmons executives to be perhaps the greatest inducer of functional obsolescence in the bedding industry in almost forty years. Anxious to capitalize fully on this innovation, the executives were searching for ways to improve the promotional programs of both the company and its retail dealers. The vice president of sales, Mr. Robert W. Bailey, Jr., was assigned the responsibility for developing a total marketing program for the successful consumer acceptance of the new mattress products.

The Simmons Company, founded in 1870 in Kenosha, Wisconsin, was the largest manufacturer of mattresses in the world. The company also was the largest and one of the oldest firms in the home furnishings fields. Beautyrest mattresses and Hide-A-Bed sofas were two of the company's best-known brands. Simmons also produced mattresses and box springs to meet the specifications of certain large retailers. In addition, Simmons sold furniture to the institutional market (hospitals, nursing homes, hotels, school dormitories) and also marketed draperies, metal caskets, and juvenile furniture. Company sales volume in 1968 was $238 million, with bedding products accounting for $150 million, or 64 percent of this total.

Sizable physical distribution costs for mattresses make long-distance shipments and long channels of distribution impractical. Consequently, the firm had decentralized both its production and its marketing operations. Fourteen mattress manufacturing plants were located throughout the United States. In addition, the company maintained product warehouses in about 65 cities where there were no manufacturing facilities. A sales organization of about 180 salesmen and 20 sales managers was used to sell bedding products (mattresses, box springs, and Hide-A-Bed sofas) directly to retailers. In addition, some thirty salesmen were assigned to the contract division where they serviced large institutional accounts.

In 1967 there were about 3,000 producers of bed mattresses in the United States. Simmons's only major competitor covering the national market was the Englander Company, a division of Union Carbide, Inc., with sales of about $20 million in 1967. However, the relatively small capital investment needed to start a mattress manufacturing firm had attracted many smaller firms into the industry. Competition also was furnished by several franchise operations; that is, various local and regional independent mattress manufacturers were franchised to market under one brand, which then could be advertised nationally. Sealy and Serta were probably the best known of these brands.

At the retail level the mattress industry generally priced its products at $10 intervals from $39.50 to $99.95, the price for a 54-inch Beautyrest. The box spring usually sold with a mattress was priced at the level of the mattress. The bedding industry was highly price-competitive, especially in the lower price lines. With well over 50 percent of total sales at the $39.50 level, there apparently was an elastic demand for mattresses in general.

Simmons depended heavily upon the sales skill of its retailers. Mattresses are not easily differentiated products because of their similar appearance. Thus while a manufacturers's advertising may play some role in the consumers' decision processes, the salesmanship of the retailer is especially significant. Consequently, the Simmons Company was constantly striving to increase the effectiveness of its retail promotion and distribution.

Since the 1920s the Simmons Company had used advertising and sales promotion extensively to establish and improve its market position. The company sought to project an image of dependability and high quality to consumers. Because the firm had been generally successful in building this image, the retail salesmen had experienced success in trading up customers to the Beautyrest mattress. More specifically, Simmon's advertising usually emphasized the comfort, restful sleep, back support, and durability provided by the independent coil-spring action in the mattress.

Because bedding products accounted for such a large share of the company's total business, they received by far the largest percentage of Simmons's total expenditures for advertising and sales promotion. In 1969, for example, the company budgeted $5.8 million (almost 4 percent of 1968 sales of $150 million) for the advertising and sales promotion of bedding products. Of this total, about $1.4 million (24 percent) was allocated to television, and $1.0 million (17 percent) to national magazine space; the remaining $3.4 million (59 percent) was to be spent for trade-publication advertising. (These figures are approximations, since the company devoted a modest amount of these funds to radio, newspaper, and outdoor advertising media.) Under the retailer cooperative agreements, Simmons reimbursed its dealers for a predetermined percentage of their local Simmons advertising, or for an absolute amount.

As some indication of the general level of the company's promotional effort, Simmons received two consecutive "Clio" awards in the 1960s, given for the best television commercial in the home furnishings industry. Management's basic advertising strategy was to concentrate on the high-price end of its product line, in contrast to the strategy of most of its competitors. As noted in Simmon's 1967 statement to its stockholders:

Our general advertising strategy had made it possible for retailers across the country to sell a fair segment of the public a better quality than would otherwise have been possible had we followed the normal practice of putting our advertising dollars behind popular price bracket mattresses in our line. We feel that this policy has paid off and is demonstrated conclusively by the fact that the ordinary wage earner is by far the largest buyer of Beautyrest mattresses, despite the fact that there are lower price mattresses made both by ourselves and our competition.

In spite of the apparent success which Simmons enjoyed in the bedding products market, management in that firm was concerned about the very slow rate of growth which the industry as a whole had experienced for some time. The total annual industry output of mattresses had remained static for several years at 8 to 9 million units. Further research indicated that the average mattress in use in the United States was 10 to 11 years old.

Management believed that the reason for the static market situation lay in the consumer's buying motivation and his perception of a mattress. Mattresses are high-unit-value products purchased for functional reasons, with rarely any thought given to a style or fashion element. Mattresses are rarely replaced. Typically they are used for years, frequently even after they are worn out and sagging —which is bad in terms of both posture and sound sleep. Moreover, the executives believed that many consumers perceived that mattresses were a nondifferentiated product, i.e., that all brands were basically the same.

The promotion of larger-sized mattresses—Simmons's super-size revolution —in the mid-1960s was intended to increase the replacement rate of mattresses, to make obsolete the 54-inch-wide model, and to modify consumers' buying psychology by introducing style and fashion considerations into the buying process. Extensive sleep research conducted by Simmons indicated that couples sleeping on standard-width beds (54 inches) do not sleep nearly so well as they would if given more room. The new king-size model was 76 inches wide, and the queen-size model was 60 inches wide; both were 80 inches long, in contrast to the 75-inch length of the standard-size mattress.

The larger-sized mattresses and box springs were not priced separately. Instead, they were sold only in combination—at a retail price of $249.95 for the queen size and $359.95 for the king size. Management reasoned that a customer could buy a standard-size mattress (or box spring) separately and use it with an existing box spring (or mattress). The king- or queen-size mattress, however, would not fit older box springs or beds. So the customer normally would have to buy both a mattress and a box spring in the larger sizes, and hence the policy of pricing the two as a combination package.

There seemed to be a large potential market for these new products. In an address to the New York Society of Security Analysts in July, 1967, Mr. Grant G. Simmons, Jr., chairman of the board of directors, noted the following market estimates as being important to his company's future (add 000 to all figures):

Year	Population	Births	Deaths	Households	Housing starts
1965	194,572	3,742	1,860	56,900	1,540
1970	208,615	5,179	2,033	63,300	1,800
1975	227,929	6,060	2,167	70,001	2,200
1980	250,489	6,657	2,284	77,308	2,600

The customer's need for larger bedding to improve sleeping conditions had existed for years. Once the company finally realized that fact and designed a product to satisfy that need, the consumer was provided with a reason for replacing his ten-year-old mattress. Moreover, management recognized that larger mattresses occupy more floor space and thus become more important to the appearance and arrangement of the average bedroom. Consequently, the style and fashion of these products became more important.

In the development stages of the super-size product concept, Simmons management had foreseen a serious problem concerning the availability of complementary bedding products. That is, would there be properly modified sheets, bedspreads, pillows, and bed frames to fit the new queen- and king-size beds? The problem was solved on two levels. First, through common interests in the National Bedding Association, the Simmons Company worked closely with manufacturers of complementary bedding products in an effort to coordinate marketing strategies and production schedules. After all, the introduction of the super-size mattress was potentially as profitable for other related bedding-product companies as it was for Simmons. Second, on the retail level, Simmons turned the size problem into an attractive promotional aid by offering its customers a free larger bed frame with the combination purchase of a super-size mattress and box spring. To those people interested in buying a standard-size mattress and box spring, the company offered a free "adapto-rail," thus providing the customer with the opportunity to move up to a super-size mattress at a later date without having to pay the extra cost of a new bed frame.

In view of the relatively higher prices of the super-size models, Simmons executives wondered whether the channels of distribution or the type of retail outlet should be any different from what had been used for the traditional models. They also pondered the question of what type of promotional program and strategy should be used for the larger-sized mattresses. A program was developed in two related parts. One concerned the company's advertising at the national level, and the other concerned the retailers' promotional efforts at the local level.

The consumer's product perception and his buying problems meant that he depended upon brand advertising and particularly upon the retail salesman for product information. Consequently, management recognized the critical importance of well-informed retail salesmen and attractive, well-planned bedding departments in retail stores. They also realized that the traditional bedding section in a department store or furniture store typically had a cold, cluttered, uninviting atmosphere.

QUESTION

1. What should be Simmons's promotional strategy for its super-size mattresses at the national level and at the local (retail) level?

CASE 21. INSTANT PRODUCTS DIVISION*

Promotional allowances and the Robinson-Patman Act

The Instant Products Division of the Southern Farm Belt Foods Corporation had marketed its wide line of dried (dehydrated) soups for a little over three years. An unusually heavy advertising and promotion campaign which accom-

*Case prepared by Prof. Neil H. Borden, Jr., University of Virginia. Reproduced with permission.

panied their introduction had won approximately 80 percent effective national distribution. Management was particularly pleased with this distribution success because dry soups had not been a very popular item with the supermarket trades. Store movement on the few existing brands had been considered quite low, and product quality was usually not the quality of canned soups.

Initial consumer sampling was quite heavy. Sales for the first fourteen months, backed by the heavy introductory program, were considered quite encouraging. Turnover rates (averaging all varieties) were about equal to the supermarket average for dry grocery products, that is, 20 times per year. This rate did not hold up, however. As advertising and promotion expenditures were adjusted to the planned sustaining rates, the stockturn started to deteriorate despite adjustments made in many store inventories. The rate sank to about 11 times per year in representative chains, at which point it had held steady for about the last year. Instant Products management claimed that this stockturn rate was not bad when compared to turn rates on many other grocery items, the small amount of shelf space the line occupied (about 4 linear feet), and the high gross margins available (24 percent) compared to the grocery average of 19 percent. They knew, however, that soup buyers would consciously or subconsciously compare dry soup sales results with the more popular canned soups. Canned soups had a stockturn rate of about 35 times per year, yielded a gross margin of about 16 percent, and occupied over 30 shelf feet in many stores. The canned soups section yielded supermarkets about $420 in revenue per week, while sales of all dry packaged soups were approximately $50 per week.

In most markets Instant Products dry soup mixes had two competitors— Excelon, an old brand stocked by most firms, and Myers, a relatively new entry which had achieved about 50 percent effective distribution. The Excelon Company was large and reputable, but most of its sales came from products in categories other than soup. Its strength was in coffee and tea. Excelon dry soup was packaged in only five varieties, compared to eight varieties of Instant. Myers was primarily a specialties company. It was best known for its extracts, condiments, and gravy mixes. Myers soup mixes were packaged in four varieties; the onion soup was also packaged as a snack dip mix. Neither Excelon nor Myers put much advertising money behind their soups.

As sales slacked off on Instant soup mixes, many supermarket firms notified the sales representatives of dry soup companies that unless sales performance improved, one of the three brands would be discontinued. Many supermarket firms did take such action. Instant Products management estimated that about 40 percent of supermarket firms (with 11 or more units) carried all three major brands; 40 percent stocked two brands, and 20 percent shelved only one brand. About two-thirds of the firms which stocked one brand carried Excelon. Instant's effective distribution had dropped to 63 percent. Product management thought that national advertising efficiency would be seriously reduced by any further loss of distribution.

The Southern Division of Solomon Supers has been threatening to discontinue Instant soups for six months. (Myers had been dropped almost twelve months before.) This Solomon Division was the major chain (32 percent share of market) in a large and competitive metropolitan area of three million people. Solomon had the reputation in the trade of being exceptionally tough to deal with. They restricted their assortments, price promoted on practically all allowances, gave as little performance as possible on advertising contracts, and would use their private labels as a wedge to force concessions from suppliers. In this area only Solomon, two regional chains, and two voluntaries carried Instant, yielding an effective distribution rate of 71 percent. Many small supermarket firms in the area followed Solomon's lead in stocking items.

The Solomon soup buyer had complained of low soup movement in many of the weekly calls made by the Instant district sales manager. He had also complained about the 48 pack, saying this was too high, and could Instant pack 24 or go to assorted packs. In response to this common complaint, Instant had switched to 24 packs, although some 48 packs were still in both company and store inventories.

On one recent call the situation reached a head. The Solomon buyer announced that he was about ready to firm up a decision to drop Instant, because he could not afford to reduce his department's stockturn by having too many items in dry soup. The Instant district sales manager argued that Solomon customers needed the selection, that many of the customers were loyal Instant users, and that if a cut had to be made, Solomon should stick with the advertised brand and drop Excelon. There was some discussion on whether Instant or Excelon had a higher following of loyal users. The Solomon buyer would not reveal his chain's sales of Excelon soups, but he inferred that they were at least equal to the sales of Instant.

The sales manager said that he was sure sales would improve if he were allowed to install shelf talkers and shelf extenders in all Solomon stores. He also said that he would have his retail men adjust stocks among the stores since he was sure some inventories were unbalanced.

The buyer did not answer this proposal, but made one of his own. He said that maybe dry soups did not get enough sampling, and that many people probably did not know of the great strides made in improved quality and taste in recent years. He said, "As a last resort, what I'll do is let you put some demonstrators in our stores for a few weeks, and sample our customers. Maybe this'll bring sales up. We need a little more activity in the stores anyway, something different than the competition. You go talk it over with your boss—tell him how important it is—and let me know tomorrow."

The Instant district sales manager wondered what he should suggest to the regional sales manager and the product manager.

QUESTIONS

1. What course of action should the Instant district sales manager recommend to his superiors?
2. With respect to the Robinson-Patman Act, what are the implications in the buyer's proposal regarding demonstrators?

PART SEVEN

MARKETING IN
SPECIAL FIELDS

MARKETING OF SERVICES

As we developed a marketing program for an individual company in Parts 3 to 6, our thoughts were focused largely on the domestic marketing of manufactured goods. The marketing programs in two additional fields will be considered separately, although briefly, in this chapter and the next one. The areas to be discussed are the marketing of services and the marketing of American products in foreign countries. In each case, we are still concerned with building a marketing program around the constituent parts of the marketing mix—the product, the price structure, the distribution system, and the promotional program.

In the first chapter of this book, we defined marketing as a system designed to plan, price, promote, and distribute goods and *services* to markets. Then we promptly devoted the intervening twenty-three chapters largely to the marketing of *products,* dealing with such things as credit, delivery, and management advice only when they were associated with, and incidental to, the sale of goods. Now we shall rectify that imbalance a bit.

Some students may question the usefulness of a separate chapter on the marketing of services, however, believing that *fundamentally* there is no difference between product marketing and service marketing. In bare-bone outline, it is true, the two are the same in that marketing research is used to develop a marketing mix which will profitably reach a predetermined market. Moreover, often there are substantial similarities in the flesh put on these bones. At the same time, however, significant differences do exist between product marketing and service marketing. Consequently, the marketing planning—the strategies and tactics—often must be substantially different, so the marketing of services does well deserve separate attention.[1]

NATURE AND IMPORTANCE

Out of every dollar that we as consumers spend, about 42 cents goes for services, and services provide about two-thirds of all private, nongovernmental jobs. Furthermore, the forecast is that these figures will increase, rather than decrease. Yet relatively little has been published in the way of a conceptual, all-encompassing study to guide marketing executives in service concerns.[2]

DEFINITION AND SCOPE OF FIELD

No common boundaries have been set to delimit the field of services. The American Marketing Association defines service as "activities, benefits, or satisfactions which are offered for sale, or are provided in connection with the sale of goods."[3] Under this interpretation, we would include (1) intangible benefits offered for sale independently of other goods or services (insurance, legal service); (2) intangible activities which require the use of tangible goods (amusement, house rentals, transportation service); and (3) intangible activities purchased jointly with products or other intangible activities (credit, training dealer salesmen). This definition is too broad for useful marketing analysis. Particularly, we should separate out those services which exist *only* in connection with the *sale* of a product or another service. Thus, when we talk about the marketing of services, using the above three-way classification, we are talking only about those activities in parts (1) and (2).

Consequently, in this chapter we shall define *services* as separately identifiable, intangible activities which provide want satisfaction when marketed to consumers and/or industrial users and which are not necessarily tied to the sale of a product or another service. Therefore, we include such services as medical care, insurance, repair service (but not the repair parts purchased), and entertainment; we exclude credit, delivery, and packaging services which exist only when there is a sale of an article or another service.

The definitional problem will continue and some statistics on services may be misleading because it is becoming more difficult to separate products and services in our economy. Actually, we rarely find situations (as in legal services) where we market services with no product involvement whatsoever. "Most goods, whether consumer or industrial, require supporting services in order to be useful;

---

[1]See Robert C. Judd, "Similarities or Differences in Product and Service Retailing," *Journal of Retailing*, Winter, 1968, pp. 1–9.

[2]For two noteworthy exceptions to this statement, see Donald D. Parker, *The Marketing of Consumer Services*, University of Washington, Business Study Series, no. 1, Seattle, 1960; Eugene M. Johnson, *An Introduction to the Problems of Service Marketing Management*, University of Delaware, Bureau of Economic and Business Research, Newark, 1964.

[3]Committee on Definitions, *Marketing Definitions: A Glossary of Marketing Terms*, American Marketing Association, Chicago, 1960, p. 21.

most services require supporting goods to be useful.''[4] It is this product-service mix which really is growing in importance in our economy.

We are concerned primarily with the services sold by some business or professional firm with profit-making motives—commercial services—in contrast to those sold by nonbusiness organizations such as churches, public schools, and the government. One useful classification of commercial services is given below. No attempt is made to separate these services according to whether they are sold to household consumers or industrial users. In fact, most are purchased by both market groups.

1. Housing (includes rentals of hotels, motels, apartments, houses, and farms)
2. Household operations (includes utilities, house repairs, repairs of equipment in the house, landscaping, and household cleaning)
3. Recreation (includes rental and repairs of equipment used in participating in recreation and entertainment activities; also admission to all entertainment, recreation, and amusement events)
4. Personal care (includes laundry, dry cleaning, beauty care)
5. Medical and other health care (includes all medical service, dental, nursing, hospitalization, optometry, and other health care)
6. Private education
7. Business and other professional services (includes legal, accounting, management consulting, and marketing consulting services)
8. Insurance and financial (includes personal and property insurance, credit and loan service, investment counseling, and tax service)
9. Transportation and communications (includes freight and passenger service on common carriers, automobile repairs and rentals, and telephone service)

GROWTH AND CURRENT IMPORTANCE OF SERVICES

The United States is moving beyond the industrial-economy stage to the point where it is becoming the world's first service economy. (See Fig. 24-1) This shift is true at least to the extent that two-thirds of the private, nongovernmental labor force is engaged in supplying services, and almost one-half of consumer expenditures are for the purchase of services. Furthermore, government projections to 1980 indicate that services will attract an even larger share of consumer spending and employment. (See Fig. 24-2.)

Many product manufacturers, preparing to capitalize on this emerging service economy, are diversifying into services. (See Fig. 24-3.) Product retailers are doing likewise. Sears—the nation's largest retailer—now operates the nation's largest stock casualty insurance company (Allstate), a car rental agency, a mutual fund, and a savings and loan association. Broadway-Hale department stores, headquartered on the West Coast, also market home cleaning, insurance, income-tax counseling, and driving lessons.

Even assuming some definitional and measurement problems, the statistics on expenditures for *consumer* services alone tell quite a story. With few exceptions since 1950, service expenditures have increased each year at a more rapid rate than expenditures for durable or nondurable goods. See Table 24-1. As a percentage of the gross national product, consumer service expenditures rose from 22 to 26

---

[4] John M. Rathmell, "What Is Meant by Services?" *Journal of Marketing,* October, 1966, p. 33.

THE SERVICE ECONOMY

For a fee, there are now companies that will balance your budget, baby-sit your philodendron, wake you up in the morning, drive you to work, or find you a new home, job, car, wife, clairvoyant, cat feeder, or gypsy violinist. Or perhaps you want to rent a garden tractor? A few cattle? Some original paintings? Or maybe some hippies to decorate your next cocktail party? If it is business services you need, other companies will plan your conventions and sales meetings, design your products, handle your data processing, or supply temporary secretaries or even executives.

Figure 24-1. *Source:* "Services Grow while the Quality Shrinks," *Business Week,* Oct. 30, 1971, p. 50.

percent during the period 1950–1973. Services accounted for 42 cents of the personal consumption dollar in 1973, as against only 33 cents in 1950.

We should use some caution, however, as we interpret these statistics on service expenditures. First, even with the growth in demand for services since 1950, we still are only returning to the goods-to-services ratio which existed in consumer buying patterns in 1930. That is, about the same share of the consumer dollar went for services in 1970 as in 1930. This percentage declined considerably in the 1930s and 1940s, but has been rising ever since. Second, much of the increase in the services sector of consumer expenditures reflects the fact that the prices of services have increased at a much faster rate than the

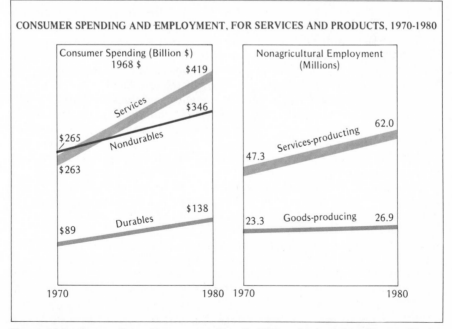

CONSUMER SPENDING AND EMPLOYMENT, FOR SERVICES AND PRODUCTS, 1970-1980

Figure 24-2. *Source: Sales Management,* Mar. 6, 1972, p. 24; based on Bureau of Labor Statistics projection.

Coca-Cola introduced a multimedia learning system which eventually will be sold in the education market.

Singer (sewing machines) Corp., already possessing teaching expertise based on years of teaching women to sew, is moving into the preschool education market.

Searle & Co., pharmaceutical manufacturer, created a new service, Project Health, to market preventive medicine programs to industry.

Gerber (baby food) Products is moving into nursery schools and insurance.

Maytag introduced a plan to lease its washing machines.

Each of the above is a case illustrating a product firm's capitalizing on market opportunities presented by the emerging services economy.

Figure 24-3. *Source:* Thayer C. Taylor, "Selling the Services Society," *Sales Management,* Mar. 6, 1972, p. 23.

prices of products, especially since 1960. In fact, measured in constant (real) dollars, consumer outlays for services have increased only fractionally faster than total consumer spending since the 1960s.[5]

Third, the rate of growth has not been uniform for all categories of consumer services. As disposable personal incomes have increased and life-styles have changed over the past 20 years, the demand for some services has grown relatively faster than that for others. Attendance at movies has declined as people have turned to television. Expenditures for municipal transportation have declined relatively as people use their private autos. On the other hand, expenditures for household utilities, domestic airline travel, and foreign travel have enjoyed well-above-average growth since 1955. Table 24-2 shows the percentage increase in expenditures for various services, in relation to the increase in disposable personal income from 1955 to 1970. In the same table we can also observe the annual growth rate for these years as well as the growth projected to 1980.

When we say that over 40 percent of the average consumer's income is spent for services, we still grossly understate the economic importance of services. These figures do not include the vast amounts spent for business and industrial services. By all indications, spending for business services has increased even more rapidly than that for consumer services. The truth of the matter is that we do not have accurate measurements reflecting total sales of services. This lack of complete statistical data is traceable, in part at least, to the definitional problems just discussed. Nonetheless, it seems quite clear that there has been a significant growth in the market for services over the past two decades.

To understand the reasons for this boom in services, we must understand what has been happening in our economy during the past quarter of a century. The long period of prosperity has meant higher incomes, increased leisure time, and generally a rise in living standards. In the early stages of a period such as this, people first expend their rising incomes on goods. This was particularly true after World War II,

[5]Fabian Linden, "The Consumer Market in the 1980s: Services," *Conference Board Record,* May, 1972, p. 50.

Table 24-1. Expenditures for personal services as a percentage of the gross national product and total personal consumption expenditures, for selected years, 1947–1973, in billions of current dollars.

The share of consumer dollars spent on services has increased rather steadily since World War II (42 percent in 1973, as against 33 percent in 1950). How do you account for this increase? Is there likely to be a continued increase in the expenditure percentage devoted to services?

Year	Services	Personal consumption expenditures	Gross national product	Service expenditures as percentage of:	
				Personal consumption expenditures	Gross national product
		(in billions of current dollars)			
1947	$50	$161	$231	31.0%	21.5%
1950	62	191	285	32.7	21.9
1955	91	254	398	35.9	22.9
1960	129	325	504	39.6	25.5
1965	176	433	685	40.8	25.8
1970	263	618	977	42.6	26.0
1973	337	804	1,289	41.9	26.1

Source: Data for 1947–1965 from *Business Statistics: 1969.*
Data for 1970, 1973 from *Survey of Current Business,* Feb., 1974, pp. 8, S-1.

when there was a huge backlog of demand for products denied to consumers in the 1930s because of the Depression, and in the early 1940s because of the war. As the years went by, the average consumer was sated with goods, and these products declined as status symbols. Instead, the consumer has increasingly turned to services which heretofore he either could not afford or did not desire—services such as travel, education, personal grooming, and medical care.

In the business field also, services have grown in importance. Business has become increasingly complex, specialized, and competitive, and as a result management has been forced to call in experts to provide services in research, taxation, advertising, labor relations, and a host of other areas.

One theory of economic growth holds that there are three observable stages of development.[6] In the primary stage (low-level economies), agriculture, forestry, hunting, and fishing occupy the population's attention. In the secondary stage, the major emphasis is on manufacturing. In the tertiary stage, the important activities involve trade, transportation, finance, communication, construction, and professional and governmental fields. Since most of these activities are services, an economy in the third stage of development should experience an increasing share of expenditures in the services sector.

[6]Colin Clark, *The Conditions of Economic Progress,* 3d ed., Macmillian & Co., Ltd., London, 1957, p. 491, as cited in William J. Regan, "The Service Revolution," *Journal of Marketing,* July, 1963, pp. 57–62.

Table 24-2. Discretionary effect of rising income on expenditures for selected consumer services, 1955–1970, with growth projections to 1980.

Expenditures for some services are growing more rapidly than those for others. As aggregate disposable personal income went up 1 percent, expenditures for foreign travel rose 1.61 percent—that is, outlays for that particular service grew 61 percent more than total personal income. All figures are based on constant dollars.

	Percentage rise in service expenditures, related to 1 percent rise in personal income	Average annual growth (percent)	
	1955–1970	1955–1970	1970–1980 (projected)
Disposable personal income	1.00	4.2	4.4
Total consumer services:	1.04	4.4	4.6
Shelter	1.16	4.9	5.1
Gas and electricity	1.27	5.3	5.6
Telephone and telegraph	1.69	7.1	7.5
Domestic help	— .34	−1.4	−1.5
Transportation:	.56	2.4	2.5
Automotive services	.69	2.9	3.0
Intercity travel	1.30	5.4	5.7
Domestic airline	2.68	11.3	11.8
Medical services	1.16	4.9	5.1
Personal care	.76	3.2	3.4
Foreign travel	1.61	6.7	7.1
Higher education	1.55	6.5	6.8

Source: Fabian Linden, "The Consumer Market in 1980: Services," *Conference Board Record,* May, 1972, p. 51.

CHARACTERISTICS OF SERVICES

Services possess distinctive characteristics which create marketing problems and result in marketing programs which are often substantially different from those found in the marketing of products.

INTANGIBILITY

Services are intangible. The impossibility of a customer's tasting, feeling, seeing, hearing, or smelling a service before he buys it places some strain on the marketing organization. This burden falls mainly on a company's promotional program, where the salesmen and advertising department must concentrate on the benefits to be derived from the service, rather than emphasizing the service itself. An insurance company will promote service benefits such as guaranteed payment of the children's college expenses, protection against losing one's life's savings in a damage suit resulting from an auto accident, or a retirement income of so many dollars a month. The telephone companies in their advertising tell us how companies can cut selling and inventory costs, and often save a sale, by using long-distance calls.

On the other hand, the factor of intangibility offers some competitive advantages to a firm. Problems of physical distribution are eliminated. There is nothing to store or handle. There is no inventory to control, and a company will never be faced with losses from a decline in inventory values.

INSEPARABILITY

Services often cannot be separated from the person of the seller. A corollary to this point is that some services are often created and marketed simultaneously. For example, a beauty operator is creating the service of a haircut and dispensing the service at the same time. Of course, preparation and training may be done in advance.

From a marketing standpoint, inseparability means that frequently direct sale is the only possible channel of distribution, and a seller's services cannot be sold in very many markets. This characteristic also limits the scale of operation in a firm. One person can repair only so many autos in a day or treat only so many medical patients. Also, because each person—that is, each "service institution"—is a specialist, the service company often cannot add a variety of other services to its line, the way a department store or supermarket can.

As a modification of the inseparability feature, there may be a tangible representation of the service by someone other than the creator-seller. A travel agent, insurance broker, or rental agent, for instance, may represent and help promote the service which will be sold by the institution producing it.

HETEROGENEITY

It is impossible to standardize output among several sellers of presumably the same service. As a matter of fact, it is not possible to standardize completely even the output of one seller. A railroad does not give the same quality of service on each trip. All repair jobs a mechanic does on automobiles are not of equal quality. Complicating this characteristic is the fact that often it is difficult to judge the quality of a service. (Of course, we can say the same for some products.) It is particularly difficult to forecast the quality in advance of buying a service. A person pays to see a ball game without knowing whether it will turn out to be an exciting one, well worth the price of admission, or a low-quality, dull performance.

In light of these problems of standardization and quality evaluation, the service company should pay particular attention to the "product-planning" stage of its marketing program. Management must do all it can to ensure consistent and high-quality performance. In this way, the company can build the customer confidence and good reputation that are so vital to repeat business and to favorable word-of-mouth advertising.

PERISHABILITY AND FLUCTUATING DEMAND

Services are highly perishable, and they cannot be stored. Unused electrical power, empty seats in a stadium, and idle repairmen in a garage all represent business which is lost forever. Furthermore, the market for services fluctuates considerably by seasons, by days of the week, and by hours of the day. Many ski lifts lie idle all summer, and golf courses in some areas go unused in the winter. College football stadia are used mainly in the fall, and then only one day a week. Use of city buses fluctuates within a day.

The combination of perishability and fluctuating demand offers product-planning, pricing, and promotion challenges to executives in a service company. They might look for new uses for idle plant capacity in off-seasons. Through advertising, they can show consumers the advantages of using city transportation facilities during nonpeak hours. In an attempt to level demand, telephone companies price at lower rates on nights and weekends.

THE MARKETING CONCEPT AND SERVICE MARKETING

The growth in services has generally been attributed to the maturation of our economy and the rising standards of living in our affluent society, but not to marketing developments in the service industries. Traditionally, executives in service companies have not been marketing-oriented. They have lagged behind sellers of products in accepting the market concept. Service organizations have also generally been slow in adopting promotional methods, "product" strategies, and other marketing techniques. With a few notable exceptions, such as the insurance industry and, more recently, the telephone companies, marketing management in service firms has not been especially creative. Innovation has come typically from product-associated companies.

To illustrate, the major impetus for the increased use of electrical power has come from appliance manufacturers, not electric utilities.[7] The laundry and dry-cleaning industry stood still, despite increased competition from home laundry equipment and coin-operated dry-cleaning establishments, and despite the development of wash-and-wear and permanently pressed fabrics. The repair industry has left a trail of dissatisfied and even irate customers for years.

Perhaps we can identify the reasons for this lack of a marketing orientation. No doubt the intangibility of services poses more difficult marketing problems than those which product sellers face. In many service industries—particularly professional services—the sellers think of themselves as producers or creators, and not as marketers, of the service. They are proud of their ability to repair a car, diagnose an illness, fly a plane, sing a concert, or give a good haircut. They do not think of themselves as businessmen. It is not "ethical," for example, for a doctor or a lawyer to advertise. Failure of management to recognize that competition existed may

---

[7]An appreciation of the marketing concept in gas-electric companies would affect their budgeting, promotional spending, and organizational structure, according to William E. Reif and William A. Knoke, "The Marketing Concept for Combination Gas and Electric Companies," *Public Utilities Fortnightly,* Oct. 22, 1970, pp. 33–39. This article also considers some common misconceptions about the utility industry (e.g., lack of competition, nature of demand, concept of product, engineering approach to pricing) which impede the adoption of the marketing concept.

account for lack of interest in marketing in some industries—banking, railroads, and public utilities, for instance.

The all-encompassing reason, however, seems to be that top management has yet to recognize how important marketing is to the success of a firm. This failure is reflected in three areas of weakness.[8] First, these executives have a limited view of the marketing function and of the business they are in. They equate marketing with selling and fail to consider other parts of the system. Movie producers thought of themselves as being in the business of making movies; instead, they were really marketing entertainment. Railroad executives saw their task as running a railroad, instead of marketing a transportation system or a total materials-handling system. The second point—a consequence of the first—is that management fails to recognize that many of its problems are marketing problems. And once this fact is recognized, management may still not act quickly. Finally, there has been insufficient coordination of all marketing activities in service firms. Many service firms lack an executive whose sole responsibility is marketing—the counterpart of the vice president of marketing in a goods-producing company.

Fortunately, this total situation seems to have improved markedly over the past decade.[9] While there may still be a long way to go in some service fields (perhaps in repair services, personal grooming, and others where small businesses predominate), the overall future prospects look good for the recognition and acceptance of the marketing concept in service industries.

The banking industry provides an interesting example of a service industry which in the past has been very much *non*marketing oriented, but which is struggling to make the transition to modern times. For years commercial banks made a customer feel as if they were doing him a big favor by holding his money in a checking account with no interest but with a service charge, or in a savings account at very low interest rates. Loans were granted grudgingly to consumers. Banks were marble mausoleums; tellers were faceless people behind protective bars, and the banker was a "black hat," stereotyped in song and story.

In recent years, however, many banks have been striving to change those images, because the market situation in banking has changed appreciably. Competition both from within and also from outside the industry has intensified. Bankers are beginning to realize that money is a highly standardized, nondifferentiated product. One bank's money is no crisper or greener than another's. Large industrial and commercial customers are diverting idle cash funds into treasury notes and other high-yield investments, rather than leaving these funds in banks at low interest rates. Today the problem facing banks is more likely to be how to *acquire* funds, rather than how to lend or otherwise *employ* them. So banks increasingly are looking to the consumer market (called the "retail" market in banking) as a source of funds.

To meet these challenges, many banks finally are starting to do a little marketing. In fact, some banks are trying to shorten the transition period by pirating

---

[8]Eugene M. Johnson, "Marketing Is Key to Success in Service Business," *Sales/Marketing Today,* November, 1964, pp. 8–11.

[9]For some examples, see David L. Bickelhaupt, "Trends and Innovations in the Marketing of Insurance," *Journal of Marketing,* July, 1967, pp. 17–22; Thomas R. Wotruba, "The Role of Marketing in a Gas or Electric Utility: A Perspective," *Southern Journal of Business,* October, 1968, pp. 26–34; "United Charts a New Flight Plan," *Business Week,* Aug. 14, 1965, p. 128; and "'A Hell of a Way to Run a Railroad,'" *Sales Management,* Mar. 4, 1966, p. 28.

marketing executives from consumer-product companies such as Sara Lee, Midas Mufflers, Ford, and Ampex.[10] Banks are establishing marketing departments, conducting sales training programs, engaging in marketing research, shifting from institutional advertising to hard-sell "product" ads, expanding their services (product) mix, and sending their people to bank-marketing executive development programs.

Banks are making concerted efforts to attract retail (consumer) business. Buildings and internal layouts are designed to project an image of warmth, friendliness, and informality. Drive-in service and bank credit cards have been added for consumer convenience (and incidentally, additional revenues). Other new services include insurance, no-charge checking accounts, travel service, personal financial counseling, payment of customers' utility bills, and 24-hour outside-wall depositories.

Admittedly most banks have quite a way to go before anyone would call them a full-fledged marketing company, but the progress is encouraging. Perhaps soon some banks may even abolish "bankers' hours" and introduce "customers' hours" by staying open and providing full services during the evenings and on Saturdays and Sundays just like other retailers intent on serving their customers. The cashless, checkless economy is anticipated by many bankers, although consumer resistance to the unknown and the consumers' inability to fully control his payments may delay the full implementation of that innovation. When a cashless, checkless system is in effect, however, it will provide banks with a vast fund of information for use in planning, evaluating, and controlling marketing activities in both consumer and industrial markets.[11]

A PROGRAM FOR MARKETING OF SERVICES

Because we are dealing with intangibles, the task of determining the marketing-mix ingredients for a total marketing program in a service industry is perhaps more difficult and thus requires more skill than is true in product-marketing firms.

MARKET ANALYSIS AND MARKET PLANNING

Procedural considerations involved in market analysis and planning are essentially the same whether a firm is selling a product or a service. A marketer of services should understand the components of population and income as they affect the market for his services. In addition, he must carefully analyze his customers' motivation for buying his services—that is, *why* do they want his services, and does each segment of his market have the same or different motives? Also, the seller must determine the buying patterns for his services—when, where, and how do customers buy, who does the buying, and who makes the buying decisions? Essentially the same psychological determinants of buying behavior—attitudes,

---

[10]"Now Banks Are Turning to the Hard Sell," *Business Week,* June 24, 1972, p. 78; see also "Tyros in the Marketing Game," *Business Week,* Sept. 15, 1973, p. 129; and Martin Everett, "See the Bankers Selling," *Sales Management,* July 9, 1973, p. 16.

[11]For examples of marketing activities which banks could then engage in, see Robert H. Myers, "Profiles of the Future: Marketing Opportunities," *Business Horizons,* Feb., 1972, pp. 12–14.

perceptions, personality, etc.—are as pertinent in the marketing of services as in product marketing. In like manner, the sociological factors of social-class structure and small-group influences are market determinants for services. The fundamentals of the adoption and diffusion of product innovation are also relevant in the marketing of services.[12]

Some of the trends pointed up in Chapters 3 to 7 are particularly worth watching because they carry considerable influence in the marketing of services. As an example, increases in disposable income and discretionary buying power mean that consumers can buy more than basic personal and household necessities. Consequently, they become a growing market for more medical care, insurance, or transportation service. The increasing number of working women means greater markets for many services. Women will now pay for services such as laundry or household repairs which formerly they performed themselves. Shorter working hours have resulted in increases in leisure time. More leisure time plus greater income means increased markets for recreation and entertainment services.

A service industry may be able to segment its market on some basis and then use an appropriate marketing strategy to reach each segment more effectively. The airlines, for instance, identified the youth market (ages twelve to twenty-two) as a separate unit and then established a youth fare (half price with a membership card or on a space-available basis) to reach that market segment.[13]

PLANNING AND DEVELOPING THE SERVICE

Product planning and development should have its counterpart in the marketing program of a service industry. Management should use an organized, systematic procedure to determine (1) what services will be offered, (2) what the company's policies will be with respect to the length and breadth of the service line offered, and (3) what, if anything, needs to be done in the way of service attributes such as branding or providing guarantees.

Unfortunately, planning and developing the service has been a neglected activity in most service firms until very recent years, and it is still ignored in too many cases. The basic reason for this neglect goes back to the lack of a marketing orientation in service industries and their narrow view of what business they are in. A motion picture firm which thinks its job is to "make movies" (instead of marketing entertainment) is not apt to get involved in creating and marketing a filmed comedy series for television. By taking the broad view of its service offerings, a company may stay in business long after narrower firms have disappeared. An electric utility which thinks of its business as marketing energy (instead of producing electricity) will not be dismayed when solar radiation or atomic energy is used as a source of power.

New services are just as important to a service company as new products are to a product-marketing firm, even though service companies may not face the problem of obsolescence to as great an extent. Similarly, improving exist-

---

[12]For a study of the diffusion of three life insurance innovations through the industry, see Robert A. Peterson, William Rudelius, and Glenn L. Wood, "Spread of Marketing Innovations in a Service Industry," *Journal of Business,* October, 1972, pp. 485–496.

[13]See Kit G. Narodick, "What Motivates the Consumer's Choice of an Airline?" *Journal of Retailing,* Spring, 1972, pp. 30–38ff; also see William R. Darden and Warren A. French, "Selected Personal Services: Consumer Reactions," *Journal of Retailing,* Fall, 1972, pp. 42–48.

ing services is every bit as important as improving existing products. Certainly much of the procedure for developing new products and many of the criteria for selecting new products (as discussed in Chapter 8) are equally applicable in a service firm.

A service industry can expand or contract its "product line," alter existing services, and trade up or down—in the same way that a product-marketing organization does. Dry cleaners, for instance, have expanded into laundry services, mothproofing, storage, dyeing, and clothing alterations and repairs. Auto insurance firms have added life and fire insurance. The reasons for these line expansions are familiar—the company wants to increase its total volume, reduce seasonal fluctuations in volume, cater to changing buying patterns such as the desire for one-stop shopping, etc. Some railroads have simplified their line by dropping passenger service or by abolishing freight stations at some small, unprofitable locations. Some service firms have effectively expanded their line by working jointly with companies selling related services. Automobile rental firms have working arrangements with airlines and hotels, so that when a customer flies to his destination, a car will be ready for his use at that point, and he will have a hotel room reserved. Travel agencies combine many transportation and recreation services in one package.

In some respects, policy making is easier for services than for products. Tasks related to packaging, color, labeling, and style are virtually nonexistent in marketing services. However, in other areas—branding and standardization of quality, for instance—the job in service industries poses greater problems. Branding is difficult because consistency of quality is hard to maintain and because the brand cannot be physically attached to a service.

Standardization of quality in a service is an extremely important goal to strive for. In some fields such as beauty care, medical care, and some of the recreation industries, no attempt is made to mass-produce a service. Instead, the sellers often offer custom-tailored service for each customer. Even in these case, however, the customer wants consistency of quality, and this consistency is very difficult to achieve because the service is produced and sold in individual units—one haircut, one appendectomy, or one dance lesson.

PRICING OF SERVICES

Perhaps nowhere in the marketing of services is there greater opportunity for managerial creativity, skill, and imagination than in the area of pricing. Price determination is critically important here because of the discretionary nature of customer buying. In the case of most services, personal or business, the customer may postpone his purchase or even perform the service himself. Only rarely does a buyer face the situation where he needs a service immediately and the number of sellers is quite limited. Another factor to consider is that markdowns are not possible in many cases. If there are empty seats at a given concert or athletic contest, it is not possible to hold them over and offer them at a lower price later.

These considerations suggest that the elasticity of demand for a service should influence the price set by the seller. Interestingly enough, sellers often recognize an inelastic demand. Then they charge higher prices. But they fail to act in opposite fashion when faced with an elastic demand, even though a lower price would increase unit sales, total revenue, utilization of facilities, and probably net profit.

The basic methods of price determination for services are generally the same as those for products. Cost-plus pricing is used for various kinds of repair service where the main ingredient is direct labor and the customer is charged on an hourly basis. The price equals the repairman's wages plus an amount to cover overhead and profit. For other services (rentals, entertainment, legal counseling, management consulting) the prices are determined primarily by market demand and competition. It is pretty much a case of what the traffic will bear.

Certainly perfect competition does not exist to any extent, if at all, in the pricing of services. Because of the inability to standardize quality, services are highly differentiated, and it is virtually impossible to have complete market information. Also, in any given market, such as a neighborhood, there are geographic limits within which a buyer will seek a service, and consequently there is not a large number of sellers. The heavy capital investment required to produce many services (transportation, communications, medical care) limits the freedom of entry considerably.

In some service industries, the private seller will establish a price, but it must be approved by a regulatory agency of the state or federal government. This public regulation of prices, however, need not stifle the opportunity for imaginative, skillful pricing designed to stimulate sales. Lower rates for long-distance telephoning on nights and Sundays and different prices which benefit large-volume users of electricity are examples of creative pricing to increase market penetration.

Sometimes a trade or professional association is a price setter within an industry. Barber unions set the price on haircuts, and a laundry and dry-cleaning association sets the price on cleaning a suit of clothes. Fees charged by doctors, architects, accountants, and advertising agencies are frequently influenced strongly by professional associations.

Many of the areas of pricing policies discussed in Chapters 13 and 14 must also be considered by executives in a service firm. Thus we see quantity discounts in the pricing of electrical power, and cash discounts are offered if you pay your auto insurance premium once a year instead of quarterly or semiannually. Doctors and management consultants use a variable-price policy, whereas a movie theater has a one-price policy at any given time of day. A motel or apartment owner offers multiple services (one bedroom, two bedrooms, suites), and he must price one service in relation to another. Geographic pricing policies may be involved, although the variable here is time, not freight charges. A repairman will charge more if he must go out of town, and a doctor will charge more for house calls than office calls.

CHANNELS OF DISTRIBUTION FOR SERVICES

When developing a distribution system for his services, a seller is concerned only with the transfer of ownership. No problems of physical distribution such as bulk breaking, transportation, or warehousing are involved. Most services are sold directly from producer to consumer or industrial user. No middlemen are used because the service cannot be separated from the person of the seller, nor is it feasible to use a tangible representative of the service. Public utilities, medical care, repair service, and others are typically sold without middlemen. The only other channel frequently used involves one agent middleman. We see this channel used in the sale of securities, transportation, housing rentals, labor, and entertainment.

Sometimes dealers are trained in the production of the service and then are franchised to sell it, as is the case with the Sanitone dry-cleaning process, Fred Astaire dance studios, Kelly Girl part-time office help, and Holiday Inn motels.

Whether the seller markets directly or uses an agent to reach his customers, the seller's or agent's *location* with respect to the potential market is all-important. Services cannot be delivered to a customer, so the seller should select a convenient, accessible location where there is maximum customer traffic. Many motels and restaurants have gone out of business because a new highway drew away traffic when it bypassed their formerly good locations. Banks have increased their business by moving the tellers' windows to a location accessible to autos on a drive-in basis.

The inability to use middlemen to any great extent limits the geographic market that a service seller can reach. On the other hand, it gives this seller a chance to serve his customers better. It also provides him with a golden opportunity to get customer feedback quickly and in sufficient detail so that he can improve his marketing program.

PROMOTING THE SERVICE

Management's task is especially difficult when the company must build a promotional program around intangible service benefits. It is so much easier to sell something which can be seen, felt, and demonstrated. In the marketing of services, we find that personal selling, advertising, and indirect forms of promotion are all used extensively.

Personal selling is important because of the close relationship between the buyer and the seller. Brands are not used extensively, so brand preferences and loyalties often cannot be depended upon. Also, self-service or automatic vending has limited application. Whether selling consumer or industrial services, the salesman can often build or destroy customer goodwill toward the firm. Consequently, it is imperative that management do a careful job in selecting, training, and otherwise managing the sales force. In most service industries where personal selling is the main promotional tool used, high-caliber salesmen are usually required.

Not much more needs to be said here about advertising because the principles and procedures are generally the same as those developed in Chapter 23. Small firms can often make effective use of local advertising. Also, a group of small local firms can participate in joint advertising ventures. National trade associations (laundry, dry cleaning, and others) have done considerable national advertising to stimulate primary demand for their services. Even though a service is intangible, store displays that show the results of using the service can be effective.

Many service firms, especially in the recreation-entertainment field, benefit considerably from free publicity. Sports coverage by newspapers, radio, and television media helps in this matter, as do newspaper reviews of movies, plays, and concerts. Travel sections in newspapers have helped sell transportation, housing, and other services related to the travel industry.

As an indirect means of promotion, doctors, lawyers, and insurance men may participate actively in community affairs as a means of getting their names before the public. Other service firms (banks, utilities, railroads) may advertise to attract new industry or more population, knowing that anything which helps the community grow will automatically mean an expanded market for them.

A promotional program in a service company should have two major goals. One is to portray the service benefits in as appealing a manner as possible. The other is to build a good reputation. Because the firm is marketing intangibles, a good reputation is perhaps even more important in a service company than in a product-marketing business. Advertising campaigns can stress dependability of the service—its consistent, high quality. Ads can also emphasize the courteous, friendly, efficient service.

A service firm's promotional effort can be even more effective if the seller can tie in with something tangible—a distinctive color, as used by Howard Johnson or Holiday Inn, or a personal symbol like Smokey the Bear, Reddy Kilowatt, or Wolley Segap (to promote use of the yellow pages in telephone books).

FUTURE OUTLOOK IN SERVICE MARKETING

NEED FOR INCREASED PRODUCTIVITY

In recent years the boom in the services market has been accompanied by a deterioration in the quality of many services. In general, service industries have been plagued by poor management, inefficiency, and low productivity.[14]

This inefficiency—and the need to increase productivity—is probably the biggest problem facing service industries in general. The productivity problem also has significant implications for the health of the total economy. Because service industries are very labor-intensive compared with manufacturing, wage increases in the service sector of the economy have a significant impact on price levels and inflation. While wage increases in service industries have kept pace with, or even surpassed, those in manufacturing, productivity increases in service industries have lagged behind manufacturing.

Perhaps the key to increasing efficiency in service industries is for the management to adopt a "manufacturing attitude."[15] The concept of "providing a service" traditionally conjures visions of personal ministration and attendance on others. To improve performance meant simply to try harder, but essentially to continue performing a task in the same old way. In contrast, the concept of manufacturing (or efficiently producing) benefits or results enables us to focus on new performance methods, and to apply manufacturing technology, planning, and organization changes to the task at hand—but all this at a price of less humanism.

Four manufacturing concepts being applied in service industries to increase productivity are mechanization, assembly-line standardization, specialization, and organizational consolidation. The use of *mechanization* to implement hand labor has increased per-man output in laundry and dry cleaning, for example. Machines have increased service output in commercial dishwashing and floor sanding. Machines help auto repairmen to do more effective work. *Assembly-line* technology has proven fruitful in such diverse service fields as fast-food retailing (Kentucky Fried Chicken and McDonald's hamburgers) and mass physical examinations for corporations and labor unions, using mobile health units and automated test equipment.

---

[14]See "Services Grow while the Quality Shrinks," *Business Week,* Oct. 30, 1971, p. 50.
[15]Theodore Levitt, "Production-line Approach to Service," *Harvard Business Review,* September–October, 1972, pp. 41–52.

Several service firms have made labor more productive by *specialization* of effort. The medical field abounds with specialists. Auto repair firms specialize in brakes, transmissions, or mufflers. Even management consultants and firms in the advertising field have started to break their work forces into specialized elements in order to cut costs and increase efficiency. *Consolidation* as a means of improving productivity is being practiced when a major airline (TWA, United, Continental, American) adds hotels to its service mix, or when Manpower, Inc. (temporary workers) branches into travel agencies, home care for the elderly, income-tax preparation, day-care centers, and distribution of new-product samples. The development of chain organizations (Ramada Inn, Howard Johnson) is another useful form of consolidation in service firms. Finally, the advent of large product firms into service fields (see Fig. 24-3) is a type of organizational consolidation which should make for more efficient service performance.

PROSPECTS FOR GROWTH

There is every reason to believe that services will continue to take an increasing share of the consumer dollar, just as they have done generally over the past 25 years. This forecast seems reasonable even if we should experience periods of economic decline, for history shows that the demand for services is less sensitive to economic fluctuations than the demand for products. It also seems reasonable to expect that the demand for business services will continue to expand as business and industry become even more complex and as management increasingly recognizes its need for business-service specialists.

We should temper these optimistic forecasts with some caution, however, because there are forces both external and internal to service industries which potentially could limit growth in these fields.[16] Perhaps the most obvious external competitive factor is the customer's alternative of performing the services himself. Another growth deterrent comes from product manufacturers who produce (1) goods with built-in features replacing former reliance on service industries —wash-and-wear shirts instead of commercial laundry service, for example, or television sets which substitute for commercial entertainment—or (2) goods which help the consumer to perform the service himself, as in the case of home appliances, home hair permanent sets, etc. The expanding role of government services is becoming an increasingly significant external force to consider.

Internal barriers to future growth in service industries are (1) the small size of the average service firm; (2) the shortage of people with specialized skills—doctors, for instance; and (3) the limited competition in many service industries—transportation, medicine, communication, education. These barriers limit internal price competition and sometimes limit entry into the field. Perhaps the overriding internal growth deterrent is managerial deficiencies—the lack of creativity and marketing innovation, the little emphasis on research and development in many service fields, and the general failure to recognize the importance of marketing in any business.

One student of service marketing has posed the following series of five propositions supporting the forecasts for growth.[17]

---

[16]See Eugene M. Johnson, *Our Service Economy: Trends and Implications,* working paper published by Marketing Science Institute, Cambridge, Mass., 1968, pp. 38–57.
[17]Regan, "The Service Revolution," *op. cit.,* pp. 60–62.

1. We have exhausted much of the growth potential in domestic markets for goods, so manufacturers are turning to markets which are more difficult to serve but which have higher rates of return. These are markets where commodity-associated services provide utilitarian satisfactions to business and functional satisfactions to household consumers. Also, higher incomes and higher consumption levels will provide bigger markets for service industries such as medicine, education, travel, and research.

2. Mass-production techniques are being developed which will routinize services so they can be provided faster, more conveniently, and at lower unit costs for the mass markets. In this respect, we have seen how data-processing systems have been developed successfully for communications and information services. Language laboratories, teaching machines, and programmed learning systems are mechanizing the field of education services.

3. As a wider market is reached by means of technologies in service systems, we can expect a growing impersonalization of these services.

4. The impersonalized attention and substitution of manufactured equipment will encourage a reduction in the extrinsic values of a service, even though the intrinsic values may be the same or higher. In the medical field, for instance, technology may improve the accuracy of the diagnosis and the quality of the remedy (intrinsic essentials). The delivery of these services to more and more people will probably result in a decrease in the extrinsic elements such as abundant personal attention from the family doctor.

5. In the long run, however, we can expect a proliferation of services which are adaptable to a wide variety of tastes, just as the mass production of commodities has led to a diversity in product choice today.

QUESTIONS AND PROBLEMS

1. When defining services, from a marketing standpoint why is it useful to exclude the group of services (credit, delivery, training dealer salesmen, etc.) which exist only in connection with the sale of a product or another service?

2. How do you account for the substantial increase in expenditures for services relative to expenditures for products since the end of World War II?

3. What are some of the marketing implications in the fact that services possess the characteristic of intangibility?

4. Why are middlemen rarely used in the marketing programs of service firms?

5. Services are highly perishable and are often subject to fluctuations in demand. In marketing its services, how can a company offset these factors?

6. Cite some examples of service marketers who seem to be customer-oriented and describe what these firms have done in this vein.

7. "Traditionally, marketers of services have *not* been marketing-oriented." Do you agree? If so, how do you account for this deficiency?

8. Present a brief analysis of the market for each of the following services. Make use of the components of a market as discussed in Chapters 3 to 7.
   a. Laundry and dry-cleaning firm located in a shopping center adjoining your campus
   b. Four-bedroom house for rent at a major seashore resort
   c. Bowling alley
   d. Nursing home

9. What are some of the ways in which each of the following service firms might expand its line?
   a. Advertising agency
   b. Telephone company
   c. Automobile repair garage
10. Explain the importance of demand elasticity in the pricing of services.
11. "Personal selling should be the main ingredient in the promotional mix for a marketer of services." Do you agree? Discuss.
12. When athletic contests are televised, the area within 50 or 75 miles of the event is often "blacked out." When there is a sellout on seats for the event, should the blackout restriction be removed?
13. In what ways does the marketing of services differ from the marketing of products?

INTERNATIONAL MARKETING

"More than ever before, the economic future of the United States is vested in the marketing process—and future American progress will be determined largely by marketing management's success on the new frontier—the world market."[1] The president of a large manufacturer of business machines (Burroughs) concluded these remarks on our future economic growth with the observation that ". . . international marketing is the number-one problem of our time, the number-one challenge, and the number-one opportunity." While some people may believe that these are overstatements of the position of international marketing, we cannot deny the fact that multinational companies are evolving in our socioeconomic system, as firms integrate their domestic and foreign operations into world enterprises.

Basically, marketing fundamentals are universally applicable. Whether a firm sells in Toledo or Timbuktu, its marketing program should be built around a good product or service properly priced, promoted, and distributed to a market which has been carefully analyzed. We devote a separate chapter to international marketing, however, because there are considerable differences in the strategic and tactical implementation of marketing programs for foreign as against domestic markets. These modifications become necessary because of the environmental differences which exist between and within the many nations.

A company operates its marketing program within the economic, political, and

---

[1]Ray R. Eppert, "Passport for Marketing Overseas," *Journal of Marketing,* April, 1965, p. 6.

cultural environment of each of its markets—foreign and domestic—and none of these environments is controllable by the firm. Consequently, an executive should try to understand this environment and anticipate its effect on his marketing program. What complicates this task in international marketing is the fact that the environment—particularly the cultural environment—often consists of elements very unfamiliar to, and perhaps not even recognized by, the marketing executives.[2] Further, complicating the situation is the tendency for a person unconsciously to use his own cultural values as a frame of reference for solving problems centered in a foreign environment.

IMPORTANCE OF INTERNATIONAL MARKETING

Among companies in the United States, there seems to be a growing awareness of international marketing opportunities and an increasing willingness to enter foreign markets. As domestic markets become saturated, American producers—even those with no previous international experience—now look to foreign markets as outlets for surplus productive capacity, and as sources of wider profit margins and higher returns on investment.

The two rounds of devaluation of the U.S. dollar in the early 1970s, and the accompanying higher valuation of currencies in Japan and European countries, also served to make international marketing more attractive to U.S. firms. These revaluations generally decreased the price of U.S. products in foreign markets and increased the price of Japanese and European goods in the U.S. In the travel industry, for example, after the dollar devaluations there was a substantial increase in the number of Europeans who visited the United States. On the other hand, the currency revaluations plus substantial price increases in Europe presented some real financial barriers to Americans planning to travel in Europe.

The world market—huge and expanding—often offers greater growth and profit opportunities than the domestic market. The indication of continued increases in buying power, gross national product, and capital investment in many foreign nations makes it almost inevitable that these countries will constitute profitable growth markets (as well as strong competition) for many consumer and industrial products. During the decade of the 1960s, as just one example, the population of Western Europe increased only about 10 percent, while the overall gross national product went up 70 percent. The net result has been a rising standard of living and a larger potential market. Furthermore, from 1970 to 1980 the total output of goods and services (gross national product) in the United States is expected to increase about 60 percent, in comparison with projected growth rates of 70 percent in the European Common Market, 100 percent in Russia, and over 200 percent in Japan during this same decade.

Sales and profits in foreign markets are a significant part of the lifeblood of many American companies. Tables 25-1 and 25-2 show the percentage of total corporate sales and profits generated in foreign markets by some large U.S. firms. A more detailed financial analysis in many companies would show that foreign sales and profits are increasing at a more rapid rate than domestic sales and profits. Also, for

---

[2]For an expansion of this thesis and a more complete treatment of international marketing using the environmental approach, see Philip R. Cateora and John M. Hess, *International Marketing*, rev. ed., Richard D. Irwin, Inc., Homewood, Ill., 1971.

Table 25-1. Foreign sales as percentage of company total, 15 largest multinational firms, 1971.

Note the especially high percentage of foreign sales for European firms (Shell, Unilever, and British Petroleum).

Company	Total sales ($ billions)	Foreign sales (% of total)
General Motors	28.3	19
Exxon	18.7	50
Ford	16.4	26
Royal Dutch/Shell	12.7	79
General Electric	9.4	16
IBM	8.3	39
Mobil Oil	8.2	45
Chrysler	8.0	24
Texaco	7.5	40
Unilever (Britain-Netherlands)	7.5	80
ITT	7.3	42
Gulf Oil	5.9	45
British Petroleum	5.2	88
Philips Lamp (Netherlands)	5.2	NA
Standard Oil of California	5.1	45

NA = Not available.
Source: United Nations data, as reported in *Business Week,* Aug. 18, 1973, p. 26.

many firms, their foreign sales are more profitable than domestic business. That is, a dollar of foreign sales earns a higher percentage of profit. International marketing is a two-way street, however. The same expanding foreign markets which offer fine growth opportunities for American firms also have their own producers who, in turn, are providing substantial competition both in the United States and abroad.[3] See Table 25-3. American consumers have responded favorably, for example, to Japanese radio-TV products (Sony) and motorcycles (Honda), to Italian clothes, and autos (Fiat), to German cameras (Leica) and autos (Volkswagen), and to Dutch petroleum products (Shell) and electric razors (Norelco). Especially strong competition is coming from Japan and the countries in the European Economic Community (EEC), more popularly known as the European Common Market. This is a group of nine Western European nations (Belgium, France, Italy, Luxembourg, the Netherlands, West Germany, Great Britain, Ireland, and Denmark) which have banded together in a multinational economic union. Ultimately, tariffs and other trade barriers will be erected around it. Competitive challenges are also being encountered from the member units of other multinational economic organizations such as the Latin American Free Trade Association

[3]See "The New Competition from Foreign-Based Multinationals," *Business Week,* July 7, 1973, p. 56.

Table 25-2. Profits from foreign operations, as percentage of corporate totals, for selected U.S. companies.
If increases in fuel prices should undermine the economies of foreign countries, consider the effect on these multinational U.S. firms.

Company	Percent of earnings from foreign operations
Burroughs	41
Coca-Cola	55
Dow Chemical	48
Gillette	51
Hoover	60
IBM	54
International Flavors & Fragrances	52
Merck	44
NCR	53
Pfizer	57
Revlon	38
Richardson-Merrell	43
Rohm & Haas	33
G. D. Searle	40
Sperry Rand	50
Sunbeam	38
Xerox	46

Source: *Business Week,* Jan. 12, 1974, p. 53.

(LAFTA), and even the Council for Mutual Economic Assistance (COMECON)—Russia and other Communist European nations.

In summary, it seems likely that the factors of surplus productive capacity, shrinking domestic profit margins, and intensified foreign competition—added to the lure of rapidly expanding, attractive foreign markets—are combining to encourage (and even force) American firms to devote more effort to the vigorous development of their international marketing programs.

ALTERNATIVE ORIENTATIONS TOWARD INTERNATIONAL OPERATIONS

Four separate stages may be identified in the evolution of international operations in a firm, and each phase has its own set of managerial attitudes and philosophies.[4] These stages and their accompanying attitudes form a conceptual framework which may serve as a starting point for guiding a company in devel-

---

[4]This section is adapted from Yoram Wind, Susan P. Douglas, and Howard V. Perlmutter, "Guidelines for Developing International Marketing Strategies," *Journal of Marketing,* April, 1973, pp. 14–23; see also Howard V. Perlmutter, "The Tortuous Evolution of the Multinational Company," *Columbia Journal of World Business,* January–February, 1969, pp. 9–18.

Table 25-3. The 20 largest industrial companies outside the U.S., ranked by sales, 1973.
Lux soap, Shell gasoline, Mercedes and Datsun autos, and other names familiar to American consumers are in this list.

Rank Company	Country	Industry
1. Royal Dutch/Shell Group	Netherlands-Britain	Petroleum products, natural gas, chemicals
2. Unilever	Britain-Netherlands	Food, detergents, toiletries, feed
3. Philips Gloeilampenfabrieken	Netherlands	Electronics, electrical equip-ment, chemicals
4. British Petroleum	Britain	Petroleum products, chemicals
5. Nippon Steel	Japan	Iron, steel
6. Volkswagenwerk	Germany	Automobiles
7. Hitachi	Japan	Electrical equip., appliances, machinery
8. Farbwerke Hoechst	Germany	Chemicals, pharmaceuticals
9. Daimler-Benz	Germany	Automobiles
10. Toyota Motor	Japan	Automobiles
11. Siemens	Germany	Electrical equipment, electronics
12. BASF	Germany	Chemicals
13. ICI (Imperial Chemical Indus.)	Britain	Chemicals
14. Mitsubishi Heavy Industries	Japan	Machinery, shipbuilding, aircraft, autos
15. Nestlé	Switzerland	Food products
16. Nissan Motor	Japan	Automobiles, trucks
17. Renault	France	Automobiles, tractors, machine tools
18. Bayer	Germany	Chemicals
19. Montedison	Italy	Chem., syn. fibers, phar-maceuticals
20. Matsushita Electric Industrial	Japan	Electrical & electronic equip., appliances

Source: Fortune, August, 1974, p. 176.

oping its market strategies. The four stages are: ethnocentrism (home-country orientation), polycentrism (host-country orientation), regiocentrism (a regional orientation), and geocentrism (a world orientation).

In the *ethnocentric* stage, foreign operations are treated as secondary to domestic operations. Planning for foreign markets is done in the home office, using the same procedures as for domestic markets. Marketing personnel are primarily home-country nationals. The marketing mix follows domestic patterns. No major changes are made in the products sold abroad. In pricing, overseas distribution costs are simply added to home prices. Promotion and distribution strategies are essentially the same as at home. The sales force is hired and trained at home, and operates from a home-country base.

The ethnocentric position is likely to be adopted by a small company just entering the international market, or by a larger firm whose foreign sales are insignificant. For these companies, the cost of extensive foreign marketing research or the cost of tailoring products and marketing programs to specific foreign market requirements simply is not justified in terms of anticipated revenue.

In the *polycentric* stage, each foreign country is treated as a separate entity with its own autonomous subsidiary organization. Each of these foreign subsidiaries does its own marketing planning and research. Products are changed to meet local needs. Each subsidiary does its own pricing and promotion. Distribution is through channels and a sales force native to the country in question.

Today most international executives probably view the polycentric position as the most desirable one. In marketing, even more so than in finance or production, it is so important to adapt to country-by-country differences, and to use local nationals of the country in doing a marketing job. Polycentrism, however, is likely to lead to problems of coordinating and controlling the marketing activities among the several countries.

In the *regiocentric* and *geocentric* stages, a given region or the entire world is treated as a single market, regardless of national boundaries. Marketing plans and programs are set for the entire region, or the world. Personnel can come from anywhere. Standardized products are used throughout the entire market—region or world. Channels and promotion are developed on a regional or global basis to project a uniform image of the company and its products.

A regiocentric approach is probably more economical and manageable than a worldwide program. From a practical point of view, however, national environmental constraints (laws, currencies, culture, life-styles, etc.) may severly limit either one of these broad marketing approaches.

STRUCTURE FOR OPERATING IN FOREIGN MARKETS

Once a company has decided to market in foreign countries, management must select a method or organizational structure for operating in those markets. There are four separately identifiable methods of marketing entry, each successively representing an increased international involvement, leading ultimately to a truly multinational firm. These alternatives reflect, and parallel to some extent, the philosophies expressed in the conceptual framework discussed in the preceding section.

A company may progress from one method to another, or management may bypass some stages. The same firm may be using several operating methods at the same time. To illustrate: depending upon a company's familiarity with a given foreign market, the maturity of economic development in the foreign nation, and the country's political stability, this company may export products to one country, establish a licensing arrangement in another, and build a manufacturing plant in a third.

The simplest way of operating in foreign markets is by *exporting through foreign trade agent middlemen.* Management's effort in the exporting venture may be somewhat sporadic—up when there are excess inventory stocks to be marketed, and down when the domestic market can assimilate the manufacturing output. The company may establish the position of export manager, and he will use various export-import middlemen to reach the foreign markets; or the domestic sales manager may be assigned the responsibility of contacting these foreign trade middlemen. At this point, very little risk or investment is required. Also, little time or effort is required on the part of the exporting producer. On the other hand, the exporter must pay tariffs, and he has little or no control over his agent middlemen. Furthermore, these middlemen are generally not aggressive marketers, and normally they do not generate a large sales volume.

To counteract some of these deficiencies, management will move to the second stage—*exporting through company sales branches* or other sales subsidiaries located in foreign markets. Bypassing the export-import agent middlemen enables a company to promote its products more aggressively, to develop its foreign markets more effectively, and to control its sales effort more completely. Of course, the firm is still exporting, with the attendant drawbacks. Also, management now has the time- and money-consuming task of selecting, training, and otherwise managing a sales force of (1) foreign nationals unfamiliar with the product and the company's marketing practices or (2) American middlemen unfamiliar with the market.

As foreign markets expand and as our company gains experience in international marketing, management may enter *licensing* arrangements, whereby foreign manufacturers are authorized to produce the articles. To distribute this foreign-produced output, the company may still rely on foreign trade middlemen, or the company's own sales branches may be established in major foreign markets.

Licensing offers a manufacturer a flexible arrangement with a minimum investment whereby he can still enjoy the advantages of his patents, research, and know-how. Through licensing, he can enter a market which might otherwise be closed to him as an exporter because of exchange restrictions, import quotas, or prohibitive tariffs. At the same time, by licensing, a manufacturer may be building a future competitor who will learn all he can from the manufacturer and then proceed independently when the licensing agreement expires.

In the fourth method, the company builds or otherwise acquires its own production facilities in foreign countries. The structure may be a *joint venture or a wholly owned foreign subsidiary*. A joint venture is a partnership arrangement where the foreign manufacturing or marketing operation is owned in part by the American company and in part by the local nationals (company or individuals) of the foreign country involved. Share of foreign ownership may be any percentage—more than, less than, or exactly 50 percent. Obviously, when controlling interest in a joint venture is owned by the foreign nationals, the American firm has no real control over any of the marketing or production activities. Decision-making authority accompanies ownership control. At the same time, a joint venture may be the only structure (other than licensing) through which an American firm can enter a given foreign market. Nationalistic tendencies in the form of exchange restrictions, tariffs, or plain political exclusion of foreign-owned companies may preclude any operation other than a joint venture or one in which there is a licensing arrangement.

Wholly owned manufacturing and marketing subsidiaries in foreign markets are commonly found in companies which have evolved to an advanced stage of international business. Even then, however, this international division is typically still separate from, and second in importance to, the domestic operations. With a wholly owned foreign subsidiary, a company has maximum control over its marketing program and production operations. This type of international structure, however, requires a substantial investment of money, manpower, and managerial attention. Thus, a large-volume operation is usually needed to justify the investment. As noted earlier, nationalistic tendencies on the part of foreign governments may preclude this type of structure. Also, organizational problems may arise when there is an attempt to coordinate the international and domestic divisions.

This leads us to the final evolutionary stage—and one reached by very few companies as yet—the emergence of the truly *world enterprise.* Both foreign and domestic operations are integrated and no longer separately identified. In this type of multinational venture, one plant may be in Bombay, a second in Brussels, and a third in Boston. The regional sales office in Atlanta is basically the same as the one in Athens (Greece, not Georgia or Ohio).

PROBLEMS IN DEVELOPING AN INTERNATIONAL COMPANY

A company faces significantly greater risks when it sets up an international marketing organization than it does when this task is performed at home. In the domestic market, company management is usually more familiar with the environment—and politically and economically this environment is usually more stable. Executives are acquainted with the institutional structure for distribution. Their experience is an aid in forecasting competitive strategies. And their marketing intelligence provides a relatively high level of knowledge concerning consumer motives and habits.

EXTERNAL PROBLEM CONDITIONS

Aspects of *exchange controls* and *other currency regulations* constitute a major problem to consider when expanding into a foreign market. Many nations set limits on the amount of earned or invested funds which may be withdrawn from the country. These exchange controls may be established because the country has a balance-of-payments problem or a shortage of foreign exchange. Limits may also be set in order to prevent the flight of domestic capital, to protect local industry, or to aid in the socialization of the economy.

Tariffs, import quotas, and other import restrictions are another problem area hindering international business. While these limits are established to stimulate national self-sufficiency and to encourage the development of domestic enterprise, the net result is still a significant obstacle to transnational operations. In some countries, the *political uncertainty* occasioned by social unrest, forthcoming elections, recent or impending independence, extreme programs, and even armed conflict is a deterrent. Sometimes high tax levels, tax discrimination, or other *unsatisfactory tax conditions* in a country will discourage foreign business activity. Another impediment is some form of *restriction on foreign companies and/or personnel.* Perhaps a nation requires that executives and other personnel of a foreign firm operating within the country be local citizens or that majority ownership be held by nationals of the country. *Labor problems* —strong unions, shortages of qualified personnel, required profit sharing, limits on a firm's authority to reduce the work force by layoffs—all act as an obstacle to foreign expansion.

Counterfeiting of products is a hazard faced by U.S. firms in some countries. Pirated copies of Levi's jeans are produced in more than 25 foreign countries. In Asia, Colgate toothpaste competes with Coalgate, Goalgate, Goldkey, and Goldcat brands.[5] *Archaic distribution systems* plague American marketing programs in many foreign markets. Even in Japan, for example, where the manufacturing system has achieved high levels of efficiency, some Japanese businessmen admit that some of their distribution systems have changed very little over several centuries.[6]

INTERNAL MANAGEMENT PROBLEMS

Notwithstanding these substantial external roadblocks, companies may experience a greater incidence of *internal* rather than external, problems in the management of an international business. One major internal problem is *orientation,* that is, the problem of getting the top executives to manage the firm as a single, integrated world enterprise rather than thinking in terms of a domestic company with a separate international division. *Organization* is a second, and perhaps corollary, problem area. Organizational difficulties arise when the international division is appended to the domestic operations, instead of the two being integrated. When established separately, the international operation tends to be isolated, and top management accords it stepchild status. This leads to another problem—*staffing.* Failure to organize as an integrated world company leads to a failure to develop truly international executives. To an important extent, the success of an international company will depend upon the type of people selected as marketing executives.[7] Another staffing consideration is the difficulty of selecting and training foreign nationals for executive and lower-level jobs. Finally, in the area of managerial control, questions arise as to whether *control* of operations should be centralized in corporate headquarters or whether, and to what extent, it should be vested in decentralized foreign locations. Perhaps the best course is an "interactive" approach to marketing planning, rather than either an ethnocentric or polycentric stance.[8] In an interactive approach, foreign subsidiaries would be responsible for marketing, production, and personnel activities related to unique factors in each national market. Headquarters staff at regional or world levels would be responsible for strategic planning, financial control, and the coordination of product, pricing, and promotional programs.

DEVELOPING AN INTERNATIONAL MARKETING PROGRAM

Firms which have been eminently successful in marketing in the United States have no assurance whatsoever that the same pattern will be duplicated in foreign markets. A key to satisfactory performance overseas lies in gauging which aspects of American marketing techniques should be retained, which ones adapted, and which ones abandoned in foreign markets.

---

[5]"Why a Global Market Doesn't Exist," *Business Week,* Dec. 19, 1970, p. 144.

[6]"Japan's Remarkable Industrial Machine," *Business Week,* Mar. 7, 1970, p. 73.

[7]For a report showing that, except for the president, the marketing executive is the most influential man in today's European firm, see *European Top Management Comparison Report,* American Management Association, New York, 1969, as reported in *Sales Management,* Oct. 1, 1969, p. 36.

[8]Warren J. Keegan, "Multinational Marketing: The Headquarters Role," *Columbia Journal of World Business,* January–February, 1971, pp. 85–90.

One analysis of the experiences of American firms successful in multinational marketing identified some basic concepts around which these companies built their marketing programs.[9] First, outstanding marketers have learned to export their approach to decision making—their analytical marketing techniques—rather than their domestic marketing practices. The ability to identify a problem, analyze it, and select the best alternative is the American firm's differential advantage. A specific marketing practice may be useless abroad, but the analytical technique for developing this practice is universally exportable. The successful marketer also realizes that foreign countries, and even sections within a country, usually have environmental and cultural differences which can affect virtually every aspect of his marketing program. Finally, a successful company is sensitive to the differences in its competitive position at home and abroad, and will change its marketing strategies accordingly. A company which enjoys 30 percent of the American market for a product will need a different marketing program in a foreign country where it is fighting for a 3 percent share of the market.

INTERNATIONAL MARKETING RESEARCH

As important as a marketing information system may be in the domestic market, it would seem to be even more essential in foreign markets because the risks are so much greater. Actual practice is to the contrary, however. Only limited facilities and modest funds are invested in marketing research in foreign countries as compared with expenditures in the United States. The several reasons advanced to account for this disparity can perhaps be distilled into one basic point. Because of the differences in the problems encountered in foreign as against domestic marketing research, the costs relative to the value received are greater abroad than at home. Consider just two illustrations of this point. Each of the many heterogeneous foreign markets is usually quite a bit smaller than the domestic market. Yet, when conducting a research study which involves sampling in these smaller markets, the sample size needed to ensure statistical validity and reliability does not decrease in proportion to the market size. Consequently, the cost of the research project, relative to market size, is greater for the smaller markets. As another example, consider the many types of market information (population, buying power, weather data, etc.) which are readily and inexpensively available in the United States, but which must be collected at some cost in each foreign market.

The extent of use of foreign marketing research and the nature of the facilities seem to vary somewhat in relation to the level of economic development achieved in the country. Apparently, marketing research is used very little in underdeveloped countries, whereas considerable and sometimes very sophisticated use is made of this tool in countries with advanced economies.[10]

---

[9]*International Enterprise: A New Dimension of American Business,* McKinsey & Company, Inc., New York, 1962, pp. 18–19.

[10]For some of the difficulties in applying research techniques in less-developed countries, see Roman R. Andrus, "Marketing Research in a Developing Nation—Taiwan: A Case Example," *University of Washington Business Review,* Spring, 1969, pp. 40–44; and Harper W. Boyd, Jr., Ronald E. Frank, William F. Massy, and Mostafa Zoheir, "On the Use of Marketing Research in the Emerging Economies," *Journal of Marketing Research,* November, 1964, pp. 20–23. See Reed Moyer, "International Market Analysis," *Journal of Marketing Research,* November, 1968,

To understand the problems of research in international marketing, an executive should try to understand how the environmental conditions in each foreign market affect the following four basic elements of research: systematic analysis, customer information, statistical data, and operational economy.[11] Fundamental to marketing research is the idea that problems should be solved in a *systematic, analytical manner.* Unfortunately, an orderly, rational approach runs counter to the instincts of most people throughout the world. In many parts of the world, the cultural personality—tempered by aspects of religion and education—is such that people are guided by intuition, emotional reaction, or tradition. None of these is particularly conducive to the scientific approach. A second and related element in marketing research—*customer information*—is dependent upon the ability and willingness of people to respond accurately and completely when researchers pose questions involving attitudes, buying habits, motives, etc. In many foreign societies, the suspicion of strangers, the distrust of government, and the individualistic personality which believes these things are "none of your business" all serve to compound the problems of gathering information.

The scarcity of *reliable statistical data* may be the single biggest problem in some foreign markets.[12] Figures on population, personal income, and production may be only crude estimates. Few studies have been made on such things as buying habits or media coverage. In the design of a research project, the lack of reliable data makes it very difficult to set up a meaningful sample. Lack of uniformity makes intercountry comparisons very unreliable. The element of *operational economy* was mentioned earlier as a partial explanation of why less money is spent on foreign than domestic marketing research.[13]

ANALYSIS OF FOREIGN MARKETS

Nowhere in a company's total marketing program is the influence of the cultural and economic environment seen more clearly than in the analysis of consumer and industrial market demand. Market demand in all countries is determined by population, economic ability to buy, and buying behavior—motives and habits. Also, human wants and needs have a basic universal similarity. People need food, clothing, and shelter. They seek a better life in terms of lighter work loads, more leisure time, social recognition and acceptance, etc. But at about this point, the similarities in foreign and domestic markets end. Furthermore, significant differ-

pp. 353–360, for some quantitative techniques for estimating present and future market demand in underdeveloped countries.

For a picture at the other end of the scale, see Edward L. Brink, "The State of Marketing Intelligence in the United Kingdom," in Peter D. Bennett (ed.), *Marketing and Economic Development,* American Marketing Association, Chicago, 1965, pp. 72–78.

[11]John Fayerweather, *International Marketing,* 2d ed., Prentice-Hall, Inc., Englewood Cliffs, N.J., 1970, pp. 90–93.

[12]For sources of secondary data on foreign markets, see Cateora and Hess, *op. cit.,* pp. 653–657; and Gordon E. Miracle and Gerald Albaum, *International Marketing Management,* Richard D. Irwin, Inc., Homewood, Ill., 1970, pp. 225–234.

[13]For a model of a proposed international business information system, see J. Alex Murray, "An Inquiry into International Business Intelligence Systems," in Boris W. Becker and Helmut Becker (eds.), 1972 *Combined Proceedings,* American Marketing Association, series no. 34, Chicago, 1973, pp. 249–256; also see J. S. Downham, "Marketing Research in a Multinational Corporation (Unilever)," in Becker and Becker (eds.), *ibid.,* pp. 179–182.

ences exist between and within foreign countries, thus forcing us to segment and define each market carefully.

A cosmetics firm selling in a Latin-American country, for example, may segment its market by upper-, lower-, and middle-income groups and by urban and rural areas. The same marketing program will not reach each segment because these markets have different potentials and characteristics. The upper-income class wants high-grade products sold through exclusive stores and advertised in high-quality newspapers. In rural markets, the products must be inexpensive. There may even be a need to promote primary demand because cosmetics are not fully accepted in this market.

When analyzing the economic ability to buy on the part of consumers in a given foreign market, management may first study the broad measures such as gross national product or per capita national income. Three other economic factors which perhaps are more meaningful in each market are (1) distribution of income, (2) rate of growth of buying power, and (3) extent of available consumer financing. Large portions of the population in the emerging economies have very low incomes. A much different income-distribution pattern—with resulting differences in marketing programs—is found in the industrialized markets of Western Europe, where there are large groups of working classes and a burgeoning middle-income market. Thus, many of the products commonly in demand in Belgium or the Netherlands would find very small markets in some African or Asian countries. See Fig 25-1. Japan, of course, is an exception in Asia. Rising incomes in Japan have generated huge markets in pursuit of travel, bowling, skiing, golf, and other leisure-time activities. In response, shops in London, Paris, and Rome display window signs indicating that "Japanese is spoken here."[14]

An understanding of the cultural environment in a given market will, in turn, help in understanding the buying motives and habits of consumers in that market. Some of the cultural elements to identify and to analyze for their effect on a firm's marketing program include (1) the family system, (2) other social groups and institutions, (3) the educational system, (4) the language, and (5) the religious system.[15] A country where the *family* is a close-knit unit will attract a different type of advertising campaign from the one appropriate in a society where the family members more frequently come and go independently, and it will constitute a market for different products. In India and other cultures where parents often arrange the marriages of their children, marketing programs are different from those in the United States and other countries where youths are free to find and select their own mates. Examples of the cultural differences in *social groups and institutions* in Japan and other countries are shown in Fig. 25-2 and 25-3.

The *educational system* affects the literacy rate, which in turn influences advertising, branding, and labeling. The brand may become all-important if the potential consumers cannot read and so must recognize the article by the picture on the

---

[14] See "The Frantic Race for a Leisurely Life," *Business Week,* Aug. 1, 1970, p. 28.
[15] See Maneck S. Wadia, "The Concept of Culture," *Journal of Retailing,* Spring, 1965, pp. 21–29ff.; Montrose Sommers and Jerome Kernan, "Why Some Products Flourish Here, Fizzle There," *Columbia Journal of World Business,* March–April 1967, pp. 89–97; Yoram Wind, "Cross-cultural Analysis of Consumer Behavior," in Reed Moyer (ed.), *Changing Marketing Systems,* American Marketing Association, Chicago, 1968, pp. 183–185; and Cateora and Hess, *op. cit.,* chap. 4, "Cultural Dynamics in Assessing World Markets."

EUROPE'S SPENDING SPREE

In the 1960s and 1970s Western Europeans were spending like Americans did in the late 1940s and 1950s. Some of the results (in percentage of family ownership):

Household appliances: electric irons (81%), refrigerators (72%), washing machines (57%).

Leisure time increased; so did television sets (75%).

Buying power brought mobility: autos (47%) and portable radios (54%).

Households in the original Common Market countries spent more heavily on laborsaving devices, while families in places like Austria, Portugal, Sweden, Norway, and Switzerland showed higher ownership of products linked with affluence and leisure time.

About half the families own their own home in Sweden, Denmark, Luxembourg, France, and Norway.

Buying power is not evenly distributed among the nations; median family income in Scandinavia and Switzerland is six times greater than in Portugal.

Figure 25-1. *Source:* Based on "A Survey of Europe Today" by *Reader's Digest* magazine as reported in *Sales Management,* Mar. 15, 1971, p. 28.

label. *Language differences,* too, pose problems. Literal translations of American advertising copy or brand names may result in ridicule of, or even enmity toward, American products. Even some English words have different meanings in England, Australia, and the United States. See Fig. 25-4. The *religion* in a country has a tremendous influence on the value systems and behavioral patterns of consumers. In countries where the Protestant ethic (hard work and frugal living) is prevalent, we find less of a market for laborsaving devices and prepared cake mixes. Moslems disapprove of liquor, and Hindus de-emphasize material goods.

A few examples may illustrate how buying habits are influenced by cultural elements. One-stop shopping is unknown in most parts of the world. In many foreign markets people buy in small units, sometimes literally on a meal-to-meal basis. Also, they buy in small specialty stores. To buy food for a weekend, a housewife in West Germany will visit the chocolate store, the dairy store, the meat market, the fish market, a dry grocery store, the greengrocer, the bakery, the coffee market, and possibly some other specialty food stores. While this may seem to be an inefficient use of time, we must recognize that a shopping trip to that housewife is more than just a chore to be done as fast as possible. To her it is a major part of her social life. She will visit with her friends and neighbors in these shops. Shopping in this fashion is simply a foreign version of the American woman's bridge club or neighborhood coffee break. Only in recent years in some Western European countries have we seen the advent of the supermarket. Another buying habit to contend with in many foreign markets is the absence of the one-price system. Consumers expect to haggle and bargain over each purchase. It is a way of life which must be acknowledged in a marketing program.

Often the question of "who buys" is related to the cultural factors in a market. In many Moslem countries, wives are kept in seclusion, and yet they play a major role

FOR THE TRAVELING EXECUTIVE—
THOSE UNWRITTEN SOCIAL RULES REGARDING:

TIME

South Africans expect on-the-dot promptness; the unawareness of time in
some tropical countries is legendary.

Japanese may excuse tardiness for a business meeting but expect promptness at a social event; Swedish executives expect you to show up on
time for either business or social meetings.

Businessmen in Yugoslavia routinely schedule appointments at 7 A.M.; in
Mexico City a foreign visitor may be received at 10 P.M.

SPACE

Arabs, when relaxed and confidential, get very close to the persons they are
talking to; Japanese prefer to keep more distance between themselves
and visitors.

Handshakes are not customary in some foreign countries, especially with
women.

MANNERS

A Swedish executive likes plenty of notice (about 3 weeks) when a visit is
forthcoming.

In Southeast Asia it is a mark of disrespect to sit with legs crossed so the
bottom of a foot is showing.

The U.S. custom of having family photos on the desk is rarely practiced in
foreign countries.

Figure 25-2. *Source: Fortune,* January, 1971, p. 52.

JAPANESE BEHAVIORAL CHARACTERISTICS THAT INFLUENCE
NEGOTIATIONS WITH U.S. EXECUTIVES

THE JAPANESE:

1. Possess greater emotional sensitivity than do Americans.
2. Hide their emotions, but their feelings about a person are important in business dealings.
3. Dislike the bold use of raw power; they are more discreet.
4. Trait of *amaeru* (longing to be looked after and protected), and
   the resultant lifetime employment system, affects personnel
   relations.
5. Prefer to work as members of a group, not individually.
6. May take a long time to make a decision.
7. Believe very much in "saving face."
8. Go out of their way to avoid directly saying "no" to a person.
9. Place great value on friendship.
10. Are very reluctant to argue or retort when challenged, even when
    they feel they are right.

Figure 25-3. *Source:* Howard F. VanLandt, "How to Negotiate in Japan," *Harvard Business Review,* November–December, 1970, pp. 45–56.

MARKETING PROBLEMS ARE CREATED
BY CULTURAL DIFFERENCES IN:

LANGUAGE

Is Chevrolet's Nova a good brand name? In Spanish, *no va* means "it doesn't go."

In German, 3M's "Scotch" tape becomes "Scotch" schmuck.

In Japanese, General Motors' "Body by Fisher" translates as "Corpse by Fisher," and 3M's slogan "Sticks like Crazy" comes out "Sticks Foolishly."

COLOR

In Malaysia, a green-colored product suggested illness.

Blue is considered feminine and warm in Holland, but in Sweden that color is associated with masculinity and coldness.

In Germany, consumers said a new menthol cigarette in a brown package tasted much better than the same product in a blue package.

White indicates mourning in China and Korea.

Red is popular in China, but not in some African countries.

DESIGN PREFERENCES

In Britain, products like Jell-O are preferred in solid-wafer or cake form.

Germans usually buy salad dressing in tubes.

Most of the industrialized countries outside the United States employ the metric system for measurements.

Figure 25-4.

in managing the family's economic life. In other countries where women enjoy freedom and liberties not available to Moslem women, the men of the house may make the buying decisions. In still other foreign markets the buying is done by servants. Each situation requires a different approach to the person who buys.

In this chapter, we have stressed the point that significant environmental differences exist between and within foreign countries. Perhaps we have overstressed this point or at least have neglected to note a countervailing development. On the horizon we can see a trend toward standardization of tastes, wants, and habits, expecially in the Western European countries. Travel, television, and trade are proving to be effective homogenizers of European culture. Signs indicate that European consumers are developing into a mass market. Now let us be sure we understand this situation. A German is still a German, a Swede knows he is still a Swede, etc. In Europe's uncommon market, there is no such thing as a Mr. and Mrs. European—yet. The *Reader's Digest* survey (see Fig. 25-1) showed that the British watch more TV, buy more life insurance, eat more canned food, and use more soap than any other Europeans. German teen-agers drink more Coca-Cola than any other country's teen-agers. People from Sweden and Luxembourg go abroad for their holidays, while most Britons stay home.

However, while the cultural differences are still very much present, the old order is changing, and we can see increasingly cosmopolitan demands. Pizzerias do business in Germany, lasagna is sold in a Stockholm supermarket, British fish-and-chips are wanted on the Continent, and whiskey sales are large in France.

People from many countries have a common demand for better housing, cars, appliances, and opportunities to travel. An alert marketing executive should certainly watch this developing "Americanization of tastes."[16]

PRODUCT PLANNING FOR INTERNATIONAL MARKETS

Most companies would not think of entering a domestic market without careful and often extensive product planning. Yet typically an American firm enters a foreign market with essentially the same product it sells in the United States. Even when a product is changed expressly for an international market, the modification is apt to be minor—converting an appliance to 220-volt electrical systems, or painting and packaging the product to protect it against the destructive tropical climate and insects, for example.[17]

One key to success in product planning has a familiar ring—that is, adapt to the cultural tastes and economic characteristics of the particular foreign market, rather than try to sell the American-market product abroad. In Europe, a 6-cubic-foot refrigerator is the most popular size, in contrast to the larger units preferred in the United States. While the cost difference is a factor, the basic reasons for the Europeans' choice lie in the cultural behavior patterns of the consumers. As noted earlier, to many European housewives a food-shopping trip is a social event. They go daily and thus do not buy large quantities which must be stored for a few days in a refrigerator. Also, if they have no car, they walk to the store and cannot carry large quantities. As yet, frozen foods are not purchased to any extent, so large freezer space for storage is not needed.

Warren Keegan has identified five alternative strategies for adapting a product and its related marketing communications to a foreign market.[18] The first of these strategies is *one product, one message—world wide.* Pepsi-Cola and Coca-Cola have used this alternative successfully, but on balance there probably are more market failures than successes with this approach. When Campbell's tried to market its U.S. tomato soup to the British, this introduction was not successful because the English prefer a soup with a more bitter taste. Problems with consumer preferences can also occur when entering the U.S. market. When Corn Products Company introduced Knorr dry soups (popular in Europe) into the U.S., the move was a failure because Americans did not want to take the 15 to 20 minutes to cook the soup.[19]

---

[16]For a brief report on the "Westernizing" of two Eastern European countries—Yugoslavia and Romania, see Arthur A. Benson, "Letter from Eastern Europe," *Sales Management,* Sept. 1, 1971, p. 42; in this context "Westernizing" means more consumer goods, improved channels of distribution, and modernized retailing.

[17]For a promising approach to international trade which is closely related to the product-life-cycle concept, see Louis T. Wells, Jr., "A Product Life Cycle for International Trade?" *Journal of Marketing,* July, 1968, pp. 1–6. For many products the following four-stage "trade cycle" may be identified: (1) the United States is an exporter, (2) foreign production starts, (3) foreign production is competitive in export markets, and (4) the United States faces import competition.

[18]The discussion of these strategies is adapted from Warren J. Keegan, "Multinational Product Planning: Strategic Alternatives," *Journal of Marketing,* January, 1969, pp. 58–62.

[19]For a report on U.S. consumers' reactions to another set of imported products, see Ralph Gaedeke, "Consumer Attitudes toward Products 'Made In' Developing Countries," *Journal of Retailing,* Summer, 1973, pp. 13–24.

The second strategy, *same product, but modified communications,* is practical when the same product can be used to fill different needs in foreign markets. The same outboard motors used for recreation in the U.S. may be used for commercial fishing or transportation abroad. In this instance, the advertising copy would be quite different in the various countries, depending upon the product use being promoted.

Under the third strategy, *product adaptation–communications extension,* the marketer uses essentially the same promotional messages abroad as at home, but the product is changed to meet local conditions. To illustrate, a soap formula is changed to adapt to local water conditions. Chemical fertilizers are altered to fit soil conditions. Voltage requirements alter appliances, and climatic factors make for packaging changes.

The fourth strategy, *dual adaptation,* involves changes in both the product and the message—in effect a combination of the second and third alternatives.

The fifth strategy is *product invention* wherein a company develops a new product in response to foreign market demands. For markets with low buying power, one firm "invented backwards" by developing an inexpensive, hand-operated washing machine with the tumbling action of an automatic machine.

Often in a foreign-market product-planning situation, a company is faced with this problem: Can we afford to modify the design, quality, or some other feature of our product. That is, will the demand offset the additional costs of producing and marketing the modified products? Answers to these questions are not easy to come by. Sometimes management can compromise by making a relatively inexpensive change, such as selling pharmaceuticals by the individual capsule or packaging razor blades singly rather than in multiple units.

Branding is especially important in foreign marketing. As suggested above, the brand picture may be the only part of the product that a consumer can recognize. Foreign consumers' preference for American products often overcomes their nationalistic feelings, so in many instances a company can use the same brand that is used in the domestic market. The legal aspects of brand registration and ownership in foreign countries may create problems. In some nations, a local firm or person may "pirate" an American brand name and thus block its use by the American company in that foreign country.

PRICING IN INTERNATIONAL MARKETS

In earlier chapters, we recognized that determining a basic price and establishing various pricing policies are complex tasks, often involving trial-and-error decision making. These tasks become even more complex in international marketing because management must contend with additional variables such as currency conversion problems, a myriad of possible bases for price quotations, and often a lack of knowledge or control of middlemen's pricing. The principles and methods of price determination in multinational marketing are quite similar to those discussed in Chapters 11 to 14.

Cost-plus pricing is probably used to a greater extent in export marketing than at home. The cost-plus approach, coupled with additional cost factors not found in the domestic market (tariffs, shipping costs, larger margins for middlemen, etc.), can result in some startling differences between foreign and domestic prices on the same article. An example of this "price escalation" is shown in Table 25-4. Some manufacturers try to reduce these differentials by (1) accepting a lower net price on

Table 25-4. Causes and effects of price escalation.

The price paid by the foreign consumer at retail can greatly exceed the manufacturer's net when we use cost-plus pricing and include the many extra costs to be covered in international marketing. Why is the retail price in example 4 ($4.79) so much higher than the $2.58 price in example 1?

	Domestic example	Foreign example 1: assuming the same channels with wholesaler importing directly	Foreign example 2: importer and same margins and channels	Foreign example 3: same as 2, but with 10 percent cumulative turnover tax	Foreign example 4: long channels, larger retail margins, no turnover tax
Mfg. net	$ .95	$ .95	$ .95	$ .95	$ .95
Transport, c.i.f.	x	.15	.15	.15	.15
Tariff (20%)	x	.19	.19	.19	.19
Importer pays	x	x	1.29	1.29	1.29
Importer margin when sold to wholesaler (25% on cost)	x	x	.32	.32 +.13 turnover tax	.32
Wholesaler pays landed cost	.95	1.29	1.61	1.74 .58	1.61
Wholesaler margin (33⅓% on cost)	.32	.43	.54	+.17 turnover tax .54	.54
Local foreign jobber pays jobber	x	x	x	x	2.15
Jobber margin (33⅓% on cost)	x	x	x	x	.72
Retailer pays	1.27	1.72	2.15	2.49 1.25	2.87
Retail margin (50% on cost)	.63	.86	1.08	+.25 turnover tax	1.92 (66⅔% on cost)
Retail price	$1.90	$2.58	$3.23	$3.99	$4.79

Note: (1) All figures in United States dollars; (2) x means this cost is not applicable in this example; (3) the exhibit assumes that all domestic transportation is absorbed by the middleman; (4) transportation, tariffs, and middleman margins vary from country to country, but for purposes of comparison only a few of the possible variations are shown.

Source: Philip R. Cateora and John M. Hess, *International Marketing*, rev. ed., Richard D. Irwin, Inc., Homewood, Ill., 1971. p. 678.

exported goods, (2) establishing overseas manufacturing operations to escape tariffs, (3) modifying the product to get it into a lower tariff classification, or (4) eliminating some of the middlemen in the trade channels.[20]

Sometimes a firm's foreign price may be *lower* than its domestic price. The price may be lowered in order to meet foreign competition, to dispose of outmoded products, or to remove supply from the home market and thus preserve the home-market structure. Sometimes governments engage in the practice of "dumping." That is, government action supports the domestic price at a level above the international market price. Then when these products are exported, they are sold below the domestic price. Through the years the surplus production of several raw materials has led to government control of world market prices. Individual governments have tried to stabilize the prices of coffee, nitrates, sugar, and rubber. Also, governments of several countries have established joint agreements covering the price of such commodities as tin, potash, cocoa, and wheat.

Foreign middlemen often are not aggressive in their pricing policies and strategies. They prefer to maintain high unit margins at the expense of low sales volume, rather than develop large sales volume by means of lower prices and smaller margins per unit sold. In fact, there is considerable rigidity in price structures in many foreign markets. In some cases, inflexibility stems from the combinations of firms which tend to restrain independent action in pricing and other marketing activities. The rigidity is sometimes engendered by price-control legislation which prevents retailers from cutting prices substantially and at their own discretion. American producers should be aware that combinations among manufacturers and middlemen are tolerated to a far greater extent in many foreign countries than in the United States, even when the avowed purpose of the combinations is to restrain trade and reduce competition. Recognizing this, Congress passed the Webb-Pomerene Act in 1918, allowing American firms to join in a trade combination in a foreign country without being charged with a violation of the American antitrust laws. Probably the best known of these international marketing combinations is the cartel. A *cartel* is a group of companies which produce similar products and which have combined to restrain competition in manufacturing and marketing. Cartels exist to varying degrees in steel, aluminum, fertilizers, electrical products, petroleum products, rayon, dyes, and sulfur. Originally they were formed to regulate competition in industries faced with conditions of chronic overproduction. Later they expanded their activities to include maintaining prices, setting up sales territories, establishing uniform documents, and even doing centralized selling.

Another area of pricing practices peculiar to foreign trade relates to aspects of price quotations. With respect to shipping, insurance, and related export charges, three bases of price quotations used extensively in foreign trade are f.o.b., f.a.s., and c.i.f. When a shipment is priced f.o.b. (free on board), the f.o.b. point is usually the inland point of departure of the port of shipment. When a shipment is priced f.a.s. (free alongside ship, at port of export), the seller pays all charges to deliver the goods to the dock within reach of the ship's tackle, but not on board. All shipping activities, costs, and risks from that point are the responsibility of the buyer. Under a price quotation of c.i.f. (cost, insurance, freight) at a given point of destination, the seller pays all costs up to the arrival of the shipment at the foreign port.

---

[20]Cateora and Hess, *op. cit.,* pp. 679–680.

Prices may be quoted in United States dollars or in the currency of the foreign buyer. Here we become involved in problems of foreign exchange and conversion of currencies. When prices are quoted in United States dollars, exchange controls by foreign governments may impede the conversion of foreign currency to dollars, thus delaying the collection of invoices. As a general rule, a firm engaged in foreign trade—whether it is buying or selling, exporting or importing—prefers to have the price quoted in its own national currency. Risks from fluctuations in foreign exchange—that is, devaluation of the currency of the other country—then are shifted to the other party in the transaction. In addition, an importer can readily determine his resale price, compute his profits, and compare offerings from sellers in different countries. Sometimes a foreign importer will prefer to have the price quoted in the currency of the exporting nation if he sees an opportunity to speculate profitably in exchange fluctuations, or if he thinks that he can buy at a lower price by assuming the risks of fluctuations. The decision on whether to quote prices in the national currency of the importer or the exporter depends on the bargaining power of each and on how badly each wants the sale to be made.

INTERNATIONAL DISTRIBUTION SYSTEMS

Perhaps nowhere else in the marketing program do we find it as difficult to categorize international marketing patterns as in the area of distribution systems. The conglomerate nature of *domestic* middlemen and their functions is found to an even greater degree when we examine *international* distribution patterns.

Understanding the environment in a foreign market helps in understanding the middlemen and the distribution system because these marketing institutions are a product of their environment. In foreign markets, just as in the United States, consumer buying habits are a major factor in shaping distribution channels and middlemen's activities. The perceptive, and thus usually successful, retailers, for example, will capitalize on environmental change by introducing innovations which anticipate trends in the environment. Thus, when supermarkets were introduced in some Western European countries, they were accepted enthusiastically because enough of the market was ready to change from the practice of shopping at several small, limited-line stores. In fact, several European retailers have done a good job of innovating. Within a relatively few years they have moved from the stage of "mom and pop" stores to a variety of retailing concepts as advanced as anything in the U.S. In so doing, these innovative retailers simply telescoped time and leapfrogged several stages of institutional development.[21] In mass retailing, the *hypermarché* in France and the *verbrauchermarkt* in Germany are huge self-service combination superstores operating very profitably and at much lower gross margins than similar U.S. stores. France's largest *hypermarché* operator (Carrefour) plans to expand into the U.S. At the other end of the size scale, Europeans also have been innovative in small specialty shops retailing shoes, clothing, and other products.

Environmental changes in Japan—rising incomes and industrialization, for

---

[21]Ralph Z. Sorenson II, "U.S. Marketers Can Learn from European Innovators," *Harvard Business Review*, September–October, 1972, pp. 89–99; also see Eugene D. Jaffe, "The Growth and Performance of Self-service Food Shops in Israel: A Study of an Adoption of an American Innovation in a Developing Country," *University of Washington Business Review*, Summer, 1968, pp. 60–66.

instance—are having an impact on Japanese department stores. They are employing sales training and better inventory control, and broadening their lines of products and services. At the same time they must contend with rising costs, in-store congestion, and other new problems.[22] An increasing number of both American and foreign-based retailers are responding to growth opportunities by crossing national boundaries. These international retailers are increasing their own profits and also changing the competitive structures of the countries they enter.[23]

Middlemen used in foreign marketing. Four groups of middlemen to be recognized in foreign trade include (1) American foreign trade middlemen, (2) foreign trade middlemen located abroad, (3) wholesalers and retailers operating within foreign markets, and (4) manufacturers' sales branches and offices located in foreign countries.

American foreign trade middlemen. Many foreign trade middlemen located in the United States engage in such a wide variety of activities today that they defy accurate titling or meaningful classification. They are simply American middlemen engaged in foreign marketing. Any narrower descriptive title may be misleading or erroneous. One company may do both importing and exporting as an independent merchant and at the same time act as a manufacturers' export agent. Another importer-exporter may also own and operate sugar plantations, manufacturing plants, a bank, or a steamship line.

The "export house" is probably the most popular term used to describe all American foreign trade middlemen, with the possible exception of brokers. The term is even used to include those firms which *import* products into the United States. The operations of "export and import brokers" are much the same as those of brokers in domestic marketing. In foreign trade these middlemen are especially active in the marketing of staple commodities such as grain, cotton, wool, sugar, and coffee.

Foreign trade middlemen located abroad. In most foreign countries there are independent middlemen (importers, exporters, brokers, and some wholesalers) who are engaged in foreign trade and who operate in essentially the same way that American-based foreign trade firms do. For an American producer, however, the main outlets abroad for manufactured goods are *agents and distributors.* These are firms which act as sales representatives for the American firms in foreign markets. Agents and distributors differ primarily in two respects: Agents do not take title to the goods and normally do not carry inventory stocks. These two types of middlemen are so important in the distribution system that often a

---

[22]Paul O. Grokë, "How Japanese Department Stores Are Meeting the Challenge of a Rapidly Changing Environment," *Journal of Retailing,* Fall, 1972, pp. 72–80. Also see "Spaniards Say 'Si' to Department Stores," *Business Week,* May 28, 1966, p. 176.

[23]See Stanley C. Hollander, *Multinational Retailing,* Michigan State University, East Lansing, International Business and Economic Studies, 1970; Bruce J. Walker and Michael J. Etzel, "The Internationalization of U.S. Franchise Systems: Progress and Procedures," *Journal of Marketing,* April, 1973, pp.38–46; "Britain's Retail Champ (Marks and Spencer) Takes on the World," *Business Week,* Nov. 3, 1973, p. 88; and "Carrefour: A Superdiscounter Eyes the U.S.," *Business Week,* Dec. 15, 1973, p. 78.

manufacturer will grant them exclusive territorial rights. They perform a wide variety of services, including personal selling, advertising, providing market and credit information, making repairs, billing, settling disputes, and collecting invoices. In addition, distributors perform the functions of warehousing and bulk breaking.

Channels of distribution. When selecting the channel of distribution to be used in foreign marketing, an executive probably will use one of the following five alternatives. Two of these are indirect, involving the use of middlemen all the way, and the other three involve direct selling to some extent, along with the establishment of foreign sales offices or branches by the manufacturer.

1. Manufacturer—foreign trade middlemen (exporters) in the United States—foreign trade middlemen (importers) abroad—wholesalers and/or retailers in foreign countries—consumers or industrial users.
2. Manufacturer—foreign trade middlemen in the United States—wholesalers and/or retailers in foreign countries—consumers or industrial users
3. Manufacturer—foreign trade middlemen in foreign countries—wholesalers and/or retailers—consumers or industrial users
4. Manufacturer—wholesalers and/or retailers abroad—consumers or industrial users
5. Manufacturer—consumers or industrial users

The main problem at this point is to decide whether to engage in direct selling and, if so, to what extent. Middlemen operating *within* foreign countries are, in general, less aggressive and perform fewer marketing services than their American counterparts. The foreign marketing situation, however, usually argues against by passing foreign middlemen. Often the demand is too small to warrant the establishment of a sales office or branch. Also, the wage structure and selling methods tend to give foreign middlemen an advantage. Government controls frequently preclude the use of an American sales organization abroad. Thus, middlemen in foreign countries ordinarily are used in the channel structure, whether the American seller exports directly to sales offices abroad or uses American exporting middlemen.

When foreign middlemen are used, the American seller usually advertises extensively and furnishes point-of-purchase display materials to strengthen the efforts of the middlemen. Missionary salesmen are sometimes employed. If the product requires mechanical servicing or installation, the American manufacturer must provide reliable repair service. This means training local middlemen, sending in American service representatives, or both. Local middlemen often require financial assistance. If retailers cannot get bank credit, the manufacturer must meet this need.

Physical distribution. In foreign marketing, various aspects of physical distribution are quite different from anything found on the domestic scene. In general, the total cost of physical distribution is a much larger share of the final selling price in foreign markets than in domestic markets. Packing requirements, for example, are more exacting for foreign shipment. Problems caused by humidity, pilferage, breakage, and inadequate marking of shipments must be considered. Requirements of commercial shipping documents and governmental documents complicate the paper work in foreign shipping. Marine insurance and the traffic management of international shipments are specialized fields involving facilitating agencies ordinarily not used in domestic marketing. In conclusion, the new capabilities in logistics control plus the faster rates of change in international marketing point up the need for an enlarged, higher-level physical distribution activity.

ADVERTISING IN FOREIGN MARKETS

Any analysis of international promotional programs should encompass the management of international sales forces, sales-promotional techniques, and advertising programs. Because of space limitations, however, our brief discussion is confined only to advertising as illustrative of the managerial problems in international promotion. Advertising is selected because it is probably used by more firms in international marketing than either a company sales force or some of the sales-promotional techniques. Many companies without their own international sales force—they use foreign trade middlemen—will advertise internationally.

In international advertising, one controversial issue is the extent to which advertising can be standardized in foreign markets. In years gone by, the consensus was that a separate program (copy, appeals, media, etc.) had to be tailored for each country or even regions within a country. While nobody is recommending complete uniformity, today we are finding much support for the idea that a commonality can exist successfully in international campaigns. Many companies are using basically the same appeals, theme, slogan, colors, copy, layout, etc., in all their international advertising—particularly in the Western European countries. Certainly standardization of advertising is spurred by the fact that (1) hordes of Europeans travel from one country to another while on vacation; (2) many radio and TV broadcasts from one country reach audiences in another country; and (3) the circulation of many European magazines and newspapers crosses national borders.

Perhaps the issue comes down to this point: The goal of advertising is essentially the same at home and abroad, namely, to communicate information and persuasive appeals effectively. The basic approach to developing an advertising campaign can be the same in every country. It is only the media strategy and specific messages which must be attuned to each country's cultural, economic, and political environment.[24] For some products the appeals are sufficiently universal and the market sufficiently homogeneous so as to permit the use of uniform advertising in several countries. Standardization undoubtedly will increase, being propelled by such factors as increasing international communications and rising standards of living.[25]

Attitude of foreign markets and governments toward advertising. In many countries the traditionally negative attitude toward marketing in general and toward advertising in particular is a hardship for American firms. The "build a

---

[24]Gordon E. Miracle, "International Advertising Principles and Strategies," *MSU Business Topics,* Autumn, 1968, pp. 29–36.

[25]For an exchange of views on the standardization of international advertising, see Arthur C. Fatt, "The Danger of 'Local' International Advertising," *Journal of Marketing,* January, 1967, pp. 60–62; and James H. Donnelly, Jr., and John K. Ryans, Jr., "Standardized Global Advertising: A Call as yet Unanswered," *Journal of Marketing,* April, 1969, pp. 57–60.

better mousetrap" theory still prevails to a great extent throughout Europe and the rest of the world. Some foreign consumers feel that a product is of dubious value if it has to be advertised. People in many foreign countries object particularly to American "hard sell" advertising. Many countries have stringent laws regulating advertising copy and media. In West Germany, for example, a seller cannot make product comparisons in his advertising. As a general rule, advertising must be factual and must employ a "soft sell" approach. On the other hand, some markets—Latin America, for example—treat and accept advertising much as we in the United States do. Where the government regulates the use of radio and television for advertising and where newspapers are government-controlled, this too affects their use as advertising media.

Choice of media. Essentially the same types of advertising media are available in foreign countries as in the United States, with the exception of television in some markets. Some print media, such as *Time* and *Reader's Digest,* which are published in the United States are also published abroad in foreign languages.

In foreign markets American exporters encounter problems related to media selection which are not normally met in the United States. One factor peculiar to foreign marketing is the low rate of literacy in many areas. A seller might ordinarily prefer print media to show a colored picture of his product and explain its merits. If he is selling in a market where 90 percent of the people cannot read and do not buy magazines or newspapers, however, he may be forced to use radio, which on other counts may be a far less effective medium for his product. Another major problem is the unavailability of accurate information regarding the quantitative and qualitative nature of media circulation. Sometimes the rates paid for media space are determined on a bargaining basis. Sometimes the rates for American sellers are higher than those for native firms. Political and religious considerations are more important determinants of newspaper readership in many foreign markets than in the United States.

Preparation of advertisements. Most of the mistakes in writing copy and preparing individual advertisements may be traced to lack of intimate knowledge of the foreign market. As we have said, the wrong use of color or a poor choice of words can completely nullify an otherwise good ad. Illustrations are of prime importance in many markets because of the illiteracy factor. They are, of course, effective in all markets, but they must be accurate, believable, and in accord with local cultures. If agencies and advertisers could have qualified people from the individual foreign markets check every advertisement before it reaches the public, many mistakes could be prevented. The translation of the advertising copy into the appropriate foreign language is a major problem. Here the advertiser especially needs someone both adept and current (an expatriate often will not do) in the idioms, dialects, and other nuances of the foreign language.

Management of foreign advertising. The advertising program in foreign markets can be coordinated in three general ways: Control may be centralized in the home office of the American seller; it may be exercised jointly by the home office and the foreign representatives; or it may be delegated entirely to the seller's foreign representatives. On balance, the best arrangement seems to be centralized control. It is difficult to exert budgetary control over an internationally decentralized operation. Better advertising talent and more advertising specialists are available in the home office than in any single foreign market. The home office can work with American advertising agencies that have foreign offices. Thus it can have some of the advantages of local market contacts but still retain basic control. Economies can be realized through centralized creation and production of the individual advertisements. Also when international media are used, some centralized control is necessary. Finally, centralized management of the advertising program makes it easier to coordinate advertising with other aspects of the company's promotional and marketing programs. Of course, centralized management means that the American seller loses the tremendous advantage of having personnel closely acquainted with local cultures, languages, and buying habits.

THE FUTURE: A WORLD MARKETING ENTERPRISE

For countless American companies, the marketing opportunities of the future lie in international marketing. This conclusion seems inevitable as management views its saturated home markets, its excess productive capacity, its shrinking profit margins, and the intensified competition in the United States coming from both domestic and foreign firms. This broadening of marketing horizons, however, will be a new experience in most cases. When exports are measured as a percentage of gross national product, the United States ranks *last* among the major trading nations in the world, although we do rank first in dollar volume of trading. Most companies in the United States have never realized that export markets provide them with an opportunity to increase sales and profits significantly. Even the increasing competition from foreign imports has usually served only to intensify American seller's competitive efforts at home, rather than turning their interest to international markets.

But the winds of change are awakening American executives to the opportunities in multinational marketing.[26] To make the most of these opportunities a company is urged to think big and plan ahead—clichés, yes, and perhaps trite, but useful admonitions nevertheless. A country-by-country market analysis is becoming increasingly common and is certainly better than going abroad with a one-shot, unplanned approach because some random opportunity has presented itself. Better than a country-by-country analysis, however, is a global planning approach. A company that takes a total global systems approach is not apt to be blocked later on by some decision made earlier in another country.

INTERNATIONAL TRADE BALANCES

To conclude this chapter, let us move from the micro level of international marketing in the individual firm to the macro level of international trade in the total economy. To maintain equilibrium in our balance of international payments, we

---

[26]See David S. R. Leighton, "The Internationalization of American Business—the Third Industrial Revolution," *Journal of Marketing,* July, 1970, pp. 3–6; and Donald S. Henley, "Multinational Marketing: Present Position and Future Challenges," in Becker and Becker (eds.), *op. cit.,* pp. 41–47.

Table 25-5. Increases in consumer prices and unit labor costs in U.S. and other countries, 1964–1970. Prices in Japan increased 40%, compared to 25% for the U.S. Labor costs in Germany (26%) and Britain (33%) rose more than in the U.S. (20%).

Country	Percentage increase in	
	Consumer prices	Unit labor costs
United States	25	20
Canada	24	29
Germany	17	26
Great Britain	31	33
France	27	16
Italy	21	18
Japan	40	12

Source: Prices—U.S. Bureau of Labor Statistics; Labor costs— International Monetary Fund.

need to generate a substantial favorable balance of merchandise trade (exports must exceed imports) to offset the negative balances stemming from foreign aid, military expenditures abroad, and U.S. tourist travel abroad. Up to the mid-1960s, the U.S. generally had a sufficiently large balance of product trade. But since then, this favorable balance of product trade has declined to the point where it is not sufficient to offset the outpayments for other purposes. The net result has been a deficit balance of payments for the United States. This situation has had serious economic and political repercussions not only in the U.S. but internationally as well.

What has caused this substantial decline in our merchandise trade balance? It is commonly alleged that U.S. products are being priced out of world markets because of our high cost structure. The facts, however, do not fully support this allegation. It is true that wage rates in the United States are higher than the pay for similar jobs in Canada, Japan, and Europe. However, a significant differential in labor costs existed even before the mid-1960s when the U.S. enjoyed a very favorable balance of product trade. From 1964 to 1970 the percentage increases in (1) consumer prices and (2) unit labor costs in the U.S. were about the same as, or even less than, the increases experienced by our major trading partners. (See Table 25-5.) So the causes of America's trade problem would seem to lie elsewhere.

More realistically, four other factors seem to be affecting our balance of trade. The first is the fact that in *productivity gains* (manufacturers' output per man-hour), the U.S. increase from 1965 to 1970 was the lowest among the major free-world nations. Our 2 percent annual rate of increase compares with 5 percent in Germany and 14 percent in Japan. (See Table 25-6). Also, this 2 percent annual increase since 1965 compares with a gain of about 3 percent per year in the U.S. for all years since World War II.

Productivity gains are related to another factor—*the state of technology*—which influences the trade balance. The "technology gap" between the U.S. and other

Table 25-6. Average annual increase in productivity, U.S. and other countries, 1965–1970.
The rate of increase in manufacturer's output per man-hour was about seven times higher in Japan than in the U.S. How do you account for the low rate of productivity gains in the U.S.?

Country	Annual increase (in percentages)
Japan	14.2
Netherlands	8.5
Sweden	7.9
Belgium	6.8
France	6.6
Switzerland	6.2
West Germany	5.3
Italy	5.1
United Kingdom	3.6
Canada	3.5
United States	1.9

Source: *U.S. News & World Report,* Oct. 4, 1971, p. 25, from U.S. Department of Labor data.

major industrial countries is narrowing. The U.S. does not enjoy the same differential advantages in this area as was the case prior to the 1960s.

Many business executives believe that *government policies* in foreign countries seem to aid and encourage international trade, more so than is the case in the U.S. While domestic prices in foreign countries increased at about the same rate as in the U.S. from 1964 to 1970 (Table 25-5), the same situation did not prevail for prices on exported products. In the U.S., the export price index went up almost as much (20 percent) as did domestic prices (25 percent). In Japan, on the other hand, export prices increased only 8 percent as against a 40 percent increase at home. France and England each had a spread of about 20 points between increases in the domestic and export price indexes.

In other words, many foreign countries have been able to keep down the prices on products entering international markets, even though prices within these countries do go up. The question is: How can these countries achieve such results? One way is for a government to devalue its currency, as England and France both did in the 1960s, and as the U.S. finally did in the early 1970s. Devaluation has the effect of stimulating exports because of their reduced prices, and limiting imports because foreign goods then cost more.

Another government policy stimulating exports is to nationalize or subsidize industries which cannot compete on a private basis. Thus many countries have a national airline (Lufthansa, Air France, Alitalia, SAS, BOAC, etc.) that is owned in total or in part by the government. Similar situations exist in the steel, commercial aircraft, computer, and jet engine industries.

The tax structure is another aspect of government policy which can play a significant role in international trade. Some countries impose substantial tariffs or other border taxes (as high as 30 to 40 percent) on imports of some products. Some foreign countries derive a substantial revenue from indirect taxes (such as value-added tax) which are waived or rebated when a product is exported. Thus it reaches the U.S. at a lower price. In the U.S., on the other hand, the main source of revenue is the income tax which is *not* rebated for exports. So the American product is shipped abroad at a price including income tax. Then when it reaches the foreign border, the indirect taxes are further added on. The net result is that the selling price on U.S. goods in the foreign country ends up pretty high as compared with the price of a foreign product being marketed in the U.S.

The fourth factor affecting the balance of trade is the relative *marketing capabilities* in the U.S. vis-à-vis other countries. Marketing skills and aggressiveness are increasing among foreign firms. At the same time, it seems that not enough American companies have applied their know-how of marketing management when selling abroad. These firms often seem preoccupied with production and financial problems in foreign markets, and have neglected to adopt a marketing orientation in their foreign ventures.

Another interesting macro marketing situation is occurring in some Third World countries in Asia, Africa, and South America. It is becoming apparent that the rate of economic growth in less-developed nations will depend largely upon how effective are the marketing systems established in these countries. Typically in these countries (as was true earlier in the United States) the economic development effort has been concentrated in production. Now these governments are beginning to recognize the role which marketing can play in their national economic growth. This enlightened attitude offers countless marketing opportunities (but not without attendant problems) to the internationally oriented business firm. Particularly, a marketing executive must understand the government's role in business in each country.[27]

QUESTIONS AND PROBLEMS

1. In what fundamental respects is international marketing different from domestic?

2. Report on *export* marketing activities of companies in the state where your school is located. Consider such topics as the following: What products are exported? How many jobs are created by export marketing? What is the dollar value of exports? How does this figure compare with the value of foreign-made goods imported into the state?

---

[27]For discussions of the increased attention being paid to marketing and economic growth in emerging economies, see, for example, Charles C. Slater, "Marketing Processes in Developing Latin American Societies," *Journal of Marketing,* July, 1968, pp. 50–55; James E. Littlefield, "The Relationship of Marketing to Economic Development in Peru," *Southern Journal of Business,* July, 1968, pp. 1–14; Harry A. Lipson and Douglas F. Lamont, "Marketing Policy Decisions Facing International Marketers in Less-developed Countries," *Journal of Marketing,* October, 1969, pp. 24–31; and Reed Moyer and Stanley C. Hollander (eds.), *Markets and Marketing in Developing Economies,* American Marketing Association, Chicago, 1968.

3. A United States luggage manufacturer with annual sales over $20 million has decided to market his products in Western Europe. Evaluate the alternative organizational structures which this company should consider.

4. Select three countries—one in Europe, one in South America, and one in Africa—and assume that a U.S. manufacturer of auto and truck tires plans to market his products in these countries. What problems will this manufacturer face in each of the following areas?
   a. Exchange controls
   b. Tariffs on tires
   c. Restrictions on foreign companies or personnel

5. Select one product—manufactured or nonmanufactured—for export and the country to which you would like to export it. Then prepare an analysis of the market for this product in the selected country. Be sure to include the sources of information which you used.

6. If there are foreign students on your campus, interview some of them to determine how their native buying habits differ from ours. Consider such patterns as when, where, and how people in their country buy. Who makes the family buying decisions?

7. Many countries unfortunately have a low literacy rate. In what ways might a company adjust aspects of its marketing program to overcome this problem?

8. Why should special attention be devoted to labeling and branding when selling U.S. products in foreign markets?

9. Describe the role of the export house in foreign marketing.

10. If an American manufacturer uses foreign middlemen, he must usually stand ready to supply them with additional financial, technical, and promotional help. If this is the case, why is it not customary to bypass these middlemen and deal directly with foreign buyers?

11. Why does an American exporter normally prefer to have prices quoted in U.S. dollars? Why should the foreign importer prefer that the quotation be in the currency of his country?

12. "Prices of American products are always higher in foreign countries than at home because of the additional risks, expenses of physical distribution, and extra middlemen involved." Discuss.

13. Carefully distinguish between f.o.b., f.a.s., and c.i.f. as bases for price quotations in foreign marketing.

14. Study the advertisements in the foreign newspapers and magazines available in your college or city library. Particularly note the advertisements for American products and compare these with the advertisements for the same products in American newspapers and magazines. In what respect do the foreign ads differ from the domestic ads? Are there significant similarities?

15. What are some of the media selection problems faced by American exporters in foreign markets?

16. Is the U.S. manufacturer being priced out of world markets because of his high cost structure?

CASES FOR PART

CASE 22. **MEDICAL-DENTAL FINANCIAL PLANNING, INC.**

Pricing and promoting a new service

Mr. Donald Heaton, the president of Medical-Dental Financial Planning, Inc., believed that his company offered a service which so far was being marketed by very few companies in the United States. At the same time he believed that there was a huge potential market for his company's service, and that only a minute portion of that market as yet had been tapped. Consequently, Mr. Heaton was wondering what type of promotional program would be most effective in (1) reaching additional portions of this large market and (2) strengthening his firm's competitive position in the market. He also was uncertain about how to price some segments of his company's financial planning service.

The service being marketed by Medical-Dental Financial Planning, Inc., was a relatively new concept—it was a total financial management program for physicians and dentists. Mr. Heaton established this "financial clinic" in 1968 after observing that doctors needed help in planning and managing their financial affairs. Heaton said, "Nine out of ten doctors are in deep financial trouble. They earn good money, but nobody misuses his funds like a physician or a dentist. They make lousy businessmen."

Currently Medical-Dental had two offices in California (Los Angeles and San Francisco), two in Canada (Toronto and Montreal), and one each in Denver, Colorado; Hartford, Connecticut; New York City; and Washington, D.C. The company managed the total financial affairs of about 1,200 clients and provided more limited, specific financial services for about 4,000 other clients. The company was in sound financial condition and it enjoyed fairly high profits. The board of directors of the company included physicians, certified public accountants, attorneys, and experts in the fields of insurance, banking, mutual funds, and real estate.

The operational manner in which Medical-Dental produced its financial service was relatively simple. One of its sales representatives lined up a prospect, and then reported on the prospect's financial situation, ambitions, and personality to the company's home office. There a six-man advisory committee, which included specialists in taxation, insurance, real estate, mutual funds, and banking, worked out a program suited to the client's needs. In many cases it obtained for the client unsecured bank loans for capital or personal investments. When the client had saved funds or had large cash values in his insurance policies, the money was put into mutual funds or real estate investments. The firm, in turn, made its money from commissions and fees, plus a share of the profits from its real estate dealings.

"We're not interested in making our clients into millionaires," said Heaton. "Our goal is to take care of many of the financial things they don't have the time or the talent for, to solve their tax problems, and help them accumulate a small amount of wealth. We custom design a complete financial program suited to the professional man's particular needs. We feature one-stop shopping with expert advice. We're interested in increasing an individual's total net worth. Usually a doctor has several financial advisors (insurance men, real estate brokers, bankers), each of whom is competing for his funds. We use the systems concept."

Because the concept of total financial planning for doctors was relatively new, Medical-Dental had very little direct competition from similar types of organizations. However, the company did have considerable competition from the insurance, mutual fund, real estate, and "estate planning" industries.

The firm felt it had a natural advantage over all these competitors because of its comprehensive approach versus their limited-service approaches. It fully expected, however, to face stiff competition, beginning in the near future, from enterprises such as itself. As one company executive said, "Our approach is the coming thing. We've got to expect competition soon." He went on to explain the pioneering work the company had done to firmly establish itself and to prepare for coming competition. He was especially pleased with Medical-Dental's success in lining up banks which were willing to make large (up to $30,000), unsecured loans to doctors.

Mr. Heaton viewed his company's potential market as including virtually all the physicians and dentists in the United States and Canada—in effect, an almost unlimited market with a great geographic dispersion. Medical-Dental's major problem with respect to that market was how to gain access to the doctors. As a general rule, doctors were extremely busy and sheltered from business contacts. It was hard to reach them through advertising, and contacts through personal selling usually were difficult to make because of the doctors' inaccessibility and the newness of Medical-Dental's service.

Mr. Heaton and some of his top executives were trying to figure out the best way to promote their company's financial management services. They believed they had better than a 50-50 chance to sell a doctor on their total service package if they could get the prospective client to sit down seriously with a Medical-Dental representative for a period of time and listen attentively and without interruption to the representative's message. Medical-Dental had salesmen working out of each of the company's offices. The men were paid a salary and a commission. They called on doctors in the doctors' offices, and they tried to make contacts with the doctors at country clubs, downtown athletic clubs, and similar places.

Some of the Medical-Dental executives felt the company should do some advertising, but they were not certain as to what media to use, how much to spend, or what type of sales message to use in the ads.

The executives were also wrestling with the problem of whether to charge a fee for working up a financial program as part of the company's initial contact with a prospective client. Presently, the company worked up a comprehensive program for each prospective client who showed enough interest to provide the salesman with the basic information. There was no charge for this service, and the doctor could become a client, use the advice on his own or with the help of others, or forget the whole thing. If he became a client, the firm charged commissions and fees for the transactions it conducted in his behalf, and shared in any real estate profits.

Some members of the firm believed it would be a better marketing strategy to charge a fee for the initial professional advice and services rendered. The sales manager, Mr. Clark Irwin, felt that professional men recognize the value of professional advice and would prefer to pay a fee for it. This would be more in keeping with the practices they themselves employ. He also pointed out that if a fee were charged to all those who requested that a program be worked up for them, then the ones who became clients would not feel they were subsidizing the ones who do not by bearing all the costs of this service. "I think it would help separate us as professional financial managers from the quacks and piece-meal estate planners who are trying to compete with us," Irwin added. "Our professional image would be strengthened if we charged a fee."

Other executives argued that many prospective clients would be turned away by this initial fee. They pointed out that the new physician or dentist trying to set up private practice needs financial advice and might make an excellent client in the long run, but at the moment he can ill afford to pay the fee. Therefore, he would be discouraged from ever becoming a client and would probably wind up with a piece-meal financial program worked up by competing bankers, brokers, insurance salesmen, and the like. They thought that the "free service, with no obligation" approach allowed the company to explain its services to many more prospective clients than would be possible if a fee were charged for the initial advice.

The cost of working up the initial program normally ranged from $250 to $500 for time, materials, and professional services. Between 60 and 80 percent of all doctors who have programs worked up for them did become clients. The company normally earned between $1,000 and $5,000 in commissions and fees during a client's first year with Medical-Dental.

Mr. Irwin believed that the *principle* of the fee was more important than the *amount*. He suggested that the fee could be based on actual costs to the company for each individual program prepared; it could be a standard fee for all, based on average costs; or, it could be only a token fee, not intended to cover the costs of the service. If the doctor became a client, the company could apply the amount of the fee against the commissions it normally charged, if this practice was deemed desirable.

Mr. Heaton was anxious that his company employ the best marketing strategy possible, in order to become as strong as it can and to corner as large a share of the market as it can before competition becomes severe.

QUESTIONS

1. Design a promotional program for Medical-Dental to reach and attract new clients.

2. Should Medical-Dental charge a fee for its initial advisory service?
   a. If so, what should be the price?
   b. If charged, should the fee be reimbursed to those who become clients?

CASE 23. **WORLD WIDE PUBLISHERS***

Marketing greeting cards in Germany

World Wide Publishers, a long-time leader in the greeting card industry in the United States, began its international operation in the 1930's when a salesman began selling its line of products in Canada. Realizing the potential greeting card market in Canada, the firm soon established a subsidiary to handle the Canadian operation. Shortly following the success in Canada, another subsidiary was established in Leeds, England. The English operation was very successful and the World Wide name was considered to have an excellent reputation in the English greeting card industry.

A few years ago, World Wide investigated the feasibility of entering the continental market and engaged a Swedish marketing consulting firm to do research on the question. As a result of the favorable findings, World Wide formed three separate subsidiaries in France, Germany, and Italy.

There were marked differences between German and American greeting cards with respect to product design and quality. Traditionally the German greeting card was either of the single fold or postcard variety. A great deal of workmanship went into the design of these cards, but seldom was any text or message required since it was customary in Germany for buyers to write their own message on the inside or back of the card. World Wide introduced written verse to the German greeting card market. A prepared verse on the inside of the card was something new and different in this market.

In addition to product innovations, World Wide established an entirely new approach to greeting card merchandising in Germany with the introduction of the American-type, floor-stand rack which held 120 cards. Prior to the innovation of this floor-stand rack, merchandising of greeting cards had been carried on in a haphazard manner. A counter 4½ ft. to 6 ft. in length usually held all the cards in the store. The lower-priced cards were piled in a bin in the center of the counter. All the cards were individually wrapped in cellophane and the more expensive cards were laid out flat at the ends of the counter often under glass and had to be asked for specifically.

The management of World Wide believed that the new merchandising program in Germany was very successful. They had found it possible to employ in their German subsidiary many of the techniques proven successful in the United States where World Wide was considered outstanding in the quality of its product and in its retail merchandising innovations.

The main retail outlets that sold greeting cards in Germany were the chain stores and the department stores. To these retail outlets the firm introduced its highly successful stock control program. This program was in effect an automatic stock rotation and reordering system that freed the retailer from concern about inventory control and selection of merchandise when reordering.

The only advertising carried on by World Wide was through trade journals. The company placed its main emphasis and reliance on personal selling. The sales force was made up of 12 native German employees trained and supervised by the sales manager. The territories were geographically divided according to the distribution of population. The sales manager was formerly a salesman with the parent company. He had a strong German background, as his parents had lived in the country. He spoke fluent German.

The American military market in Germany was completely divorced from the German subsidiary. This market was handled by the parent company with products shipped from the United States directly to a sales representative based in Germany. Management felt the subsidiary was unable to handle this market, because its line was not extensive enough nor did it have the facilities to print in English.

The company thought its pricing policy was competitive despite the fact that its prices were slightly higher than those of German manufacturers. Most of World Wide's line was priced at one mark (about 40 cents) or less. It was discovered that the one-mark, 40-pfennig cards and the two-mark cards (55 cents and 80 cents) did not sell well in the German market. Management attributed its slightly higher price line to the fact that the cards offered by local German competitors were smaller and had little or no verse. The retailers' markup in both Germany and the United States was 50 percent of the retail price.

When approaching retailers with their line, World Wide was faced with two obstacles. The first one was that German manufacturers always supplied with each card a tissue envelope with a colored lining. World Wide, however, supplied a regular white envelope without colored lining or tissue.

The second obstacle that World Wide ran into was the long-established practice of the German firms to wrap their cards individually in cellophane. This was done because traditionally greeting cards had been a low-turnover item, and therefore the cellophane protected the inventory while it was in stock. World Wide packaged their cards, with individual, white envelopes, in lots of 6, 12, or 24, depending on the card, and wrapped them in a brown envelope. The retailer then removed the cards from the brown envelope and displayed them on the rack.

To overcome the German traditions, World Wide told greeting card retailers that the company was introducing cards with verse into the market, and therefore the cards had to be read and could not be wrapped in cellophane.

World Wide felt the envelope was not as important as the card and stressed the idea that they were putting more quality into the card rather than the envelope which was thrown away after opening.

By last year the product line in Germany had been expanded to incorporate a variety of everyday cards (birthday, anniversary, etc.) and seasonal cards (Christmas, Easter, etc.). The line was not as extensive as in the United States, but was considered adequate by management for the German market.

The procedures used by the German subsidiary to produce cards was to copy successful cards marketed by the parent firm in the United States. The designs were a replica of the United States cards with a German translation of the American text printed on the card. Many times a text would lose something in the translation. For example, a card that was humorous in English would not always be humorous in German. Also, because of cultural differences between the two nations, a text appealing to Americans would not necessarily appeal to prospective German customers. Sentimental design and text was never a big seller, and long flowery verses did not sell well in Germany. Verses had to be kept to a minimum of one or two lines to be at all successful.

Since it was important that the cards be adequately adapted to the German language and cultural sensitivities after translation—particularly in an industry where in the words of one World Wide executive, "The message is our most important product"—management was constantly searching for a better means of choosing which American cards to use.

By last year, however, despite the high levels of prosperity characterizing the market areas serviced by the German subsidiary, its sales of greeting cards were significantly less than originally anticipated. The high administrative and initial start-up costs incurred to launch the German subsidiary and required to continue the product and merchandising innovations that had been introduced by it were of increasing concern. Company executives believed that the introduction of prepared verse and of effective merchandising practices and controls at the retail level to the German greeting card industry had been steps in the right direction. They also believed, however, that factors other than product design and retail merchandising methods were operating in the German greeting card market to limit prospects of any immediate increase in the rate of sales growth.

Germans, for one thing, do not send each other as many cards as Americans do because they are by custom and tradition a more formal people. As a result, card sending is more of an occasion, a fact which might relate to the preference and frequent insistence upon individually wrapped cards. Current analyses of the German market were suggesting, however, that there had been a gradual shift to the informal, partly due to contacts the German people have had with the many Americans living in their country.

The company now was re-examining the Germany greeting card market and the opportunities for further progress and growth in it. A number of possibilities were under consideration. Among these was the possibility of negotiating the sale of the German subsidiary to a German publishing company. Under the proposed terms of sale, World Wide would recoup a significant proportion of its unamortized administrative and initial costs. World Wide executives felt the German firm had a good reputation, was familiar with the market and temperament of the German greeting card purchaser, and could easily carry on the operations of the firm. The German firm would continue to use the American cards, for which World Wide would receive a royalty, and there would be a sharing of profits and expenses at a ratio not yet worked out.

QUESTIONS

1. Should World Wide sell its German subsidiary?
2. If not, what should the company do to increase its sales and growth rate?

CASE 24. LEVI STRAUSS & COMPANY *

Production and distribution for international markets

Levi Strauss & Co., a San Francisco clothing manufacturer, was well established in the export business with sales reaching into most parts of the world. Levi's overall—the company's rugged, tight-fitting blue jean—is the most important garment manufactured by the company and had been the mainstay of the company since its founding in 1850. Over the years additional items were added to the product assortment; so that by 1963 the company was producing and marketing eight lines of men's and women's clothing.

Although export sales accounted for a relatively small percentage of the company's dollar volume, this percentage was based on a total that was both substantial and expanding. Thus, export sales represented an appreciable absolute dollar volume with—in the view of the company management—considerable growth potential. The problem confronting management, therefore, was no longer how to enter foreign markets. Rather, it was how to allocate long-run expansion resources between domestic and export business, and among the alternative foreign markets themselves, and how to employ the allocated resources within each market.

Export sales were being handled through an International Division, headed by the International Director. This person was directly responsible to the president of the company and was located in the company's home office in San Francisco. The company also had a bonded warehouse in Antwerp, Belgium, under the control of the International Director and, in turn, of his European resident manager. This warehouse stocked all fast-moving items and could make delivery to any European point within two to three days.

Europe accounted for a large share of the export volume with the principal markets being France, Western Germany, and Great Britain. The Far East, primarily Japan, was also an important market. It, plus Africa, Australia, and Latin America, made up most of the remaining export volume. Foreign sales were largely from the Levi's line and the new White Levi's line. The latter line was formally set up in late 1962 and included selected colors of cotton twill jeans using the Levi's jean pattern. These garments, with their unique cut and the traditional images of the American West and the American teenager associated with that cut, enjoyed a ready market among the teenagers of most countries. Other lines such as the casual line were also exported; however, these lines met more market resistance. Close substitutes manufactured domestically were frequently available. Furthermore, these garments carried no cherished image for any major market segments such as did the Levi's jean for the teenagers.

*Case prepared by Prof. Harry E. Allison, California State College at Hayward. Reproduced with permission. Data, and at times management opinions and decisions, have been altered in order to protect confidential information and/or to focus the case problem along a particular line.

In Europe and the Far East, sales were typically handled through distributors, equivalent to domestic jobbers, who were fully responsible for local warehousing and reselling to retailers. These distributors were billed directly for all merchandise shipped. Levi Strauss & Co. exercised no direct control over distributor selection of retail accounts or credit policies. However, it did strongly recomment its own domestic policies of dealing primarily with department stores and independent retailers and of striving for a stable, uniform resale price among retail accounts. Promotional expenditures were on a 50–50 basis. Therefore, Levi Strauss & Co. required home office approval of distributor plans and procedures although their proposals were typically accepted with little modification. Distributors could, and frequently did, handle related lines such as western boots and/or hats, but they could not sell competing clothing items. Pricing to the distributors was on the basis of a common price schedule for all distributors regardless of their country. This, of course, resulted in widely varying retail prices from country to country owing to variations in import restrictions as well as in local market conditions.

Distributors were now limited to no more than one per country. In some cases, several small countries—e.g., Belgium, Luxembourg, and The Netherlands—were combined under one distributorship. Initially more than one distributor had been taken on in some of the larger countries. However, enough interdistributor squabbles resulting almost inevitably in price cutting and hard feelings had arisen from such arrangements that they had been discontinued.

In Africa and Australia sales were made through agents located within the various countries. These agents carried no inventory. Shipments were typically made direct to the retail accounts with the agent being responsible for any extension of credit. Most of the Central and South American countries had restrictions against importing goods that were also manufactured locally. Thus, sales to these countries were generally closed off. However, some of the Levi Strauss & Co. merchandise sold to domestic exporters did find its way into the Central and South American markets.

From a long-run point of view two major decision areas now confronted the management of Levi Strauss & Co. in the company's international operations. The first involved the question of whether the company should move into foreign production and, if so, in which markets and under what type of arrangement, i.e., outright ownership and operation, some type of joint venture, or a licensing agreement. The International Director made several observations relevant to this decision area. First, two of the company's major competitors in the domestic market—Lee and Blue Bell—already had pilot plants operating in Belgium. Second, although technological change was on the move in the clothing industry, scale economies in quality clothing production were still so slight that when distribution costs and service were taken into account, relatively small plants could be justified. Such plants gave greater flexibility in that capital could be committed in relatively small chunks and in a more or less experimental manner. Also, scattered small units gave the investor better protection against political instability, tariffs, duties, etc. and better adaptability to local consumer tastes and preferences. Third, trade restrictions between individual foreign countries were often far less than those existing between these countries and the United States. As noted earlier, many of the Central and South American countries barred foreign-made goods that competed directly with domestically manufactured items. These barriers, however, had been collectively negotiated away among members of the Latin American Free Trade Association (LAFTA) so that most goods produced by a plant located in one LAFTA country could readily enter another LAFTA market. Fourth, the type and quality of denim insisted upon by Levi Strauss & Co. for its Levi's jean were not available within the individual foreign markets. Furthermore, production scale economies at the textile mill level would generally dictate that the denim be purchased from the United States mills even though the garments were manufactured overseas. And fifth, the "Made in U.S.A." label had both positive and negative merchandising considerations that had to be evaluated individually for each product, company, and country.

The second major decision area was concerned with the channel of distribution. Should Levi Strauss & Co. build its long-run foreign sales program around independent distributors? Or, should such distributors be viewed as transitory stepping stones in the path of market development with the long-run foreign distribution system being similar to the company's domestic system— i.e., company salesmen contacting retail accounts directly? Some company personnel maintained that considerations of control and sales effectiveness would eventually bring about direct selling to retailers in the primary foreign markets. Management realized that there was value in being represented by an accepted and established local firm that not only had knowledge of the market but also had a cultural feel for its behavior. Under a direct-selling arrangement, local foreign nationals would still do the selling to retailers but they would do it as Levi Strauss & Co. employees rather than as employees of independent distributors.

Contingent to dealing with the two long-run decision areas was the need to make a general appraisal of the long-run export demand. The current strong export demand rested primarily on the desire of foreign teenagers to identify with the American West and American teenagers, and on the image of the Levi's jean as the traditional garment of American Westerners and American teenagers. Was such a demand stable from a long-run perspective, and if not, what were the prospects for stabilizing it? Export sales may merely be riding a fad that might be largely wiped out by a rise of anti-Americanism, or might die simply because the next generation of foreign teenagers did not follow in the footsteps of their predecessors.

The more optimistic members of the management team noted that Westernism had persisted for some time among American youth. Furthermore, with skillful merchandising the American Western and American teenager images of the Levi's jean could be exploited in gaining market entry. Then gradually these images could be replaced with the more stable image of the company's blue jean as a rugged garment of top-quality construction capable of standing up under extremely heavy wear. The latter image also had merit in that it could be tied to—and therefore in time identified with—local living patterns. Furthermore, once established, the quality image had possibilities for positive transference to other non-Western lines, such as matched work sets and casual wear, thereby facilitating the entry of these lines into foreign markets. These executives did not maintain that native substitutes such as lederhosen would disappear, but rather that blue jeans were now being purchased by an increasingly wide segment within most of the foreign markets. Furthermore, once tried, the basic utility and serviceability of the garment would assure a high rate of repeat purchasing.

The more pessimistic executives granted that the above market penetration procedure had worked well in the domestic market as the company expanded from regional sales into a nationwide market. They pointed out, however, that American Western and American teenager living patterns were of foreign source to those making up the export market. As such, the images based on these patterns were likely to be much more fragile than similar images held in the domestic market. Furthermore, they noted that differences in the cultural orientation of the foreign markets gave little validity to projecting the company's domestic success to the export market or, for that matter, to projecting experience accumulated in any one foreign market to another foreign market. Finally, because of the basic unpredictability of most foreign markets (both their internal political instability and their changing external relationships such as tariffs, exchange rates, special taxes, etc.), the more pessimistic management personnel felt it would be prudent to go slow in foreign expansion. Meanwhile, they noted, the potential of these markets could continue to be tapped successfully along the current lines without any major commitment of company personnel or capital to foreign locations.

QUESTIONS

1. Should Levi Strauss & Co. go into foreign production of its garments?
2. If yes, under what type of production arrangements, and in what countries?
3. Should the company set up its own sales force to sell direct to retailers within the major foreign markets?

PART EIGHT

PLANNING AND EVALUATING THE MARKETING EFFORT

A MARKETING
INFORMATION SYSTEM
AND MARKETING RESEARCH

"Half the cost of running our economy is the cost of information. No other field offers such concentrated room for improvement as does information analysis."[1] This quotation highlights a fundamental point which has been stated or implied frequently throughout this book—namely, management's need for more, better, and current information for problem solving and decision making. Now that we have some background in marketing, perhaps we can better understand the function of managing information in a marketing system. The next three chapters relate to this subject. In this chapter we discuss a marketing information system and the related activity of marketing research. Chapter 27 is devoted to marketing planning and demand forecasting. In Chapter 28 we cover the managerial activity of performance evaluation, especially as related to a company's sales volume and its marketing costs.

NEED FOR A MARKETING INFORMATION SYSTEM

Today many environmental forces, plus changing conditions within a company, are making it imperative that a firm must develop the best possible arrangements for managing its marketing information. Let's consider just a few of these external and

---

[1]"Today's Office: Room for Improvement," *Dun's Review,* September, 1958, p. 50.

internal factors and their relationship to information management. First, there is a *shortening of the time span allotted to an executive for decision making.* Product life cycles frequently are shorter than they used to be, and companies are being forced to shorten their entire new-product-development process. Also being shortened are test-marketing periods—periods during which a company runs a limited-market test of a price, a package, an ad, or some other feature in a marketing program before introducing it to the full market. In summary, the time available to an executive to gather and analyze information is less than it used to be.

Second, *marketing activity is becoming much more complex and broader in its scope,* thus putting further strain on information gathering and processing. Competition continues to intensify and firms engage more and more in nonprice competition. Companies are expanding their product offerings and their markets—even to the point of broadly engaging in multinational marketing. Our insights into buyer behavior and psychological and sociological market segmentation, while limited, are still sufficient to tell us there is a world of behavioral data we need to acquire and understand. *Shortages of energy and other raw materials* are calling for more efficient use of materials resources and manpower. A company needs to know which of its products, territories, and customers are profitable, which ones need different treatment, and which ones should be eliminated.

Growing *consumer discontent* often is intensified because management lacks adequate information about some aspect of its marketing program. Maybe the firm does not realize its product is not up to consumer expectations, or its middlemen are not performing adequately, or its advertising is creating ill will. Finally, the knowledge explosion—*the information explosion*—itself is just fantastic. Management somehow must learn how to cope with the abundance of information. An executive must not be swamped by it. In effect, we have more than an adequate supply of information. We simply need to figure out what to do with it—how to control it—how to manage it.

Fortunately, computers and other data processing equipment continue to improve, thus providing management with fast, inexpensive means of processing masses of marketing information. In the same vein, mathematically oriented people are developing sophisticated models and other quantitative techniques for analyzing these data. At the same time, however, it is unfortunate that a sizable number of companies seem unaware of the importance of managing information in a more sophisticated fashion. In spite of what would seem to be an obvious need to develop a better system for managing information, even today a significant number of firms have no marketing research department. Another reasonably large segment of firms has only a small (sometimes one person) marketing research department whose scope of activity typically is limited to sporadic surveys, some sales-volume analysis, and other modest data-gathering efforts.

WHAT IS A MARKETING INFORMATION SYSTEM?

In firms that are conscious of the need for better information management, there is a shift from a fact-finding, information-gathering activity to a problem-solving and action-recommending function. In today's business setting, a company needs to add a new dimension to its information management, predicated on the systems approach to marketing management. A marketing information system would emphasize the continuing interaction and integration of information in the decision-making process.

A *marketing information system* (MkIS) may be defined as an interacting, continuing, future-oriented structure of people, equipment, and procedures designed to generate and process an information flow in order to aid managerial decision making in a company's marketing program.[2]

Implicit in this definition are several useful considerations. One point to note is the broad, systems concept of information handling. The system starts with the *determination* of what data are needed. Then it provides for the *generation* or gathering of this information. The information is then *processed,* with the aid of statistical analysis, model building, and other quantitative analytical techniques. Finally, there is provision for the *storage* of the data and future *retrieval* of desired information. A second point is that a marketing information system is future-oriented. It is intended to anticipate and prevent problems, as well as to solve them. The system serves as a prognosis as well as a diagnosis; it is preventive as well as curative medicine for marketing. Third, the system operates on a continuing basis. It is not a sporadic, intermittent sort of thing. Finally, the emphasis is on the total system—the process—and not just on the analytical techniques or data processing equipment used in the process.

We are involved in a marketing intelligence operation. To some extent it resembles a military or diplomatic intelligence operation in that we are gathering, processing, and storing potentially useful information which currently exists in fragmented, unorganized—but open and available—fashion in several locations both inside and outside the company. In an MkIS, however, we are *not* suggesting the use of any undercover intelligence methods such as industrial espionage, bribery, hiring competitors' personnel to learn their secrets, etc. In most cases a company does not need to rely on such clandestine methods. Frequently they are valueless or even counterproductive. Moreover, all the information which a company needs usually is open and available by socially acceptable means if the firm will just establish a reasonably simple marketing information system.

A marketing information system is especially characterized by its involvement with the computer and with personnel possessing quantitative analytical capabilities. A modern MkIS would not be possible without a computer because of the masses of data to be handled. Essentially in an MkIS we are using the management scientist and his abilities to apply model building and other operations research techniques to the management of marketing information.

The typical informational input for a company's MkIS may be divided into four broad categories—two external and two internal. One area of external information relates to the economic, social, and political environment—general economic conditions, the labor market, social conditions, international situation, political considerations, etc. The other external area pertains to external aspects of a company's marketing system—its middlemen, competition, and all data pertaining to its customers. Internally a marketing information system depends upon input from the marketing department itself and from other functional areas—primarily accounting, but also the departments which are responsible for purchasing, inven-

---

[2]Definition adapted from Samuel V. Smith, Richard H. Brien, and James E. Stafford, "Marketing Information Systems: An Introductory Overview," in Smith, Brien, and Stafford (eds.), *Readings in Marketing Information Systems,* Houghton Mifflin Company, Boston, 1968, p. 7.

tory management, production scheduling, customer credit arrangements, and order filling.

BENEFITS AND USES OF AN MkIS

Unless management consciously establishes some communication system to process information gathered from within and outside the company, it is unlikely that the company is using its marketing information effectively. Unfortunately, experience has shown that information flowing from these primary sources is frequently lost, distorted, or delayed.

A marketing information system is of most obvious value in a large, multidivisional company where information is likely to get lost or distorted as it becomes widely dispersed. However, case experiences have shown that use of integrated information systems can also have beneficial effects on management's performance in small and medium-sized firms.[3]

For most small companies, however, a formal, computer-based system probably will not provide sufficient benefits to offset the costs of establishing and operating it. But a small firm can effectively adopt an arrangement which embodies the concept of systematized information handling. Only the small company will probably use less complex and less formal techniques in the various stages of its MkIS. The optimal arrangement probably is a noncomputer system which includes (1) coordinated efforts at information gathering and processing by various departments in a firm, (2) the use of data processing equipment other than a computer —mechanized accounting and billing equipment, office copiers, tape recorders, etc., and (3) the periodic, but frequent, use of outside marketing research firms to provide informational aid in problem solving and decision making.

Some of the possible benefits accruing from an effective marketing information system are as follows:[4]

1. It may provide more information within the firm's time constraints, thus leading to improved managerial performance.
2. Large, decentralized firms may gather information which is scattered in many places, and integrate it meaningfully.
3. Management may exploit the marketing concept more fully.
4. Users may retrieve information on a selective basis, taking only what they want or need.
5. Management may recognize developing trends more quickly.
6. A company may make far better use of information which is ordinarily collected

---

[3]For a report on the effects in small retailing firms, see Cyrus C. Wilson and Charles D. Greenidge, "The Effect of an Integrated Information System on Management Performance," in Reed Moyer (ed.), *Changing Marketing Systems*, American Marketing Association, Chicago, 1968, pp. 113–117. For a five-part case example illustrating in a medium-sized industrial company the development, organzation, and implementation of an information system, see Richard L. Pinkerton, "How to Develop a Marketing Intelligence System," *Industrial Marketing*, in 1969, April, p. 41; May, p. 48; June, p. 60; July, p. 62; August, p. 54.

[4]Conrad Berenson, "Marketing Information System," *Journal of Marketing*, October, 1969, pp. 17–18.

in the course of its business operations; for example, sales by products, territories, or customer groups.

7. Management may be able to better control its marketing plan by receiving and heeding early warning signals.

8. It may prevent important information from being easily suppressed; for example, indications that a product should be withdrawn from the market.

The notion of a marketing information system is consistent with the philosophy of the marketing concept, which emphasizes the coordination and integration of all marketing activities in order to maximize the effectiveness of a company's marketing program. See Fig. 26-1.[5] A marketing information system might serve, for example, as a basis for *setting goals* and *formulating a marketing plan.* Research would be used to *predict* the results of alternative courses of action—e.g., reliance primarily on salesmen rather than advertising in promoting a product. (See the "A" feedbacks in Fig. 26-1.) Then later the information system would serve as the basis for *evaluating* the results of the marketing program ("B" feedbacks). Findings in the evaluation stage would then be the basis for reformulating goals and plans for the succeeding stage of the marketing program. "B" feedbacks (evaluative) from stage 1 would in effect become "A" feedbacks (formulative) for stage 2 in the ongoing marketing process.

In an earlier landmark study, Cox and Good pointed out that an effective MkIS has three operating subsystems related to (1) the control of marketing operations, (2) the planning of marketing activities, and (3) the basic research on particular marketing problem areas.[6] For each of these three subsystems, Fig. 26-2 illustrates some typical uses, benefits, and examples.

In another example Fig. 26-3 illustrates how the full information cycle can be used to improve marketing activities. In this figure we observe three marketing activities—sales forecasting, maintaining a central file on customers, and sales-force management. In sales forecasting, the information system is being used to improve the accuracy of the annual sales forecast. In the sales-force-management project, the goal is to develop better quotas for a new compensation plan for salesmen. As the full information cycle is applied to each marketing project, we can see that the different projects each may emphasize some parts of the information cycle more than others.

As a company embraces the concept of a marketing information system, we can expect some changes in its organizational structure. The information system will become the nerve center of the entire marketing activity. Kotler envisions an organizational unit which will broaden the marketing research function and will improve the accuracy, timeliness, and comprehensiveness of marketing information services. This "Marketing Information and Analysis Center will function as the

---

[5]The discussion of Fig. 26-1 is adapted from Brien and Stafford, "Marketing Information Systems: A New Dimension for Marketing Research," in Smith, Brien, and Stafford, *op. cit.,* pp. 19–21.

[6]See Donald F. Cox and Robert E. Good, "How to Build a Marketing Information System," *Harvard Business Review,* May–June, 1967, pp. 145–154. For later reports on the status of MkIS, see The Conference Board, *Information Systems for Sales and Marketing Management,* report no. 591, New York, 1973; and Richard H. Brien, "Marketing Information Systems: The State of the Art," in B. W. Becker and H. Becker (eds.), 1972 *Combined Proceedings,* American Marketing Association, Chicago, series no. 34, 1973, pp. 19–27.

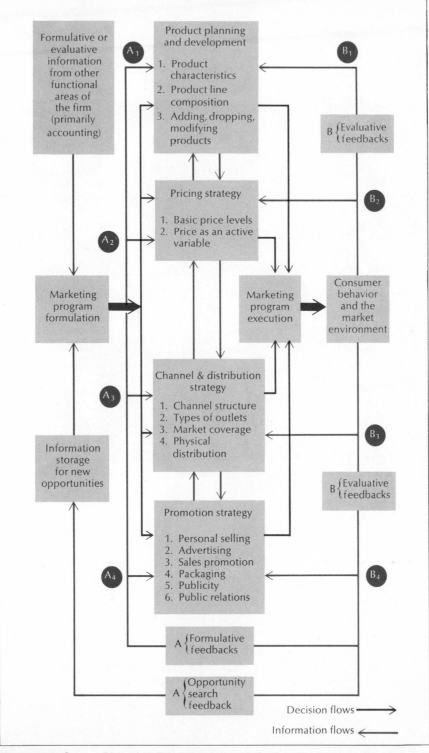

THE MARKETING MANAGEMENT PROCESS AND INFORMATION FLOW

Figure 26-1. *Source:* Richard H. Brien and James E. Stafford, "Marketing Information Systems: A New Dimension in Marketing Research," *Journal of Marketing*, July, 1960, p. 20.

EXAMPLES OF BENEFITS AND USES OF A MARKETING INFORMATION SYSTEM

	Typical Applications	Benefits	Examples
Control Systems	1. Control of marketing costs	1. More timely computerized reports	1. Undesirable cost trends are spotted more quickly so that corrective action may be taken sooner
	2. Diagnosis of poor sales performance	2. Flexible on-line retrieval of data	2. Executives can ask supplementary questions of the computer to help pinpoint reasons for a sales decline and reach an action decision more quickly
	3. Management of fashion goods	3. Automatic spotting of problems and opportunities	3. Fast-moving fashion items are reported daily for quick reorder, and slow-moving items are also reported for fast price reductions
	4. Flexible promotion strategy	4. Cheaper, more detailed, and more frequent reports	4. On-going evaluation of a promotional campaign permits reallocation of funds to areas behind target
Planning Systems	1. Forecasting	1. Automatic translation of terms and classifications between departments	1. Survey-based forecasts of demand for complex industrial goods can be automatically translated into parts requirements and production schedules
	2. Promotional planning and corporate long-range planning	2. Systematic testing of alternative promotional plans and compatibility testing of various divisional plans	2. Complex simulation models both developed and operated with the help of data bank information can be used for promotional planning by product managers and for strategic planning by top management
	3. Credit management	3. Programmed executive decision rules can operate on data bank information	3. Credit decisions are automatically made as each order is processed
	4. Purchasing	4. Detailed sales reporting permits automation of management decisions	4. Computer automatically repurchases standard items on the basis of correlation of sales data with programmed decision rules
Basic-research Systems	1. Advertising strategy	1. Additional manipulation of data is possible when stored for computers in an unaggregated file	1. Sales analysis is possible by new market segment breakdowns
	2. Pricing strategy	2. Improved storage and retrieval capability allows new types of data to be collected and used	2. Systematic recording of information about past R & D contract bidding situations allows improved bidding strategies
	3. Evaluation of advertising expenditures	3. Well-designed data banks permit integration and comparison of different sets of data	3. Advertising expenditures are compared to shipments by county to provide information about advertising effectiveness
	4. Continuous experiments	4. Comprehensive monitoring of input and performance variables yields information when changes are made	4. Changes in promotional strategy by type of customer are matched against sales results on a continuous basis

Figure 26-2. *Source:* Donald F. Cox and Robert E. Good, "How to Build a Marketing Information System," *Harvard Business Review,* May–June, 1967, p. 146.

USE OF FULL INFORMATION CYCLE TO IMPROVE MARKETING ACTIVITIES

Marketing activity	Assessment of information needs	Data measurement and collection	Storage retrieval and transmission	Format, display, reporting	Analytical technologies and models	Data utilization; new concepts
1. Sales forecasting	More accurate annual sales forecasting	Customer industry information Salesmen probability estimates on contracts Competition product and marketing effort	More current updating of recent sales	Graphical display of actual sales vs. previous forecasts	Simulation model for evaluation of forecasts Statistical extrapolation methods	Relative product and marketing advantage; rating our firm relative to the prime competitor
2. Central file on customers	Learn which types of marketing efforts work most effectively with customers	Demographic, psychological, sociological, behavioral, and sales data on each customer	Creation of a new file		Experimental design Statistical evaluation	Measuring the impact of competitive actions on our sales
3. Sales-force management	Better quotas for new compensation program	Territory potential indicators Territory competitive pressure	New files	Computer reports	Computerized compensation formulas, sales-call routing Automated direct mail follow-up for efficient "holding" of customers	Optimal level of effort for both prospecting and holding Segmentation: match type of letter by type of customer

Figure 26-3. *Source:* Robert E. Good, "Managerial Design of Information Systems: The Full Information Cycle," in Jack L. Taylor, Jr., and James F. Robb (eds.), *Fundamentals of Marketing: Additional Dimensions*, 2d ed., McGraw-Hill Book Company, New York, 1975.

marketing nerve center for the company and will not only provide instantaneous information to meet a variety of executive needs but also will develop all kinds of analytical and decision aids for executives."[7] Of course, essential to the success of any marketing information system and any related organizational structure is the full support of top management.

RELATIONSHIP OF MARKETING INFORMATION SYSTEMS AND MARKETING RESEARCH

It may be a bit risky to generalize on this relationship, because it is perceived quite differently by various people. Some folks see an MkIS as simply a logical, computer-based extension of marketing research. The first marketing information systems were developed generally in the 1960s, while marketing research as a separately identified activity predates this by some 50 years. Other students of the situation see the two as distinctly different activities, related only to the extent that they both deal with the management of information. Firms without an MkIS will perceive a broader role for their marketing research group. If a company has a formed MkIS, then the marketing research activity (whether departmentized or not) is probably treated as just one part of the information system.

The essence of what we mean by "marketing research" is contained in Richard Crisp's definition of the term. Crisp has called marketing research "the systematic, objective, and exhaustive search for and study of the facts relevant to any problem in the field of marketing."[8] This definition suggests a *systematic* activity, thus sounding like the essence of an MkIS. Yet, as traditionally practiced, marketing research has tended to be *unsystematic*. (See Fig. 26-4 for a polarization of characteristics of the two activities.)

Marketing research tends to be conducted on a project-to-project basis, with each project having a starting point and an end. These projects often seem to deal with unrelated problems on an intermittent, almost "brush-fire" basis, as contrasted to the continuous information flow for decision making in a marketing information system. Marketing research tends to stress the collection of past data to solve problems. Information systems are future-oriented activities designed hopefully to prevent problems from arising. Marketing research is involved primarily with handling external data. Accounting departments and other nonmarketing areas in the firm typically gather and process internal marketing data, as when they analyze sales volume or marketing costs to evaluate performance in various sales territories or product lines.

Parenthetically we should recognize that many marketing research practitioners probably would not agree with the distinctions in the above paragraph and in Fig. 26-4. They would contend they already are doing much of what we have attributed to an MkIS. And they may be correct *if* the firm has no formal MkIS. Then the scope of the marketing research activity is likely to be much broader. It may well include some sale volume analysis, marketing cost analysis, demand forecasting, etc.

---

[7]Philip Kotler, "A Design for the Firm's Marketing Nerve Center," *Business Horizons,* Fall, 1968, p. 70.

[8]Richard D. Crisp, *Marketing Research,* McGraw-Hill Book Company, New York, 1957, p. 3.

CONTRASTING CHARACTERISTICS OF MARKETING RESEARCH AND A MARKETING INFORMATION SYSTEM	
Marketing research	Marketing information system
1. Emphasis on handling external information	**1.** Handles both internal and external data
2. Concerned with solving problems	**2.** Concerned with preventing as well as solving problems
3. Operates in fragmented, intermittent fashion—on a project-to-project basis	**3.** Operates continuously—is a system
4. Tends to focus on past information	**4.** Tends to be future-oriented
5. Noncomputer-based	**5.** Is a computer-based process
6. Is one source of information input into a marketing information system	**6.** Includes other subsystems besides marketing research

Figure 26-4.

In firms that have an MkIS, the separate marketing research activity can be extremely valuable. Marketing research projects are a significant source of data entering an MkIS. Also the marketing researcher's contact with the external environment may provide an expertise which is a useful complement to the quantitatively oriented computer specialists so vital in a marketing information system.

Consequently, at this point we shall turn to the subject of marketing research and discuss its scope, the typical procedure in a marketing research investigation, the organizational structures typically used for marketing research, and the current status of the field.

SCOPE OF MARKETING RESEARCH ACTIVITIES

For over 50 years there has been a steady growth in marketing research departments, thus reflecting management's recognition of the importance of this activity. In a broad-based study sponsored by the American Marketing Association in 1973, about 60 percent of the companies reported having a formal (more than one person) marketing research department. This figure ranged from 61 percent in medium-sized firms to 81 percent among the large companies. The research departments were most commonly found among manufacturers of consumer products (70 percent), followed by publishing and broadcasting firms (66 percent), manufacturers of industrial goods (59 percent), and retailers, wholesalers, and advertising agencies (53–54 percent). Also, about half of these formal departments had been established just during the preceding decade. The broad scope of marketing research activities and the percentage of firms engaging in each are summarized in Table 26-1. The most common activities were determination of market characteristics, measurement of market potentials, market-

Table 26-1. Marketing research activities of 1,322 companies.
Most common activities are determination of market characteristics, measurement of market potentials, market-share analysis, and sales analysis. Note the large number participating in corporate-responsibility research.

Research activity	Percent doing
Advertising research	
Motivation research	33
Copy research	37
Media research	44
Studies of ad effectiveness	49
Business economics and corporate research	
Short-range forecasting (up to 1 year)	63
Long-range forecasting (over 1 year)	61
Studies of business trends	61
Pricing studies	56
Plant- and warehouse-location studies	47
Product-mix studies	51
Acquisition studies	53
Export and international studies	41
Company-employees studies	45
Corporate-responsibility research	
Consumers' "Right to Know" studies	18
Ecological-impact studies	27
Studies of legal constraints on advertising and promotion	38
Social values and policies studies	25
Product research	
New-product acceptance and potential	63
Competitive-product studies	64
Testing of existing products	57
Packaging research: design or physical characteristics	44
Sales and market research	
Measurement of market potentials	68
Market-share analysis	67
Determination of market characteristics	68
Sales analysis	65
Establishment of sales quotas, territories	57
Distribution-channels studies	48
Test markets, store audits	38
Consumer panel operations	33
Sales compensation studies	45

Source: Dik Warren Twedt (ed.), *1973 Survey of Marketing Research,* American Marketing Association, Chicago, 1973, p. 41.

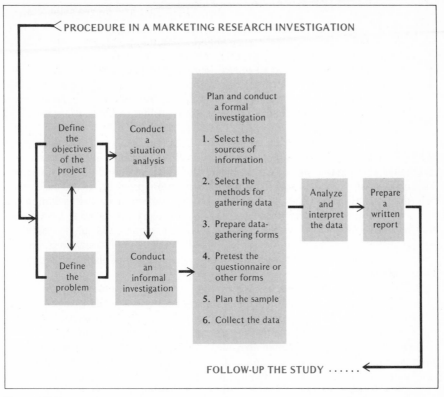

Figure 26-5.

share analysis, and sales analysis. It is interesting to note the sizable number of firms now engaging in research on corporate responsibility.[9]

PROCEDURE IN A MARKETING RESEARCH INVESTIGATION

In marketing research no two tasks are exactly alike, nor is there any single procedure that can be followed in all investigations. The general procedure illustrated in Fig. 26-5, however, is applicable to most projects. Some of the steps listed here are interrelated, some overlap, and some are not needed in every project.

DEFINE THE OBJECTIVE AND THE PROBLEM

A researcher should have a reasonably clear idea of what he is trying to do in a research job. Usually this means defining a problem. However, the objective of a

---

[9]Dik Warren Twedt (ed.), *1973 Survey of Marketing Research,* American Marketing Association, Chicago, 1973, pp. 11–13, 21–23, 40–44. This survey covered 1,322 firms representing a diverse assortment including manufacturers, retailers, wholesalers, advertising agencies, publishers and broadcasters, banks, and public utilities.

research job is not always to *solve* a problem. Often the purpose of a sales analysis is to determine whether the company *has* a problem and, if so, in what territory, product, or class of customer it lies. To illustrate, a manufacturer of commercial air-conditioning and refrigeration equipment had been enjoying a steady increase in sales volume over a period of years. Management decided to make a sales analysis, and this research project uncovered the fact that although the company's volume had been increasing, its share of the market had declined. In this instance, marketing research uncovered a problem which management did not know existed.

When marketing research ascertains that a problem does exist, the objective of the project is to determine exactly what the problem is and to attempt to solve it. Normally, a company starts with a broad, tentative statement of its problem. Through investigation it is able to pinpoint the problem precisely. In the case of the refrigeration equipment manufacturer, the broad problem was why this company's share of the market had decreased and how its position could be improved. To get this into manageable form, we can state the problem in parts. We can, for instance, ask: Have the company's product policies been the cause of its declining share of the market, or have weaknesses in the company's channel of distribution policies been the cause?

The case history of the Aurora Electronics Company (an actual company, but a fictitious name) may be used to illustrate the first three steps in a marketing research project, namely, problem definition, situation analysis, and informal investigation. The Aurora Company was a small electronics manufacturer, with the engineering department located in Chicago and the production plant and the president's office located in Phoenix, Arizona. Annual sales volume was $3 million, with 90 percent of this coming from contracts with the federal government. The other 10 percent came almost entirely from sales of the electronic component part used in automatic garage-door openers. This component was sold directly to a large door manufacturer. Joseph Stacy, the president, was an engineer, and his company had an excellent reputation. The firm had no marketing department, no sales manager, and no salesmen. It had a fine engineering department; the entire company was heavily engineering-oriented. At the time of the case, the firm was interested in diversifying its product line and its market so as to reduce its heavy dependence on government contracts. The engineering department developed an FM auto radio—a tuner and amplifier unit which could be connected to the regular AM auto radio and could use the AM speaker.

The general problem, as presented to an outside marketing research firm, was to determine whether the company should add this product to its line. Breaking the problem down into parts which could be handled by research resulted in the following specific questions:

1. What is the market demand for such a product?
2. What product features are desired, such as push-button tuning or signal-seeking tuning?
3. What channels of distribution should be used for such a product?
4. What should its price be?
5. What changes or additions in the company's organizational structure would be required if the product were added?

With this tentative restatement of the problem, the researchers were ready for the next procedural step, the situation analysis.

CONDUCT SITUATION ANALYSIS

The situation analysis involves getting acquainted with the company and its business environment by means of library research and extensive interviewing of company officials. The researchers try to get a "feel" for the situation surrounding the problem. They analyze the company, its market, its competition, and the industry in general.

In the situation analysis the researchers also try to define the problem more clearly and develop hypotheses for further testing. In research the establishment of hypotheses is a valuable step in problem solving. A *hypothesis* is a tentative supposition or a possible solution to a problem. It is something which is assumed or conceded merely for purposes of argument or action.

In the Aurora Company case, the situation analysis suggested the following hypotheses:

1. The company organization is inadequate to take on a consumer product.
2. The market for FM radios is limited geographically to a radius of 25 miles from FM stations. (This distance is the approximate sending or receiving limit for FM broadcasting.)
3. Marketing channels should be the same as those used for AM auto radios; distribution patterns for home radios are substantially different.

CONDUCT INFORMAL INVESTIGATION

Having gotten a feel for the problem, the researchers are now ready to conduct an informal investigation. To some extent this step overlaps the preceding one, which involves getting background information from *within* the company or from a library. The informal investigation consists of talking to people *outside* the company—middlemen, competitors, advertising agencies, customers, and men in the industry.

In the Aurora case, the researchers talked with many people. FM station owners and managers were of considerable help. Wholesalers and retailers of automobile radios were consulted, as were repairmen for auto radios. Long interviews were held with automobile dealers handling German FM auto radios—the Blau Punkt and the Becker. Consumers who had purchased these imports were interviewed. Helpful information was derived from talks with sales representatives of the Motorola Company. (This source was extremely valuable since there were rumors in the trade that Motorola had already engineered and produced models of an FM auto radio. As it turned out, the rumors were true, and a year later Motorola introduced such a product to the market.) Advertising agencies were consulted regarding their possible future use of FM stations as an advertising medium—the idea being that an increase in their use of FM stations would in time increase the quantity of FM programming and thus make set ownership more attractive.

This important step in a research project will often determine whether further formal study is necessary. Decisions regarding the problem are frequently made after the informal investigation is completed. As a matter of fact, at this point Aurora executives decided *not* to market the FM auto radio.

PLAN AND CONDUCT FORMAL INVESTIGATION

After the problem is defined and the informal investigation shows that the project is economically feasible, the company determines what facts are needed. The next step for the researcher is to plan how and where to get the desired data.

Select the sources of information. First the investigator must determine what sources of information he will use. He may use primary data, secondary data, or both.

Primary data are original data gathered specifically for the project at hand. *Secondary data* are those already existing, having been collected originally for some other purpose. Thus when a researcher stands in a supermarket and observes whether people use shopping lists and in what order they go to the various departments, he is collecting primary data. When he gets information from the Census of Population, a Ford Foundation report, or a library, he is using secondary sources.

One of the biggest mistakes made by many people in marketing research is rushing out to get primary data before exhausting the information already available in secondary sources. Ordinarily, secondary information can be gathered much faster and at far less expense than primary data.

At the same time, secondary sources of information must meet certain standards of accuracy in order to be of optimal usefulness. First, the information must be sufficiently *current*. If quotas for salesmen in Florida or Arizona in 1976 are set on the basis of data found in the 1970 Census of Population or the 1972 Census of Business, the quotas will be understated because these are areas of rapid growth in market potential. The information should be *classified in a manner useful* to the researcher. He may want to make a study of college students, but then find that his desired secondary source classifies the data by age groups of 10-19 and 20-29.

To be useful, the data must be *valid* (relevant). For instance, sales of ski equipment in Texas is not a valid measure of the size of the Texas ski market, because many Texans who ski in Colorado or New Mexico will buy some equipment at the ski resort. Secondary information also must be *reliable;* that is, it must be based on a sampling procedure which is statistically sound. Finally, accuracy in the information implies that the original source generated the data in an *impartial* manner. In order to determine the validity, reliability, and impartiality of secondary information, the researcher may have to investigate the organization that collected the data and the methods it used in making its study.

Sources of secondary data. Several readily available, excellent sources of secondary information are at the disposal of a marketing researcher.[10]

---

[10]For a good discussion of the major sources of secondary data, see Harper W. Boyd, Jr., and Ralph Westfall, *Marketing Research,* 3d ed., Richard D. Irwin, Inc., Homewood, Ill., 1972, pp. 247–265.

1. Internal company records. Companies regularly maintain orderly records of salesmen's daily reports, call reports, sales orders, and customers' complaints. Companies also usually keep sales records for each territory, product, and class of customer. When a problem must be solved, the first place a company should go for information is to its own files. In many cases, this source may well be the only place where the needed information can be found.

2. Government. The federal government furnishes more marketing data than any other single source in the nation. These data are available at very low prices, even though there is a tremendous cost involved in collecting them. Also, the government has access under the law to types of information (company sales and profits, personal income, etc.) which are impossible for a private company to get. The decennial Census of Population, for example, published by the Department of Commerce, contains economic, market, and sociological data in addition to a count of people by state, county, city, metropolitan area, and census tract in big cities. The Census of Business, usually taken every five years, provides detailed information about the number of establishments, sales, expenses, employment activity, and other business indicators for retailing and wholesaling institutions and service trades. The Census of Manufactures, also taken usually every five years, furnishes an extremely detailed industrial classification, including the number of establishments, the value added by manufacturing, employment figures, etc., for each industry.

   The Department of Commerce publishes various summaries of statistics. The most inclusive is the annual *Statistical Abstract of the United States*. The monthly *Survey of Current Business* furnishes data on a wide variety of topics. The *County and City Data Book* is ordinarily published every three years and includes a variety of statistics for all counties and all cities with populations over 25,000. The *Minerals Yearbook* (Department of the Interior) is a comprehensive annual report on mining activities.

   The U.S. Department of Agriculture is a fine source of information on agricultural activity. Reports issued regularly cover crop estimates, acreage yields, and acreage planted. The Department also publishes many excellent reports on marketing methods, channels, consumption patterns, prices, packaging, and the like. *Agricultural Statistics,* published annually, furnishes information on production, consumption, price, and trade of most agricultural products and minerals both in the United States and in many foreign countries.

   The Deptartment of Labor, particularly the Bureau of Labor Statistics, is another good source. Its *Monthly Labor Review* carries data on wages, employment, unemployment, and price indexes. The *Monthly Catalog of United States Government Publications* lists all federal government publications according to the agency or department which prepared them.

   State and local governments provide a wide variety of sources of information, but normally they are not so well catalogued or easy to locate as the federal sources. Data stemming from tax records, license applications, and other registration systems furnish much of the state and local information.

3. Trade, professional, and business associations. Associations are excellent sources of information for their members. They also supply data for outside groups. Through trade journals and periodic reports, members of associations can also keep up to date on activities in their given trades.

4. Private business firms. Private marketing research firms, advertising agencies,

and individual manufacturers or middlemen may be able to provide information needed by a researcher. Companies such as the A.C. Nielsen Company (the largest marketing research firm in the world) conduct various kinds of marketing research. Their findings are published and are available to persons who subscribe to the companies' publications. The Nielsen Company, for example, prepares a food-drug index giving information on a client's retail sales and his competitors' sales for particular products. Data regarding inventories, retail prices, and promotional activity at the retail level are also published. The Daniel Starch Company regularly measures readership of advertisements in various magazines and newspapers.

5. Advertising media. Many magazines, newspapers, radio and television stations, and outdoor advertising companies publish information that marketing researchers may not find available elsewhere. *Sales Management* annually publishes its "Survey of Buying Power," which covers population, retail sales, income, and effective buying power for all states, counties, metropolitan areas, and cities with populations over 10,000. Many media publish circulation data, station coverage maps, and statistics on their trading areas.

6. University research organizations. Most large universities operate research bureaus and publish findings which are of value to the business community. Bureaus of business research play a leading role in this activity, although marketing people may also obtain useful reports from a bureau of agricultural research or social research.

7. Foundations. Nonprofit research foundations and related groups carry out many kinds of research projects. Statistical analyses and reports on special topics are published by such groups as The Conference Board, the American Management Association, and the Committee for Economic Development. While the Ford, Carnegie, Russell Sage, and similar foundations are not limited to business research, many of their reports are of interest to marketing people.

8. Libraries. Lest the student forget, a good library is probably the best single, all-around source of secondary information. It will contain publications from practically all the sources mentioned here. The ability to use bibliographies, card indexes, and periodical indexes is virtually a prerequisite for anyone hoping to do any kind of research.

Sources of primary data. After exhausting all reasonable secondary sources of information, the researcher may still lack sufficient data. Then he will turn to primary sources and gather the facts himself.

1. Company salesmen. Frequently a marketing analyst will interview salesmen in order to get pertinent market information, or he will ask the salesmen to interview middlemen, customers, or representatives from competitors. Salesmen can often supply quite current and detailed information from their territories and at a low marginal cost. These same data, if available at all from secondary sources, might come several months later.[11] Management should not, however, use expensive sales personnel in research capacities if this diverts them from their

---

[11]For a report on how salesmen for manufacturers of technical industrial products can be used effectively to gather information for a company's marketing program, see Frederick E. Webster, Jr., "The Industrial Salesman as a Source of Market Information," *Business Horizons*, Spring, 1965, pp. 77–82.

primary job of selling. Also, salesmen are not trained field researchers, and the information they collect may be biased.

2. Middlemen, consumers, and others. Manufacturers can seek information from their wholesalers and retailers. Wholesalers, in turn, can use their retail customers as primary sources. Middlemen may be asked their opinion of a given product, company policy, or program. Sometimes middlemen can give a manufacturer a good indication of the feelings of the ultimate consumer or industrial user, but sellers may have to go directly to the household consumer or the industrial user to get the facts about attitudes, motives, and buying habits.

In some cases a firm's competitors may provide primary information. It may be gathered surreptitiously by having salesmen query the competitors' salesmen, or it may be gathered openly through the trade association. A firm may approach a competitor directly on matters of mutual interest. For instance, all supermarket operators or used-car dealers in a city may have a meeting to discuss the question of keeping their establishments open on Sundays.

Determine methods for gathering primary data. There are three widely used methods of generating primary data: survey, observation, and experimentation. Normally, not all three are used on one project. The choice of method will be influenced by the availability of time, money, personnel, and facilities.

Survey method. A *survey* consists of gathering data by interviewing a limited number of people (a sample) selected from a larger group. A survey has the advantage of getting to the original source of information. In fact, this may be the *only* way to find out the motives, opinions, or buying intentions of a group.

While the survey is still the most widely used method of collecting primary data, there may be a trend away from it. Not only have methods of observation and experimentation been improved and their value more fully realized, but the survey method contains certain inherent limitations. Surveys require careful planning, and there are opportunities for error in the construction of the questionnaire, in its editing, and in the interviewing process. Surveys may be very expensive, and they are time-consuming. Often the process is slow, and the researcher may need facts immediately. Another key weakness is that respondents often cannot or will not give correct answers. This is particularly destructive when a marketing analyst is searching for reasons underlying a respondent's behavior. There also are indications that researchers' access to one especially rich data base—business corporations—is declining and will continue to do so unless ways can be found to alleviate growing friction between businessmen and researchers (particularly academicians).[12] Business respondents object to the sheer number and complexity of questionnaires received, as well as to the misuse of information.

The interviewing or data gathering in a survey may be done by the researcher in person, by telephone, or by mail. These three types of interviews may be evaluated on the following bases: (1) flexibility, (2) amount of information to be obtained, (3) accuracy, and (4) speed, cost, and administration.

Personal interviews are more flexible than the other two types because the interviewer can alter his questions to fit the situation as he sees it. He is able to

---

[12]Thomas L. Reuschling and Michael J. Etzel, "The Disappearing Data Source," *Business Horizons,* April, 1973, pp. 17–22; also see "The Public Clams Up on Survey Takers," *Business Week,* Sept. 15, 1973, p. 216.

probe more deeply if he is not satisfied with the answer. (Of course, there is a danger that a bias may be introduced into the survey if the original questions are altered.) Ordinarily, it is possible to obtain more information by personal interview than by telephone or mail. Virtually every subject lends itself to a personal interview. Also, the interviewer can by observation obtain data regarding a respondent's socioeconomic status—his home, neighborhood, and apparent standard of living. Finally, a statistically sound sample is more easily obtainable with personal interviews.

The major limitations of this method of interviewing are its relatively high cost, the length of time needed to plan and execute the survey, and the opportunity to introduce errors in the interviewing process. When the personal interview method is used on a broad geographic basis, as in a national survey of magazine readership or shaving habits, the advantage of flexibility pretty much disappears. Interviewers in these situations ordinarily must follow an exactly prescribed procedure. Probing becomes difficult, questions should not be reworded, and very little is left to the interviewer's discretion.

In a *telephone survey* the respondent is approached by telephone, and the interview is completed at that time. Telephone surveys can usually be conducted more rapidly and at less cost than either personal or mail surveys. Wide geographic areas can be covered without any traveling. Telephone surveys are less flexible than personal interviews but more flexible than mail surveys. Since a few interviewers can make any number of calls from a few central points, this method is quite easy to administer. Many of the problems involved in the management of interviewers in personal surveys are not present here. Another significant advantage is that a telephone survey may be timely. For instance, people may be asked whether they are watching television at the moment and, if so, the name of the program and the sponsor.

One limitation of the telephone survey is that interviews must be short. Normally, lengthy interviews cannot be conducted satisfactorily over the phone. Also, it is difficult to ascertain the socioeconomic characteristics of the respondents. It is virtually impossible to get a complete cross section of the public because some people do not have telephones, others have unlisted numbers, many are not at home when the interviewer calls, and finally some refuse to respond in this type of survey.

Interviewing by mail involves mailing a questionnaire to potential respondents and having them return the completed form by mail. Since no interviewers are involved, this type of survey is not hampered by interviewer bias and problems connected with the management of interviewers. Mailed questionnaires are more economical than personal interviews and are particularly useful in broad, national surveys. Respondents may answer the questions at their leisure, so the replies may be carefully thought out. Also, if the respondent remains anonymous, he will probably give true answers because he does not feel the need to impress the interviewer. Finally, it is easier to reach some groups by mail than by either of the other two methods.

A major problem with mail questionnaires is the compilation of a good mailing list, especially in a broad-scale survey. If the sample can be drawn from a limited list, such as property taxpayers in certain counties or subscribers to a certain magazine, the list presents no problem. Another significant limitation concerns the sample reliability of the questionnaire returns, particularly when the returns are anonymous. If the respondents have characteristics which differentiate them from the nonrespondents, this factor would negate the validity of the survey results. A mail survey may lack timeliness; respondents are often slow about returning the questionnaire. Furthermore, the questionnaire must be reasonably short and the questions very simple; there is no way to elaborate or explain a puzzling question. There is also no opportunity to get additional data by observing the respondent. Often the representativeness of the sample is quite doubtful because the rate of returns on mail questionnaires is so low.

Observational method. In this research method the data are collected by observing some action of the respondent. No interviews are involved, although an interview may be used as a kind of follow-up to get additional information. For example, a customer may be observed buying beer in cans instead of bottles, and then he may be asked why he preferred one form of packaging to another. The consumer is unaware that he is being observed, so presumably he acts in his usual fashion. This is a valuable research tool, but unfortunately it is often underrated in favor of the interview technique.

Information may be gathered by personal or mechanical observation. In one form of personal observation, the researcher poses as a customer in a store. This technique is useful in getting information about the caliber of the salesman or in determining what brands he pushes. In another situation, an observer may watch customers at a discreet distance and notice what motivates a purchase. One study was made to determine how people buy beer in a retail store. To some, price was important. ("What do you have on sale this weekend?" "What is a good low-priced beer?") Some had brand preferences. ("Give me a six-pack of _____.") Others needed help in selecting a brand. ("What brand do you recommend?") Suburban shopping centers have used the observation technique to determine where their customers come from. The investigators record the license numbers of cars in the parking lot, and the addresses of owners are then traced through license bureaus. Mechanical observation is illustrated by the use of an electric cord stretched across a highway to count the number of cars that pass during a certain time period. A mechanical recorder may be attached to a radio or television set. This device will record whether the set was on and to what station it was tuned. Hidden cameras are also useful in gathering data by observation.

The observation method has several merits. It can be highly accurate; often it removes all conjecture about what the consumer does in a given matter. If a researcher over a period of several weeks traces the license numbers of cars parked in a suburban shopping center, he has a pretty good idea of the area from which this center is drawing customers. The observation technique reduces interviewer bias, but the possibility of bias is not completely eliminated as long as field observers are used. Devices such as mechanical recorders or hidden cameras supply more detailed data than normally can be gathered by surveys.

A major drawback to the observation method, which has already been mentioned, is that field observer bias may creep in. However well trained an observer may be, mistakes are possible. A second disadvantage is that the technique is limited in its application. Observation tells *what* happened, but it cannot tell *why*. It cannot delve into motives, attitudes, or opinions. Finally, this technique may be expensive. Observers must be posted at a given location for a certain period of time.

During part of the time, however, they may be just waiting for a consumer to perform the act to be observed.[13]

Experimental method. This method of gathering primary data involves the establishment of a scale model or a controlled experiment which simulates the real market situation as much as possible. The theory is that the small-scale experiment will furnish valuable information in designing a large-scale marketing program.

The experimental method may be used in several different ways and countless situations. In one instance, a firm may manufacture a few units of a product and give them to employees or consumers to try out. Probably the major application of the experimental method has been in market testing. This technique consists of establishing (1) a control market, in which all factors remain constant, and (2) one or more test markets, in which one factor is varied. A firm may be trying to determine whether to change the color of its package. In city A, the product is marketed in its traditional color; in each of cities B, C, and D, a different color is used. All other factors are presumably kept constant. Thus by measuring the sales in the four markets over a period of time, the manufacturer hopes to tell which color is best.

The outstanding merit of the experimental method is its realism. It is the only one of the three methods of gathering primary data which affords actual market tests and simulates an actual market situation. In testing the relative values of different advertisements or the value of an entire campaign, only the experimental method will tell which advertisement or campaign sold the most merchandise. Furthermore, this method holds great promise for the future as marketing research people improve their techniques. For instance, the method lends itself nicely to the use of mathematical models as a device for quantitative measurement.

Two big problems are encountered in market testing: selecting the control and test markets and controlling the variables. It is difficult—though necessary—to select markets that are identical in all significant socioeconomic factors. Experimental models, which have recently been developed, may be helpful in solving this problem. Some variables are really uncontrollable, and these may upset the comparability of results. Competitors may get wind of the test and try to confuse the picture by suddenly increasing their advertising, for example. Company salesmen or retail dealers may act abnormally if they find out that a test is being run. Furthermore, the experimental method is expensive; it requires long, careful planning and administration. Tests frequently cover six months—two months during which activity in the test and control centers is measured before anything new is introduced, two months during which the variable being tested (new color, new price, new advertising) is placed in the market, and two more months to allow for sales which may have been motivated by the test variable but were not made until sometime after it was removed.

Prepare data-gathering forms. Regardless of whether the interviewing or observation method is used to gather primary data, the researcher must prepare

---

[13]See Louis C. Wagner, "The Use of the Observational Method in Marketing Research," *University of Washington Business Review,* Autumn, 1968, pp. 18–24, for a more detailed review of some possible uses of this method, along with an analysis of its advantages and limitations.

standard forms to record the information. The importance of the questionnaire, however, and the difficulty of designing it cannot be overemphasized. In fact, most of the problems in data collection, whether by personal, mail, or telephone survey, center around the preparation of the questionnaire. Marketing research textbooks devote whole chapters to this subject, and in at least one instance an entire book has been devoted to only part of the task.[14]

Ordinarily a questionnaire designed for a telephone survey will be short. A mail questionnaire typically can be longer. It may run one or two pages, or on rare occasions even longer. Personal interviewing provides an opportunity for flexibility in (1) the length of the questionnaire, (2) the degree to which it is structured (standardized), and (3) the use of projective techniques as in motivation research.[15]

Extreme care and skill are needed in designing questionnaires in order to minimize bias, misunderstanding, respondent anger, misleading answers, etc. Even in a carefully prepared questionnaire, mistakes are bound to occur. This is one good reason for pretesting a questionnaire. (See next section.) Some of the typical errors occurring in questionnaire design are as follows:

1. The respondent feels the information is none of your business: What is your family's income? How old are you? What percentage of your house remains to be paid?
2. Questions lack a standard of reference: Do you like a large kitchen? (What is meant by "large"?) Do you attend church regularly?
3. The respondent does not know the answer: What is your wife's favorite brand of lipstick?
4. The respondent cannot remember, so he guesses: How many calls did you (as a salesman) make on office supply houses during the past year?
5. Questions are asked in improper sequence. Save the tough, embarrassing one for late in the interview. By then some rapport ordinarily has been established with the respondent. A "none-of-your-business" question asked too early may destroy the entire interview.

Pretest the questionnaire or other forms. No matter how good a researcher thinks his questionnaire is, it still should be pretested. This process is similar to

---

[14]Stanley L. Payne, *The Art of Asking Questions,* Princeton University Press, Princeton, N.J., 1951. One procedure for questionnaire construction set forth by Boyd and Westfall, *op. cit.,* pp. 288–316, is as follows: (1) Determine what information is wanted, for example, quantitative market characteristics (number, age, sex, income, geographic location) of people visiting Alaska for a vacation only; (2) determine the type of questionnaire to be used (mail, telephone, or personal interview); (3) determine the content and necessity of each question and try to determine whether the respondents can and will answer it; (4) determine the type of question to use—open-end ("What did you like about Alaska as a vacationland?") or multiple-choice or dichotomous ("Should the capital of Alaska be Juneau or Anchorage?"); (5) decide on wording of questions; (6) decide on sequence of questions; (7) determine the physical form, layout, and method of reproduction; (8) prepare a preliminary draft and pretest it; (9) revise the questionnaire and prepare a final draft.

[15]For an explanation and appraisal of the standardized (structured) versus the nonstandardized (nonstructured) types of questionnaires, both when the objective of the questionnaire is clear to the respondent and when the objective is disguised, see Boyd and Westfall, *op. cit.,* pp. 136–143.

field testing a product. Obviously, an engineer thinks a new model of his automobile is perfect; otherwise he would not have sent it away from the drawing board. But he knows from experience that the only way to test the automobile is to use it. The researcher must test in three areas. First, he wants to make sure that the questions are clear and are in the proper order. Second, he wants to find out whether the instructions to the interviewers are adequate. Finally, he wants to uncover any problems which may arise in the course of tabulating the questionnaires. The method used in pretesting consists simply in trying out the questionnaire on a small sample of people similar to those who will be interviewed. It is wise to let the research person do some interviewing. By observing the reaction of a few respondents, he may be able to catch a number of unforeseen problems.

Plan the sample. Normally it is unrealistic and unnecessary to survey or observe every possible person who could shed light on the research problem. Before the data can be gathered, therefore, the researcher must determine from whom he is going to seek the information. He must plan or establish a sample. As is true of research in general, sampling is no stranger to us because we employ it frequently in our everyday activities. We often base our opinion of a person on only one or two conversations with him. We often take a bite of food before ordering a larger quantity.

Actually, the fundamental idea of sampling is that "if a small number of items or parts (called a sample) are chosen at random from a larger number of items or a whole (called a universe, or population) the sample will tend to have the same characteristics, and to have them in approximately the same proportion, as the universe."[16] In marketing research, sampling is another procedural step whose importance is difficult to overestimate. Sampling is a source of errors in many survey results. In one study, an opinion on student government was derived from interviewing a sample of fraternity and sorority members. With no dormitory students, off-campus residents, or commuting students included, this was obviously a biased, nonrepresentative sample of student opinion.

One of the first questions asked regarding sampling is: How large should the sample be? To be statistically reliable, a sample must be large enough to be truly representative of the universe or population. There are other generalizations which a researcher should keep in mind, however. First, size is by no means the main source of sampling errors. Second, huge increases in sample size are needed to produce small increases in the statistical reliability of the sample. Third, in the mathematical determination of statistical reliability the size of the universe is *not* a factor to consider. Finally, the size of the sample is often determined by such practical factors as the time and money available and the amount of cross-classification of data desired.

To be statistically reliable a sample must be proportionate. That is, all types of units found in the universe must be represented in the sample. Also, these units must appear in the sample in approximately the same proportion as they are found in the universe. Assume that a manufacturer of power lawn mowers wants to know what percentage of families in a certain metropolitan area own this product. Further assume that in this market one-half of the families live in the central city and the other half in the suburbs. Relatively more families in the suburbs have

---

[16]Richard D. Crisp, *op. cit.*, p. 95.

power mowers than in the city. Now, if 80 percent of the sample is made up of suburban dwellers, the percentage of families owning power mowers will be overstated because the sample lacks proportionality.

Innumerable sampling techniques may be used in marketing research. Many of these are quite similar, and many are used only infrequently. We should be able to get a basic understanding of sampling by considering three types: (1) simple random sample, (2) area samples, and (3) quota samples. The first two are probability samples, and the third is a nonprobability sample.

In *simple random sampling,* the sample is selected in such a way that every unit in the predetermined universe has a known and equal chance of being selected. Thus if we wished to use a random sample to determine department store preferences among people in Denver, Colorado, we would need an accurate and complete listing of all people within the city limits. If we wanted to use a random sample to determine feed and seed preferences among farmers in the Great Plains states, we would first decide what states to include and then get an up-to-date listing of all farmers in those states.

A variation of a simple random sample which is widely used is an *area sample*. Where it is not economically feasible to obtain a full list of the universe, an area sample may be used. In the above example of a study covering department store preferences among Denver residents, one way to conduct an area sample would be to list all the blocks in the city and then select at random a sample of the blocks. Then every household or every other household in the sample blocks could be interviewed. In this sampling method, the researcher needs only a list of the city blocks, not a listing of all Denver residents.

A *quota sample* is both a nonprobability sample and a stratified sample. Randomness is lost because proportionality is "forced." Every element in the universe does *not* have a known chance of being selected. To select a quota sample, the researcher must first decide which characteristics will serve as the basis of the quota and then determine in what proportion these characteristics occur in the universe. Thus in selecting a quota sample from among the people who went to Alaska for a vacation, the researcher may decide that the quota will be based upon the state of residence. In one study, it was found that 30 percent of the tourists to Alaska came from California, 10 percent from the state of Washington, and 15 percent from the East North Central census region (Illinois, Indiana, Ohio, Michigan, Wisconsin). The sample was forced to the extent that it was stratified on a nonprobability basis according to the home state of the tourist. Consequently, of the people included in the final sample, 30 percent were from California, 10 percent were from Washington, and so forth. In some studies, as many as four or five quota characteristics, such as age, sex, income, education, geographic area, and city size, are established to delimit the sample.

Probability sampling has one big advantage: it is the only method that enables the reliability of the results to be measured with mathematical exactness. The mathematical theory of probability may be employed to estimate the size of the sampling error. Furthermore, it does not require a considerable fund of detailed information regarding the universe. On the other hand, probability sampling can be very expensive and time-consuming, particularly when there is wide geographic dispersion of the units in the sample. Adequate listings of units may not be available, and much skill in selecting the sample is required. In simple random sampling these limitations are accentuated.

In quota sampling much reliance is placed on the judgment of those designing and selecting the samples. There is no mathematical way of measuring the accuracy of the results.

Collect the data. The procedural stage during which the primary data are actually collected in the field—by interviewing, observation, or both—normally constitutes the weakest link in the entire research process. Ordinarily, in all other steps reasonably well-qualified people are working carefully to ensure the accuracy of the results. Great care goes into preparing the survey questionnaire and considerable planning underlies the selection of the sample. Then the fruits of these and earlier labors may be entirely lost if the fieldworkers (data gatherers) are poorly selected or inadequately trained and supervised. The management of fieldworkers is a difficult task because they are usually part-time workers with little job motivation and their work is done where it cannot be observed, often at many widely separated locations.

A myriad of errors may creep into a research project at this point, and poor interviewers only increase this possibility. Bias may be introduced because people in the sample are not at home or refuse to answer. Errors occur because the interviewers do not follow the prescribed sample. In some instances, fieldworkers are unable to establish rapport with respondents, or they revise the wording of a question and thus elicit untrue or inapplicable responses. Considerable error may be introduced by improper interpretation or recording of answers. Finally, some interviewers just plain cheat in one way or another.[17]

ANALYZE DATA AND PREPARE WRITTEN REPORT

The final steps in a marketing research project are to analyze the data, interpret the findings, and submit a written report. Today the availability of sophisticated electronic data-processing equipment enables a researcher to tabulate and statistically analyze masses of data quickly and relatively inexpensively.

The end product of the investigation is the researcher's conclusions and recommendations, supported by any necessary detailed analyses, and submitted in written form. It typically is helpful if an oral discussion can be held shortly after the written report has been submitted. Then the report can be expanded and explained as the recipients raise questions. Whatever form is used for transmitting the recommendations, suffice it to say that the researcher has "a message for Garcia," and he should put it in such a form that Garcia will be sure to read and understand it.

FOLLOW UP THE STUDY

For his own best interests, a researcher should follow up his study to determine whether his recommendations are being followed, and if not, then what are the reasons. So often the follow-up is omitted. Actually the analyst's future relations

---

[17]See Harper W. Boyd, Jr., and Ralph Westfall, "Interviewers as a Source of Errors in Surveys," *Journal of Marketing,* April, 1955, pp. 311–324. Ten years later, and again fifteen years later, another survey of the subject was made by the same authors. They observed that some significant gains had been achieved in dealing with interviewer bias, but they also concluded that the same problems still existed to a major degree and that relatively little was being done to solve them; see Harper W. Boyd, Jr., and Ralph Westfall, "Interviewer Bias Once More Revisited," *Journal of Marketing Research,* May, 1970, pp. 249–253.

with the company can be influenced seriously by this step, whether he is in the firm's own marketing research department or working for an outside agency. Unless there is a follow-up, the company may not pay much real attention to the report; it may be filed and forgotten.

ORGANIZATIONAL STRUCTURE FOR MARKETING RESEARCH

When a firm wishes to carry out a project, there are two ways it can get the job done: by the company's own personnel or by an outside organization.

WITHIN THE COMPANY

The American Marketing Association study indicated a strong trend toward companies' having a separate marketing research department, with the manager of this department reporting either to the chief marketing executive or directly to top management. From an organizational standpoint, the separate marketing research department is usually a centralized unit. The field sales force and branch personnel may be involved in data gathering—as in the "sales-force-composite" method of sales forecasting—but typically the analysis and action determination are accomplished in the central department. A case may be built, however, for decentralizing the research function to the extent that field sales management and personnel may perform certain organized research tasks in their respective territories. Strategic and tactical benefits are to be gained when branch managers can analyze their markets, make on-the-spot decisions, and adjust quickly to changing market and competitive conditions.[18]

When marketing research is done within the company, the researchers are well versed in company policy and procedures and know what information is available. Also, the firm is more apt to use its research facilities fully. On many problems, executives might not bother to call in an outside agency, while they might—if the firm had a research department—present the same problems to it. Using company manpower and facilities can be expensive, however, and unless the company has adequately qualified full-time personnel, needed research projects may be unavoidably delayed.

OUTSIDE THE COMPANY

An interesting mark of maturity in marketing research is the fact that despite the comparative youth of the field, it has already developed many institutions from which a company may seek help in marketing research problems. One group of organizations, which is regularly available for hire in research projects, includes advertising agencies and marketing research or management consulting firms such as the A. C. Nielsen Company or McKinsey and Company. A second group includes, for example, railroads, public utilities, and advertising firms which engage in marketing research in order to promote the services they are selling. A third type of outside organization includes trade associations, university bureaus of business research, and government agencies which conduct marketing research on common problems faced by a group of companies.

---

[18]Louis W. Stern and J. L. Heskett, "Grass Roots Market Research," *Harvard Business Review,* March–April, 1965, pp. 83–96.

Some companies have in their normal setup the nucleus of a marketing research department which can on occasion work with an outside agency on problems calling for a larger staff and more facilities than the companies themselves maintain.

These outside agencies employ highly qualified specialists in the marketing research field. Also, they have an objective; impartial approach. (Rarely does one hear of an actual case in which the agency seeks to retain its business by parroting what management wants to hear.) Finally, the agencies are experienced in their own right; they may bring to a given case the experiences of many other clients who had similar problems. Outside organizations do, of course, lack that intimate, continuing knowledge of a firm which can come only from a permanent employee relationship.

STATUS OF MARKETING RESEARCH

American business is just beginning to realize the full potential of marketing research. Many firms have long since passed beyond the nose-counting data-gathering stage—the stage where management was hindered by an insufficiency of information. Significant advances have been made in both quantitative and qualitative research methodology, to the point where researchers are making effective use of the behavioral sciences and mathematics. At the same time, however, we realize that far too many companies are still spending dollars on research for engineering and manufacturing their products, but only pennies, if anything, to determine the market opportunities for these products. In the American Marketing Association study mentioned earlier, about 40 percent of the firms did not have a formal marketing research department, and about one-quarter did not have even one person formally assigned to the activity. These firms apparently are making very limited use of marketing research and are simply treating it as an information-gathering activity.[19]

Several factors account for this less-than-universal acceptance of marketing research. Unlike the results of a chemical experiment, the results of marketing research cannot always be measured quantitatively. The research director cannot do a given job and then point to x percent increase in sales. Also, because management is not yet convinced of the value of marketing research, it will not always spend the amount of money necessary to do a good job. Good research costs money. Executives may not realize that they cannot always get half as good a job for half the amount of money.

Marketing research is far from perfect. We have noted several limitations of marketing research and several areas where major opportunities for error can occur—in sampling, field interviewing, etc. Even when marketing research is accurate, it is not a substitute for judgment. Research gathers, analyzes, and interprets facts, but the executive himself must make the decision.

Marketing research cannot predict future market behavior accurately in many cases, yet often that is what is expected of it. In fact, when dealing with consumer behavior, the researcher is hard pressed to get the truth regarding *present* attitudes or motives, much less those of next year. Predicting future market behavior obviously is loaded with risk. Can you imagine how many research projects

---

[19]Dik Warren Twedt (ed.), *1973 Survey of Marketing Research, op. cit.*, p. 11.

predicated on estimates of the future were rendered invalid by the oil embargo imposed by Arab countries in 1973? In that situation the oil embargo was so well publicized that inaccuracies in marketing research predictions probably were accepted by management. But consider the many other cases where future estimates (and thus the marketing research conclusions) proved to be inaccurate, and management's reaction was that marketing research is just no good!

Even in firms with a sophisticated research capability and a good track record, the predictions of the future can be expensively inaccurate. Witness, for example, the multimillion dollar market failures of Ford's Edsel, Du Pont's Corfam (man-made substitute for leather), and RCA's venture into computers. In all three of these projects, the estimates of future market behavior proved to be inaccurate by the time the products were marketed. Ford's market predictions in connection with its later cars—Mustang, Maverick, and Pinto—proved to be quite good, however. The main point here is that when management is making decisions based on estimates of the future, these decisions must be based on executive opinions, assumptions, and judgment, and not on "hard data"—known facts.

Possibly a more fundamental reason for the modest status of marketing research has been the failure of researchers to communicate adequately with management. Admittedly, there is poor research and poor researchers. Moreover, sometimes the mentality of the direct, quick-acting, pragmatic, decison-making executive may be at odds with the cautious, complex, hedging-all-bets mentality of a marketing researcher. However, the researchers, like many manufacturers, are often product-oriented when they should be market-oriented. Thus, they concentrate on research methods and techniques, rather than on showing management how these methods can aid in making better marketing decisions. Executives are willing to invest heavily in technical research because they are convinced there is a "payout" in this activity. Management has not been similarly convinced of a return on its investment in marketing research.[20] To communicate more effectively, the marketing researcher must let management know what he is doing for the company. He must take the initiative in communicating with management, talk their language, and be willing to make recommendations rather than straddle the fence on issues.[21]

In management's relationship with marketing research today, another basic problem is the apparent reluctance of management (1) to treat marketing research as a continuing process and (2) to relate marketing research and decision making in a more systematic fashion. Too often marketing research seems to be viewed in a fragmented, one-project-at-a-time manner. It is used only when management realizes it has a marketing problem.

---

[20]For a method of forecasting the return on investment of research dollars, see Lee Adler, "Profiting from Marketing Research," *Sales Management,* Nov. 10, 1970, p. 34. For some guidelines in evaluating research proposals, see A. B. Blankenship and Raymond F. Barker, "The Buyer's Side of Marketing Research," *Business Horizons,* August, 1973, pp. 73–80.

[21]For a survey of marketing research directors in large corporations, reporting on the role and effectiveness of the marketing research department as perceived by the director, his immediate superior, and other executives who use the department's services, see James R. Krum, "Perceptions and Evaluations of the Role of the Corporate Marketing Research Department," *Journal of Marketing Research,* November, 1969, pp. 459–464. This study identified (1) some ambiguities in the role of marketing research and (2) the areas of disagreement between marketing research directors and other executives.

One reason why many executives have been unable to relate research and decision making more closely is their unfamiliarity with modern decision-making processes and the informational sources available from related business and nonbusiness fields. Some executives resist the use of research because they fear it is a threat to their personal status. That is, research implies an evaluation of their effectiveness, and it may also invalidate many beliefs fondly held. Organizational defects such as the failure to identify clearly the company's goals and the lack of systematic marketing planning tend to limit the productive use of marketing research.

Regarding these basic problems, Newman observed:[22]

Reflecting executives' lack of understanding of research and its potential contribution to decision making is the fact that research departments have tended to be technical job shops to which operating people could bring requests if they chose to do so. The weakness of this system is that it depends on the initiative of executives who are unfamiliar with research and who typically are unable to identify their problems well enough to ask for the help they need.

Research departments which work only on requests brought to them tend to be occupied with routine, short-range operating problems. They are unlikely to be contributing to policy formulation, planning, and innovation. They cannot become an integral part of the decision-making process because line executives do not look to research for that sort of participation. Without a close relationship with the decision makers, research cannot play much of an educational role.

THE FUTURE: A MARKETING INFORMATION SYSTEM

The critical remarks in the preceding section bring us full circle in marketing research and back to the need for a marketing information system. Today a mass of information flows from external sources and also from within a firm. That information must be gathered, processed, and the findings disseminated in a meaningful way to executives so they can manage their firms' marketing programs. To effectively manage this mass of information, a company needs more than the traditional marketing research activity—a company needs an MkIS. A marketing information system is future-oriented, whereas traditional marketing research, with some exceptions, has been concerned largely with explaining why something in the past happened as it did. It is true that we can learn from the past. We should study the past, however, not for its sake alone but because it can guide us in the future. The expansion of temporal horizons focuses management's attention on forecasting and long-range planning. The importance of this future orientation is summed up well in the following statement: "To manage a business well is to manage its future; and to manage the future is to manage information."[23]

---

[22]Joseph W. Newman, "Put Research into Marketing Decisions," *Harvard Business Review*, March–April, 1962, pp. 109–110.

[23]Marion Harper, Jr., "A New Profession to Aid Management," *Journal of Marketing*, January, 1961, p. 1.

QUESTIONS AND PROBLEMS

1. Why does a company need a marketing information system?

2. Give some practical examples showing how a firm might use a marketing information system.

3. *a.* What is a marketing information system?

    b. How does it differ from marketing research?

4. "The marketing information executive—rather than an operating, decision-making executive—should be the one to identify marketing problems, delineate the area to be studied, and design the research projects." Do you agree? Explain.

5. Should the director of marketing information report directly to the chief marketing executive or to the president?

6. A large wholesaler of electrical supplies and equipment located in the Midwest wanted to learn as much as possible about the potential market for an electric milk cooler. This was essentially a chestlike container which could hold ten regular-sized farm milk cans.

    Many small farmers stored their cans of fresh milk in cool well water. Before the cans were collected by a local dairy, processor, or shipper, the temperature of the water—and the milk—might fluctuate considerably. Heat tended to raise the bacteria count in milk. In some cities and states milk having more than a certain level of bacteria count could not by law be processed for human consumption.

    The manufacturer of the electric cooler approached the wholesaler with the hope that he would add the product to his line. Before making a decision, the wholesaler wanted to do some informal investigating of the product's market possibilities. What should this informal investigation consist of?

7. A group of wealthy businessmen regularly spent some time each winter at a popular ski resort—Aspen, Colorado; Sun Valley, Idaho; Snow Valley, Vermont; or Squaw Valley, California. These men were intrigued with the possibility of forming a corporation to develop and operate a large ski resort in the Colorado Rockies. This would be a totally new venture and would be on U.S. Forest Service land. It would be a complete resort with facilities appealing to middle- and upper-income markets. What types of information might they want to have before deciding whether to go ahead with the venture? What sources of information would be used?

8. Acquire the following information for the most recent year available, using secondary sources. In each case, cite your source of information and list alternative sources where the information is also available.

    a. Tons of coal mined in Pennsylvania

    b. Wholesale sales in Illinois

    c. Value of cotton produced in California

    d. Population of Dade County, Florida

    e. Total number of new housing units started in the East-North-Central geographic region

    f. Gross-margin percentage of the Johns-Manville Company

    g. Total labor force in the United States—annual average

    h. Number of shoe stores in Texas

    i. Operating expense ratio for jewelry wholesalers

    j. Consumer expenditures for personal services and for durable goods

    k. Consumer price index—for any given month or the annual average

9. A manufacturer of a liquid glass cleaner competitive with Windex and Glass Wax wants to determine the amount of the product which he can expect to sell in various markets throughout the country. To help him in this project, prepare a report which shows the following information pertaining to your home state and also, if possible, your home city or county. Carefully identify the source you use for this information and also state other sources which provide this information.

    a. Number of households or families

    b. Income or buying power per family or per household

    c. Total retail sales in the most recent year for which you can find reliable data

    d. Total annual sales of food stores, hardware stores, and drugstores

    e. The number of food stores

10. A wholesaler of air-conditioning and refrigeration equipment for both domestic and commercial use wants to analyze his marketing costs in each territory to determine the relative profitability of each district. Specifically, what types of internal data would he use in this study?

11. Evaluate surveys, observational techniques, and experimentation as methods of gathering primary data in the following projects:

    a. A sporting goods retailer wants to determine college students' brand preferences for skis, tennis rackets, and golf clubs.

    b. A supermarket chain wants to determine women shoppers' preferences for the physical layout of fixtures and traffic patterns, particularly around check-out stands.

    c. A manufacturer of conveyor belts wants to know who makes buying decisions for this product among present and prospective users.

12. Carefully evaluate the relative merits of personal, telephone, and mail surveys on the bases of flexibility, amount of information obtained, accuracy, speed, cost, and ease of administration.

13. What kind of a sample would you use in research projects designed to answer the following questions?

    a. What brand of shoes is most popular among the female students on your campus?

    b. Should the department stores in or near your hometown be open on Sundays?

    c. What percentage of the business firms in the large city nearest your campus have automatic sprinkler systems?

14. What criteria should a manufacturing firm use or what questions should its executives ask in selecting an outside research organization to aid in marketing research work?

MARKETING PLANNING AND FORECASTING

We may recall from Chapter 2 that the management process involves developing a plan, operating (executing) it, and evaluating the results. Parts 3 to 6 were devoted to operating and directing a marketing program. This and the following chapter will emphasize planning and evaluation.

Three planning activities—marketing planning, sales forecasting, and budgeting—are closely interrelated. Marketing planning is the comprehensive activity. Forecasting demand then is the cornerstone of successful planning. One type of forecasting—sales forecasting—is the basis of all budgeting and operations (production as well as marketing) in a firm. Budgeting is the process of activating a marketing plan. That is, a budget is an operating plan expressed in dollars.

PLANNING IN THEORY AND PRACTICE

A careful student of marketing has referred to planning in marketing as "the exercise of analysis and foresight to increase the effectiveness of marketing activities."[1] Another writer states that "the purpose of planning is to manipulate the present systematically in order to be prepared for the future."[2] In simple English,

---

[1] Wendell R. Smith, "The Role of Planning in Marketing," *Business Horizons*, Fall, 1959, p. 54.
[2] Mark E. Stern, *Marketing Planning*, McGraw-Hill Book Company, New York, 1966, p. xi.

planning is drawing from the past to decide in the present what to do in the future. Or, let's decide now what we're going to do later, when and how we are going to do it, and who will do it.

In Chapter 2, planning was discussed as a management function separate from that of establishing objectives. Actually, marketing planning, broadly viewed, starts with the determination of marketing goals. It then involves a determination of how the goals will be reached. Several alternative courses of action may be followed, and management must apply problem-solving processes to select the best of the alternatives. Thus planning is also concerned with the operating system—the strategies and tactics—through which the goals are reached, the quantity and quality of effort needed to attain the goals, and, finally, the firm's ability to generate this effort.

Planning may also be viewed as an extension of the input-output theory developed by Prof. Wassily Leontief, of Harvard: "Most planning is the attempt to exercise such foresight with respect to the anticipated outputs of an organization so that the inputs can be utilized with maximum efficiency."[3] Once management forecasts its desired output—that is, sets a goal—then through careful planning it can determine what input factors will be needed to attain the output goal. To illustrate, assume that management wants to enter a new geographic market and attain a sales volume of $2 million in this market by the end of the second year. Through input-output analysis, management can estimate what inputs are necessary in the form of advertising, personal selling, production facilities, financing, and personnel to reach the goal. Management may find that the required inputs are beyond the firm's capacity. Then the output goal must be altered along more modest lines. Thus availability of inputs may actually set limits on output. In essence, planning involves a matching of means and ends, or inputs and outputs.

IMPORTANCE OF PLANNING

Planning may be done formally or informally—in a simple, crude fashion or in a scientific, sophisticated manner—but, nevertheless, planning is inevitable when a firm is confronted with alternative courses of action. The concept of planning is not new, but the growing importance of the marketing concept in our economy has resulted in an increased recognition of the value of formal, organized planning. As one writer said, "The hard core of the so-called marketing concept . . . is effective and scientific use of market planning."[4] Truly, any success which management has in increasing the profitability of marketing operations depends in large part upon the nature of the marketing planning. Formal marketing planning is one of the most effective *management tools* available for risk reduction.

The dynamic nature of our economy, the growing fierceness of competition, and the shrinking profit margins are forcing management to focus more attention on marketing planning. Careful, formal planning is essential for maximizing the chances of success: in new-product development, in setting up an international marketing program, in establishing a distribution system, and in countless other aspects of a total marketing program. In this age, forward-looking competitors are

---

[3] Wroe Alderson, *Marketing Behavior and Executive Action*, Richard D. Irwin, Inc., Homewood, Ill., 1957, p. 414.

[4] Smith, *op. cit.*, p. 57.

adopting the systems approach to marketing. Computer technology is being employed to help management optimize its use of quantitative analytical techniques such as PERT, linear programming, input-output analysis, probability theory, etc. In such a competitive setting, a company may be committing economic suicide if it relies on haphazard, informal planning.

Many other advantages accrue from organized planning. It can save a considerable amount of executive time and effort. With a formal staff group assigned to planning tasks, line executives can be freed for other revenue-producing work. Also, internal coordination and communication can be improved, and executives can be provided with some framework for day-to-day decisions. Formal planning should also elicit disciplined thinking because executives must put their thoughts in writing before acting. Good planning forces a firm to do advance scheduling. As a result, management by crisis and expediency can be reduced to a minimum, and short-term disturbances can be placed in a proper perspective.

OBSTACLES TO SUCCESSFUL PLANNING

Despite the many benefits to be gained, most firms still do not employ formal marketing planning. Moreover, only "about 20 percent of the major industrial companies that are thought to be good marketing planners *are* good marketing planners."[5] This summary observation was based on a study (conducted by McKinsey & Company, a management consulting firm) which covered marketing planning in large industrial companies. The following four common administrative weaknesses in marketing planning were identified in this study:

1. Failure of the chief executive to establish and communicate major corporate goals
2. Inability to assess realistically the capabilities and probable strategies of competitors
3. Lack of internal coordination and communication with the firm
4. Overstructured planning process, generating unnecessary paper work and irrelevant details which obscure the critical problem areas

Other obstacles may be observed in the path leading to successful planning.[6] Often marketing strategies are based on goals which are unrealistic, conflicting, or too numerous. Many top-level executives claim they do not have time for formal planning activities. Yet these same administrators often seem reluctant to delegate authority to a staff planning group, pleading that staff people lack experience. Our limited abilities in interpreting consumers' attitudes and motivation also hinder successful marketing planning. Sometimes plans go awry because they are based on inadequate data. Another limitation has been the failure of marketing management to make effective use of the computer as an aid in developing marketing plans.

In a firm that has enjoyed a favorable rate of growth, the executives may see no need for organized planning. Planning is often absent also in a small firm where one man—frequently the founder—has dominated. Actually, if such a company is

---

[5] "Shortcomings Predominate in Marketing Planning," *Industrial Marketing,* July, 1967, p. 60.
[6] "Long-range Planning: Séance or Science?" *Sales Management,* Jan. 15, 1969, p. 31.

successful, often the guiding executive is fundamentally a good planner. He just does not recognize planning as a formal activity. In both of these nonplanning situations, executives will claim that their operations change so frequently and so quickly that advance planning—especially long-range planning—is not feasible. Regardless of how substantial all the above difficulties may seem, they cannot negate the proved value of sound planning.

SCOPE OF PLANNING ACTIVITIES

The length of time for which planning is done serves as one basis for classifying planning. Long-range planning, for three, five, ten, or twenty-five years, is probably more important than short-range planning. Top management and special planning staffs are involved in long-range planning, and the resultant policy decisions cover broad, far-reaching topics, such as plant, market, or product expansion. Short-term planning usually covers periods of three months, six months, or a year. It is done at the operational level by lower- and middle-echelon executives and is concerned with such things as adjusting prices to meet current competition, buying for the coming season, handling the day-to-day problems of a sales force, and selecting middlemen in a new market.

For purposes of clarity we should distinguish among three planning concepts: (1) total company planning, (2) marketing planning, and (3) the annual marketing plan. *Total company planning* involves setting broad, but basic, company goals over the long run and then developing long-range strategies to achieve these goals. These long-range goals and strategies then become the framework within which departmental plans are developed. In company planning, attention is devoted to financial requirements, production goals, manpower needs, and research and development efforts as well as to the determination of market targets and the marketing programs needed to reach these targets.

The emphasis and starting point in company planning have shifted as firms have evolved from a production to a marketing orientation. In the past, company planning was concerned first with the production facilities and financial resources needed to generate what management estimated the company would sell. (Even today, financial planning dominates in industries such as oil, steel, and telephones where new production facilities require such huge capital investments.) As the marketing concept is implemented in a firm, however, marketing becomes the focal point in planning in that company. Now planning starts with (1) an identification of market objectives and opportunities, then (2) a determination of the marketing program needed to capitalize on those opportunities, and finally (3) the planning encompasses the plant and financial resources needed. As marketing influences both short-term and long-range company policies, total company planning and marketing planning tend to merge.

Short of that merger, however, we can identify long-range *marketing planning* as a distinct concept. This activity involves setting goals and strategies for the marketing effort in the firm. Marketing planning is done within the framework of the total company planning, and yet the marketing planning is recognized as being separate from similar activity in finance, production, and other major departments in a firm. Marketing planning would include the development of long-range programs for the major ingredients in the marketing mix —

the product, the distribution system, the pricing structure, and the promotional activities. Separate planning might be done for subdivisions within these major ingredients—subdivisions such as product groups, market segments, or advertising, as separate from sales-force activities. In Parts 3 to 6 of this book, the major ingredients in the marketing mix were considered in consecutive order. Realistically, however, the planning in each of these areas must be done concurrently and be carefully coordinated because each element in the mix interacts with every other element.[7]

Whereas marketing planning is done on a continuing basis, the *annual marketing plan* reflects one time segment of the ongoing planning process. Thus management will develop a master plan covering a year's marketing operations. The overall plan will consist of several coordinated subplans in marketing. More attention can be devoted to tactical details in the annual plan than is feasible in longer-range planning. As an example, long-range marketing planning related to the product may set as a goal the introduction of truly innovative products. The marketing plan for 1976, however, may strive to correct an inventory imbalance by especially promoting the sales of one product which is in the declining stage of its life cycle. Long-range planning may speak of the role of personal salesmen in the promotional mix, while the annual plan for 1976 speaks of increased college recruiting as a source of salesmen.

THE PLANNING PROCESS

One series of steps which management can fruitfully follow in developing a marketing plan will be considered briefly at this point. A key point to remember in relation to the marketing planning process is that the final product—any marketing plan —should appear in detailed, *written* form. The first step in the planning process might be called the *situation analysis.* At this point management makes a thorough analysis of the company's existing situation—its markets, its competition, the product, the distribution channels, and the promotional programs. With this background management can set its *goals* in some detail. Recalling Chapter 2, we are reminded that these goals should be realistic, specific, and mutually consistent. Problems uncovered in the situation analysis should draw attention to the limitations and opportunities facing the company and thus should influence the goals. Next, the planning executives can examine alternative *strategies* and select the ones which, when implemented by an effective marketing mix, will offer the best potential for achieving the goals. The fourth step is to select the most appropriate *tactics.* These are the specific operational details which direct the plan in action. Finally, an effective planning process should provide for a periodic audit or *evaluation* of the operating results. In this way mistakes can be corrected, and the plan can be adjusted to its current environment.[8] See Figure 27-1.

---

[7]For some findings from a five-year study on the accuracy of corporate planning in some 60 companies, see Richard F. Vancil, "The Accuracy of Long-Range Planning," *Harvard Business Review,* September–October, 1970, pp. 98–101.

[8]For a review of some 30 publications on various aspects of planning, see Robert J. Mockler, "Theory and Practice of Planning," *Harvard Business Review,* March–April, 1970, pp. 148–150ff. The reviewed publications were selected on the basis of being most useful to executives in the management of their planning activities.

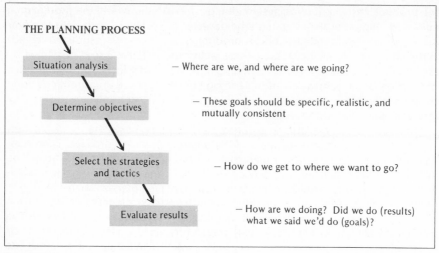

THE PLANNING PROCESS

Situation analysis — Where are we, and where are we going?

Determine objectives — These goals should be specific, realistic, and mutually consistent

Select the strategies and tactics — How do we get to where we want to go?

Evaluate results — How are we doing? Did we do (results) what we said we'd do (goals)?

Figure 27-1.

FORECASTING MARKET DEMAND

The cornerstone of successful marketing planning is the measurement and forecasting of market demand. The key figure we need is the sales forecast because it is the basis for all budgeting and operations in the firm. A company can forecast its sales by using either of two basic procedures—a "top-down" or a "buildup" approach.

Using the "top-down" (or "breakdown") approach, management generally would:

1. Start with a forecast of general economic conditions, as the basis to
2. Determine the industry's total market potential for a product. Then
3. Measure the share of this market the firm is getting. The measurements in items 2 and 3 form the basis for
4. Forecasting the sales of the product. The sales forecast, in turn, is the basis for all
5. Budgeting and other operational planning in the firm.

In the "buildup" technique, management generates estimates of future demand in various segments (territories or customer groups) of the market or from various organizational units (salesmen or branches) in the company. Then management simply accumulates the individual estimates into one total forecast.

As the need arises in this discussion, we shall define several terms—"market potential," "sales potential," "market share," and others—which often are used loosely in business. At this point we should understand the meaning of the terms "market factor" and "market index."

A *market factor* is an item or element which exists in a market, which may be measured quantitatively, and which is related to the demand for a product or service. To illustrate, the number of cars three years old and older is a market factor underlying the demand for replacement tires—that is, affecting the market potential for replacement tires. In Chapter 3 we spoke of population and income factors which affect the market for consumer products. In Chapter 7 we mentioned some of the market factors which affect the demand for industrial goods.

A *market index* is simply a market factor expressed in percentages or in some other mathematical term. Sometimes more than one market factor is combined into a single index number. A market factor or market index may be developed for the entire national market or for any segment of it. To illustrate, in 1972 the index representing expenditures for personal services in the United States was 165 with the year 1960 serving as the base period of 100. The index was computed in constant dollars, so increases in the price level did not affect the index numbers. Thus, from 1960 to 1972 there was a real increase of 65 percent in expenditures for services. If sales of our product are related directly to expenditures for personal services, then our 1972 sales (in constant dollars) should be about 65 percent above the 1960 level.

GENERAL ECONOMIC FORECAST

Forecasting sales or determining the market potential for many products frequently starts with a prediction of things to come in the national economy. Trends in the gross national product, disposable personal income, or some other macroeconomic measure may be the best indicator of future market demand for automobiles or other consumer products. The supply of money, interest rates, and rates of family formation are factors useful in estimating the future market demand for housing. Consequently, an early step in forecasting sales in many firms is to develop a forecast (or to study an already prepared forecast) of the relevant indicators of general economic conditions.

DETERMINATION OF MARKET POTENTIAL AND MARKET SHARE

The *market potential* for a product may be defined as the expected combined sales volume for all sellers of that product during a stated period of time in a stated market. Implicitly in this definition we assume the existence of a given set of environmental constraints such as technology, general economic conditions, a politico-legal situation, etc. *Market share* (synonymous with *sales potential* or *market penetration*) is "the ratio of a company's sales to the total industry sales on either an actual or potential basis."

Thus we may speak of the "market potential" for automatic washing machines, but the "market share" (or sales potential) for one company's brand. In the case of either market potential or market share, the market may encompass the entire United States, or even the world, or it may be limited to some part segmented by income, by geographic area, or on some other basis. For example, we may speak of the *market potential* for washing machines on the Pacific Coast or the *market share* for General Electric washers in homes with incomes of $7,000 to $10,000. The market potential and market share will be the same when a firm has a monopoly in its market, as in the case of a telephone company or some other public utility.

For some products the market potential can be derived from a national economic forecast because the market factors most predictive of future sales of these products are part of the forecast of the national economy and general business conditions. Thus, when a rise of 4 percent in the gross national product is forecasted for next year, the market potential for given products can be expected to increase at the same level. In determining the market potential for many other products, however, management can effectively bypass the step of preparing or studying a national economic forecast, because the key market factors most directly predictive of future sales of these products normally are not a part of the forecast of the national economy. For instance, the market potential for textbooks in a beginning advertising course is a function of the number of schools offering such a course and the total number of students enrolled.

Ordinarily a company will determine the market potential for its product in a given market, and then from this figure determine its market share (sales potential). If a company's sales are a minor segment of the industry total, it may start directly with a determination of sales potential and not compute the total industry market potential at all. In some industries the trade association gathers data from all member firms, and from this information a firm can rather easily determine the market potential or its market share. When a firm must compute these measures all by itself, several basic techniques are available. These will be explained briefly later in this chapter.

SALES FORECASTING

While a sales forecast ordinarily can be made more intelligently if the company first determines its market and/or sales potential, actually many firms start their marketing planning directly with the sales forecast.

The American Marketing Association defines a sales forecast as:[9] "An estimate of sales, in dollars or physical units for a specified future period under a proposed marketing plan or program and under an assumed set of economic and other forces outside the unit for which the forecast is made. The forecast may be for a specified item of merchandise or for an entire line."

The sales forecast and the marketing plan. We should note in the above definition that a sales forecast is influenced by a company's proposed marketing program. Unfortunately, the relationship between the sales forecast and the marketing plan in a firm is often misunderstood. Some executives speak of developing a marketing plan based on their annual sales forecast, for example. This is reversing the proper order of things. Perhaps the confusion arises because of the variety of demand forecasts we are dealing with. It is true that a forecast of the national economy or an estimate of market potential should precede the development of a marketing plan. However, the marketing goals and broad strategies—the core of a marketing plan—must be established before a sales forecast is made. That is, the sales forecast is dependent upon these predetermined goals and strategies. Certainly a different sales forecast will result, depending upon whether the goal is to liquidate an excess inventory of product A or to expand the firm's market share by aggressive advertising.

Now, once the sales forecast is prepared, it does become the key controlling factor in all *operational* planning throughout the company. The forecast is the basis of sound budgeting. Financial planning for working-capital requirements, plant expansion, and other needs is based on anticipated sales. Scheduling of

---

[9]Committee on Definitions, *Marketing Definitions: A Glossary of Marketing Terms,* American Marketing Association, Chicago, 1960, p. 20

all production resources and facilities, such as setting manpower needs, purchasing raw-materials, and determining the rate of production output, depends upon the sales forecast.

The sales forecast and sales potential. Because a sales forecast is dependent upon a company's marketing plan, it is not an estimate of sales under ideal conditions. This would be more like the calculation of sales potential. In some cases a sales forecast and a sales potential may be the same, but usually a sales forecast is less. The company's existing production facilities may limit its opportunity to sell more units during the coming year. Or the company might be able to bring its forecast nearer to its sales potential if funds were available to devote to sales-force expansion and a more intensive advertising campaign.

Sales-forecasting periods. One year is probably the most widely used period for sales forecasting, although many firms prepare forecasts for periods of three or six months. Also, many firms review their annual forecasts monthly or quarterly. Annual sales forecasts tie in with annual financial planning and reporting, and are often based on estimates of the coming year's general economic conditions.

Short-run forecasts of less than a year may be desirable when activity in the firm's industry is so volatile that it is not feasible to look ahead a full year. As a case in point, many firms engaged in fashion merchandising, producers and retailers alike, prepare a forecast which covers only one fashion season.[10]

In some instances, long-range forecasts (more than one year) are helpful in financial planning and in planning for long-term plant, equipment, and materials needs. These long-range estimates are really estimates of sales potentials rather than sales forecasts. They usually indicate maximum sales opportunity and are related to the firm's marketing program.

METHODS OF FORECASTING MARKET DEMAND

Predictions of future market demand—whether they are sales forecasts or estimates of market potential—may be based on techniques ranging from uninformed guesses to sophisticated statistical methods requiring the assistance of specialists. Marketing executives do not need to know how to do the statistical computations. However, these administrators should understand enough about a given technique to appreciate its merits and limitations, know when it is best used, and be able to ask intelligent questions regarding the assumptions underlying the method.[11]

Separate estimates should be prepared for each article or product line. Then each total product forecast should be subdivided in as much detail as possible. That is, a forecast should be prepared in dollars and/or units for each territory, customer group, or other meaningful sales unit. The itemized forecast can then

[10]As an example of short-run forecasting done by one such company—a manufacturer of seasonal, fashion sportswear—see Carl Vreeland, "The Jantzen Method of Short-range Forecasting," *Journal of Marketing*, April, 1963, pp. 66–70.

[11]See Stanley J. PoKempner and Earl L. Bailey, *Sales Forecasting Practices: An Appraisal,* The Conference Board, Experiences in Marketing Management, no. 25, New York, 1970; and John C. Chambers, Satinder K. Mullick, and Donald D. Smith, "How to Choose the Right Forecasting Technique," *Harvard Business Review*, July–August, 1971, pp. 45–74.

be used in operational levels of planning, such as setting sales quotas or allocating the advertising appropriation.

Market-factor analysis. For most companies the analysis of market factors is probably the best forecasting method to use because it is the most reliable and valid. The fundamental thesis underlying this method is that the future sales of a given product depend upon the behavior of certain factors related to the market demand for the product. Thus if we can determine what these factors are and can measure their relationship to sales activity, we can forecast future sales simply by studying the behavior of the factors. If the market-factor behavior occurs prior to the period covered by the forecast, there is a lead-lag situation.

The key to the successful use of this method lies in the selection of the appropriate market factors. Management must be certain that a relationship does exist between the selected factor and the market for the product. It is also important that the researcher minimize the number of market factors used. The greater the number of factors, the greater the chance for erroneous estimates, and the more difficult it is to tell the extent to which each influences the demand for the article. The two procedures used to translate the market-factor behavior into an estimate of future sales are the direct-derivation method and the correlation-analysis technique.

Direct derivation. As an illustration of the use of this method to estimate market potential, suppose that a manufacturer of automobile tires wants to know the market potential for replacement tires in the United States in 1976. The main market factor is the number of automobiles on the road. The first delimitation is the estimate of how many cars are likely prospects. Assume that the seller's studies show that the average passenger car is driven about 10,000 miles a year and that the average driver gets about 25,000 miles from a set of four tires. This means that all cars which become 2½ years old during 1976 can be considered a part of the potential market for replacement tires during that year. Reasonably detailed information regarding the number of cars sold between July 1, 1973, and June 30, 1974, is readily available from state and county licensing agencies and also has been compiled by private organizations. In addition, a similar count must be established for cars reaching 5, 7½, and 10 years of age during 1976. These ages are multiples of 2½. That is, a 5-year-old car presumably would be ready for its second set of replacement tires. The number of cars in these age brackets times 4 should give a fair approximation of the market potential for replacement tires in 1976. We are, of course, dealing in averages. Not all drivers will get 25,000 miles from a set of tires, and not all cars will be driven exactly 10,000 miles a year.

The seller then must determine his share of this market. Here the analysis becomes more subjective. He must consider the quality of his product in relation to competitive products, the strength of his distribution system and promotional program, the extent of competition, his market share in past years, his plans for market expansion, and many other factors.

The market-factor-derivation method has much to recommend it. It is relatively simple and inexpensive to use, and it requires relatively little statistical analysis. It is reasonably easy to understand, so that non-statistics-oriented executives can follow the method and interpret the results. Usually the factors selected are those for which detailed, reliable data are available.

Correlation analysis. This technique is simply a mathematical refinement of the market-factor-derivation method. When correlation analysis is used, the variations in the potential sales of the product are mathematically correlated with the variations in the measurements of the market factor. In effect, correlation measures the variations in two series of historical data. Consequently, this method can be used only when a lengthy sales history of the industry or the firm is available, as well as a history of the market factor's measurement.

Probably the major advantage of correlation analysis is the exactness of the estimate of market demand, assuming, of course, that the elements in the statistical estimating equation are accurate. By placing the measure of the market factor into the estimating equation, the researcher can come up with an accurate estimate of the market or sales potential. This is a more precise measure than the one developed through direct derivation, where the correlation analysis is implicitly assumed to be a perfect + 1.00. Rarely does this perfect relationship exist between a market factor and the sales of a product. Also, correlation analysis allows a researcher to incorporate more than one factor into the formula.

There are at least two major limitations to this method. First, as suggested above, a lengthy sales history must be available. To do a really good job, a researcher needs about twenty periods of sales records. Also, he is assuming that approximately the same relationships have existed among the variables during this entire period and, furthermore, that this relationship will continue throughout the period for which potentials are being estimated. This may be a highly unrealistic assumption. The other major drawback is that very few marketing executives understand correlation analysis and can actually do the necessary computations. Thus a statistical staff may be necessary. Even then, because of their lack of comprehension, the executives may suspect the results.

Survey of buyer intentions. Another commonly used method of forecasting is to survey a sample of potential customers, asking them how much of the stated product they would buy at a given price during a specified future time period. This technique is used for both consumer and industrial products. The sample of buyers may be ultimate users or middlemen. Some firms maintain consumer panels on a continuing basis to act as a sounding board for new-product ideas, prices, and other product features.

A major problem is that of selecting the sample of potential buyers. For many consumer products a very large, and thus very costly, sample would be needed. Aside from the extremely high cost and large amount of time that this method often entails, there is another very serious limitation. It is one thing for a consumer to say he *intends to buy* a product, but quite another for him *actually to buy it.* Surveys of buying intentions inevitably show an inflated measure of market potential. They are widely used, however, particularly where there are inadequate data for a market-factor derivation or a correlation analysis.

Surveys of buying intentions are probably most effective when there are relatively few buyers, when they are willing to express their buying intentions, and when their past record shows that their follow-up actions are consistent with their stated intentions.

Test marketing. In using this technique, a firm markets its product in a limited geographic area and, from this sample, projects the company's sales potential (market share) over a larger area. Test marketing is used frequently for new products in deciding whether sufficient profitable sales potential exists to warrant introducing the item. The technique also serves as a basis for evaluating various product features and alternative marketing strategies. The outstanding benefit of test marketing is that it can tell management how many people *actually buy* the product, instead of only how many *say they intend* to buy. If a company can afford the time and money for this method and can run a valid test, it will find that this is the best way of measuring the full potential for its particular product. Management estimates do not play as big a role here as they do in the other techniques for determining market potential.

These are big "ifs," however. Test marketing is expensive in time and money. Great care is needed to set up and control the test-marketing experiment and to arrange for informational feedback from these markets. Once a competitor learns you are test marketing, he usually is adept at "jamming" your experiment. That is, by unusual promotional or other marketing effort, he can create an artificial situation so that your test results are not meaningful.

While test marketing is still being used very widely, many marketers are questioning (1) the time and costs needed for testing and (2) whether test results can be projected to reflect the total market. As a result, alternatives are being considered, and some trends are observable. For one, companies are testing in (1) an entire region, (2) large cities (Chicago), or (3) mini-markets (Lima, Ohio, or Yakima, Washington). Traditionally, only medium-sized cities (pop. 200,000– 500,000) were used. See Fig. 27-2. Very large or very small cities were considered taboo because of their high cost or atypical results. The length of the test period also is being cut from months to weeks. Pretesting is being used to replace full test marketing.[12]

Past sales and trend analysis.   A favorite method of forecasting is to base the estimate *entirely* on past sales. This technique is used frequently by retailers whose main goal is to "beat last year's figures." The method consists simply in applying a flat percentage increase to the volume achieved last year or to the average volume of the past few years. The same rate of increase is anticipated for every product in the company's line.

This technique is simple, inexpensive, and easy to apply. For firms operating in a reasonably stable market situation, where their market shares have remained constant for a period of years, it is possible that past sales can be depended upon as the sole indicator of future volume. On balance, however, the method is highly unreliable. Most firms operate in a dynamic market. Also, it is unrealistic to assume that each article in the product mix will enjoy the same rate of growth. Finally, changes in the marketing program can have varying effects on future sales and destroy the relationship with past sales activity. In some of the other sales forecasting methods, management considers past sales to be one of several influencing factors.

Trend analysis is a variation of the forecasting method based on past sales, but it is a bit more complicated. It involves either a long-run projection of sales trends

---

[12] For two articles reporting on trends, ideas, and case histories in test marketing, see Sally Scanlon, "Test Markets: Is the Chemistry Changing?" *Sales Management,* Apr. 16, 1973, p. 21; and "Test Marketing: Who's Got the Pulse of the Customer?" *Sales Management,* Mar. 1, 1971, p. 19. See also Jack Abrams, "Reducing the Risk of New Product Marketing Strategies Testing," *Journal of Marketing Research,* May, 1969, pp. 216–220.

TEST MARKETS FREQUENTLY USED BY THREE MARKETING RESEARCH COMPANIES, 1972.

Standard markets
 Used by Audits & Surveys:
  Atlanta, Ga.
  Boston, Mass.
  Cleveland, Ohio
  Dallas/Forth Worth, Texas
  Fort Wayne, Ind.
  Grand Rapids, Mich.
  Indianapolis, Ind.
  Minneapolis, Minn.
  Rochester, N.Y.

 Used by Burgoyne Index:
  Albany-Schenectady-Troy, N.Y.
  Atlanta, Ga.
  Dallas, Texas
  Denver, Colo.
  Fort Wayne, Ind.
  Grand Rapids, Mich.
  Kansas City, Mo.

Mini markets
 Used by Market Facts:
  Binghamton, N.Y.
  Fort Wayne, Ind.
  Lima, Ohio
  Madison, Wis.
  Quad cities: Davenport and
   Bettendorf, Iowa; Rock
   Island and Moline, Ill.
  Rockford, Ill.
  South Bend, Ind.
  Spokane, Wash.
 Used by Burgoyne Index:
  Binghamton, N.Y.
  Dayton, Ohio
  Erie, Pa.
  Fort Wayne, Ind.
  Fresno, Calif.
  Grand Rapids, Mich.
  Nashville, Tenn.
  Orlando, Fla.
  Spokane, Wash.
  Wichita, Kans.

Figure 27-2. *Source: Sales Management,* April 16, 1973, p. 21.

computed by the statistical technique known as the *least-squares method* or a short-run projection (forecasting for only a few months ahead) based upon a seasonal index of sales. Adding the statistical sophistication in long-run trend analysis does not really remove the inherent weakness of basing future estimates only on past sales activity. Short-run trend analysis may be acceptable if the firm's sales follow a reliable seasonal pattern. Thus if sales reach 10,000 units in the first quarter (January–March) and, historically, the second quarter is always about 50 percent better, we can forecast sales of 15,000 units in the April–June period.

Sales-force composite. This is a buildup method which may be used to forecast sales or to estimate market potentials. As used in sales forecasting, it consists of collecting from each salesman or each middleman an estimate of sales of various products in his territory during the future period to be covered in the forecast. The total composite of these separate estimates is the company's sales forecast. This method may be used advantageously if the firm has competent, intelligent, high-caliber salesmen and if it is selling to a market composed of relatively few, but large, customers. Thus a sales forecast based on this method would be more applicable to large electrical generators than to small general-use motors.

The sales-force-composite method has the merit of placing responsibility for forecasting upon the shoulders of the men who must meet their own target. Also, it takes advantage of the salesmen's specialized knowledge of their own market, and it should make them more willing to accept their assigned sales quota. On the other hand, it takes salesmen away from their main task—selling. Furthermore, salesmen are not trained or qualified to do the research needed in forecasting. They are in no position to see the "big picture," that is, the total company operations and the socioeconomic conditions which influence future sales volume.

Executive judgment. This method covers a wide range of possibilities. Basically it consists of obtaining opinions regarding future sales volume from one or more executives. If these are really informed opinions, based on other valid factual measures such as market-factor analysis, then this type of executive judgment is desirable. Certainly all the previously discussed forecasting methods should be tempered with sound executive judgment. Forecasting should not be done solely by computer or mathematical model. On the other hand, forecasting by executive opinion alone is a risky technique. In some instances, it is simply intuition or guesswork.[13] See Fig. 27-3.

DETERMINING TERRITORIAL POTENTIALS

After a company has determined its sales potential or sales forecast for its entire market, management typically wants to establish these demand estimates for each territory assigned to its salesmen or its middlemen. Forecasts of territorial market demand may be used for several purposes, such as setting sales quotas, determining territorial boundaries, evaluating performance of sales units, or allocating advertising effort.

Once the potentials are calculated for the total market, it is ordinarily easy to compute territorial potentials. Management simply uses a pertinent market index which has been determined for small geographic areas such as counties or cities. For example, assume that a manufacturer of machine tools estimates his market share for a given year to be $12 million: the market factor he uses is the number of employees in manufacturing establishments. Referring to his information sources, he can get the number of manufacturing employees in each county. He determines that 9 percent of the total manufacturing employees are located in his western region and 6 percent in his southern territory. The potentials in these territories are then calculated at $1,080,000 and $720,000, respectively.

QUESTIONS AND PROBLEMS

1. "Planning involves the matching of means and ends—of matching inputs and outputs." Explain how this concept may be applied in a practical fashion to the promotional program in a firm. To new-product development.
2. Explain some of the ways in which formal marketing planning serves as an effective form of risk management in marketing.
3. What are some of the reasons why some firms do no formal planning? Which of

---

[13]See Richard Staelin and Ronald E. Turner, "Error in Judgmental Sales Forecasts: Theory and Results," *Journal of Marketing Research,* February, 1973, pp. 10–16.

A WHIMSICAL VIEW OF SALES FORECASTING

Gather 'round children, and I shall tell you the story of the Sales Forecast. Like the fruit fly, the Forecast has a brief life and is usually abandoned by its parents the day after birth. Like us, the Forecast has one mother, and her name is Computer. But unlike us, the computer has a whole rookery of husbands who deny they're the father. Every Forecast has all its anonymous father's bad features and its mother's precise, beautiful profile.

Mating season is between September 15th and November 15th, give or take requested extensions. Gestation can be a matter of electronic seconds or several weeks depending on the skill of the obstetrician, the treasurer. Often the treasurer has difficulty decoding the seeds of wisdom ejaculated by the fathers, a rather ordinary breed called salesmen, district sales managers, regional sales managers, general sales managers, and perhaps even a marketing vice president (if he's not in a meeting).

Conception by the Computer takes place when the thousands of little numbers manufactured by the Fathers are inserted via interoffice memo into the Computer. You can tell when a Computer is ready for mating, because it does a fan dance with its blank punch cards and makes a whirring sound that sounds like "Shoot the data to me, Dada."

When a Forecast is born, it can be either black, which is beautiful, or red, which makes everybody sick just to look at it.

Treasurers always throw up when they see a red Forecast, especially if it looks like last year's annual report (which is really a Forecast that's grown up and thus become hopelessly out of date). A red Forecast has a very tough time being adopted by any nice family, especially families with names like Stockholder, Director, or President.

Usually, a red Forecast's birth results in the arrest, conviction, and execution of suspected fathers who haven't already slit their own throats.

Black Forecasts, on the other hand, create joy and merriment for all concerned. The treasurer especially beams with a grin implying that he is not only the obstetrician but perhaps even the father. When all the possible fathers enthusiastically invite a paternity suit, you *know* the Forecast was born black. It's ironic, but encouraging, that even companies in the South seem to love black Forecasts.

But, Forecasts, like children, don't always turn out so well. Though everybody knows a Forecast is just a promise when it's born, all hell breaks loose when it doesn't act like it said it would.

This sometimes happens. The Forecast is the only gambling device legalized in all 50 states with avid players even among bankers, but its principal characteristic is its vacillating personality. As a result, Forecasts are at the doctor's constantly having their insides altered and their columns straightened.

Every business should have a Forecast. It employs lots of people, puts iron in the blood, and self-destructs in 30 days.

Source: Jim Lavenson, "Meet Rosemary's Other Baby," *Sales Management*, Aug. 15, 1971, p. 26. Reprinted by permission of *Sales Management*, © 1971.

Figure 27-3.

these obstacles are reflections of administrative weaknesses, and which ones are likely to occur even with good management?

4. Distinguish between marketing planning and an annual marketing plan.

5. What are the steps which usually should be followed in the process of writing a marketing plan?

6. Using examples of consumer or industrial products, carefully distinguish between market potential and sales forecast.

7. Why is the sales forecast usually smaller than the sales potential?

8. What companies—manufacturers or middlemen—might be interested in forecasting sales on a weekly or a monthly basis?

9. What effect would each of the following occurrences have on the market potential for furniture? For a manufactured grocery product?
   a. Establishment of a 10 percent federal sales tax accompanied by a major cut in federal income tax rates
   b. Increase in minimum wages to $2.50 per hour

10. What are some logical market factors which you might use in estimating the market potential for each of the following products?
    a. Central home air conditioners
    b. Milking machines   d. Sterling flatware
    c. Golf clubs   e. Safety goggles

11. How would you determine the market potential for a textbook in a beginning course in marketing?

12. What are some of the problems a researcher faces when using the test-market method for determining market or sales potentials?

13. If a firm bases its sales forecasts on estimates compiled by its salesmen, should a salesman be rewarded financially for correctly forecasting the sales in his territory during the coming year?

14. "No company should forecast its sales without making some use of the executive-judgment method, and yet this method never should be used to the exclusion of other methods." Discuss.

15. A grocery products manufacturer estimates that sales of his new cereal will reach $15 million next year. How much should he expect to sell in the state in which your school is located?

ANALYSIS OF SALES VOLUME AND MARKETING COSTS

After a firm's plans have been set in operation, the results should be evaluated as promptly as possible. Without an evaluation, management is in no position to tell whether its plan worked, to what degree it was successful, and what the reasons were for success or failure. Planning and evaluation are interrelated activities. Evaluation logically follows planning in that planning sets forth what should be done, and evaluation shows what really was done. Sometimes a circular relationship exists: plans are made, the operational results are evaluated, and new plans are prepared on the basis of this appraisal.

Earlier in the book we discussed briefly the topic of evaluation as it related to separate parts of our marketing program—the product-planning process, the performance of our salesmen and middlemen, and the effectiveness of our advertising program, for instance. At this point, we want to make a study of the results of our total marketing effort in the form of an analysis of our sales volume and our marketing costs.

THE MARKETING AUDIT: A TOTAL EVALUATION PROGRAM

To appreciate fully the managerial activity of evaluation, we shall first consider the concept of a marketing audit as a total evaluation program.[1] Audits are not new to

---

[1] The "marketing audit" concept is presented in *Analyzing and Improving Marketing Perfor-*

business management. Traditionally, they have carried the connotation of a review and evaluation of some business activity. They have long been used in accounting and financial operations, and we are also accustomed to personnel audits. Really all we are doing here is applying the concept of an audit to our marketing operations and the marketing program.

A *marketing audit* may be defined as *"a systematic, critical, and unbiased review and appraisal of the basic objectives and policies of the marketing function and of the organization, methods, procedures, and personnel employed to implement the policies and achieve the objectives."* [2] In this definition six areas in marketing are identified for appraisal—objectives, policies, organization, methods, procedures, and personnel. To qualify as a marketing audit, any appraisal must include all six, along with the underlying philosophies upon which the activities are based. A fragmented appraisal of some marketing activities may be useful, but it is only one part of an audit. To be classed as a marketing audit, the appraisal must be a coordinated study of the total marketing program, and it should be done at one time.

Although an audit suggests an after-the-fact review of a business structure, a marketing audit includes an evaluation of the effects of alternatives *before* a decision is reached. Thus the audit becomes an aid in decision making. In addition to identifying weaknesses in a company's program and suggesting means to eliminate them, marketing audits should include reviews of successful operations so that management may capitalize on its strong points. Furthermore, an audit should anticipate future situations. An audit is intended for "prognosis as well as diagnosis. . . . It is the practice of preventive as well as curative marketing medicine." [3]

SCOPE OF EVALUATION ACTIVITIES

A complete marketing audit is something of an ideal. Rarely does a firm conduct a full audit of its total marketing program because the cost and difficulty of the task are great. Instead, management usually appraises individual components of the marketing mix. Such an evaluation is desirable if a full-scale audit is impossible. A major shortcoming, however, is the possible lack of integration among the several areas studied. For instance, a recommendation stemming from a review of the distribution system may have serious implications in pricing or promotion.

The evaluation process is essentially the same three-stage task regardless of which area is being appraised. First, management must gather the facts and compare the actual results with the budgeted figures in order to determine the extent of the variations. Next, it must determine what specific factors in the marketing program are responsible for the program's results. Finally, it must develop plans and procedures with the intent of improving unsatisfactory conditions and capitalizing on favorable ones. To summarize, the administrator's job is to find out

---

mance: *"Marketing Audits" in Theory and Practice,* American Management Association, Management Report no. 32, New York, 1959. Much of this section is based on this source. See especially Abe Shuchman, "The Marketing Audit: Its Nature, Purpose, and Problems," pp. 11–19; and Alfred R. Oxenfeldt, "The Marketing Audit as a Total Evaluation Program," pp. 25–36.

[2] Oxenfeldt, *op. cit.,* p. 26.
[3] Shuchman, *op. cit.,* p. 14.

what happened, and *why* it happened, and then to decide *what to do* about it.

MISDIRECTED MARKETING EFFORT

One of the primary benefits of evaluation activities is that they can help correct misdirected or misplaced marketing effort.[4]

THE "80-20" PRINCIPLE

A company does not enjoy the same rate of net profit on every individual sale. In most firms a large proportion of the orders, customers, territories, or products account for a small share of the profits. This relationship between selling units and profits has been characterized as the "80-20" principle. That is, 80 percent of the orders, customers, territories, or products contributes only 20 percent of the net sales, gross margin, or net profit. Conversely, 20 percent of these selling units account for 80 percent of the volume or profit. The 80-20 figure is used simply to epitomize the misplacement of marketing efforts. Actually, of course, the percentage split varies from one situation to another.

The basic reason for the 80-20 situation is that some misdirected or misplaced efforts are found in most marketing programs. Marketing efforts and costs follow the *number* of territories, customers, products, or other selling units rather than the actual or potential sales volume or profit. In a retail sale which is to be charged and delivered, approximately the same order-filling, billing, and delivery expenses are involved whether the sale is a mink coat or a necktie. Manufacturers may assign one salesman to each territory, and yet there may be substantial differences in the volume and profit returns from various districts.

REASONS FOR MISDIRECTED MARKETING EFFORT

Many businessmen are unaware of the misdirected marketing effort in their firms. They do not know what percentage of total sales and profits comes from a given product line or customer group. Ordinarily they do little or nothing about evaluating their marketing operations. They have relied upon sales volume as the sole criterion for measuring the success of a marketing program. The increasing acceptance of the marketing concept should blunt this emphasis on sales volume. It still exists, however, among manufacturers who set sales volume quotas for their salesmen, among wholesalers who pay their salesmen a commission on net sales, and among retailers who base their sales goals on the preceding year's sales volume figures.

Frequently executives cannot uncover their misdirection of effort because they lack sufficiently detailed information. The analogy of an iceberg in an open sea has been used to illustrate this situation. Only a small part of an iceberg is visible above the surface of the water, and the submerged 90 percent is the dangerous part. The figures representing total sales or total costs on an operating statement are like the visible part of an iceberg. The detailed figures representing sales, costs, and other

---

[4]The term "misdirected marketing effort" was first noted in Charles H. Sevin's writings on distribution cost analysis. See Charles H. Sevin, *Distribution Cost Analysis,* U.S. Department of Commerce, Economic Series, no. 50, 1946; and Charles H. Sevin, *How Manufacturers Reduce Their Distribution Costs,* U.S. Department of Commerce, Economic Series, no. 72, 1948.

performance measures for each territory, product, or salesman correspond to the important submerged segment.

Total sales or costs on an operating statement, or other figures representing total performance, are too general for a marketing executive interested in evaluation. In fact, the total figures are often inconclusive and misleading. More than one company has shown satisfactory overall sales and profit figures, but when these totals were subdivided by territory, products, or some other basis, serious weaknesses were discovered. A manufacturer of rubber products showed an overall annual increase of 12 percent in sales and 9 percent in net profit on one of his product lines one year. But when he analyzed his figures more closely, he found that the sales change within each territory ranged from an increase of 19 percent to a decrease of 3 percent. In some territories, profits increased as much as 14 percent, and in others they were down 20 percent. This is a practical example of the "iceberg principle."

An even more important cause of misplaced marketing effort is that marketing executives must make decisions even though their knowledge of the exact nature of marketing costs is woefully inadequate. In other words, management lacks (1) knowledge of the disproportionate spread of marketing effort and (2) reliable standards for determining what should be spent on marketing and what results should be obtained from the expenditures.

As an illustration, a marketing executive really does not know how much to spend on advertising, marketing research, or sales training. Even more troublesome is the fact that, after the money is spent, there is no satisfactory yardstick to determine whether the results are satisfactory. If a company spends $250,000 more on advertising this year than last year, management ordinarily cannot state what the resultant increase in sales volume or profits should be. Nor do the executives know what the results would have been if an equivalent sum had been devoted to new-product development, management training institutes for middlemen, or some other aspect of the marketing program.[5]

ANALYSIS OF SALES VOLUME

An *analysis of sales volume* is a careful study of the internal records of a firm as they are summarized in the net sales section of the operating statement. A researcher studies the dollar and/or unit sales in total and analyzes these sales on the basis of such subdivisions as territories, product lines, time periods, customer groups, and order sizes. A sales volume analysis may be extended to include a study of the cost of goods sold and the resultant gross margin, also divided into various product and market bases. A *marketing cost analysis* is a detailed study of the operating expense section of the profit and loss statement in an attempt to determine the relative profitability of each product line and various market segments. A sales volume analysis and a marketing cost analysis are thus closely related activities. Together they constitute a detailed study of a company's operating statement.

---

[5]For some contributions which accounting and financial management tools can make toward a more effective allocation of marketing effort, see V. H. Kirpalani and Stanley S. Shapiro, "Financial Dimensions of Marketing Management," *Journal of Marketing*, July, 1973, pp. 40–47.

LIMITATIONS OF VOLUME ANALYSIS

There are two major limitations to using a sales volume analysis as a basis for decision making. The first is that the necessary detailed data are usually not readily available in a form useful to the analyst. Accumulating and processing these essential facts can be a tedious, expensive task. Fortunately, the advent of the computer and other electronic data processing equipment has greatly facilitated the information-gathering step and has opened tremendous new opportunities for management to analyze sales data.

The second limitation is that even a completely reliable sales volume analysis may, if used alone, be misleading. A volume analysis alone may show that sales of a certain product or sales in a given region are steadily increasing as a percentage of market potential. A study of gross margin or marketing costs, however, may show that the firm is enjoying a "profitless prosperity." Nevertheless, we hasten to point out that while a full marketing cost analysis is more desirable than a volume analysis alone, certainly a volume analysis is better than nothing.

BASES FOR ANALYZING VOLUME

There are many bases upon which a company may analyze its sales volume. These include total sales volume, territories, product lines, customer groups, and size of orders. To illustrate some aspects of a volume analysis and show what can be done with the results, we shall build our discussion around a hypothetical firm—the Great Western Office Furniture Company. This firm sells in 13 Western states, including Alaska and Hawaii. The market is divided into four territories. The company's product mix is divided into four broad categories: desks, chairs, filing and safekeeping equipment, and accessories (wastebaskets, desk sets, desk pads, clothes trees). Some of these products are manufactured by the Great Western Company, and others are purchased from outside sources but sold under Great Western's brand.

Total sales volume. There are two trend figures related to total sales volume that we should study. The first is the trend in the company's total sales volume over a period of years, and the second is the trend in the company's share of the market. As we know, a company's sales may increase steadily while its share of the market actually decreases.

An analysis of total sales volume is probably the easiest of all the usual types of marketing analyses made by management. Figures on the company's total volume ordinarily are readily available from the firm's accounting records. All an executive needs in addition is an accurate estimate of total industry sales in the geographic market covered by the company. Trade associations and government agencies are excellent sources for industry volume statistics in many fields.

Table 28–1 shows the information necessary to start an analysis of total sales volume in the Great Western Office Furniture Company. The company's annual sales doubled (from $18 million to $36 million) during the 10-year period ending in 1974. Furthermore, they increased each year over the preceding year, with the exception of 1971. Thus far the company situation is very encouraging. When industry figures are introduced for comparison, however, the picture changes.

Table 28-1. Annual sales volume of Great Western Office Furniture Company, industry volume, and company's share in thirteen-state market.

This table gives the basic data needed for a sales volume analysis in a single firm. In this case, the company's volume doubled in 10 years, but its share of the market declined from 15 to 12 percent. What factors might account for this decreasing market share? Is a sales volume analysis sufficient to detect situations characterized as "80-20" or "iceberg"?

Year	Company volume, in millions of dollars	Industry volume in company's market, in millions of dollars	Company's percentage share of market
1974	36.0	300	12.0
1973	34.7	275	12.6
1972	33.1	255	13.0
1971	30.4	220	13.8
1970	31.7	235	13.5
1969	28.0	200	14.0
1968	24.5	170	14.4
1967	22.5	155	14.5
1966	21.8	150	14.8
1965	18.0	120	15.0

During this decade, the industry's annual sales have increased from $120 million to $300 million (a 250 percent increase), with the result that the company's share of market declined from 15 to 12 percent. In summary, the company's annual sales increased 200 percent, but its market share declined 20 percent. We have now concluded the first of the three steps in the analytical procedure—we know *what* happened.

The next step is to determine *why* Great Western's market position declined. The number of possible causes is almost limitless, and this is what makes management's task so difficult. A weakness in almost any aspect of Great Western's product line, distribution system, pricing structure, or promotional program may have contributed to the loss of market share. It may be that the real culprit is competition. There may be more strong competitors in the market, who were attracted by rapid growth rates in market potentials, or competitors' marketing programs may be more effective than Great Western's own excellent program.

Sales by territories. While a study of total sales volume may be a good place to start a sales analysis, it is usually insufficient because of the workings of the iceberg principle. To uncover activity in the submerged segments of the market, administrators will analyze sales volume by territories. This type of analysis may also bring to light the existence of the 80-20 principle in that a large share of volume may be coming from a small number of territories.

Let's look briefly at one four-step territorial sales analysis procedure which is reasonably simple and need not be expensive. The first step is to determine what share of the company's total sales volume should come from each territory. This involves selecting a market index which can be used to establish territorial potentials. (The use of market indexes to determine territorial potentials was discussed in the preceding chapter.) For instance, one firm used an index of residential building permits issued. If 15 percent of the total residential building permits issued in the nation during one year were issued in the company's Midwestern region, then 15 percent of the company's sales volume should be obtained from that area. If the firm's total market covers only part of the country, then the total annual building permits issued in that limited area would be equated to 100 percent. Thus if a company operated only in the six New England states and if 28 percent of the building permits issued in that six-state area were issued in Massachusetts, then management should expect 28 percent of its total sales volume from that state.

The next step is to determine the actual total sales made during the period under review. The third step is to multiply each territorial index by the actual *total* sales in order to establish the goal or par for each district. Finally, the actual sales figure in each territory is compared with the predetermined standard of performance for the region, and any variation is tabulated.

This procedure is illustrated in Table 28–2. The company has set up four sales territories to cover its 13-state market. By applying a pertinent market index chosen by management, we find that 30 percent of the total sales should have been obtained from territory A, 25 percent from territory B, etc. Applying these percentages to the total annual volume of $36 million, we find that the dollar *goal* was $10.8 million in region A, $9.0 million in region B, etc. The *actual* territorial sales are tabulated in column 4, and the dollar *variation* is listed in column 6.

The critical column is the one entitled Performance Percentage. The percentages are derived by dividing the actual sales by the territorial goal. A performance percentage of 100 means that the territory did exactly what was expected of it. Thus from the table we see that territories B and C did just a little better than was expected, territory A passed its goal by a wide margin, and territory D was quite a disappointment.

When management knows what has occurred in each territory, it must find the reasons for the performances and then take constructive action based upon the findings. Consequently, a careful study should be undertaken to find out why area D did so poorly. The fault may lie in one or more aspects of the marketing program in that area, or competition may be particularly strong there. An attempt should be made to determine what accounts for A's success and whether this information can be helpful in the other regions. Also, the executives should analyze territorial volume by products and customer groups. Even though area A did well, the iceberg principle may be at work within the region. The fine total performance within A may be covering up weaknesses in separate product lines.

Sales by products. Management may use any of several types of volume analyses by product lines. One type is simply a tabulation of the annual sales by individual products or related groups of products for the past several years. This tabulation shows the percentage of total volume obtained from each line. From it, management can ascertain any trend in sales by products.

It is particularly helpful if industry figures are available for each product line. Then the executives can compare the firm's sales record with industry figures, as was done in Table 28 – 1 for total sales. If the company's sales in one product are decreasing, this is not so bad if industry sales for this article are also de-

Table 28-2. Territorial sales volume in four territories of Great Western Office Furniture Company, 1974.

Here the iceberg principle is at work. Territory D is $2.4 million below its sales goal, while the performances in the other three regions are above par. How did management derive the figures in the market-index column?

Territory	Market index, percent	Sales goals, in millions of dollars	Actual sales, in millions of dollars	Performance percentage	Dollar variation, in millions
A	30	10.8	12.5	116	+1.7
B	25	9.0	9.6	107	+ .6
C	21	7.6	7.7	101	+ .1
D	24	8.6	6.2	72	−2.4
Total	100	36.0	36.0		

clining. If one product accounts for a very small part of the company volume, management can evaluate this situation better if industry figures are available for comparison.

Another type of product sales analysis is made by studying the sales of each product *in each territory* over a period of years. Through such a study, management can determine in what geographic market each product is relatively strong or weak. Great Western may find, for instance, that its total sales of desks increased 14 percent last year but that sales of this product declined 2 percent in territory B.

To study product sales in each territory, we can use the method illustrated in Table 28–2 in connection with the territorial analysis. That is, through the application of appropriate market indexes, management can establish sales goals for each product line in each territory. Then actual sales can be compared with these goals. In Table 28–2, we saw that territory A reached 116 percent of its goal, or an excess of $1.7 million; territory D was short of its goal by 28 percent, or $2.4 million. What actually occurred in these two districts is identified more specifically by the type of product sales analysis illustrated in Table 28–3. Selected market indexes were applied to each product line to establish product sales goals in each territory. Thus in A, the total goal was $10.8 million, with $4.5 million expected from sales of desks, $3.4 million from sales of chairs, etc. In district A, almost two-thirds of the $1.7 million excess over quota came from sales of desks, and one-third was contributed by the line of filing equipment. While the region as a whole surpassed its goal by 16 percent, the sales of chairs declined about 3 percent ($100,000). In fact, sales of chairs were below par in both territories.

MARKETING COST ANALYSIS

An analysis of sales volume on the several bases discussed earlier in this chapter can be quite helpful in appraising a company's marketing efforts. A volume analysis, however, does not tell us anything about the *profitability* of a territory, product line, salesman, or group of customers. In order to determine the relative profitability of the various selling units, management may conduct a marketing or

Table 28-3. Sales volume in two territories of Great Western Office Furniture Company, 1974.

In Table 28-2, we saw that territory A exceeded its sales goal by $1.7 million (16 percent), while territory D was 28 percent below par. Now we can see more of our iceberg by determining which products accounted for these variations. Sales of desks were $1,150,000 above the goal in territory A and $1,400,000 below the forecast in territory D. Note also that A was well above its market target in filing equipment, while D fell off considerably in sales of chairs.

Product line	Territory A ($000)			Territory D ($000)		
	Goal	Actual	Variation	Goal	Actual	Variation
Desks	$ 4,500	$ 5,650	+$1,150	$3,800	$2,400	−$1,400
Chairs	3,400	3,300	− 100	2,400	1,420	− 980
Filing equipment	2,100	2,700	+ 600	1,800	1,900	+ 100
Accessories	800	850	+ 50	600	480	− 120
Total	$10,800	$12,500	$1,700	$8,600	$6,200	−$2,400

distribution cost analysis.[6] In the literature, the term "distribution cost analysis" seems to be preferred. "*Marketing* cost analysis" is more representative of the full scope of the analytical activity and is more in line with the concept of marketing management. The two terms are used synonymously in this chapter.

NATURE AND SCOPE OF MARKETING COST ANALYSIS

A marketing cost analysis is a detailed study of a firm's entire distribution cost structure. For the various cost items, management may establish a budgetary goal, and then analyze the cause of variations between the actual and the budgeted expenses.

Marketing cost analysis can be used by the individual business firms to determine the cost of performing marketing activities such as outside selling, billing, advertising, and warehousing. It can be used to determine the expenses and profits of the company's various products, customer classes, territories, and order sizes. This is an extremely important use in relation to the Robinson-Patman Act because this law requires firms to justify their discount schedules on the basis of cost differentials. Marketing cost analysis may also be used to establish and appraise various marketing policies and procedures.

Like a sales volume analysis, a marketing cost analysis is more concerned with analysis than with accounting practices. Furthermore, cost analysis is frequently performed on a sporadic or sampling basis, whereas the accounting system is maintained on a routine, continuing basis. We may analyze territorial costs in only half the districts or study the cost of selling various products for only a six-month period. The cost analysis, however, is closely related to the accounting system in

---

[6]Several fine books and journal articles cover the more technical phases of marketing cost analysis. For example, see Donald R. Longman and Michael Schiff, *Practical Distribution Cost Analysis,* Richard D. Irwin, Inc., Homewood, Ill., 1955; or J. Brooks Heckert and Robert B. Miner, *Distribution Costs,* 2d ed., The Ronald Press Company, New York 1955.

one very important way. A detailed system of ledger accounts is a virtual necessity if management wishes to do a thorough cost analysis, because many of the raw data for a cost analysis come from the accounting records.

Some significant differences exist between marketing cost analysis and production cost accounting. First, their scope differs. In production cost accounting, management is interested in determining the costs per unit of product. In marketing cost analysis, the administrators are interested not only in marketing costs for each product but also in the marketing expenses attached to geographic market segments, separate customer classes, and various order sizes.

Most production expenses are related to the operation of machines or to men who are subject to constant personal supervision. Consequently, it is possible to measure rather accurately the cost of producing a unit of the product. On the other hand, marketing expenses are incurred by salesmen whose job is not completely repetitive and whose activities are not constantly observed by a supervisor. Therefore, usually it is not possible to determine the time, effort, and resultant costs related to individual marketing activities.

A third, and probably more important, difference exists. With respect to production activities, the costs are a function of volume ($C = fV$). That is, the costs react to a change in volume. To illustrate, if the factory output is increased 15 percent, then as a *result* there is an accurately measurable change in costs. In marketing, on the other hand, volume is a function of costs ($V = fC$). That is, the sales volume output reacts to a change in input cost factors. Volume will ordinarily increase, for example, *as a result* of adding more salesmen or spending money for advertising.

In these relationships, management can foretell quite accurately what will happen to production expenses when there is, say, an increase of 10 percent in the volume produced. A marketing executive is not in a correspondingly advantageous position. He cannot say, for instance, exactly how much increase in volume should be expected when the advertising budget is increased 10 percent or when two new salesmen are added in territory A.

PROBLEMS INVOLVED IN COST ANALYSIS

Management must realize the need for marketing cost studies, have some understanding of the techniques involved, and be able to interpret the results. A cost study will require a considerable amount of manpower, time, and money. Even if the company uses data processing equipment, the cost may still be high.

Classifying marketing expenses. Once management decides which of its costs can be categorized as marketing expenses, it must organize the costs into useful classifications. In the accounting systems of most companies, the operating expenses are classified according to the direct object of the expenditures. Thus we find ledger accounts for rent, salesmen's commissions, taxes, salaries, office supplies, etc. These are often called "natural" expenses. For purposes of a marketing cost analysis, administrators usually find it necessary to reclassify these expenses according to the marketing functions involved. Then all costs pertaining to one activity, such as advertising or warehousing, are grouped together.

To regroup the various natural (ledger) expenses, management should first determine which functional classifications will be most useful and then allocate the natural expenses to the appropriate function. There is no standard list of functional classifications. The following groupings, however, can apply to many firms:

1. Selling—direct costs (salesmen's compensation, travel, etc.)
2. Selling—indirect costs (sales training, marketing research, sales statistics, etc.)
3. Advertising and sales promotion
4. Warehousing
5. Transportation and shipping, including order filling and packing
6. Credits and collection (bad-debt losses, credit office expenses)
7. Order processing and billing
8. Marketing administrative expenses

Allocating costs. Undoubtedly one of the most difficult problems in cost analysis, whether it is an analysis of marketing or of production expenses, is that of cost allocation. In a marketing cost analysis, this problem occurs in two places. First, the ledger expenses must be allocated to appropriate activity cost groupings. Then these functional cost totals must be allocated to individual territories, products, or some other market segment. The choice of unreasonable cost allocation bases can distort the results and mislead management.

Operating expenses can be divided into direct and indirect expenses. (These are sometimes called "separable" and "common" expenses.) Direct, or separable, expenses are those which are incurred totally in connection with one market segment or one unit of the sales organization. Thus the salary, commission, and travel expenses of the salesman in territory A are a direct expense for that territory. The cost of media time or space to advertise product C is a direct cost of marketing that product. The task of allocating direct expenses is easy. They can be apportioned in their entirety to the marketing unit, such as a product or territory, for which they were incurred.

The allocation problem really arises in connection with indirect, or common, costs. These are expenses which are incurred jointly by more than one marketing unit and therefore cannot be apportioned totally to one product, territory, or other market segment.

A given cost does not remain permanently in either the direct or the indirect category. Its classification depends upon the type of cost analysis being made. If a firm is analyzing costs by territories, then salesmen's salaries are direct expenses chargeable entirely to the territory in which they work. If the company conducts a cost analysis by products, however, and each salesman sells the entire line of products, then salaries are indirect expenses and should be prorated according to the estimated time salesmen devote to each product.

Within the category of indirect expenses, some costs are more indirect than others. That is, some of the activity cost groupings are *directly* related, to some extent, to the territories, products, or other marketing units being studied. For instance, the total cost for advertising, order filling, or shipping would *decrease* if some of the products or territories were eliminated. By the same token, they would *increase* if some territories or product lines were added. These functional costs might be called *partially* indirect. On the other hand, activity groups covering marketing administrative expenses are *totally* indirect. Total expenses for maintaining the chief marketing executive, his staff, and his office would remain about the same, whether or not the number of territories or product lines was changed.

A study of business management today will disclose that different companies follow fundamentally different philosophies in allocating totally indirect costs such as administrative overhead expenses. One approach is to allocate these expenses equally among all territories, products, or other units being studied. This is an easy method, but it is obviously inadequate and in no way related to actuality.

Another approach is to allocate these expenses in proportion to the sales volume obtained from each segment being analyzed. This method is also sometimes used to apportion partially indirect expenses, such as billing, shipping, and order filling. The philosophy is that the expense burden should be placed where it can best be borne. The large-volume territories or products are thus charged with the bulk of these expenses. Although this philosophy has some merit, it does not accurately reflect the real situation.

A third allocation system is simply to prorate the indirect costs in the same proportion as the direct expenses. If one territory has been charged with 20 percent of the total direct expenses, it is also assigned 20 percent of the indirect costs. Sometimes partially indirect expenses such as billing and shipping are allocated to the marketing unit on some reasonable basis. Then the totally indirect expenses of administrative overhead are prorated in the same proportion as the sum of the direct plus partially indirect costs.

In Table 28–5, which we shall discuss later, we shall see some of the better, more precise bases which are suggested for allocating a specific functional cost to various product groups or sales territories.

Full-cost versus contribution-margin controversy.   One approach to the allocation of indirect costs is known as the *contribution-to-overhead* or the *contribution-margin* method. Under this system, management determines the gross margin of each marketing unit being studied. Then the direct expenses which have been allocated to each unit are deducted from the gross margin. These are the costs which presumably would be eliminated if the corresponding marketing unit were eliminated. After deducting these separable costs, the remainder is the amount which that unit is contributing to cover total overhead or indirect expenses.

There is a basic point of conflict between the contribution-margin approach and the full-cost approach to the allocation of costs. In the full-cost approach, all indirect expenses are allocated among the marketing units being analyzed. Proponents of the full-cost approach contend that the purpose of a marketing cost study is to determine the *net* profitability of the units being studied. They feel that the contribution-margin approach does not fulfill this purpose.

Under the contribution-margin system no attempt is made to allocate indirect costs, especially the *totally* indirect ones such as administrative expenses. Advocates of this approach contend that it is not reasonably possible to make an accurate apportionment of these items among organizational units or market segments. Furthermore, items such as administrative costs are not at all related to any one territory or product, and therefore the unit should not bear any of these costs. Contribution-margin supporters also state that management is not concerned with fixed, indirect costs when making decisions affecting short-run situations. They suggest that management is then concerned only with alternative courses of action where cost structures are variable. Finally, they point out that a full-cost analysis may show a product or territory with a net loss, whereas this unit may be contributing something to overhead. Some executives might recommend that the losing department be eliminated, overlooking the fact that the unit's contribution to overhead would then have to be borne by other units. Under the contribution-margin approach, there would be no question about keeping this unit as long as no better alternative could be discovered. On balance, it seems that both methods, contribution margin and full cost, are useful in marketing cost analysis.[7]

TYPES OF MARKETING COST ANALYSES

Three types of marketing cost analyses are commonly used by business. One is an analysis of costs as they appear in ledger accounts; another is a study of marketing expenses grouped into functional classifications; and the third is an analysis of marketing costs after they have been allocated to territories, products, or other marketing units.

Analysis of ledger expenses. The simplest and least expensive way to make a marketing cost analysis is to study the object-of-expenditure costs as they appear in the accounting ledgers. The researcher simply lists expense totals for delivery salaries, salesmen's travel expenses, advertising salaries, telephone and telegraph, etc. These costs may be compared with similar totals for past years, and each expense may be expressed as a percentage of net sales. If at all possible, the company's expense ratios should be compared with industry figures. Many trade associations publish median figures and other measures of central tendency for the industry as a whole.

Analysis of functional expenses. When a marketing executive wants additional information in order to help him control the cost of various marketing functions, such as advertising or warehousing, he should make an analysis of marketing expenses classified into groups representing these activities.

The procedure in a functional cost analysis is to decide what activity groups will be used and then allocate each ledger expense among the appropriate activities. An expense distribution sheet is often useful in this procedure (Table 28–4). The ledger expenses listed in the left-hand column are prorated among the appropriate columns which represent the functional groups. Some items such as the cost of advertising media space (newspapers) can be apportioned directly to one activity (advertising and sales promotion). For other expenses, the cost can be prorated only after management has established some reasonable basis for allocation. Rent or property taxes, for instance, may be allocated according to the proportionate amount of floor space occupied by each department. Thus, if the warehouse accounts for 30 percent of the total square feet of floor space in the firm, the warehousing function would be charged with 30 percent of the rent or property taxes. A columnar total represents the full cost of each function. In Great Western's case, advertising and sales promotion cost $169,750 and warehousing costs $200,000.

---

[7]For more on this notion that either method may be appropriate, depending upon the situation, see John J. Wheatley, "The Allocation Controversy in Marketing Cost Analysis," *University of Washington Business Review,* Summer, 1971, pp. 61–70. See also Leland L. Beik and Stephen L. Buzby, "Profitability Analysis by Market Segments," *Journal of Marketing,* July, 1973, pp. 48–53; and W. J. E. Crissy, Paul Fischer, and Frank H. Mossman, "Segmental Analysis: Key to Marketing Profitability," *MSU Business Topics,* Spring, 1973, pp. 42–49.

Table 28-4. Expense distribution sheet, Great Western Office Furniture Company, 1974.

The worksheet is a useful tool when allocating ledger-account expenses among the various groups of activity costs. Why is the salesmen's travel expense allocated entirely to direct selling, while the office supplies expense is prorated among all activity groups? What is a good basis for allocating the property tax expense among the functional cost groups?

Ledger expenses	Totals	Selling—direct costs	Selling—indirect costs	Advertising and sales promotion	Activity Cost Groups				
					Ware-housing	Transportation and shipping	Credits and collections	Order processing and billing	Marketing administrative
Salesmen's salaries	$ 2,500,000	$2,500,000							
Salesmen's travel	570,000	570,000							
Salesmen's commissions	2,400,000	2,400,000							
Media space	1,200,000			$1,200,000					
Dealer displays	200,000			200,000					
Advertising salaries	175,000			175,000					
Office supplies	180,000		18,500	25,500	$ 15,000	$ 19,500	$ 15,000	$ 52,500	$ 9,000
Telephone	90,000		9,000	6,750	1,500	5,250	9,000	6,000	10,500
Administrative salaries	615,000		100,000		55,000	40,000	60,000	110,000	100,000
Property taxes	240,000		20,500	12,500	128,500	18,000	13,500	23,500	15,500
Bad debts	30,000						30,000		
Freight out	1,500,000					1,500,000			
Total	$9,700,000	$5,695,000	$147,000	$1,169,750	$200,000	$1,583,750	$127,500	$192,000	$135,000

A functional cost analysis gives an executive more information than he can get from an analysis of ledger accounts alone. By comparing expense distribution sheets for several periods, management can ascertain which particular ledger expenses are responsible for significant changes in the cost of an activity. Finally, an analysis of activity expenses in total provides an excellent starting point for management to analyze costs by territories, products, or other marketing units.

Analysis of functional costs by market segments. The third and most beneficial type of marketing cost analysis is a study of the costs and profitability of each segment of the market. Common practice in this type of analysis is to divide the market by territories, products, customer groups, or order sizes. Cost analysis by market segment will enable management to pinpoint trouble spots or areas of satisfactory performance much more effectively than can be done with an analysis of either ledger-account expenses or activity costs.

The procedure for making a cost analysis by market segments is quite similar to the method used to analyze functional expenses. The total of each functional cost is prorated on some appropriate basis to each product or market segment being studied. By combining a sales volume analysis with a marketing cost study, a researcher can, in effect, prepare a complete operating statement for each of the product or market segments. In a territorial analysis, for example, all he needs to do is classify sales by territories and then determine the cost of purchasing or making the merchandise which was sold in each region. The difference between the sales and cost figures is the territorial gross margin. The third step is to allocate each activity expense among the territories. If only the direct expenses are allocated, the figure arrived at by subtracting expenses from gross margin is the territory's contribution to overhead. If all expenses are allocated and then subtracted from gross margin, the final result is the territory's net profit.

Table 28–5 presents examples of some reasonable bases for allocating groups of functional costs among sales territories and among product groups.

USE OF FINDINGS FROM COMBINED VOLUME AND COST ANALYSIS

The findings of a combined volume and cost analysis may be used by management in making decisions on many aspects of the marketing program.

Territorial decisions. Once marketing administrators know the net profit (or contribution to overhead) and the sales volume of the territories in relation to potential, they should throw their major effort into the weakest district because the greatest opportunity for improvement lies there.

Territorial boundaries may need adjustment to bring them into line with current potential. Often a company lets its territorial limits remain untouched long after shifts have occurred in market potential. As a result, some districts have more potential business than one salesman can effectively develop, whereas others have insufficient potential to support a salesman.

Territorial problems may stem from weaknesses in the distribution system, and changes in channels of distribution may be needed. Some firms which have been using manufacturers' agents may find it advisable to establish their own sales forces in growing markets. Other businesses may try to bypass wholesalers in some districts and sell directly to retailers or industrial users. Territorial problems may call for changes in selling methods. A company might use mail or telephone selling

Table 28-5. Bases of allocating functional cost groups to sales territories and to product groups.

A given functional cost group may be distributed among territories or products on the basis of some measurable characteristic which bears a "causative" relationship to the total amount of that functional cost group. Explain, using numbers, how advertising media costs would be allocated to territories.

Functional cost group	Basis of allocation	
	To sales territories	To product groups
1. Selling—direct costs: sales salaries, incentive compensation, travel, and other expenses	Direct	Selling time devoted to each product, as shown by special sales-call reports or other special studies
2. Selling—indirect costs: field sales-office expense, sales-administration expense, sales-personnel training, marketing research, new-product development, sales statistics	Equal charge for each salesman	In proportion to direct selling time or time records by projects
3. Advertising: media costs such as TV, radio, billboards, newspapers, magazines, etc.; advertising production costs; advertising department salaries	Direct; or analysis of media circulation records	Direct; or analysis of space and time by media; other costs in proportion to media costs
4. Sales promotion: consumer promotions such as coupons, premiums, etc.; trade promotions such as price allowances, point-of-purchase displays, cooperative advertising, etc.	Direct; or analysis of source records	Direct; or analysis of source records
5. Transportation: railroad, truck, barge, etc.; payments to carriers for delivery of finished goods from plants to warehouses and from warehouses to customers; traffic department costs	Applicable rate times tonnages	Applicable rates times tonnages
6. Storage and shipping: rent or equivalent costs for storage of inventories in warehouses; insurance and taxes on finished goods inventories; labor and equipment for physical handling, loading, etc.	Number of shipping units	Warehouse space occupied by average inventory. Number of shipping units.
7. Order processing: preparation of customer invoices; freight accounting; credit and collection; handling cash receipts; provision for bad debts; salary, supplies, space and equipment costs	Number of order lines	Number of order lines

Source: Adapted from Charles H. Sevin, *Marketing Productivity Analysis,* McGraw-Hill Book Company, New York, 1965, pp. 13–15.

rather than personal salesmen in unprofitable districts. Intensive competition may be the cause of unprofitable volume in some districts, and changes in the promotional program may be advisable.

Of course, a losing territory might be abandoned completely. If an abandoned region has been contributing anything to overhead, however, even though a net loss was shown, management must recognize that this contribution must now be carried by the remaining districts.

Product decisions. When the relative profitability of each group of products is known, management may take action to improve the situation. A product line may be simplified by eliminating slow-moving, unprofitable styles, sizes, or colors. The salesmen's compensation plan may be altered to encourage the sale of high-margin items. Commissions may be reduced on low-margin items to deter the men from devoting an inordinate amount of effort to them. Channels of distribution may be altered. Instead of selling his complete group of products directly to industrial users, for example, a machine tools manufacturer shifted to industrial distributors for standard products of low unit value. Advertising appropriations may be altered in order to develop more effective advertising for some line of merchandise. Changes in product policies themselves may be effective. For instance, multiple packaging may increase unit sales and thereby reduce the unit cost of order filling, billing, and shipping. Changes in physical distribution methods may enable a company to employ less expensive packaging materials and processes.

Pricing policies and practices with respect to each product should be reviewed carefully to determine whether price changes upward or downward may increase total revenue and net profit.

In the final analysis, management may decide to discontinue handling a product. Before this is done, however, consideration must be given to the effect this decision will have on other items in the line. Often a low-volume or unprofitable product must be carried simply to round out the line. Customers expect the seller to carry the article, and if he does not, he may lose business in his other products.

Decisions on customer classes and order sizes. By combining a volume analysis with a cost study, the executives can determine the relative profitability of each group of customers. If a substandard rate of net profit is coming from one group, changes in the pricing structure used for these accounts may be required. The prices may be raised to cover costs more effectively. Or, if competition is severe and there is an elastic demand, the prices may be reduced. Perhaps accounts which have been approached directly should be turned over to middlemen.

Marketing cost analysis by *size of order* is often helpful in connection with customer-classification cost studies. Management can determine its break-even point with respect to order size and can ascertain the amount of sales volume and net profit obtained from each order-size classification. A common problem plaguing many firms today is that of the small order. Many orders are below the break-even point. The revenue from each of these is actually less than the allocated expenses because several costs, such as billing, accounting, or direct selling, are the same whether the order amounts to $10 or $10,000.

Small-order accounts create a difficult decision-making situation. Management's immediate reaction may be that no order below the break-even point should be accepted and that small-volume accounts should be dropped from the customer list. Actually, such a decision may be erroneous and harmful. Management should determine first *why* certain accounts are small-order problems and then adopt procedures to correct the situation. Proper handling can very often turn a losing account into a satisfactory one.

There are several reasons why a customer may be a small-order problem. He may be new and growing. (However, eventually he may become a profitable account.) He may be buying a sufficient total volume of merchandise, but on a hand-to-mouth basis. That is, he may send in many small orders instead of a few large ones. He may be spreading his purchases among many different suppliers, thus creating small-order problems for all of them. Sometimes the accounting method determines whether a customer or order is profitable. If a customer is charged only with the appropriate *marginal* costs required to do business with him, he may be a profitable customer, but if he is charged with his share of all costs—that is, if an average cost basis is used—his account may show up as a net loss.

A multitude of practical suggestions may be made to aid management in reducing the costs of small orders or increasing the size of the order. Management may initiate customer education, establish minimum order sizes, change the price structure, use multiple packaging, turn to direct-mail or telephone selling, or use wholesalers instead of direct selling.

FUTURE OF COST ANALYSIS

The use of marketing cost analysis has increased considerably in the past 30 years. Refinements in technique have come rapidly, and the future is highly promising. If there is any real problem in the area of cost analysis, it is the shortage of skilled personnel. This shortage will undoubtedly be alleviated as college instruction in the field is increased and as trade and professional associations in business administration place added emphasis on marketing cost studies. The situation will also be helped as marketing and accounting people come to realize that they have mutual problems in this area and can benefit from more closely coordinated efforts.

QUESTIONS AND PROBLEMS

1. The iceberg principle has been likened to a medical diagnosis where the patient's complaint is different from the real problem. Explain.
2. "A sales volume analysis is of very little value unless it is accompanied by a marketing cost analysis." Discuss.
3. A sales volume analysis by territories indicates that the sales of a manufacturer of roofing materials have increased 12 percent a year for the past three years in the territory comprising South Carolina, Georgia, and Florida. Does this indicate conclusively that the company's sales volume performance is satisfactory in that region?
4. A manufacturer found that one of his products accounted for 35 to 45 percent of the company's total sales in all but two of the eighteen territories. In each of

those two districts, this product accounted for only 15 percent of the company's volume. What factors might account for the relatively low sales of this article in the two districts?

5. Explain how the results of a territorial sales volume analysis may influence a firm's promotional program.

6. What effects may a sales analysis by products have on training, supervising, and compensating the salesmen?

7. "In production, costs are a function of volume; in marketing, volume is a function of costs." Explain.

8. "The Robinson-Patman Act served as the greatest stimulus ever for the development and widespread use of marketing cost analysis." Explain.

9. Are the following expenses properly classified as marketing or production costs? Does the nature of the company or the nature of the product influence your decision?

a. Credit
b. Shipping
c. Packaging
d. Labeling
e. Repair service
f. Styling and designing
g. Engineering
h. Inventory control

10. What is an unprofitable sale? Explain carefully, keeping in mind the various kinds of costs such as total, marginal, average, etc. Should a company ever intentionally accept unprofitable business? Explain.

11. A national manufacturer of luggage and other leather products, such as briefcases, wallets, attache cases, and pocket notebooks, employs 30 salespeople. Each salesperson has a particular territory, and each one sells the entire group of products. The company calls directly on department stores and specialty luggage stores. The marketing department wishes to make a territorial cost analysis. What bases do you recommend they use for allocating each of the following costs?

a. Salespeople's salaries
b. Salespeople's commissions paid on net sales
c. Sales training expenses
d. Newspaper advertising
e. National magazine advertising
f. Marketing research
g. Shipping
h. Billing
i. Manager of the sales force and his office expenses
j. Marketing manager's salary and office expenses

12. Of what value is an analysis of ledger expenses? What are some marketing policies which might be based on this type of analysis?

13. "Firms should discontinue handling losing products." Discuss.

14. Do you agree with the following statements?

a. "Customers whose annual purchases are large never present a small-order problem."
b. "Small-order problems are always created by small-annual-volume customers."

15. Should a company discontinue selling to an unprofitable customer?

CONSUMERISM AND SOCIALLY ORIENTED MARKETING

In the first two chapters of this book we introduced the broader, societal dimension of marketing, and we examined briefly the role of marketing in the total economy. For the most part, however, we have used throughout the book a micro approach and a managerial orientation as we studied the problems facing an individual producer or middleman in the management of his marketing activities. Now in these two concluding chapters, once again we will step back and take a look at marketing from a broader societal perspective.

In the 1970s there is clearly emerging a social orientation in marketing which both broadens and complements managerial marketing. Since the 1960s our socioeconomic goals and cultural values have been changing, thus leading to consumer discontent with the then-existing system. This discontent—labeled "consumerism"—in turn has led to a more socially oriented system of marketing (called "social marketng"). Now social marketing is resulting in management's awareness of its broadening social and ethical responsibilities.

CONSUMERISM

Before we consider the forces leading to consumerism, and the government and business responses to this phenomenon, let's first explain what consumerism means.

MEANING AND SCOPE OF CONSUMERISM

If social upheaval is too strong a term to describe consumerism, then at least it is a social movement—a social "happening"—of the 1960s and 970s. Furthermore, this phenomenon shows every indication of growing stronger, rather than abating, in the years ahead.

Some definitions. We may define *consumerism* as the actions of individuals and organizations (consumer, government, and business) in response to consumers' dissatisfactions arising in exchange relationships. Consumerism is (1) a protest against perceived business injustices and (2) the efforts to remedy those injustices.[1]

In exchange relationships between buyers and sellers, the feeling clearly exists on the part of consumers that the balance of power lies with the sellers. Consumerism is an expression of this opinion and an attempt to achieve a more equal balance in the power of buyers and sellers.[2] Consumers are considered to have certain rights, and consumerism encompasses the activities designed to protect those rights. In 1962 President Kennedy identified the following four rights of the consumer:

1. The right to safety
2. The right to be informed
3. The right to choose
4. The right to be heard

These four rights have served as a foundation for consumerism. We shall talk more about them later in this chapter.

Scope of consumerism. The accepted scope of consumerism today broadly envelopes three areas of consumer dissatisfaction and remedial efforts. The original, and still dominant, focus of consumerism involves the discontent generated in direct buyer-seller exchange relationships between consumers and business firms, especially in their marketing activities. Marketing is singled out as the

---

[1]For a sample of other discussions of consumerism—its meaning, causes, actions, and prospects, see David W. Cravens and Gerald E. Hills, "Consumerism: A Perspective for Business," *Business Horizons*, August, 1970, pp. 21–28; Rom J. Markin, "Consumerism: Militant Consumer Behavior: A Social and Behavioral Analysis," *Business and Society*, Fall, 1971, pp. 5–17; Robert O. Herrmann, "Consumerism: Its Goals, Organizations and Future," *Journal of Marketing*, October, 1970, pp. 55–60; Richard H. Buskirk and James T. Rothe, "Consumerism—An Interpretation," *Journal of Marketing*, October, 1970 , pp. 61–65; John F. Willenborg, "The Emergence of Consumerism as a Social Force," *Business and Economic Review*, December, 1971, pp. 2–6; Boris W. Becker, "Consumerism: A Challenge or a Threat?" *Journal of Retailing*, Summer, 1972, pp. 16–28; and Philip Kotler, "What Consumerism Means for Marketers," *Harvard Business Review*, May–June, 1972, pp. 48–57.

For two good collections of articles on consumerism, see David A. Aaker and George S. Day (eds.), *Consumerism, Search for the Consumer Interest*, 2d ed., The Free Press, New York, 1974; and William T. Kelley (ed.), *New Consumerism*, Grid, Inc., Columbus, Ohio, 1973.

[2]For the notion that both consumerism and environmentalism are on the brink of acquiring social power, see Charles G. Leathers, *"New Dimensions of Countervailing Power:* Consumerism and Environmentalism," *MSU Business Topics*, Winter, 1972, pp. 64–72.

main target of consumer discontent with business, because marketing is that part of a company's total program which is closest to the consumer, is most visible to him, and is the easiest for him to contact.

In the second of our perspectives on consumerism, we recognize that consumerism is *not* limited to discontent with business alone. Remembering the term "exchange relationship" in our prior definition of consumerism, we now see that "consumerism is concerned with protecting consumers from *all* organizations with which there is an exchange relationship.[3] (Italics added.) Therefore, consumerism (dissatisfactions and remedial effort) may arise from a consumer's relations with such diverse organizations as hospitals, schools, athletic clubs, or government agencies (police department, trash collectors, tax assessors, street maintenance department, etc.). This broader concept of consumerism is in line with our societal definition of marketing (recall Chapter 1), where we recognized that the essence of marketing is an exchange transaction in any field of interpersonal endeavor, not just business alone.

Today the dimensions of consumerism have been expanded even further to include enviromental matters affecting our quality of life. In this context consumerism is part of the broader social and political discontent of an activist generation. Perhaps basically consumerism falls in the same category as various group protests against a series of social crises such as "inadequate educational systems, hardcore unemployment, hazardous pollution of natural resources, antiquated transportation, shameful housing, insufficient and ineffective public facilities, lack of equal opportunity for all, and a highly dangerous failure of communication between young and old, black and white."[4] That is, people see things which they feel are wrong, and they are vocal and even active as they seek to change the situation.

The unusual feature of this third phase of consumerism is that we are dealing with an *indirect* impact on one social unit (person, business, etc.) stemming from an exchange relationship between two other people of organizations.[5] Consumer Jones buys steel from company A. But in producing the steel for that exchange, the mill pollutes the river used by Consumer Smith for fishing and swimming, so Smith protests. Or, one group of consumers buy drinks in throwaway containers and then litter the highway with them, thus reducing the quality of life for another group who enjoy driving through a litter-free countryside.

In other words, the exchange between two people or groups creates a problem for a third group. This problem situation is intensified by the fact that individuals have very little incentive to change their behavior, because the action of a single buyer or seller will have no observable impact on the enviroment. One person using a litter bag in his car, one firm hiring disadvantaged workers, one advertiser removing billboards, or one group using a car pool—each will have no noticeable effect on our total environment or quality of life. To get the concerted action on the part of enough individuals to produce the desired enviromental change typically requires government action.

---

[3]Aaker and Day, *op. cit.*, p. xvii.

[4]David Rockefeller, president of New York's Chase Manhattan Bank, as quoted in "The War that Business Must Win," *Business Week,* Nov. 1, 1969, p.63.

[5]Aaker and Day, *op. cit.*, pp. xv, xx.

Consumerism yesterday and today. Consumerism really is not a new phenomenon. In the early 1900s and again in the 1930s there was a "consumer movement," in which efforts were made to protect the consumer from harmful products and from false and misleading advertising. Several laws were passed in connection with this movement.

There are three significant differences, however, between the earlier movements and that of today. First, the socioeconomic settings are vastly different. In the 1930s there was a depression, incomes were very low, and we did not talk of an economy of abundance. Today's consumerism arose within an environment of high incomes, full employment, and subsistence needs largely filled. It is an unfortunate paradox that, on the one hand, our advanced technology can provide us with so many mechanical marvels but that, on the other, it is the very complexity of these advancements which often creates service and quality-control problems. In a way, we are spoiled. We demand high levels of performance and are critical of imperfections, and yet the average level of performance is still far above what it was, say 10 or 20 years ago. In the same vein, on the one hand our high level of affluence enables us to buy products which were impossible to obtain with incomes of 30 or 40 years ago, and yet on the other hand, this very same affluence makes us choosier about what we buy and quicker to complain about these products when they do not perform as expected.

The second differentiating feature is the nature and purpose of the legislation related to the two consumer movements. In the 1930s the guiding political philosophy was to keep everyone in business and to protect small businessmen from the giant companies, especially the corporate chain-store organizations. Legislative emphasis was placed primarily upon the protection of competition, and consumer protection (when there was any) occurred as a buy-product. (There were some exceptions—the Pure Food and Drug Act and various labeling laws, for example.) In today's political atmosphere the goal of consumer legislation is quite different—the laws first and foremost are intended to protect the consumer.

The third distinguishing aspect of today's consumerism is that it is much more likely to continue and to grow, because it has generated an institutional structure to support it. Not only have consumer-oriented laws been passed, but government agencies have been established at the federal, state, and local levels to administer these laws and to generally represent and protect consumer interests.

CONDITIONS LEADING TO CONSUMERISM

One may wonder why consumerism happened to occur in the 1960s when the factors of social and economic discontent (pollution, unsafe products, criticisms of advertising, urban decay, low-income consumers, etc.) had been with us for some time previously. In view of the cultural and economic changes taking place in the U.S., a new consumer movement was inevitable—the time was ripe. It just so happened that a whole series of inflammable issues converged in the mid-1960s to touch off a real "social conflagration"—namely, consumerism.

Broad cultural changes. Four broad cultural changes occurred in the U.S. in the 1960s to provide the setting for consumerism. The first was a dramatic *shift in the social and economic goals of American consumers.* In the decades pre-

ceding the mid-1960s, we were concerned with building an affluent society—
an economy of abundance. After the years of "doing without things" during the
Great Depression of the 1930s and the Great War of the early 1940s, our emphasis was on improving our material standard of living. We were busy acquiring—
we were "things-oriented."

Having reached these material goals, we now are raising two questions.
First, are these material things that we *really* want, and second, are these things
worth the price we are paying for them in terms of pollution, depleted resources,
poverty in the midst of plenty, etc.

Since the mid-1960s, our goals have been changing. Today we are seeking
broader societal goals. We are concerned more with our physical environment
and the quality of our life. We worry more about a *qualitative* standard of life,
rather than a *quantitative* material standard of living. Our orientation is shifting
from things to people.

This change in goals is a real-life application of Maslow's theory regarding a
hierarchy of human needs. (Recall discussion in Chapter 4.) After a person satisfies
his subsistence needs, he moves up the hierarchy to social needs, and then on to
self-esteem and self-fulfillment needs. With some notable exceptions, American
consumers have achieved a measure of affluence and we have developed our
product technology to an advanced stage. It is a natural evolution now to turn from
individualistic, materialistic goals to social, quality-of-life goals. With their
materialistic needs more or less taken for granted, consumers have time to be
sensitive to social and environmental needs.[6]

The second broad change—a corollary of the first—is that we are *entering
a more advanced stage of cultural-economic development* in the U.S. One
theory of economic growth holds that there are three observable stages of development: First a subsistence stage featuring agriculture, fishing, and hunting,
then a secondary stage emphasizing manufacturing and product acquisition,
and finally a tertiary stage where services (trade, education, transportation, government fields, communication, etc.) are paramount.[7] In the U.S. we are moving
into the third stage. In this stage people are more willing to take the time,
money, and effort to be concerned about other people and their physical environment. Manufacturing industries tend to decline in relative importance,
and service-oriented industries (communication, knowledge, government) become more important. As a result, the balance of power in society tends to shift
toward consumers, because service industries are a more people-type operation than are manufacturing industries.

The third cultural change underlying consumerism is the *active role of young
people.* As a group, young people have probably always tended to be more
idalistic and humanistic than older age groups, or at least it has seemed that
way on the surface. And certainly the under-30 group in the 1960s was no exception. Compared with previous generations of young adults, however, today's
young people definitely are different in that they are better educated, more
articulate, and more inclined (less afraid) to speak out and take action.

---

[6]For more on how the shift in consumer priorities and goals has invalidated products and
procedures of the past, see W. Thomas Anderson, Jr., Louis K. Sharpe, and Robert J. Boewadt,
"The Environmental Role for Marketing," *MSU Business Topics*, Summer, 1972, pp. 66–72.

[7]Colin Clark, *The Conditions of Economic Progress*, 3d ed., Macmillan & Co., Ltd., London,
1957, p. 491.

The fourth cultural development has been the *growing visibility of, and concern for, environmental problem situations.* Low-income consumers, for example, achieved visibility through riots and fires in some urban ghettos and through other less violent, yet very concerted, efforts to achieve equal rights. In other situations environmental pollution simply got so bad that it was no longer possible to ignore it.

Consumer discontents and frustrations.[8] To continue our tracing of the rise of consumerism, we shall use the analagous situation of building and lighting a fire. (In view of the actual fires and riots in the 1960s, perhaps this analogy is more real than we would like.)

Into the cultural setting just described came a series of highly inflammable issues which generated much consumer discontent and frustration. *Economic discontent* was fostered by the steady inflation. The Vietnam War, racial conflict, and awareness of conditions facing consumers below the poverty level all contributed to *social discontent. Ecological* discontent was generated by hazardous pollution, traffic congestion, overcrowded cities, etc. *Political* discontent stemmed from the belief that political, legislative, and other governmental institutions were either unresponsive to consumer needs or unequipped to handle them.

In the business area, *discontent with the marketing system* was particularly strong and widespread. The marketing conditions which have fostered modern-day consumerism possibly can be summed up in this single observation: Consumers are frustrated, dissatisfied, and indignant because of unfulfilled promises, unrealized expectations, and unstated dangers in the products and services they have purchased. And nobody seemed willing to listen to the complaints or to do anything about them.

In the following sample of consumer complaints against marketing, there is a general parallel with the four consumer rights stated by President Kennedy.

Right to safety: unsafe products; unstated dangers in products; unrealized expectations regarding product performance; inadequate repair service.

A consumer can't see, smell, touch, or taste the radiation emanating from his television set or the pesticide residue in his food. Power lawn mowers have injured countless people; dangerous toys and unsafe tires have been sold. Much attention has been directed to the benefits of contraceptive pills and some wonder drugs, but the advertising programs have had little to say about possible side effects of using these products. It was on this point of dangerous products that today's consumerism was launched when Ralph Nader started his crusade to increase the safety of automobiles.

While not directly related to product safety, a major product complaint is poor product quality backed up by confusing and worthless warranties. Moreover, consumers too often are led to expect higher performance levels than the product delivers. Parts fall off cars, zippers jam, meat products are adulterated, commuter trains run late, telephones do not work, wash-and-wear clothing really needs ironing, appliances do not perform as advertised, etc., etc. Probably the number of such occurrences is a small percentage of total units sold. Nevertheless, these

---

[8]The organizational structure in this and the next section is adapted from Philip Kotler, "What Consumerism Means for Marketers," *Harvard Business Review*, May–June, 1972, pp. 51–52.

occurrences are sufficiently frequent to arouse consumer wrath. Related to the problem of product quality is the poor repair service provided by many manufacturers and middlemen.

Right to be informed: inadequate and misleading information; deceptive advertising; deceptive packaging; misleading warranties; insufficient information on product contents, operating instructions, or care of product; deceptive personal selling tactics; deceptive pricing, deceptive credit terms.

Right to choose: confusing assortment of products, brands, and package sizes; lack of real competition; collusion among business firms; prices are fixed among "competing" sellers.

Right to be heard: business firms unresponsive to consumers' grievances; impersonal attitude in selling; we can't get past the computer and deal with real people.

The president of the Grocery Manufacturers of America observed: "The trend to self-service and super stores brought the consumer great dollar savings, but it also left her with no one to talk to about the weather, no one who could advise her on a product choice, and no one who would take responsibility if the product failed. The gulf between the consumer and the product manufacturer is even wider."[9] Did you ever try to get someone to listen to you when you want a company to correct the mistakes in a charge account messed up by a computerized accounting system, or when you want someone to straighten out an error in order filling and shipping?

"Lighting the fires" of consumerism. During the 1960s there was a growing belief (expressed in the writings of social critics, in some congressional activity, and in the efforts of consumer educational organizations) that something should, and could, be done to remedy the causes of consumer dissatisfaction. However, something still was needed to ignite the combustible mass of issues. That "something" was provided by two issues. The first centered around Ralph Nader, General Motors' unsuccessful attempt to investigate and discredit him, followed by Nader's successful attack on the unsafe aspects of GM's Corvair automobile. The second igniter was a widespread series of unplanned housewives' boycotts of supermarkets.

Once lit, the fires of consumerism burned brightly with fuel from several sources. Mass media gave front-page and prime-time coverage to the activities of consumer advocates. Politicians in droves got on the consumer bandwagon. The social movement became increasingly institutionalized as new and existing organizations moved in the direction of consumer protection. Businessmen inadvertently were a big help to consumerism, because so many of them ignored the movement or actively resisted it. In the early stages even the state and federal legislatures seemed slow to respond to expressed needs of the consumers.

ACTION RESPONSES TO CONSUMER DISCONTENT

Significant action-oriented efforts to remedy the conditions leading to consumerism have come from the consumers themselves, from governmental ac-

---

[9]"The U.S.'s Toughest Customer," *Time*, Dec. 12, 1969, p. 89.

tivities, and from business organizations. The response from each of these three groups has, of course, been quite different, because of the differences in their attitudes and perceptions about consumerism.

Responses of consumers and consumer organizations. Consumers have reacted in a wide variety of ways to vent their frustrations and to correct what they consider to be injustices. These responses have been as individuals or in organized groups. They have ranged from refusing to buy a product or shop at a certain store, all the way to burning and looting business establishments. Many consumers are more active politically than ever before. They support consumer-oriented candidates. They write letters to editors, legislators, and business executives.

Consumers are becoming increasingly, and better, organized in their social and economic protests. In recent years many organizations such as church groups, the PTA, and student groups have become involved in consumer issues, whereas in previous years their efforts were in quite different directions.

Consumers are simply too heterogeneous a group to generate much uniform action. Conflicts and contradictions are bound to occur. We want clean air and no traffic congestion, but we also want unlimited use of our own auto. We want clean water, but we do not want to close the local factory and lose its jobs. Through all the heterogeneity, nevertheless, several common themes do emerge which give direction to the consumer movement, as witness some conclusions from one study:[10]

1. Most consumers recognize and value highly many aspects of the free enterprise system.
2. Many consumers are skeptical about certain business policies and are discontented with specific marketing activities such as advertising.
3. Many people concede that some of the imperfections in the marketing system result from consumer ineptness, carelessness, and apathy.
4. Respondents think that consumer problems are important and deserve more attention than they now receive.
5. Overwhelming support is voiced for additional government regulation as a means of solving consumer problems. This attitude is expressed by both liberals and conservatives.

Government responses. Consumerism is not likely to fade away; instead, it probably will grow stronger in the coming years. The main reason for this forecast is that today it is politically popular to support consumers. Politicians may have generally been unresponsive to consumer needs in the years prior to the mid-1960s. Since then, however, consumer-oriented activity at both the federal and state levels has been at an unprecedented rate. Almost all the states and many cities have created some kind of office for consumer affairs. Provisions now exist whereby a *group* of consumers allegedly injured in substantially the same manner can file a "class-action" suit against one firm or a group of com-

---

[10]Hiram C. Barksdale and William R. Darden, "Consumer Attitudes toward Marketing and Consumerism," *Journal of Marketing*, October, 1972, pp. 28–35.

panies. This provision is in response to the feeling that poor or even middle-class consumers, acting individually, do not have anything resembling an equal chance for justice in a court suit against a large business firm.[11]

The scope of governmental activity in consumerism covers three areas —presidential support, legislation, and an expanded role for government regulatory agencies.

Presidential support. Starting with President Kennedy and continuing through the administrations of Presidents Johnson and Nixon, the executive office has provided strong and explicit support for consumer interests. Many legislative measures supporting consumers have been sponsored by the Presidents. They have proposed new programs, established new agencies (e.g., The Office of Consumer Affairs in the White House), and urged the strengthening of existing programs and agencies closely related to the consumer.

Legislation. For the first time, state and federal legislatures are passing laws whose primary purpose is to aid the consumer. In contrast, so often in the past marketing legislation was generally business-oriented, not consumer-oriented. To repeat a point made earlier, often the intent of legislation was to protect competition or to benefit some segment of business, and any benefit or protection to the consumer occurred as a by-product, if it occurred at all. In contrast, in some of the recent biannual sessions of the U.S. Congress, over 500 consumer-interest bills affecting product sales have been introduced, and a substantial number have been passed.

A significant group of these laws is designed to protect the consumers' "right to safety"—especially in situations where he cannot judge the risk himself. Thus, we have the auto-safety law, the toy-safety law, and several others regulating textiles, tires, foods, drugs, cigarettes, cleaning fluid, and many other products.

In the opinion of the author and others, however, the most significant product-safety law is the Consumer Product Safety Act (1972). This act might well be the most powerful consumer-oriented law ever passed. Moreover, the Consumer Product Safety Commission (CPSC), created by the act, could well be the most powerful regulatory agency ever established by our government.[12] The commission has authority to set mandatory safety standards for practically all consumer products. (The CPSC has no authority over autos, foods, drugs, tobacco products, and some other products covered by separate laws or other agencies.) The Commission can name brands and companies when publishing information regarding injurious products. It can ban the distribution of these products without a court hearing. Top management of offending companies is liable for criminal, not just civil, charges.

In its first year of existence the CPSC quickly made its presence known by issuing a "most wanted" list of nearly 400 product categories which were con-

---

[11]For some implications and possible dangers to legitimate businesses from class-action suits, see Buskirk and Rothe, *op. cit* ., p. 64.

[12]For the historical development of this law, its contents, and its implications for management, see Walter Jensen, Jr., Edward M. Mazze, and Duke Nordlinger Stern, "The Consumer Product Safety Act: A Special Case in Consumerism," *Journal of Marketing*, October, 1973, pp. 68–71.

sidered hazardous in some way.[13] The list, called a Product Hazard Index, was based on the frequency and severity of injuries as reported by a group of hospitals. The number-one spot in the index was held by bicycles. The top 16 were as follows:

THE TOP 16 CATEGORIES OF HAZARDOUS PRODUCTS*

1. Bicycles
2. Stairs
3. Doors
4. Cleaning agents
5. Tables
6. Beds
7. Football equipment
8. Playground equipment

9. Liquid fuels (lighter fluid, etc.)
10. Architectural glass
11. Power lawn mowers
12. Baseball equipment
13. Nails and tacks
14. Bathtubs and showers
15. Space heaters
16. Swimming pools

*Products like autos, cigarettes, and some foods and drugs would have made the top group if they were under jurisdiction of the CPSC.

One controversial area of product-safety legislation is the paternalistic type of law that is intended to protect the consumer, whether or not he wants that protection. Thus, it is mandatory to equip autos with seat belts that must be in use before the car will start, regardless of whether the consumer wants those seat belts. In effect, somebody else is forcing a consumer to accept what that other person feels is in the consumer's best interests—truly a new and broadening approach to consumer legislation.

Another series of laws supports the consumers' "right to be informed." These measures help in such areas as reducing the confusion and deception in packaging and labeling (Fair Packaging and Labeling Act), identifying the ingredients and nutritional content in food products, interpreting the price per unit (ounce, pint, pound, etc.) of food products (unit pricing laws), and determining the true rate of interest (Truth-in-Lending Act).

At the state legislative level there also has been considerable interest in consumer-support laws. Several states, for example, have passed some variety of "no-fault" auto insurance laws, and almost all states and several cities now have some form of "cooling-off" law affecting door-to-door selling. The latter are regulations providing for a "cooling-off" period (usually three days) during which the buyer of goods or services in a door-to-door sale may cancel the contract, return

---

[13]See "A 'Most Wanted' List of Hazardous Items," *Business Week,* Sept. 29, 1973, p. 34; James D. Snyder, "Washington's Product Safety Crew Is Loaded with Clout," *Sales Management,* Oct. 15, 1973, p. 37; "'We're Going for Companies' Throats,'" *Dun's Review,* January, 1974, p.36; and "More Muscle in the Fight against Unsafe Products," *U.S. News & World Report,* Mar. 11, 1974, p. 49.

any merchandise, and obtain a full refund. In effect, you can say "no" to the company even after you have said "yes" to its salesman.[14]

Government regulatory agencies. The strengthened and expanded role of regulatory agencies involved in consumer affairs has been a significant government response in the consumer movement. New agencies have been established—the Environmental Protection Agency, the Consumer Product Safety Commission, for example, and the Office of Consumer Affairs in the White House. At the time this was being written, Congress was moving toward establishing an independent Consumer Protection Agency which would encourage testing of product performance, handle consumer complaints, and represent the consumer—as sort of a consumer advocate or ombudsman—in proceedings involving other government agencies. Its potentially far-reaching effects were drawing strong objections from business groups, so compromises were being sought.

Existing agencies such as the Food and Drug Administration (FDA) and the Federal Trade Commission (FTC) have been given expanded powers and have become more aggressive in their activities. FDA approval is required in a variety of product categories—drugs, pesticides, products with toxic chemicals, for example—before a new product can be put on the market. An expanded field staff has enabled the FTC to search more intensively for deceptive business practices. The FTC has issued trade regulations covering a number of marketing practices—product warranties door-to-door selling, "cents-off" pricing, etc.—which the Commission considers to be misleading.[15] The FTC has required documented substantiation of advertising claims made by manufacturers of autos, electric razors, air conditioners, tires, toothpaste, cough-and-cold remedies, and TV sets.[16] In cases of misleading advertising, the FTC can require the firm to run a certain amount of "corrective advertising" for a period of time.[17] A "corrective ad" is one in which the company states that specified claims in previous ads were incorrect or may have left the wrong impression.

---

[14]For an analysis of the role of cooling-off legislation and its effectiveness in protecting consumers, particularly those with low-incomes, see Orville C. Walker , Jr, and Neil M. Ford, "Can 'Cooling-off Laws' Really Protect the Consumer?" *Journal of Marketing*, April, 1970, pp. 53–58; for summaries of the state laws, see "Cooling It, State by State," *Sales Management*, Oct. 2, 1972, p. 16, and Oct. 16, 1972, p. 32.

[15]The commission has even noted that the potential for deception exists when an advertiser uses certain indicators such as colors, symbols, or endorsements to imply that his product possesses certain features which in reality it does not. See Dorothy Cohen, "Surrogate Indicators and Deception in Advertising," *Journal of Marketing*, July, 1972, pp. 10–15.

For suggestions on how the FTC might amend its framework for regulating advertising by recognizing behavioral characteristics of consumers, see Dorothy Cohen, "The Federal Trade Commission and the Regulation of Advertising in the Consumer Interest," *Journal of Marketing*, January, 1969, pp. 40–44.

[16]See Robert E. Wilkes and James B. Wilcox, "Recent FTC Actions: Implications for the Advertising Strategist," *Journal of Marketing*, January, 1974, pp. 55–61.

[17]See Robert F. Dyer and Philip G. Kuehl, "The 'Corrective Advertising' Remedy of the FTC: An Experimental Evaluation," *Journal of Marketing*, January, 1974, pp. 48–54; and H. Keith Hunt, "Effects of Corrective Advertising," *Journal of Advertising Research*, October, 1973, pp. 15–22.

Effectiveness of government action. How effective have governmental efforts been in improving the consumer's position? The consumers' answer might start with that cigarette slogan, "You've come a long way, baby," and then would add, "but you still have a long way to go." Just as consumerism started with unrealized expectations from *business* performance, now the consumer is experiencing unrealized expectations from *government's* performance. Consumers expected much from the laws covering truth in packaging, credit practices, reduction of pollution, product safety, and many other topics. The results from these laws, however, have often been disappointing to consumer groups. Water and air pollution remain high and the energy crisis generated efforts to postpone or weaken the pollution-reduction legislation. The truth-in-packaging and truth-in-lending laws proved to be less than anticipated.

Certainly the consumers' position has been greatly improved, but the pace of improvement is still too slow to satisfy many consumer advocates. However, even with this criticism, consumers still have decidedly more confidence in government-enforced action than in voluntary business efforts. Consumers want more, not less, government intervention in the marketplace, according to various opinion polls and research studies.

Several factors account for the government's performance level being lower than consumers expected. One is that business lobbyists still are effective at getting amendments to a bill that will temper a strong antibusiness bias. A corollary factor is that compromise often is necessary to get any kind of a consumer bill passed. Often the strong consumer advocates fail to see all the long-run problems and implications contained in their requests. Then there are the interest conflicts within the body of consumers. They want the Environmental Protection Agency to fight air pollution, for example, but then they complain to their congressmen when that agency proposes a parking tax to discourage urban commuting.

On balance, it is becoming apparent that legislation and government agencies are not the total answer to consumer complaints about business and social conditions. While governmental action has helped considerably, it is not a cure-all. So let's see how business has responded to consumer discontent.

Business responses. As responses to consumerism, we know that business apathy, resistance, or token efforts simply increase the probability of more government regulation. It is as simple as this today—consumerism is a sufficiently entrenched, vocal, and well-organized force in the market place so that consumer complaints will be answered. The only question is: Answered by whom?—business or government? If business cannot or will not do the job, the only alternative is additional government intervention.

> "The reaction of many businessmen who have been caught by consumerism, is like good old Charlie Brown's bafflement when his team lost its 43rd consecutive game: 'How can we lose when we're so sincere?' Good intentions don't impress anyone. The public wants good intentions translated into effective action, and they're going to get it, one way or another."
>
> *Source*: Elisha Gray II, chairman of Whirlpool Corporation, as quoted in *Newsweek*, July 26, 1971, p. 44.

Yet, unfortunately, studies show that the business response "has tended to be superficial, negative, unplanned, and uncoordinated—even among the largest companies in the country.[18] These reactions are reflected in remarks such as, "Consumerism has nothing to do with us because we are industrial manufacturers," or "This consumerism is nothing new and anyway it doesn't apply to us because we've always been customer-oriented." These attitudes, held by a wide segment of business executives, simply overlook the facts that (1) the new consumerism is rooted in changing consumer goals, attitudes, and values, and (2) basic changes are occurring in the marketing environment as a result of legislation, more powerful regulatory agencies, and the growing legitimacy earned by consumer advocates. Failure to understand the nature and scope of consumerism has the potential to cost industry untold sums of money (1) in actions forced by the government and (2) in lost sales to disenchanted customers.

Positive responses of individual firms. The above gloomy picture is offset somewhat by a growing executive awareness of the dangers accompanying a negative response to consumerism. Consequently, we are seeing an increasing number of programs that are positive and substantive responses to consumer needs and problems. Consumerism is forcing businessmen to reexamine their social roles and to look at problems they previously ignored.

Perceptive businessmen now see that the *long-run* net results from consumerism can be social and economic gains for the consumers and businessmen alike.[19] First, better-informed consumers normally are more efficient to their purchasing, and thus able to buy more goods and services in total. Second, if manufacturers have to absorb the costs of reducing the pollution caused by their products, then the prices on these goods will rise and the demand will shift to low social-cost goods. This will mean lower government expenditures—and lower tax rates—to clean up the environment. Third, everybody wins when consumerism results in fewer unsafe products and thus more satisfied and healthy consumers. Finally, perhaps the most promising benefits to businessmen are the unlimited market opportunities awaiting (1) the marketers of new products and services to satisfy environmental demands and (2) the firms which reorient their marketing programs to reach the environmentally and socially conscious consumers.

More specifically in the short run, individual firms have developed responses to consumerism which relate to five areas in marketing. Some of these are voluntary efforts, and others are in response to legislation or rules set down by regulatory agencies. The first group of actions involves *better communication with consumers.* Many of the consumers' complaints can be summed up as a failure to recognize the consumers' "right to be heard." Consumers often are frustrated simply because they cannot get anyone in the huge, impersonal, remote corporation to listen to them when they need some information, the prod-

---

[18]This paragraph is adapted from Frederick E. Webster, Jr., "Does Business Misunderstand Consumerism?" *Harvard Business Review*, September–October, 1973, pp. 89–97, especially pp. 89–92.

[19]These points are developed in Kotler, *op. cit.*, pp. 53, 55.

uct needs repairing, or something else goes wrong. The individual consumer needs to be able to communicate with, and be answered by, a company.[20]

Many firms have responded positively to this need in a variety of ways. Whirlpool (appliances) Corporation established a 24-hour "cool line" enabling customers to call free of charge from anywhere in the country in order to register a complaint, ask about service, or get product-usage information. Similar systems were set up by Avis and Chrysler. Other firms (Scott lawn products, Pan Am Airways, Nabisco, Johnson & Johnson, Pillsbury) have speeded up and otherwise improved their responses to consumers' written inquiries or complaints.

In response to one of the major areas of consumer criticism, many companies today are generating *more and better information for consumers.* Point-of-sale information has been improved by a number of firms. Manufacturers are publishing instructional booklets on the use and care of their products. Labeling is more informative than in the past in many instances. Several supermarkets, even where not required to do so by law, have instituted unit pricing. The ads run by several firms carry far more informational-type copy than in the past.

In the area of *product improvements,* companies have introduced many product-safety changes and pollution-reduction measures. Warranties have been simplified and strengthened. Nutritional elements have been added to some foods, and lead removed from some gasolines. *Advertising* is being more carefully scrutinized than ever before. Many advertisers are extremely cautious in approving agency-prepared ads, in sharp contrast to past procedures for approval. Advertisers are involving their legal departments in the approval process. They are very sensitive to the FTC's possible demand for substantiation of claims. The advertising industry, especially through the National Advertising Division (of the Council of Better Business Bureaus) and the National Advertising Review Board, is doing a more effective self-regulation job than ever before.[21] Corporate leaders are working closely with advertising agency executives and the ad-creating people to develop some useful goals and guidelines. Advertisers are urged to "tell it like it is" and to "cool" the type of promotion which leads to exaggerated, and subsequently unrealized, expectations.[22]

Finally, many firms are *putting pressure on offenders or rewarding excellence in compliance.* Allstate Insurance Co. (Sears) offered premium discounts on cars that met certain safety standards. The company also offered discounts on collision insurance on cars that could withstand a 5-mile-per-hour crash into a test barrier without front- or rear-end damage. Some retailers refuse to handle products that are deceptively advertised or priced. Other retailers have rewarded ecologically desirable products with good shelf locations and in-store promotion.

---

[20]See William G. Nickels and Noel B. Zabriskie, "Corporate Responsiveness and the Marketing Correspondence Function," *MSU Business Topics*, Summer, 1973, pp. 53–58.

[21]See "The (Advertising) Industry Gets a Controversial Watchdog," *Business Week*, May 12, 1973, p. 130; and "Madison Avenue's Response to Its Critics," *Business Week*, June 10, 1972, p. 46.

[22]See Rolph E. Anderson and Marvin A. Jolson, "Consumer Expectations and the Communications Gap," *Business Horizons*, April, 1973, pp. 11–16.

Organizing for effective response. Many firms have made organizational changes to implement their response programs. Most of these moves have been to establish an "ombudsman" position—sometimes a high-level executive and sometimes a separate department of consumer affairs. The responsibilities of this department typically are (1) to serve as a listening post for consumer inquiries and complaints, and to see that they are answered, (2) to represent the consumers' interests when policies and programs are being formulated, and (3) to ensure that the firm maintains the necessary degree of societal orientation in its planning.

The ombudsman position or department must be an independent unit, preferably reporting directly to the chief executive. Placing consumer affairs in the marketing department is ordinarily a mistake, because when profit or competitive crises arise, marketing executives too often are short-run oriented and do not place the consumer's interests foremost in their decision making.

A consumer affairs department that cannot act effectively in processing consumers' inquiries and representing consumers' interests in executive councils is probably worse than none at all. If the role of the ombudsman is only cosmetic—if the consumer affairs department is simply a public relations operation, then the company's position further deteriorates. Experience so far shows that consumers' reactions to consumer affairs representatives are mixed. Some programs get high ratings, and others are looked upon simply as "paper consumerism" and "corporate hypocrisy."[23]

Trade-association responses. Many trade associations have moved positively to respond to consumer dissatisfaction. From that position they can play a real leadership role in four basic areas:[24]

1. Coordinating and disseminating research among the association members.
2. Stimulating consumer and dealer education.
3. Developing *(a)* product standards for safety, quality, and performance, and *(b)* standards for advertising and promotion.
4. Establishing a system for processing consumer complaints.

Many of the trade associations have been active in one or more of the above areas. Of course, trade associations also have not been neglecting their time-honored activity as congressional lobbyists. In that role they are viewed by businessmen as seeking moderation in government anti-business legislation, and by consumer advocates as negative defense mechanisms striving to defang needed consumer-oriented legislation.

Limitations to business self-regulation.[25] Self-regulation is an obvious alternative to government regulation, and just as obviously, it is an alternative preferred

---

[23]"More Talk than Action on Consumer Complaints," *Business Week,* May 9, 1973, p. 66. For an in-dept look at the consumer affairs executive, see Milton L. Blum, John B. Stewart, and Edward W. Wheatley, "Consumer Affairs: Viability of the Corporate Response," *Journal of Marketing,* April, 1974, pp. 13–19.

[24]David A. Aaker and George S. Day, "Corporate Responses to Consumerism Pressures," *Harvard Business Review,* November–December, 1972, pp. 120–121.

[25]For a fine analysis of the topic, see Louis L. Stern, "Consumer Protection via Self-Regulation," *Journal of Marketing,* July, 1971 , pp. 47–53.

by businessmen. Generally speaking, unfortunately, the efforts at self-regulation have not been too successful, at least not in the eyes of consumer advocates. Many of the business responses already noted have come only as result of government prodding by law or regulatory agency.

If an industry depends upon the *voluntary* compliance of its members toward meeting industry standards, the results are likely to be ineffective. For self-regulation to have any real chance of success, an industry must be able to *force* its members to comply with the industry standards. The problem is, however, that any enforcement measure strong enough to be effective (a boycott against an offender, for example), is likely to be a restraint-of-trade violation of the Sherman Antitrust Act. One reasonable solution here is some form of industry-government cooperation whereby the industry sets its own standards, and once accepted by the government, the government then enforces these standards.

Two additional situations limit the effectiveness of self-regulation. The first is that often it is difficult to get a consensus among industry members regarding an acceptable set of product or promotion standards. The net result is that the industry settles for the least common denominator as the level for its standards. A second limitation is that executives often fail to see anything wrong in various business practices in their industry—practices which are highly criticized by outside observers. Thus the cause of self-regulation suffers when industry members openly condone questionable practices such as distorting a competitor's test market, deceptively advertising price savings "up to" some amount, unsubstantiated ad claims, deceptive consumer contests, etc.[26]

Effective self-regulation by business can serve as a countervailing force in relation to consumer advocates and governmental action in setting and enforcing industry standards. For business to be effective in this respect, however, means that it must generate a much higher confidence level among the consumers than presently is the case.

Conclusion. It should be quite clear by now that consumerism is here to stay, and the negative business responses of the past are totally inadequate. No longer can business executives argue that a little puffery in advertising, a few bad products, a few crooks in marketing, and a little pollution here and there is really a small price to pay for the marketing system which has generated an affluent society in an economy of abundance.

Instead, business needs to develop strong, positive programs that will serve as a satisfactory response to consumerism.[27] These programs must generate (1) adequate consumer information, (2) safe products whose performance meets advertised expectations, (3) consumer satisfaction, and (4) a socially desirable environment. Striving for these goals may mean that some businesses will suffer *short-run* losses. Hopefully any opposition arising from these loss situations will not deter

---

[26]*Ibid.*, p. 51.

[27]For the contention that to formulate appropriate marketing policies we need a better understanding of the relationship between consumerism and consumer behavior, see Jerome E. Scott and Lawrence M. Lamont, "Consumerism: A Theoretical Framework for Analysis," in B. W. Becker and H. Becker (eds), *1972 Combined Proceedings*, American Marketing Association, Chicago, 1973, pp. 241–248; also see Cravens and Hills, "Consumerism: A Perspective for Business," *op. cit.*

business from *(a)* its *long-run* goals of consumer interests, and *(b)* the emerging societal orientation in its marketing programs.

EMERGING SOCIAL ORIENTATION IN MARKETING

Out of consumerism and our changing consumer goals has emerged a new orientation in the practice and study of marketing—it is a social orientation. (This point was discussed briefly in the opening chapter.) This new approach—social marketing—is both a broadening and a logical extension of the managerial systems approach to marketing.[28]

SOCIAL MARKETING AND MANAGERIAL MARKETING

Social marketing is a broadening, but not a replacement, of managerial marketing. In social marketing we still have to develop a marketing program which will plan, price, promote, and distribute products and services to satisfy consumers' wants. But we also must go further and consider the social consequences of this marketing program. In managerial marketing we are concerned with marketing automobiles to people. In social marketing, in addition, we worry about the societal aspects of auto production and marketing—air pollution and traffic congestion, for example.

In managerial marketing the criteria for evaluating success are sales volume, costs, and profits. In social marketing we consider the social benefits and social costs. By means of a "social audit" we conceptually measure social products and the generating of social wealth. It is when the sales and profit criteria conflict with the social criteria that marketing management has a problem for which we somehow must find acceptable compromise solutions.[29]

CONFLICTS IN CONSUMER GOALS

The broadening of both consumer goals and a company's market targets creates some real problems for marketing management. The consumers' shift

---

[28]For some perspectives and viewpoints on social marketing—its meaning, the forces underlying it, government and business responses to it, and its relation to a managerial marketing mix—see William Lazer and Eugene J. Kelley, *Social Marketing*, Richard D. Irwin, Inc., Homewood, Ill., 1973; and Leonard L. Berry and James S. Hensel (eds.), *Marketing and the Social Environment*, Petrocelli Books, New York, 1973. Also see Laurence P. Feldman, "Social Adaptation: A New Challenge for Marketing," *Journal of Marketing*, July, 1971, pp. 54–60.

[29]For some ideas on developing and applying a set of "social indicators"—i.e., a data base of factors which would measure the social values in a firm's output, see Robert S. Raymond and Elizabeth Richards, "Social Indicators and Business Decisions," *MSU Business Topics*, Autumn, 1971, pp. 42–46; and Polia Lerner Hamburger, *Social Indicators–A Marketing Perspective*, American Marketing Association, Chicago, 1974.

For some suggestions as to what should be included in a social audit and who should do this job, see George A. Steiner, "Should Business Adopt the Social Audit?" *Conference Board Record*, May, 1972, pp. 7–10; and Raymond A. Bauer and Dan H. Fenn, Jr., "What *is* a Corporate Social Audit?" *Harvard Business Review*, January–February, 1973, pp. 37–48.

THE CHANGING PRIORITIES IN MARKETING EDUCATION

"The marketing graduate of 25 years ago learned, basically, to sell soap. The comparable graduate in recent years has learned to sell soap and to understand computer analyses of the soap market. Today's graduate in a growing number of schools completes a curriculum in which he examines both these areas of marketing. He also learns to evaluate the effect of that 'soap,' and the massive resources committed to its commercial success, on issues which lie beyond the traditional income statement."

Source: Betsy D. Gelb and Richard H. Brien, "Survival and Social Responsibility: Themes for Marketing Education and Management," *Journal of Marketing,* April, 1971, p. 3.

---

to societally oriented goals is not proving to be a simple or easy transition, because by no means have we abandoned our desire for things—we have simply tempered this desire with a special concern.

Here is the difference, possibly oversimplified, between the pre-1960s goals and today's goals. Then, we wanted big cars that would go fast. We paid little attention to the air pollution, traffic congestion, depleting oil resources, polluted streams from mills making steel for autos, etc. Now today we still want autos, but we also want clean air, no traffic jams, clean water, and no dependence on foreign oil resources. Certainly the former goal—autos only—was much easier to achieve, because the element of conflict in goals was largely absent.

As a firm broadens its market targets (the publics it deals with), it becomes more difficult to satisfy them all, because often the goals and values of the different publics are in conflict. One group may want a mill closed because it pollutes the air and water. But another of the target markets wants it kept open because it provides jobs.

In trying to understand this problem of goal-conflict, perhaps a key point to keep in mind is that we are dealing with consumers—human beings—with all of their attendant contradictions, inconsistencies, and self-interests. Thus we criticize business for a lack of consumer information, but we often do not use the information when it is provided. We cry out for safer autos, but given the chance, a large percentage of people do not use their seat belts. We want more energy-generating facilities, but don't build an oil refinery or a power plant in my town. We decry the waste in federal spending. As a Colorado resident, my solution to this is to eliminate some government projects in New York, Georgia, California, or anywhere except the Colorado projects—those are necessary and beneficial. We want social benefits (clean air) until we find out the price we must pay (factory closed or auto use restricted). At that point we may have second thoughts on whether the benefit is worth its price.

Truly, there are no easy answers to the goal-conflict problems. And the situation often is further complicated when the groups involved seem to take an overly simplistic perspective. *However, there has been one significant accomplishment by business.* Today many marketing executives recognize that they have some social problems. Formerly they were concerned only with producing and marketing profitable products, and they never considered the social costs. Now these executives are awakening to the concept of social values, and the need for a societal orientation in their marketing programs.

ETHICAL AND SOCIAL RESPONSIBILITIES OF MARKETING MANAGEMENT

A recurring theme in this chapter has been the broadened perspectives in marketing. Continuing in this vein, we now want to focus on the ethical and social responsibilities of marketing executives, looking at both the conceptual and operational aspects of the subject. In so doing we shall repeat, and perhaps better tie together, some points mentioned earlier in the chapter.[30]

THE CONCEPT OF BUSINESS ETHICS

The dictionary defines "ethics" as the science of moral duty or the science of ideal human character. Ethics are moral principles or practices; they are professional standards of conduct. Thus, to act in an ethical fashion is to conform to some standard of moral behavior.

Importance of long-run viewpoint. At times, the pressures to follow an unethical course of action may seem almost irresistible to a marketing manager. If he feels that his personal interests or the success of his company is at stake, he may revert to the law of survival, and ethical considerations will be forgotten. It is easy to be ethical when no hardship is involved.

A key factor for an executive to remember when considering the ethics of a situation is to take a long-run point of view. He should understand that ethical behavior is not only morally right but, over the long run, also realistically sound. Too many administrators are shortsighted; they do not see the possible backlash from many of their activities. If the buyer was deceived or high-pressured, they seem to think this is unimportant, as long as the sale was made. These executives apparently do not realize that by continuing such practices, they can lose customers, invite public regulation, or both.

Problem of determining ethical standards. It is easy to say that a marketing executive should act in an ethical fashion, but it is far more difficult to put this axiom into practice. Each manager as an individual usually has his own standards of conduct, which he believes to be ethical, and he abides by them in the administration of his duties. It is doubtful that many people, marketing executives or otherwise, consciously engage in unethical practices. That is, most of us believe we are acting ethically *by our own standards.* However, ethical standards are set by a group—by society—and not by the individual. Thus the group evaluates the individual's judgment of what he thinks is ethical.

---

[30]For an excellent "state of the art" assessment of social responsibility as it relates to marketing, see Thaddeus H. Spratlen, "Marketing: A Social Responsibility," in B. W. Becker and H. Becker (eds.), *1972 Combined Proceedings,* American Marketing Association, Chicago, 1973, pp. 65–75.

Now, the problem at this point is that the group (society) lacks commonly accepted standards of behavior. What is considered ethical conduct varies from one country to another, from industry to industry, and from one situation to another. The guidelines of personal conscience are also relative and individual, even among people with a common ethical tradition.

WHAT IS SOCIAL RESPONSIBILITY?

A marketing executive has a threefold responsibility—to his company, to his workers, and to his customers. For his company, his job is to provide a satisfactory net profit over the long run. To his employees, his responsibility is to provide a good working enviroment. For his customers, the executive's job is to maximize their standard of living by marketing want-satisfying goods and services at the lowest reasonable cost. In these relationships the marketing executive typically views any ethical considerations on a person-to-person basis.

The substance of social responsibility is much broader, however. It emphasizes an executive's institutional (company) actions and their effect on the entire social system. Without this broader viewpoint, personal and institutional acts tend to be separated. A marketing executive can lead a model personal life, but can continue to justify his company's pollution of a river because there is no direct personal involvement. To him, river pollution is a public problem to be solved by governmental action. The concept of social responsibility, however, requires him to consider his acts within the framework of the whole social system, and it holds him responsible for the effects these acts may have anywhere in that system:

> When a man's primary frame of reference is himself, he may be counted upon for antisocial behavior whenever his values conflict with those of society. If his values are limited primarily to a certain group or organization, he tends to become a partisan acting for that group. But, if he thinks in terms of a whole system, he begins to build societal values into his actions, even when they are for a certain organization. *This is the essence of social responsibility.* For the manager it means realizing that the business system does not exist alone and that a healthy business system cannot exist within a sick society.[31] [Italics Supplied]

Organizational location for social responsibility. To be effective, any program for social responsibility in a firm must start with top management—the chief executive officer and his board of directors. Unless the program has their wholehearted support in spirit and action, it is likely to be a token, lip-service type of effort.[32] However, the accountability for socially responsible actions also must permeate all executive echelons in a firm. Unfortunately, it does not always happen this way. Top management may have a strong commitment to this responsibility, while at the same time the executives at operational levels may be practicing just the opposite. The advertising manager may have approved a price-comparison advertisement which is misleading; a purchasing agent may be pressuring a small supplier in order to get an especially low price; or a sales-

---

[31]Quotation and preceding paragraph from Keith Davis, "Understanding the Social Responsibility Puzzle," *Business Horizons*, Winter, 1967, p. 46.

[32]See Kenneth R. Andrews, "Can the Best Corporations Be Made Moral?" *Harvard Business Review*, May–June, 1973, pp. 57–64.

man may offer a free trip to Europe to a state government official if he will buy an expensive computer system from that salesman.

REASONS FOR CONCERN ABOUT SOCIAL RESPONSIBILITY

The best reason why a marketing executive should have a high degree of social responsibility is simply that it is the morally right thing to do. We grant that this is an easy reason to conceptualize, but far more difficult to put into operation. Now let's look at four points which have a more pragmatic flavor.

Price of economic freedom and flexibility. Marketing executives must conduct their activities in a socially desirable manner in order to justify the privilege of operating in our relatively free economic system. No worthwhile privilege or freedom comes without a price. Our economic freedoms sometimes have a high price, just as our precious political freedoms do. Moreover, it is very much in management's self-interest to be concerned with social problems. A business cannot remain healthy if its social enviroment is sick. Also, a concern for the quality of life may very well lead to change, and this change may present opportunities for new business.

Minimize government intervention. When a marketing executive fails to act in a socially responsible manner, society's penalty typically is to restrict his freedom of operation. Indeed, most of the governmental limitations placed on marketing executives' activities throughout the years have been the result of management's failure to live up to its social responsibilities. Moreover, once some form of governmental control is established, it is rarely removed. So the wise course of action would seem to be to fulfill a social responsibility, thus minimizing additional government intervention.

The power-responsibility equation. Perhaps the concept that social power equals social responsibility helps to explain why business executives have a major responsibility to society. Marketing executives do have a great deal of social power as they influence markets and speak out on matters of economic policy. In business, we see many practical applications of the idea of reasonably balanced power and responsibility. Business executives urge labor leaders to be responsible; a management axiom holds that authority and responsibility should be matched. Now, if responsibility arises from power, then we may reason that the avoidance of social responsibility will lead to an erosion of social power. That is "those who do not take responsibility for their power, ultimately shall lose it."[33]

Marketing department represents company. Procter & Gamble put this point nicely in an annual report: "When a Procter & Gamble salesman walks into a customer's place of business—whether he is calling on an individual store or

---

[33]Keith Davis, *op. cit.*, p. 49, as cited in Keith Davis and Robert L. Blomstrom, *Business and Its Environment*, McGraw-Hill Book Company, New York, 1966, p. 174. Also see Richard H. Brien, Betsy D. Gelb, and William D. Trammell, "The Challenge to Marketing Dominance: Will Social Responsibility Be Recognized?" *Business Horizons,* February, 1972, pp. 23–30.

keeping an appointment at the headquarters of a large group of stores—he not only represents Procter & Gamble, but in a very real sense, he is Procter & Gamble." Therefore, as the public see these men and their activities, so does the public judge the concern.

Ordinarily the public does not meet the production and office workers in a company. Consequently, a firm is rarely judged by the actions of these employee groups. In fact, the marketing department often is blamed for mistakes (such as a defective product or an incorrect bill) made by these other groups simply because the marketing personnel are the only employees who have contact with the public.

BUSINESS IS BEST QUALIFIED TO SOLVE SOCIAL PROBLEMS

In the past, the social responsibility of business executives was generally translated as the way they spent their companies' spare money and their own spare time. Direct dealings with social problems were considered outside the scope of business acitivity. Now there is the demand that the quality of life become the business of business.[34]

We might ask why business should be given this responsibility—why not the government or various local community groups, for example? (Drucker did note parenthetically that business is not the only institution with this responsibility; the same obligation is laid at the door of the government, educational institutions, labor unions, medical institutions, etc.) The chief executive of a large appliance corporation stated that business can and should be the catalyst to begin social reforms because it has the resources to get things done. That is, it can create jobs, it has the managerial skills to develop programs, and it can work at the local level.[35] A business executive with experience in constructing and marketing a low-income housing project in a ghetto said: "Government has been overly oriented toward *control*—not geared to results and achievement. Community leaders are—all too often—interested in personal power and pressing ideological points at the expense of genuine accomplishment."[36]

Within the business system, this same executive believes, marketing people are the logical management group to act as the catalyst for needed change. They are trained in persuasion and communication; they are people-oriented. As generalists, they relate effectively to other fields, and they have proved they can get things done—and on time. Most of all, as one advertising executive observed, a marketer is inherently a radical—a revolutionary—in that his real forte is the management of innovation, that is, the management of change.[37]

---

[34]Peter F. Drucker, "Business and the Quality of Life," *Sales Management,* Mar. 15, 1969, p. 31.

[35]Elisha Gray II, "Changing Values in the Business Society," *Business Horizons,* August, 1968, pp. 21–26.

[36]Leonard Sucsy, as quoted in Roy Alexander, "The Marketer in the Ghetto," *Industrial Marketing,* October, 1969, pp. 57–72; quotation on p. 72. This article also lists a series of practical guidelines for business-social interaction.

[37]Leo Bogart, "The Marketer as a Radical," *Conference Board Record,* October, 1968, pp. 20–25.

Role of profit in social action. We need to consider the profit factor, however, when stating that business is the best-qualified institution to tackle our social problems. It used to be that profit-making alone was sufficient justification for a firm's existence. Certainly profit making was the management's primary goal and the foundation for its strategic planning. Not so any more! Today society demands a broader outlook. However, let's make one point quite clear. Profit is still an absolutely essential element in a company's existence. It no longer is the *only* guide for management, but it still is a necessary one. A company with fine, socially responsible programs, but with no profits, will soon be out of business. In fact, one belief held by some people close to the scene is that business cannot solve our social problems until we figure out some way to make these solutions a profitable venture for business managers.[38]

ACTION PROGRAMS REGARDING SOCIAL PROBLEMS

A marketing executive who wants to work toward solving major social problems will find many useful courses of action open to him, both within his firm and also in his company's dealings with the community.[39] Just a sample of some possible actions within the firm's marketing program are listed below. Many firms, of course, have been active in these areas for some time with varying results.

1. Increase the efficiency of marketing operations, so as to lower distribution costs and selling prices, enabling consumers to maximize their purchasing power.
2. Properly interpret and anticipate consumer demand, whether it is an active or latent demand, thus better supplying want-satisfying goods and services.
3. Refuse to do business with unethical suppliers or customers.
4. Increase control over operating personnel—particularly salesmen and advertising people—to ensure higher social standards of operation.
5. Cooperate with trade associations, Better Business Bureaus, and other business groups interested in raising business standards.
6. Earlier we spoke of programs to *(a)* increase product safety, *(b)* minimize defective products, *(c)* repair those that need it, *(d)* improve warranties, and *(e)* develop more informative packaging and labeling.

In the community, marketing can play an active role in: hiring and training disadvantaged people; contributing to education and the arts; urban renewal; improving the physical environment; removing discrimination against women, old people, and minority groups; the marketing problems of low-income consumers. In a moment we shall discuss briefly some practical examples of marketing's involvement in two of these problem areas.

But first a reminder to marketing executives regarding the importance of communicating their social-action programs and accomplishments to the public. With all the criticism being heaped on business today, it is not enough just to *do* some

---

[38]David B. McCall, "Profit: Spur for Solving Social Ills," *Harvard Business Review*, May–June, 1973, pp. 46–48 ff.

[39]For a report on the activities of major U.S. corporations in the area of social responsibility, see Henry Eilbert and I. Robert Parket, "The Current Status of Corporate Social Responsibility," *Business Horizons*, August, 1973, pp. 5–14.

good in the social arena. Business executives must start to *tell* people about it instead of hiding their light under a bushel. In the past, many presidents and other executives went out of their way to maintain a low profile. Now they are urged to be more visible in their community and in the public media. Let the public know what you are doing to improve the quality of life as well as the standard of living.[40]

Marketing problems of low-income consumers. Most of the public discussion, research, proposed corrective programs, and actual business response regarding low-income consumers has been related to black ghetto markets. (Here we define a *ghetto* as an urban geographic area, most of whose inhabitants have extremely low incomes and usually, but not always, are members of one racial or ethnic group. But let's not overlook the fact that a sizable portion of the low-income market in the U.S. includes other segments—the elderly poor, the rural poor, American Indians (also typically a rural market), and Spanish-speaking consumers (Americans of Mexican, Puerto Rican, or Cuban heritage)—both in urban and rural locations. In a 1970 special Presidential message to Congress, for example, the American Indians were identified as the most deprived and isolated minority group in our nation. Their per capita income was one-third of the national average, and their unemployment rate (40 percent) was 8 to 10 times the national average. About 80 percent of the reservation Indians had incomes below the government-defined poverty level.

Certainly the efforts of many companies to hire and train disadvantaged people is a major thrust in the fight against poverty, and these efforts must be continued. Yet the benefits can be largely nullified when these people enter the retail marketplace. There they often encounter higher prices, inferior-quality merchandise, unethical and illegal retailing practices, and a degrading shopping environment. It is little wonder—and surely more than a random happening—that retail stores were the target of most of the damage and looting which occurred in the urban riots of the 1960s. Even the retailers who do try to serve the customers and treat them fairly are faced with abnormally high operating costs, excessive losses from pilferage, and frequently bitter resentment from the community.[41]

A particularly incendiary issue is whether the inner-city residents—primarily black and primarily poor—pay higher prices than more affluent white suburbanites. After countless studies and reports on this question, the answers still are mixed. When fewer store services, higher credit costs, and poorer product quality are included in the "bundle of utilites" being purchased with the product, then the low-income consumers typically do pay more. In these markets, chain-store units are scarce. The predominant retailing institution is the small-scale, independent

---

[40]Some executives have resorted to taking lessons on how to handle themselves on television or in interviews with the press. See "Adjusting to a More Visible Role," *Business Week*, May 4, 1974, p. 49.

[41]See Frederick P. Sturdivant, "Better Deal for Ghetto Shoppers," *Harvard Business Review*, March–April, 1968, pp. 130–139.

[42]For a review of price-comparison studies and the retailing system in low-income markets, see Stephen W. Brown and Lee Richardson, *The Unique Problems of Low-Income Consumers*, College of Business Administration, Louisiana State University, Baton Rouge, Occasional paper no. 15, 1973; and Leonard L. Berry, "The Low-Income Marketing System: An Overview," *Journal of Retailing*, Summer, 1972, pp. 44–63 ff.

merchant who typically lacks the managerial ability and financial capital to serve his market effectively.[42] Business has a vested interest in the retailing problems in low-income markets, because the most direct and impressionable contacts between the poor and the business community occur at the retail level. This, in turn, means that the retail marketers serving poverty areas have the greatest opportunity (and perhaps responsibility) for improving the daily economic lives of the ghetto residents. Businessmen must understand that "To ignore . . . the market system serving low-income neighborhoods is to ignore a problem that daily affects the well-being of the poor and, rather directly, the well-being of society."[43]

Fortunately, there is evidence of increasing action by business to solve some of the marketing problems in low-income areas. Several of the nation's largest retail chains have quietly, but increasingly, started consciously to do something about these problems. These companies are making changes, where and if necessary, in product lines, labor force, consumer credit, etc., to adjust effectively to the low-income market. Manufacturers are also active in such ways as helping minority-race businessmen to establish dealerships and to become soundly financed and well managed. Starts have also been made toward providing management-consulting services to businessmen located in ghetto markets.[44] Moves to broaden the base of "black capitalism" have run into some problems, however, and some of the initial ventures did not meet expectations.[45] But the concept of expanded black management and ownership is still a sound one, and a goal to be pursued.

There still is a long, long way to go, of course. Some large retailers are phasing out ghetto locations. Others are only adjusting existing stores, but are not yet opening new ones in the ghetto. Perhaps the most encouraging sign is that something is being done, and that is better than nothing. Whether this "something" is enough and on time, or too little and too late, remains to be seen. In any case, one can hope that the action will speed up. One significant factor keeping apparent progress moving at a modest pace is a lack of enough solid information on the market behavior of the ghetto consumer—his wants, attitudes, shopping habits, preferences, etc.[46]

For a survey of 15 price-comparison studies on food, see Donald E. Sexton, Jr., "Comparing the Cost of Food to Blacks and to Whites—A Survey," *Journal of Marketing*, July, 1971, pp. 40–46; also see A. Coskun Samli and Larry J. French, "De Facto Price Discrimination in the Food Purchases of the Rural Poor," *Journal of Retailing*, Fall, 1971, pp. 48–60.

[43]Frederick P. Sturdivant (ed.), *The Ghetto Marketplace,* The Free Press, New York 1969, p. 3. This well-selected assortment of timely readings discusses (1) the characteristics of low-income consumers, (2) the practices and problems of ghetto merchants, (3) price and quality differentials between ghetto and nonghetto stores, (4) the conflict between consumers and merchants, (5) the special case of the Jewish merchant in black communities, and (6) possible solutions to the consumers' plight and the retailers' problems.

[44]See Fred C. Allvine, "Black Business Development," *Journal of Marketing*, April, 1970, pp. 1–7.

[45]See Thaddeus H. Spratlen, "A Black Perspective on 'Black Business Development,'" *Journal of Marketing*, October, 1970, pp. 72–73; and Frederick D. Sturdivant, "The Limits of Black Capitalism," *Harvard Business Review*, January–February, 1969, pp. 122–128.

[46]For two excellent bibliographies of research already done on the subject, see Sturdivant, *The Ghetto Marketplace*, pp. 291–305; and Robert J. Holloway and Frederick D. Sturdivant (eds.), *Bibliography on Marketing to Low-income Consumers,* U.S. Department of Commerce, 1969.

Marketing and environmental pollution. One of the major social problems facing us today is the pollution of our physical environment. Our ecology—i.e., the relationship of people to their environment—is being disturbed, and in some cases seriously, by air, water, or noise pollution.

Who are the polluters? Marketing has contributed to the pollution problem. By stimulating a demand for products and by satisfying consumers' wants, marketing has helped to build mountains of solid wastes. Making and using these products pollutes our air and water. Promotional efforts in marketing have generated a "throwaway" society and have contributed to a "no-deposit, no-return" behavioral pattern.

However, we must understand this about our ecological problems—they are far more complex than many people realize. Marketing alone did not cause pollution. Production and engineering technology are responsible for air and water pollution from steel mills, chemical plants, paper mills, oil refineries, and utility power plants. Cattle feed lots and various mining operations contribute their share of wastes. Various government agencies have inadequate control over their own pollution-producing operations—and the critics of business want the government to control pollution. Selfish consumer behavior adds to the problem. We want clean air but we won't pay to tune up our auto engines. As a group, we demand highway beautification, but as individuals we toss stuff out of the car window and often leave some picnic grounds a shambles. We abandon old cars on city streets.

We are dealing with a complex assortment of technological, political, economic, and even cultural and psychological factors. Furthermore, contrary to the belief held by many critics, pollution is *not* the exclusive province of a capitalistic economy and big business. Pollution is a by-product of an industrialized urban society whether it is capitalistic, socialistic, or communistic.

The factor of goal conflict is certainly involved in ecological issues. We want to drive cars, and we also want clean air and no traffic jams. One reason we have an energy shortage is because our desire for a clean environment leads us to oppose the building of more energy-generating facilities in our city. We don't want mosquitoes, but we also do not want the DDT residue (from insecticides) laced through our soil and water. Now if only someone would invent a *silent* snowmobile.

Marketing's contributions to pollution reduction. Because of the complexities in ecological problems, effective solutions will require cooperation from producers, marketers, and consumers, with the government serving as a coordinating and enforcement agency. The costs of pollution reduction and control are enormously high. Prices will have to be increased to pay for these efforts. To ensure that all companies comply, government regulation will be necessary.

For a sample of subsequent studies see Gerald E. Hills, Donald H. Granbois, and James M. Patterson, "Black Consumer Perceptions of Food Store Attributes," *Journal of Marketing,* April, 1973, pp. 47–57; Carl E. Block, "Prepurchase Search Behavior of Low-Income Households," *Journal of Retailing,* Spring, 1972, pp. 3–15; John V. Petrof, "Attitudes of the Urban Poor Toward Their Neighborhood Supermarkets," *Journal of Retailing,* Spring, 1971, pp. 3–17ff; and Leonard L. Berry and Paul J. Solomon, "Generalizing about Low-Income Food Shoppers: A Word of Caution," *Journal of Retailing,* Summer, 1971, pp. 41–51 ff.

Otherwise, some firms will clean up their operation and have to raise prices, while others who do nothing will have an unfair competitive advantage.

Just as marketing alone did not cause pollution, so too marketing alone cannot cure it. But marketing can, should, and is contributing to the "solution of pollution." To do so is simply part of our social responsibility. We also can attract purely profit-oriented people to our cause, because there are many profitable business opportunities in pollution abatement. Pollution reduction is *not* limited to shut-down-the mill, don't-drive-your-car, and return-that-bottle type of negative alternatives. Some illustrations of positive efforts by marketers revolve around product planning, channels of distribution, and promotion.

The major polluting industries and many of the lesser culprits provide golden market opportunities for new pollution-control products. Marketing is also challenged to develop products which will *not* contribute to solid waste matter. The disposal of solid wastes is a monumental problem, and one way to cope with it is not to accumulate so much waste in the first place. Thus, biodegradable or recyclable products, and returnable or reusable containers, are desirable. In fact, it may be necessary at the national level to follow the lead of Oregon, which banned the sale of drinks in nonreturnable containers. A little innovative thinking also helps. As we run out of land for garbage dumps, some cities are generating electricity by using solid wastes for fuel.[47]

Recycling—the reprocessing of waste products—is another area where marketing is reducing solid-waste pollution. The key to success in recycling is to develop an effective channel-of-distribution system which will move the waste products from consumer back to a producer who can use them as raw materials in manufacturing new products. Marketing's challenge is to find the incentive needed to stimulate the consumer to start this reverse channel movement.[48]

Marketers can use their skills in promotion and persuasion to urge consumers to conserve our natural resources by using them in a more efficient, less wasteful manner. Promotion also can be the tool to impress upon consumers the seriousness of our pollution and waste-disposal problems.

QUESTIONS AND PROBLEMS

1. Do you think that self-regulation by business will prevent, or correct, the abuses that led to consumer discontent?
2. In what ways is the consumerism phenomenon of the 1970s different from the consumer movement of the 1930s?
3. Bring to class two advertisements which contain no product information and two which contain inadequate information.
4. What information do you think should be included in advertisements for each of the following products or services?

   a. Lipstick   *d.* Breakfast cereals
   b. Auto tires   *e.* Public accounting firm
   c. Typewriters   *f.* Personal loan (finance) company

---

[47]See "U.S. Finds a Rich Resource: The Nation's Trash Pile," *U.S. News & World Report*, May 13, 1974, p. 63.

[48]See William G. Zikmund and William J. Stanton, "Recycling Solid Wastes: A Channels-of-Distribution Problem," *Journal of Marketing*, July, 1971, pp. 34–39.

5. What suggestions do you have for an applicance manufacturer who wants to improve the servicing of his products? An automobile manufacturer?

6. What is the annual rate of interest charged by department stores and mail-order firms on their revolving credit accounts?

7. What suggestions do you have for a wife who wishes to minimize the cost of the following, and yet at the same time get want satisfaction in her purchases?

   a. Food for the family
   b. Clothes for herself
   c. Furniture for the house

8. Should the federal government establish a "Department of the Consumer" to aid and protect the consumer?

9. What is the social and economic justification for the "paternalistic" types of laws—like the auto-seat-belt regulations—which require us to do something because the government says it is in our best interests?

10. What proposals do you have for resolving some of the consumer goal-conflict situations discussed in this chapter?

11. Discuss the relationship between illegal and unethical marketing practices. For instance, are illegal acts always unethical? Are unethical marketing activities always illegal? Give examples in each case.

12. Some salesmen in your company have increased their profitable sales volume considerably by employing slightly unethical practices. If you, as the sales manager, sanction these practices, you will meet your responsibility to your company and its stockholders. But you will be failing to meet your social responsibilities. What would you do in this case? Is management's social responsibility incompatible with its responsibility to its stockholders?

13. You are vice president of marketing in a company heavily involved in outdoor advertising. Your company owns billboards and handles the outdoor advertising for many manufacturers. Currently in your state legislature there is a bill pending which would eliminate all outdoor advertising on all state and federal highways in your state. Several key members of the committee considering the bill have received major campaign contributions from your company over the years. Should you tell them that your firm will cut off further financial support if they approve the bill? Assume they do approve the bill; then what position should your company take at the next election when these legislators seek your campaign contributions?

14. Why is it marketing's responsibility to reduce air, water, and noise pollution?

MARKETING: APPRAISAL AND PROSPECT

In this concluding chapter we shall develop in summary form a marriage of three topics—an appraisal of (1) marketing in the American economy, (2) the government's role in marketing, and (3) the outlook for the future of marketing.

Our frame of reference is the present-day economic system of the United States: a free enterprise but *imperfect* economic system. Price is the prime determinant of resource allocation. We call our system imperfect, however, because the market is not composed of elements basic to the theoretical model of perfect competition —elements such as great numbers of well-informed buyers and sellers, always acting rationally, each so small that his individual activity has no appreciable influence on total supply, demand, or price. Another imperfection is the structural rigidity of our system. There is probably greater freedom of exit and entry in the retailing part of our market structure than in any other segment, but even here some rigidities exist. Also, in the interests of the general welfare, the various levels of government often act so as to affect the free play of market forces.

Another point to keep in mind is that the American economic system contains many freedoms, but for every freedom—whether it is political, economic, religious, or social—we pay a price. For example, one economic privilege we have is freedom of choice; we are offered a wide variety of products and often a considerable number of brands of each product. The price we pay for this freedom is the burden of making up our minds—of making a marketing decision about which products and brands we will buy with our limited resources.

EVALUATION OF MARKETING SYSTEM

Anything so important and all-pervasive as marketing is bound to draw a share of censure. In some cases, criticism is leveled at marketing in the individual firms, while in other situations the target is the role of marketing in the economy. We can summarize the major charges at this point, but it will not be possible within the scope of this book to discuss them in detail.

In order to appraise our marketing system, we need some yardsticks for measurement. First, what is the objective of the system? Throughout this book we have stressed the philosophy of the marketing concept. The goal of the marketing concept is to develop a customer orientation on the part of management. In line with this philosophy, it seems reasonable to establish as a goal the satisfaction of consumers' wants, as they are expressed by the consumers themselves. Then marketing should be appraised on the basis of how well it achieves this goal, that is, how effectively it satisfies consumers' wants. We grant that this goal is a questionable one in the minds of many people. Some feel that the consumer does not know what is good for him—that some group (usually the government) should take over the responsibility for setting standards. Others believe that the social and economic goals should be to build a country's military strength, to promote the growth of its underdeveloped segments, or to perpetuate the great wealth and high social position of a favored few. Regardless of these other possible goals, however noteworthy some people think they are, *we shall evaluate marketing in light of its ability to satisfy consumers' wants, as the consumers themselves define or express these wants.*

Next we must try to establish objective, quantitative yardsticks for measuring the extent to which marketing has achieved this goal. In an *individual company* the effectiveness of marketing can be measured generally by the company's financial status. This is measured on the bases of operating costs, net profits, operating ratios, comparisons with similar firms, and so on. Tools have been developed to measure the profitability of various products, territories, channels, salesmen, and advertising media within a given firm.

A different situation prevails when we attempt to measure quantitatively marketing's contribution to consumer want satisfaction in *our economy.* Input-output analysis may be employed, although it is difficult to assign objective values to the various factors in input and output unless we use the market value of these factors. For instance, in the marketing system we can measure quantitatively the value of such inputs as newspaper space used in advertising, time and program costs for television advertising, freight carloadings, marketing research costs in developing the brand and package, salesmen's compensation and expenses, and others. The output factors may be summarized as consumer want satisfaction. But of course, so far no one has been able satisfactorily to impute objective values to this output. Market price indicates what consumers are willing to pay, but it does not accurately measure satisfaction received. Consequently, much of our evaluation of marketing's contribution to consumer want satisfaction in our economy must be done on a subjective basis.[1]

---

[1]For a conceptual measurement of costs and benefits to producers, consumers, and society in marketing transactions, see Richard E. Homans and Ben M. Enis, "A Guide for Appraising Marketing Activities," *Business Horizons,* October, 1973, pp. 20–30.

For a conceptual framework to assess the contribution of the distribution system to our

CRITICISMS OF MARKETING

Critics of our marketing system have raised many thought-provoking questions and generated many lively discussions. In order to summarize the major charges of the critics, we shall group them according to their relationships to the four components of the marketing mix—the product, the distribution structure, the price system, and promotional activities. Some of these complaints are a repeat of those noted in the discussion of consumerism in the preceding chapter.

With respect to the *product,* critics allege that many products are of poor quality; for the price the seller charges, the products and services should be better. Furthermore, heavily promoted product improvements are often trivial. Planned style obsolescence encourages consumers to get rid of products before they are physically worn out. Besides, there are too many different types of goods and too many different brands of each type. As a result, the buyer is confused; he is unable to make accurate buying decisions.

Probably the main objection to the *distribution structure* is that it is unnecessarily complex and includes too many middlemen. This is a two-part charge: there are too many different types of middlemen and too many of each type. Regarding the *price system,* we hear that prices are too high or too inflexible or that they are controlled by the large firms in an industry. Some people feel that price competition has been largely replaced by nonprice competition.

The strongest and most bitter indictments leveled against marketing are in the area of *promotional activities*—especially in personal selling and advertising. Most of the complaints about personal selling are at the retail level, where we find both consumers and businessmen disenchanted with the poor quality of retail salesmanship. Objections are also voiced against the poor services offered by many retailers, even by stores whose high prices would seem to reflect a service-oriented policy.

The general criticisms against advertising may be divided into two groups—social and economic. From a *social* point of view, advertising is charged with overemphasizing our material standard of living and underemphasizing our cultural, spiritual, ethical, and moral values. Advertising also is charged with manipulating people—making them want to buy things they should not have, cannot afford, and do not need. Advertising, in effect, is being charged with being a major tool in the business system's management of consumer demand.[2]

A major social criticism of advertising today, and one that has some justification and should be considered by marketing men throughout our economy, is that advertising is often false, misleading, deceptive, or in bad taste. Exaggerations, conflicting claims, overuse of sex and fear appeals, jarring commercials, inane claims, excessive numbers of commercials on radio and television, and poor choice of the placement of commercials are some examples of this

---

economic and social welfare, see Louis P. Bucklin, "Marketing Channels and Structures: A Macro View ," in B. W. Becker and H. Becker (eds.), *1972 Combined Proceedings,* American Marketing Association, Chicago, 1973, pp. 28–40. This article also contains an extensive bibliography on the subject.

[2]See Stephen A. Greyser, "Advertising: Attacks and Counters," *Harvard Business Review,* March–April, 1972, pp. 22 ff., for an adapted version of Greyser's testimony to the FTC concerning the social issues and social impact of advertising. Also see John A. Howard and Spencer F. Tinkham, "A Framework for Understanding Social Criticism of Advertising," *Journal of Marketing,* October, 1971, pp. 2–7.

general point of censure.[3] As with most criticisms in marketing, this one applies to a small segment of advertising. The main offenders are advertisers of a limited number of consumer goods, and the advertising medium causing most of the furor is television. The charge of false, misleading, and offensive advertising is rarely made against advertisers of industrial products or companies which advertise consumer products in trade journals. Most of our retail department store display advertising is not subject to this charge, nor is most of the newspaper classified advertising.

Advertising is charged with causing a misallocation of our resources. This criticism is related to the assertion by John K. Galbraith and others that advertising has contributed significantly to an imbalance of expenditures between the private and public sectors of our economy. For instance, these people believe that American business promotes frills on automobiles when it should be concerned with clearing slums, improving our schools, and eliminating air and water pollution. Furthermore, these critics believe that more of our national output should be diverted from the private to the public sector.[4]

The *economic* criticisms of advertising have taken an interesting turn in recent years. We still hear that advertising costs too much—that it increases the cost of marketing and therefore raises the prices of products. In the past, much criticism was devoted to the competitive nature of advertising and the attendant economic waste which is claimed to result from generating imaginary brand differentials. Recently, however, the economic charge drawing the most interest is somewhat the opposite—namely, that advertising leads to restraint of competition, economic concentration, and monopoly. While certainly not a new criticism, this point received revived attention when it was espoused by Prof. Donald F. Turner in his role as head of the Antitrust Division of the Department of Justice.[5]

The line of reasoning in the economic-concentration complaint goes something like this.[6] (1) The big companies can afford to spend the most on advertising to differentiate their products, and thus they are able to acquire a large share of the market; (2) in this way advertising creates a barrier to market entry by new or smaller firms; (3) a high level of market concentration then results; (4) the firms enjoying this protected position can charge high (monopoly) prices, which in turn lead to high (monopoly) profits.

The refutation of the economic-concentration charges was carefully spelled out by Prof. Jules Backman in a study he conducted under the sponsorship of the Association of National Advertisers.[7] This report was based on Backman's empiri-

---

[3]For suggestions of five types of research to help reduce irritation in advertising, see Stephen A. Greyser, "Irritation in Advertising," *Journal of Advertising Research,* February, 1973, pp. 3–10; also see S. A. Greyser and Bonnie B. Reece, "Businessmen Look Hard at Advertising, *Harvard Business Review,* May–June, 1971, pp. 18ff.

[4]See John K. Galbraith, *The Affluent Society,* Houghton Mifflin Company, Boston, 1958; for a different point of view, see, for example, John W. Lowe, "An Economist Defends Advertising," *Journal of Marketing,* July, 1963, pp. 16-19; and V. E. Boyd, *Advertising and Public Service: Not-so-strange Bedfellows,* American Association of Advertising Agencies, Nov. 19, 1964.

[5]Particularly in a speech to the Federal Bar Association in Washington, D.C., in June, 1966.

[6]Alex Groner, *Advertising: The Case for Competition,* Association of National Advertisers, Inc., New York, 1967, pp. 5-6.

[7]Jules Backman, *Advertising and Competition,* New York University Press, 1967. See also Jean C. Halterman, "Can Advertising Build a Monopoly? Some Current Opinions," *Business*

cal studies plus those of other researchers. He concluded that there is no relationship between advertising intensity and high economic concentration. Nor does there seem to be any link between advertising intensity and (1) price increases or (2) high profit rates. Advertising is highly competitive, Backman states, not anticompetitive.

Undoubtedly the economic arguments will continue as long as respected professional researchers differ in their conclusions. Whatever approach may be used in the future as we research the still unanswered questions, we can hope that it will (1) cease to evaluate advertising against the unrealistic backdrop of perfect competition and (2) consider advertising in terms of operational alternatives.

IMPORTANCE OF UNDERSTANDING TRUE NATURE OF CRITICISMS

When evaluating charges against marketing, we should be careful to recognize the differences in the nature of the various points. We should understand what fundamentally is being criticized. In a company, is it the marketing department or some other department which is the cause of the complaints? In the economy, is it the marketing system or the general economic system which is being criticized? It is also helpful to sort out the points wherein the critics (1) are misinformed, (2) are unaware of the services performed by the marketing system, or (3) are trying to impose their own objective value judgments on consumers. That is, the critics do not agree that the goal of the marketing system should be consumer want satisfaction as the consumers *themselves* define and express their wants.

In some cases the criticisms of marketing are fully warranted; they point out weaknesses and inefficiencies in the system and call for improvement. By most people's standards, there are instances of deceptive packaging and of misleading and objectionable advertising. There are weaknesses in marketing, just as there are in any system developed and operated by human beings. The real key to the evaluation of our marketing system lies in the answers to two fundamental questions. First, is the present system of marketing achieving its goal (that is, satisfying consumers' wants as the consumers themselves express these wants) better than any other known alternative could? The answer is an unqualified "yes." Second, is constant effort being devoted to improving the system and increasing its productivity and efficiency? Generally speaking, the answer to this question is also a strong "yes."

Progress sometimes may seem slow. Companies that operate in a socially undesirable manner even over a short-run period of time are harmful. Price-fixing and objectionable advertising are intolerable and inexcusable. Instances of this nature, though widely publicized, are in a small minority, however, when the total picture of marketing is viewed. In essence, we are saying that weaknesses exist in marketing and that a continuing effort must be devoted to their elimination. However, at the same time, we should not overlook the improvements in marketing and consumer want satisfaction over the years. The way to correct existing weaknesses is not to destroy or seriously regulate the existing system.

Horizons, April, 1968, pp. 87-95; and L. G. Telser, "Some Aspects of the Economics of Advertising," *Journal of Business,* April, 1968, pp. 166-173.

DOES MARKETING COST TOO MUCH?

Many of the censures of marketing may be summarized in the general criticism that marketing costs too much. It is estimated that the total cost of marketing for all products is about 50 percent of the final price paid by ultimate consumers. Admittedly, total marketing costs are a substantial proportion of total sales value of all products. However, the question of whether marketing costs too much is in many respects somewhat academic because we do not have sufficient information to make comparisons. We do not know how the costs of marketing compare with the costs of manufacturing, mining, and other activities which create form utility. Even if we had accurate data on marketing costs, we would still have no objective criteria for determining whether these expenses are too high or not high enough. As we said in Chapter 28, we have not yet developed adequate tools for measuring the return (output) that is derived from a given marketing expenditure (input). To say that marketing costs are too high implies that one or more of the following situations prevail: marketing institutions are enjoying abnormally high profits; more services are being provided than consumers and businessmen demand; marketing activities are performed in a grossly inefficient manner; consumption is declining; and total costs (production plus marketing) are increasing. Actually, there is no reasonable evidence that any of these conditions exist.

It is granted that total marketing costs have risen substantially both absolutely and relatively over the past 100 years. At the same time, careful studies indicate that these costs have been leveling off for the past three or four decades. Still, it is important that we understand the reasons for this increase in marketing expenses. Certainly it would be a mistake simply to jump to the conclusion that the cost increase indicates growing inefficiencies in marketing. Actually, the rise in marketing expense is traceable to several factors, some of which are external environmental influences. As an example, one reason for the increase in the number of people employed in marketing relative to the number employed in production is simply that the workweek in marketing has been shortened relative to that in production. In the latter part of the nineteenth century, people employed in wholesaling and retailing worked about 66 hours a week; those employed in production worked about 52. Today, both groups work about 40, and this shift toward equality has meant that relatively more employees were added in marketing.

Another reason why the number of workers and costs in marketing have increased is that consumers are demanding more services and more marketing refinements today than in the past. Consumers today demand credit, delivery, free parking, attractive stores, merchandise return privileges, and other services. A related point is the rise in consumer demand for products emphasizing style, and for merchandise assortments covering considerable breadth and depth. Certainly we could cut marketing costs and problems substantially if consumers would buy on a cash-and-carry, no-returns-permitted basis in stores displaying small quantities of standardized merchandise on pipe racks or in wooden boxes.

Sometimes the seeming increase in distribution costs is really the result of a more careful classification of business expenses. If a small businessman or farmer produces his goods and sells them himself, all his operating expenses are classed as production expenses (creation of form utility) because he is classified as a producer. Once this businessman or farmer employs the advantages of specialization of labor, however, or once his markets expand, he will probably use independent middlemen to help in the marketing process. Immediately the costs are separated into production and marketing classifications. Marketing expenses seem to have increased substantially, even though there may have been no real change in the total cost picture. In a large company which adopts the marketing concept, many expenses (such as new-product development, inventory control, transportation, and warehousing) which formerly were classified as production costs will now be shown as marketing expenses simply because the expense-generating activity is now the organizational responsibility of the marketing manager.

It is a mistake to study the trend in marketing costs alone. A total cost approach should be adopted. In many instances, a firm can reduce its total costs by increasing its marketing costs. To illustrate, an increase in advertising and personal selling expenditures may so expand a firm's market that the unit production cost can be reduced more than the marketing costs have increased. Thus the net effect is to reduce the total expenses. In another situation, production economies can result when a company locates near sources of raw materials or low-cost power; yet marketing costs (transportation) may be increased in the new location.

One approach to a better understanding of the role of marketing in the economy is to apply the concept of "value added by marketing" as a counterpart of the already-accepted concept of "value added by manufacturing." "Value added by marketing" is a much more accurate term than "cost of marketing" to describe the output or utilities created by marketing.[8]

It is understandable that productivity in marketing may never match the level attained in manufacturing or agriculture. Marketing offers far fewer opportunities for mechanization. It is one thing to control the input and output value of machines, but it is quite another problem when the activity largely involves dealing with people. To the extent that the marketing system is not perfect and that marketing costs have not reached a theoretical minimum, we may say that marketing does cost too much. Until we can define this perfect system objectively, however, and until a better system for satisfying consumer wants is proposed, we shall continue with the existing system. Its benefits in both the private and public sectors of our economy are bounteous by almost any measure used. American business must continue to improve the efficiency of marketing, to measure accurately its cost, and most important of all to explain to the American public the essential role marketing plays in our economy.

GOVERNMENT'S ROLE IN MARKETING

In many situations the government probably rates second to the consumer in importance as an external environmental influence on marketing. Anything that is so much a part of our economic system as marketing is bound to be influenced directly by governmental action. Throughout this book, major legislation and other

---

[8]Prof. Theodore N. Beckman, of Ohio State University, developed the "value-added" concept in marketing. See his "The Value Added Concept as Applied to Marketing and Its Implications," in Stewart H. Rewoldt (ed.) *Frontiers in Marketing Thought,* Indiana University, Bureau of Business Research, Bloomington, 1955, pp. 83-99; or his "Value Added by Distribution," *Twenty-eighth Boston Conference on Distribution,* Boston Chamber of Commerce, Boston, 1956, pp. 43-47.

governmental actions were discussed when pertinent to particular areas of market-ing. At this point we shall make a few summary observations regarding the role our government plays in marketing.

At all times a marketing executive must be aware of the impact which his internal decisions have on the external environment of his firm. Particularly should he consider the political or governmental appraisal of his internal policy making. In most companies, the marketing department, more than any other, feels the inter-vention of the government—federal, state, or local. This in no way suggests that regulation of nonmarketing activities is unimportant.

Governmental intervention takes two forms. First, the government offers aid on a voluntary basis to businesses in an effort to foster competition and to increase business efficiency. Countless examples of such aid could be cited. Federal agen-cies such as the U.S. Department of Commerce and the U.S. Department of Agriculture publish many different sorts of information of considerable value to marketing men. The Small Business Administration has published many marketing aids for small businesses. At the state level, many states offer programs in distribu-tive education (retailing) with federal support through the George-Dean Act.

The second form of governmental intervention involves regulation and control. A study of our business history shows rather clearly that governmental regulations come about because (1) private industry is either unable or unwilling to accept its responsibility for acting in the public interest or (2) special-interest groups foster the legislation.

As examples of governmental action resulting from the inability or refusal of private business to accept its responsibilities, we have the various antitrust laws, laws prohibiting unfair competition, and the legal restrictions on advertising. In the late nineteenth century, society felt that monopolistic practices were contrary to the public interest, so the Sherman Antitrust Act was passed. Later, when private industry did not accept its responsibilities in matters of labeling and selling food and drugs—when it sold adulterated products and used deceptive labels—Congress passed the Pure Food and Drug Act (1906). In years following, short-sighted businessmen found ways to circumvent this law, and it was strengthened by further restrictive amendments in 1938.

In some areas, government engages in business itself, directly competing with private enterprise. Often the original reason for such government activity was that private enterprise could not or would not meet consumer demand. This reason lies behind the government's development of water resources and its activity in financ-ing home mortgages.

In some cases, a private business group seeks government intervention to support the group's self-interest. We see the results of this form of activity in such legislation as the state fair-trade laws, unfair-practices acts, laws restricting in-terstate trade, chain-store taxes, and municipal Green River ordinances regu-lating door-to-door selling. The stated purpose of these laws is to protect com-petition. In effect, however, they protect *competitors* rather than *competition,* and there is a substantial difference between the two. Some of these legal mea-sures actually penalize the low-cost, low-selling-price, generally efficient oper-ations of chain stores and large-scale independents, while at the same time protecting the high-cost, inefficient retailers. In such cases these laws tend to injure competition.

Often a marketing executive who seeks legislation favoring his own special interest will profess to be an advocate of free competition, when in actual fact he is attempting to combat strong, but entirely fair, competition. Sometimes it seems that a marketing man's only criterion of fair competition is whether it allows him to beat a competitor. Unfair competition is, of course, any situation in which he loses. Marketing management must realize that it is not possible to regulate one segment of the economy and let other parts go unrestrained. Regulation usually begets more regulation.

From the consumers' point of view, marketing legislation in the past has had two weaknesses. One is that in general it has been business-oriented rather than consumer-oriented. (There were some exceptions, of course, such as the Pure Food, Drug, and Cosmetic Act, the various labeling laws, and some provisions of the Wheeler-Lea Amendment to the FTC Act.) The other weakness was the absence of federal "watchdogs." That is, under most laws a suit must be brought by an injured party, and not by an agency of the government. A corollary to that weakness is the absence of speedy, inexpensive means for the redress of consumer grievances.

Since the 1960s a dramatic shift has occurred relative to the first of those two weaknesses—namely, there has been a significant amount of consumer-oriented legislation. Regarding the second problem, the situation today is moderately improved. Some of the regulatory agencies—the FDA, the FTC, and the CPSC, for example—are quite active in protecting consumers' interests. The problem of slow, expensive redress of grievances, however, still has not been noticeably improved.

BROADENING THE MARKETING CONCEPT

In the preceding chapter we developed the theme that changing cultural values led to consumerism, and subsequently to a societal orientation in the field of marketing. This emerging orientation, in turn, highlighted the ethical and social responsibilities of marketing executives. This sequence inevitably leads us to review the marketing concept which we have espoused throughout this book. We must analyze it critically to determine: (1) Is it an outmoded concept? or (2) Is it still viable? That is, is it workable in today's socioeconomic system—is it compatible with a socially oriented marketing perspective?[9]

In Chapter 1 we explained that the marketing concept is a three-part philosophy—namely, that a company should (1) develop an integrated marketing program (2) to generate profitable sales volume (3) by means of satisfying consumers' wants.

By virtue of the fact that the phenomenon of consumerism exists in the United States today, the marketing concept has to some extent failed. Peter Drucker (a professor, a management consultant, and certainly not an antagonist of business) referred to consumerism as "the shame of the total marketing concept." The customer-orientation theme in the marketing concept implies that business should look at the world from the buyer's end, find out what he wants, and then

---

[9]See Bent Stidsen and Thomas F. Schutte, "Marketing as a Communication System: The Marketing Concept Revisited," *Journal of Marketing,* October, 1972, pp. 22–27; Lynn J. Loudenback, "Social Responsibility and the Marketing Concept," *Atlanta Economic Review,* April, 1972, pp. 38–39; and E. Laird Landon, Jr., "The Invisible Backhand or the 'New Marketing Concept' Must Be Turning Adam Smith in His Grave," *Journal of the Academy of Marketing Science,* Fall, 1973, pp. 132–137.

Also see brief discussion of this subject in Chapter 1.

try to satisfy those wants in a profitable manner. Consequently, carried to their logical extremes, consumerism and the marketing concept are mutually exclusive; if one exists, the other does not. Yet most businessmen probably would claim that they are consumer-oriented, and that they do try to satisfy their customers. They look on in wounded surprise at the wave of consumer discontent that is engulfing them.

Okay, then, what went wrong? Is it simply that the marketing concept has outlived its usefulness and is not compatible with today's societal orientation in marketing? In this author's opinion there is nothing wrong with the marketing concept that a broader interpretation won't cure. It is as viable as it ever was. It is quite compatible with a societal orientation to marketing and with a marketing executive's social responsibility.

However, three things did occur which have hurt the credibility and acceptability of the marketing concept. The first is that too many marketing executives, while professing wholehearted agreement and support of the philosophy, were in actual practice giving it only token or lip-service implementation. In some cases these executives may have meant well, but they were simply too production- or engineering-oriented to fully comprehend the idea of customer orientation. To them, customer satisfaction was achieved by building a better mousetrap. In other cases the short-run crises forced line-operating executives to put their self-interest ahead of consumer satisfaction, even though top management may have been preaching consumer orientation. This point was discussed in the last chapter.

The two more fundamental factors affecting the full implementation of the marketing concept revolve around the narrow interpretation of consumer want satisfaction. Who is a consumer, and what is meant by want satisfaction? Answers to both of these questions have been too narrow and too short-run-oriented. Most of us as human beings—whether in our role as producer or consumer—tend to be short-run-oriented in most situations. We fail to see the boomerang effect—the long-run implications of our actions. Thus, I may want certain foods, and be satisfied when marketers cater to these wants. But these foods may be fattening or low in nutritional value, so there is a negative personal want-satisfaction effect on me in the long run. My wants for a TV set, or for some kind of medicine, or for cigarettes may be satisfied by companies. But the long-run effects may be radiation damage from the TV set, bad side effects from the medicine, and heart and lung damage from the cigarettes.

If the consumer-orientation goal of the marketing concept is defined as want satisfaction *in the long run,* then the marketing concept is more in line with the societal perspective of marketing. Of course, the problem of goal conflict (as discussed in the preceding chapter) crops up here again. To sell me the fattening foods is contrary to society's view of socially desirable want satisfaction. But to market nonfattening foods to me (while socially desirable and healthy for me) is just not what I want tonight, so the marketer loses my business. My short-run wants and long-run interests conflict.

Besides extending the *time* dimension in the marketing concept, we need to extend its *breadth* dimension. To view consumers as being only the direct buyers of a company's product—a view generally held in the past—is too narrow a dimension. We must broaden our definition of the markets to be satisfied to include groups affected by the direct buyer-seller exchange. Thus I may buy an auto and be satisfied with it. But the negative social effects of pollution and traffic congestion from my auto displease other groups. So in the broader context, we have not generated customer satisfaction and thus have not successfully implemented the marketing concept. A steel producer can sell a good product, reasonably priced——thus satisfying its direct customers. But if that mill is polluting the air and water when making that steel, then from the broader societal perspective, the marketing concept is not being implemented.

In conclusion, the marketing concept is compatible with a societal perspective of marketing when we define the marketing concept as a philosophy whereby a company strives (1) to develop an integrated marketing program (2) to generate long-run profitable sales volume (3) by means of satisfying the long-run wants of (a) product-buying customers and (b) the parts of society affected by the firm's activities.

MARKETING IN AN ERA OF SHORTAGES

Seemingly all of a sudden, around 1973–1974, our economy of abundance developed several spots of scarcity. The oil shortage which triggered the so-called energy crisis generally epitomized the shortage situation. However, in the mid-1970s shortages seemed to occur suddenly not only in oil-based industries (plastics and other petrochemicals) but also in many other industries (wood, paper products, farm products, for example) where the shortages were not triggered by cutbacks in energy availability. This is not the place to argue the political and economic causes underlying the shortages, but we should recognize the impact they have on marketing in our economy.

To paraphrase an article title, marketing is not dead but it sure is going to be different in these shortage situations.[10] Because shortages could last for many years in some product categories, the face of marketing is likely to be different for a long time in these industries. In our discussion of the marketing implications in shortages, first we shall consider some "don'ts" for management and then some positive action proposals.

DON'T REDUCE MARKETING'S ROLE

Faced with a limited supply of its product and a situation where the company can sell all it can produce, the two biggest mistakes management can make are (1) to reduce the role of marketing in the firm and (2) to mistreat its customers.

It is bad enough, but perhaps understandable, when financial and production executives want to reduce the role of marketing during periods of shortages. Unfortunately, these executives seem to think that their functions are needed all the time, but that marketing is necessary only when supply exceeds demand. But what is really incomprehensible is when *marketing* executives talk about cutting sales forces, reducing advertising, and otherwise lessening their marketing effort.

These executive opinions reflect both a shortsighted point of view and a nonunderstanding of the role of marketing. Budget cuts and other reductions in marketing effort can hurt whether the scarcities are short-lived or long-lasting. If they end

---

[10]With apologies to Carl Rieser, "The Salesman Isn't Dead—He's Different," *Fortune*, November, 1962, p. 124, an article about the changing role of salesmen.

soon, management needs experienced people to maintain a competitive position in a market. As long as the shortages continue, experienced people in sales, advertising, and marketing research can play vital roles in solving problems and seeking new marketing opportunities.

Business executives need to recognize the true role of marketing in relation to demand. In the past, marketing's job was seen as finding customers for existing products, or developing new products for unmet wants. In either situation marketing was *stimulating* demand. A more useful perspective is to consider marketing's job as one of *managing* demand. Then excess demand becomes as much of a marketing problem as excess supply. "The tasks of coping with shrinking demand or deliberately discouraging segments of the market call for the use of all the major marketing tools. As such, marketing thinking is just as relevant to the problem of reducing demand as it is to the problem of increasing demand."[11]

DON'T MISTREAT CUSTOMERS

With the shift to excess demand and a seller's market, some companies may be tempted to abandon the customer-orientation keystone in the marketing concept. It probably would be only human for salesmen and sales executives to release their resentments and try to "get even" for the real and imagined mistreatment they have suffered at the hands of purchasing agents during the long periods of excess supply and a buyer's market.

Any such ideas are simply stupid at best and suicidal at worst, for several reasons. First, good customers—market franchises—are a major asset for any firm. They are harder to acquire than most assets, and you don't go around destroying customer relationships any more than you destroy the firm's plant or machinery. Second, the shortages in many areas may prove to be short-run, but ill-treated customers have long-run memories. Third, customer complaints today fall on receptive ears in Washington and in state legislatures, as we noted in the preceding chapter.

POSITIVE PROGRAMS FOR MARKETING MANAGEMENT DURING SHORTAGES

Far from being discouraged or abandoning a customer orientation, marketing executives should look upon this period as a time to rethink their marketing programs, adapt to changing priorities, and capitalize on the new opportunities generated by the scarcities. In a general marketing management sense, for example, executives can pursue alternative marketing strategies, depending upon their assessment of the demand for their product in relation to its supply. Increasing demand and adequate supply may call for a growth strategy, while increasing demand coupled with inadequate supply suggests a market retention strategy.[12]

---

[11]This paragraph is adapted from Philip Kotler and Sydney J. Levy, "Demarketing, Yes, Demarketing," *Harvard Business Review,* November–December, 1971, pp. 74–80, quote from p. 75.

[12]For additional strategy-action guidelines, see David W. Cravens, "Marketing Management in an Era of Shortages," *Business Horizons,* February, 1974, pp. 79–85.

One interesting development with major marketing implications is the emergence of a barter economy as a means of acquiring vital materials now in short supply. Company A will sell a scarce item to company B, if B can pay its bill, not in cash, but in another scarce item which A needs.[13]

More specifically, management can analyze its customer list and then consider actions pertaining to each of the four components of the marketing mix. A marketing cost analysis by customer groups, checking on present and potential profitability, will enable a seller to prune out marginal customers. If shipment priorities are to be set up, obviously the high-profit customers should get preferential treatment. However, a seller also has to consider the antitrust implications in these moves. As we saw in the early stages of the oil shortages, the major firms could not simply eliminate selling gas to the small independents.

In product planning, companies have been slimming their product mix by eliminating low-margin products. Planned obsolescence may be de-emphasized in some firms. In planning new products, look for markets expanded by the shortages. Less building heat means more sweaters, and less gasoline means more bicycles, books, and home entertainment. Regarding pricing policies and strategies, the combination of shortages and inflation pose real challenges for marketing management.[14] Marketing cost analyses by channel of distribution may result in eliminating some middlemen, employing a more selective distribution policy, or even restructuring the basic channels used by a firm.

In the promotional areas of advertising and personal selling, several adjustments to shortages are being made. Advertising is shifting to more informational ads. "Status" appeals are giving way to "utilitarian" appeals. (One interesting consumer backlash to current oil-company advertising is the query, "How come the companies waited till now to tell us how to save gas, get better mileage, etc.?") Perhaps most important of all, from a societal viewpoint, is that advertising can play a major role in stimulating economic and behavioral change in getting consumers to husband rather than squander our resources.[15]

The role of the personal salesmen will change dramatically in shortage-ridden companies, and there may be cutbacks in the size of some sales forces. The shortage-era salesman will work more on servicing good accounts, educating customers and middlemen, helping customers solve their shortage-induced problems, and particularly on providing product and market information to customers.[16]

In conclusion, the forces of shortages and inflation are changing the lifestyle of U.S. consumers in many instances. During the next decade, consumers may decide to live more simply, cut back on their product acquisitions, and generally conserve resources. These attitudes will have a significant impact on the marketing programs in many companies.

---

[13]See "The Sultans of Swap," *Time,* Mar. 11, 1974, p. 87; and "Wanna Swap?" *Wall Street Journal,* Feb. 13, 1974, p. 1.

[14]See "Pricing Strategy in an Inflation Economy," *Business Week,* Apr. 6, 1974, p. 43.

[15]See "Advertising: New Role in 'Unabundant' Economy," *Grey Matter,* February, 1974.

[16]See Michael B. Rothfeld, "A New Kind of Challenge for Salesmen," *Fortune,* April, 1974, p. 156. *Sales Management* magazine devoted an entire issue (Jan. 21, 1974) to a series of questions regarding how to keep a sales force running in a crunch economy.

ADDITIONAL PROSPECTS FOR THE FUTURE

What does the future hold for marketing? We just discussed two of the prospects—a socially oriented marketing concept and marketing during shortages. Now to finish this book, let's briefly summarize some of the other broad forces which will reshape marketing in the final two decades of the twentieth century. The crystal ball seems reasonably clear regarding many of these projections because they are a continuation of trends which have been in evidence for some years now. As we move into the 1980s, perhaps the overriding feature we can expect is an accelerated rate of change.

TOMORROW'S CONSUMERS WILL BE DIFFERENT

Perhaps the most significant prospect is that the markets of the 1980s will be quite different from those of today. Consumers will be better educated and more critical. Their goals will be more socially oriented, and they will expect marketers to play a greater role in solving our environmental and social problems. Population growth will slow down. The role of women will change dramatically with consequent effects on marketing. Family structures are changing toward smaller, less permanent institutions (the divorce rate is rising). There will be further movement toward a rental (rather than product ownership) economy and a growth in the services sector. Consumers will be less concerned with status, hard work, competition, and material success. Instead, their attention will swing more to personal fulfillment and achievement measured quite differently from past generations. These value differences are highlighted in the following comparison of attitudes held by (1) college seniors in the Boston area and (2) college graduates ten years after graduation. See Fig. 30-1. The authors of that study predicted that the value systems of today's graduating seniors are permanent, not transitory. These values may be modified over time, but today's seniors are not going to settle down in the value mainstream as it has existed for the past 20 to 30 years.

USE OF SYSTEMS APPROACH AND MARKETING PLANNING

Throughout this book we have advocated the use of the systems approach in the philosophy and practice of marketing management. Even our definition of marketing back in Chapter 1 embodied the systems concept. We can anticipate a growing appreciation of the value of treating marketing as a total system, composed of several subsystems such as a marketing information system, a channel system, a physical distribution system, etc.

The acceptance of the systems approach to marketing implicitly carries with it several attendant trends. One is the recognition of the indispensable value of marketing planning, especially as firms become larger, more complex, and more decentralized. Second, the various marketing activities within a firm are becoming better integrated with one another, and marketing in total will be better coordinated with the other major functions (finance, production, etc.) in a company.

Third, we may expect the marketing programs in many firms to acquire an international perspective. Moreover, this international dimension will be integrated with the domestic arm, thus forming a global marketing enterprise. This trend will develop, if for no other reason, simply because in many companies the best

THE CONTRASTING VALUES OF COLLEGE SENIORS AND THE GRADUATES OF 10 YEARS EARLIER

10-year graduates	College seniors
The system works, with reservations	The system does not work, but used to
Competition is a positive element	Competition is negative, "anti-humanist"
Hard work brings society's rewards	Hard work isn't worth the rewards it brings
Work itself is an important value	Work is a questionable value
Material success is desirable and attainable	Material success is questionable and no longer attainable for everyone
Success means accumulation	Conventionally defined success means accumulation
Material success and status go together	Material success and conventionally defined status are questionable values
Personal self-fulfillment comes with material success	Personal self-fulfillment may have no relation to material success
Freedom comes with money— the more money the more freedom	Freedom is a state of mind, it requires only minimum money. Hunting after money and success curtail freedom
Whatever cuts the incentive to work hard is dangerous for the system and its values	Working too hard and devoting too much attention to work is dangerous for the individual

Source: Scott Ward, Thomas S. Robertson, and William Capitman, "'What Will Be Different about Tomorrow's Consumer?'" in Fred C. Allvine (ed.), *1971 Combined Proceedings*, American Marketing Association, Chicago, 1972, p. 373.

Figure 30 – 1.

opportunities for growth lie in foreign operations. Finally, the adoption of a systems approach in marketing should facilitate the growth of vertical marketing channel systems as the dominant distribution network in our economy. This newer system will largely replace the traditional channel arrangement consisting of loosely aligned, independent, frequently conflicting assortments of manufacturers, wholesalers, and retailers. (For a review of major trends in retailing institutions, the final section of Chapter 16 could be reread profitably at this point.)

SCIENTIFIC MARKETING AND INTERDISCIPLINARY CONTRIBUTIONS

Enough groundwork has been laid to predict that marketing management in business is on the threshold of a new era in problem solving—an era which would abandon the heavy reliance on subjective executive judgment in favor of an approach based on knowledge from mathematics, the behavioral sciences, and other nonbusiness fields. Marketing executives traditionally have not been trained in the scientific approach, and they have resisted change in this area. For example, many of them have not made much effective use of a computer. But a new day is coming—it may not come quickly, but it is coming. We can expect companies increasingly to implement the concept of a marketing information system as a continuing system of information management to aid in problem solving.

As a separate field of study, marketing evolved from the general discipline of economics. However, marketing men now recognize that they can draw profitably from many other disciplines. The behavioral sciences—psychology, sociology, anthropology—have contributed much to an understanding of consumer behavior. Statistics and mathematics, as well, have contributed to quantitative measurement in marketing. Demography, geography, and ecology have contributed to an understanding of markets and market movements. Looking to the future, we can expect marketing men to become better trained in the use of the tools of other disciplines and to be more cognizant of their value in marketing.

As part of this interdisciplinary approach, we are seeing a melding of the work of behavioral scientists and quantitative analysts. Unlike the separatism of the past, today we see psychologists and sociologists making extended use of quantitative techniques, while the mathematicians are trying to apply their theories to practical problems. This interdisciplinary activity is bearing fruit in many marketing areas, but especially in terms of broadening and deepening our understanding of buyer behavior.[17]

A major spur to scientific problem solving in marketing has been the developments in computer technology. The use of a computer can increase a firm's marketing efficiency tremendously because executives are able to analyze the marketing effort and conduct many other types of marketing research projects in greater detail, at less expense, and with more speed than has been possible heretofore. An obvious prediction is that as newer, more analytically trained people appear in marketing executive positions, companies will make substantial strides toward realizing the potential for computer use in marketing.[18]

GROWING SOCIETAL ORIENTATION IN MARKETING

Up to this point our crystal-ball gazing has centered largely on the role of marketing in the individual firm, that is, in the *private* sector of our economy. Now in shifting our attention to marketing's future role in the *public* sector, we should recall the discussion in the preceding chapter. Consumerism will prob-

---

[17]See John A. Howard, "Buyer Behavior and Related Technological Advances," *Journal of Marketing,* January, 1970, pp. 18–21.

[18]See Philip Kotler, "The Future of the Computer in Marketing," *Journal of Marketing,* January, 1970, pp. 11-14; and Paul E. Green, "Measurement and Data Analysis," *Journal of Marketing,* January, 1970, pp. 15–17.

ably loom larger, thus posing greater challenges for marketing to help consumers fulfill their expectations. Marketing must, and undoubtedly will, assume a key role in improving the economic situation for low-income consumers. After all, "creating and delivering a standard of living" is one definition of marketing. Marketing also will become increasingly involved in solving the problems of environmental pollution. We will increasingly question the value of continued economic growth when it is accompanied by the use of nonreplaceable natural resources. Marketing will play a major role in developing the effective use and conservation of these resources. The concept of demarketing will get more attention.

As societal values change, marketing may come under more criticism. In considering the marketability of a new product, rather than asking, "Can it be sold?" a marketing executive may be asking, "Should it be sold? Is it worth its cost to society?" In effect, we may see a shift from the marketing concept to the human concept. Or perhaps these can be one and the same if business can interpret the marketing concept as being societally oriented over the long run.[19]

QUESTIONS AND PROBLEMS

1. Some people feel that too much power is concentrated in big business in the United States and that large firms should be broken up. Yet these same people will drive a General Motors car, buy groceries at a large chain supermarket, buy home appliances made by a giant in the industry, wash with a brand of Procter & Gamble soap, and brush their teeth with the leading brand of toothpaste. How do you reconcile the behavior of these people with their opinion concerning big business?

2. Name some products which you feel are marketed under too many different brand names. About how many should be eliminated? How should we go about the elimination process?

3. "Middlemen make unfairly high profits." Do you agree?

4. Some people belive that there are too many gasoline service stations in their communities. Suggest a method for reducing the number of stations. Are there too many in your college community? How many should be eliminated?

5. Evaluate the following criticisms of advertising:
   a. Advertising creates a false sense of values.
   b. Advertising costs too much.
   c. Advertising is in bad taste.
   d. Advertising is false, misleading, and deceptive.
   e. Advertising tends to create monopolies.

6. What proposals do you have for regulating advertising?

7. What specific recommendations do you have for reducing the costs of marketing?

8. List the major federal laws affecting marketing. Indicate in each case whether the law's principal purpose is to aid business or regulate it. Briefly describe the intent and provisions of each measure.

---

[19]Leslie M. Dawson, "The Human Concept: New Philosophy for Business," *Business Horizons,* December, 1969, pp. 29–38.

9. Besides the examples given in this chapter, can you name some fields of business which the government entered because private enterprise was unable to meet, or refused to meet, consumer demand?
10. Is the marketing concept compatible with a societal orientation in marketing?
11. "When a company can sell all it can produce (during periods of product shortages), management should cut expenses by reducing its sales force and advertising expenditures." Discuss.
12. Assume that a manufacturer's sales force is paid a salary plus a commission on sales volume. How can management motivate these people during periods of product shortages when they cannot get enough of the product to sell?
13. What can a manufacturer do to hold together his good retail distribution system when, because of shortages, he cannot supply these retailers with all the product quantities they order?

CASES FOR PART

CASE 25. RELWAY APPLIANCES, LTD.*

Designing a marketing research project

In the fall of 1967, Relway Appliances, Ltd., decided that some consideration should be given to adding a new product line. The company was manufacturing and marketing a range of small appliances which included electric frying pans, toasters, steam irons, and broilers. A survey done by one of the leading appliance trade journals gave the yearly sales figures (in units) for various appliances in Canada. (See the table at the top of page 717.)

Although Relway was obtaining sales roughly in proportion to the market trends, management felt that the company had the facilities to manufacture and market an additional line. Sales of many small appliances were seasonal; for example an estimated 45 percent of all mixers and electric blankets were sold in November and December.

After some consideration, Relway management felt that the addition of a line of air conditioners would help to offset some of the problems of seasonal demand.

Relway was considering two possibilities as to the type of product they would

*Maurice Archer and William J. L. Clark, *Canadian Marketing,* McGraw-Hill Company of Canada, Ltd., Toronto, 1969, pp. 280–282.

	1963	1964	1965	1966
Frying pans	103,000	159,000	218,000	298,000
Toasters	287,000	279,000	256,000	265,000
Mixers	70,000	85,000	92,000	93,000
Steam irons	143,000	218,000	265,000	302,000
Electric blankets	65,000	90,000	120,000	121,000
Air conditioners	32,000	57,000	68,000	75,000
Broilers	15,000	17,000	13,000	12,000

*Maurice Archer and William J. L. Clark, Canadian Marketing, McGraw-Hill Company of Canada, Ltd., Toronto, 1969, pp. 280–282.

manufacture. The first was to produce three conventional types of air conditioners that could be installed in the window of a house or office. These would include a 4,500 Btu unit capable of cooling a small room, an 8,500 Btu unit for cooling an average-size bedroom, and a 12,000 Btu unit for cooling a large room such as a living room. The price of the units would range from $150 to $500. The prices would be competitive with comparable products already being sold.

The basic philosophy behind the marketing of three models was that the consumer could, if desired, air-condition an entire house using a combination of the models from the line. If air conditioning of one room was required, it was also felt that the range of three models was sufficient to accommodate most consumer requirements.

Before investing the large amount of money required for manufacturing machinery for the air conditioners, Relway felt it wise to investigate the market further. They found that two large national appliance manufacturers had approximately a 65 percent share of the home air conditioner market. The remaining share was divided among eight smaller manufacturers. Three of the small firms had a product which was considered by the trade to be excellent. Due to lack of promotion, the products of these firms were not nationally known. In their own local area, however, each of the three had developed a market share of approximately 30 percent.

Relway felt that there would be an expanding market for home air conditioners for some years to come. They were, however, concerned about the amount of competition they would encounter.

In an attempt to assess competition, Relway had each of their ten salesmen call on ten retail outlets for air conditioners to record dealer reaction towards a new line of air conditioners. The following table indicates the results obtained.

Numbers of dealers carrying one line of air conditoners	32
Number of dealers carrying two lines of air conditioners	28
Number of dealers carrying three lines of air conditioners	38
Number of dealers carrying more than three lines of air conditioners	2

Generally speaking, the attitude of the dealers was very negative towards adding a new line of air conditioners. They indicated that Relway would have to manufacture a product which would incorporate some definite improvement over existing air conditioners before they would consider carrying the Relway line. The dealers also indicated that if Relway blasted into the market with heavy consumer advertising, they would consider carrying the new line if the consumer demand was great enough.

At this point, the general manager of Relway reviewed the facts and figures concerning the proposal to market air conditioners to ascertain whether or not he had sufficient information to allow him to make a decision properly. He thought he probably needed more data, but he was not certain what information was still needed nor how to get it. He realized that further surveys could be costly. He also was anxious to make a decision as quickly as possible.

QUESTION

1. Does the general manager have enough information to make a decision on whether to add the line of air conditioners?
   a. If so, what course of action should he recommend to his board of directors?
   b. If not, explain what information is needed and how you would go about getting it.

CASE 26. STURDI-WEAR CLOTHING COMPANY*

Analysis of sales volume

The Sturdi-Wear Company was founded in January, 1959. The owners of the firm were experienced in the manufacture and sale of men's and boys' clothing. Mr. Sam Smith, president, had been the production manager for an old-line clothing company prior to his present venture. His partner and vice president, Mr. John Adams, had been an outstanding salesman and was associated with the same firm as Smith. Sturdi-Wear was successful primarily for two reasons. Mr. Smith was able to produce quality clothing at competitive prices, and Mr. Adams was successful in transfering the business of a nucleus of his old customers to the new firm. Particularly pertinent was a contract negotiated in 1970 with two of the leading chain department stores headquartered in Chicago, Illinois. The firm had been selling to these chain organizations for the past three years.

The firm manufactured and sold men's and boys' suits, sports coats, and slacks. These items were manufactured for the low-price market, but were of good quality and style. Mr. Adams had an unusual ability to select the styles and patterns most desired by the market.

This firm had restricted distribution to the states of Indiana, Illinois, Iowa, and Missouri. The owners believed that there was sufficient opportunity for sales within the four-state area to absorb the maximum output of the plant. In addition, the plant was located centrally so that close contact with the accounts was possible, reorder shipments could be received by the accounts within four days from the date of order, and transportation costs were relatively small.

The firm employed six salesmen who were assigned as follows: (1) Two men covered the Chicago area which consisted of Cook, DuPage, and Kane Coun-

---

*Case prepared by Prof. Donald W. Scotton, Cleveland State University. Reproduced with permission.

ties. (2) One salesman traveled the remaining portion of Illinois. (3) The other three salesmen were assigned one state each consisting of Indiana, Iowa, and Missouri. The three-county Chicago area was divided between the two salesmen working there so that one was responsible for all activity within the Chicago city limits, and the other traveled the other sections of Cook County and all of DuPage and Kane Counties.

The salesmen sold directly to large retail accounts and to wholesalers to obtain coverage of smaller retail outlets. The Chicago city salesman was responsible also for servicing the two chain organizations mentioned above. Although chain accounts were solicited, the salesmen had not been successful in obtaining others.

Sales trends. Sturdi-Wear sales for the year 1959 were $2,000,000 and increased approximately at the rate of $2,000,000 per year until 1969. The 1969 sales were $20,000,000. Sales from 1970 through 1972 were:

Year	Chain sales	Non-chain sales	Total sales
1970	$1,000,000	$21,000,000	$22,000,000
1971	2,000,000	22,000,000	24,000,000
1972	2,600,000	17,400,000	20,000,000

The management of the firm was concerned about the decline in sales between 1971 and 1972 and decided that an analysis of sales might be helpful. Although the owners knew a great deal about their customers, they recognized that continuous study of sales segments might be necessary.

Mr. William Brown was hired in January, 1973, to fill the newly created position of Marketing Analyst. The owners were aware that it would take some time to install a satisfactory system of market analysis and control, and suggested that Mr. Brown review 1972 sales first. It was hoped that this analysis would serve as a beginning point in understanding the problem and possibly reveal some areas for further study and correction of weaknesses.

Mr. Brown selected counties as geographical control units. He experimented with various general indexes and found that a coefficient of correlation of .95 existed between his firms's *total* sales and the *Sales Management* magazine's Buying Power Index. He believed that some geographic segment analysis within each of the states would be valuable. Thirty counties were selected at random to discover the correlation between county sales of his firm and the "Survey of Buying Power Index." This testing demonstrated that the general index was not sufficiently correlated to firm sales at the *county* level. So he made a statistical study of market factors affecting the sales of the firm's products. It was found that an index consisting of population (weighted 1), effective buying income (weighted 2), and total retail sales (weighted 3) had a coefficient of correlation of .92 when related to county sales of Sturdi-Wear products. On the basis of these findings it was decided that the sales analysis of the four states would be made using the *Sales Management* magazine's *general index* and that the *specific index* would be employed in the analysis of county sales.

In preparing 1972 sales for analysis it was noted that billings were:

Illinois	$12,600,000
Indiana	2,000,000
Iowa	1,600,000
Missouri	3,800,000
Total	$20,000,000

Because the Illinois sales were large, it was decided that this area should be analyzed further. In addition, it was believed that the sales to the chain store organizations should be examined as a possible influence on the other states. Finally, Mr. Adams suggested that Chicago area sales were of sufficient magnitude that they should be examined separately from the Illinois state totals.

To facilitate the analysis, the following information was gathered:

1. Chain-store sales were made at Chicago in the amount of $2,600,000. The chains reported that the goods represented by these sales were shipped and sold in their stores as follows: Illinois 40%, Indiana 30%, Iowa 20%, and Missouri 10%.

2. The chain groups indicated that all the Illinois sales of Sturdi-Wear clothes were made as follows:

Cook County	70%
DuPage County	20%
Kane County	10%
Total	100%

3. Other sales in the Chicago area which included Cook, DuPage, and Kane Counties, consisted of $4,000,000 to large independent retail stores in Cook County and $4,000,000 to wholesalers.

4. The Chicago area wholesalers reported that the Sturdi-Wear sales to retailers were distributed (at manufacturer's sale price) as follows:

Cook County	$2,400,000
DuPage County	1,000,000
Kane County	600,000
Total	$4,000,000

The sales analysis computations were presented in Tables 1 through 5 by Mr. William Brown. Messrs. Adams and Smith were interested in the findings, but they expressed doubt as to the adequacy of the analysis. Specifically, they suggested that a more comprehensive analysis follow this first effort. In addition, they requested that a plan be drawn for interpreting the results and taking corrective action.

QUESTIONS

1. Appraise the job of sales volume analysis which Mr. Brown performed.
2. What conclusions may be drawn from the results of the sales volume analysis?

Table 1. Sales management buying power index and related variables, by state, 1972.

State	Population (000)	Effective buying income $(000)	Retail sales $(000)	SMBP index	State % of index total
Illinois	11,285.7	48,946,224	25,891,375	5.9207	48.88
Indiana	5,314.3	19,587,623	11,504,622	2.5235	20.83
Iowa	2,894.6	10,672,932	6,854,337	1.4144	11.68
Missouri	4,802.1	16,947,895	10,707,150	2.2543	18.61
Total	24,296.7	96,154,674	54,961,484	12.1129	100.00

Source: Sales Management, Survey of Buying Power (annual issue), July 23, 1973.

Table 2. Efficiency index by states, 1972.

Outlets by state	Buying power index	Sales Actual $(000)	Par $(000)	Excess or deficit $(000)	Efficiency index
Illinois					
Chain		1,040			
Wholesale & retail		10,000			
Total	48.88	11,040	9,776	1,264	112.93
Indiana					
Chain		780			
Wholesale & retail		2,000			
Total	20.83	2,780	4,166	−1,386	66.98
Iowa					
Chain		520			
Wholesale & retail		1,600			
Total	11.68	2,120	2,336	−216	90.71
Missouri					
Chain		260			
Wholesale & retail		3,800			
Total	18.61	4,060	3,722	338	109.08
Totals	100.00	$20,000	$20,000	-0-	

Table 3. Specific index variables for Illinois counties, 1972.

Illinois counties	Population (000)	Population Percent of 4-state total	Effective buying income $(000)	Effective buying income Percent of 4-state total	Retail sales $(000)	Retail sales Percent of 4-state total
Cook	5,572.7	22.93	26,074,695	27.16	12,791,370	23.25
DuPage	511.9	2.11	2,729,985	2.84	1,500,933	2.73
Kane	252.1	1.04	1,099,233	1.15	697,587	1.27
All others	4,949.0	20.37	19,042,311	19.83	10,901,485	19.82
Total	11,285.7	46.45	48,946,224	50.98	25,891,375	47.07

Source: Sales Management, Survey of Buying Power (annual issue), July 23, 1973.

Table 4. Specific index computation for Illinois counties, 1972.

Illinois counties	Population[1] +	Effective buying income[2] +	Retail sales[3] ÷ 6	Specific = index
Cook	1 (22.93) +	2 (27.16) +	3 (23.25) ÷ 6	24.50
DuPage	1 (2.11) +	2 (2.84) +	3 (2.73) ÷ 6	2.66
Kane	1 (1.04) +	2 (1.15) +	3 (1.27) ÷ 6	1.19
All others	1 (20.37) +	2 (19.83) +	3 (19.82) ÷ 6	19.91

[1]Population weighted 1.
[2]EBI weighted 2.
[3]Retail sales weighted 3.

Table 5. Efficiency index of Illinois counties, 1972 (based upon the specific index).

Outlets by county	Specific index	Sales		Excess or deficit $(000)	Efficiency index
		Actual $(000)	Par $(000)		
Cook					
Chain		728			
Wholesale		2,400			
Retail		4,000			
Total	24.50	7,128	4,900	2,228	145.47
DuPage					
Chain		208			
Wholesale		1,000			
Retail					
Total	2.66	1,208	532	676	225.19
Kane					
Chain		104			
Wholesale		600			
Retail					
Total	1.19	704	238	466	295.80
All others					
Total	19.91	2,000	3,982	−1,982	50.22

CASE 27. THE ARGENTINE DRUG CAPER*

Marketing cost analysis

Bill Cool, the general manager of the International Division of the Far Flung Drug Co., finds himself faced with an extremely difficult competitive situation in Argentina. A Japanese competitor is underpricing him on his major product ("super pill") in the Argentine market, and he is faced with total loss of all Argentine sales for this product. "Super pill" is manufactured in one of Far Flung Drug's United States plants from which the International Division purchases them.

Bill's problem, as he sees it, is a matter of meeting his competitor's price. "Super pill" and the Japanese competitive product are basically equal from the point of view of quality and performance. Delivery and credit terms are also similar. The basic financial facts are as follows:

Prices:
   Super pill $1.00 per gross
   Japanese pill $.60 per gross
Annual Volume:
   5,000,000 gross plus an estimated 5% annual growth factor
Manufacturing Cost:
   (Including transportation) $.70 per gross

In this situation Bill felt that he could not afford to meet the competitive price of $.60, since his division would then show a loss of $.10 per unit. He then remembered, somewhat vaguely, a discussion he got involved in while attending an executive development program. The discussion revolved around the idea that manufacturing costs were best thought of as consisting of two separate components, i.e., fixed and variable. The fixed costs were then described as a "kind of handicap" which a company tried to overcome by generating a sufficient profit contribution, i.e., the difference between sales and variable costs.

Bill wondered if these concepts might be applicable to his situation. As a result of a cable to his company's main office in Atlanta, Bill found that the accounting staff of Far Flung Drugs did not separate variable and fixed costs in its cost accounting system. However, they turned Bill's question over to a cost analyst who estimated that $.30 of the $.70 per unit manufacturing cost represented fixed costs.

Based on the above information, Bill calculated variable costs per gross as $.40 and a profit contribution of $.20 per gross if the competitive price was met. With these facts in hand Bill went to Atlanta to discuss his problem with the headquarters pricing policy staff.

In Atlanta, all agreed that the company's other products were covering the fixed costs and capacity was available for the foreseeable future to produce sufficient amounts of "super pill." All also agreed that the competitive price had to be met and could be met without any adverse effects and with a $.20 per

---

*Case prepared by Prof. William L. Ferrara, Pennsylvania State University. Reproduced with permission.

gross profit contribution. Thus, Bill Cool went home satisfied that he could retain his Argentine "super pill" business at a price which would be profitable to Far Flung Drugs.

A few months later Bill noticed that reports concerning the profitability of South American sales were getting worse and worse. He could not understand this since everything seemed to be going well from a volume and cost point of view.

Bill decided that he had to uncover the causes of his poor showing, so he started to take apart the profit report for South America. To his surprise he found that the headquarters accounting staff was charging his Argentine sales of "super pill" with a manufacturing cost of $.70 rather than $.40. His anticipated profit contribution of $.20 per gross was in effect turned into a loss of $.10 per gross. An expected annual profit contribution of $1,000,000 ($.20 × 5,000,000 gross) was being turned into a loss of $500,000 ($.10 × 5,000,000 gross) by a group of accountants.

Bill then tried to explain his poor South American showing to the company's executive committee at a special meeting called by the executive committee. They could not understand his explanation due to the fact that they were as concerned as the accountants with the "full cost" of manufacturing. Bill left the meeting, muttering to himself, "I make a sound and profitable decision and the accounting department makes me look like a bum. I guess they and the executive committee are really telling me to give up the Argentine market for 'super pill.'"

QUESTIONS

1. Assuming that "super pill" is a profitable product at the $.60 price, how would you adjust the profit report for South American sales to conform with Bill Cool's decision?
2. Was Bill Cool's decision really sound? That is, was there anything wrong with the analysis which preceded Bill's decision?

MARKETING ARITHMETIC

Marketing involves people—customers, middlemen, and producers. Much of the business activity of these people, however, is quantified in some manner. Consequently, mathematical figures are used as tools for the analysis of their quantitative relationships. Some knowledge of the rudiments of business arithmetic is essential for decision making in many areas of marketing. Since most students taking this course have already had a beginning course in accounting, this appendix is intended as a review. In marketing, we frequently use the following accounting or business arithmetic concepts: (1) the operating statement, (2) markups, and (3) analytical ratios. Another useful concept—discounts and terms of sale—was reviewed in Chapter 13 in connection with price policies.

THE OPERATING STATEMENT

An operating statement—often called a "profit and loss statement" or an "income and expense statement"—is one of the two main financial statements prepared by a company. The other is the balance sheet. An *operating statement* is a summary picture of the firm's income and expenses—its operations—over a period of time. In contrast, a *balance sheet* shows the assets, liabilities, and net worth of a company at a given time, for example, at the close of business on December 31, 1976.

The operating statement shows whether the business earned a net profit or suffered a net loss during the period covered. It arranges in orderly fashion a summary of the income and expense items which resulted in this net profit or loss. From the information in a profit and loss statement we also may compute several ratios useful in a financial analysis or a marketing analysis of the company's operations.

An operating statement may cover any selected period of time. Because of income tax requirements, virtually all firms prepare a statement covering operations during the calendar or fiscal year. In addition, it is common for businesses to prepare monthly, quarterly, or semiannual operating statements.

Figure A-1 is an example of an operating statement for a wholesaler or retailer. The main difference between the operating statement of a middleman and that of a manufacturer is in the cost-of-goods-sold section. A manufacturer shows a net figure for cost of goods *manufactured,* whereas the middleman's statement shows net *purchases.* If additional detail is desired, one can look to the accounting records and other supporting data upon which the operating statement was based.

MAJOR SECTIONS

From one point of view, the essence of business is very simple. A company buys or makes a product and then sells it for a higher price. Out of his sales revenue, the seller hopes to cover the cost of the merchandise and his own expenses and have something left over, which he calls "net profit." These relationships form the skeleton parts of an operating statement. Sales minus cost of goods sold equals gross margin; gross margin minus expenses equals net profit. An example based on Fig. A-1 is as follows:

Sales	$80,000
Cost of goods sold	48,000
Gross margin	32,000
Expenses	27,000
Net profit	$ 4,800

Sales. The first line in an operating statement records the gross sales—the total amount sold by the company. From this figure, the company deducts its sales returns and sales allowances. In virtually every firm at some time during an operating period, customers will want to return or exchange merchandise. In a sales return, the customer is refunded the full purchase price in cash or credit. In a sales allowance, the customer keeps the merchandise, but is given a reduction from selling because of some dissatisfaction. The income from the sale of returned merchandise is included in a company's gross sales.

After sales returns and allowances are deducted from gross sales, the resulting amount is net sales. This is the most important figure in the sales section of the statement. It represents the net amount of sales revenue out of which the company will pay for the products and all its expenses. The net sales figure is also the one upon which many operating ratios are based. It is set at 100 percent, and other items are then expressed as a percentage of net sales.

Gross sales		$87,000
Less: Sales returns and allowances	$ 5,500	
Cash discounts allowed	1,500	7,000
Net sales		$80,000
Cost of goods sold:		
Beginning inventory, January 1 (at cost)		18,000
Gross purchases	49,300	
Less: Cash discounts taken on purchases	900	
Net purchases	48,400	
Plus: Freight in	1,600	
Net purchases (at delivered cost)		50,000
Cost of goods available for sale		68,000
Less: Ending inventory, December 31 (at cost)		20,000
Cost of goods sold		48,000
Gross margin		32,000
Expenses:		
Salesmen's salaries and commissions		$11,000
Advertising		2,400
Office supplies		250
Taxes (except income tax)		125
Telephone and telegraph		250
Delivery expenses		175
Rent		800
Heat, light, and power		300
Depreciation		100
Insurance		150
Interest		150
Bad debts		300
Administrative salaries		7,500
Office salaries		3,500
Miscellaneous expenses		200
Total expenses		27,200
Net profit		$ 4,800

Figure A-1. Alpha-Beta Company, operating statement, for year ending December 31, 1974.

Cost of goods sold. From net sales, we must deduct the cost of the merchandise which was sold, as we work toward discovering the firm's final net profit. In determining cost of goods sold in a retail or wholesale operation, we start with the value of any merchandise on hand at the beginning of the period. To this we add the net cost of what was purchased during the period. From this total we deduct the value of whatever remains unsold at the end of the period. In Fig. A-1 the firm started with an inventory worth $18,000, and purchases were made which cost $50,000. Then the firm had a total of $68,000 worth of goods available for sale. If all were sold, the cost of goods sold would have been $68,000. At the end of the year, however, there is still $20,000 worth of merchandise on hand. Thus during the year, the company sold goods which cost $48,000.

In the preceding paragraph, we blithely spoke of merchandise "valued at" a certain figure or "worth" a stated amount. Actually, the problem of inventory valuation is complicated and sometimes controversial. The usual rule of thumb is to value inventories at cost or market, whichever is lower. The actual application of this rule may be difficult. Assume that a store buys six footballs at $2 each and the next week buys six more at $2.50 each and then places them, jumbled, in a basket display for sale. Then one is sold, but there is no marking to indicate whether the cost of goods sold was $2 or $2.50, and the inventory value of the remaining eleven balls may be $27.50 or $28. If we multiply this situation by thousands of purchases and sales, we may begin to see the depth of the problem.

Another figure which deserves some comment is the net cost of delivered purchases. A company starts with its gross purchases at billed cost. Then it must deduct any purchases which were returned or any purchase allowances received. The company should also deduct any discounts taken for payment of the bill within a specified period of time. Deducting purchase returns and allowances and purchase discounts gives the net cost of the purchases. Then freight charges paid by the buyer (called "freight in") are added to net purchases to determine the net cost of *delivered* purchases. In some accounting systems, firms place their purchase discounts near the bottom of the operating statement in a section called "other income," thus treating these discounts as a reflection of financial ability to pay bills promptly. The preferred location of this income item in retail and wholesale operating statements today is in the cost-of-goods-sold section, so that management may see the net cost of its purchases.

In a manufacturing concern, the cost-of-goods-sold section takes on a slightly different form. Instead of determining the cost of goods *purchased,* the company determines the cost of goods *manufactured.* Cost of goods manufactured is added to the beginning inventory to ascertain the total goods available for sale. Then after the ending inventory of finished goods is deducted, the answer is cost of goods sold. To find the cost of goods *manufactured,* a company starts with the value of goods partially completed (beginning inventory of goods in process) and then adds the cost of raw materials and parts, direct and indirect labor, and factory overhead expenses incurred during the period. By deducting the value of goods still in process at the end of the period, management knows the cost of goods manufactured during that span of time.

Gross margin. Gross margin is determined simply by subtracting cost of goods sold from net sales. Gross margin, sometimes called "gross profit," is one of the key figures in the entire marketing program. When we say that a certain store has a "margin" of 30 percent or that a salesman's compensation plan is set up to encourage the man to push the "high-margin" products, we are referring to the gross margin.

Expenses. Operating expenses are deducted from gross margin to determine the net profit. The operating expense section includes marketing, administrative, and possibly some miscellaneous expense items. It does not include cost of goods purchased or manufactured. These expenses have already been deducted. Expenses may be itemized in several different ways.

MARKUPS

It is common practice for retailers and wholesalers to use the concept of markup when determining the selling price of an article. Normally the selling price must exceed the cost of the merchandise by an amount sufficient to cover the operating expenses and still leave the desired profit. The difference between the selling price and the cost of the item is the markup. Sometimes it is termed the "mark-on."

The markup is closely related to the gross margin. It will be recalled that gross margin is equal to net sales minus cost of goods sold. Looking below the gross margin on an operating statement, we find that gross margin equals operating expenses plus net profit. Normally the initial markup in a company, department, or product line must be set a little higher than the overall gross margin desired for the selling unit because ordinarily some reductions will be incurred before all the articles are sold. For one reason or another, some items will not sell at the original price. They will have to be marked down, that is, reduced in price from the original level. Some pilferage and other shortages may also occur.

Typically, for convenience in computation and for other reasons, markups are expressed in percentages rather than dollars. The first problem is to determine the *base* for the percentage. That is, when we speak of a 40 percent markup, what do we mean—40 percent of what? Markups may be expressed as a percentage of either the cost price or the selling price. To determine markup percentage when it is based on cost, the formula is:

$$\text{Markup percentage} = \frac{\text{dollar markup}}{\text{cost}}$$

When the markup is based on selling price, the formula is:

$$\text{Markup percentage} = \frac{\text{dollar markup}}{\text{selling price}}$$

It is important that all interested parties understand which base is being used in a given situation. Otherwise the results can differ considerably. To illustrate, Mr. A runs a clothing store and claims he needs a 66⅔ percent markup to make a small net profit. Mr. B, who runs a competitive store, says he needs only a 40 percent markup and that A must be inefficient or a big profiteer. Actually both merchants are using identical markups, but they are using different bases. Each man buys hats at $6 apiece and sets the selling price at $10. This is a markup of $4 per hat. Mr. A is expressing his markup as a percentage of cost—hence, the 66⅔ percent figure (⁴⁄₆=66⅔ percent). Mr. B, in quoting a 40 percent markup, bases his on the selling price (⁴⁄₁₀ = 40 percent). It would be a mistake for Mr. A to try to get by on B's 40 percent markup, as long as A uses cost as his base. After buying the hats at $6, Mr. A would end up with a selling price of $8.40 if he used B's markup but his own (A's) cost basis. That is, 40 percent over $6 equals $2.40. This $2.40 markup on the average over the entire hat department would *not* enable A to cover his usual expenses and make a profit. *Unless otherwise indicated, markup percentages are always stated as a percentage of selling price.*

The computation of selling price is simple if we know dollar cost and the desired percentage markup. The following diagram, along with some examples, should help you understand the various relationships between selling price, cost, and markup, whether the markup is stated in percentages or dollars and whether the percentages are based on selling price or cost:

	$	%
Selling price		
—Cost		
Markup	$	%

In these examples, the markups are based on selling price. A merchant buys an article for $90 and knows he must get a markup of 40 percent. What is his selling price? By filling in the known information in the diagram, we see the following picture:

	$	%
Selling price		100%
—Cost	90	
Markup	$	40%

It is easy to see that the percentage figure representing cost is 60 percent. Thus the $90 cost equals 60 percent of the selling price. The selling price is then $150. ($90 equals 60 percent times selling price. Then $90 is divided by .6 or 60 percent to get the answer of $150.)

Another common situation facing a merchant is to have competition set a ceiling on selling price, or possibly he must buy an item to fit into one of his price lines. Then he wants to know the maximum amount he can pay for the item and still get his normal markup. For instance, assume that the selling price of an article is set at $60 (by competition or by the $59.95 price line). The retailer's normal markup is 35 percent. What is the most he should pay for this article? Again, let us fill in what we know in the diagram.

	$	%
Selling price	$60	100%
—Cost		
Markup		35%

The dollar markup is $21 (35 percent of $60), so by a simple subtraction we find that the maximum cost the merchant will want to pay is $39.

It should be clearly understood that markups are figured on the selling price *at each level of business* in a channel of distribution. A manufacturer applies a markup to determine his selling price. The manufacturer's selling price then becomes the wholesaler's cost. Then the wholesaler must determine his own selling price by applying his usual markup percentage based on his—the wholesaler's—selling price. The same procedure is carried on by the retailer whose cost figure is the wholesaler's selling price. The following computations should illustrate this point:

Retailer's selling price	$20 ⎱ Retailer's markup = $8, or 40 percent
Retailer's cost	$12 ⎰
Wholesaler's selling price	$12 ⎱ Wholesaler's markup = $2, or 16⅔ percent
Wholesaler's cost	$10 ⎰
Producer's selling price	$10 ⎱ Producer's markup = $3, or 30 percent
Producer's cost	$7 ⎰

If a firm is used to dealing in markups based on cost—and sometimes this is done among wholesalers—the same diagrammatic approach may be employed that was used above in the examples of markup based on selling price. The only change is that cost will equal 100 percent, and the selling price will be 100 percent plus the markup based on cost. As an example, assume that a firm bought an article for $70 and wanted a 20 percent markup based on cost. The markup in dollars is $14 (20 percent of $70), and the selling price is $84 ($70 plus $14).

Even though it is customary to compute markups on the basis of selling price, a marketing executive should understand the relationships between markups on cost and markups on selling price. For instance, if a product costs $6 and sells for $10, there is a $4 markup. This is a 40 percent markup when based on selling price, but a 66 2/3 percent markup when based on cost. An executive should also be able to convert from one base to another. The following diagram may be helpful in understanding these relationships:

Selling price = 100%   Cost = 100%

                    40% { Markup =   } 66⅔%
                         $4.00
$10 = 100% $10 = 166⅔%

                    60% { Cost =   } 100%
                         $6.00

These convertible relationships may be expressed in the following formulas:

(1) Percentage markup on selling price = $\dfrac{\text{percentage markup on cost}}{100\% + \text{percentage markup on cost}}$

(2) Percentage markup on cost = $\dfrac{\text{percentage markup on selling price}}{100\% - \text{percentage markup on selling price}}$

To illustrate the use of these formulas, let us assume that a retailer has a markup of 25 percent on cost and wants to know what the corresponding figure is, based on selling price. In formula (1) we get

$$\frac{25\%}{100\% + 25\%} = \frac{25\%}{125\%} = 20\%$$

A markup of 33 1/3 percent based on selling price converts to 50 percent based on cost, by using formula (2) as follows:

$$\frac{33^{1}/_{3}\%}{100\% - 33^{1}/_{3}\%} = \frac{33^{1}/_{3}\%}{66^{2}/_{3}\%} = 50\%$$

ANALYTICAL RATIOS

From a study of the operating statement, management can develop several ratios which will be useful tools in evaluating the results of its marketing program. In most of these cases, net sales is used as the base of 100 percent. In fact, unless it is specifically mentioned to the contrary, all ratios reflecting gross margin, net profit, or any operating expense are stated as a percentage of net sales.

GROSS MARGIN PERCENTAGE

This is the ratio between gross margin and net sales. Referring to Fig. A-1, the gross margin percentage is $\frac{\$32,000}{\$80,000}$ or 40 percent.

NET PROFIT PERCENTAGE

This ratio is computed by dividing net profits by net sales. In Fig. A-1 the ratio is $\frac{\$4,800}{\$80,000}$ or 6 percent. This percentage may be computed either before or after federal income taxes are deducted, but the answer should be labeled adequately to reflect which it is.

OPERATING EXPENSE PERCENTAGE

When total operating expenses are divided by net sales, the result is the operating expense ratio or percentage. In Fig. A-1 the ratio is 34 percent $\frac{\$27,200}{\$80,000}$. In similar fashion, we may determine the expense ratio for any given cost. Thus we note in Fig. A-1 that the rent expense was 1 percent, advertising was 3 percent, and salesmen's salaries and commissions were 13.75 percent. Frequently in its operating statement, a company will add a percentage column at the right. This column will start with net sales being 100 percent and will show for each item on the statement its percentage in relation to net sales.

RATE OF STOCKTURN

Management often measures the efficiency of its marketing operations by means of the stockturn ratio. This figure represents the number of times the average inventory is "turned over," or sold, during the period under study. The ratio is computed on either a cost or a selling-price basis. That is, both the numerator and the denominator of the ratio fraction must be expressed in the same terms, either cost or selling price.

On a cost basis, the formula is as follows:

$$\text{Rate of stockturn} = \frac{\text{cost of goods sold}}{\text{average inventory at cost}}$$

The average inventory is determined by adding the beginning and ending inventory and dividing this answer by 2. In Fig. A-1 the average inventory is $\frac{\$18,000 + \$20,000}{2} = \$19,000$. The stockturn rate is $\frac{\$48,000}{\$19,000}$ or 2.5. Because inventories usually are abnormally low at the first of the year in anticipation of taking physical inventory, this average may not be representative. Consequently, some companies add the book inventories at the beginning of each month and divide this sum by 12.

If the inventory is kept on a retail basis, as is done in most large retail organizations, the stockturn rate equals net sales divided by average inventory at selling price. Sometimes the stockturn rate is computed by dividing the number of *units* sold by the average inventory expressed in units.

Wholesale and retail trade associations in many types of businesses compile and publish figures showing the average rate of stockturn for their members. A firm with a low rate of stockturn is apt to be spending too much on storage and inventory expenses. Also, the company has a higher risk of obsolescence or spoilage. If the stockturn rate gets too high, this may indicate that the company maintains too low an average inventory. Often a firm in this situation is operating on a hand-to-mouth buying system. In addition to incurring high handling and billing costs per order, the company is apt to be out of stock on some items.

MARKDOWN PERCENTAGE

Sometimes a retailer is unable to sell an article at the originally posted price, and he reduces this price in order to move the goods. A *markdown* is the reduction from original selling price. Management frequently finds it very helpful to determine the markdown percentage and to analyze the size and number of markdowns and the reasons for them. Retailers, particularly, make extensive use of markdown analysis.

Markdowns are expressed as a percentage of net sales and *not* as a percentage of original selling price. To illustrate, assume that a retailer purchased a hat for $6 and marked it up 40 percent to sell for $10. The hat did not sell at that price, so he marked it down to $8. Now it is true that his advertisement or display sign may advertise a price cut of 20 percent. Yet in our calculations, his markdown is stated at $2, or 25 percent of the $8 selling price.

Markdowns in a department or in an entire company are computed for a given period of time by dividing total dollar markdowns by total net sales during that period. Two important points should be noted here. The markdown percentage is computed in this fashion, regardless of whether the markdown items were sold or are still in the store. Also, the percentage is computed with respect to total net sales and not only in connection with sales of marked-down articles. As an example, assume that a retailer buys ten hats at $6 each and prices them to sell at $10.

He sells five hats at $10, marks the other five down to $8, and sells three at the lower price. His total sales are $74, and his markdowns are $10. He has a markdown ratio of 13.5 percent.

Markdowns do not appear on the profit and loss statement because they occur *before* an article is sold. The first item on an operating statement is gross sales. That figure reflects the actual selling price, which may be the selling price after a markdown has been taken.

A refinement in the computation of the markdown percentage involves sales allowances. Actually, these allowances are added to markdowns in determining the markdown percentage. The formula is:

$$\text{Markdown percentage} = \frac{\text{dollar markdown} + \text{dollar sales allowances}}{\text{total net sales in dollars}}$$

The reasoning here is that, in effect, an allowance is simply a markdown taken after the sale was made. In the hat example above, if the retailer saw that a hat was soiled, he would mark it down $2. Assume that he did not notice the defect and that he sold the hat for $10. The customer later saw that the hat was soiled and voiced his dissatisfaction. He kept the hat, but was given a $2 allowance. Allowances here should not be confused with sales returns where the customer returns the article and is refunded the full purchase price.

RETURN ON INVESTMENT

A commonly used measure of managerial performance and the operating success of a company is its rate of return on investment. We use both the balance sheet and the operating statement as sources of information. The appropriate formula for calculating return on investment (ROI) is as follows:

$$\text{ROI} = \frac{\text{Net profit}}{\text{Sales}} \times \frac{\text{Sales}}{\text{Investment}}$$

Two questions may quickly come to mind. First, what do we mean by "investment"? Second, why do we need two fractions? It would seem that the "sales" component in each fraction would cancel out, leaving net profit/investment as the meaningful ratio.

To answer the first query, consider a firm whose operating statement showed annual sales of $1,000,000 and a net profit of $50,000. At the end of the year the balance sheet reported:

Assets	$600,000	Liabilities		$200,000
		Capital stock	$300,000	
		Retained earnings	100,000	400,000
	$600,000			$600,000

Now, is the investment $400,000 or $600,000? Certainly the ROI will be different depending upon which figure we use. The answer depends upon whether we are talking to the stockholders or to the company executives. The stockholders are more interested in the return on what they have invested—in this case, $400,000. The ROI calculation then is:

$$\frac{\text{Net profit} \quad \$50,000}{\text{Sales} \quad \$1,000,000} \times \frac{\text{Sales} \quad \$1,000,000}{\text{Investment} \quad \$400,000} = 12\tfrac{1}{2}\%$$

Management, on the other hand, is more concerned with the total investment, as represented by the total assets ($600,000). This is the factor which the executives must manage, regardless of whether the assets were acquired by stockholders' investment, retained earnings, or loans from outside sources.[1] Within this context the ROI computation becomes:

$$\frac{\text{Net profit} \quad \$50,000}{\text{Sales} \quad \$1,000,000} \times \frac{\text{Sales} \quad \$1,000,000}{\text{Investment} \$600,000} = 8\tfrac{1}{3}\%$$

Regarding the second question, we use two fractions because we are dealing with two separate elements—the rate of profit on sales and the rate of capital turnover. Management really should determine each rate separately and then multiply the two. The rate of profit on sales is influenced by marketing considerations—sales volume, price, product mix, advertising effort, etc. The capital turnover is a financial consideration not directly involved with costs or profits——only sales volume and assets managed.

To illustrate, assume that our company's profits doubled with the same sales volume and investment because management operated an excellent marketing program this year. In effect, we doubled our profit rate with the same capital turnover:

$$\frac{\text{Net profit} \quad \$100,000}{\text{Sales} \quad \$1,000,000} \times \frac{\text{Sales} \quad \$1,000,000}{\text{Investment} \quad \$600,000} = 16\tfrac{2}{3}\%$$
$$ 10\% \quad \times 1.67 \quad = 16\tfrac{2}{3}\%$$

In another example let us assume that we earned our original profit of $50,000 but that we did it with an investment reduced to $500,000. We cut the size of our average inventory, and we closed some branch offices. By increasing our capital turnover from 1.67 to 2 we raise the ROI from 8⅓ percent to 10 percent, even though sales volume and profits remain unchanged:

$$\frac{\$50,000}{\$1,000,000} \times \frac{\$1,000,000}{\$500,000} = 10\%$$
$$ 5\% \quad \times \quad 2 \quad = 10\%$$

---

[1] In fact, it has been suggested that the term "assets employed" or "assets managed" be used in the formula instead of "investment" when using the ROI concept as a measure of managerial performance. See Michael Schiff, "The Use of ROI in Sales Management," *Journal of Marketing*, July, 1963, pp. 70–73; and J. S. Schiff and Michael Schiff, "New Sales Management Tool: ROAM (Return on Assets Managed)," *Harvard Business Review*, July-August, 1967, pp. 59–66.

Assume that we increase our sales volume—let us say we double it—but do not increase our profit or investment, the cost-profit squeeze is bringing us "profitless prosperity." The following interesting results occur:

$$\frac{\$50,000}{\$2,000,000} \times \frac{\$2,000,000}{\$600,000} = 10\%$$
$$2\frac{1}{2}\% \quad \times \quad 3.33 \quad = 8\frac{1}{3}\%$$

The profit rate was cut in half, but his was offset by a doubling of the capital turnover rate, leaving the ROI unchanged.

QUESTIONS AND PROBLEMS

1. Construct an operating statement from the following data and compute the gross-margin percentage:

Purchases at billed cost	$15,000
Net sales	30,000
Sales returns and allowances	200
Cash discounts given	300
Cash discounts earned	100
Rent	1,500
Salaries	6,000
Opening inventory at cost	10,000
Advertising	600
Other expenses	2,000
Closing inventory at cost	7,500

2. Prepare a retail operating statement from the following data and compute the markdown percentage:

Rent	$ 9,000
Closing inventory at cost	28,000
Sales returns	6,500
Gross margin as percentage of sales	35%
Cash discounts allowed	2,000
Salaries	34,000
Markdowns	4,000
Other operating expenses	15,000
Opening inventory at cost	35,000
Gross sales	232,500
Advertising	5,500
Freight in	3,500

3. What are the percentages of markup on cost which correspond to the following percentages of markup on selling price?

a. 20 percent   c. 50 percent
b. 37½ percent   d. 66⅔ percent

4. What are the percentages of markup on selling price which correspond to the following percentages of markup on cost?

a. 20 percent   c. 50 percent
b. 33⅓ percent   d. 300 percent

5. A hardware store bought a gross (twelve dozen) of hammers, paying $302.40 for the lot. The retailer estimated his operating expenses for this product to be 35 percent of sales, and he wanted a net profit of 5 percent of sales. He expected no markdowns. What retail selling price should he set for each hammer?

6. Competition in a certain line of sporting goods pretty well limits the selling price on a certain item to $25. If the store owner feels he needs a markup of 35 percent to cover his expenses and return a reasonable profit, what is the most he can pay for this item?

7. A retailer with annual net sales of $2 million maintains a markup of 66⅔ percent based on cost. His expenses average 35 percent. What is his gross margin and net profit in dollars?

8. A company has a stockturn rate of five times a year, a sales volume of $600,000, and a gross margin of 25 percent. What is the average inventory at cost?

9. A store has an average inventory of $30,000 at retail and a stockturn rate of five times a year. If the company maintains a markup of 50 percent based on cost, what is the annual sales volume and cost of goods sold?

10. From the following data, compute the gross-margin percentage and the operating expense ratio:
Stockturn rate = 9
Average inventory at selling price = 45,000
Net profit = $20,000
Cost of goods sold = $350,000

11. A ski shop sold 50 pairs of skis at $90 a pair, taking a 10 percent markdown in so doing. All the skis were originally purchased at the same price and had been marked up 60 percent on cost. What was the gross margin on the 50 pairs of skis?

12. A men's clothing store bought 200 suits at $90 each. The suits were marked up 40 percent. Eighty were sold at that price. The remaining suits were each marked down 20 percent from the original selling price, and then they were sold. Compute the sales volume and the markdown percentage.

13. An appliance retailer sold 60 radios at $30 each after taking markdowns equal to 20 percent of the actual selling price. Originally all the radios had been purchased at the same price and were marked up 50 percent on cost. What was the gross-margin percentage earned in this situation?

14. An appliance manufacturer produced a line of small appliances advertised to sell at $30. The manufacturer planned for wholesalers to receive a 20 percent markup, and retailers a 33⅓ percent markup. Total manufacturing costs were $12 per unit. What did retailers pay for the product? What were the manufacturer's selling price and his percentage markup?

15. A housewares manufacturer produces an article at a full cost of $1.80. It is sold through a manufacturers' agent directly to large retailers. The agent receives a 20 percent commission on his sales, the retailers earn a margin of 30 percent, and the manufacturer plans a net profit of 10 percent on his selling price. What is the retail price of this article?

16. A manufacturer suggests a retail selling price of $400 on an item and grants a chain discount of 40-10-10. What is the manufacturer's selling price? (Chain discounts are discussed in Chapter 13.)

17. A building materials manufacturer sold a quantity of his product to a wholesaler for $350, and the wholesaler in turn sold to a lumberyard. The wholesaler's normal markup was 15 percent, and the retailer usually priced the item to include a 30 percent markup. What is the selling price to the consumer?

18. From the following data, calculate the return on investment, based on a definition of "investment" which is useful for evaluating managerial performance:

Net sales	$800,000	Markup	35%
Gross margin	$280,000	Average inventory	$75,000
Total assets	$200,000	Retained earnings	$60,000
Cost of goods sold	$520,000	Operating ex- penses	$240,000
Liabilities	$40,000		

NAME INDEX

SUBJECT INDEX